The American Clipper
Ship, 1845–1920

ALSO BY GLENN A. KNOBLOCK
AND FROM MCFARLAND

Weathervanes of New England (2018)

*African American Historic Burial Grounds and
Gravesites of New England* (2016)

*Historic Iron and Steel Bridges in Maine,
New Hampshire and Vermont* (2012)

*African American World War II Casualties and Decorations
in the Navy, Coast Guard and Merchant Marine:
A Comprehensive Record* (2009)

*Black Submariners in the United States
Navy, 1940–1975* (2005; paperback 2011)

*"Strong and Brave Fellows": New Hampshire's
Black Soldiers and Sailors
of the American Revolution, 1775–1784* (2003)

The American Clipper Ship, 1845–1920

A Comprehensive History, with a Listing of Builders and Their Ships

GLENN A. KNOBLOCK

McFarland & Company, Inc., Publishers
Jefferson, North Carolina

The present work is a reprint of the illustrated case bound edition of The American Clipper Ship, 1845–1920: A Comprehensive History, with a Listing of Builders and Their Ships, *first published in 2014 by McFarland.*

LIBRARY OF CONGRESS CATALOGUING-IN-PUBLICATION DATA

Knoblock, Glenn A.
The American clipper ship, 1845–1920 : a comprehensive history, with a listing of builders and their ships / Glenn A. Knoblock.
p.   cm.
Includes bibliographical references and index.

ISBN 978-1-4766-9421-4
softcover : acid free paper ∞

1. Clipper ships—United States—History.
2. Merchant marine—United States—History—19th -century.
3. Merchant marine—United States—History—20th century.
4. Shipbuilding—United States—Atlantic Coast—History.   I. Title.

VK23.K57 2023   387.2'24—dc23   2013042895

BRITISH LIBRARY CATALOGUING DATA ARE AVAILABLE

© 2014 Glenn A. Knoblock. All rights reserved

No part of this book may be reproduced or transmitted in any form or by any means, electronic or mechanical, including photocopying or recording, or by any information storage and retrieval system, without permission in writing from the publisher.

Front cover: *The Clipper Ship* Southern Cross *Leaving Boston Harbor, 1851* (© 2023 PicturesNOW)

Printed in the United States of America

*McFarland & Company, Inc., Publishers
Box 611, Jefferson, North Carolina 28640
www.mcfarlandpub.com*

To my sisters,
Debbie and Lisa,
With love and admiration
For two of the
Most creative people I know!

Table of Contents

Acknowledgments   viii
Introduction   1

PART ONE: THE HISTORY OF THE CLIPPER

    I.   *Westward Ho:* The Coming of the Clipper   6
    II.   *Challenge:* The Design of a Clipper Ship   17
    III.   *Young Mechanic:* The Building of a Clipper Ship   39
    IV.   *Architect:* The Clipper Ship Builders   70
    V.   *Intrepid:* Clipper Ship Commanders, Crew and Passengers   80
    VI.   *Wild Rover:* Clipper Ship Voyages and Trade   129
    VII.   *Titan:* Clipper Ship Owners and Agents   159
    VIII.   *Sweepstakes:* Fast Passages and Record Setting Voyages   193
    IX.   *Hurricane:* Shipwrecks and Other Noteworthy Clipper Events   206
    X.   *Twilight:* The End of the American Clipper Ship Era   232

PART TWO: CLIPPER BUILDERS AND THEIR SHIPS BY STATE   255

Bibliography   355
Index   359

Acknowledgments

During the course of writing this book I have received assistance from many individuals. First and foremost, I would like to thank my wife, Terry, for all her love, understanding, and encouragement, not just for this work, but for all my historical endeavors over the years.

On the professional side, the following individuals have been particularly helpful during the course of my research: Leanne Kubicz, reference librarian, Hoboken Public Library (NJ); Martin Blasco, special collections librarian, Gardiner Public Library (ME); Bonnie Healy, president, Trescott Historical Society (ME); Kevin Johnson, photo archivist, Penobscott Maritime Museum (ME); Captain Jim (James) Sharp, Sail, Power, and Steam Museum, Rockland, ME; and Megan Good, director, J. Welles Henderson Archive & Library, Independence Seaport Museum, Philadelphia, PA.

Special thanks go out to Robert J. Alesbury (Bethesda, MD) and A. William Alesbury (Acton, MA), who are direct descendants of the New York shipbuilder Jabez Williams; they were kind enough to supply copies of period photos and pages of shipyard record books that help to document the Williams shipyard. These illustrations are an important addition to this work as I've placed a great amount of emphasis on the clipper ship builders, and thus it was quite interesting to make this direct family contact. I am even told that Robert in particular bears a strong resemblance to Jabez Williams, which I hope to verify in person someday if distance and circumstances allow!

Finally, in keeping with that traditional disclaimer stated by many a historical author, though I've received assistance from many quarters over the years that this work was conceived, researched, and written, any mistakes that may appear are strictly my own.

Introduction

The clipper ship era, lasting from approximately 1845 to 1860, marked the high point of America's maritime achievements during the age of sail. It was a time noted for the California gold rush and our nation's correspondingly rapid growth westward, expanding worldwide trade, as well as the boundless energy, technological innovations, and outstanding feats of seamanship that accompanied them. The clipper ships were the stars of the day, heralded in newspaper accounts and the lithograph prints of Currier and Ives alike for their beauty and speed. And not just in America; wherever these ships appeared in ports around the world, they elicited great praise for their form and function. Indeed, there was no national representative at the time that better symbolized the driving spirit of America than these ships that sailed under the Stars and Stripes. However, the heyday of the clipper ships also came about at a tumultuous time in our nation's history, a period when the country suffered a great economic downturn during a financial panic that was the first to occur on a global level, while at the same time on the political front, America, though not everyone realized it yet, was slowly spiraling downward towards a civil war. Given all this, it may truly be said that the decade of the 1850s was one of great highs but also great lows, and the clipper ships were an important part of the national story.

This book seeks to tell the full story about the American clipper ships in a comprehensive fashion from their first development in the 1840s, the full height of their activities and achievements in the 1850s, and down through their later operations into the early 20th century. It was written with the general reader in mind, including both the nautical novice with a limited but perhaps budding interest in the subject, and those maritime enthusiasts who have already immersed themselves in the subject of the clippers but want to know more. Indeed, this is what has inspired me to write this book; having read everything about the clippers I could find over the years by some of America's most noted maritime historians, I was always left with some unanswered questions. In the beginning chapters, the reader will learn how shipbuilding in America evolved over the years, and how, and by whom, these fast ships eventually came to be designed, and in turn, how these designs changed during the 1850s. Succeeding chapters offer details about the construction of these ships, including the men who built them, the locales at which they were built, the cargos they carried, the captains and crews that that operated them, and shipboard life during the day of the clippers. Another important facet of this book, and something that has been but little touched upon in previous histories, is the business aspect of owning and operating a clipper ship; just how much did these ships cost, how were they insured and regulated, what cargos did they carry and why, and what kinds of profits did they make for their owners? These are all details that offer fascinating historical insights into a period when

America's maritime commerce was at an all-time high. Continuing onward, this work also covers the later day aspects of the clipper ships and their life histories; though their reign effectively ended in 1857 and the last American clippers were built in 1859, this class of ships continued in operation for many decades, including their involvement with events during the Civil War that were both interesting and, at times, destructive; the subsequent sale of many of them to foreign countries; and, finally, to their last days when many once proud but now aged clippers served as workaday vessels and tramp ships seeking a cargo wherever one could be found. Despite their high pedigrees, many of these ships, forced to earn a living wherever and whenever they could, drifted into some of the most controversial trades of the day. Finally, this work is ended with a state by state accounting of every known builder and their clipper ship productions, compiled from a variety of authoritative sources, and their ships, from those built at Robbinston in Downeast Maine in northern New England to the lone clipper built in the deep south at Key West, Florida, along with a list of what I consider to be the most significant clippers constructed in each state where multiple vessels were built. If this should, by chance, spark a revival of the debates of old when the merits of clippers from differing locales, especially Boston and New York, were hotly discussed by both mariners and businessmen, then I will have accomplished my goal.

There have been many fine and authoritative works published in the past documenting the clipper ship era; the works of Captain Arthur H. Clark, Octavius Howe and Frederick Matthews, and Carl Cutler come immediately to mind. This book is not an attempt to supplant these classics, and indeed it would be foolish to even try such a thing, as each offers a unique perspective of the American clipper. However, when these works were authored, between 1911 and 1930, the events of the clipper ship era had not only taken place within the memories of those still living men and women who had been participants, but also the clippers themselves were still a part of our recent past, and many communities where they were built still took great pride in the achievements of their hometown builders. Today, other than perhaps that most famous of all clippers, the Boston-built *Flying Cloud*, who among us has ever heard of the exploits of such ships, famous (or infamous) in their own day and renowned countrywide, as the *Challenge, Nightingale, Andrew Jackson,* or *Dreadnought*? The story of these fast ships, their operations, the races they took part in, and the records they set is an exciting one, but I have here in these pages placed less overall emphasis than the works previously mentioned on the discussion of sailing records and times. Discussions of such details in the past were entirely appropriate when there were those still living that had experienced such voyages, but they have less meaning for the modern reader. In a day when one can make it to Europe by jet in mere hours, the fact that the clipper ship *Phantom*, to cite one random example, made a record passage from New York to Rio de Janeiro in 23 days is largely irrelevant to today's reader.

Today, over a century and a half after the last clipper ship was built, their place in our national history and, more specifically, our transportation history may have faded a bit, but the interest in the sailing ships of old in general is still of great interest to young and old alike, as evidenced by the huge crowds of people that have visited the many Tall Ship events that have taken place over the years, no matter where they may appear. In this modern retelling of the clipper ship era, while sailing records and times have their place, I have tried to take a detailed approach to the *everyday* lives of these ships and the men, and, yes, in a few cases some extraordinary women, who built and operated them. If the devil is in the details, as the old saying goes, so too is that where the most interesting of the facts regarding the clippers may be found, and their story is still a compelling one to this day.

A Note About Sources and Illustrations

In this expanded story of the clipper ship era I have consulted a wide variety of works to give the fullest picture possible; all of them are listed in the bibliography at the end of this book. However, it will here be appropriate to discuss five major works on the subject that have been previously published, almost all of which (those by William A. Fairburn and William L. Crothers excepted) have been primary reference works on the subject for all subsequent authors and historians since 1930.

The first of these is Captain Arthur H. Clark's *The Clipper Ship Era*, which was first published in 1910 and has been in and out of print over the years. Clark grew up around ships in New England and later became a ship's captain, and was thus thoroughly qualified to write about this era. His accounts of the sailors of the day especially, taken from his own experiences under sail and from many who had sailed aboard the clippers themselves, are particularly interesting, and I have not hesitated to quote him on many details of seafaring life. This book, one of my personal favorites, I consider to be a classic in American maritime history, an essential part of any maritime library, and eminently readable.

The next and most invaluable work to come along was *American Clipper Ships, 1833–1858* by Octavius T. Howe and Frederick C. Matthews, published by the Marine Research Society, Salem, Massachusetts, in two volumes in 1926 and 1927. This encyclopedic work has been *the* source for all subsequent writers about clipper ships, giving as it does the life histories of 352 clippers, since its first appearance. I have not only quoted this work many times, but also have used it as the primary source for all the clipper ship voyages, cargo details, and life events of these ships that I have discussed unless otherwise noted. For the reader who has an interest in a specific clipper and wants to know most of what can be found about the vessel, this is the work to consult. This work was compiled over the course of many years by two outstanding marine historians who gathered their information from newspapers and ship's logs, as well as the family papers of seafaring families and personal accounts of those still living participants of the clipper ship era; unfortunately, Howe and Matthews cite very few of these sources in detail. That these writers, perhaps understandably so, had a favorable bias toward Boston-built clippers is subtle in presentation, except in their discussion of the *Flying Cloud* versus *Andrew Jackson* debate! However, the organization and scope of this work is also what inspired me to write my own history; because Howe and Matthews' work was a reference one by apparent design only, it offers little or no detailed analysis of the clipper ships or their historical background as a whole, and to read the work through and through offers a sometimes dry, sometimes exciting account of each clipper with a plethora of dates and details that are out of context with one another. Despite this minor criticism, this work, too, is a classic and one that not only saved many details about these ships from being lost to history, but without which my own book would have been impossible to write.

The third major work on the clipper ships to make its appearance was Carl Cutler's *Greyhound of the Sea: The Story of the American Clipper Ship*, published in 1930. Cutler (1878–1966) was an eminent marine historian who was one of the founders of the Marine Historical Association and Museum at Mystic, Connecticut. His works, including the subsequent *Five Hundred Sailing Records of American Built Ships* (1952), were the first to offer an unbiased, sometimes critical, and thoroughly analytical view of the clipper ship era and is also a classic. The narrative of the clipper ship years is quite interesting and many details regarding fast passages are offered, though it suffers from a lack of operational details about the ships and their cargos. Cutler, a most diligent historian, consulted many ship's logs housed at the National Archives, as well as many other records and newspaper sources. Most valuable are the appendices in Cutler's earlier work, expanded in part with his later work on sailing records, that detail record-setting sailing passages, as well as those listing the California voyages and all clippers or reputed clippers built from 1850 to 1859. These I have not hesitated to consult, and I consider Cutler, as do many other maritime historians, to be the final word on the subject of sailing records and fast passages.

Finally, there are two other works that are also helpful to the clipper ship historian. William Armstrong Fairburn's *Merchant Sail* is a massive six-volume work that was published from 1945 to 1955 but was distributed, free of charge, only to academic institutions and marine historical societies and was never made available to the general public. Fairburn (1876–1947) was a naval architect and marine engineer with an interest in history and began compiling records and notes on the subject in 1891. His work covers the marine history of the United States from colonial days down to the end of the age of sail and certainly gives the clippers their fair share of attention, albeit in a somewhat disjointed fashion. Fairburn is most effective in documenting many of the lesser known clippers through the use of local custom house records and, as might be expected, given his background, he gives the clipper builders greater attention than any of the works listed above. Though he was born in England and educated in Scotland, Fairburn came to Bath, Maine, at an early age and here worked in the shipbuilding industry for many years; his bias in favor of Maine-built clippers in particular is quite noticeable. Lastly, William Crothers' *The American-Built Clipper Ship 1850–1856* (1996) is a technical work, richly illustrated with detailed drawings, that highlights the construction elements of the clippers in all their varying aspects. Those with a background in marine architecture or an interest in model building will find this work of great appeal. I have used it as a reference work in my discussion on clipper ship design and construction, but have avoided discussing those very technical details that are likely beyond the interest of most of my readers. For those who want the complete clipper story from shrouds and backstays down to the sternpost and keelson assemblies, this is the work to consult.

These are the main sources which I have drawn upon to tell the story of the clipper ships, but there are many other fine works to be found in the bibliography that will interest the reader. Having discussed the biases of some of the maritime writers above, it is only fair that I here disclose the fact that not only am I a resident of New Hampshire, but also a former resident of Portsmouth (and still a frequent visitor), where twenty-eight clipper ships were built from 1850 through 1859. It may be that some favorable bias, entirely unintended, has crept into this work in this regard, and if that is the case, I hope that those partisan readers from elsewhere (the state of Maine, Boston, Mystic, New York, and Baltimore come to mind) may forgive me! Finally, in regards to illustrations for this book, all, with a few exceptions which are noted and credited, come from my own collection. I have given particular emphasis to contemporary illustrations, particularly the Currier and Ives prints and newspaper illustrations in woodcut form from both domestic and British publications, which depict these ships (and their forerunners) as they were presented to the American and overseas public at the very height of their popularity. In most cases these are some of the most accurate portrayals of the clippers to be found as they were created by artists who actually viewed their subjects in person and had access to data and models from their builders and owners.

Finally, for comparing the worth of the U.S. dollar in the 1850s to its current value, I consulted the Measuring Worth website: www.measuringworth.com.

Part One: The History of the Clipper

I

Westward Ho
The Coming of the Clipper

To gain a sense of where the American clipper came from we must first take a brief look at America's maritime past for the clipper did not just spring to life at a definitive point in time, but rather it evolved over many years. It was not just the physical form of the ship that evolved, but also the maritime practices and ideals involving the concept of speed. We in the modern world now know about speed all too well, fully realizing that what may have been considered fast five, ten, or even fifty years ago is vastly different than it is today. Marine architect and historian Howard Chapelle: "In all forms of transportation an increase in speed of movement has been sought and has been accepted as a fundamental indication of progress" (Chapelle, p. 3). So it was with the decades running up to the appearance of the first California clipper ships; a great amount of progress in ship design had been achieved. The need for fast ships was ever growing from the 1820s onward, but in the immediate years after the California gold rush of 1849 it exploded to unprecedented heights; records for travel by sailing ships in the early 1850s in some cases were not to be broken until the late 20th century, long after the age of the American sailing ship had ended.

The Evolution of American Ship Design

The earliest merchant vessels in American history were built on European models, primarily English, Dutch, and Spanish, not with speed in mind, but for carrying capacity and durability. A look at such historic craft as Christopher Columbus' *Nina, Pinta* (the fastest of the three), and *Santa Maria*, which participated in the discovery and exploration of America in the 1400s, and the earliest ships to carry colonists to America, including the *Susan Constant* to Jamestown, Virginia, in 1607 and the *Mayflower* to Massachusetts in 1620, shows that all have several features in common. All had rounded hull forms with a bluff, "apple-cheeked" bow form and the high stern castles that were a throwback to earlier times when ships used such structures for defensive purposes. These vessels were also three-masted with square sails on the fore and main masts, and a lateen (triangular) sail on the mizzen mast. None of these ships, which were sizeable for the day, exceeded 120 tons burden, although larger merchant and naval ships were being built. Though important to America's founding, none of these craft were built in America. The first vessel known to have been built in British North America (earlier vessels may have been built in Spanish-controlled Florida) was the pinnace *Virginia*, a small, 30-ton two-masted craft built by settlers at the Popham Colony in Maine. This small settlement, located on the coast at the mouth of the Kennebec River, was established in 1607, and its members built the *Virginia* not only for their own needs, but also to demonstrate the feasibility of establishing such an industry in the New World. While the colonists were correct in this particular, the Maine winter was not kind to them and the colony was abandoned after a year's time.

From the time of the settlement of these first colonies and throughout the seventeenth and eighteenth centuries in America, shipbuilding increased, at first slowly, and by 1700 at a more rapid pace, though most of the vessels built were small in size, and by the time of the American Revolution was well established. When larger vessels were built, they were usually for the Royal Navy, including the 372-ton *Bedford Galley* (1699) and the 863-ton *America* (1749), both built in New Hampshire.

A Baltimore clipper topsail schooner. Fast and rakish armed craft like this were used extensively during the American Revolution to combat the British on the high seas (courtesy of the U.S. Navy).

Two of the locales in America where the fastest ships were developed over the years were the Chesapeake Bay area, including the major port of Baltimore, and Essex County, Massachusetts, located north of Boston and encompassing the major ports of Marblehead and Gloucester. Both regions were (and still are) known for their fishing activities that took their men far from home. These operations not only required speed to get their catches home and to market in good time, but also to provide protection from the many pirates that preyed upon them on the open ocean. Unlike coasting vessels which sailed close to shore and could depend upon some degree of protection from local naval vessels, the small ships in the fisheries could not depend on such protection and so had to develop fast sailing ships to outrun piratical craft. The former area was known for its fast sailing, two-masted craft, the schooner (with fore and aft sails on both masts) and brigantines (with a square-rigged foremast and fore and aft rigged mainmast), and the variant topsail schooner (which carries a square rigged sail, sometimes two, on the foremast). These craft are thought to have had their origin in the Caribbean islands (possibly by way of England), where fast and nimble craft were needed to sail in and among the many small islands and inlets of a region that was home to many pirates from the fifteenth century down to modern times. In Essex County, Massachusetts, the famed Marblehead schooner was developed over many years and gained such a reputation for speed that a number were either built for or acquired by the Royal Navy in the early 1760s (Chapelle, p. 83). This type of schooner, likely also evolved from the Caribbean version, has been described as being "sharp" in hull form (think of a "V" shape when looking at it dead on, rather than the broad "U" shaped hull of a conventional merchant ship), but not to the extreme as it still had to carry large quantities of fish. The popularity and widespread use of these vessel forms, from the Chesapeake to New England, not only proved to be an early influence in the future development of fast ships, but also by their foreign influence serve to demonstrate that American shipbuilders learned and refined their trade from the ships of many countries. Desirable traits from some foreign vessels were adopted for use, yet others tried and discarded for one reason or another. Indeed, to say that the American clipper ship was of a purely home-grown design is wildly inaccurate; we have already mentioned the Caribbean and English influence (via the study of French, Italian, and Spanish designs) for the Baltimore clippers and Marblehead schooners; additionally the American maritime trade brought merchants and shipbuilders into contact with a wide range of foreign vessels, aspects of which were sometimes copied or adopted with some modification. This practice would continue, albeit in reverse and often in more formal surveys, when American clippers in the early 1850s arrived in England and had *their* lines copied while in dry dock so that the secrets behind their fast sailing qualities might be divined. Chapelle, once again, states it best when he writes that "ships themselves are the best and most common means of conveying information on their design to a foreign area" (Chapelle, p. 33).

To give a full account of American maritime activities that led up to the final development of the clipper ship of the 1850s would be both lengthy and redundant, as many other historians have written on this subject in authoritative fashion. Below are listed some of the major influences on clipper ship design in the period from approximately 1740 to 1849. However, it should be understood that none of these influences developed in a vacuum and that the many different trades over time experimented with the hull forms described below. Some were indeed successful for a given trade, while others were not suitable for one reason or another.

The Privateers of the Revolution and the War of 1812

In both these wars, the American Navy was either totally outclassed and outnumbered (the Revolution) or simply outnumbered (the War of 1812) by the British Royal Navy and its large fleet of frigates and ships of the line. However, there was one force that helped to defeat the British war effort at sea in both conflicts and that was the privateers. As their name implies, privateers were privately owned merchant ships that were granted a document, called a *letter of marque*, which allowed them to be armed and make voyages to capture combatant ships. While many merchant ships were converted for use as privateers in both wars, the financial windfalls that resulted from the sale of goods from captured enemy vessels soon made it profitable to commission the building of specially designed fast sailing ships for privateering. These ships were incredibly successful in their cruises and dealt a serious blow to the long British supply chain that stretched across the Atlantic from the British Isles to North America, as well as from the Caribbean northward. The one advantage that these sharp ships had was that cargo carrying was not the overriding concern. Heavily armed with anywhere from one to twenty cannons, and sometimes even more, their method was not to engage enemy warships, but to capture enemy merchantmen intact, man them with American sailors, and send them into an American port where their cargos could then be sold and the prize money subsequently divided among the privateer's crew and owners. Speed, of course, was vital to a privateer; not only did they need to be fast enough to overtake a fleeing merchantman, but, as was often the case, they needed to be able to elude British warships to avoid capture. During the Revolution nearly 1,700 privateers were commissioned, which captured over 1,300 British ships. One notable privateer during this war was the 22-gun *Hampden*, commissioned out of New Hampshire; this vessel, a sizeable one among privateers, fought a larger, 26-gun British Indiaman to a draw in a fierce, three hour battle, and when it was later captured by the British during the Penobscot fiasco up in Maine, it was found to be such a good vessel it was put "into the king's service" (MacLay, p. 135). What type of craft this was is unknown, but another Revolutionary War privateer, the *Rhodes* of Salem, Massachusetts, was also captured and surveys of her show that she was a sharp-built craft. During the War of 1812, over 500 privateers were commissioned, capturing about 1,300 British ships. Among the famed privateers in this war were the 16-gun *Chasseur*, nicknamed the "Pride of Baltimore," and the New York–built 18-gun *Prince de Neufchatel*. This later privateer was so successful and fast that after her eventual capture in 1814 by the Royal Navy, her lines were copied and a ship based on her model was ordered to be built, but with the end of the war a year later the plan was abandoned. In both wars, the fastest of the privateers were the sharp and rakish schooners, brigs, and other similar rigged craft that were legendary for their speed and maneuverability. Like the clippers of the 1850s which they inspired, many of these privateers had raked masts and were heavily sparred for their size and had sharp bow lines that helped them sail through the water at a fast clip. Many also had the V-shaped hull forms that were used by some of the earliest sharp-built clippers.

American-Built Naval Vessels

Many of America's early naval vessels, built without cargo carrying capacity in mind and with speed as a desirable quality (both to pursue and capture enemy craft, as well as to outrun them when they were out-gunned), were built with V-shaped hulls having a great deal of deadrise (the angle between the hull, or floor, of a ship and its widest beam) that were influenced by French practices dating back even prior to the American Revolution. One example from the American Revolution is the 32-gun frigate *Hancock*, built at Newburyport, Massachusetts, in 1776 as one of the original thirteen commissioned American naval ships. This fast ship was captured by the British in 1777 and taken into their navy, subsequently described as the Royal Navy's fastest vessel. By the time of the construction of the first American naval vessels after the American Revolution, including the U.S.S. *Constitution* (launched in 1797), the French frigate form was an accepted standard and would remain so for the first decades of the 19th century (Chapelle, p. 139). These ships, too, were distinguished by their lofty spars and large sail plans.

The Packet Ships

The packet trade, so named for its original purpose of carrying packets of mail and newspapers from port to port, was carried on in two different areas; coastal packets traded between American port towns and cities all along the eastern seaboard from Maine to New Orleans, while the transatlantic packet trade involved sailings to European ports, primarily those in England, but also to France and Holland. The coastal packet trade typically employed smaller vessels, usually under 100 tons in the early days, that sailed on well-established routes fairly close to shore, while the transatlantic packets were generally larger ships, 300 tons and upwards early on and soon evolving to those that were 1,000 tons or more, that had to brave the open seas of the often stormy North Atlantic. Because of the Gulf Stream current, the eastbound passage to England could often be made in quick time, but the westbound passage back to America could be a killer. On this portion of the round trip, a packet had to buck the prevailing seas and currents even on a good passage, and when a passage was being made in stormy weather, the conditions were even more brutal for sailors and passengers alike. Prior to 1818, the transatlantic packet trade, conducted since the end of the American Revolution in one fashion or another, was intermittent and was conducted on an informal basis, the same generally being true for coastal packets. However, with the formation of the soon-to-be-famous Black Ball Line of packets, running from New York to Liverpool beginning in January 1818, the trade was dramatically changed. The Black Ball ships, the first of which were not specially built for the line and already had been in service for a number of years, were the first American merchant ships to sail at regularly established intervals, whether full with cargos and passengers or not, and soon proved to be invaluable to those businessmen and merchants who came to depend on their reliable service. As one historian states, "In no other respect did they [the ships of the Black Ball Line] furnish better accommodations or superior service" (Cutler, p. 58). While the

The packet ship *Cornelius Grinnell*. Loftily sparred packet ships like this one, built by Donald McKay in 1850, were important in the development of the clipper ships of the 1850s (*The Illustrated London News*, August 31, 1850).

first Black Ball ships were above average size for their day, they were more noted for their speed; the plans and models for these early vessels have not survived, but they were undoubtedly fast. Captain James Rogers, commander of one of these inaugural ships, the 384-ton *Pacific* (built prior to 1811), would later state in 1851 that "the little *Pacific* would be fast among clippers" (Cutler, p. 59). Following the establishment of the Black Ball Line, trade with England and the competition on the transatlantic route grew at a quick pace and rival packet lines were soon established, mainly in New York, but also several out of Boston. Though New York shipbuilders led the way in building packet ships, many others were constructed at yards all the way from Maine and New Hampshire in the north and at many other locales down the New England coast. Indeed, the famed clipper builders of the 1850s, men like William Webb (New York), Donald McKay (Massachusetts), and George Raynes (New Hampshire), were all building noted packet ships in the 1840s.

While the earliest packet ships were not noted for their sharp designs, their design evolved over the years from 1818 to the 1830s as more speed in these regular sailing ships was sought by each line in order to gain an edge over their rivals. It is perhaps ironic that the biggest influence came not from the European packet trade, but from the conditions in one branch of the coastal packet trade. During this period, when cotton was king in the South, New Orleans was a major port for the shipping of cotton to the textile mills of New York and New England. However, the sandbars at the mouth of the Mississippi River had always proved an impediment to merchant shipping. As a result, a new kind of hull form developed, one that had a long, flat floor, enabling it to negotiate the shallow waters, rather than a V or U-shaped hull. While small vessels with this type of hull had previously been built for sailing in local waters, the flat-floored hull was always considered a working-class feature and not one that would enhance a vessel's speed capabilities. One such flat-floored packet ship on the New Orleans run was the *Huntsville*, which was owned by New York shipping magnate E.K. Collins and commanded in the early 1830s by Captain Nathaniel Palmer, a noted mariner of the day who would soon prove to be a major influence in the evolution of the clipper. While the voyage between New York and New Orleans normally took about 18 days, Palmer in his several runs in *Huntsville* cut this down to two weeks and thereby came to believe that the flat-floored hull design was a factor in his success. To that end, when Collins decided to establish his own line of Liverpool packets, the Dramatic Line, and chose Palmer to help design his ships, Captain Palmer chose to go with the long, flat-floored hull design. The ships *Garrick, Sheridan,* and *Siddons* (all named after famed actors of the day) were subsequently built in 1836 and 1837. All these ships were identical in design and measured 927 tons, while a fourth Dramatic liner, the *Roscius,* was built in 1839 and, at 1,009 tons, was the largest merchant ship built in America up to that time. All these ships were a smashing success; not only could they carry more cargo because of the flat floor, but they were quite speedy, their westward runs on the difficult route from Liverpool to New York averaging only 28 days versus the 40 day average of the famed Black Ball Line ships (Cutler, p. 96). Later on, by the 1840s, the flat floored hull would be combined with the sharp bow and lofty sail plans in many packets, features that the clippers of the 1850s would also embody, one of the most noted of these ships being the *Yorkshire*, a packet built by William Webb in 1843.

Finally, the packet trade was also important to the later-day clipper ship era because it was the proving ground for many future clipper ship commanders. Among the men that gained valuable experience in driving ships to the utmost performance in all kinds of conditions in this service that later served as clipper captains were Robert Waterman, John "Jack" Williams, Oliver Mumford, Asa Eldridge, and Nathaniel Palmer, to name just a few. These hard driving commanders carried sail in all weather conditions, in direct contrast to the sailing practices of old when most merchant captains would take in sail at night or during periods of heavy weather. Such practices were outdated now that regularly scheduled sailings were advertised and the quest for speed was ever greater.

The China Traders

America's trade with China and the Far East had a long tradition dating back to 1784 when the first merchant ships conducted such voyages from New York. Previously, during colonial times, China trade goods were brought to America, but usually via England due to the monopoly held on this business by the British East India Company. However, once independence was achieved, American merchants, slowly at first, began to finance these trading voyages and by 1800 the China trade was a substantial one. Ships plying the China trade routes had many variables to contend with, including monstrous storms and typhoons, periods of light weather, many uncharted reefs and small islands, as well as the pirates that operated from many of the small island groups in the Pacific and the China Sea. As a result, the early China trading vessels ran the gamut from large and full-built ships to small and fast schooners. Speed was required not only for protection, but also to get perishable goods to market quickly, as well as the overall desire of every merchant to get his goods to market first, thereby setting the price. It was a tradition for many years, as more and more packet ships were built, to send older packets into the China trade. Many of these made quite good runs home from China, but perhaps the most stunning was that made by Captain Robert Waterman in the old New Orleans packet *Natchez* (built way back in 1831), bringing her home to New York from Macao in 1845 in the "world beating time of 78 days" (Cutler, p. 114).

However, despite this remarkable achievement, due both to the old packet's hull plan and Captain Waterman's hard driving abilities, even before this run other, sharper ships with a greater amount of deadrise, were being built for the China trade in the early 1840s, influenced by the particular sailing circumstances that arose on that run. Among these notable ships were the *Helena* (1841) and the *Montauk* (1844), both of which were built at New York by William Webb. Though these vessels and others like them built during the 1840s were by no means true clippers, they were fast and bridged the gap between the sharp-built China clippers that would soon follow. Though New York builders led the way, Massachusetts was not without her contributions in this field; in Medford, the ship *Paul Jones* was launched in 1843 and made some fast passages under Captain Nathaniel Palmer. Among the subsequent pioneer clipper ships that were built for the China trade, all built at New York, were the *Houqua* (1844), *Rainbow* (1845), and *Sea Witch* (1846); the former was built by Brown & Bell, while the later ships were designed by John Griffiths, a pioneer marine architect who believed in the sharp bow form with a great amount of deadrise, and built by Smith & Dimon. That the *Sea Witch* was a true clipper is undisputed, though there is some debate among maritime historians as to the status of the former ships mentioned. Given the performances of *Houqua* and *Rainbow*, there should be no doubt that these ships too were true clippers. These ships will be discussed at greater length further on. In the late 1840s a number of other clippers intended for this trade would also be built, the most notable of which were the *Samuel Russell* (1847) and *Oriental* (1849), both built for the large China trading firm of A.A. Low & Brother of New York, and *Memnon* (1848), built by Smith & Dimon of New York and designed by John Griffiths. As can be seen from the above, New York was clearly the leader early on when it came to the building of the clipper ships for the China trade. Finally, the China trade, too, was noted for its many captains who would later become noted clipper ship commanders, among whom were the previously mentioned Robert Waterman and Nathaniel Palmer, as well as Josiah Cressy (commander of the *Oneida*), John Land (the original captain of *Rainbow*), and Freeman Hatch, again to name just a few. As with the packet trade the new breed of captains in the China trade were sail carriers in every sense of the word. We will hear more about these men later on.

The California Gold Rush of 1849

What may have happened with American ship design had the California gold rush never occurred is an interesting exercise in speculation. On one hand, the European packet ships were being built bigger and faster by the mid–1840s, while sharp built and ever larger clippers were already being built, as discussed above, for the China trade. With new growth in the China trade even further stimulated by changes in British trade laws that now allowed American ships to export tea, grain, and most any other product to England without restriction, the prospect for even faster ships was high. The sky may have seemed the limit to the American wooden ship-building industry, but this was in fact not the case; steamships were now being built that were increasing in size every year and the end of the merchant sailing ship, though not yet written in stone, was certainly looming on the horizon. While the state of Maine led the way in wooden shipbuilding as the decade of the 1850s approached (the state's output was nearly double that of second place New York), steamships were being built at New York in ever increasing numbers. Despite this advance, America was far behind Britain when it came to the development of the steamship; the Great Western Steamship Company operated a packet line between England and New York beginning in 1839, while in 1840 Boston became a stop on Samuel Cunard's British and North American Royal Mail Steam-Packet Company mail line that operated between Britain, Canada, and the United States. More importantly, this venture was subsidized by the British government with guaranteed yearly payments. Five years after Cunard established his steamship line, the American postal service in 1845 did the same, offering a contract for delivering mail on the New York–Bremen run, and four years after this offered a ten year subsidized mail contract for the New York–Liverpool route. By 1848, steamships were being built at a rapid rate in New York while the construction of sailing ships was starting to lag; in early 1848, just as gold was being discovered in California, New York had eleven steamships, some of them over 2,000 tons in size, under construction, but only one sailing ship (Cutler, p. 131). Indeed, prominent shipbuilders such as Smith & Dimon and William Webb, already famous for their notable sailing ships, were also building steamers,

The port of San Francisco before the California Gold Rush. Prior to 1849, only a few ships a month made an appearance at this unimportant seaport town (*The Illustrated London News*, 1851).

and not half-heartedly. Webb built his first steamship, a small ferryboat of under 200 tons, back in 1842, but in 1848 his yard was a busy one; he launched the 1,857 ton *United States,* his first oceangoing steamer, the 1,057 ton *California,* and the 1,139 ton *Panama* (a nearly identical vessel), both for the Pacific Mail Steamship Company (a third steamer for this line, the *Oregon,* was built by Smith & Dimon), as well as the steamers *Cherokee* and *Tennessee* for the New York & Savannah Steam Navigation Company.

Given this type of building activity, the evidence was probably clear to many in the shipping trade, merchants and builders at first to be sure, that the days of the merchant sailing ship had probably seen their peak by 1847 and were now on a slow but steady downward trend. However, a strange and wonderful thing happened on the road to the inevitable decline of the merchant sailing ship in favor of the steamship; on a January day in 1848, one John Marshall was working on building a lumber mill on the American River, north of Sacramento, California, for pioneer farmer John Sutter when he saw a glint of metal. Once tested, the sample of rock turned out to be gold, and while Sutter preferred to keep the discovery a secret, by March 1848 word of the discovery had gone public. News of the discovery spread initially on the West Coast at a steady rate and the first of the miners that came to the area to seek their fortune came from Oregon and Washington territory, as well as Hawaii and even Peru and Chile in South America. The first reports of the gold strike did not hit New York until August 1848, and it was not until December 1848 that President James Polk gave an address to Congress regarding the event. With news of the gold rush, the first in America, now having traveled worldwide, the rush was on to get to California with the hopes of striking it rich. During the subsequent years of the gold rush, which lasted from 1848 to 1855, about 300,000 people came to California from all corners of the world, 90,000 during the year 1849 alone, thus gaining the nickname "49'ers." Of these fortune seekers, half arrived via travel overland from the east on the California Trail, a journey fraught with danger due to varying weather conditions, harsh terrain, and sometimes attacks from the Native Americans whose territory they had to cross to get to California. The other half chose to go by sea, where two routes were used; the first was to take a sea voyage from an eastern port south to the Isthmus of Panama, where future miners disembarked and crossed overland via horse or mule to the Pacific side where they could then catch a ship to take them the rest of the way to the port of San Francisco, the jumping-off point for miners headed toward the Sacramento area. While the sea portion of this route was relatively easy, though not without the hazards and perilous possibilities of any such voyage, it was the crossing of the isthmus that was problematic; the trek through the jungle to get to the Pacific side was not an easy one and many "argonauts," as the travelers to California were called, succumbed to tropical diseases. The other alternative, which is where the clipper ships would soon make their mark, was to embark on a sailing ship at an eastern port and make the entire trip by sea via the Atlantic south to Cape Horn at the tip of South America, and after rounding the cape driving up the Pacific northward to San Francisco. This was a voyage along a route that measured about 18,000 miles and though it was one that was well-known to mariners, it was no sure or easy bet. The southern tip of the South American continent was a difficult and stormy place where the Atlantic and Pacific oceans meet with violent force, and the waters off Cape Horn were the final resting place for many a ship gone missing. Despite this difficult passage, countless miners were soon departing from ports all over the East Coast in vessels of all kinds, some of them newly-built, but many of them old or worn out ships that, though purchased at a high price due to the heavy demand by companies of miners, had no business trying to make such a voyage. The sea voyage around Cape Horn for the average tub could take anywhere from five to eight months, if they could make it all. However, once the clippers came on the scene, the voyage was cut down to as little as three months.

During the California gold rush it was the port of San Francisco that soon became the epicenter for the mining trade. This sleepy port town saw little shipping activity prior to 1848, maybe a few

The port of San Francisco in 1851. The Gold Rush changed everything for this formerly sleepy port. By 1850 thousands of ships were sailing for San Francisco every year, transforming the town into the most important city on the West Coast, its population rising from 1,000 in 1848 to over 25,000 by 1850 (*The Illustrated London News*, July 5, 1851).

ships a month, and only had about 200 residents in 1846. However, with the gold rush on, the port city had grown by leaps and bounds and in 1852 had a population of 36,000. In 1849 hundreds of ships arrived every month, many of them simply run ashore and abandoned by their crews in their hurry to get to the gold fields. However, while many men went to the gold fields, many others, men such as William T. Coleman (of whom we will hear more about later on), came to California to establish businesses to capitalize on the demand created by the mining industry. While the demand for nearly every commodity in these early days was very high, California itself could not supply these items as it had no manufacturing base, and very little, at least early on, in the way of agricultural activity that could support this sudden population influx. Thus it was that from the years 1849 to 1852 items from the East of every kind, from clothing and housewares to flour, liquor, and lumber were in high demand, and those who could supply them could make astronomical profits the likes of which had never been seen before. It truly was a boon economy, and it was the clipper ships that helped make it happen.

The First California Clippers

With the breaking of the news of the California gold rush on the East Coast, New York and New England shipbuilders lost no time in laying down fast sailing craft, but in the meantime many merchants diverted clippers

The whaling ship *Maria* of New Bedford. Ships like this, with its full modeled hull and apple-cheeked bow, were built for capacity and the requirements of their specific trades rather than speed (*Gleason's Pictorial Drawing Room Companion*).

previously built for the China trade. Indeed, of the first six clipper ships that made it to California in 1849, three of them, *Grey Eagle* (arriving in May, and the fastest of the year, 113 days), *Greyhound* (arriving in June, 116 days), and *Architect* (128 days), were all Baltimore-built (in 1847 and 1848) and well upheld the fast sailing traditions of the Chesapeake Bay area. The other clippers arriving in 1849 were the *Memnon* (122 days) from New York, the Donald McKay–built *Reindeer* (122 days, arrived in April) from Boston, and the first clipper to arrive in 1849, the aptly named *Argonaut* (March, 133 days), also out of Boston. Given her name, the Medford-built *Argonaut* was probably on the building ways when news of the gold rush reached the Boston area, but none of these ships were designed with the California run in mind. Of the eleven clippers that reached California in 1850, four (*Samuel Russell, Houqua, Sea Witch,* and *Memnon*) were designed for the China trade, while the remainder (*Celestial, Mandarin, White Squall, Seaman, Surprise, Sea Nymph,* and the bark *Race Horse*) were built for the California gold rush conditions. The *Celestial* was the first ship, built at New York by William Webb, designed specifically for the California run, but *Surprise* (96 days, 15 hours) and *Sea Witch* (97 days) made the fastest passages and set a high bar early on with their record performances. A relative few of the later clippers that were built would shave a week off this time, but no more. Most of these builders putting over clippers in 1850 and 1851 followed the hull forms of the pioneer China clippers like the *Rainbow*, and the even more sharply-built *Sea Witch*, but to the extreme, building ships with an even greater amount of deadrise and the sharp bow form. However, just as in times past, the form of the clipper, too, would evolve as conditions changed in the 1850s, albeit at a more rapid pace. How and in what form these changes took place will be discussed in the next chapter.

II

Challenge
The Design of a Clipper Ship

The ideas as to what characteristics made a clipper ship a clipper ship have been the subject of much discussion ever since the full development of this type of ship during the era of the California gold rush. For years now experts have debated and argued about which ships were clippers and which were not. Boston native Captain Arthur Clark, a mariner who knew some of these ships and their commanders quite well, in his later years wrote an excellent history of the clipper ship era that is fairly conservative, identifying fewer than 180 clipper ships built from 1850 to 1856. Maritime historian and author Carl Cutler lists over 249 clipper ships and barks built from 1850 to 1859, readily admitting that all were probably not true clipper ships, while historians Octavius Howe and Frederick Matthews identify 352 clippers built from 1833 to 1858 in their encyclopedic work. Marine architect and later-day historian Howard Chapelle is the most conservative of the clipper ship historians, citing the clipper ship era as lasting from 1845 to 1855. Because of a lack of plans, models, and other documentary evidence, he even goes so far as to question whether all of the so-called clippers built in 1850, in direct response to the California gold rush, were true clipper ships.

In fact, the question as to what defines a clipper ship is best approached in a dual fashion, from both a marine architecture (technical) viewpoint and a performance-based (practical experience) viewpoint. In defining a clipper ship in technical terms, vessels of this type, whether ship or bark-rigged, all had one characteristic in common, namely that of being deliberately designed with speed in mind, willfully sacrificing some cargo capacity to that end. Merchant ships had formerly sometimes been designed to carry as much cargo as possible with little regard for how long it took to get the cargo to its destination. American whaling ships were one type of merchant ship and were strictly working-class vessels that were stoutly built for the rigors of finding whales, killing them, and processing their carcasses for their bone, blubber, and oil while at sea. Their voyages were measured, not in weeks or months, but years. On the more glamorous end were the previously mentioned packet ships that operated in the north Atlantic between England and America, as well as the coastal packets that ran from northern ports such as New York to southern ports like New Orleans and Mobile. These ships sometimes made fast passages due to their hard driving captains and developing hull form but were built first and foremost as carriers. The first clipper ships, however, were built expressly for the purpose of getting their tea cargos home from China in quick order, and they were followed in a few short years by the extreme California clippers; getting their cargos to San Francisco as quickly as possible was the most important consideration. The amount of freight they carried was less of a concern, as ships like *White Squall* (New York), *Surprise* (Massachusetts), and *Seaman* (Maryland) sometimes paid for themselves, or came close to doing so, on their first cargo runs. Indeed, the *Surprise*, built by Samuel Hall of East Boston, loaded freight

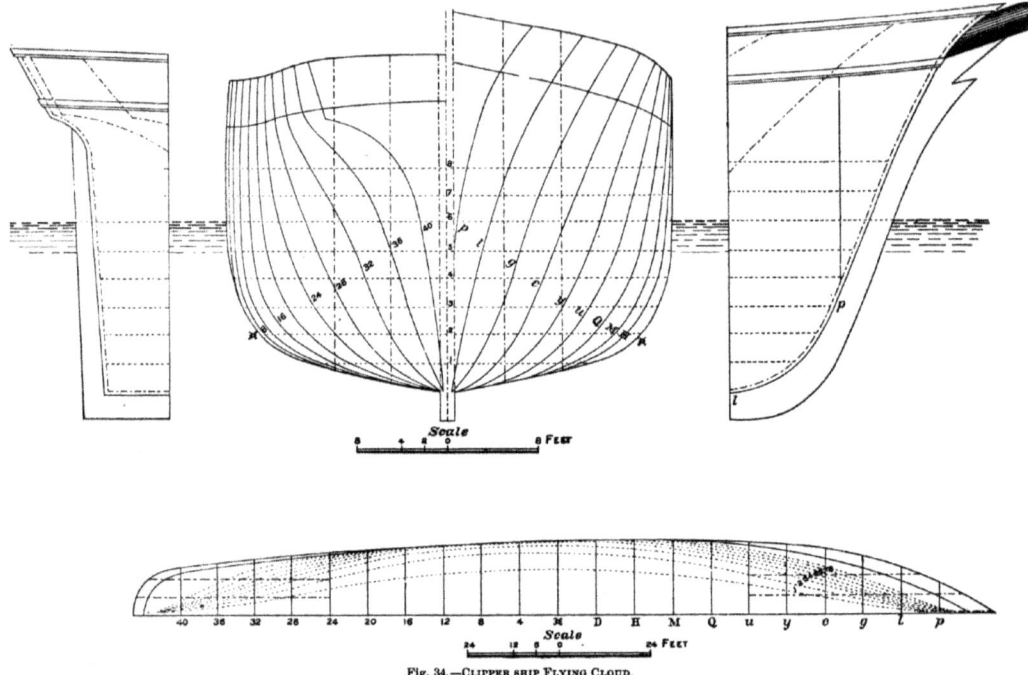

Fig. 34.—CLIPPER SHIP FLYING CLOUD.

Hull line drawings of the *Flying Cloud*. These drawings illustrate the sharp hull forms used by the early California clippers and, as seen at upper right, the great amount of deadrise they employed (Henry Hall's *Report on the Ship-Building Industry of the United States*, 1885).

valued at nearly $80,000 on her first California voyage, and subsequently cleared a $50,000 profit above and beyond her building costs on her first roundtrip voyage from New York to San Francisco, and from thence to Hong Kong and home to New York via London. As the old saying goes, time *was* money in the early clipper ship days. The extreme clipper ship type was built for a few years before more moderate business practices prevailed once again and subsequent versions of the clipper ships, termed medium and half clippers, combined both speed and cargo carrying capacity.

Beyond sacrificing cargo capacity for speed, the characteristics of the clipper ships varied when it came to their hull form. The clipper ship was distinguished by its bow portion being considerably lengthened and very much sharpened and hollowed above the waterline. Previously, merchant ships were traditionally bluff bowed (sometimes called "apple-cheeked") with a rounded or bulging form designed more for floating on the waves and pushing the seas aside while making their way rather than slicing through the water like the clipper ships did. These earlier ships were often designed to resemble a fish in form, having a rounded bow (the head of the cod fish), a wide midsection (the body of a fish) that enabled the vessel to carry a large cargo, and tapering aft toward the stern (the tail of a mackerel). While this form worked well for nature's sea creatures that live *under* water, it was not the best, in terms of speed, for ships making their way on the surface of the world's seas.

Not only did the clippers have sharp bow sections, but their hulls were the subject of great debate and experimentation during the clipper ship era, often being widest not at their midsection, as in the merchant ships of the days of old, but just aft of their midsections. As to form, the hulls of the early extreme clippers followed previous marine traditions that held that in order for a ship to be speedy its bottom had to be V shaped. This resulted in a great amount of deadrise; usually measured in inches, this is a measurement of the angle that the bottom of a vessel rises to meet the side (in modern terminology *chine*) of the ship. Clipper ships such as the New Jersey–built *Hurricane*, with 40 inches of deadrise, and William Webb's *Flying Dutchman*, with 36 inches, were extreme models that, though usually fast, were limited economically. This narrow bottomed configuration lessened a ship's cargo carrying capacity and had been traditionally used only in those vessels where speed was the overriding concern, including naval frigates, and the vastly smaller pilot boats and pleasure yachts. However, by 1854 the fad for extreme clippers was done and many subsequent clipper ships were flat floored, highlighting a change in ideas that, while employed in colonial era ships, were revived in the 1830s, led in part by Captain Nathaniel Palmer, with ships in the packet service, where speed and carrying capacity were both important. The lines of the clipper ships, especially the later medium and half-clipper varieties launched after the California trade became more competitive, combined the best of these two hull types, the sharp bow and the flat floor, to create a class of ships that were both speedy and good cargo carriers. Many later clipper ships were built with less than twenty or even as little as ten inches of deadrise; J.O. Curtis's Medford-built *Ocean Express* had 14 inches of deadrise, and the Briggs brothers of South Boston built the *Alarm* with 12 inches, making both of them good carriers, while George Thomas up in Rockland, Maine, built the *Defiance* with ten inches of deadrise. The consistently fastest clipper ship on record, Donald McKay's famed *Flying Cloud*, had 30 inches of deadrise, but the clipper ship that holds the all-time record for the passage between New York and San Francisco, the *Andrew Jackson*, was but a medium clipper with a much flatter-floored hull model. While full specifications for the *Jackson* are unavailable, her deadrise was probably at least half of that of the *Flying Cloud*, if not a little less.

It is at this point that the system for measuring the size of a clipper ship (and all ships, whether sail or steam) should be discussed, as they have a direct correlation to the issues of hull type and

The bark *Moses Kimball*. This so-called half-clipper, built by Columbus Carter at Belfast, Maine, in 1853, is illustrative of the many forgotten smaller clippers that employed the economical bark rig (***Gleason's Pictorial Drawing-Room Companion***, 1853).

deadrise just detailed. The cargo carrying capacity of a ship (not the weight of the ship itself) is measured in terms of tonnage. This system of measurement began in England during the Middle Ages, established for purposes of assessing a tax on those ships in the cargo carrying business and was based on how many tuns, or casks of wine, could be carried by a given ship. Furthermore, since a tun was a standard shipping unit (each holding 252 gallons of wine and weighing 2,240 pounds), the cargo carrying capacity of a ship could be measured. This was the derivation of the idea of tonnage measurement, but this changed drastically over the centuries as cargos changed. In the 1720s in England what is now called the builder's Old Measurement (OM) rule came into common use (but not put into law until 1773), whereby a ship's cargo capacity was measured on a mathematical formula that was based on the length of a ship's keel and her maximum breadth (width to a landlubber). While this was the tonnage formula that was used by American shipbuilders until well into the 1850s, in England a new system, the Moorsom System, was adopted in 1849. This system for measuring tonnage was adopted due to the advent of the steamship, and was an important change because it calculated the actual internal carrying volume of any given ship, making allowances for subtracting the volume of non-revenue generating space that was required for such things as a ship's boiler system and the coal that was carried to operate it. While this new and much more accurate system for measuring tonnage (put into law in England in 1854) was uniquely suited for measuring steamships (again, as always, for taxing purposes), it was also applied to many American clipper ships, mainly those sold foreign in the late 1850s and beyond. Thus it is that in the life histories of many clipper ships we find designated their cargo carrying capacity in two figures, "old" and "new" measurement. The differences in these, once understood, are quite revealing and show just how sharply built some of the earliest clippers really were. Here are a few examples of how the clipper ships fared under the two tonnage systems. The Massachusetts-built *Archer* (1852) was an average clipper of 1,095 tons old and 905 tons new measurement, a 17 percent difference in actual carrying capacity; the McKay-built *Flying Cloud* (1851) was an extreme clipper of 1,782 tons old but 1,139 tons new measurement, a 36 percent difference; and finally, the Newburyport-built *War Hawk* (1855) was a medium clipper of 1,067 old and 1,015 new measurement, a 5 percent difference. As can clearly be seen, once their carrying capacity was more accurately measured in the modern system, all clippers suffered a reduction of some sort, with the medium clippers faring much better. With this in mind, the case can be made that all clipper ships sacrificed some cargo capacity for speed, but to a widely varying degree and a correspondingly lesser or greater economic impact. For consistency's sake, as well as the fact that new measurements are not available for all the clippers discussed herein, all tonnage measurements given for clippers under discussion are of the old type unless otherwise indicated.

The clipper ships of all types were also distinguished by their stern sections as well; while older merchant vessels typically had square shaped sterns, the fine lines of the clipper ships usually terminated in a stern section that was more rounded or elliptical in form (referred to in technical terms as a *counter stern*), possibly with the idea that it created less drag and water resistance, though as one historian states, "According to sailing records none of the configurations had a significant effect on the sailing ability or performance of the vessels" (Crothers, p. 43). This change first came about in naval vessels in the early 1800s but was not used in merchant ships until the 1840s and was such a striking and graceful change from the boxy end form of ships from an earlier generation that these curved forms were often called a "champagne glass" stern because of its strong resemblance to that fine type of glassware. Once again, however, though the elliptical form predominated in the clipper ship era, many clippers were built using the more traditional square form, among them the long-lived *Dashing Wave*, built at Portsmouth, New Hampshire, the unlucky and short-lived *Flying Arrow*, built at Frankfurt, Maine, and the New York–built *Black Hawk*.

Finally, the clipper ships were also well-noted for their sail configurations. Indeed, the striking

II. Challenge: *The Design of a Clipper Ship* 21

Sail plan of the *Sovereign of the Seas*. This Donald McKay–built Boston clipper, like most of his productions, was loftily sparred. The primary sails of the heavily canvassed clippers were named as follows: A. Spanker sail B. Mizzen course C. Mizzen topsail D. Mizzen topgallant E. Mizzen royal F. Main course G. Main topsail H. Main topgallant I. Main royal J. Main skysail K. Fore course L. Fore topsail M. Fore topgallant N. Fore royal O.-P.-Q. Flying jibs (Hall's *Report on the Ship-Building Industry of the United States*, 1885, with additions by the author).

appearance of the clipper ship under sail epitomized to many, both in their own time and down to our modern age, the ideal form of a sailing ship. Typically referred to as "heavily sparred," nearly all clippers were ship rigged, that is to say that they were equipped with square sails on all three masts. Only one clipper ship, the giant *Great Republic* built in 1853, had four masts. There also was a second type of clipper ship that was built in the late 1840s and 1850s, the clipper bark (also sometimes spelled "barque"). These also were three-masted vessels, but with square sails on the fore and main masts, while the mizzen mast carried a lateen sail. These clipper barks were much smaller (generally less than 400 tons), yet were also, for their size, heavily sparred. The masts of the clipper ships towered in size and carried a large amount of "canvas" (sails), more than any other merchant sailing ship designed before or since. Because the center of gravity of the clippers was further aft, the mast placement differed than was traditionally the case in earlier generations of square-rigged ships, with the foremast no longer placed in the extreme bow of the ship, the main mast placed just aft of the middle portion of the hull, and the mizzen mast correspondingly placed further aft. This configuration gave the clipper ships a very beautiful and rakish look whose appearance alone held out great promise in terms of speed. The sail plans of the clippers were necessarily large as wind was the engine that drove them; the clipper *Sweepstakes*, built by the Westervelts in New York in 1853, carried nearly 13,000 yards of sail, a large spread but one that was exceeded by other clippers. To that end, each mast on a clipper generally carried four or five tiers of sails, and sometimes a sixth, under peak performance conditions, while older and smaller traditional square riggers utilized only two or three sails per mast depending on their size. The sails carried were larger at the lower tier and decreased in size the higher up the mast they were located. For example, the sails on the mainmast were termed, from bottom to top, the mainsail, the main topsail, the main topgallant, the main royal, and, if so equipped, the main skysail. Many clippers crossed skysail yards, as it were, on all three masts, giving them a lofty sail plan, but not all did so; the Portsmouth-built *Noonday* had only one skysail, that on her mainmast, while the Medford-built *Queen of the Seas* and the Newburyport-built *Racer* had no skysails or, in nautical terminology, "had no flying kites" (Howe & Matthews, p. 494). However, the clippers sometimes went even a step further, having an additional smaller set of sails aloft that were given the very descriptive name of moonsails. A mate on the clipper *John Stuart*, built in New York in 1851, later described his clipper's model and "said that above the sky-sail she carried a main moonsail and above that, consecutively, a cloud-cleaner, a stargazer, a sky-scraper and an angel's footstool, the latter however, being set only in dead calms, when the watch on deck were not allowed to cough or sneeze for fear of carrying it away" (Howe and Matthews, pg. 317). Despite this humorous bit of sailor hyperbole, some clippers did indeed carry a moonsail above the skysail, although they were seldom employed in most clippers and soon proved impractical. Among the clippers so equipped with moonsails was the Portland, Maine–built *Phoenix*, which carried such sails on both her main and fore masts. Clippers, however, did have yet another set of sails to give them added speed, the studding sails. These were rigged on booms that extended from the yardarms, most often from the main or fore masts and as high up as the royals. These sails, when in place, projected over the sides of the ship, giving the clipper under full sail the appearance of a bird on the wing. Studding sails, which were used on ships before the clipper ship era, were generally used under extended ideal weather conditions because they were difficult to set, and even more difficult to take down in stormy weather. Finally, there were also additional smaller sails used on clippers, as with most other square-rigged

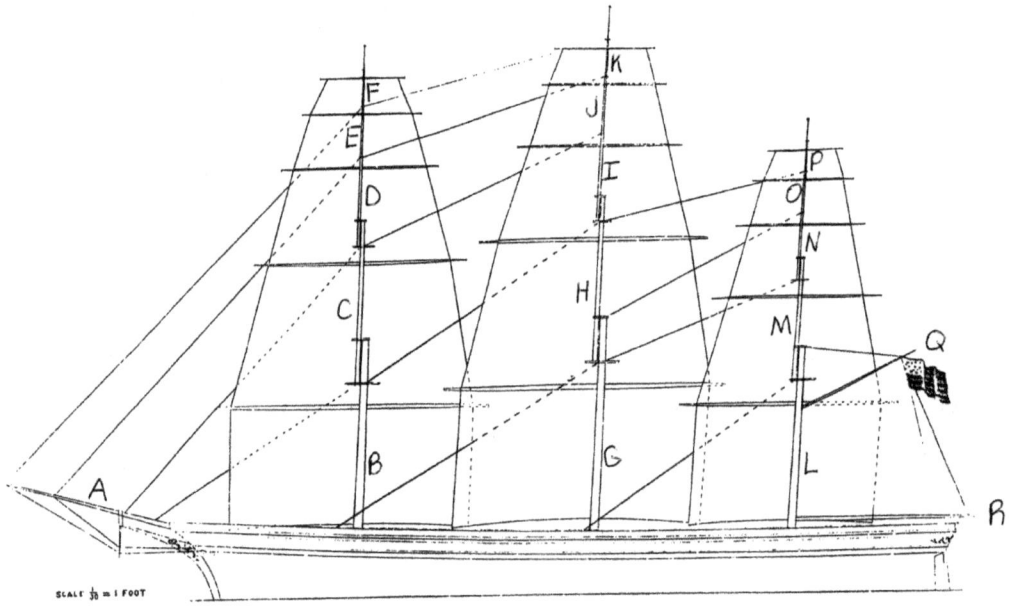

Spar plan of the *Lightning*. The masts and spars that supported the sails of a clipper ship consisted of many components, the most common being as follows: A. Bowsprit B. Foremast C. Fore topmast D. Fore topgallant mast E. Fore royal mast F. Fore skysail mast G. Mainmast H. Main topmast I. Main topgallant mast J. Main royal mast K. Main skysail mast L. Mizzen mast M. Mizzen topmast N. Mizzen topgallant mast O. Mizzen royal mast P. Mizzen skysail mast Q. Spanker gaff R. Spanker boom (diagram from John Griffiths' *Monthly Nautical Magazine* 3, 1855, with additions by the author).

ships of the day. These included the jibs, often called a flying jib, which was a single sail or series of sails carried forward of the foremast that were rigged to the bowsprit; the staysails, which were triangular shaped sails rigged in between the main and fore masts and the main and mizzen masts; and, finally, the spanker sail, either singly or a pair (upper and lower) aft of the mizzenmast. All of these sails in combination were intended to capture even the slightest wind available to send a clipper on her way. During the 1850s there were many improvements and innovations in how a ship's sails, especially the topsails, were handled or configured so that they could be managed with less manpower and greater efficiency and safety. These include Cunningham's roller reefing (the term used for gathering in sail, usually during severe weather) or self-reefing topsails, the Forbes double-topsail rig (which divided the topsail into an upper and lower sail for easier handling), and Howe's Patent Rig, also a double topsail system. One or more of these systems were used on a large number of clippers and especially gained in popularity toward the end of the 1850s when ships were forced to operate on leaner budgets with less manpower.

No matter how they were configured, the large sail plan and heavy spars of the clipper ships were instrumental in enabling them to make fast passages, but they were sometimes problematic; early clippers often suffered great damage to their spars and sails both due to heavy weather conditions, as well as design flaws and inferior materials, and otherwise speedy voyages to California were delayed when captains were forced either to heave to and make repairs at sea or, even worse, put into such foreign ports as Rio de Janeiro (Brazil), Montevideo (Uruguay), or Port Stanley (the Falkland Islands) to seek repair options which were expensive and time consuming. Interestingly, of the first group of thirteen California clippers built in 1850, six of them, the *Game Cock* (Boston), *John Bertram* (Boston), *Sea Serpent* (Portsmouth, NH), *Stag Hound* (Boston), *White Squall* (New York), and *Witchcraft* (Chelsea, MA) suffered severely damaged masts and spars during their maiden voyages to California. The *John Bertram* had difficulties that forced her to put into Valparaiso, Chile, for repairs that took seventeen days, while *Witchcraft* had to put in at Rio de Janeiro. Often these spar problems were due to heavy weather; the *Sea Serpent* was battered by storms for two weeks off Cape Horn that resulted in damaged spars and split sails, but this was not always the case. *White Squall* lost all three topgallant masts within 50 hours of departing from New York on her maiden voyage, while *Stag Hound* had her main topmast broken within six days of departure, which also carried away the clipper's three topgallant masts in their fall. Luckily, *Stag Hound* carried extra spars that allowed her to make repairs at sea. The damage incurred on both these clippers may have been the result of poor or hasty workmanship, or the use of wooden material that was not durable enough, but soon enough clipper ship builders realized that these hard-driven ships needed stout timbers to do the job. However, these vast sail plans were very much in doubt at the beginning of the clipper ship era, even by those well-versed in maritime matters; in speaking about the *Stag Hound*, one marine underwriter remarked to Captain Josiah Richardson prior to the maiden voyage that "I should think you would be somewhat nervous in going so long a voyage in so sharp a ship, so heavily sparred" (Howe and Matthews, v.2, pg. 615).

The Evolution of Clipper Ship Design

Bringing a clipper to life, from an idea in the mind of the shipbuilder to a reality on the building ways, was a process that involved many steps, the first being the conception of a hull form. In colonial days ships were built by rule of thumb, much the same as were houses, barns, and wooden bridges; though the form a shipbuilder had in mind may have been roughly sketched out or perhaps a rough model was whittled out of a scrap of wood, there were no formal methods used to design a ship. However, this changed in 1794 (some accounts state 1796) when young Orlando Merrill, the son of shipbuilder James Merrill of Newburyport, Massachusetts, invented the lift model. He

Half-hull model of the *Spitfire*. This speedy clipper was designed by Samuel Pook and built by Captain James Arey at Frankfurt, Maine. This hull model was likely retained by her Boston owners and their descendants for many years and has only recently come to light (courtesy Penobscot Marine Museum, Searsport, Maine).

was helping his father build ships by at least 1784 and later became a noted regional shipbuilder in his own right, probably best known for co-building the U.S. Navy's 509-ton sloop-of-war *Wasp* at his yard with William Cross in 1813. The type of model developed by Merrill was no small affair, but was built to scale, measuring almost two feet long for the smaller tonnage ships built in the early 1800s and, most importantly, was segmented in form, with the individual model layers held together by dowel rods or screws. By taking the model apart, the hull form of a proposed vessel could be measured at any number of points on the waterline. From this model, then, the lines of the hull form of a ship from keel to deck could be drafted and converted into templates from which full sized ship components were formed. This type of model became commonly used in New England shipyards, but was not used by New York shipbuilders until many years later; the first such model in New York was probably crafted before 1820 by apprentice Stephen Smith, later a partner in the shipbuilding firm Smith & Dimon, the first shipyard in the country to build a clipper ship (Dunbaugh and Thomas, pg. 23). By the time of the clipper ship era, lift models ranged from about four to six feet in length, depending on the size of the clipper being built. Interestingly, there are a number of folk stories from the clipper ship era regarding these models, including one for the *Houqua* whose model was said to have been whittled by Captain Nathaniel Palmer while he was sailing as a passenger, and one carved by a young boy that was the son of a Maine shipbuilder that later inspired the building of the downeast clipper named, appropriately enough, the *Young Mechanic*. Some historians question the veracity of these stories because of the fact that accurate lines for a clipper could not have been drawn from a small, crudely carved model, which is certainly true. However, just as many great inventions over the years were first conceived in the mind of a dreamer, so too is it plausible that the spark of an idea for any number of clippers may indeed have come from the random whittlings of a sailor passing the time at sea or a boy following in his father's footsteps. Whatever the circumstances surrounding their creation, and despite their common usage, relatively few of these models have survived. Those that have, including a number from clippers built in Portsmouth, Boston, and New York, clearly illustrate how they were instrumental in the ship designing process. One reason that few of these models have survived is that they were often kept by builders and used multiple times if the design was a good one. Like other skilled mechanics of the day, shipwrights usually kept their best designs to themselves, so the half-hull models were seldom made public. Despite their beautiful form, even after the age of sail was at an end few of these half-hull models survived; when shipyards closed, many of their models were simply discarded, considered outdated tools of a dying trade. Those that did survive the closure of a shipyard were seldom recognized for their potential historical value; after the great clipper ship builder Donald McKay retired and moved to a farm in Hamilton, Massachusetts, the half-hull models he kept were stored in a barn, most of them later chopped up and used for firewood in the years after his death!

While these technical models, and in rare cases, line drawings, were employed to plan the lines of a proposed clipper ship, what about the men behind these ideas? In the late 1830s and 1840s there were no formal schools to learn the trade of shipbuilding and design and, indeed, there were no trained marine architects because the profession did not yet exist. Instead, young men in their teens (usually beginning at age 15) learned the trade by becoming an apprentice at a local shipyard. In return for being taught the secrets of the shipbuilding trade by an experienced builder, the apprentice signed a contract agreeing to serve his master for a fixed number of years, usually terminating by the age of twenty-one. The contract stipulated a weekly pay the apprentice would receive for working, on average, a twelve hour day; in New York in the 1830s this averaged about $2.50 a week. The apprentice also either received room and board and had his meals provided for, or in lieu of this was paid a yearly stipend to cover these expenses. The work performed by the apprentice was demanding and encompassed all aspects of the shipwright's trade; one day he might work in the mold loft, where the templates for a ship's components were drawn, another day he might work sawing the heavy timbers for the ship, and on yet another he might be employed as a caulker helping to seal the seams of a ship with oakum and hot tar. In short, the apprentice learned his prospective craft by working and mastering all aspects of the trade, no matter how much dirt or drudgery was involved!

While there were no naval architecture schools before the era of the clipper ship, the 1830s and 1840s were a crucial time that marked the beginning of the scientific development of design theories and burgeoning use of mathematical formulas as they applied to ship building and how a ship might move through the water in the most efficient manner possible. These scientific advances regarding sailing vessels corresponded with other advances in the transportation field taking place at the same time, including the development of the steamship at sea and the railroad ashore, as well as the pioneering work done by naval officer Matthew F. Maury in mapping and better understanding how the world's wind and ocean current systems operated. Though no one individual invented the clipper ship, five men that stand out for their influence in developing these fast ships in all their varied forms are John Griffiths, Nathaniel B. Palmer, William Webb, Donald McKay, and Samuel H. Pook. All of these men were noted ship builders or designers and are today synonymous with the clipper ship era. Three of them started their careers in New York; it has often been written, and rightly so, that the shipyard of Isaac Webb in that city, established in 1818, was the cradle of the great clipper ship builders. Here it was that Webb trained his son, William H. Webb, in the art of shipbuilding. William Webb would later become the most versatile and successful shipbuilder of his time. Isaac Webb also employed as apprentices another New Yorker, John Griffiths, in the 1820s and Nova Scotian Donald McKay in the 1830s, giving both men a sound foundation for their future shipbuilding activities in New York and Massachusetts. Captain Nathaniel B. Palmer was an experienced mariner from Connecticut who was influential in the building of the first clipper ships of the 1840s in the China trade based on his vast reservoir of seafaring knowledge, while Samuel H. Pook, the youngest of this group of important men, was a native New Yorker who grew up in New England. He was the namesake son of a prominent builder for the U.S. Navy and by 1851 was the nation's first independent marine architect. The clipper ships advocated for, designed, and built by these men are among those vessels that are considered the finest and fastest sailing ships ever built in America. What follows is a brief biography of each of these men.

John Willis Griffiths

Griffiths was born in New York City in 1809, the son of shipwright John Griffiths. At which shipyard the elder Griffiths was employed is uncertain, but he may have worked at one time in the yard of Charles Brownne when the historic vessel *North River Steam Boat* (often mistakenly referred to as the *Clermont*) was launched in 1807. By the mid–1820s the younger Griffiths was following in his father's footsteps, serving as an apprentice to Isaac Webb. Upon learning the shipbuilding trade, Griffiths sought his fortune in the South, going to work at the Gosport (Norfolk) Naval Shipyard in Virginia, where he was employed during the 1830s. In 1831 and 1832 he began working on the navy's project to rebuild the frigate *Macedonian*, tasked with drawing the lines of the new vessel. While in Virginia he also began to publicize his own theories on naval architecture through a series of newspaper articles. Griffiths returned to New York by 1840 and worked as a draftsman for the Smith & Dimon shipyard. He was also active in exploring the latest advances in marine engineering of the day, building his own testing tank to replicate the experiments of the Englishman Mark Beaufoy regarding the resistance of objects as they moved through water. In 1841 Griffiths exhibited a half-model with a sharper bow design than was the norm at the time at the American Institute in New York, and "as a result of the arguments over his model, Griffiths gave a series of lectures in the American Institute on the science of ship design and construction. These lectures were the first held in the United States dealing with naval architecture" (Chapelle, pgs. 322–23). The fact that John Griffiths was both passionate about ship design theory and somewhat eccentric was recognized by his contemporaries, but there is no question that his designs had real merit. In 1843 his model attracted the attention of the New York mercantile firm of Howland & Aspinwall and they subsequently contracted with Smith & Dimon to build them a ship on Griffiths' design for use in the China tea trade. The ship that was eventually built and launched in 1845 after nearly two years of delay was named *Rainbow* and is considered by many historians the first true clipper ship to be built. As the 757-ton *Rainbow* gained its form on the building ways, it was said to be the subject of much comment on the waterfront by experienced sailors; while *Rainbow* was a medium clipper compared to the later, much sharper extreme clippers that were built beginning in 1850, many thought that her sharp and hollow lines forward would cause her to dive to the bottom of the sea on her maiden voyage. Was the form of *Rainbow* really that revolutionary? Yes and no; while her sharp form had been previously used on much smaller yachts and pilot boats, it had never been employed in a large merchant ship designed to make long-distance voyages to China and back. Griffith's design for *Rainbow* was said to have been inspired by one of Howland & Aspinwall's previous vessels, the Baltimore-built *Ann McKim*, which is a ship sometimes cited by maritime enthusiasts as the first true clipper. However, a comparison of the hull plans for both vessels shows that the *Ann McKim*, while a speedy ship, was not near as sharply-built as *Rainbow*. Though Griffiths' patrons seemed to have second thoughts about the design of *Rainbow* and delayed her completion for a time while they sought foreign advice on the placement of her masts (which advice was never followed by Griffiths and Smith & Dimon), they were not to be disappointed in their investment. While the ship was nearly lost by her hard-driving commander, Captain John Land, just four days out of New York on *Rainbow*'s maiden voyage due to being over-sparred, the round-trip voyage to China and back was made in the then record time of seven months and seventeen days. Howland & Aspinwall were hooked and soon ordered another ship designed by John Griffiths and built by Smith & Dimon. Had Griffiths designed the *Rainbow* alone, his place in the history of marine architecture would still have been well secured, but he was not done yet; with his next production, the 907-ton *Sea Witch* in 1846, he gained immortal status. While *Rainbow*'s classification as a true clipper is in dispute, there are no such doubts about *Sea Witch*. This loftily-sparred and beautiful ship shattered the record for a voyage from China to New York, making the trip in just 77 days, and in early 1850 set the standard for the voyage from New York to San Francisco, making the trip in the then record time of 101 days. She was, in the popular phrase of the day, an *out and out* clipper.

Following the design of *Rainbow* and *Sea Witch*, John Griffiths would design no more clippers directly, but influenced many a shipbuilder during the era. From 1847 to 1849 he presided over his own marine architecture school, and in 1850 his important work *Treatise on Marine and Naval Architecture or Theory and Practice Blended in Ship Building* was first published, with a fourth edition in print by 1854. While some have criticized the sometimes florid prose in this otherwise technical work, it is nonetheless indicative of Griffiths' enthusiasm for his subject. He followed up these works with other practical guides for shipbuilders, including *The Ship-Builder's Manual* (1853) and *The Progressive Ship-Builder* (1875–76). He also was a co-owner and editor of the short-lived *Nautical Magazine* from 1856 to 1858, one of the few public forums for the shipbuilding profession during the clipper ship era and one that published many ship plans and offered commentary on recently built vessels. Griffiths later edited the weekly journal *American Ship* in New York from 1879 to 1882. Though he may not have been designing clipper ships after finishing *Sea Witch* (though he did design one clipper, name unknown, for German owners), Griffiths' publications were important; they were the only technical ones of their kind and were an excellent resource for builders when it came to current theories and shipbuilding practices and techniques. Despite his continued work in advancing wooden shipbuilding, John Griffiths was also mindful of the future and was active in steamship design and construction, building for the U.S. Navy the screw-sloop USS *Enterprise* in 1874 and patenting a number of steamship improvements in his later years. He died in Brooklyn, New York, in 1882 having outlived the historic clippers he designed by many years.

Captain Nathaniel B. Palmer

Palmer is somewhat unique among the clipper ship pioneers, for he was the only one of the five men here discussed who had extensive seafaring experience. What Palmer learned in the practical areas of ship handling and business operations over many years he later used quite successfully when it came to formulating the ideals of that perfect ship that combined speed and carrying capacity. It is significant that he is only one of three clipper ship captains that had a clipper ship named in his honor (the others were the *Rainbow* skipper, John Land, and Asa Eldridge of the *Red Jacket*) and at the same time one of only two clipper ship designers (along with Donald McKay) to be so honored.

Nathaniel B. Palmer was born in the seaport town of Stonington, Connecticut, in 1799, the son of a shipbuilder. The Palmer shipyard built small ships, sloops and schooners, and from a young age Nathaniel had a chance to observe the building process; one biographer states quite succinctly that "he began to absorb a knowledge of hulls and spars before he went to school to learn his letters" (Spears, pg. 2). Despite his father's trade, Palmer went to sea at the age of fifteen in 1814, sailing on a coaster between New York and Portland, Maine. While details are lacking, he clearly was a quick study and by the age of eighteen was master of the schooner *Galena*. With a solid reputation as a sailor, he was subsequently offered a job as second mate aboard the sealing ship *Hersilia*, departing Stonington in July 1819 to take part in a privately financed expedition to explore the waters around Cape Horn and find new hunting grounds. Gaining experience as an officer, Palmer made a subsequent voyage in 1820 to 1821, this time as master of the small, 44-ton schooner *Hero*, which served as a supply tender to the *Hersilia* and other vessels in the expedition. It was on this trip that Palmer explored the Antarctic coast, discovering new lands that were subsequently named Palmerland in his honor. He would make yet another exploring and sealing voyage to the Antarctic as master of the sloop *James Monroe* and, despite his youth, was undoubtedly a sailor of the highest skill. Palmer continued his shipping activities as captain, returning to the Antarctic in a private expedition organized and financed by Jeremiah Reynolds in 1830 and 1831 as skipper of the *Annawan*.

Upon his return home, Captain Nathaniel Palmer was hired by the Collins Line of packets, sailing between New York and New Orleans as captain of the ship *Huntsville*. This was a vast change in stature for Palmer, as the packet captains of the 1830s were among the most renowned and best paid masters in the merchant service. When owner E. K. Collins gave thought to opening a packet line between New York and Liverpool, England, he sent Palmer to England and, upon receiving his report, made a decision in the affirmative. The first four ships in Collins' Dramatic Line, all named after famous actors of the day, were the *Garrick, Sheridan, Siddons,* and *Roscius*. All of these ships were built at the Brown and Bell shipyard in New York from 1836 to 1839, all were designed by Palmer, and all were commanded by him on their maiden voyages. As historian Carl Cutler states, these ships, with their long and flat-floored hull models, "may be taken to mark the period which definitely separated the old packet service from the new" (Cutler, pg. 98). In the later clipper ship era, as previously discussed, it was the flat-floored carrier that would eventually come to prevail.

Captain Palmer, due to health concerns, took a hiatus from commanding ships for Collins in 1839, but returned in 1840 to make a fast westward passage in *Siddons* before leaving the packet service for good. In 1843 he took command of the Boston-owned China trader *Paul Jones*, a newly-built vessel. While homeward bound from China he carried as a passenger one William Low, of the New York firm of A.A. Low and Brothers, a company involved in the China tea trade. William Low was also part of the mercantile firm of Russell and Company in Hong Kong, and during the voyage home Low and Palmer talked about the China trade, the type of ship that would be best suited for the trade, and the possibility of partnering up on such a project. Upon arriving back in New York in October 1843, Palmer met the head of the firm, A.A. Low, and was subsequently given the authorization to contract for a ship. The ship that was subsequently built by the firm of Brown & Bell in 1844, modeled by Palmer, was the *Houqua* and is considered by many, including Palmer's contemporary John W. Griffiths, the first clipper ship ever built. While other marine historians categorize *Houqua* as more of a proto-clipper, it is clear that this handsome and speedy ship was an early influence in the building of clipper ships for the tea trade that preceded the California clippers. The history behind this clipper's early days, however, are something of a mystery; though designed by Palmer, the 581-ton ship was originally built not as a merchant ship, but as a warship to be sold to the Chinese government, and had eight gun ports on each side. When *Houqua*, named after a prominent Hong merchant in Canton, was deemed to be too small to serve as a warship by the Chinese, A.A. Low retained ownership and employed the ship in the China trade for many years. Palmer commanded the fast and successful clipper on its first voyage and was succeeded in turn by his brothers Alexander and Theodore.

Nathaniel Brown Palmer (1799–1877). This outstanding mariner hailed from Stonington, Connecticut, and was a leading figure in the development of the clipper ships. Not only did he design several early clippers, he was also a clipper commander and had one clipper named in his honor (photograph from John Spears' *Captain Nathaniel Brown Palmer: An Old-time Sailor of the Sea,* **1922).**

II. Challenge: *The Design of a Clipper Ship*

Following the building of *Houqua*, Nathaniel Palmer superintended the subsequent building of the next clippers for the Low fleet, the *Samuel Russell* in 1847 and the *Oriental* in 1849, commanding both ships as well on their maiden voyages. Both were similar in design to *Houqua*, but on a larger scale. The *Oriental* was an influential ship in that she was the first American clipper to be seen in England; arriving there in late 1850 with 1,600 tons of tea from China, the beautiful ship was thronged by visitors hoping to get a glimpse of her and her lines were even taken off by Admiralty surveyors while in drydock. The Lows would build other, bigger and more extreme clippers to add to their fleet, including the *N.B. Palmer*, *Contest*, and *David Brown*, but it is unknown to what extent, if any, Palmer was involved in their design. While one biographer claims Palmer designed these notable ships, it is more likely that he superintended their building on behalf of the Lows. No matter what his involvement may have been in designing these later clippers, Palmer's influence as a designer of the early clippers is indisputable, yet sometimes forgotten. He is even connected to that most famous of clipper ship builders, Donald McKay, in a significant way. Once McKay had built the largest clipper ship ever built (also the largest merchant ship in the world), the 4,555 ton *Great Republic*, he had her towed to New York to load her first cargo for Liverpool in late 1853. However, on the day after Christmas, a large fire broke in the waterfront district of New York, where ashes and cinders from the fire were carried by a strong wind to the wharf where the *Great Republic* was loading. In these days of sail, a ship's rigging was tarred to give it weather protection, but it also made the ship highly flammable; the rigging of the great clipper subsequently caught fire and quickly spread throughout the ship. Though efforts were made to save the ship, including scuttling the ship at its moorings, the *Great Republic* was burned to the waterline, resulting in a huge loss to McKay, who owned the ship and had it under-insured. The wreck was subsequently bought as was by Nathaniel Palmer, acting on behalf of but without prior

The clipper *Oriental* of New York. This early China clipper, built at New York by Jacob Bell in 1849, turned the British merchant shipping world upside down when she sailed to England in 1850. Not only did the public turn out in large numbers to view the sleek ship, but naval authorities took off her lines in dry dock, while those involved in maritime trade gloomily predicted the demise of British shipbuilding (*The Illustrated London News*, December 21, 1850).

knowledge, of A.A. Low. Palmer subsequently superintended the rebuilding of the massive clipper, cutting it down in size to 3,356 tons. The ship would remain in the Low fleet for many years before being sold to Canadian interests in 1866.

With all his experience, it is perhaps not surprising that Captain Nathaniel Palmer was a believer in the wooden sailing ship through and through, more akin to Donald McKay in this regard rather than Griffiths, Webb, or Pook. When the iron hulled tea clippers were being built in England, Palmer "laughed at them. He looked at the iron plate and said he could fire a musket ball through it" (Spears, pg. 248), and indeed was able to do so when a friendly wager was made. Palmer subsequently commanded an iron-hulled vessel for one voyage, but upon returning to New York gave up his seafaring career. During his retirement years, however, the old sailor could not give up the sea entirely and was intimately involved with the New York Yacht Club, designing, building, and sailing yachts. Quite fittingly, the last voyage Palmer made, albeit as a passenger, was to China. He died soon after his return to San Francisco in June 1877 and his body was subsequently shipped home to Stonington, Connecticut, for burial. If ever there was a man whose experience covered all aspects of the clipper ship era, from ship design and building to the sailing and business end of things, it was Nathaniel B. Palmer.

William H. Webb

Being the son of one of New York's premier shipbuilders, Isaac Webb, it might be presumed that William Webb, born in 1816, was destined to follow in his footsteps. However, this was not exactly the desire of Isaac Webb; one historian has stated that Webb "was beginning to view his own profession as a great deal of hard work with relatively small remuneration. He wanted his son to pursue a career that was both more respectable and more financially rewarding" (Dunbaugh and Thomas, pg. 16). To that end, Isaac Webb placed a high priority on his son's formal education and sent him to the prestigious Columbia College Grammar School. However, Isaac Webb was fighting a losing battle when it came to directing William in his career choice; academically, William Webb did quite well and was particularly adept in the subject of mathematics, but in his free time he was drawn to his father's shipyard, where he built his own small boat at the age of twelve (and in subsequent years continued to build other boats on his own) and also helped his father and shipyard employees construct a forty-foot model of a ship for use on a float in New York's Fourth of July parade one year. When Webb was a young man, both John Griffiths and Donald McKay were employed in his father's yard; whether Webb had any interaction with these men is undocumented but certainly likely.

In the summer of 1831, William Webb went to work at his father's shipyard with the expectation that he would attend Columbia Grammar in the fall, but Webb never did go back to school, preferring the mold loft to the classroom. He soon was immersed in learning the trade of a shipwright, working long hours by day and studying at night. That he was a skilled ship designer was evident early on, for he helped his father to design the successful 495-ton packet ship *Oxford* in 1834 for the owners of the Black Ball Line, and built a ship of this exact same design months later for the Havre Line. In 1837 William Webb's apprenticeship with his father ended, but he continued to work with his father and had a good reputation for the design and construction of packet ships, building four good ships from 1837 to 1839. To build his ships was alone not enough for William Webb; he made a sea voyage on one of his ships to see her in action and learn how to improve on his designs, and in 1839 resolved to make a trip to Europe. While this voyage was partly meant to restore his poor health, William Webb also wanted to see firsthand how ships were built in Europe. Sadly, while he was overseas in early 1840, his father died and he was forced to return to New York to take over the operations of the Webb and Allen shipyard.

William Webb quickly took over control of his father's shipyard and its day to day activities. While the yard was in poor shape financially, he eventually got it on a solid footing and took over sole control in 1843 when John Allen retired. William Webb's establishment from here on out would go on to become the dominant shipyard in New York for the next twenty-five years. While other shipyards specialized in only one size or type of ship, Webb did it all, building not only large packet ships such as the celebrated *Yorkshire* and the great clippers *Swordfish* and *Young America*, but also the bark *Snap Dragon* and other small craft such as brigs and schooners. Unlike many wooden shipbuilders of the time, Webb was smart enough to realize that steamships were the wave of the future, not sailing ships, and as early as 1842 he was building small steam ferry boats. This versatility would not only help Webb amass a large personal fortune but benefited his workers as well; in times of economic downturn, the Webb shipyard was seldom idle.

Even in his own time, William Webb was recognized not just as an accomplished shipbuilder, but also as a pioneer in the field of marine architecture. He was personally involved in every phase of ship construction, especially in his early days, to the extent that he carved the yard's half-models and made line drawings of every ship he built, a rarity at this time. Webb was also adept at utilizing the advanced ideas of the day when it came to hull design and reached his own compromise between speed and carrying capacity. Two of his early ships are considered important designs in the pre-clipper ship period, the *Helena* and the *Montauk*. The former was built in 1841 for the China trade and had the flat-floored hull form of a packet ship but was heavily sparred like the later clippers and was noted for her fast passages. The *Montauk* was also a speedy vessel; built in 1844 for the China trade she made several record times on her runs that would subsequently be eclipsed in the clipper ship era.

Even after the day of the clipper ships was over, William Webb continued building until he closed his shipyard in 1869. A man with a sterling reputation, Webb was also courted by the Republican Party to run for mayor of New York, but this was not to his liking, nor did it suit his subdued personality. Instead, he pursued a number of maritime business ventures, some of which proved unprofitable, but also more profitable activities in the fledgling oil business in Pennsylvania. In 1889 he established Webb's Academy and Home for Shipbuilders, an institution charged with the dual purpose of educating young men in the shipbuilding trade as well as providing a retirement home for aged shipbuilders of little or no means. This institution became a reality in 1894 and Webb was heavily involved right up until his death in 1899. The Webb Institute of Naval Architecture in Glen Cove, New York, is today one of the premiere schools of its type in the nation. At about this time, in 1893, William Webb was also one of the prime movers in the establishment of the Society of Naval Architects and Marine Engineering. Right up to his last days he was actively involved in the field of naval architecture.

Donald McKay

While the era of the clipper ship was an American one in many aspects, it is quite ironic then that one of the premier clipper ship designers and builders, the man whose name is most recognizable even today in this regard, was a native of Canada. Born in Shelburne, Nova Scotia, in 1810, he was the son of farmer Hugh McKay. Like many young men in Nova Scotia, McKay was drawn to the sea at a young age and when he was sixteen years old shipped as a crewman on a *bluenose* (as Nova Scotia vessels were referred to in the days of sail) schooner destined for New York. Upon arriving in New York, McKay quickly found employment in the shipyard of Isaac Webb and soon thereafter, in early 1827, was indentured to Webb as an apprentice for a term of four and a half years. His pay was two dollars and fifty cents a week, with a stipend of forty dollars a year to cover meals, lodging, and clothing. Donald McKay proved to be a talented and hard-working shipwright and learned his new profession rapidly. Perhaps anxious to start his independent career, McKay requested an early release from his master, which the kindly Isaac Webb graciously allowed. From here, McKay went to work for the rival New York shipbuilding firm of Brown & Bell for a time before going to work at the Brooklyn Navy Yard; here, the "exceptional ability" of McKay was quickly recognized, but "at that time a strong native American party-feeling prevailed among the mechanics and, because McKay was not born under the 'Stars and Stripes,' they bullied him out of the yard" (McKay, pg. 14).

One aspect of McKay's early life in New York, and its impact on his future career, that is sometimes forgotten is that of his marriage in 1833 to his first wife, Albenia Boole. She was the daughter of shipwright John Boole, and her two brothers were also shipbuilders and thus, just like William Webb, Albenia had had a life-long exposure to ship construction. Indeed, as a McKay family historian relates, "she not only understood much about ship construction, but could draught and quite expertly 'lay off' plans for a vessel. This capable woman became the mentor and teacher, who imparted to Donald McKay not a little of his knowledge of marine architecture at the beginning of his career" (McKay, p. 10). The drafting skills that McKay learned from his wife were vital to his future career and are indicative of the adage that behind every great man there stands an equally great woman. Indeed, one can almost picture the two of them together early on practicing the design calculations for some unknown vessel. While Albenia Boole McKay died after a brief illness in 1848, before her husband began building clipper ships and reached the pinnacle of his fame, "she had continually assisted him in his work. Night after night, together they toiled, planning and designing sailing craft" (McKay, pgs. 56–57), perhaps by checking his calculations, or suggesting a change here or there, in some of his pre-clipper productions. Interestingly, it is even stated by Donald McKay's biographer that "the *McKays* [the italics are mine] had completed plans for a clipper ship" (McKay, p. 57).

Donald McKay (1810–1880). This Canadian shipbuilder got his start in New York, but soon migrated to Massachusetts where, at his modern East Boston shipyard, he built some of the fastest and most famous sailing ships of the clipper ship era, including *Flying Cloud*, *James Baines*, and *Lightning* (McKay's *Some Famous Sailing Ships and Their Builder Donald McKay*, 1928).

Following his time in New York, Donald McKay turned his attention to New England. He first went to Maine while employed with Brown and Bell to check on some of the ships there being built for New York interests, but McKay stayed in New England for good. Perhaps he was a restless wanderer, but more likely McKay was looking for a good opportunity. This he would find in Newburyport, Massachusetts, in 1840, where he gained employment in the shipyard of John Currier, Jr. Here he worked on the ship *Delia Walker*, whose owner would be quite satisfied with the new vessel, but it is said that "what he [McKay] did to the *Delia* did not please John Currier" (Cheney, pg. 55). Likely this ship was built utilizing some of the newer hull principles being espoused at the time by younger shipwrights like John Griffith, but the exact details as to why Currier was displeased have been lost to history. Interestingly, another account of McKay's time with Currier, written by a McKay descendant, states just the opposite, that Currier was so happy with McKay that he offered him a five-year contract that was turned down. Whatever the circumstances, Donald McKay subsequently built one ship on his own in the city before forming a partnership with William Currier in 1841. Though the firm of Currier and McKay lasted just two years, three ships were completed, the last of which was the 380-ton *Courier*. This ship was used in the Brazilian coffee trade and was so fast that it gained considerable attention, many wondering how such a ship could have been built outside of Baltimore or New York. Once again, however, McKay's partner "would have none of her," the ship being "a radical departure from the established and proven designs" of the day (Cheney, pg. 55). The two men parted ways and in the process split their assets in half, both literally and financially; even the waterline models were sawn in half so that each man could retain a piece of their work. One wonders what William Currier did with his half of the model for *Courier*, given the fact that he was opposed to her design! McKay, however, continued his work in Newburyport, soon forming a partnership with W. B. Pickett. They subsequently built three packet ships in 1843 and 1844, two of them for New York owners. Their final ship was the inaugural packet ship for Enoch Train of Boston and his new White Diamond Packet Line. Train was so impressed with his new ship, and with further encouragement from Dennis Condry, the owner of McKay's first Newburyport production, the *Delia Walker*, he encouraged Donald McKay to move to Boston and set up his own shipyard there with his financial backing. In the end, though the details are not known, it is clear that Donald McKay's time in Newburyport helped solidify not only his reputation as a builder of fast ships, but as a man with vision. McKay may not have impressed the old time builders in Newburyport, but he did learn from them. One of the most interesting friendships he formed during his time there was with Orlando Merrill, the inventor of the waterline model, and it is interesting to speculate on what discussions these two men may have had regarding hull design.

In short time, Donald McKay found a suitable location in East Boston and established his own shipyard, one that would soon be among the most modern in the United States for wooden shipbuilding, and likely the most modern by far in New England. While McKay was not the first wooden shipbuilder to turn to modern construction methods (New York shipyards led the way in this regard), he embraced them fully. His East Boston yard utilized a modern steam powered sawmill and large derricks to lift heavy timbers into place rather than manual labor. McKay also utilized a lathe machine to make the treenails, wooden pegs that helped hold a ship together. These time saving devices would not be used elsewhere in New England for many years to come; as one early historian remarked in 1884, "It was long before Bath, Maine, bought even a bevel saw, and the first that went there was the one previously used by Donald McKay, which was sold after he had built his last ship" (Hall, pg. 87).

Within a short time of establishing his shipyard in 1846 Donald McKay built the largest merchant ship in the world, the 1,404-ton appropriately named *New World*; this packet ship was also the first three-decked ship to be built for the merchant trade. Just five years later McKay would build the 1,782-ton *Flying Cloud*, a ship that would prove to be the fastest clipper afloat, and two years after that he would build the largest clipper ship of them all, and the largest merchant ship in the world, the 4,555-ton *Great Republic*. One thing that is most notable about McKay's ships is that he often built on a grand scale, and though this was sometimes to his financial detriment, the results of his work cannot be overlooked. Like William Webb, John Griffiths, and Samuel Pook he adhered to the flat-floored hull principles that defined the later clipper ship era, but McKay ships also derived much of their speed due to their size and length. Indeed, while it was known even in the previous century that the length of a ship has a direct correlation to the maximum speed a vessel can achieve, this design factor was limited because the techniques to build a long and strong enough hull form that could stand the ocean pounding it would have to bear was not fully attainable until the advent of the clipper ship era. Now, with improved construction techniques and the use of iron strapping to further strengthen a vessel, larger and longer vessels were possible and Donald McKay took advantage of these advances to the extreme right from the start. Indeed, McKay's first California clipper, the 1,534-ton *Stag Hound*, was not only the largest merchant ship in the world, at least for a short time, it was also the longest.

Once the mania for clipper ships had died down, Donald McKay's yard was idled for several years and, unlike William Webb, he did not turn to building smaller vessels or steamships on a consistent basis. While McKay did build several schooners and steam powered vessels, including several ships for the navy, he obviously preferred designing and building the grand wooden sailing ships that were his passion. In 1859 McKay even contemplated the idea of authoring a book on the theory and practice of naval architecture, a work that, had it been completed, would have given historians an even more thorough understanding of the clipper ship era from one of its greatest proponents. Regrettably, though a prospectus for this work was drafted in London, the plan never reached fruition (McKay, pg. 356). Though McKay's yard stayed open until 1875, his last great production was the medium clipper ship *Glory of the Seas*, built in 1869, a ship that was both fast and successful for many years. Upon his retirement, Donald McKay moved to a farm in Hamilton, Massachusetts, and died a few years later in 1880. It is perhaps appropriate that he was buried at Oak Hill Cemetery in the city, Newburyport, where he got his start in building fast ships.

Samuel Hartt Pook

Like John Griffiths, Nathaniel Palmer, and William Webb, Pook was the son of an experienced shipbuilder. His father, Samuel Moore Pook, was a very successful naval architect who was employed by the U.S. Navy for many years and was the designer of a number of vessels, including the City-class of ironclads during the Civil War. He also wrote a treatise entitled *A Method of Comparing the Line and Draughting of Vessels propelled by Sail or Steam* in 1866. His son, often referred to as "young Sam Pook," was born in Brooklyn, New York in 1827 but spent the later part of his youth in Portsmouth, New Hampshire, where his father was employed at the naval shipyard. Samuel H. Pook graduated from the Portsmouth Academy in 1843 and subsequently served an apprenticeship under his father as a naval architect from 1843 to 1850 at the Charlestown Navy Yard in Massachusetts. While we know less about Pook and the details of his life than the other clipper ship pioneers discussed above, it is clear that at a young age he, too, was well-versed in the latest developments in hull design and embraced many of these advanced concepts. Perhaps wanting to establish his own reputation as a designer separate from his father, Pook became an independent ship designer after the end of his naval apprenticeship in 1850 and concentrated for a time solely on the design of merchant ships. In fact, the timing of the commencement of Pook's career as an independent marine architect, perhaps the first ever, could not have come at a more exciting time, coinciding as it did with the beginning of the clipper ship era.

At first, Samuel Pook appears to have been employed as a draftsman at the shipyard of Samuel Hall in East Boston, one of the best known and skilled shipbuilders in all of New England. Though the details are unclear, it seems that Pook came to Hall looking for work and was soon employed by him in making models for the clipper barks *Race Horse* and *Mermaid* and the clipper ships *Surprise* and *Game Cock*. Pook was also involved in laying down the lines of these ships and creating the molds. All of these ships were built at the Hall shipyard in 1850 and early 1851. It is interesting to note that within months of these ships being built much of the credit for their designs was given to Pook, a young man described as having made "great scientific attainments" (*The Boston Daily*

Atlas, May 10, 1851). However, Samuel Hall publicly disputed the idea that the ships in question were entirely Pook's design and stated that he was the guiding force behind Pook's work, offering advice as to changes and alterations in his original models before their final acceptance. While Pook himself apparently made no public comments on this minor Boston-area brouhaha, it is clear that the *Race Horse* was modeled after the design of an earlier Hall production, the bark *Coquette*, but that the *Surprise* was probably his work. The fact that Pook was the one who kept the line drawings of this clipper in his possession for some years after *Surprise* was built, a privilege usually only reserved for the true designer of a ship, is a good indicator that the clipper was his work, though with some input from Hall. The *Game Cock*'s design is also disputed by Hall but is usually credited to Pook, and the same may be true of *Mermaid*.

Whatever the case may have been regarding these early collaborative works, Pook's association with Samuel Hall was over within a year and he thenceforth designed a number of clipper ships on an independent basis. Though "Pook's designs were not radical" (Chapelle, pg. 362), he was unique in the way he worked as an independent designer, offering his service to all comers, likely ship owners rather than builders, who were interested in constructing a ship of his design. His ships had a good reputation for speed but could also carry a fair amount of cargo, and in this aspect he was not much different than William Webb and Donald McKay, though his designs, combining speed and carrying capacity, turned out to be more influential than the model advocated by Griffiths. How many ships Pook truly designed is unknown, but among those credited to him, in addition to those that he designed while employed with Samuel Hall as discussed above, are the Maine-built clippers *Red Jacket*, *Defiance*, *Ocean Chief*, and *Spitfire*, the New Hampshire–built clipper *Typhoon*, and the Massachusetts-built clippers *Northern Light*, *Fearless*, *Telegraph*, *Belle of the West*, *Witchcraft*, *Ocean Telegraph*, *Challenger*, *Winged Racer*, *Golden West*, and *Herald of the Morning*. Among those builders he worked closest with were Paul Curtis (*Witchcraft* and *Golden West*) between 1850 and 1852 at Chelsea and East Boston, J.O. Curtis (*Ocean Telegraph* and *Telegraph*) at Medford in 1851 and 1854, Robert E. Jackson (*Challenger* and *Winged Racer*) at East Boston in 1852 and 1853, and Deacon George Thomas (*Defiance* and *Red Jacket*) at Rockland, Maine, in 1852 and 1853. Pook's designs were also built by several other Boston area shipyards, including the Sampson brothers of East Boston, Hayden and Cudworth at Medford, the Briggs brothers at South Boston and, further afield, the Shiverick brothers at East Dennis on Cape Cod. Unfortunately, the details of Pook's design methodology are unknown; he likely created his models and drafted the lines of these well-known clippers of the day at his own workshop in Boston, with subsequent approval given by the ship's owners or their representatives, but how much interaction he had with the individual shipyards that built his designs is unknown. In the case of the clipper *Typhoon*, New Hampshire shipwright Frederick Fernald is said to have gotten the plans from friends at the Portsmouth Navy Yard, where Pook's father was employed (Brighton, pg. 70), but the plans for masting the ship came from the ship's owners in New York. In this more informal situation, it is unknown if Pook was even paid for his work. In fact, it is likely that a number of clippers were built off of Pook's designs without payment or credit given to him by the shipbuilders listed above, as there was nothing to prevent them from using plans from one ship for subsequent vessels. Thus, it is highly likely that the number of Pook influenced clippers that were built is much greater than those ships normally credited to him. Some possibilities include the famed clippers *Blue Jacket*, built in 1854 by Robert E. Jackson at East Boston for the same firm that owned the Pook-designed *Red Jacket*, and the *Nightingale*, built at Portsmouth, New Hampshire, in 1851 by Samuel Hanscomb, Jr. Of this later ship, one historian, William A. Fairburn, credits the design definitively to Pook, while historians Howe and Matthews credit Hanscomb as *Nightingale*'s designer; which one is correct is uncertain. Indeed, the debate over which clippers may, or may not, have been designed by Pook will likely never be fully resolved at this late date.

Returning to the design process, for those clipper ships built outside Pook's home area, how much direct involvement he had is unknown. Might he, for example, have made the trip to Rockland, Maine, to work with the shipyard workers in George Thomas's mold loft to lay down the lines of the *Red Jacket*? Or did he serve as merely a long-distance designer and consultant, perhaps making the trip only if called upon to check on a ship's progress? It does seem likely that, at least for his Boston area productions, Pook probably was on the scene at least at the early stages, and likely in the later stages on a more informal basis to see how construction was progressing.

Samuel H. Pook's star burned brightly for five years from 1850 to 1854 and the ships built from his designs were among the most outstanding of the clipper fleet. The 1,021-ton *Northern Light* set the speed record for a voyage from San Francisco to Boston that would not be eclipsed by another sailing vessel (a 6-ton tri-hulled catamaran) until 1993, while *Red Jacket* set a speed record for a sailing voyage from New York to Liverpool, England, that stands to this day. How personally profitable Pook's work really was, however, is questionable; like Webb and Griffiths, Pook knew that steamships would be the future and once the fervor for clipper ships began to subside, he had the wisdom to return to his career origins as a naval architect where the work (and pay) was more regular. From the 1860s onward he worked first as an assistant naval constructor, then chief naval constructor at the navy yards in New Haven, Connecticut; Portsmouth, New Hampshire; Mare Island, California; Boston; Washington; and New York until his retirement in 1889. He died in 1901 at his home in Washington, D.C., still renowned for the beautiful ships he helped create a half-century before.

In closing this discussion on the design aspect of building a clipper ship several other interesting points are also worthy of discussion. The first of these has already been alluded to in the discussion of Samuel Pook's career, namely that ship designs traveled, so to speak, from one locale to another. The use of Pook's designs in shipyards in Massachusetts and over one hundred miles away in Maine is just one example of this practice. Another possible example is that of the famed clipper *Neptune's Car*; the plans for this ship may have originated in New York and were provided by her owners, the New York shipping firm of Foster and Nickerson, to the shipyard of Allen & Page in Portsmouth, Virginia. A final example, found in Maine, are the molds and model of a 750-ton clipper made by Donald McKay, which were offered for sale by a Portland businessman. It seems likely that the famed 742-ton Maine clipper *Snow Squall*, launched in 1851 by Alford Butler at his shipyard in Cape Elizabeth (now South Portland), came from these plans (Dean and Switzer, p. 27). The reasons for this sharing, pirating, or purchase of designs were varied; the desire to build clippers was so high, and the designs of both McKay and Pook were so admired that builders had no qualms about using them. For those clipper ships that were contracted for outside of Boston or New York, such as *Neptune's Car*, that used these design plans, this was probably because a ship's owner became enamored of a particular model and simply wished for the builder to follow it, or because builders outside of the large shipbuilding centers, while generally less expensive (which is why they were contracted with in the first place), were likely viewed as slightly less qualified or experienced in designing a clipper ship. In fact, the practice of owners providing models to a builder and asking them to build a ship on their preferred design happened even in New York; master shipbuilder William Webb built the extreme clipper ship *Gazelle* in 1851 to the specifications given to him by the owners, Taylor and Merrill, but pointedly disavowed having anything to do with her design, the sharpest ever to emerge from his shipyard.

Finally, though the most important of the clipper ship designers have been highlighted above, it must not be thought that they were the only men of skill and vision when it came to the design of clipper ships. While Samuel Pook plied his trade throughout New England, and Donald McKay and William Webb were the deans of Boston and New York (respectively) clipper ship builders, helping to spur the great maritime competition that existed between the two cities, a number of other shipbuilders also stand out as quite capable designers. The Westervelt family (father Jacob and sons Daniel and Aaron) of shipbuilders, and the firm of Perrine, Patterson, and Stack, both of New York, were not far behind when it came to the clippers they built. Aaron Westervelt was a very capable ship designer, though no details of his background are known. On his own he built the 760-ton *Aramingo*, and in partnership with his brother Daniel built the noted extreme clipper *Sweepstakes*. Perrine, Patterson, and Stack built the little beauties *Wide Awake* and *Ino*, the later being one of the fastest clippers. Meanwhile, just across the way in Hoboken, New Jersey, Isaac Smith came out of nowhere to design and build *Hurricane*, the most extreme clipper of them all. In New England, too, Donald McKay had his rivals; in Mystic, Connecticut, there was Charles Mallory and the firm of Irons and Grinnell. Mallory, with master-builder Peter Forsyth, built the fine clippers *Pampero* and *Twilight,* while Dexter Irons and Amos Grinnell built the famed *Andrew Jackson*. Even within a short distance from McKay's yard there were some fine builders, including the previously mentioned Samuel Hall and Robert E. Jackson, both of East Boston. Hall's work with Pook has already been discussed, but later on he built his solo masterpiece, the clipper *Wizard*, while the lesser known but equally capable Jackson built the noted clippers *Blue Jacket, Swallow, Endeavor*, and *Queen of Clippers*. Another capable designer was clipper ship owner Captain James Huckins of Boston; he modeled the form for his ship *Bonita*, built by the Briggs brothers at South Boston, and perhaps did so for two of his other clippers, the *Golden Light* and *Meteor*, launched by the same builders (Howe & Matthews, pg. 47). Farther north in New England there were also many well designed clippers; George Raynes and the firms of Fernald and Petigrew and Tobey and Littlefield all worked out of Portsmouth, New Hampshire. Raynes' designs included the well known early clippers *Sea Serpent* and *Witch of the Wave*, as well as the noted flyer *Wild Pigeon*, Frederick Fernald and William Petigrew's productions include the fast extreme clipper *Typhoon* and the long-lived *Dashing Wave*, while Stephen Tobey and Daniel Littlefield built the largest ship ever launched in Portsmouth, *Sierra Nevada*, and the fine extreme clipper *Morning Light*. Maine shipyards, always active in the age of wooden sailing ships, continued to increase their already dominant position in the building of sailing ships during the clipper ship era; Metcalf and Norris of Damariscotta,

A New Jersey shipyard. Though no clippers were built at this Millville yard, it nonetheless is an example of the simple type of shipyards that dotted the New England and mid–Atlantic coastline from Maryland to Maine, from which were launched over 200 clippers in the 1850s. As can be seen in this view, yards like this built a variety of craft, including square-rigged ships, schooners, and many smaller craft used in the fishing and coasting trades (Stewart's ***Combination Atlas Map of Cumberland County, New Jersey,*** 1876).

Maine, built the extreme clipper *Flying Scud*, a large and fast ship, and the speedy *Talisman*, while Trufant and Drummund of Bath, Maine, built the fast clippers *Monsoon* and *Flying Dragon*, as well as the large clipper packet *Emerald Isle*. Finally, the home of the original American clipper, Baltimore, Maryland, must also be mentioned. Among the noted builders in this port were the brothers William and George Gardner, who built the clippers *Atalanta*, *Napier*, and *Sirocco*, all of which were fast vessels; John Robb, a former apprentice of New York builder Henry Eckford who later went to Baltimore to ply his trade; and John J. Abrahams, who built a trio of C-named clippers, the finely modeled *Canvasback* and *Carrier Dove*, and the big *Cherubim*. These are just a few of the notable clipper ship designers nee builders whose names have now largely faded into oblivion, except, perhaps, in the immediate locales where they practiced their trade. These shipbuilders, and many others, will be discussed at greater length below.

III

Young Mechanic
The Building of a Clipper Ship

Once a model was made or line drawings were completed, the task of turning an idea for a ship into reality could begin. The shipyards where clippers were built can be generally divided into two categories; the first of these were the modern and large shipyards of builders like William Webb, Samuel Hall, and Donald McKay. By the time of the coming of the clippers such yards were well established and organized and utilized a number of specialized buildings or shops, and though they may have varied in their complexity depending on the size and nature of the shipyard, the basic tasks these were intended for was the same. Lest we think that all of these modern shipyards were located in Boston or New York, this description of the Currier & Townsend shipyard in Newburyport, Massachusetts, for sale after the builders went bankrupt in 1856, tells another story:

> This yard has 210,000 square feet of land between Merrimac St. and the river and three other parcels of land on the other side of Merrimac St. The most spacious steam mill in New England with a forty horse power engine. The building is 110 feet by 40 feet three and one half stories high with a mold loft on the top story. Included in the machinery are two runs of up and down saws, circular saws, turning out saws, treenail machines and machines for making treenail wedges. In fact everything that can be done by steam. There are now three good slips with foundations for building and launching with additional room for three more and a solid filled wharf for tying up vessels while fitting out [Cheney, pg. 62].

However, while shipyards were slowly becoming the complex manufacturing sites that we know today, this was not always so in the era of wooden shipbuilding. True, the large shipyards of New York and Boston were more akin to modern day shipyards, but many of the other yards where clippers were constructed, especially in Maine, were more spartan in nature. In fact, wooden ships could be built wherever there was a suitable site for launching the vessel on a river or ocean inlet. All a shipwright needed was his basic tools, which were easily portable, men to help him out, and the supplies to build the ship transported to the site and he was all set. Historian Admont Clark's book about the Shiverick brothers, builders of five fine clippers, including the *Belle of the West* and *Kit Carson*, on Cape Cod at East Dennis is quite aptly titled *They Built Clipper Ships in their Backyard*, for that is truly what they did. Lest we think that all these shipyards were strictly utilitarian in looks and setting, contemporary accounts sometimes tell us a different story. To look at the site of the Raynes shipyard today in Portsmouth, for example, it is hard to visualize that the area, which occupied the site of the estate of colonial merchant and shipbuilder George Boyd, was a site to behold and, as one historian states, "The original beauty of the grounds was preserved so far as possible, and this was perhaps the most beautiful and picturesque shipyard of modern times" (Clark, A.H., pg. 53).

Getting back to the building of the clippers, the established yards utilized a number of specialized buildings or shops, and though they may have varied in their complexity depending on the size and nature of the shipyard, the basic tasks these were intended for was the same; there was a mold loft, a blacksmith shop for forging the ship's iron components, a general carpentry shop, the steaming plant for bending the ship's timbers, a joiner's shop, and a caulking shop. The first step in building a clipper was laying out the lines for the proposed ship's components. This work was undertaken in a large building called the mold loft, where the life-size lines of the ship were drawn out in chalk on the floor. These lines were accurately laid out with the use of flexible strips of wood, called battens, which were pinned to the floor. While to the untrained eye the resulting chalk outlines might look like a swirling jumble of lines, to the shipwright they were the patterns from which templates, or molds, for the ship's ribs and other components were fashioned. As previously discussed, these molds were saved by the builder if the ship was a successful craft and could be used to fashion the timbers for future ships. Though no two wooden ships built during the age of sail were ever exactly alike, through the multiple use of these molds some ships were virtual sister ships. Examples of clipper ship sisters include Donald McKay's *Chariot of Fame* and *Star of Empire* and Medford, Massachusetts, shipbuilders Elisha Hayden and William Cudworth's *Electric Spark* and *Thatcher Magoun*.

With the making of the molds complete, now the hewing of the ship's timbers could begin. In the larger yards in Boston and New York, timber was generally stockpiled and readily available to be worked, having been previously harvested or purchased from lumber dealers. One historian, in describing the waterfront of New York, commented that "coming along the East River, one saw many fine vessels on the stocks and great piles of lumber" (*Ships and Shipping of Old New York*, pg. 46). However, in the smaller shipyards located outside of the major urban centers, especially those in New England, shipwrights often made trips to local forests to pick out prime trees from which to fashion a ship's major components, such as the keel and ribs. Several example of this include the building of the medium clipper *Noonday* by Fernald and Petigrew in Portsmouth, New Hampshire, during the winter of 1854 and 1855. It is said that the selection and cutting of the white oak timber used in her construction was supervised by the ship's Boston owner personally during a trip into the woods of either New Hampshire or Massachusetts, depending upon which account you believe, and subsequently accompanied by him during its shipment to Portsmouth. Another example of local wood going into the use of a clipper was the *Southern Cross*, built by the Briggs brothers at East Boston in 1850 and 1851. In describing the oak knees and stanchions of the ship, it is stated that it came from "the growth of Worcester county in this State [Massachusetts], and is considered equal to most of the live oak of Florida" (Howe and Matthews, pg. 590). A final example is that of the Shiverick brothers' shipyard at East Dennis on Cape Cod; family tradition states that the oak and pine timber for the five clippers they built, *Hippogriffe*, *Belle of the West*, *Wild Hunter*, *Kit Carson*, and *Webfoot*, was mostly cut in Maine, personally chosen by Paul Shiverick and shipped to their yard by sea (Clark, Admont, pg. 13).

As to the types of wood used in building the American clipper ship, a number of varieties were used. Rock maple, white oak, live oak, hackmatack, chestnut, pine, and locust were the woods most commonly used in fashioning the components that needed the most strength, such as the keel, keelson, ribs, and hanging knees (braces) that supported the deck. Most of these grew plentifully in New England, while live oak came from forests in southern states, especially Virginia, Maryland, and Georgia. Clippers built in New York (whose forests had been harvested many years prior) and farther south bought their timber from dealers who supplied these southern woods, while clippers built in Connecticut and Massachusetts, especially large yards like that of Donald McKay and Samuel Hall, probably used a combination of local timber and timber from the South, but the smaller yards in these states, as well as New Hampshire and Maine, usually used timber that was grown locally or regionally. No matter where these trees were cut, all were suitable for use if treated and seasoned properly. Well-built clippers used trees that were felled in the winter months

THE "GREEN TREE."

SPECIFIC GRAVITY OF TIMBER FRESH FROM THE FOREST—NONE OF WHICH WAS FELLED MORE THAN TEN DAYS BEFORE THE SPECIFIC GRAVITY WAS OBTAINED.

SQUARE LIVE OAK.		SQUARE WHITE OAK.		SQUARE YELLOW PINE.	
MONTH FELLED.	SPECIFIC GRAVITY.	MONTH FELLED.	SPECIFIC GRAVITY.	MONTH FELLED.	SPECIFIC GRAVITY.
	lbs. oz.		lbs. oz.		lbs. oz.
September 15th	1.242 = 77 10	September 15th	1.037 = 64 13	September 15th	.665 = 41 9
October 15th	1.273 = 79 9	October 15th	1.059 = 66 13	October 15th	.662 = 41 6
November 15th	1.274 = 79 10	November 15th	1.058 = 66 2	November 15th	.653 = 40 13
December 15th	1.283 = 80 8	December 15th	1.083 = 67 11	December 15th	.689 = 39 15
January 15th	1.283 = 80 3	January 15th	1.068 = 66 12	January 15th	.625 = 39 1
February 15th	1.252 = 78 4	February 15th	1.066 = 66 10	February 15th	.673 = 42 1
March 15th	1.261 = 78 13	March 15th	1.044 = 65 4	March 15th	.581 = 36 5
April 15th	1.244 = 77 12	April 15th	1.071 = 66 15	April 15th	.683 = 42 11
May 15th	1.258 = 78 10	May 15th	1.102 = 68 14	May 15th	.583 = 36 7
June 15th	1.257 = 78 9	June 15th	1.032 = 64 8	June 15th	.595 = 37 3
July 15th	1.239 = 76 15	July 15th	1.123 = 70 3	July 15th	.655 = 40 15
August 12th	1.245 = 77 13	August 15th	1.082 = 67 10	August 15th	.639 = 39 15

ROUND LIVE OAK.		ROUND WHITE OAK.		ROUND YELLOW PINE.	
MONTH FELLED.	SPECIFIC GRAVITY.	MONTH FELLED.	SPECIFIC GRAVITY.	MONTH FELLED.	SPECIFIC GRAVITY.
	lbs. oz.		lbs. oz.		lbs. oz.
September 15th	1.144 = 71 10	September 15th	.950 = 59 6	September 15th	.828 = 51 12
October 15th	1.173 = 73 5	October 15th	.997 = 62 5	October 15th	.764 = 47 12
November 15th	1.182 = 73 14	November 15th	.996 = 62 4	November 15th	.777 = 48 9
December 15th	1.186 = 74 2	December 15th	1.018 = 63 10	December 15th	.765 = 47 13
January 15th	1.194 = 74 10	January 15th	1.015 = 63 7	January 15th	.823 = 51 7
February 15th	1.178 = 73 5	February 15th	1.014 = 63 6	February 15th	.789 = 49 5
March 15th	1.187 = 74 5	March 15th	1.070 = 67 7	March 15th	.782 = 48 14
April 15th	1.193 = 74 9	April 15th	1.013 = 63 5	April 15th	.795 = 49 11
May 15th	1.182 = 73 14	May 15th	1.021 = 63 18	May 15th	.744 = 46 8
June 15th	1.154 = 72 2	June 15th	1.005 = 62 13	June 15th	.792 = 49 8
July 15th	1.148 = 71 12	July 15th	1.089 = 68 1	July 15th	.751 = 46 15
August 12th	1.176 = 73 8	August 15th	1.054 = 65 14	August 15th	.772 = 48 4

Tree gravity chart. The selection of the timber that went into the building of a clipper was the most important aspect in the early phases of a clipper's construction. Though this task had been practiced for hundreds of years before the coming of the clippers through trial and error and by accumulated experience, by the 1850s science would become a part of the equation (John W. Griffiths' *Treatise on Marine and Naval Architecture*, 1854).

so that they had less sap in them, and any that remained was subsequently removed by soaking the timber in water and allowing it to dry. Yet other established and proven methods used to treat ship timbers to prevent decay, in use well before the days of the clipper, were the varied techniques known as *salting*. In some cases, ship timbers were soaked or washed with brine, while the more common method involved filling the lower spaces of the hull (those areas most subject to dampness and subsequent rot) with rock salt between the frames as the hull was being planked. Woe to the builder who failed to follow these time-tested methods or to the owner who insisted on too much haste in getting his ship built. The resulting clipper would then be built of unseasoned or green wood and would soon succumb to rot and would have to be rebuilt or scrapped altogether within a few short years. While this surely did occur on some occasions, the practice was not widespread, despite contemporary English descriptions which often derided American clippers as soft-wood vessels that were susceptible to rot. As will be amply demonstrated later on, the American clippers were staunchly-built of quality hard woods and held up remarkably well to the hard driving they were subject to. Other varieties of wood utilized include white pine, which was suitable for use as deck planking, as well as cedar, hickory, cherry, and fir. One of the few southern clippers, the Key West–built *Stephen Mallory*, was notable for being constructed of mahogany, the only clipper to utilize this material on a large scale.

Pine was one of the most important of the woods used in building the clipper ship. Not only was hard pine used for the ship's ribs, deck planking and other applications, but it was especially important in the fabrication of the masts. Each of a clipper's three masts, the foremast, the

Red Jacket **framing model. The timber framing that made up the skeleton of a clipper ship was massive in size, as shown by this full-sized dimensional replica. It measures over two stories high and represents just one rib of the famed Rockland, Maine–built clipper *Red Jacket*, built by Deacon George Thomas in 1853. The actual timbers for each of the ribs was thicker than those shown here (photograph by Captain Jim Sharp, courtesy Sail, Power & Steam Museum, Rockland, Maine).**

mainmast, and the mizzenmast, consisted of a number of sticks of wood, not just one piece. The lowest portion of a mast was the mainmast; it had the greatest diameter and length and was thus the sturdiest, being seated in place at the keel. Above the mainmast were, in order, the top mast, the topgallant mast, the royal mast, and, if so equipped, the skysail mast. The mainmasts alone of many clippers measured close to 100 feet in length and were usually fashioned not from one single piece of pine alone, but were termed "made sticks," consisting of three, four, or even five pieces held together at their junctions by strong iron hoops. The main mast of the McKay-built clipper *Bald Eagle* measured 90 feet long, while the Webb-built clipper *Challenge* had a mainmast measuring 97 feet in length. Add to this the height of the ship's upper masts and the result was, as in the case of the *Challenge*, masts that towered some 230 feet skyward in total, greater than the height of a twenty-story building! Along with the discussion of the masts, we must also look at the yardarms from which the sails were hung. Constructed in proportion to the masts which supported them, the yardarms, too, were massive in size. On the 1,289-ton clipper *Storm King*, built by John Taylor at Chelsea, Massachusetts, in 1853, the main yardarm measured 78 feet long on a mainmast that measured 86 feet in height, while the 2,421-ton McKay-built clipper *Sovereign of the Seas*, a ship nearly twice the size of *Storm King*, had a main yardarm that measured 90 feet in length and was two feet in diameter on a mainmast that was 93 feet high. Pine was the ideal material from which to fashion masts and their corresponding yardarms due to its strength and flexibility, thus making it able to both carry the weight of the vast spread of canvas carried by the clippers, and stand up to the incredible winds that would both drive and batter the ship. Indeed, the great pine trees of

American forests, especially New England's, had been used in this application since the early colonial days, when designated pine trees were marked by government surveyors with an axe mark known as the "King's broad arrow," an indicator to all that that particular tree was reserved for use by the Royal Navy. These trees were later cut down and hauled down paths or *mast* roads where they could subsequently be transported to a local port for shipment to England. By the time the clipper ships were being built, though many pine trees had been harvested over the intervening years since the American Revolution, there was still much timber to be had.

The first portion of the ship to be laid down was the keel, the backbone of the ship. This consisted of several joined pieces of large timbers of the strongest and hardest wood available, rock maple or live oak. The joints where the pieces of the keel came together were fastened by iron bolts measuring about three feet long. The keel itself was laid out on a series of blocks that rested on the building ways, the crib of timbers that supported the ship during construction and slanted down to the waterway where the clipper would eventually become waterborne. The timbers of the building ways were greased with animal tallow so that, when the blocks were knocked out from under the keel on the day of launching, the finished hull would slide down the ways and into the water. Once the keel was laid, the ship's many giant u-shaped ribs were then hauled into place, one by one, with the hull form soon rising to form the skeletal outline of the ship. The curve of these ribs was also formed out of wood hewn to match the ship molds, this being done by a team of the shipyard's carpenters while another team of men, carpenters and joiners, worked on laying the keel.

The idea of utilizing teams of specialists to form the ship's components and complete other skilled tasks during the building process was a relatively new concept during the clipper ship era. Before this time, ships took much longer to build because, in most shipyards, a single shipwright did all the work, but now the work was done in something that came closer to resembling an assembly line, with groups of carpenters, joiners, caulkers, and dubbers all performing their specialized tasks. This way of working, along with the overall urgency to get a cargo to California as quickly as possible, cut the construction time down considerably, and some clippers were built in sixty days or less, an amazing achievement for the time. The increased speed in shipbuilding that resulted from this differentiation of labor was also a necessity from a business standpoint; with the great demand for ships during the clipper ship era, ships had to be completed in quick-time so that future ship orders could be taken. While the bigger shipyards of William Webb in New York and Donald McKay in Boston would have no problem gaining commissions due to their prestige and could afford all the modern conveniences, smaller shipyards outside these areas realized that the clipper ship craze would be short lived and that this outside business would not last forever. In order for them to compete, they, too, had to build clippers in a timely fashion with a larger and more specialized workforce. Among those provincial builders that constructed a large number of fine ships were the Massachusetts-based Captain James Hood, who built nine clippers, including the *Governor Morton*, *Archer*, and *Raven* in his Somerset shipyard, and William Currier and James Townsend of Newburyport, who built a number of clipper packets for the Red Cross Line, including the fast but ill-fated trio of *Highflyer*, *Racer*, and *Driver* (all wrecked or lost in 1855 and 1856), as well as the most famed clipper-packet of all, the *Dreadnought*, known as the "Wild Boat of the Atlantic." Farther north in Portsmouth, New Hampshire, George Raynes had no trouble finding work, building nine clipper ships (six for New York and two for Boston owners) before his death in 1856, including the famed *Sea Serpent* and *Witch of the Wave*, as well as the long-lived *Coeur de Lion* and the speedy little *Tinqua*. All of these locales, and a number of others not yet discussed, had a long-standing tradition of shipbuilding but did not build large ships until the coming of the clipper ship era.

In continuing this discussion of a clipper's construction, I will here highlight some of the main details and components that will be of interest to the general reader, leaving out some of the more technical aspects regarding such things as moulded offsets, beam mould, the many types of scarphfs used in joining ship timbers, stem and sternpost assemblies, and the like. Those readers desiring to delve further into these more complex details are advised to consult the bibliography at the end of this work.

Once the ship's ribs were hauled into place, another large series of strong timbers, known collectively as the *keelson*, were bolted into place on the ship's center line to secure the ribs snugly against the keel. A number of clippers were so strongly built they had double, or even triple keelsons that were many inches thick. With this ship's skeleton in place, teams of men worked inside and outside the ship; deck beams were installed, reinforced at the point where they met the ribs of the ship by angled timbers, cut from a single piece of wood, called *knees*. The staunchest of the knees were those in the lower hold of the ship made of oak, while those in the upper holds sometimes used lesser woods. Meanwhile, outside the hull of the ship, scaffolding was built that supported the men who attached the ship's exterior planking to the ribs. Built to take the constant battering of the waves, this planking was sometimes as thick as seven or eight inches. Among the men working on the planking were men known as *dubbers*, who used an adze to flatten parts of the framework so that the planking would fit snugly against the ribs. Other men then came along using an augur to bore the holes in the planking for the treenails that would secure it to the framework of the ship, while others followed using a mallet to pound the treenail fasteners into the planking, and yet another man was employed in sawing off those portions of the treenails that stuck out, making each finished connection flush with the planking of the ship. Treenails were also used to secure deck planking, while in many cases iron strapping was also used to strengthen the interior of the hull. Among the many clippers that utilized iron strapping and diagonal bracing were a number of William Webb's productions, including *Comet, Flyaway,* and *Flying Dutchman.* The 1,278-ton *Panther,* built by Paul Curtis at Medford, Massachusetts, in 1854, also had the added strength and expense of diagonal iron bracing. This was likely based on the trade for which the clipper was intended as *Panther*'s first three cargoes consisted of railroad iron bound from England to India.

It is at this point that we might take a look at some of the fastening methods used by shipbuilders during the construction process. Iron bolts, spikes, and copper drift pins were utilized to hold a clipper together. The drift pins were heated up before being driven into the planking that covered a ship's ribs, and once they cooled shrank into the wood, creating a strong and solid bond, making the ship a "copper fastened" one. However, one of the simplest and most time-tested methods used to fasten a ship's components together were the treenails (pronounced "trunnels"). Simply put, these were wooden pegs that were pounded into the round hole drilled by the man called the borer; the resulting connection was a simple one, but one that was very strong, durable, and flexible. Trunnels were fashioned from a variety of woods and in the olden days were fashioned by hand, and still were by many smaller shipyards during the clipper ship era, though the more advanced shipyards used lathes to fashion them by the thousands. When they were made by hand, they were generally octagonal shaped, while those that were machine made were round, and no matter how they were fashioned all were seasoned and dried out before being used (Crothers, pg. 61). Once driven into the holes that were pre-bored, the round, machine-fashioned treenails had a small wedge driven into them at either one or both ends, depending on their location, but wedging was not needed for the handmade treenails that were octagonal shaped as this was the equivalent of, as the old saying goes, "a square peg in a round hole" that resulted in a strong connection all on its own. Of course, the use of treenails was not confined to shipbuilding, but was also used from early colonial days to join the timbers in American homes, barns, and covered bridges.

Another important aspect of the shipbuilding process was the transportation and lifting of the heavy timbers used. Many of the smaller yards used the old-fashioned method of manually hauling the timbers to the building way, using gangs of men to aid in directing the final placement of key components. More advanced yards, however, used derricks and teams of oxen to perform this back-breaking work. They also utilized steam driven power saws when less advanced yards used two-man pit saws to get this heavy work done. Finally, another device that is of interest is the steam box or oven. This large enclosure was heated to create an environment in which the timbers which required a curve, such as the ship planking covering the hull, could be heated and subsequently bent to shape during the building process.

To continue on with the construction of a clipper ship, with the framing of the hull well underway, many other tasks remained to be done below deck. Located amidships, a cast-iron cylindrical water tank (and sometimes two such tanks) was installed, with a typical

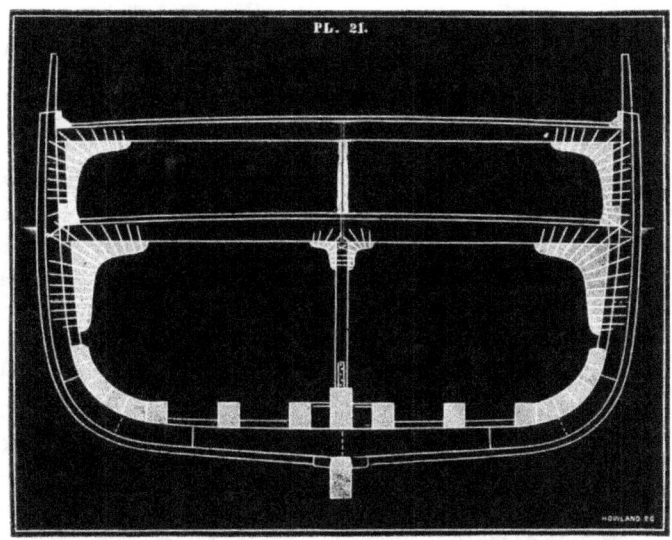

Hull components diagram. This drawing illustrates a few of the key support elements in the hold of a wooden sailing ship. The highlighted angled components on each side are the hanging knees, which were the major support for the ship's decks, while at center are shown the stanchions (note that the top one is turned and somewhat resembles a table leg or spindle) that offered additional deck support. At bottom center are highlighted the square timbers that make up the ship's keelson assembly (John W. Griffiths' *Treatise on Marine and Naval Architecture*, 1854).

capacity of nearly five thousand gallons that provided enough water to last the crew and passengers for a long voyage. Prior to the 1840s, merchant ships were either single or double-decked below, but many clippers were three-deckers, including the *Challenge* and *Sierra Nevada*, while McKay's *Great Republic* was the only four-decked clipper. Clippers like these had cavernous spaces below with plenty of room for passengers, provisions, and huge amounts of freight; the lowermost area of storage, termed the hold of the ship, held both cargo and the ship's ballast, while the area between the lower and upper decks in a two-decked ship was called the *tween decks*. In a three-decked ship, the cargo spaces above the hold between the lower, middle, and upper decks were termed, successively, the lower tween decks and the upper tween decks. This terminology was not just applied to the clippers, but was traditional nautical speak that had been in use for many years In the case of some of these larger two- and three-decked ships, it is interesting to note that while clipper ships were built at the height of the age of sail powered ships, some owners were apparently mindful that the future would be steam propulsion. Of all the clippers built, at least one (and probably others) was built with this possibility in mind; when the *Typhoon* was contracted for in Portsmouth, New Hampshire, in 1850 by her New York owners, Daniel and Ambrose Kingsland, they wrote to builders Fernald and Petigrew, "We are undetermined whether we shall put machinery into the ship, but should like to have her framed in such a manner that we can do so if we are so disposed" (Brighton, pg. 70). This provision turned out to go unfulfilled and when the ship was lost in the China Sea twenty years later, the former *Typhoon* (now under the British flag) was still a sailing ship. In concluding this discussion of a ship's below-decks cargo space, there are several interesting features that are worthy of consideration. The deck beams below, which held either immigrant passengers or cargo, were structurally supported in two ways; first, on either side of the hull, where these beams met the ribs, by the previously mentioned hanging knees. These were bracket-like pieces of timber, fashioned from strong wood pieces that were made utilizing the natural angles and curves found in the crooks of the trees from which they were hewn, and secondly by stanchions, or wooden posts, that were placed along the centerline of the ship above the keel and were bolted into place. These stanchions acted in the same supportive manner that the upright posts often found in the basements of older houses do, but they had to be judiciously placed so as not to interfere with cargo or passenger spaces. It is interesting to note that the stanchions used in pure cargo spaces were simply squared posts, with nothing decorative about them, while those stanchions that were located in passenger spaces were often more decoratively turned, made "to suit the eye of the designer" (Crothers, p. 215). To this end, the Portsmouth-built *Witch of the Wave*, a beautiful ship in every way, was unusual in that all her turned stanchions were secured in cast iron sockets.

Finally, in concluding this discussion about a ship's below deck spaces for cargo, one may wonder just how these spaces were accessed. Most clippers had three hatches, which were accessible from the weather deck, the ship's uppermost deck on which her sailors worked exposed to the elements; these were the forward hatch, which was the smallest due to its location in the narrower bow portion of the ship, just forward of the foremast; the main hatch, which was the largest cargo hatch (about ten feet long), located amidships, just forward of the mainmast; and a final hatch, located toward the stern of the ship, forward of the mizzenmast. These three hatches allowed a ship's cargo to be loaded efficiently and evenly, with less maneuvering in the restricted spaces below. All hatches were framed with raised openings called a coaming, the hatch coaming preventing the water which ran on the weather deck from pouring into the hold; of course, when a ship was at sea these hatches had covers that were well secured which also prevented water from entering a ship's hold in times of heavy weather, though they could easily be removed for ventilation or inspection purposes. Further, some clippers, including the *John Gilpin, Champion of the Seas,* and *Ellen Foster*, had additional access to cargo spaces via cargo ports that were cut into the side of a vessel or, among those vessels those working in the timber trade, in their stern quarters. The use of such ports was not common, usually found only in larger ships, primarily because it affected the watertight integrity of the hull. These ports were typically about four feet high and resembled the gunports of a naval vessel. When a ship was at sea these ports had to be strongly secured and sealed so as to keep water out, though some were hinged just like real gunports and could be opened when ventilation was required (Crothers, p. 321).

In looking at the construction details on the weather deck, there was also much work to be done here by the builder. One task was the laying and finishing of the decks; made of pine or hackmatack, they had to be slanted just so, so that water would run off in the scuppers located along the deck's edge and back into the sea. To prevent water from seeping below decks, the deck had to be sealed by a team of caulkers; this dirty job consisted of forcing bits of tar-soaked rope (called *oakum*) deep into the seams between each deck plank. The oakum was driven into the cracks by a two-man team using a long-handled wedge called a *hawsing iron* which was struck by a special mallet called known as a *hawsing beetle*. Once the oakum was in place, another man followed behind pouring hot tar into the crack to complete the watertight seal. Other above deck tasks included the construction of the several deck houses. These houses either sheltered the entrance to the crew, captain, or passenger's quarters that were located just below decks, or, on some clippers, the quarters themselves were located above deck. Some vessels also had a small deck house aft that gave shelter to the wheelsman. The captain's and passenger cabins were usually located amidships and toward the aft-end of the ship. These were quite elaborately finished during the age of the clipper ships and rivaled that of any fine room in a mansion ashore. The furnishings in these rooms will be described at length further on when discussing the voyages these ships made. Even the captain's quarters were well appointed, despite the fact that, depending upon the nature of the voyage, a captain might have precious little time to spend below. As for the crew's quarters, located in a central deck house or forward in the forecastle or *focs'le*, these were more spartan in nature and had none of the finery found aft. Those ships that were built specifically for the passenger trade also were sometimes equipped with the modern convenience of a water closet or two.

Yet another job in the construction of a clipper was to step the masts of the ship. In many cases, the ship was launched with just the mizzenmast, mainmast, and foremast in place, giving the ship a stumpy look that belied her future beauty. The topgallant and topgallant pole masts, along with yardarms, running rigging, and a set of sails would later be added at the rigger's wharf. Sometimes this was done in the port where the ship was launched, but often this took place in the larger ports, such as Boston and New York, where many experienced riggers, rope makers, and sailmakers were located. Just as the masts of a clipper, as previously discussed, were massive in size, so too were the sets of sails and the yardarms on which they were set. The most commonly used material in sailmaking was canvas duck cloth made from cotton. While linen was the main material in the earlier days of sail, cotton was not only more readily available, but was lighter in weight, an important consideration as the size of sails increased on American ships. The cotton duck cloth was carded in varying sizes; the clipper *Challenge* had sails fashioned from cloth that measured 16 inches wide. Prior to the early 1800s, sailcloth was woven by hand and the weave of the resulting fabric was loose and uneven so that sails often lost their shape and did not hold the wind that well. However, by the 1830s sailcloth was woven by power looms, resulting in a more tightly woven and thus stronger product that kept its form. Perhaps the most prominent supplier of duck cloth was John Colt of Paterson, New Jersey; he was the first to make cotton duck cloth, beginning in 1824, and by the 1830s his mills were the U.S. Navy's main supplier for their ships. Many clippers carried sails made out of Colt cloth. The duck cloth was made into sails at the loft of the skilled sailmaker; every port city where clippers were built had at least one such team of skilled sewers who could craft a set of sails for a vessel of any size or rig. Indeed, the amount of canvas carried by the clippers to power them on their voyages to California and beyond was impressive; the *Game Cock* carried 8,000 yards of sail, *Don Quixote* 9,000, and the *James Baines* 13,000 yards of canvas. Perhaps the most impressively sparred and canvassed clipper was the diminutive *Ino*; measuring but 895 tons, she carried nearly 9,500 yards of sail, a figure close to or greater than clippers that were almost twice her size. The most heavily canvassed ship during the clipper ship era, however, was Donald McKay's *Great Republic*; as she was originally built the four-masted clipper (the only four-masted clipper to be built) carried 15,653 yards of sail.

In regards to rigging, here too the American clipper ship used the finest materials available. The rigging was of the strongest hemp and was spun into rope of varying degrees of thickness, usually four strands, and standard lengths of about 1,000 feet long at a manufacturing facility known as a ropewalk. Most cities where the clippers were built had a ropewalk. The main building of the ropewalk was huge, measuring over a thousand feet long, and was where the long strands of material, typically Russian or Manila hemp, were twisted into rope. There was also a tarring room, where the hemp strands that would make the rope were coated with tar in order to protect it from the elements. Indeed, the ropewalk, with its vast amounts of hemp dust and flammable tar was a dirty and dangerous place to work, but not long after the clipper ship era ended they would soon become a thing of the past when wire rigging eventually replaced rope. In addition to the sailmaker and rope maker, other allied trades in the shipbuilding business included the block maker, a carpenter who fashioned the wooden pulleys, or guides, through which the hemp rigging was run, and the pump maker, who fashioned the copper pumps that clippers were equipped with so as to keep their holds free of water that came aboard during a voyage. During the era of the clipper ship, it was not uncommon for a ship to be launched after being fully masted, rigged, and equipped

The launching of the *Challenge*. This infamous clipper was built at the New York shipyard of William Webb in 1851. Note that the ship was launched with just its lower masts in place, and also the two other sailing ships in varying stages of completion in the background. In the foreground at the bottom of the ship's hull can be seen the timber cradle that supported the ship during its building (*Gleason's Pictorial Drawing Room Companion*, 1851).

with sails on the building ways. Such was the case with two New England clippers launched in 1854, the Marblehead, Massachusetts-built *Mary* and the Portsmouth, New Hampshire–built *Express*. When this was done, seldom was a grander nautical sight ever to be seen.

After a ship was launched, there was still much work to be done. This included the installation of a wide number of deck fittings and equipment, including pumps, windlass, capstans, anchors, the steering gear, ventilators, and lifeboats. Most of the clipper ships also had their hulls coppered; sometimes this was done while the ship was still on the builder's ways, sometimes after launching. This process, which came into common usage on merchant ships in the 1840s, involved sheathing the lower portion of the hull in copper sheets and was done to impede marine growth on the ship's bottom. This accumulated growth, consisting of barnacles and plant life, over time affected the ship's movement through the water and reduced speed considerably. The copper sheets also provided protection from teredos (shipworms) that fed on wooden hulls in warmer waters and, to a lesser extent, gave some protection when a clipper suffered minor groundings or collisions. A common alternative to the copper used in this sheathing process by clipper ship builders was yellow metal or brass, an alloy consisting of about 70 percent copper and 30 percent zinc metals.

The Launching of a Clipper Ship

Once the ship's hull form was completed on the builder's ways, then the launching day, the time when the ship would take to the water for the first time, was soon at hand. From the days when ships were first built in the ancient times down to the present, the launching of a ship is a notable event. During the clipper ship era, the launching of one of these celebrated and much-an-

III. Young Mechanic: The Building of a Clipper Ship 49

The launching of the *Great Republic*. This, the largest sailing ship in the world at the time in 1853, was perhaps meant to be builder Donald McKay's (depicted on horseback in top hat) finest creation, here with at least 30,000 people present at her launching. Note the giant eagle figurehead adorning her bow, and the lack of anything above deck. The clipper would be towed to New York for masting and rigging in October and November 1853 but would be greatly damaged by a dockside fire before making her first voyage (***Gleason's Pictorial Drawing-Room Companion***, October 1853).

ticipated ships turned into a holiday, where local businesses and schools were closed so that the population could attend the launch and politicians and merchants made speeches. At the shipyard, the hull to be launched stood on the building ways all decked out in patriotic bunting and from her masts banners and flags were flying. Dignitaries, including the ship's owners, their family and friends and local politicians, were usually on hand, with the most distinguished guests being on the clipper's deck and riding the ship as it slid down the ways and hit the water. While many launchings took place during the daytime, there were those occasions where a nighttime launching occurred, usually because of the prevailing tides, presumably accompanied by the anxiousness on the part of both owner and builder to set their creation afloat. One such nighttime event was the midnight launching of the *Gem of the Ocean* at Medford on August 4, 1852, due to the prevailing tides on the Mystic River. Of this launching it is said that "each man brought his lantern" and that builder William Cudworth's seventy-year-old mother visited from Scituate, "never having witnessed a launch ... a great one for her" (Wooley, p. 97). How many townsfolk turned out for this launching is unknown, but those that did were certainly treated to what must have surely been an unusual spectacle.

As has been the custom for hundreds of years, just prior to a launching, the ship was officially christened with its name by an individual associated with the ship (the owner, owner's wife or other family member) whose ceremonial duty was to break a bottle of liquid on the ship's bow. While champagne has been the liquid of choice in ship launches since the late 1800s, before this time (and during the clipper ship era) a variety of liquids were used, including water, whisky, and wine. Whatever liquid was used, its ceremonial significance dated back to ancient times, when newly-built ships were baptized by having water poured over the bow, masts, and other important portions of the ship. During the 1850s some clippers were christened with water in deference to the many temperance organizations that were then in existence. One clipper possibly christened with water was the Newburyport, Massachusetts–built *Charmer* in 1854, "whose figurehead was described by the reporter who attended her launch as that of a snake with the tongue hanging out of its mouth, as if it had had a drink of Cochituate water and did not like it" (Howe and Matthews, pg. 88–89). It is unknown, however, if this may have been a general commentary on the use of water, rather than liquor, to launch the ship or whether it was a thinly-veiled criticism about the quality of water supplied to the city of Boston (the *Charmer*'s owners were Boston-based) from the nearby Cochituate reservoir! Whatever liquid was used to launch a ship, liquor was almost certainly present at the shipyard, as it was a tradition to give shipyard workers the rest of launching day off and treat them to copious amounts of food and drink, usually rum or whisky, as a reward for their good work. For the owners of a newly-launched clipper and their more prominent guests, it was tradition to host a lavish post-launching banquet at a local hotel, where further speeches were made and toasts to honor the future glory and success of the ship were made.

The launchings of clipper ships, and details about their finely crafted construction were covered in detail by local newspapers in port cities, with the marine reporter a common fixture at such events. The articles that these reporters wrote about the new clipper ships were almost always positive when it came to the qualities of the new ship, and sometimes downright gushing in their praise for builders and owners alike. The details that they offered their readers about construction and finish details were often minute and in this sense may be compared to the comprehensive new automobile reviews of our modern times. However, here the comparison ends, for seldom in these reviews does one find a new ship, its model, or her owners criticized in any way. Indeed, marine reporters like Duncan McLean of the *Boston Atlas* were the greatest and most public proponents

The *Telegraph* in dry dock. This clipper was launched at Medford, Massachusetts, by James Curtis in 1851 and subsequently completed her fitting out at the naval dry dock in Charlestown. Notice the men on the scaffolding at the bow of the ship, while the lighter color of the lower portion of the hull shows that the clipper's bottom was already sheathed in yellow metal. The ship has not yet been given her masts or rigging (*Gleason's Pictorial Drawing Room Companion*, June 14, 1851).

of the builders in their cities, and it is McLean who was not only a friend of Donald McKay, but in many ways also his greatest public promoter. Given this state of media affairs, so to speak, at the time is it any surprise that there was in fact a clipper ship, launched by Paul Curtis at East Boston in 1854, that was named *Reporter*? This ship, which was lost in a storm off Cape Horn in 1862, came complete with a figurehead of a full sized member of the media taking notes, though this image "was not considered very artistic" (Howe and Matthews, pg. 519)!

Clipper ship launches were so commonplace in the early 1850s that sometimes even marine reporters recognized the predictability of the celebrations; writing of the launching of the clipper ship *Morning Light* at Portsmouth in August 1853, one commentator observed, "The announcement of the launching ... drew together a large number of people, on Saturday afternoon, to see a common but always interesting occurrence. A larger company than usual were attracted as the ship to be launched from a new yard, by a new firm — this being the first vessel built by Tobey & Littlefield.... Everyone pronounced it the most splendid launching they ever saw — a verdict that has been rendered at every launching within memory of the oldest inhabitant" (Brighton, pg. 108). However, not all launchings went off so smoothly or predictably. When the *Red Rover* was launched at Portsmouth in October 1852, she collided with an inbound Canadian schooner and subsequently hit a nearby dock but escaped serious damage. The summer of 1853 was not a good one in terms of launches for the Westervelt family of shipbuilders in New York; when Daniel and Aaron Westervelt launched the family's largest clipper ever, the 1,735-ton *Sweepstakes*, it only partially made the water before slamming to a halt halfway down the builder's ways because of a lack of clearance between the ground and the clipper's keel. The ship subsequently swung wildly to the side and struck the staging for the nearby clipper *Kathay* that was under construction and many spectators were thrown into the water. Though there were some upset, bruised, and wet spectators and certainly wounded egos on the part of the builders, luckily no one was killed. However, the mishap was a costly one as the *Sweepstakes* was really stuck and it took over three days and two barge derricks to free the ship. Upon subsequent examination at the nearby Brooklyn Navy Yard it was found that repairs to the tune of $20,000 were required to make *Sweepstakes* seaworthy again. Later on, with all this mess over, the owners were still a bit sensitive about their ship and when a toast was made at a banquet held in advance of its first voyage, an attendee offered, "Here's hoping that the ship is all right, with a good captain and crew and that she may have a fair wind and no accident." The owners churlishly responded, "The ship is all right, the captain is all right, the crew shall be all right. It's our business to see to this and we've done it. You needn't ask for anything but a fair wind and no accident"(Howe and Matthews, pg. 647). Sailors are a superstitious lot by nature and such an inauspicious beginning for any ship was usually viewed as a bad omen, but there is no evidence to show that *Sweepstakes* was a jinxed ship because of her launching misfortune. Though the ship had a short life, being scrapped at Batavia after going ashore in 1862, it was a profitable ship that was driven hard with excellent results, making the eighth fastest time on record (95 days) from New York to San Francisco in 1856.

Even before the *Sweepstakes* departed on its first voyage, there was yet another launching miscue at the Westervelt yard, once again involving the *Kathay*. On the day of its intended launching, August 11, 1853, the extreme summer heat had melted completely the tallow that greased the ways and the ship refused to budge an inch. The launching delayed, the ship over the next four days was lifted using levers and jacks and the building ways were re-laid and fresh tallow applied, after which the launching went off without a hitch. Given the several events surrounding the launching of *Kathay*, one might suppose that she was an unlucky ship. In fact, the clipper had a successful, if mundane, career before being sold foreign in 1863, and was subsequently lost, with no loss of life, after being driven on a reef at Howland's Island in 1867. In all fairness to *Kathay* it must be noted that extreme weather conditions often caused launching problems and delays; the aptly-named New Hampshire clipper *Granite State* was scheduled to be launched on December 7, 1853, but a snow and ice storm caused the ship to become iced on the stocks and stuck solid, a problem in direct contrast to that of *Kathay* but one that ended up with the same result. To get the *Granite State* freed, the workers at Samuel Badger's shipyard had to build huge fires next to the wooden ship to melt the ice, surely a dicey situation to manage. In fact, launching problems were a common occurrence and were simply one of the many hazards of the shipbuilding trade. However, even after a ship was launched, mishaps sometimes occurred during the final phases of masting, rigging, and getting in ballast. The first *Golden Fleece*, launched by Paul Curtis at Boston in 1852, capsized while at the rigger's wharf, possibly due to a problem with her ballast, but the ship suffered no damage, while the previously mentioned *Red Rover* suffered another accident before leaving Portsmouth when a careless rigger cast off a rope that caused the top mast to fall to the deck, splitting a beam before falling overboard.

Once a ship was launched, as mentioned previously, the finishing details as to masting, rigging, ballasting, and outfitting were quickly attended to in order to get the clipper completed and ready for its first voyage. We have already discussed details about a ship's rigging and masts, but what about ballast? Almost all commercial ships, even those operating today carry ballast to help stabilize the vessel. Today, strategically placed water tanks serve this purpose in cargo-carrying merchant ships, but in the days of sail, iron bars, called *kentledge* in marine terminology, as well as gravel and stone were used. Those clippers with a great amount of deadrise, resulting in a V-shaped bottom, needed the most ballast to keep them upright and maneuverable. Without such ballast the loftily sparred clippers would have been grossly top-heavy and impossible to operate. The 1,174-ton *Eagle Wing* was typical of many clippers, requiring 600 tons of ballast to keep her stable when empty of cargo. However, the more ballast a ship needed meant in turn that less paying cargo could be loaded. This was yet another reason that the extreme clippers of the early 1850s soon gave way to the flat-floored medium and half-clippers of the later clipper ship era. Most clipper ships probably used stone as ballast that was easily obtainable at the port city in which it was built. The ballast stones, deliberately arranged in the hold of a given ship, came in a variety of sizes, ranging from pebble size to those the size of a brick. Piles of ballast stone from the clipper *War Hawk*, built in 1855 at Newburyport, Massachusetts, and sunk in Puget Sound in 1883 after catching fire, can still be seen by recreational divers today marking the wreck site off Mill Point.

Before heading off on their first paying voyages, ships built in northern New England, like the New Hampshire clippers *Coeur de Lion*, *Morning Light*, and *Nightingale*, were usually towed to Boston or New York. The same was true of Maine-built clippers, including the Rockland-built *Red Jacket*, which was towed to New York for masting and rigging. The Portsmouth-built *Witch of the Wave* was towed to its official homeport of registry in Massachusetts, though builder George Raynes, who was aboard for the festive occasion, talked the ship's captain into laying on some sail while the ship was under tow to see what she could do. The *Witch* quickly sped up to nearly ten knots and caught up with her towing vessel, the celebrated and powerful Boston steam tug *R.B. Forbes*! While most clippers built in outlying areas were towed to ports like Boston or New York to take on their first cargo, this was not always the case; the Portsmouth-built *Wild Duck* sailed to New York under her own power, while the Maine-built *Live Yankee* sailed from Rockland to New York. One of the relatively few ships to take on a cargo and depart fully loaded from one of these outlying ports was the Portsmouth-built *Express*, which loaded a cargo of ice from the newly formed Portsmouth and South Berwick Ice Company bound for New Orleans!

A small number of clippers built in these outlying ports are also of interest in that they were owned by their merchant-builders, the most important by far being Charles Mallory of Mystic, Connecticut, and thus had closer ties to their ports of origin for a longer time than was the norm.

The Mallory shipyard built eight clipper ships, of which five were owned by Charles Mallory himself. Occasionally his ships would return to their port of building for repairs and overhaul, as happened with *Twilight* in 1862. Other examples of the builder-owner model which kept a clipper tied to its port of building was the *Wizard King*, built by Thomas Southard at Richmond, Maine, and the medium clipper *Golden Horn*, built by Clark & Wood of Wiscasset, Maine, and owned in part by Henry Clark. Both these locally owned and operated Maine clippers were eventually sold foreign, going to British interests in 1863. Despite these exceptions, and a few others, the fact remains that once a clipper left such places as Portland, Bath, Damariscotta, Newcastle, and Rockland (Maine), Portsmouth (New Hampshire), Marblehead, East Dennis, Swansea, or Somerset (Massachusetts), Warren (Rhode Island), or Mystic (Connecticut) they would never again return to the places at which they were built, though their activities were usually closely followed in the marine columns of local newspapers.

Finely Finished: The Aesthetics of the Clipper Ship

The American clipper ship, first and foremost, represented a business investment by its owner and was thus a working ship. However, during the flush times in which they were built both owner and builder took a great amount of pride in the ships they commissioned and built and spared no expense in their outfitting. As a result, the clipper ships were among the most beautiful of American ships ever built. Nowhere is this more evident than in the outward appearance of these ships. The men that sailed them and the public alike were smitten with their clipper ships and delighted in their rakish appearance, beautiful figureheads, and lavishly decorated stern quarters. In describing the Cape Cod–built clipper *Belle of the West* and its first visits to Boston and San Francisco, one account states that "the newspapers called her the handsomest ship that had ever appeared in those harbors, saying, 'Whatever bright-eyed little flirt she is named after, need not be ashamed of her appearance,' and even clipper ship historians writing nearly 75 years later, using terms that might make a proper lady of the 1850s blush, describe this clipper as having a 'most saucy and coquettish appearance, which was further enhanced by her graceful elliptical stern'" (Howe and Matthews, pgs. 37–38). While there is more than just a little sexual innuendo in these terms, such descriptive adjectives were commonly applied to the sailing ships of old by owners and the men who sailed them.

It is to be regretted that though photography had been invented by the time the clipper ships appeared on the scene, it was not yet in common enough usage to document fully the appearance of these ships. However, detailed newspaper accounts from the era help to fill the gap, as do contemporary marine lithographs and paintings, commissioned by owners and captains, by such artists as Currier & Ives, Fitz Henry Lane, J.E. Buttersworth, and many other lesser known but equally skilled artists working in foreign ports, particularly in China and Hong Kong. So, just what kind of finish details did the American clipper ship have? Nearly all the clipper ship hulls were painted black, which contrasted nicely with their brass deck fittings, and had a white stripe running the entire length, while lower masts were often painted white. Some vessels varied from the norm just enough to make them distinctive; the New York–built *Challenge*, the masterpiece of William Webb, had a gold stripe running the length of her black hull and had the lower portion of her masts also painted black, which gave the ship the smart look of a naval vessel, while the Portsmouth-built *Sea Serpent* had a yellow line running the length of her otherwise black hull. The clippers of the William F. Weld & Co. fleet of Boston, on the other hand, including the clippers *Fearless, Competitor, Orpheus,* and *Galatea,* were painted a distinctive dark green, sometimes also called a tea color (Howe and Matthews, pg. 173). In speaking of the masts of the clippers, these too were sometimes ornamented, as on Donald McKay's *Sovereign of the Seas*, with gilded balls topping them off, giving them some resemblance to a flag pole or lightning rod. Sails, too, were sometimes decorated; the fore mainsail on the *Dreadnought* bore a large red cross as the clipper was the flagship of the Red Cross Line of packets, *Hurricane* had its name printed boldly across its foretopsail, while *Galatea*, and probably other clippers of the same owner, bore the black horse emblem of the Weld fleet on one of its foresails. Aboard ship, most clipper deckhouses were painted white, as were cabin interiors and bulwarks, while waterways were painted a variety of colors, including pearl, lead, light blue or buff color. The deck fittings of the clippers were also quite lavish at times; the helmsman's platform on the *Jacob Bell*, built by his son Abraham Bell for A.A. Low & Company in 1852, was heart-shaped and made of solid brass. One other unusual feature on some clippers was a binnacle, the stand on which a ship's compass was mounted on deck, that was carved in the image of a sailor. When the *Champion of the Seas* was in distress and abandoned off Cape Horn in 1876, the captain of the British vessel that rescued her crew was preparing to sail away from the sinking clipper until he spotted what he thought was a man left on deck. Captain Wilson of the *Champion*, after taking a look through the spy-glass, informed the British skipper that this was no crewman, but the ship's binnacle, which was "a life-sized wooden effigy of a sailor boy ... being quite lifelike with wide pants and flap collar and painted according to life" (Howe and Matthews, pg. 75). The clipper *N.B. Palmer* also sported one of these binnacle boys, but it was eventually removed because her sailors found it more than a little creepy due to its lifelike nature.

Every ship had two canvasses, so to speak, where the marine artists of the day could show their work, the bow and stern of the ship. The artwork on the forward part of a vessel was the most distinctive; it led the ship into port and, once a vessel was moored at its berth it was on public display as the bow portion of the ship overhung the walkways where sailors and the public at large were free to roam on the waterfront. Back in the days of the sailing ship era, maritime ports were not closed off areas like they are today, but were within the communal and public areas of a city or town. One common type of bow decoration was the billethead, which was used in place of a figurehead. This type of decoration, in use on sailing ships for centuries, consisted of carved scrollwork, sometimes with a floral theme and often gilded, mounted on the cutwater. Billetheads came in countless designs and were used to adorn the bows of many clipper ships, including *Charger, Dashing Wave, Don Quixote, Flying Arrow, Gem of the Ocean, Kingfisher, Mountain Wave, Ocean Pearl, Phantom, R.B. Forbes, Raven, Westwind,* and *Young America*, to name just a few. One of the most unusual billetheads, and surely the most patriotic, was that for the clipper *Invincible*, which featured a liberty cap in front of an American themed coat of arms.

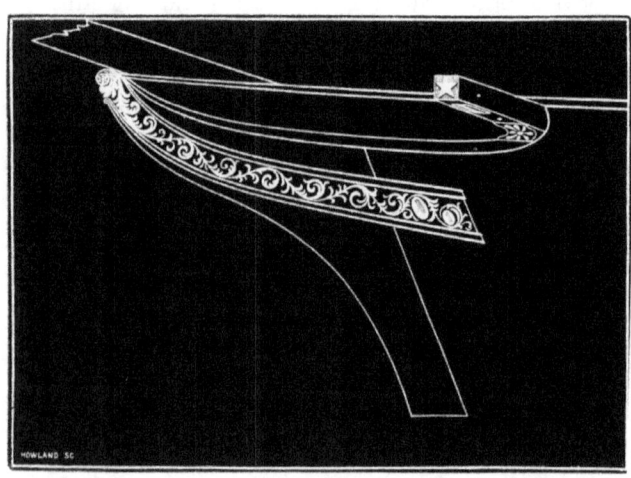

Billethead and cathead diagram. This drawing illustrates some of the typical decorative elements found on the bow of American clipper ships. The scrolled billethead was often used in place of a figurehead, while the cathead (top, right) used to support a ship's anchor was also sometimes decorated with various motifs (John W. Griffiths' *Treatise on Marine and Naval Architecture*, 1854).

In addition to billetheads and figureheads, a few clippers also had oculi, or a set of painted eyes, one on each side of the bow, on the catheads (the beams on the ship's upper bow that support the anchor) looking forward so as to give the ship a lively and lifelike appearance. Once again, the use of oculi on ships was a nautical tradition that dates back to ancient times when they were thought to impart to a ship the power to see its way safely over the ocean during a long journey. These oculi were commonly used by Arab dhows sailing in the Indian Ocean, as well as on Chinese junks sailing the Pacific. Those clippers known to have sported oculi were the New York–built *Challenge* and *Witch of the Wave* and *Wild Pigeon*, the latter pair having been built by George Raynes in Portsmouth. Other interesting design variants of the oculi used to decorate the catheads include the use of a gilded sun, sported by the *Queen of the Seas* and *Radiant*, both built by Paul Curtis at East Boston, the lion device used on the *Ellen Foster*, and the star motifs sported by the *Flying Mist, Invincible,* and *Black Hawk*. A number of other clippers are also known to have sported decorative cathead devices, but it is unknown what forms they may have taken.

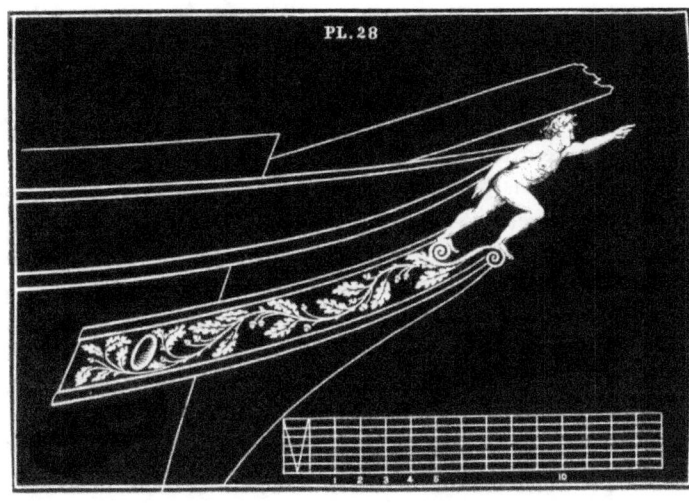

Figurehead diagram. Clipper ships sported many types of human figureheads, both male and female, in a wide variety of forms. This figurehead may be an imaginary one, or may represent that which adorned the bow of Smith & Dimon's clipper packet *Universe*, which John Griffiths helped to design (Griffiths' *Treatise on Marine and Naval Architecture*, 1854).

Of course, the most distinctive decorative feature of any clipper that had one, the one piece of marine artwork most recognized by the public today whether maritime enthusiast or not, was the ship's figurehead. This type of ship adornment had a long history, too, reaching far back into ancient times, but the art of the figurehead reached its zenith in America during the clipper ship era. While few figureheads from clipper ships have survived down through the years, those that have offer a clear portrait of this magnificent craft. Out in San Francisco at the National Maritime Museum there is the namesake image of the clipper *David Crockett*, complete with rifle and coonskin cap. Interestingly, this figurehead survived because it was carried aboard the ship and mounted only in port, never while at sea. Also surviving are several figureheads for Donald McKay–built clippers, including the giant gilded eagle head that adorned the *Great Republic* and survived its burning in 1853, and a Scottish Highland warrior, complete in tartan kilt and carrying a sword, that led the *Donald McKay*. One of the most recent finds, and probably the oldest clipper figurehead in existence, is that for the Portsmouth-built clipper ship *Nightingale*. Built in 1851, this famed ship carried a bust of the famed Swedish singer of the day, Jenny Lind. The ship was later sold to Norwegian interests and hailed from the port of Krageroe, and at one point while being refitted before her loss in 1893 had the figurehead removed. It eventually ended up in the possession of a farmer and was used as a scarecrow until 1994, when by chance of fate it was acquired by an antiques dealer and collector who became so enamored of the figurehead that he researched its origins. This figurehead was subsequently put up for auction by Sotheby's in 2008, where it sold for the low price of $120,000 due to unfair publicity about its authenticity, and it is now apparently owned by a private collector. Just as in real life the clipper *Nightingale* had a varied, interesting, and controversial career, so too has her figurehead! Other figureheads for clippers that have survived are those for the Massachusetts-built *Galatea* and one of Donald McKay's last (and least known) clippers, the *Minnehaha*, as well as the figurehead for McKay's very last clipper, the 1869-built *Glory of the Seas*.

The carving of figureheads was a specialized art and seems to have been practiced by relatively few carvers during the clipper ship era. Perhaps the most renowned were the shops of John Mason and William Gleason, both of Boston. Mason specialized in human forms, while Gleason seems to have been the animal expert, and there was plenty of work to be had during the 1850s. The finely carved, painted, and gilded works of art by Mason, Gleason, and other artists in port cities from Maine to Maryland were commissioned by many clipper ship owners. For a few clippers, records survive that detail the costs of a figurehead; the lion that adorned the bow of the 962-ton *Midnight*, built by Fernald & Petigrew at Portsmouth in 1854 was carved and gilded by Gleason for the seemingly low price of $110 (Pickett, pg. 92). However, when this amount is converted into our modern day values, that same figurehead would today cost about $3000, which gives us a much better idea of just how finely finished American clipper ships, with no expense spared, really were. Created in the woodcarving shops of their makers, these figureheads were usually carved out of one large piece of wood (Eastern pine was commonly used), though some figureheads, especially those with outstretched arms (see below for some examples) or accompanying emblems utilized additional pieces of wood and upon completion were then shipped to the builder's yard. Here they were mounted on the bow of a clipper and secured in place with drift pins and cleverly concealed braces. In some cases, as with the *David Crockett*, these figureheads were removed while at sea, but how common this practice was is unknown.

For the vast majority of clipper ships whose figureheads have not survived, there was a wide variety of subjects represented according to written accounts. While the most common were those in the figure of a woman, these were wrought in many styles. Some were lifelike in nature, like those for *Ellen Foster* (named after a Medford shipbuilder's wife) and the *Mary L. Sutton,* while others were representative of the female form in a variety of settings. The McKay-built *Flying Cloud* sported an angelic figure blowing a trumpet, as did *Chariot of Fame* and *Alarm,* while the *Northern Light* featured an angel with one arm extended holding a torch with a golden flame. The clippers *Queen of Clippers* and *Queen of the Seas*, naturally, had queenly figures, the later of which was holding a wand in one hand and was surrounded by a golden sun. The clipper *Cleopatra* had a figurehead of her historic namesake, while *Mystery* and *Syren* both featured a mermaid, the figurehead on the former depicted rising dramatically out of the ocean. The goddesses of ancient days, too, were represented among the clipper figureheads; the ship *Herald of the Morning*, quite appropriately, featured a likeness of the Roman goddess of the dawn, Aurora (it is unknown if the clipper *Aurora* did so as well), while *Meteor* featured the fleet-footed Greek goddess Atalanta picking up golden apples which, according to mythology, is how she was tricked into marriage. It is unknown if the clipper *Atalanta* featured this goddess as well. The *Whirl-*

> ☞ The clipper ship *Flying Cloud*—the swiftest craft afloat—is now upon the Sectional Dock, where the curious in nautical matters may examine her build and bottom. The *Flying Cloud*, it will be remembered, made the voyage from San Francisco in 89 days—running in one day 389 miles, a greater distance than has ever been made in the same time by any other craft, steamers included.

Flying Cloud newspaper notice. Clippers like this famed record-setter were the stars of the day in the transportation world and were visited by thousands of people wherever they put into port (*New York Times*, March 25, 1853).

wind, naturally, featured a goddess of the winds with wings of gold, holding a lighted torch in one hand. Closer to our country's history is the goddess of liberty, featured on some clippers including *Onward*, which depicted the goddess draped in an American flag and one foot resting on a globe, with one hand pointing forward and the other holding harvest related emblems. Below the status of goddess, other classical female forms in mythology were also depicted on the bows of clippers; the *Dauntless* featured a nymph with wings, adorned with a golden girdle and a ring of flowers around her head. Among those clippers figureheads that also depicted the female form, usually in flowing drapery or robes, were *Adelaide*, *Belle of the West*, *Challenger*, *Empress of the Sea* (carrying a globe in one hand, a scepter in the other), *Flying Mist*, *Grace Darling*, *Hoogly*, *Lightning*, *Ocean Telegraph* (surrounded by forks of lightning), *Romance of the Seas* (flanked by the names of the romantic poets "Scott" and "Cooper"), *Shooting Star* (with a waist circled by a ring of stars), *Swallow*, *Telegraph*, *Water Witch*, *White Swallow* (adorned with outstretched wings), and *Witch of the Wave*. Interestingly, none of the witch-related clippers named above depicted a traditional

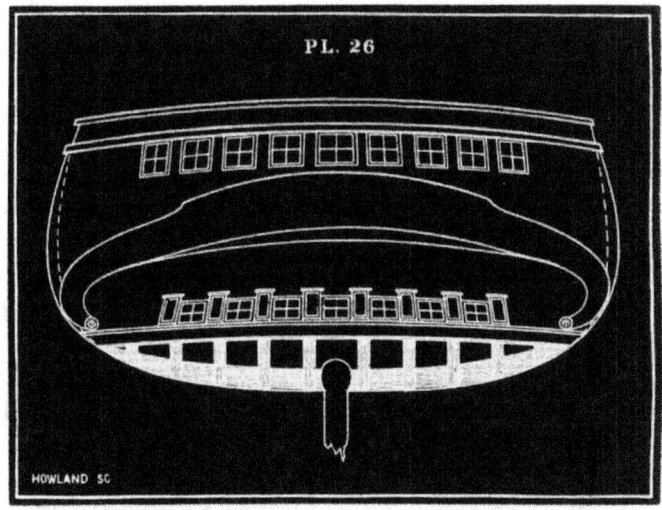

Stern diagrams. Here are shown two stern configurations, along with their accompanying decorations. The stern at top is for an unknown but finely finished vessel. Note the windows above, while at bottom is the drawing for the stern of the clipper packet *Universe*, built by Smith & Dimon at New York in 1850 and designed by John W. Griffiths (Griffiths' ***Treatise on Marine and Naval Architecture***, 1854).

hag-like witch as their figureheads, surely because it was not as attractive and perhaps would have been viewed by superstitious sailors as downright unlucky. However, the *Witch of the Wave*, whose homeport, quite fittingly, was Salem, Massachusetts, did have an elaborately decorated stern that also featured a witch — whether one that was beautiful or the more traditional kind is unstated — floating in a seashell, flanked by an imp riding on a dolphin!

While ships have traditionally been referred to in the feminine and the female figurehead was the most popular among the clipper fleet, male figureheads were also used quite regularly. Among those clippers that had figureheads of their namesakes were the *Asa Eldridge* (named after a packet ship captain), *Andrew Jackson*, *Edwin Forest* (a famed actor of the day), *James Baines* (the owner of the Black Ball Line of Australian packet ships), *John Wade* (named for Captain Wade of the Boston firm of Reed & Wade), *Malay* (a Malay chief), the previously mentioned *Reporter, Robin Hood* (with bent bow), *Saracen* (a Middle Eastern warrior), *Santa Claus* (smoking a gilded pipe and with presents in every pocket), *Thatcher Magoun* (the Medford shipbuilder), *Viking* (a Norse warrior in armor), and *Wizard* (an Oriental magician holding a book of spells). Other clippers that also carried male likenesses were *Coeur de Lion* (King Richard), *Daring* (a pirate), the second *Golden Fleece* (a knight in armor), and *Star of the Union* (famed orator and politician Daniel Webster). Naturally, the gods of the ancients and mythical figures were also represented; *Storm King* sported a figurehead of Neptune, a trident in one hand and the other pointing seaward, *Sovereign of the Seas* featured a merman blowing on a conch shell, *Starlight* also apparently featured a merman (though one account given during its building was at a loss as to what it represented, a serpent or a dragon, so perhaps it was replaced), and *Morning Light* featured a winged archer with bent bow. Not to be forgotten are those ships that depicted Native American warriors or chiefs, including *Red Jacket* (the famed Seneca chief and orator), *Westward Ho*, and *Sierra Nevada* (originally named *King of the Forest*). Finally, a number of clippers had figureheads depicting sailors in traditional sailor garb, including *Champion of the Seas* and *Blue Jacket*, whose figurehead depicted a sailor dressed in a blue jacket with yellow buttons, a square belt buckle, handkerchief around his neck, flanked by a scroll with the saying "Keep a sharp lookout." While figureheads are usually lost when a ship is lost at sea, this was not the case with *Blue Jacket*; though the ship caught fire and burned before sinking off the Falkland Islands in March 1869, the figurehead survived and subsequently washed ashore nearly three years later, in December 1871, off Fremantle, Australia.

A third category of clipper ship figureheads also prominent were those that depicted members of the animal kingdom, both real and mythological. By far the most popular was the eagle figurehead, in all its myriad forms including those that portrayed just its head and those that depicted it in flight. While the eagle was a popular symbol for figureheads prior to the clipper ship era, the time of the 1850s saw its use soar to great heights, a patriotic symbol that was emblematic of our national pride, strength, and drive to expand westward. Among those clippers with eagle figureheads, many of them obvious choices, were *Bald Eagle, Challenge, Climax, Competitor, Eagle, Fleetwing, Flying Eagle, Golden Eagle, Golden West* (with quartz rocks in its talons), *John Bertram, Nabob, National Eagle, Ocean Express, Prima Donna, Southern Cross, Spitfire,* and *Surprise*. The choice of an eagle figurehead was a curious choice for some ships, including the Portsmouth-built clippers *Sea Serpent* and *Wild Duck* and the Baltimore built clipper *Seaman's Bride*. Among the other animal-themed figureheads used by clippers, many of them also obvious choices, was the dove (*Alboni*), pigeon (*Carrier Pigeon* and *Wild Pigeon*), duck (*Canvasback*, featuring a whole flock rising in flight), dog (*Mastiff, Wild Ranger* and *Stag Hound*), fish (*Flying Fish*), hawk (*War Hawk*), tiger (*Witchcraft*, in crouching position), horse (*Flying Childers, Racer* and *Typhoon*, the latter in a leaping form, surrounded by clouds and lightning bolts), snake (*Charmer*, with tongue sticking out), bird (*Game Cock*, game bird with outstretched neck), lion (*Midnight*), gazelle (*Gazelle*, not liked by the owner and removed), dragon (*Flying Dragon, Dreadnought, Snow Squall, Sea Witch* and *Tinqua*), Pegasus, the winged horse of mythology (*Winged Racer*), and a sea monster (*Sunny South*). Finally, there were those clipper figureheads that depicted neither human nor animal forms, but were instead more emblematic in nature. The clipper *Flyaway* must have been a sight to see, with the large pair of wings that adorned its bow, while the *Golden Light* featured a golden hand grasping a torch staff. There was seemingly no limit to the artist's imagination when it came to figureheads.

In concluding this account of clipper ship adornment, the stern quarters of these finely finished ships are also worthy of consideration. This rear portion of the ship, along with the headboards and trailboards, wooden plaques often mounted on a ships hull either forward or aft (or both) that carried the ship's name or some other form of decoration, combined to provided a large canvas, so to speak, for the marine artist and resulted in many elaborate forms. Sadly, though these works of art have been well described in print, none of them have survived to this day. When a ship went down at sea, or went to the breaker's yard ashore after suffering irreparable damage, or otherwise reached the end of her productive life, this artwork was also gone, though some shipyard workers salvaged some portions to take home for use as household decorations, as happened with some pieces from unknown ships that can be found in the holdings of many nautical museums.

As with other forms of maritime art, the decoration of stern quarters had a long history prior to the day of the clipper ship, perhaps the most elaborate being found on the towering and castle-like sterns of warships like the *Wasa* of Sweden, dating from 1626, and Admiral Nelson's flagship HMS *Victory* of Britain's Royal Navy, launched in 1765 and the world's oldest commissioned warship. Closer to home, the decorative stern of the world's oldest commissioned warship still afloat, the Boston-built USS *Constitution*, with its carved eagle holding an American flag shield flanked by stars and sturdy pillars, is a notable forerunner to the later-day clipper ships. Because the clipper ship sterns were designed with speed in mind, they were not as elaborately carved as American merchant ships and naval vessels in earlier ages. However, while some clipper sterns were but sparsely decorated, others carried on the traditions of old in a lighter but equally elegant form. Among the early clippers of the 1850s there were some finely carved works to be found; the first California clipper to be launched, the *John Bertram*, carried on her stern a medallion bust of her namesake, a famous sea captain and merchant of Salem, while *Sea Serpent* sported her namesake in a green and gold color that was surely eye-catching. The use of our American symbol, the eagle, was a common stern decoration motif that continued the tradition dating back from the early days of the republic; the giant *Great Republic* featured an eagle with extended wings holding a shield that bore the ship's name and homeport, *Hurricane* had a gilded eagle's head with a ribbon flying from its beak that had the ship's name, and *Sierra Nevada* sported an eagle in flight with a scroll in its beak that had written on it the ship's name and homeport. Other clippers that featured the eagle motif were *Invincible*, *Racer*, *Whirlwind*, and *Typhoon* to name just a few. In keeping with this same theme, other clippers featured patriotic scrolls, shields and other devices. The celebrated *Challenge* had the arms of the U.S. above the ship's name and hailing port, which were done in gilded letters, while *Young America* featured trail boards that sported carvings of national emblems. In keeping with a similar theme, the clipper *Onward* featured the carving of a Native American surrounded by gilt work with the phrase "According to Law" carved in white letters above the ship's name and port. The meaning of the use of this phrase in this sea context is not entirely clear today, but perhaps refers to the general ideal that America is a country ruled by the principles of law, or, given the ship's name, may refer to the then current idea of manifest destiny and America's inevitable expansion westward.

Another popular stern decoration motif was the use of coats of arms or those that featured the national emblems of the United States, sometimes in conjunction with those of other nations. The McKay-built *Champion of the Seas* was built for James Baines and his line of England to Australia packet ships, so it is not surprising that she sported the coat of arms of Australia, while the *James Baines*, also built by McKay for the same line, featured a globe flanked by the coats of arms for the U.S. and England. This ship is said to have had the most beautiful stern of all of the clippers built by Donald McKay. On the other hand, the *Surprise*, designed by Samuel Pook and built by Samuel Hall, carried the coat of arms for the state New York, where the ship was owned and homeported. The *Saracen* featured Middle Eastern themed weapons, perhaps a scimitar, and shields on her stern. A final example of this type of motif is the escutcheon for England's King Richard, which was carved in relief on the stern of the clipper *Coeur de Lion*.

The most common type of stern adornment found during the clipper ship era, however, was the scrollwork, often carved in relief and gilded, that was executed in countless abstract designs.

Often the ship's name and homeport was also done up in fancy carved and gilded letters. Among those clippers so decorated were *Bonita, Competitor, Game Cock, Golden Light, R.B. Forbes, Southern Cross, Star of the Union, Thatcher Magoun,* and *Wizard*. The clippers *Challenger* and *White Swallow* had their fancy work carved in arched form, the former being gilded, *Silver Star* featured an arch of gilded work with a star in the center, while *Don Quixote*'s stern was "chastely ornamented with gilded branches" (McLean, October 27, 1853). While most accounts of the clippers extol their decorative virtues, not all of a ship's features were well received; the New York–built *Sunny South*, designed by famed yacht builder George Steers, was said to have a "rather ugly" stern, while the gilded carved work on the stern of Donald McKay's *Lightning* was described shortly after her launch thusly: "This, at best, is only an excrescence, and adds nothing of beauty to the hull" (Howe and Matthews, pgs. 639 and 357).

Finally, there were those ships that had decorative scenes relating to their namesake that were carved in relief on their stern. Themes from the ancient gods were of course present on the sterns of some clippers; *Morning Light* featured a golden chariot in which Aurora, the goddess of the dawn, was seated, *Galatea* showed a female figure painted white surrounded by gilt carving, while *Ocean Telegraph* featured the sea god Neptune surrounded by scroll work. Also present were themes from popular song and literature; the *John Gilpin*, named after the main character in a famous comic ballad, depicts its namesake astride a horse galloping at full speed out of control, *Nightingale* depicted the wildly popular singer of the time, the Swede Jenny Lind, in a reclining position with, what else, a small nightingale perched on her finger, the whole surrounded by the ship's name in blue and gold letters, and *Dauntless* featured a bust of a woman surrounded by a span of multi-arched and gilded carvings that was noted for its beauty of design and execution.

A popular theme, of course, for these stern mounted murals, however, were those that related directly to the ship's name itself; the *Charger* featured a mounted charger in full gallop; *Competitor* featured a carving of a hunting dog, as did the *Wild Duck*; *Stag Hound* featured a stag surrounded by other un-named emblems; *Tinqua* had trailboards that featured the tail of a dragon, an extension of its dragon figurehead; *War Hawk* (New York–built) sported a cameo of a hawk carrying off a fish; *Wild Pigeon* featured two gilded pigeons to match her figurehead; *Water Witch* depicted a seascape with three frolicking mermaids, while *West Wind* quite appropriately depicted a carved scene of a ship under full sail by the wind. Most interesting is the decoration for the multi-personality clipper *Charmer*; though its figurehead was a snake, its stern depicted a reclining female form (no doubt a "charming" one) surrounded by gilt work! Finally, the *Staffordshire* was also interesting for its stern carved scene depicting a pottery manufacturing scene from the area of its namesake on one side and a view of the counting house of Enoch Train, the packet ship's owner, on the other, flanked by lion's heads carved in relief. This combined theme of manufacturing and the riches it brought was indeed quite an appropriate theme not just for the *Staffordshire*, but for any clipper ship, for it was these vessels that carried the goods of the burgeoning industrial nations of America and England to California and all corners of the globe.

Final Reckoning; Clipper Ship Costs

The methods of designing and building having now been discussed, it is time to examine the costs and sales figures relating to building and outfitting a clipper ship. Knowing what clipper ship builders charged for a completed hull, and other details such as spars and iron work, the costs to outfit a clipper for sea, and what these ships sold for in the years after they were built helps to give a full financial picture of the clipper ship era and show just how much capital was laid out in the building of these speedy ships. By the 1830s we know that rising costs made shipbuilding in New York a much less profitable venture; Isaac Webb tried, luckily without success, to dissuade his son William Webb from following in his footsteps for this very reason. Mitigating economic factors that affected the building of a clipper (or any wooden sailing ship) included material costs, which could run anywhere from 45 percent to 55 percent of the total for iron work and timber, especially in New York as the forests around the area were long-ago depleted and timber had to be purchased from wholesale dealers who included in their prices their own profit margins, increased competition, and rising labor costs. It is interesting to note that after 1853, few clippers were built in New York, in part because of prohibitive supply and labor costs. One newspaper reporter, commenting on the slowdown in the shipyard business there in prior months, noted that builders began to "brighten up, half forgetting the losses which a sudden rise in materials and labor entailed on the contracts of last year. Materials still rate high, though somewhat under the prices of May last. The unusually fine quality of the timber in market at present has been subject of remark through the different yards, and builders anticipate much for the performance of the craft now on the stocks, as well from the quality of their 'stuff,' as the improvements in model and execution, which the experience of each year introduces" ("Our Shipyards," *New York Daily Times*, August 13, 1853).

One of the major pieces, so to speak, of the profitability puzzle, labor costs, was also one that was changing; in an earlier age, shipyard workers in New York labored on a standard day that began when the sun rose and ended sometimes at sunset, but often well into the night. However, by the late 1820s shipyard workers began to push for a ten-hour day, ideas that were advanced in part by "skilled mechanics ... mainly from Great Britain and Germany" (Morrison, pg. 66) who had fought for labor rights in their home countries. While the first labor organization for shipyard workers in New York, eventually incorporated as the New York Journeyman Shipwrights Society, was formed in 1804, this was not a union, but a benevolent society. Its members paid initiation dues and monthly dues of fifty cents, thus accumulating funds that were used to help support members and their families who were too ill, injured, or aged to work. Though this first society was short-lived, others were soon formed to take its place. When shipyard workers in New York began to agitate for reduced working hours, their efforts at first failed despite several strikes at a few shipyards. The New York Journeyman Shipwrights' and Caulkers' Benevolent Society was subsequently formed in 1833, and this united group once again asked shipbuilders to implement the ten hour day. Finally, seeing the handwriting on the wall, New York shipbuilders agreed to the ten hour day in 1834; now, shipyard workers reported for work at 6 A.M., stopped for one hour at 8 A.M. for breakfast, continued work until noontime, resumed work again at 1 P.M. and ended their work day at 6 P.M. It is interesting to note that Boston shipwrights also agitated for a ten hour work day in the 1830s, but their efforts failed and the shortened workday would not there become a reality until the 1850s. As for shipyards located elsewhere in New England, there was less of a need for labor organizations to champion worker's rights as most shipbuilding concerns were small and more community oriented in nature, employing family, friends, and fellow townsmen. One such example may be found in Pittston, Maine, located on the mighty Kennebec River. Here, the clipper *White Falcon* was put over by local builders William and Franklin Stevens, surely with the help of many other members of the Stevens family, a number of which were also in the shipbuilding trade. However, it must not be thought that labor organizations were slow in forming when it came to the smaller shipyards outside of New York and Boston, and in many places the ten hour day was in place. In 1854 the Mechanics Shipbuilding Company in Portsmouth, referred to as the Union Company, built the clipper *Morning Glory* for a consortium of local owners. The company that built the clipper was a joint stock venture consisting of forty men working in the local shipbuilding trades who purchased shares at $500 each (Brighton, pgs. 150–51). An earlier example of this type of labor company was the Bone and Muscle Society in Frankfort, Maine; formed prior to the clipper ship era, it "consisted of a dozen competent mechanics who were to build ships, do all the work, and share the profits" (Fairburn, pg. 3524). The society, however, was unsuccessful and was dissolved before its first ship was completed.

In the end, when it comes to workers' wages, this was a large part of the expense of building a clipper, comprising as much as a third of the overall initial builder's cost. New York shipwrights earned two dollars a day (twenty cents an hour) at the beginning of the clipper ship era in 1846, a figure that rose to $3.00 per day by 1853. New York shipwrights were undoubtedly the best paid such workers in the country, though the workers at Donald McKay's Boston shipyard and likely several others in the Boston area were probably not far behind. However, wages for shipyard workers in less populous areas like New Hampshire, Maine, Rhode Island, and parts of southern and northern Massachusetts were substantially lower, resulting in clipper ships that were thus built at correspondingly lower prices for both New York and Boston area owners who had no qualms in patronizing these shipyards.

While surviving records and accounts are limited in regards to specific clipper ship costs, enough information exists to offer some numbers in several areas, including labor costs, builders' contract prices, voyage ready costs, and later clipper ship selling or auction prices. These figures are often stated on a price per ton basis, which was standard in the shipbuilding trade. With some of the specific cost figures given in this section, I have included in parenthesis what these amounts correspond to in modern (circa 2010) dollars for comparison purposes. Builder costs and resulting profit margins are the most difficult to determine; just what portion of a builder's overall selling price represented a profit to the builder after paying for material and the labor to complete the job? Profit margins for New York shipbuilders were likely no higher than 10 or 15 percent during good times and during slack or extremely competitive times were reduced to less than 5 percent. In comparison, modern private shipyards in America today earn profits somewhere in the 3 percent range, showing that little has changed in 150 years. However, in the clipper ship era there were some cases where either no profit was realized by the builder, or a loss was incurred. Jabez Williams built the long-lived and fast clipper *Simoon* at his Long Island shipyard in December 1852 and received $105,000 from Mumford & Co. for his work, yet "nothing was made by building her" (Griffiths, *The Progressive Shipbuilder* 2, pg. 254). Having been a shipbuilder for over thirty years in New York, perhaps the lack of any profit for the building of *Simoon* was a factor in Williams' subsequent retirement as this was his last ship! The most extreme profit margins, though not fully documented, were surely earned in the period from 1850 to mid–1852, when the demand for ships was so great that shipyards all along the East Coast from New York to Maine were operating at full capacity. It would not be surprising if during this period some builders realized profits of 20 percent or even 25 percent on the early clippers. Given these potential earnings, it is no surprise that a number of new shipyards were subsequently established during the first years of the clipper ship era. The figures for the early clippers *Rainbow* and *Sea Witch*, both designed by John Griffiths and built by Smith & Dimon of New York, are quite interesting; the 757-ton *Rainbow* was built in 1845 and cost her owners $22,500 ($669,000), or $29.72 per ton, for the hull and spars, while the second true clipper ship ever built, the 908-ton *Sea Witch*, was launched a year later in 1846 for the same owners and cost the builders $11,739 ($345,000) in labor alone, or $16.77 per ton to build. Though the selling price of this clipper is unknown, it can be assumed that this ship was sold to Howland & Aspinwall for at least the same price per ton as *Rainbow* (and probably more) as the owners were extremely pleased with this first vessel. If this was the case, then Smith & Dimon sold *Sea Witch* for at least $27,000 and probably realized a profit that was no greater than 10 or 15 percent. It is perhaps telling that Smith & Dimon built only one more clipper after *Sea Witch* before turning their attention to steamships, likely because they were more profitable to build and demand in this area, despite the competition, intensified during the 1850s.

Another important figure to look at is the contract price agreed upon between the builder and owner and which is known for a number of clippers. In some cases these ships were contracted for before their building commenced, while in other cases the ship was built and launched before being sold to its first owner. These initial acquisition costs ranged from $30,410 ($895,000) for the 742-ton Maine-built *Snow Squall*, or $38.01 per ton, to $150,000 ($4.4 million) for the 2006-ton New York–built *Challenge*, or $74.78 per ton. Both ships were launched in 1851, and while the Maine clipper was built in an area where labor and material costs were much lower, the New York clipper was specifically built "without reference to cost" (Howe and Matthews, pg. 60) and was intended to be the best built clipper afloat. Other 1851-built clippers whose contract prices are known include the New York–built *Invincible* ($120,000 or $67.83 per ton), the Massachusetts-built *Telegraph* ($70,000 or $64.94 per ton), and the New Hampshire–built *Witch of the Wave* ($80,000 or $53.40 per ton). All of these clippers were well-built and fast ships, but from the foregoing it can easily be seen that clippers built in northern New England were decidedly less expensive. In 1852 the New York–built *Contest* was launched at a cost of $80,000 ($2.33 million), or $72.86 per ton, while the Maine-built *Flying Eagle* cost her owner $62,500, or $57.13 per ton. Another Maine-built clipper, *Rattler*, was sold by her builder in 1852 for $66,000, or $58.88 per ton. In Boston, Donald McKay built the *Empress of the Seas* in late 1852 and launched her in January 1853. He originally intended to operate the big 2,197-ton ship himself, but when it was half finished he received and accepted an offer from Baltimore interests for $125,000, or $56.90 per ton. In 1853 the Connecticut-built *David Crockett* cost her owners $93,000, or $55.39 a ton, the New Hampshire–built *Morning Light* cost $117,000 ($3.41 million), or $68.30 per ton, and the Massachusetts-built *Wizard* was sold by her builder for $95,000, or $59.34 per ton. Figures are also known for three Maine-built clippers launched in this year; the large *Black Warrior* sold for $90,000, or $49.23 per ton, the small *Anglo Saxon* sold for $50,000 or $57.60 per ton, while the big and fast *Flying Scud* sold for $100,000, or $58.38 per ton. Two of the more expensive clippers in terms of price per ton were also launched in 1853, the Boston-built *Lightfoot*, which cost $140,000 or $70.14 per ton, and the New York–built *Young America*, which cost the same and came in at $71.39 per ton. Contrast these prices with that of the Boston-built *Reporter*, which cost $80,750, a bargain price of $54.78 per ton, but lasted for only nine years before her loss off Cape Horn after springing a leak due to heavy storms. Interestingly, among these 1853-built clippers whose contract price is known, one of the least expensive, *David Crockett*, and the most expensive, *Young America*, of this group were among the best values when it came to productivity and longevity. The former ship served several owners for nearly forty years, while the latter sailed the seas profitably for over thirty years. Finally, in 1854, the last year for which some contract and initial prices are known, these figures were generally on the downward trend, but some high-priced clippers were still launched; the Baltimore-built *Napier* cost a reported $140,000, or a whopping $77.31 per ton, the New York–built clipper packet *Adelaide* cost $128,000, or $69.91 per ton, the Maine-built *Phoenix* sold for $90,000, or $61.73 per ton, and the Massachusetts-built *Asterion* sold for $67,000 ($1.79 million) or $59.03 per ton. Another Maine-built ship acquired this year was the *Nonpareil*; launched in November 1853, she was subsequently put up for sale in Boston early in 1854 and sold for $76,000 or $53.11 per ton. In contrast, two New Hampshire–built clippers cost a great deal less; *Midnight* cost her Boston owner $40,000, or $41.58 per ton, but *Noonday*, constructed by the same builder for the same owner, cost $44,000, a slightly reduced figure of $37.00 per ton. Finally, among those clippers that were initially sold to foreign interests and never made a voyage under the American flag during the height of the clipper ship era was the Maine-built *Ocean Chief*, which her builder sold to the Black Ball Line of Australian packet ships, owned by Englishman James Baines, for $85,000 or $69.22 per ton.

While the contract price for a clipper between builder and owner is interesting, that price does not represent an owner's full investment in his ship, nor does it mean that a ship was then ready to start earning its keep. Once launched, a clipper still had to be outfitted with a number of items and sometimes, as previously discussed, had to be rigged and coppered, which added significantly to the cost. Even when a contract price included these additional construction costs, an owner still had to spend money to get a clipper ready for sea. Such "voyage ready" costs included charts and nautical instruments (those for *Courser* cost $116), provisions and additional supplies, and, in a day when many supplies and food items were stored in wooden barrels, coopering costs. What data there is that is available suggests that these additional voyage ready costs added anywhere from twenty to twenty-five dollars extra per ton. The 1094-ton *Flying Eagle*, built at Newcastle, Maine, in 1852 by William Hitchcock for New York owners, had a builder's price of $62,500 ($57.12 per ton), but her final voyage ready cost came out to $85,473, or $78.12 per ton (Evans, Jr., pg. 36). Other clippers whose voyage ready costs are known (but not contract prices) include *Aurora*, $83,400 ($59.74 per ton), *Oriental*, $70,000 ($69.79 per ton), and *White Squall*, $90,000 ($80.43 per ton). The first of these was a Massachusetts clipper built in 1853 when the clipper craze was starting to subside, which is evident from her lower cost per ton, while the last two ships were both built in New York by Jacob Bell in 1849 and 1850 at the beginning of the clipper ship era and are reflective of the quickly rising demand for speedy ships in the California trade. Another clipper for which both contract and voyage ready costs are known is the Medford, Massachusetts–built *Courser*, put over by talented shipwright Paul Curtis in 1851. This ship had an initial cost of $50,000 ($48.83 per ton) and a voyage ready cost of $69.43 per ton. A final example of a clipper whose contract price and voyage ready costs are known is the New Hampshire–built *Noonday*; while her contract price came to $37.00 per ton her voyage ready cost amounted to $72,000 or $60.56 per ton. While it is unfortunate that exact figures for the clippers built by Donald McKay in Boston are unknown, after his retirement in 1870 he stated that he built "first-class ships" with voyage ready costs of between $65 and $70 per ton (Evans, Jr., pg. 36). Despite the gaps in our knowledge, the voyage ready cost of a clipper is, in the end, a more accurate and practical figure to use when considering the financial ramifications of the clipper ship era.

The final set of figures to be examined in the area of clipper ship finances are the selling prices, either outright or via auction, that were realized when a clipper was sold by her original owner. These selling prices serve to tell us not only how valuable clipper ships were overall, but also how their value fluctuated during the decade of the 1850s. These figures can be divided into two classes, namely sale prices to American interests that were realized within several years after the ship was built and those that resulted when a given clipper was sold to foreign interests after the clipper ship era had ended. These later figures came at a time when there was a great sell-off in general among American merchant ship owners due to the effects of the Civil War and are thus not germane to this discussion. In regards to the selling prices to American interests during the 1850s, perhaps the best story out there involves the fastest clipper of them all, Donald McKay's famed *Flying Cloud*; built in 1851 for McKay's financial supporter and friend, Enoch Train, the 1,782-ton ship was sold while still on the stocks to Grinnell, Minturn & Company of New York. As the story goes, the New York firm was very desirous of buying a clipper ship and inquired of Train if he would sell *Flying Cloud*. Ever the businessman, Train asked them to name their price, which they did, $90,000 ($2.65 million). Since Train had contracted with McKay to build the ship for $50,000 ($28.05 per ton), he immediately accepted the offer and the ship was sold before her first voyage, thereby realizing him an immediate profit of $40,000 without having spent one cent in operating costs! Though the sale helped the financially strapped company, Enoch Train would always regret selling the soon to be celebrated clipper. In regards to the *Flying Cloud*, while one might wonder why McKay contracted to build the ship during a period of great demand for such a low price, it must be remembered that Train had provided McKay the financial backing to establish his shipyard in East Boston just six years before, so Train received some compensation in return in the form of

III. Young Mechanic: *The Building of a Clipper Ship* 65

The clipper *Nightingale*. This famed Portsmouth ship, shown in this Currier & Ives print from 1854 getting underway off The Battery, New York Harbor, was built in 1851 in circumstances that resulted in a tangled financial mess. She never did make her intended maiden voyage for the World's Fair but nevertheless had a fascinating career (courtesy of the Library of Congress).

favorable building prices. As to other clipper ships and their early sales figures, the 587-ton *Raduga*, an early Massachusetts-built clipper, was sold at auction in 1851 when she was three years old for the relatively large sum of $32,500 ($55.36 per ton) at a time when fast ships were at a premium, while in 1853 the small Massachusetts-built clipper *Mischief* was sold after just one voyage for $22,000, or $40.15 per ton. In 1854 a number of clipper ships were sold within one to three years after their launching. The small Massachusetts-built *Sparkling Wave* was sold after a year's worth of service for $50,000 or $76.34 per ton; another Massachusetts clipper, the *Star of the Union*, sold for $70,000 or $66.23 per ton when two years old, while the well-known *Sword Fish*, built by William Webb in New York just three years prior, sold for just $55,000, or $53.09 per ton. This fast ship was one of the sharpest clippers built and was nicknamed "the Diving Bell" because she shipped a lot of water during her voyages. The low sale price was likely a result of a number of factors, despite her renowned builder and speed, including an overall decline in demand, an inability to carry a large cargo due to her sharp form, difficulties in signing a crew, and potential damage claims to her cargo, which last two factors were due to the wetness of the clipper. Finally, in 1855, with the craze for clippers coming to an end, the Maine-built *Golden Racer* was sold after three years of service for $45,000, or $53.70 per ton, not a bad price all things considered. Though clipper ship financials are lacking for later years, by 1856 and 1857 the market for these ships had bottomed out due to a number of factors, to be discussed at length in a later chapter, and by the early 1860s many clippers were sold to foreign interests and no longer sailed the seven seas under the American flag.

In the discussion of clipper ship costs and selling prices, everything may appear to have been well-ordered and cut and dried, but this was not always the case. In an era where financial regulations were virtually non-existent, builders who constructed a clipper did not always make the profits they had anticipated, nor did their owners. Sometimes owners and builders did not agree on the final product and, as with any large business transaction, sometimes deals went awry. Sometimes third parties, including ship brokers, whose work was the business of buying and selling ships, became involved in order to salvage the situation. One famous example of this type of complicated transaction involved the famed Portsmouth-built clipper *Nightingale* in 1851. The ship was contracted for between Badger Island shipwright Samuel Hanscom, Jr., and a group of investors that included Hanscom himself and Captain F.A. Miller. The beautiful, yacht-like clipper was well-built and lavishly appointed in every way, her owners intent on carrying passengers in grand style to England and exhibiting her at the World's Fair in London later in 1851 as a masterful example of American shipbuilding. However, cost overruns and the fact that few people were booking passage on the ship in advance, resulted in financial support drying up and a resulting muddled mess. Captain Miller and Hanscom disagreed on construction details and Miller refused to accept the ship, while Hanscom's shipyard workers and sub-contractors were caught in the middle and went unpaid. With all these problems, *Nightingale* was launched in June 1851, a month after she was supposed to have sailed for England. To resolve this financial disaster, businessman Ichabod Goodwin, New Hampshire's future Civil War governor, was appointed agent. The clipper was soon towed to Boston and put up for auction six weeks later. Though the details are murky, the 1,060-ton ship was sold for $43,500 ($41.04 per ton) to shipbrokers Davis & Company in an arrangement that paid off Hanscom and his workers, as well as Captain Miller. How this was achieved based on the low auction price is not known, but in terms of actual cost, of *Nightingale* it is said that "from the point of cost, no clipper built on the Piscataqua priced out at more per ton" (Brighton, pg. 127).

What's in a Name? Clipper Ship Nomenclature

As has been discussed, the clipper ship was a notable technological development during the age of sail in America; utilizing an evolving hull form, these ships soon became the fastest cargo carriers the world had ever seen. With their expansive sail plans and grandiose styling, the clipper ships were a pleasing sight to behold to sailor and landsman alike. However, it is in the names that were bestowed upon the clippers that we see reflected the state of the American mindset during this exciting period. The Baltimore-built clipper *Spirit of the Times* was one of the most aptly-named clippers of all, for that is what these ships truly represented. In fact, when it came to ship nomenclature, the clipper ship era marked a great change from American maritime traditions. In previous days, ship's names were much more down to earth, usually indicative of their commercial purposes, places of trade or hailing port, while other traditional names came from ancient mythology and the sea, or highlighted their intimate connections to a local builder or owner.

A look through American ship registry records gives us such common ship names for the first category as *Reaper, Harvest, Industry,* or *Traveler*; for the second we see such names as *Venus* or *Neptune*; while for the third such geographical names as *Hudson, Columbia, Peru,* and *America*. Perhaps the most interesting changes in naming tradition were those that occurred in regard to a ship's personal connections as relating to builders or owners. Previously, many ships were given such feminine names as *Anna, Polly, Mary,* and the like, named after a beloved daughter or wife, while many other ships had such standard masculine names (though a ship was always still referred to as a "she" by sailors) as *Two Brothers, Franklin,* or *Washington*. While the old naming traditions never fully died out, with the advent of the clipper ship era these localized naming practices changed dramatically. Now, ships were bestowed with names that signified speed and the riches to be gained in the California trade, names that spoke to America's ideals of strength, boundless energy and patriotism, those that related to the frenzied action of the sea in all its myriad forms, and those relating to the majesty and gods of the ocean. The following is a list of clippers representative of each of these categories:

Speed and the California Trade: *Golden Racer, Golden Rocket, Golden Horn, Golden Light, Golden State, Golden City, Golden Fleece, Eureka, Westward Ho, Ocean Express, Flying Arrow, Fleetwood, Fleetwing, Eagle Wing, Belle of the West, Flying Cloud, Hotspur, Meteor, Comet, Shooting Star, Stag Hound, Gazelle, Antelope, Grey Hound, Flying Dragon, Flyaway, Flying Scud, Dashaway, Challenger, Charger, Courser, Flying Mist, Racer, Whistler, Derby, Messenger, Winged Racer, Winged Arrow, Highflyer, Lightfoot, Rapid, Wings of the Morning, Flying Yankee, Sierra Nevada, Quickstep.*

American Ideals and Symbols: *Young America, Eagle, Bald Eagle, National Eagle, Flying Eagle, Chariot of Fame, Great Republic, Contest, Competitor, Climax, Challenge, Invincible, Intrepid, Onward, Champion of the Seas, Defiance, Gauntlet, Defender, Electric Spark, Endeavor, Resolute, Matchless, Fearless, Wide Awake, Victory, Union, Morning Light, Star of the Union, Star of Peace, Star of Hope, Undaunted, Sweepstakes, Telegraph, Ocean Telegraph, Surprise, Spirit of the Times, Romance of the Seas, Young Mechanic, Architect, Live Yankee, David Crockett, Andrew Jackson, Titan, Pride of America.*

Ocean Elements and Denizens: *Cyclone, Tornado, Typhoon, Levanter* and *Euroclydon* (both named after a cyclonic-type storm that appears in the Mediterranean), *Hurricane, Simoon, Sirocco, Pampero, Monsoon, Dashing Wave, Mountain Wave, Sparkling Wave, Crest of the Wave, Wild Wave, Snow Squall, White Squall, Trade Wind, Whirlwind, Fair Wind, North Wind, West Wind, Nor'Wester, Atmosphere, Northern Light, Lightning, Aurora, Starlight, Southern Cross, Guiding Star, Morning Star, Sea Serpent, Frigate Bird, Wild Duck, Seaman, Seaman's Bride, Ocean Spray, Ocean Rover, Ocean Chief, Ocean Pearl, Flying Fish, Canvasback, Webfoot, Lookout, Grey Feather.*

Ocean Majesty and Mythology: *Monarch of the Seas, Queen of Clippers, Queen of the Seas, Queen of the East, Queen of the Pacific, Empress of the Seas, Empress, Sovereign of the Seas, Storm King, Argonaut, Gem of the Ocean, Ocean Herald, Pride of the Ocean, Pride of the Sea, Neptune's Car, Neptune's Favorite, Water Witch, Witch of the Wave, Sea Witch, Sea Nymph, Flying Dutchman.*

Interestingly, another source of inspiration for the naming of American clipper ships came from the realm of literature, both the classics and popular novels of the time, as well as heroic historical figures, both male and female. From the world of literature came the clipper duo *Don Quixote* and *Sancho Panza*, both built by Samuel Lapham at Medford for John E. Lodge of Boston, thereby giving us some insight into that owner's reading habits, while up in Portsmouth there were built the clippers *Red Rover* and *Water Witch*, both for different owners, but no doubt named in honor of the great American author James Fenimore Cooper, who penned two famous stories of the same names and who had died in 1851, at the height of the clipper ship craze. Meanwhile, the *John Gilpin* was named after the main character (a rather humorous one) that was the subject of an old English ballad, while in Fairhaven, Massachusetts, the author of the famed classic *Paradise Lost* was remembered with the launching of the *John Milton*. As to historic heroic figures, there were the clippers *Robin Hood* and *Red Jacket* to cover the male domain, while in honor of historic women were named the clippers *Grace Darling* and *Cleopatra*. The former of these was most appropriate for the times, as the real Grace Darling (1815–1842) was a young English lady who helped man the Longstone Lighthouse on the Farne Islands with her father and gained fame for helping in the rescue of survivors from the shipwrecked *Forfarshire* in 1838. She would be immortalized in both novel form, as well as in poetry by William Wordsworth.

Despite the above listed colorful ship names, there were still a few clippers that retained the nomenclature of old; among the vessels named after women associated with builders and owners are included the *Mary, Kate Hooper, Ellen Foster, Mary Whitridge, Mary Robinson, Mary Bangs,* and *Emily Farnum*. Among those clippers named after prominent men in the shipping industry, including merchants, shipbuilders, and captains, were the *Osborne Howes, Asa Eldridge, Thatcher*

Magoun, N.B. Palmer, Jacob Bell, John Bertram, Joseph Peabody, Governor Morton, John Wade, John Land, and *S.S. Bishop.* One seemingly oddly named clipper was the *Harry of the West*; built by Robert Jackson at East Boston in 1855, it was given the nickname of well-known politician Henry Clay, a prominent figure in national politics in the decade prior to the Civil War. As for the geographical names of old, these too are found among the clippers; there was the *Oriental, Kathay, Celestial Empire, Panama, Indiaman, Staffordshire, Boston Light, Granite State,* and *San Francisco.* Of course, there are always those ships whose names are unusual and their owners' naming intent less obvious; we know not why the clippers *Midnight, Noonday, Mischief,* and *Mystery* were so designated, while the name *Cherubim* for the big, 1,796-ton Baltimore clipper built by James Abraham in 1855 seems also to be an odd choice. Another odd naming choice for a clipper, or any ship for that matter, was *Flying Dutchman*, built by William Webb in 1852 and named after an old mariner's legend about a ghost ship that was doomed to sail the seas for all eternity. What is even more apropos about this choice is the fact that the captain of this mythical ghost ship, named Vanderdecken, was based on a real life Dutch captain renowned for his fast passages between Holland and Indonesia while employed by the Dutch East India Company. Not surprisingly, the *Flying Dutchman*, while a fast vessel, was ill fated and had but a short career, being shipwrecked in early 1858 off New Jersey.

While all ship's names reflect the hopes, dreams, and aspirations of a ship's builder or owner in some way or another, perhaps none was more appropriate than that for the Portland, Maine, clipper *Phoenix*, launched in 1853 by shipwright Thomas C. Knight and financed by shipping merchant Nathaniel Blanchard. Knight had had a ship for Blanchard on the building ways the previous year that caught fire and burned when nearly complete, a total loss exacerbated by the fact that the ship was uninsured. Undaunted, the two men set to work again and a new ship soon rose from the ashes, financed and owned by Blanchard, and was a successful ship for some years. Ironically, the flames that began her career also proved to be the cause of the demise of *Phoenix* as well, as her service came to an abrupt end in early 1860 after catching fire at Melbourne, Australia (Fairburn, pgs. 3146–47).

Despite the change in naming practices brought about by the clipper ship era, not everyone in the shipping industry was happy with this break in tradition and some longed for a change, or perhaps the days of old. One of the best known accounts in this regard is offered up in a letter written home from Australia in 1854 by George Francis Train, the nephew of Enoch Train, founder of a Boston-based packet line and Donald McKay's backer; writing of a Maine-built clipper and her arrival in Melbourne, Train wrote to *Hunt's Merchants Magazine* that "The *Wings of the Morning* came in day before yesterday from New York but the Utter-Most-Parts-of-the-Sea has not yet been heard from. Snail, Tortoise, or Drone I would suggest for the next clipper, just for a change. I am tired of these always-a-little-faster names" (Howe and Matthews, pg. 723). It is significant to note that after the time of the clipper ships had passed by the 1870s the nomenclature of old had regained the upper hand and ships again were largely given more practical names relating to their owners rather than the high-flying names of twenty years before. However, not everyone could give up the past; the great builder Donald McKay, whose clippers of the 1850s had some of the most majestic names of all, including *Romance of the Seas, Champion of the Seas,* and *Flying Cloud*, gave his last ship, the 1869-built *Glory of the Seas*, a name reminiscent of his own past glory days. We have already discussed the aptly-named clipper *Spirit of the Times*, built near the height of the clipper ship era in 1853, but another clipper was also aptly named as the dominance of the clippers was coming to an end. The Mystic, Connecticut–built *Twilight* was launched in 1857, her name also a sure sign of the changing times.

In concluding this discussion about clipper ship nomenclature, it should also be mentioned that not every ship was launched with its originally intended name, while yet others had quick name changes. The big Portsmouth-built clipper *Sierra Nevada* was originally intended to be called the *King of the Forest*, perhaps because of her great size and the amount of timber used in her construction, while another famed Portsmouth clipper, the *Nightingale*, was originally called the *Sarah Cowles*, and was advertised as such in the local newspapers. Just who the namesake of the *Sarah Cowles* was and what her relation may have been to the clipper's owner or builder is unknown. One of the biggest name changes, in every sense of the word, may have been that for Donald McKay's *Great Republic*, the largest clipper ship ever built. The ship was launched in October 1853, but as late as May was referred to in local papers as the *King of Clippers*. This original name may have been inspired by McKay's ego and his sense of competition, as fellow East Boston shipbuilder Robert Jackson had launched his *Queen of Clippers* in March of that same year. Perhaps it was McKay's sense of patriotism that caused the name change? Yet another McKay-built clipper was also the subject of much speculation; while the *Flying Cloud* was well under construction, one report mentions that he also had begun work on another 1,800 ton clipper, said to be named the *Eternal*, and would have a figurehead of General Andrew Jackson (*Daily Alta California,*1851). In fact, no such clipper by this name was ever launched and the ship in question then under construction was undoubtedly the future 1,807-ton clipper *Staffordshire*. Why the name of the ship, if ever really contemplated, was changed is unknown, though it is rather ironic that it would be a Connecticut-built medium clipper named *Andrew Jackson* that would break the *Flying Cloud*'s record on the California run. Meanwhile, in Downeast Maine Isaac Dunham launched the *Flying Yankee* in late 1852 at Frankfurt, but the clipper was sent to Boston upon completion and quickly sold to owners there who immediately changed her name to *Flying Arrow*. While it is an old nautical superstition that changing the name of a ship would bring bad luck, this happened quite frequently in the shipping trade without great consequences. However, in the case of the *Flying Arrow*, such superstitions seemingly came true as "Her entire career, as an American ship, was one continuous series of disasters" (Howe and Matthews, pg. 183). The owners subsequently sold the clipper for a low price in Australia within three years, surely glad to be rid of a ship that caused them nothing but trouble. Another name change that is found among Maine-built clippers is the *Hyperion*, launched in 1852 at Thomaston by Joshua Morton. The 838-ton clipper's name was almost immediately changed to that of *Golden Racer* when she was put on the California run. Like the *Flying Arrow*, this ship too, though a fast one, had a short career, being lost in China when only four years old. Another interesting case of a name change also involves the Donald McKay and the Train family in Boston. George Francis Train would claim in later years in his memoirs that he intended the Donald McKay–built clipper *Sovereign of the Seas*, launched in 1852, to be named the *Enoch Train* in honor of his uncle, and that he had stated this fact to marine reporter Duncan McLean of the *Boston Atlas*. However, when this appeared in print the next day, May 25, 1852, Enoch Train is said to have called the naming of the ship "premature" and "would not discuss the matter" with his nephew, who immediately concluded "that the name should be changed at once … I decided to call her the *Sovereign of the Seas*" (ibid., pg. 607). Whether or not the younger Train, who was just nineteen years old in 1852, was really so intimately involved in the naming of the clipper is unsubstantiated, but it is interesting to note that the name of the clipper was still given as the *Enoch Train* by news accounts in the *Boston Atlas* after she was launched in June. Just two years later, Train would rail against clipper naming practices, perhaps in part as a result of this frustrating experience! A final example of a name change is that for the Connecticut-built clipper *Andrew Jackson*; originally named *Belle Hoxie* at her launching by Irons & Grinnell in 1855, she was sold to New York interests within a month and given a new name that would soon send her off on some very speedy passages under Captain John Williams.

IV

Architect
The Clipper Ship Builders

The men who built the clipper ships of the 1850s were a diverse and talented group who came from a variety of backgrounds, not only symbolic of America's entrepreneurial spirit, but also, perhaps, illustrative of that old dictum that anyone could make it in America with enough skill, hard work, and a measure of good luck. Indeed, in the boom years of 1850 to 1853, any shipwright worth his salt was not lacking for work. Some of these shipyards, like those of Samuel Lapham, James Curtis, and Jotham Stetson in Medford, Massachusetts; Jabez Williams in New York; Caleb S. Huston in Eastport, Maine; William and George Gardner in Baltimore; and George Raynes in Portsmouth, New Hampshire, were well-established nearly two decades before the clipper ship era began, others like George Greenman in Mystic, Connecticut, and William Webb in New York began their careers during the 1840s following in the footsteps of their shipbuilding fathers, still others like Donald McKay in Boston and Thomas Southard in Richmond, Maine, got their start in the 1840s when the shipbuilding business was undergoing a great period of change, and yet others — James Hood in Somerset, Massachusetts, the Briggs brothers in South Boston, Robert Jackson in East Boston and Isaac Smith of Hoboken, New Jersey, are good examples — began their careers in shipbuilding in the late 1840s or after the start of the California gold rush in 1849 and 1850.

The business arrangements of the clipper ship builders could be found in several forms; there was the singular builder, who contracted for and built and sold his ships on his own, usually on contract. This method was the most common among builders. However, building partnership models (among those men who were not related) were also popular and many examples abound, including Patten & Sturdevant (builders of two clippers, the *Peerless* and *Pride of America*) in Richmond, Maine, the firm of Perrine, Patterson, & Stack in New York, which built six clippers including the *Ino* and *Antelope*, and the firm of Foster & Booz in Baltimore, which built the clippers *Rover's Bride* and *Pride of the Sea*. Often such a partnership included a senior member who was the main financial investor (and may or may not have been a shipwright), and a junior partner who was the shipbuilding expert, as was largely the case with Trufant & Drummond in Bath, Maine, as well as Patten and Sturdevant. However, in many other cases, as with Hayden & Cudworth in Medford and Metcalf & Norris in Maine, both partners were skilled shipbuilders. In only several cases, that of Perrine, Patterson, & Stack in New York and Abrahams & Ashcroft in Baltimore, do we find an example where one of the partners (William Perrine, sole builder of the *Francis A. Palmer*, and John Abrahams, sole builder of *Carrier Dove* and *Cherubim*) built a clipper after his partnership was dissolved during the clipper ship era. This leads us to question just how formal these shipbuilding arrangements really were. A final partnership model that also existed among clipper builders was that among blood relations, whether brother, cousin, or father and son is not always clear; up in Maine there was the father and son team of Joshua and Charles Morton; in

Baltimore Richard & Edward Bell built the clippers *Seaman* and *Seaman's Bride*, while in that same city brothers William and George Gardner built a number of clippers together, including *Sirocco* and *Whistling Wind*. Once again, the business arrangement between family members was likely rather informal as William Gardner also built the clipper *Euroclydon* in partnership with yet another family member, J. Gardner. Finally, we might wonder whether independent shipbuilders ever collaborated with one another to build a clipper ship without the formation of a partnership. Such an arrangement is rare but is known to have happened in at least one instance. Captain Isaac Taylor was a shipbuilder of Chelsea, Massachusetts, who built the clipper *Matchless* there in mid–1853. However, just a year before he was up in Rockland, Maine, supervising the construction of the big clipper *Defiance* at Deacon George Thomas' shipyard (Howe & Matthews, pg. 130). While ship captains were routinely involved in supervising the construction of the clipper they would soon command, this was not the case here. There can be little doubt that the *Defiance*'s Boston-based owner wanted someone with proven abilities to make sure everything was done correctly as Thomas was heretofore an unknown builder and this clipper was far bigger than any ship he had built before.

The men that built the American clipper ships of the 1850s encompassed a wide range when it came to their age and experience. The majority of these shipbuilders were born sometime between the years 1800 and 1816 and got their independent start in shipbuilding anywhere from the 1830s to the late 1840s. The oldest known clipper ship builder on record was Richard Bell (born 1773) of Baltimore, followed by Gilbert Trufant (born 1782) of the shipbuilding firm of Trufant & Drummond in Bath, Maine, which built seven clippers from 1851 through 1854, and Mason Barney (born 1784) of Swansea, Massachusetts, who built the diminutive *Sparkling Wave* in 1853 when he was nearly seventy years old. Not far behind in age was another Maine builder, Joshua Morton (born 1789 and usually referred to in the records as J. Morton, or J.C. Morton) of Thomaston, who built two clippers with his son, and fellow shipbuilder, Charles. Incredibly, Trufant, Barney and Morton, and several others listed below who were a bit younger, were trained in the old days when bluff bowed merchant ships were the norm, and yet they were not so conservative or set in their ways so as to refrain from building the fast ships that were in demand in the 1850s. Several other of the oldest of the clipper ship builders also came from Maine, including William Hitchcock (born 1792), who built two clippers at Newcastle, and one at Damariscotta, and Johnson Rideout (born 1795) of Bath, who launched the clipper *Dashaway* at Hallowell in 1854. Other old-guard clipper ship builders who were born in the 18th century include John Robb (born 1792) of Baltimore, who built the clipper *Frigate Bird*; Samuel Badger (born 1794), who put over three clippers in Portsmouth; Jacob Westervelt (born 1794), the master shipbuilder of ten clipper ships in New York; Jacob Bell (born 1794), who built seven clippers in New York; Jotham Stetson (born 1796), the builder of six clippers at Medford and South Boston, Massachusetts; and Charles Mallory (born 1798) of Connecticut, who built eight clippers at his yard in Mystic. The output of these eleven older builders alone is significant, comprising as it does more than 10 percent of all the clipper ships built between 1844 and 1860, and serves to highlight the fact that while the clipper form constituted a revolution in ship design, progressive shipbuilders in all areas from Maine to Maryland were more than willing to adapt to the new demands of speed combined with carrying capacity.

At the other end of the spectrum, we might wonder who the youngest of the clipper ship builders were; the title for the youngest almost without a doubt must be given to the sons of Jacob Westervelt, Daniel and Aaron (born 1827 and 1830, respectively). Aaron Westervelt is credited as the builder of the small, 716-ton clipper *Aramingo* at the Westervelt shipyard in 1851 when only twenty-one years old. In 1853, Aaron and Daniel Westervelt together built the big clipper *Sweepstakes*, quite an accomplishment for two young men, even if we allow for the fact that they virtually grew up in the shipbuilding trade alongside their renowned father. Likewise, there is the career of Abraham C. Bell (born 1827), the equally gifted son of Jacob Bell. He built four clipper ships after the death of his father in the years 1852 through 1854 while still in his mid- to late twenties. Others of the younger crowd of builders includes Captain Ebenezer Thorndike (born 1827) of Thomaston, Maine, who put over the *Empire* for New York owners in 1851 at the age of twenty-four; Daniel Foster (born 1826) of Warren, Rhode Island, who built the *Pride of the Ocean* in 1853; the Briggs brothers, J. Edwin (born 1821) and Harrison O. (born 1824), who built twenty clippers, including the famed *Northern Light*; the Butler brothers, Cornelius (born 1823) and Alford (born 1822), of Cape Elizabeth, Maine, builders on speculation of the *Snow Squall*; and George H. Ferrin (born 1822) of Richmond, Maine, who launched the 1,547-ton *Wild Wave* in 1854. Indeed, the clipper ship era saw a changing of the guard in some ports; in several prominent New York shipyards, those of the Westervelts and the Bells, sons succeeded their fathers and earned a measure of fame on their own. Meanwhile, up in Portsmouth, George Raynes, Jr., built what many historians consider to be the last clipper ship ever built, the *Shooting Star* (not to be confused with the original ship of the same name built in 1851 at Medford) in 1859, four years after the death of his father.

Yet another interesting aspect of the business of building clipper ships is the little known fact that there was a degree of mobility among shipbuilders and the places in which they built and launched their vessels. A number of builders migrated to different locations to build clippers, no doubt seeking an opportunity to both make a name for themselves and earn a share of the money that was ready to be spent by merchants and shipping firms anxious to add a clipper to their fleet. We have already seen how Donald McKay built his first ships in the 1840s in Newburyport, Massachusetts, but within a short time was persuaded to move his operations to the Boston area with the help of Enoch Train, but several other shipbuilders also moved about even as the clipper ship era progressed and built ships in multiple locales. In northern Massachusetts, Benjamin Dutton of Newburyport, Massachusetts, built the small, 670-ton clipper *Victory* at Newburyport on the Merrimac River in 1851, and three years later put over the 1,148-ton *Mary* at Marblehead and two other clippers. Up in New Hampshire, Elbridge (E.G.) Pierce came down from Maine and built the *Charger* for Boston owners in 1856 at his rented shipyard on Pierce's Island in Portsmouth; though he had been building ships in Maine since the 1820s as a young man, none were even close to the size of the *Charger*, which combined both speed and cargo carrying capacity in exceptional fashion. However, despite these examples, most moves among clipper builders seem to have occurred between the states of Maine and Massachusetts. This is not surprising when we consider the fact that Maine was really the cradle of New England shipbuilders, a place where countless young men went to serve as apprentices before returning to their native states. However, the best known example of a shipbuilder moving his operations is that of the Rockland builder Deacon George Thomas. Well established as a shipbuilder in his native state before the clipper ship era, Thomas came into prominence when he built the big, 1,900-ton clipper *Defiance* and the smaller *Rattler* in 1852, and followed it the next year with the fast and highly celebrated clipper packet *Red Jacket* in 1853. However, George Thomas, in the wake of the success of the *Red Jacket*, sought a greater opportunity by moving his yard to Quincy, Massachusetts, where he would subsequently build the medium clippers *King Philip* and *Logan* in 1854 and 1856, respectively. Though Thomas' Quincy-built clippers did not live up to the reputation of his previous productions, he did continue to build some fine ships there into the 1870s. Lesser known builders who also moved about include Abner Stetson and Isaac Ewell. The former mentioned builder is somewhat of a mystery; he may be the Abner Stetson who was a Maine native that built the *Western Empire* at Newcastle in 1852 for Boston owners, or another man by the same name that built smaller craft in the South Shore area of Massachusetts; in either case, in 1854 he went to Chelsea to build the *Asterion*. What caused Stetson to come to Chelsea to build the *Asterion* is not known, nor is it known what his relation,

IV. Architect: *The Clipper Ship Builders* 73

Donald McKay shipyard diorama. This model shows a realistic likeness of the McKay yard in East Boston at the height of its activities in the 1850s. This shipyard was one of the most modern in America and employed hundreds of men at any given time. Shown here are three ships in varying stages of their building (author's collection).

if any, may have been to the Medford shipbuilder Jotham Stetson. Isaac Ewell's career is also somewhat obscure; he was a shipbuilder in Medford in 1850 and, though uncertain, may have been the brief partner of East Boston shipbuilder Robert Jackson on at least one clipper venture. In late 1850 the firm of Ewell & Jackson launched the first California clipper, the *John Bertram*. If Jackson's partner was indeed Isaac Ewell, soon after launching the *John Bertram*, Ewell moved to Pembroke, Maine, where he is known to have launched the unlucky clipper *Queen of the Pacific* for Boston owners in late 1852, and possibly the clipper bark *Comet*, also in 1852. Thereafter, Isaac Ewell moved back to Massachusetts and may have been the junior partner in the firm of Jackson & Ewell, which built the clipper *Lightfoot* in the summer of 1853. If it was not Isaac Ewell who was Jackson's partner, another strong candidate is Henry T. Ewell; he too was a ship carpenter in Medford (the junior partner in the firm of Waterman & Ewell) before later moving to Marblehead, where he helped Benjamin Dutton build a clipper.

Just as it is today with finely crafted (and high cost) handmade goods, the public reputation of a shipbuilder was also important and was pretty generally known to the public. A builder, quite simply, who put over poorly crafted vessels could not survive because of word of mouth alone. The clippers and their builders, of course, received a great amount of favorable publicity in local newspapers because of the national craze surrounding these ships, but local merchants and fleet owners also recognized a good ship when they saw one, and many tended to patronize the same clipper builders for multiple ships. We might also wonder about the crew and passengers that sailed on the clippers and their perceptions; while perhaps most passengers, especially those from inland areas, were probably uninformed, many others may have done their homework, so to speak, and taken passage on a specific ship or clipper because of the builder's reputation. One interesting anecdote in this regard is that for the clipper *John E. Thayer*, launched by Paul Curtis at East Boston in 1854 and employed as a transatlantic packet ship. When the ship was making a homeward run from Europe prior to 1858, it

> encountered an unusually severe gale lasting three days, with constantly increasing violence. The passengers became so alarmed that the captain was appealed to for assurances of safety. While he admitted the storm to be the worst he had ever known, he called the ladies to the cabin and asked them to notice the builder's name in golden letters on the white enameled panel. They read this: "Paul Curtis, builder." He assured them that no ship of his had ever foundered, no ships had so high a record for low insurance rates, no timber or bolt was introduced unless free from all defect. "I assure you ladies," he said, "I think she will ride this terrible storm safely." The ship came through the storm safely (Wooley, pgs. 98–99).

While this may or may not have been an overly dramatic account of what kind of conversation actually transpired, it does point to the importance of a builder's reputation not only to a ship owner, but also the captain, crew, and passengers that risked their lives when sailing aboard one of their ships.

As previously discussed, once a clipper was built, launched, and sent on her way, it very seldom (with the exception of New York and Boston builders) returned to the locale in which it was built. Nonetheless, there were several methods in which a builder maintained a connection with the clipper he crafted; the first and most common of such situations was when the builder himself owned a partial or minority share of the ship (usually measured in eighth, quarter, or half shares), similar to owning stock in a company. While many clippers were solely owned by shipping firms, many others were owned by a number of parties, including local merchants and shipping firms, ship captains, and builders. One example of this type of arrangement is highlighted by the 1854-built *Ocean Rover* at Portsmouth, New Hampshire; builders Tobey and Littlefield owned a share in the clipper, with the remainder being held by three private individuals, one mercantile firm, and her captain, McLauren Pickering. The shareholders retained ownership of the vessel until selling the *Ocean Rover* to a Salem, Massachusetts, company in 1863 (Brighton, pgs. 120–121). Another example of a builder having a share of the ownership of the clippers he built is found in northern Maine; in Robbinston builder James W. Cox "retained a substantial interest" (Fairburn, pg. 3595) in his ships *Dictator* and *Red Gauntlet*, which were otherwise owned by Massachusetts parties. Once again, this type of arrangement was quite common, and it seems only natural that builders would put some stock, so to speak, in the clipper they crafted with their own hands

A second business model that was commonly practiced by shipbuilders, especially during the boom days of clipper ship building up to 1853, was that of building a vessel on their own account or speculation, with the hope of selling her afterward at a handsome price. This could be a risky proposition because many factors came into play; a builder not only had to assume all risks during the course of building the ship, but also had to maintain the ship until it was sold. While many vessels were insured for damage, this did not often cover the entire cost, not to mention time, spent in building and outfitting a ship. In fact, as with any sea venture, dangers were inherent at every turn, so this arrangement was not for the builder who was faint of heart. Clippers, like any sailing ship, were prone to unforeseen accidents both at sea or in port that could severely tax or even bankrupt a builder. A clipper could become damaged while being rigged or ballasted, as we have seen, but they could also catch fire and burn at any time. The Donald McKay clipper *Great Republic* was the largest sailing ship in the world at her completion in October 1853 and was built on McKay's own account. Shortly afterward, he sent the *Great Republic* to New York for her first cargo, but luck was not with McKay; the ship was gutted by flames after a nearby baking company caught fire and the wind blew the embers the short distance toward ships at anchor in the harbor. While part of the ship was intact, much of the 4,555-ton ship was gone and McKay left the ship to the underwriters, accepting $180,000 for the vessel and $275,000 for a lost cargo that was said to be valued at $300,000. It is said that this one incident nearly bankrupted the great clipper ship builder, and the records show that it was indeed a financial blow from which he never recovered. However, not all builders were so unlucky; up in Thomaston, Maine, old-time shipbuilder Joshua Morton and his son Charles built the *Ocean Chief* on their own account in 1854 and soon after made a tidy profit by selling the 1,228-ton clipper, "in every way a beautiful ship" (Howe and Matthews, pg. 451), to James Baines & Company in England for $85,000.

A final business model which was followed by a few builders was that of being the full owner and operator of the ship they had launched. Not only did these builders build a clipper on their own account, but they did so with the full intent of outfitting and operating the vessel under their own management. This model was not as common as those previously discussed but was nonetheless practiced by enough builders that examples are not hard to come by; we have already mentioned Charles Mallory of Mystic, Connecticut, and the fortune he made from the clippers that he built and operated during the 1850s and 1860s. Up in Maine, Thomas Southard built the clipper *Wizard King* at Richmond on the Kennebec River in 1854 and reaped the profits from her voyages until he sold the ship foreign in 1863. Likewise, over in Wiscasset, Maine, Clark & Wood built the *Golden Horn* in 1854 and, just as Southard did, operated the ship until selling it foreign in 1863. In fact, with the exception of Donald McKay in East Boston, Maine shipbuilders were perhaps the main practitioners of this form of ownership, and this is not all that surprising. Maine was already a leader in shipbuilding before the clipper ship era, but it was also the home of many accomplished sea captains and maritime merchants turned builders who knew every aspect of the shipping business to the fullest. They were not averse to taking calculated risks and knew the ships they built had to be well-founded as cargo carriers, not overly large (typically about 1,100 tons), nor too heavily sparred. The same, however, cannot be said of Donald McKay; he built several ships on his own account, including the previously mentioned *Great Republic*, the *Sovereign of the Seas* (first commanded by his skilled brother, Captain Lauchlan McKay), and had intended to own and operate the *Empress of the Seas* on his own but received an offer he couldn't refuse while she was still on the stocks. While these ships were big, powerful, and heavily sparred vessels that were undoubtedly well-built, they were also costly to man and operate. Whatever profits Donald McKay may have earned in the 1850s as a builder of some of the most prominent clippers ever built, by 1860 he had little in personal holdings to show for it, especially in comparison to other clipper ship builders.

Finally, another interesting aspect of the financial picture that can help one understand just how profitable clipper ship building ventures really were during the decade of the 1850s is to track the personal finances of the builders themselves. While surviving financial records regarding the wealth (or lack thereof) of these individual builders is by no means complete, one way to gauge their comparative success is to take a look at Federal Census records for the years 1850, 1860, and 1870. One of the pieces of information often provided (by the builders themselves) in these census records is their net worth; in 1850 the financial data recorded was for real estate holdings only, while in 1860 and 1870 the total worth of their holdings or estate was broken down into real estate and personal estate amounts. This data does have several shortcomings to consider; the recording of this financial data was not uniform between the states and often varied even between cities or towns in the same state, and it must also be noted that the source of the wealth is not detailed. A number of shipbuilders in the 1850s built not just clippers, but steamships as well, and some builders may also have had income derived from other ventures and investments. Despite these issues, the information that is available regarding shipyard owners and their wealth gives us a clear enough picture of the end results of the clipper ship era.

Starting with the highest profile names of all the clipper builders, Donald McKay and William Webb, one finds the disparities in their wealth startling; while no information is recorded for either man in 1850, by 1860 Webb reported a total estate valued at $400,000. This bears out the well-

The clipper *Syren*. This ship, probably the longest lived of all the American clippers, was launched at Medford in 1851 by John Taylor, before his move to nearby Chelsea, and was still afloat in 1920 (*Gleason's Pictorial Drawing-Room Companion*, July 5, 1851).

known fact that William Webb was not only a solid and judicious businessman, but also a versatile one; not only did he build clipper ships, but he also built small craft and steamships. On the other hand, his great rival in Boston, Donald McKay, had a personal estate that was valued at only $15,000 in 1860. Now, to be sure, for the average farmer or tradesman of the time this sum was quite sizeable, but when we consider McKay's status in the shipbuilding business and the great amounts he was paid to build some of the biggest, fastest, and most celebrated ships of the time, the value of his estate is quite small. In fact, this figure, too, is indicative of McKay's poor business acumen; though his legacy as a shipbuilder is undeniable, the fact that he took great risks by building huge ships on speculation (like the *Great Republic*) and continued building clipper ships even as the era was winding down and profits had dwindled, is well reflected in his estate. Indeed, even after McKay's business began to fail, his previous reputation carried the day and, as one historian states of McKay,

> he had hoped that his assets would pay all his debts and leave him enough to resume operations again. But owing to the extreme depression of business the real estate in which most of his money was invested was found to be of insufficient value to liquidate his debts. However, his creditors, realizing that he had disbursed over $2,000,000 and given employment to thousands of Americans in the eleven years he had been in business in East Boston, took into consideration the benefit he had been to the city and agreed to accept whatever payment he could make at the time and to permit him to continue his business (Cheney, pg. 63).

In other words, to put it into language we can today understand quite easily, the shipbuilding operation of Donald McKay (builder of twenty-eight clippers) was too prestigious and too big to let fail. In contrast, it is interesting to note that most of McKay's Boston area rivals were quite a bit better off in regards to the fortunes they earned in the 1850s, as demonstrated by 1860 census data; in South Boston, the Briggs brothers built more clippers than any other such builder in

America except Donald McKay and did quite well, with J. Edwin Briggs having an estate valued at $83,000 in 1860, while his brother Harrison, worth but $2,000 in 1850, was worth $79,000 in 1860; in East Boston, Samuel Hall (builder of fourteen clippers including *Flying Childers* and *Mystery*) was worth $143,000, Robert Jackson (builder of twelve clippers including *Swallow* and *Norseman*) was worth $44,000, Daniel D. Kelly (builder of the clippers *Edwin Forrest* and *Zephyr*) was worth $45,000, but George T. Sampson, of the firm of A. & G.T. Sampson (builders of three clippers including the *Fearless* and *Peerless*), was worth only $5,000; in Chelsea, John Taylor (builder of seven clippers including the long-lived *Syren* and *Storm King*) was worth $50,500; in Medford, James O. Curtis (builder of seventeen clippers, including the *Telegraph* and *Wild Ranger*) had $9,000 worth of holdings in the 1850 Census, and for the 1860 Census is listed as living with his son George (also a shipbuilder) with no personal holdings; Joshua T. Foster (builder of six clippers including *National Eagle* and *West Wind*) had holdings worth $23,000, while William Cudworth, junior member of the shipbuilding firm of Hayden & Cudworth (builders of the *John Wade, Kingfisher*, and sixteen other clippers) was worth $28,000, though his partner Elisha Hayden was only worth $5,000; in Quincy, transplanted Mainer George Thomas (builder of six clippers, including *Red Jacket* and *King Philip*) was worth but $3,000 in 1850 while still in Maine, but had increased his wealth to $50,000 by 1860. Interestingly, of all the builders in this area whose holdings are known for 1860, only three of them are worth less than Donald McKay.

Jacob Westervelt (1800–1879). This New Jersey native served as a sailor at sea before learning the shipbuilding trade under the famed New York shipbuilder Christian Bergh. During the course of his career, Westervelt would build more vessels than any other builder of the day, including some of the best known of the early California clippers, including the appropriately named *Golden Gate* and *Golden State* (Walter Westervelt's **Genealogy of the Westervelt Family**, 1905).

In southern New England and points farther south on the Atlantic seaboard the fortunes that other clipper ship builders had earned by the 1860s were also quite favorable in most cases; in Connecticut, Charles Mallory (the builder of eight clippers, including *Pampero* and *Mary L. Sutton*) was the leader by far after William Webb, increasing his personal estate holdings from $20,000 in 1850 to $225,000 in 1860. However, in New York master-shipbuilder Jacob Westervelt (the builder of ten clippers, including *Hornet* and *Golden Gate*) was worth but $15,000, a seemingly small amount for a long-time builder. Finally, in Kensington, Pennsylvania, the founder of the long-lived shipbuilding firm of William Cramp & Sons (builders of three clippers, including the *Manitou* and *Isaac Jeanes*) had an estate valued at $15,000 in 1850, but had increased his worth to $116,500 by 1860.

In looking at the fortunes of builders north of Boston, we see similarly profitable results for the most part. While the estate holdings of these non-urban shipbuilders in Newburyport, Massachusetts, and New Hampshire, and Maine were generally on a smaller scale, they are nonetheless impressive when we consider their relative value and purchasing power, not to mention the prestige that came with it in these smaller seaport towns. Historian William Fairburn's comments are interesting in this regard when highlighting the building career (and change of locations as previously discussed) of George Thomas; "at Rockland, Maine, 'The Deacon' had been a big frog in a little pool; in Boston he was a very little frog in a big pool" (Fairburn, pg. 2964). In Newburyport, Massachusetts, the fortunes of her builders were mixed; James L. Townsend and William Currier of the firm of Currier & Townsend (builders of fourteen clippers, including the *Dreadnought* and *Driver*) were bankrupt by 1856 and later census records show no estate holdings. Similarly, George W. Jackman, Jr. (builder of nine clippers, including *Daring* and *Black Prince*), was worth $5,800 in 1850 but had only $800 worth of holdings reported in 1870. This figure is likely in error, given the fact that Jackman was building ships well into the 1870s. Perhaps it is telling that the wealthiest of Newburyport's shipbuilders, John Currier, Jr., built only two vessels (and possibly a third) classified as clippers (the *Guiding Star* and *Star of Peace*) and instead concentrated on vessels that were not overly sparred and were good carriers; he increased his estate substantially in the 1850s with holdings rising from $7,000 to $155,000 in 1860, more than ten times the worth of Donald McKay! However, just about twenty miles to the north at Portsmouth, New Hampshire, fortunes among that city's clipper builders were decidedly better. While master builders George Raynes and Frederick Fernald died in 1855, William Pettigrew, junior partner in the firm of Fernald & Pettigrew (builder of seven clippers, including *Typhoon* and *Dashing Wave*) had an estate valued at $60,000 in 1860. The men of the firm Tobey & Littlefield also did quite well; with virtually no personal wealth to their name before they established their yard in 1853, Stephen Tobey was worth $12,000, and Daniel Littlefield $11,500, in 1860. Similarly, carpenter turned shipbuilder Daniel Moulton (builder of two clippers, the *Morning Glory* and *Star of Hope*) had an estate valued at $2,200 in 1850 that increased to $5,500 by 1860.

Finally, in Maine too the clipper ship builders fared well. Thomas Southard of Richmond, who built two clippers, the *Gauntlet* and *Wizard King,* had an estate that increased in value from $15,000 in 1850 to nearly $195,000 by 1860. This income was derived not just from the ships he built on contract, but also from those that he owned and operated. Meanwhile, up in Thomaston Charles Morton, son of Joshua, was worth but $3,200 in 1850, but after building the clippers *Golden Racer* and *Ocean Chief,* as well as other ships, increased his worth to $19,400. Similarly, there is the example of William Drummond, junior partner of the Bath shipbuilding firm of Trufant & Drummond (builder of seven clippers, including the *Viking* and *Emerald Isle*), whose wealth increased from $5,000 in 1850 to $17,600 by 1860. Another shipbuilding partnership that was financially successful was the Damariscotta firm of Metcalf & Norris (builders of five clippers, including *Alert* and *Queen of the East*); senior member Benjamin Metcalf was worth at least $11,000 in 1850, but by 1870 was worth $76,000 and was still building ships, while Elbridge Norris had holdings of $2,500 in 1850 that increased to $73,000 by 1870. While 1860 data for these men are unavailable, it seems likely that the earnings from their clipper ship building days got them off to a good start. Those with either a less modest increase, or a decrease in their wealth, include Rockland master shipbuilder Horace Merriam (builder of the clippers *Live Yankee* and *Euterpe*), whose wealth increased from $2,000 in 1850 to $2,800 in 1860, and Waldoboro shipbuilder Edwin Achorn (builder of the clippers *Wings of the Morning* and *Woodcock*), whose wealth went down from $3,000 in 1850 to $1,250 by 1860.

Taken as a whole, the census financial data suggests that clipper ship builders overall made out quite well during the 1850s and earned solid profits. However, it is clear that those builders who during the clipper ship era went all in, so to speak, men like Donald McKay and possibly James Curtis of Medford, and built either nothing but clippers or speculated heavily were the ones to suffer reverses in fortune.

Finally, it is also interesting to look at the later careers of some of the clipper ship builders.

IV. Architect: *The Clipper Ship Builders*

With the era of wooden shipbuilding in America winding down by 1860, some builders still continued as independent shipwrights in their craft for a decade or two, primarily in Maine, and some worked for other shipbuilding firms or government navy shipyards. Yet other builders quit their trade altogether and gained employment with local or federal government agencies. Among those who continued to build ships on their own include William Webb, Donald McKay, James Curtis, George W. Jackman, John Currier, Jr., William Cramp, John Taylor, Robert Jackson, James Abrahams, Thomas Southard, George Thomas, and Benjamin Metcalf. Those men who worked as shipwrights at other yards include E.G. Pierce (Portsmouth Naval Shipyard), Cornelius Butler in Maine, and James L. Townsend, who moved from Newburyport to work in an East Boston yard. Those that perhaps saw the writing on the wall in the shipbuilding industry and were otherwise forced to turn to other careers or who retired altogether include Captain James Hood, builder of eight clippers in Somerset, Massachusetts; the Briggs brothers of South Boston; Jacob Westervelt and Jabez Williams in New York; Alford Butler in Maine; and J. Madison Balkans and Robert Trowbridge in Maine. After Hood lost his yard due to fire, he later moved to Illinois and, as a supporter of Abraham Lincoln, received a consular appointment overseas at Bangkok, Thailand (formerly Siam). The Briggs brothers ceased their building operations in 1865, and while J. Edwin retired from business pursuits altogether, Harrison Briggs delved into the financial markets and later was a bank president. Jacob Westervelt retired from a long career in shipbuilding and served as mayor of New York City from 1853 to 1855 during the height of the clipper ship era, while longtime competitor Jabez Williams turned the business over to his son, John T. Williams, but later became a ship surveyor for American Lloyds in New York. Up in Maine, Alford Butler, who had a clothing manufacturing business in Cape Elizabeth before building with his brother four vessels, three of them small clippers, continued his clothing business and moved to Boston. Also in Maine, J.M. Balkans, builder of the clipper bark *Francis Palmer* and possibly the small clipper *Juniper*, was a deputy customs collector by 1860, while Robert Trowbridge, a sparmaker at Rockland who built the *Yankee Ranger* in 1854, was also by 1860 the local customs inspector. Despite the fact that some builders fell on hard times after the day of the clippers had ended, the later careers of some builders, both within and without the shipping industry, are a sure indicator of the status and respect accorded these men as a result of their skill and prominence as a result of their building activities.

V

Intrepid
Clipper Ship Commanders, Crew and Passengers

Once a clipper ship was put afloat, now was the time when she went from the charge of her builders to those that would sail aboard her throughout the course of her sea life. There were several groups of individuals involved, either directly or indirectly, in the sailing activities of the clipper ships; these were the commander, the crew that operated the ship, and the captain's family and passengers that sailed aboard some of these ships. Each of these groups had their own unique experiences that offer an interesting and exciting look at shipboard life during the clipper ship era.

Clipper Ship Commanders

Other than the ships themselves, the most celebrated personalities during the clipper ship era were the men that commanded them. To be sure, even before this time commanders of large ships were celebrated for their status, as being the most elite members of a skilled and highly visible occupation, and for their exploits at sea in driving their commands on fast passages through stormy seas. As mentioned previously, the most high profile of these captains in the 1830s and 1840s were those serving in the packet trade sailing between East Coast ports and those in England and France. On the packet runs, a skilled captain had to perform many functions that required not only nautical skill, but also people skills, having to deal with all kinds of passengers, government officials, and even the public media of the day. During the era of the clipper ships this was also true; the men that drove these high-flying ships were also the source of great media attention and became household names because of the graceful ships they commanded and, often, the fast passages they made. The connection a captain had with his ship, any ship, was an intimate one for a number of reasons. Not only was it the main source of his livelihood, but it was also his home on the high seas for months and even years at a time. The performance of the ship, too, was a reflection of the captain's abilities, as was her outward appearance. And every ship was different, even those built on the same model; each had its own way of interacting with the winds and ocean that drove it on its way, and a good captain soon was able to figure out the whims and tendencies of his ship and use them to his advantage. Though the idea is politically incorrect in modern times, the beauty and capriciousness of the sailing ship is what has led them, at least in part, to be referred to in the feminine since ancient times. Someone ashore, whether company or individual, may have owned his ship, but while at sea it *was* the captain's ship in every way and it was he who reigned supreme, whether softly or with an iron fist, when it came to the decisions that had to be made every day and, in times of duress, every minute of every hour.

The captain's connection to his clipper often began at the very beginning, while his ship was still on the building ways. Owners sometimes hired experienced captains to superintend the builder in his work, effectively putting his own representative on the spot. Given the huge amounts invested in the clippers of the 1850s, such a practice, already standard, was even more important. Further, in many cases the captain that superintended the building was also the ship's first commander on her trial run. Captain N.B. Palmer not only had a hand in designing the early clippers *Houqua* and *Samuel Russell* for A.A. Low & Brother of New York, but also superintended their building and was the first commander for each of them. Likewise, Captain Pearce Penhallow of Portsmouth, New Hampshire, superintended the building and was the first commander of the big *Sierra Nevada*, while Captain Henry Steele oversaw the construction of the Newburyport clipper *Racer* and commanded that ship on her maiden voyage. A final example is that of Captain Robert "Bully" Waterman; he not only helped designer John Griffiths make the sail plan for the early clipper *Sea Witch* in 1846, but also commanded her on her first three voyages. This involvement of the captain both during the building of a clipper ship, as well as taking her out on the maiden run was vital, ensuring that not only would the builder construct the ship to the proper specifications, but also to note any deficiencies that were revealed in her first sailing, really a trial run or what could be called a test drive. Many times the results were satisfactory, but many times a captain was upset with the quality of workmanship; who oversaw the building of the Portsmouth clipper *Typhoon* in 1851 is unknown, but during her successful maiden voyage to England in near record time under Captain Charles Salter, the ship's supercargo, Edward Sise, commented that the ship "has some defects. In the first place the Iron work is constantly breaking — and certainly must be bad" and noted that the blacksmith who performed the work "will catch it from Salter — he has a bucket full" (Brighton, p.75). It is interesting to note that in modern times a newly-completed ship, whether of the naval or merchant type, is put on a trial run or shakedown cruise in waters close to home before being sent on a long-distance voyage. Such was not the case

Captain Samuel Samuels. This Pennsylvania native was the hard driving commander of the famed Newburyport-built clipper packet *Dreadnought*. He got his start as a mariner when he ran off to sea at the age of eleven, eventually rising from the forecastle to the cabin as a clipper captain. Samuels' merchant career would end when he suffered a severe leg injury when the *Dreadnought* was caught in a storm, but he later was a famed yacht skipper for the New York Yacht Club in the 1860s (woodcut from Samuels' autobiography ***From the Forecastle to the Cabin***, 1887).

with the clippers of the 1850s; short of an accident or obvious major defect (the *N.B. Palmer* leaked so badly while fitting out at her wharf that a detailed inspection revealed a hole that was left unplugged by her builders), it was on a ship's first paying voyage that her captain had to fine tune his ship.

In regards to the clipper ship captain, we might wonder about his prior experience and just how it was that he came to a position of authority in the first place. Though in the larger maritime ports there were individuals that taught seamen the art of navigation, there were not yet any full-fledged maritime schools as we know them today (such as the Maine or Massachusetts maritime academies). Instead, a young boy, depending on his family desires and feelings, was either sent for service or ran away from home to become a sailor aboard a local ship that was in need of crewmen, often starting out as a lowly cabin boy while in his early teenage years. In the days of sail there were two ways in which a future captain might gain experience prior to his first command. The most respected of these men, especially to the sailors that served beneath him, was he who "made his way through the forecastle." This colorful phrase indicates a captain who had worked his way from the bottom up, starting his career as a regular sailor, gaining experience over many voyages, rising first from cabin boy or ordinary sailor, then able-bodied seaman, and eventually to a position of junior officer (such as third mate), then to second in command (first mate), and finally to that of captain. Such a captain that had this kind of experience was usually well-respected by his crew, as he had been in their shoes before, so to speak, had put in his time and earned his way to the captain's quarterdeck. Many examples abound of this type of captain; Samuel Samuels, the colorful and skilled commander of the packet clipper *Dreadnought* took just such a path, and even proudly titled his 1887 autobiography *From the Forecastle to the Cabin*. He started out at the age of eleven as a cook and cabin boy on a schooner sailing out of Philadelphia and ten years later gained his first command after a final stint as chief officer for a number of voyages. Another renowned clipper captain that started out low on the ladder was Phillip Dumaresq, a native of Maine and later day captain of a number of clippers, including Donald McKay's *Bald Eagle* and *Romance of the Seas*. Indeed, this most celebrated of clipper commanders had started out at the age of sixteen as a regular hand after having previously worked in a shipyard at Gardiner, Maine, and, like Samuels, showed such skill that he rose to command by the age of twenty-two. Finally, we should not forget the exploits of Nathaniel B. Palmer of Stonington, Connecticut, whose career rise from sailor to captain at a young age has been previously discussed. However, just as it was on land, so it was on the sea, and there were those captains, most of them fine commanders, who did not start out at the bottom, but instead made their way to the top by "coming in through the cabin window." Once again, this colorful phrase is sailor-speak, in this case applied to a captain who gained his position due to wealth and influence. While not uncommon, commanders in these circumstances usually gained their position due to family ties, perhaps the son of a ship owner or merchant in the maritime trade. Salem, Massachusetts, native Samuel Augustus Fabens was, perhaps, an example of this scenario. Born in 1813, he first made a voyage as a cabin boy on one of his father's ships, but the following year he was serving as mate. He soon thereafter became a captain and had a long seafaring career, commanding the clippers *Golden Eagle*, *Challenge*, and *Ganges* in the 1850s and 1860s. While Fabens' time in the forecastle was short, this does not mean that he was any less skilled than those captains that rose to command the old-fashioned way. Though undocumented, we can be sure that Fabens, by virtue of being the son of a ship owner, had been around ships his entire life and certainly knew the ropes, even if, perhaps, he never suffered the discipline of a regular sailor. However, within the captain's fraternity, so to speak, there was a decided bias and those that came to command through the forecastle sometimes, often with good cause, looked down on those who rose to command in easier fashion. Charles Porter Low, the commander of four clippers owned by the family firm of A.A. Low & Brother, including the *Jacob Bell* and *Samuel Russell*, rose to command the hard way (though in quick time), and had this to say about his first commander, Captain William Howland (later commander of the clipper *Sea Serpent*): "Captain Howland was an aristocratic captain. He came on deck at stated times and always wore kid gloves.... He was a good navigator, but not much of a sailor, having taken command without going through the forecastle. He would never allow himself forward of the mainmast and very seldom spoke to a sailor, but gave all his orders to the chief mate" (Low, pg. 19). Of course, there are exceptions to every rule, and some men rose to command via a more unusual path. One such man was Captain Lauchlan McKay, a Nova Scotian and the younger brother of the great clipper builder Donald McKay. He commanded two of his brother's ships: the *Sovereign of the Seas* in 1852 and 1853 on her first voyages, where he made a name for himself as a driver, and the *Great Republic,* but only briefly for her first voyage from Boston to load cargo at New York in 1853, where she subsequently burned and was sold and rebuilt. It could be said that McKay came to his position not through the forecastle or the cabin window, but instead through the mold loft. Perhaps one of the most versatile men during the clipper ship era, and not nearly as well remembered as his brother, Lauchlan McKay started out, like his brother, as an apprentice shipbuilder in New York under Isaac Webb and later worked at the New York shipyards of Brown & Bell and Smith & Dimon, served in the U.S. Navy as a seagoing carpenter, and in 1839 wrote the first guide for American shipbuilders, *The Practical Ship-Builder* (pre-dating the work by John Griffiths). He would subsequently serve as a packet commander before coming back to work with Donald McKay and commanding his clippers. If ever there was a clipper ship renaissance man, it was Lauchlan McKay.

American clipper entering port. This woodcut shows a clipper with all sail set, getting ready to engage a pilot. The pilot boat is in the foreground, flying a starred burgee. Note the lighthouse in the background. Most captains took aboard a pilot off their arrival port, but some captains who were bold enough, and presumably familiar with local waters, sailed into port on their own (*Ballou's Pictorial Drawing-Room Companion*, October 6, 1855).

No matter how he attained his position as captain of a clipper ship, the commander's responsibility was a great one. Not only was he responsible for managing his crew, usually consisting of anywhere from twenty-five to thirty-five men (upwards of fifty men for the larger clippers), and getting his ship from one port to another quickly and safely with her cargo in good condition, but he also had to be a judicious businessman. In boom times, cargos were easy enough to procure, but as business slackened by the mid–1850s, and bottomed out by the end of the decade, a clipper captain (or any ship captain for that matter) had to decide which cargos to accept, what freight rates were acceptable, and often where to take his ship to get a prospective cargo. While a ship's owners usually gave the captain standing orders from which to work with, communicated via overseas letters, and sometimes even employed a shipboard business representative called a supercargo to conduct business matters on behalf of the ship (most often in the China trade), it was usually the captain who was on the spot and had knowledge of prevailing shipping conditions. A bad decision by him could, and many times did, cost his owners (and the captain himself) dearly, resulting in lower than expected profits and downright losses. One example of poor business judgment and disagreement between owner and ship's captain is found in the operation of East Dennis, Massachusetts, owner Prince Crowell's clipper *Kit Carson* (1,016 tons). While at San Francisco in late 1857, the *Carson*'s commander, Captain James Dillingham, Jr., accepted a charter to pick up a load of lumber at Puget Sound bound for Australia, and from thence go to Calcutta, India, and back to San Francisco with an unstated cargo, all for $25,000. Of this transaction, Crowell was furious, writing his commander, "To go to Calcutta, one of the most expensive ports in the world, and take a cargo from there in the height of the N.E. monsoons at a rate equal to $8.50 per ton for a port in the United States, exceeds by far all the miscalculation I ever heard of since I ever had anything to do with any ships" (Kittredge, pg. 241). While Captain Dillingham, stung by this criticism, disagreed with Crowell's assessment of the situation, and had previously stated his ship was "too large for the times" (Kittredge, pg. 240), it was no use; having lost faith in his captain, Crowell later relieved him of command at Liverpool in 1860, sending another captain to take his place. Such was the business life of a clipper captain, and in the end, fast passages or not, how profitably a clipper commander operated his ship was the usual way in which his performance was judged.

Captain Charles Porter Low. This commander sailed the noted clippers owned by the family firm of A.A. Low of New York, including the *Samuel Russell* and *Houqua*. A fair-minded captain who was tough when he had to be, Low was one of the most capable of all the clipper captains (Low's *Some Recollections*, 1906).

While the vast majority of the clipper ship commanders served their owners honestly, there was at least one case and probably others, rare ones to be sure, when a captain did not act honestly or in the best interest of his owner. This one known and unusual example, which later resulted in a case that went before the U.S. Supreme Court, was that of the Maine-built clipper bark *Grapeshot*. Owned by George Law of New York, this ship departed that port for Constantinople in February 1857 under the command of Captain Joseph Clark and all apparently went as scheduled, at least at first. However, by late 1857 Clark apparently decided to operate the *Grapeshot* on his own private speculation and subsequently made two voyages between the Cape Verde Islands and Rio de Janeiro carrying salt. After his final speculative voyage ended at Rio in April 1858, the ship then underwent repairs (under suspicious circumstances) and was re-supplied, all to the tune of nearly $10,000 in expenses. Captain Clark took out a bond on the clipper to finance these repairs and after these were completed departed for New Orleans, arriving there in June 1858. Once at this port, Captain Clark refused to pay the bond, resulting in the seizure of the *Grapeshot* by local authorities and her subsequent sale, along with her cargo, for nearly $14,000 in September 1858. The case was appealed by the *Grapeshot*'s owner and finally, after the end of the Civil War, ended up in the highest court of the land. George Law argued that Captain Clark was defrauding him by colluding with the parties that loaned him the money to repair the ship, stating that the clipper did not need the repairs and that Clark had embezzled the freight money and had the clipper's copper bottom stripped and the metal sold at Rio, replaced by second-hand materials. The court ultimately agreed with Law and ruled on his behalf, citing Clark's gross negligence if not outright fraud. What became of the *Grapeshot* after this incident and her sale is uncertain, but we may be sure that George Law made certain that future captains operating his vessels were carefully scrutinized.

Of course, mercantile and crew management duties were not the only worries of a clipper ship commander. How resourceful a commander was in dealing with damage at sea and getting his ship safely on her way again without having to put his ship into a foreign port for expensive repairs (and resulting claims to the ship's insurers) was also an ever looming task. Insurance companies and owners alike appreciated a captain who could both handle difficult and dangerous situations *and* save them money in the process. Captain George Cumming of the *Young America* was given $1000 in gold by the ship's underwriters in 1869 for bringing his ship into San Francisco after a 117-day passage from New York under jury rig. Hit by a whirlwind off South America that damaged much of his ship's spars and rigging, the *Young America* was repaired at sea by Captain Cumming rather than putting into Rio de Janeiro, where the clipper might have been forcibly condemned and totally lost to her owners. Similarly, Captain Charles Treadwell of that unlucky clipper *Flying Arrow* was awarded $500 in 1853 by insurance agents "for his judicious and painsworthy [sic] management of his ship under very perplexing and adverse circumstances" (Howe & Matthews, p. 183). Treadwell's ordeal occurred on the clipper's maiden voyage in 1853 when she was hit by a storm that totally dismasted her and left her in such a way that she nearly foundered until being taken up by a steamer and towed to St. Thomas, Virgin Islands. A final example of a rewarded captain may be found in Captain Charles Low while commanding the *Houqua*; upon returning to New York in 1849, he was allowed

> to pick out the finest chronometer to be had in New York, and to have a suitable silver plate put upon it ... its cost was eight hundred dollars; and a silver plate, costing fifty dollars, was engraved ... the inscription was as follows; ... Presented ... as a testimonial ... of his good conduct in saving said ship and cargo, after having been thrown on her beam ends in the Indian Ocean on the 15th of January 1848 in a violent Typhoon ... by the extraordinary exertions of the Master and crew was righted and subsequently taken by them to her port of destination, which was 3500 miles distant [Low, p. 85].

Yet another job of the captain was the business of dealing with local pilots and customs officials at ports worldwide. Once again, a commander had to know when to trust his own instincts and when to trust the local pilot, whose job it was to know the local waters around a given port and was customarily hired to guide large incoming vessels to their berths. Sometimes clipper captains either did not trust the pilots, or just wanted to save their owners pilotage fees by taking their ships into port on their own. Once again, Captain Charles Low, while in command of the heavily loaded *Samuel Russell* offers us an example in this regard, this time displaying a unique combination of Yankee frugality and the bold confidence of a young commander upon his arrival off the port of San Francisco in 109 days from New York in 1850:

> We made the Farallones early in the morning and spoke a pilot boat. I asked the price, and was told eight dollars a foot.... Now I had an excellent chart of the harbor, and I thought if I could not take my ship into such a harbor I ought not to command one, and I refused to take the pilot. He said I would have to pay half price anyway. I replied that it was better than paying full price, which would have amounted to one hundred and sixty dollars. As we entered the Golden Gate the wind increased rapidly, and we went flying in, and came to anchor just where I would have done if I had known all about it [Low, pgs. 91–92].

This display of seamanship not only saved Low's owners eighty dollars (no small sum in those days), but, along with the ship's quick passage, amazed the seafaring community there, as well as the public at large. Yes, on a day like that it surely felt good to be a clipper ship captain!

Like any seafaring occupation during the age of sail, commanding a ship could be deadly at times. There was, of course, always the risk of a ship being lost due to accident or storm, as well as by any one of a number of different and often unpredictable causes. While it is true that a captain was, in general, not directly in harm's way at the same level as those he commanded (e.g., he seldom had to go aloft during heavy weather to handle the sails and rigging), still, the burden of being a captain was a heavy one and often took its toll during the clipper ship era. Captain Eben Linnell was in command of the *Eagle Wing* in February 1864 when the clipper was struck by a heavy squall off South America. The spanker boom tackle broke free during the storm and caught Captain Linnell, throwing him against the ship's wheel, driving its spoke handles into his body, causing grievous injuries to which he quickly succumbed. Likewise, Captain John Burgess of the *David Crockett* was washed overboard and drowned in 1874 during a passage from San Francisco to the East Coast; he had decided to retire, and it was to have been his last voyage. Crew difficulties and even outright mutinies (more about this later) were also becoming a big problem during the 1850s, but few captains lost their lives because of them. Not so with Captain George Fraser of the famed *Sea Witch*; he was murdered by his first mate in 1855 while bound from New York to Hong Kong and the ship was thus forced to put into Rio de Janeiro for a new captain early in the voyage. These are just a few of the captains who failed to survive a voyage, even if their ship was able to make her destination, and this does not even count the many captains that succumbed to illness and, occasionally old age, during a passage.

The tenure of a clipper captain sailing in any one ship varied greatly during the 1850s; the average captain served for an average of three or four voyages in one clipper before either moving on to another clipper for one reason or another, retiring from sea life, or even getting out of sailing ships altogether and commanding a steamship. Some commanders served in just one clipper, but many served for at least one voyage in as many as two, three, or even four different clippers. Some commanders may have served in even more, though the records in this regard are not complete. One of the top clipper captains in all regards — experience, reputation, ability, and the number of clippers commanded — was Phillip Dumaresq (born 1804), popularly referred to as "The Prince of Captains." Of this Maine native, born on Swan Island on the Kennebec River, it is said that "all shipping firms were eager to get him to sail their vessels" (*Other Merchants and Sea Captains of Old Boston*, p. 22), with the result that he commanded four clippers for four different owners, all except the first being from Boston, from 1850 to 1859. These ships were the early clipper *Surprise* (1850–52) for A.A. Low of New York, *Bald Eagle* (1852–53) for George Upton, *Romance of the Seas* for builder and owner Donald McKay, and *Florence* (1856–59) for R.B. Forbes. Other notable captains who served in more than two clippers include Nathaniel Palmer and Charles Low (both in different times in *Houqua*, *Samuel Russell*, *Jacob Bell*, and *N.B. Palmer*), Francis Bursley (*Alert*, *Skylark*, and

Talisman), Daniel McLaughlin (*Gray Feather, Swallow, Herald of the Morning*), E.C. Gardner (*Celestial, Comet,* and *Intrepid*), John Burgess (*Governor Morton, Monarch of the Seas,* and *David Crockett*), Samuel Pike (*Meteor, Sea Serpent,* and *Mameluke*), Thomas P. Howes (*Alarm, Wild Hunter,* and *Southern Cross*), Michael Gregory (*Sunny South, West Wind,* and *Nor'Wester*), Francis Hinckley (*Winged Hunter, Leading Wind, Star of Peace*), Josiah Knowles (*Wild Wave, Charger,* and Donald McKay's last clipper, *Glory of the Seas*) and David Babcock (bark *Race Horse, Swordfish,* and *Young America*).

Given the tendency for captains to change clipper commands on a frequent basis, we might wonder about which captains served a single clipper the longest. While records, again, are not complete in this area, several men stand out for their devotion to a single ship. One of the most prominent in this category was Connecticut commander David Babcock, a native of Stonington. He commanded the William Webb–built clipper *Swordfish* on her maiden voyage in 1851 and 1852 and made a near record run of just over 90 days from New York to San Francisco. Perhaps the "Diving Bell," as this sharp clipper was soon nicknamed, did not suit Babcock's tastes, for in 1853 he took another Webb-built clipper, *Young America* (1,961 tons), on her

Captain John E. "Jack" Williams. This native of England came to America at a young age and settled in Mystic, Connecticut. He rose through the ranks to become a noted officer in the Black Ball Line of packets sailing between New York and Liverpool, but gained undying fame when he took over command of the clipper *Andrew Jackson* and set the all-time speed record on the California run in 1859 and 1860.

maiden voyage and stayed with her for six years. Having supervised the building of this clipper, one of the most notable of all American clipper ships, Babcock was surely attached to this fine ship, which was "singularly free from mishaps" (Howe & Matthews, p. 741) during her long life both due to her good model and excellent commander. Indeed, like many captains of the day, Babcock's family went to sea with him, and at least one child, son Washington Irving Babcock (later, not surprisingly, a noted marine engineer), was born aboard the *Young America* at sea. Several other commanders with long tenures include Captain Alfred Doane of Orleans, Massachusetts, who commanded the Boston-built clipper *Endeavor* (1,137 tons) from her inception in 1856 until 1868; Captain Laban Howes of Dennis, Massachusetts, who had the Medford-built *Fleetwing* (896 tons) from 1854 to 1861; and Captain Sturgis Crowell of Hyannis, Massachusetts, who had the Chelsea, Massachusetts–built clipper *Orpheus* (1,272 tons) for six years. As has already been mentioned, many captains were intimately involved with the ships they commanded. Many superintended their building, while others bought the ships they loved and operated them on their own account. Captain William Nott superintended the building of the fine Medford-built ship *Don Quixote* (1,429 tons) for her owners in 1853 and commanded her first on her maiden voyage and at various times later on before buying the ship in the early 1860s. Likewise, Captain Seth Doane of Orleans, Massachusetts, bought the Pook-designed clipper *Northern Light* (1,021 tons) in 1854 after having served aboard her as mate during the clipper's record voyage from San Francisco to Boston. Doane served as her captain and owner from 1854 to 1861, though the ship was lost the following year under a new captain. We will hear more about this clipper later on. A final captain-owned clipper worthy of mention, though there were a number of others, was the Mystic, Connecticut–built *Twilight* (1,482 tons). This clipper was built by Charles Mallory under the supervision of and for Captain Gurden Gates and was commanded by him from her launching in 1857 until her sale in 1863, all but one year of her American career before being sold foreign.

Yet another interesting aspect of the subject of the clipper ship captains and their commands is the fact that there were many family ties in the sailing business. Sometimes brother succeeded brother in the command of a clipper, other times there were several brothers in one family, each of whom rose to command a clipper and sometimes succeeding one another in the same ship. There is even one known case, though possibly there were others, where a son took over his father's command. Massachusetts captain Charles A. Ranlett (born 1804) commanded the clipper *Surprise* for many years beginning in 1852 and was succeeded by his namesake son, Charles, Jr. (born 1836), who was in command when the ship was lost off Japan in 1876, thereby ending a family connection to the clipper that had lasted twenty-four years. One of the greatest areas from which clipper ship captains originated was the Cape Cod region of Massachusetts. As historian Henry Kittredge has well documented, there were a number of families noted for the clipper commanders among them. In Yarmouth, there were John and Otis White, both of whom commanded the Medford-built *Ringleader* (1,154 tons), the latter being in command when she was lost. Yarmouth was also home to the Eldridge brothers, including Asa Eldridge (born 1809), a celebrated packet commander and captain of the packet-clipper *Red Jacket* (2,305 tons); Oliver Eldridge, commander of the early clipper-bark *Coquette* (457 tons) and later, in 1855, the then largest clipper in the world, the 1,985-ton *Titan*; and John Eldridge, commander of the Medford-built clipper *Young Brander* (1,467 tons). In West Yarmouth the Crowell brothers, Elkanah and Sturgis, both commanded the *Boston Light* (1,154 tons). In the town of East Dennis, one branch of the Howes family had three clipper captains among them; William F. Howes commanded the *Belle of the West* (936 tons), built in Dennis by the Shiverick brothers, from her launching in 1852 to 1859, and was succeeded by his brother Allison Howes, "a skillful navigator, but not a driver" (Howe & Matthews, p. 38), for several voyages. Meanwhile, another Howes brother, Levi, commanded the Boston clipper *Starlight* (1,153 tons) from 1857 to 1863, in his final year racing his brother Allison (in the *Belle of the West*) home to Boston from Calcutta, India. Finally, of the Massachusetts captains another clan worthy of mention were the Bearse brothers of Hyannis: Richard Bearse commanded the fast clipper *Robin Hood* (1,181 tons) on her maiden voyage in 1854 and 1855; Warren Bearse was the noted driver of the big Maine-built clipper *Flying Scud* (1,713 tons), in command from 1854 to 1856; and Frank Bearse commanded the speedy *Winged Arrow* (1,052 tons) from her launching in 1852 to about 1856.

From the above, it can be seen that Massachusetts predominated when it came to the number of clipper captains hailing from any one state. However, the Cape was not the only area of the state that sent her sons forth on the seas to command the clippers; the seafaring communities north of Boston also had a large share of notable captains, none more so, perhaps, than Marblehead. From this place at least eleven men, and possibly more, have been documented as serving as clipper commanders, including John Bridgeo of the *Mary* (built at Marblehead), Richard Brown (born 1809) of the *Rattler*, Richard Dixey (born 1809), a later commander of *Houqua*, Richard Evans (born 1824) of the *Archer*, Michael Gregory (born 1817) of the *Sunny South, West Wind, Nor'Wester, and Mary Kimball*, William Homan (born 1803) of *Winged Racer*, David LeCraw (born 1803) of the *Dashing Wave*, Knott Pedrick (born 1810) of the *National Eagle* and *Troubador*, George Henry Wilson (born 1820) of the *Golden Racer*, and William Creesy (born 1818, brother of Josiah) of the

Mary Whitridge. However, the most famous son of Marblehead, indeed the most famous of all the clipper ship captains during the 1850s, was Josiah Perkins Creesy (born 1814), commander of the famed and fast *Flying Cloud* for four years from 1851 to 1855. He had previously commanded the fast China packet *Oneida* and was well known as "a most competent navigator and a great driver" (Howe & Matthews, p. 190), and his owners would not be disappointed with his performance in his new command, built by Donald McKay. Creesy, with the help of his wife and co-navigator, Eleanor, drove the *Cloud* from New York to San Francisco on her maiden voyage in 1851 in just under ninety days, a then record setting mark, and followed this up with another record making passage in 1854, making San Francisco eight hours in excess of 89 days. Though historians still debate the issue today, this was the second fastest voyage on record for a sailing ship ever, and well demonstrates, even given the obvious fact that the *Flying Cloud* was truly a great clipper, Creesy's skills as a captain, the only captain to make such a fast passage twice. Creesy later served in the navy during the Civil War as a volunteer lieutenant, commanding the little clipper *Ino* and searching for Confederate raiders from 1861 to 1862, and subsequently commanded the *Archer* until his retirement.

Meanwhile, the great seafaring port of Salem, while it built no clippers, did produce a number of clipper captains, including the previously mentioned Samuel Fabens (born 1813), Samuel Very (born 1815), commander of the big *Hurricane*, and William C. Rogers, the commander of the famed and locally owned (appropriately enough) clipper *Witchcraft*, as well as the son of her owner. Other well known Salem shipmasters include Charles Porter Low (born 1824, moved to New York at a young age) who commanded many clippers as previously discussed, while Captain Benjamin Tay (born 1805) also dabbled, so to speak, in witchcraft; he commanded the clippers *Undaunted* and the Salem-owned *Witch of the Wave*, and also superintended the construction of the *Water Witch*, the last two ships both being built in Portsmouth.

As regards clipper captains hailing from other states, Connecticut's Mystic River area also produced some notable captains, including two from Stonington families that were among the most famous, David S. Babcock, commander of *Sword Fish* and *Young America*, and the Palmer brothers, Nathaniel, Alexander, and Theodore, all of whom commanded clippers for A.A. Low & Brother. Babcock (born 1822) first went to sea with Nathaniel Palmer and would later not only serve as his officer aboard a packet ship, but also became his brother-in-law. In regards to Mystic, Captain John E. "Kicking Jack" Williams (born 1816) must also be mentioned. This hard driving skipper was born in England and came to America in 1817 and eventually took up residence in Connecticut. He later rose to command in the Black Ball Line of packets running between New York and Liverpool, where he gained his nickname for the tough discipline he meted out to his "packet rat" sailors. His infamous hard driving is immortalized in the traditional sea chantey "Blow the Man Down," whose lyrics state in part, "'Tis larboard and starboard on the deck you will sprawl, to my way haye, blow the man down, For 'Kicking Jack' Williams commands the Black Ball." Of course, to "blow the man down" in this context means to strike him, a form of punishment that packet commanders had to resort to all too often. However, Captain Jack Williams really cemented his reputation when he drove the medium clipper *Andrew Jackson* (1,679 tons) on her record run from New York to San Francisco in 1859 in under 90 days, beating the record set by the *Flying Cloud* and thereby creating a controversy that lasts to this day. Finally, though not a native of the Nutmeg State, Captain Robert "Bully" Waterman (born 1808) also got his start here. He was born in Hudson, New York, but moved to Fairfield, Connecticut, at the age of eight. He began his seafaring career at age twelve and by 1829 was the first mate of the Black Ball packet *Britannia*. He first commanded the Black Baller *South America* and made a name for himself as a capable, yet tough (hence the nickname "bully") commander. He later gained fame as commander of the clipper *Sea Witch* and an infamous reputation as skipper of the *Challenge*.

Northern New England, too, had her notable captains; up in Portsmouth, New Hampshire, Captain Charles Salter (born 1824) of the clipper *Typhoon* came from a noted local sailing family, as did Captain George Blunt Wendell (1831), a commander with a merchant background who commanded the clippers *Galatea* and *Ganges* in the late 1850s and early 1860s while not yet thirty years of age. While the state of Maine was best known for the ships that were produced there, she too had her share of famed clipper ship captains; Philip Dumaresq, previously mentioned, was the best known of the Maine captains, but there were others of note. Joseph Limeburner (born 1817) worked his way up in the A.A. Low fleet, serving under Captains Palmer and Low, later commanding the *Samuel Russell* and the largest clipper ship ever built, the *Great Republic*, from 1855 to 1864. He made one of the fastest passages ever to California in 1856, making the run in 92 days. Another commander of note, though a young one whose full potential would never be realized, was Rockland native Joshua Patten (born 1827); whether he is the same Captain Patten that commanded the *Flying Scud* (1,713 tons) for a round trip between New York and Liverpool in early 1854 is unknown but likely. However, it is known that he took over a similar sized clipper, the 1,616-ton *Neptune's Car*, in late 1854. He made one fine California run of 101 days on his first passage, but succumbed to illness on his second run. The story of this tragic passage, completed by his wife, Mary Ann, will be recounted later on. Captain John W. Arey (born 1816) was also another downeaster, known as a driver, who commanded the Maine-built extreme clipper *Spitfire*; of him it is said that "he wants a mate that can jump over the fore yard every morning before breakfast" (Kittredge, pg. 10). Captain Josiah Mitchell (born 1814) of Freeport is also another notable Maine captain. He gained fame while in command of the extreme clipper *Hornet* (1,426 tons), surviving the loss of that ship in 1866 by demonstrating outstanding seamanship, while at the same time inadvertently sending Mark Twain forward on his famed literary career. Yet another notable clipper captain was Phippsburg native Jacob D. Whitmore (born 1825), who commanded two Portsmouth-built clippers, the *Tinqua* (668 tons), whose construction he supervised, and the famed *Sea Serpent* (1,337 tons) from 1855 to 1861. The *Tinqua* was a fast little clipper commanded by Whitmore during her entire career beginning in 1852, but was lost by him off Cape Hatteras in January 1855. A final downeaster worthy of mention is Captain Daniel McLaughlin, who was a native of Grand Manan Island, New Brunswick, Canada, in the Bay of Fundy, but made his home in Eastport, Maine. This skipper commanded the first Maine-built clipper, *Grey Feather* from 1850 to about 1854, later commanded the Eastport-built *Aetos* (built by C.S. Huston), and several other famed clippers, including, later in the 1880s, Donald McKay's *Glory of the Seas*.

Heavily burdened with responsibility as the clipper ship commanders were, one might wonder about how they reacted to everyday stress and their mental makeup. Like any seafaring man of the day, these captains knew that their job entailed danger and long periods of separation from their families, and it was a basic requirement of their profession to handle such situations. However, these men *were* human and sometimes had wild swings of emotion, depending on the weather situation, crew or passenger difficulties, or a simple longing for home. The high emotions of being a clipper captain were extremely high when they occurred, and the lows could be correspondingly depressing. This is well illustrated in the letters of Captain Joshua Sears (born 1817) of East Dennis, Massachusetts, while in command of the Cape Cod–built clipper *Wild Hunter* (1,081 tons, built 1855) during the years 1857 to 1860. In May 1858 Sears wrote to his wife, Minerva, back home, "We had four or five vessels in company last week and they all sail as fast as we do, and some of them outsail us. I don't know what is the matter with the old ship ... I have been almost angry enough to sink the old ship sometimes ... I am lonely, lonesome, disconsolate and low spirited and have got the blues the worst kind — Oh for a cot in some vast wilderness, but on Cape Cod will do...when you get this letter, I shall be forty-one years old — time to hang up my harp" (Kittredge, p. 210). Later, on the same voyage in the fall of 1858, Sears' spirits were considerably better, he commenting that his ship "keeps tight and she sails faster than she ever did before, since she was launched. She goes eleven knots on the wind with skysails set, and twelve or thirteen with the wind a little stiff.... She is stiff as a church, and I can carry sail on her just as long as the spars will stand, *and they will stand some I can tell you*.... I have been acting the captain this voyage thus far, and I find that I get along much better than ever I did before" (Kittredge, p. 212). However, the ups and downs of the shipping business took their toll on the *Wild Hunter*'s captain, for Sears later wrote during this same voyage, in the spring of 1859 while in the Far East, "Sometimes I feel as if I wanted to jump overboard, but now I have a great desire to live and see my home again," and continued in this same melancholy vein for the next year, writing his wife in June 1860 that "I think that I had better come home and start new, for it seems that every move I make, I get deeper in the mire.... Today when the mail arrived and no freights, I felt as if I should settle right down and be nothing left but a grease spot, and I shall have the blues for a week to come" (Kittredge, pgs. 214 and 218). To conclude the story of Captain Sears, he finally made it home with *Wild Hunter* in August 1860 and returned to Cape Cod to live with his wife, Minerva, and daughter, Louise; though sometimes asked to command another ship, Sears refused and never went to sea again. Lest one think from the above that Captain Sears was an incompetent clipper captain, this was not the case, and indeed the opposite was true; those who knew him and sailed with him commented favorably about his abilities later on, stating that he was "as accomplished a sailor ... as sailed the seas in those days. The Wild Hunter in every port was a show, so complete in every respect was she kept" (Kittredge, p. 206).

Despite the above example, it was not just stormy weather, a poor performing ship, or dreary business conditions that gave a clipper captain cause for worry; many commanders went to sea alone without their wives and families (many others did not) and simply missed their loved ones. Captain William Burgess, commander of the Medford-built clipper *Whirlwind* (960 tons) wrote to his new bride, Hannah Rebecca Burgess, in April 1853 during his first voyage since their marriage in August 1852, his sentiments being quite natural for a newly-separated couple: "Oh: if my dearest Rebecca was only with me how happy I should be how many long & now very tedious hours should I pass pleasantly and quickly away yet I am well aware that she would be deprived of many advantages of which she now enjoys" (Shockley, p. 49). However, many captains were accompanied by their spouses, and often their children; though perceived by us in the modern world as a large risk to take (it was), the idea of a captain's family accompanying him during his voyages to all corners of the globe was actually encouraged by many owners, and for good reason. With his family aboard, a captain's worries about those he left behind and their overall welfare was mitigated to a degree, though perhaps replaced in part by having to worry about them at sea when his ship was in danger. It may also be that owners thought a captain might be more prudent and take less grave risks with their expensive clipper investment if a captain had his family aboard. Finally, the presence of a captain's loved ones aboard the ship also served to provide a balance in the captain's life at sea. Though many captains had to spend days on deck during times of emergency and prolonged storms, during other times the chance for a captain to see his children provided a well-needed rest and change of pace from his normal activities and perhaps offered a renewed energy and focus when he returned to his quarterdeck duties. In fact, anyone who works today and has a family likely understands this idea very well. In addition, the presence of a captain's wife aboard the ship was certainly beneficial in many areas; from the hundreds of sea-going wives that have been documented (not all of them in clipper ships), records suggest that these brave women provided valuable support, both emotionally and physically, to their husbands during times good and bad. Whatever the circumstances may have been, the captain was privileged to have his spouse and children aboard ship if he so chose, as no other crewmen were allowed this privilege. We will hear more about the wives of some of the clipper commanders later on.

Finally, we might mention something here about the income of a clipper captain. While contemporary records are incomplete, enough facts are known to offer a look at the financial compensation received by these men. As the cream of the crop, clipper commanders in general were quite well paid and were tops in their profession, replacing the preeminent position previously occupied by the packet commanders of the 1830s and 1840s. In fact, many of the packet commanders would later move to the command of a clipper. Ship captains received compensation in several different ways, the first being that they were paid on a per voyage basis. Secondly, many of the captains also had arrangements whereby they received a percentage of the ship's profits earned on a particular voyage or earned bonuses for making a fast passage. The former practice was a smart one for owners because it ensured that commanders would make the best possible business decisions that not only affected their owner's profits, but also their own, while the latter arrangement gave ship and owners alike a great deal of publicity when a fast passage was made. Finally, commanders were also allowed to carry some cargo on their own behalf, known as the captain's dunnage, which they could sell or trade and pocket the proceeds. During the height of the clipper ship era, a commander in charge of a top-flight ship, such as Josiah Creesy in the *Flying Cloud*, could make as much as $5,000 per voyage (Shaw, p. 263), a considerable sum equaling almost $110,000 in 2010 figures. Though Creesy was likely the highest earning of the clipper captains, others surely had an opportunity to earn considerable sums. Perhaps the highest offer of a bonus was made by the firm of N. L. & G. Griswold of New York; by the time their new clipper *Challenge* came down the ways in mid–1851, they had lured the hard driving and successful Captain Robert Waterman out of retirement with the promise of a $10,000 bonus if he got his command to San Francisco in 90 days or less (Whipple, *The Challenge*, p. 117). Waterman ultimately failed to make his bonus, not for lack of trying, but with disastrous results. Of course, once the decade of the 1850s wound down, the pay was not so lucrative due to the fact that clipper ships had a more difficult time finding freight to carry and were starting to show their age and did not handle the driving they were previously subjected to.

A sailor of the day. This illustration, perhaps an idealized one, shows a sailor of the 1850s standing next to a capstan on the deck of a ship. In fact, many sailors were not as well dressed as this man and suffered terribly for their lack of appropriate clothing and gear (Captain Arthur H. Clark's ***The Clipper Ship Era,*** 1910).

Clipper Ship Crews

The men that manned the clipper ships of the 1850s were a widely diverse group and their story is, perhaps, not only one of the most ignored aspects of the history surrounding the clipper ship era, but also the most controversial. Indeed, of all the individuals involved with the clipper ships, whether it be the owners and builders, or a captain and his crew, these men by far profited the least and, often, suffered the most. No matter what trade he was involved in, whaling, coastal shipping, the North Atlantic packets, or the general freighting business, life for a sailor in the age of sail was always both difficult and dangerous. Add to this the California trade, where speedy passages were the desired outcome, achieved by the ships, their captains, and hard-driven crews, and their situation many times became even tougher.

The American clipper ship was manned in general, depending on the size of the ship, by anywhere from about twenty-five to fifty men altogether, including officers and captain. The exceptions to this rule include the small clipper barks, such as the Boston-built *Coquette* or the Maine-built *Grapeshot*, which required fewer men, approximately ten or fifteen in number, both due to their size and easier rig, while small square-rigged clippers under 1,000 tons might require anywhere from fifteen to twenty men. On the other hand, the larger extreme clippers required additional men to handle them; Donald McKay's monster *Great Republic* (4,555 tons) initially had a crew of over 130 men and boys and later, after being cut down in size to 3,356 tons, Captain Limeburner sailed with a much reduced crew of fifty men. The makeup of the crew of any ship consisted of several classes of sailors of varying levels of experience. At the bottom was the lowly boy, who was a youth without prior seafaring experience. A boy received little or no pay for the voyage he made, being paid instead by the experience he gained. This was like an apprenticeship, but one that was less formal than those on land; by his very presence aboard a ship, he would naturally be housed and fed, but beyond that there was no explicit guarantee in writing that he would be taught the ropes, or even be treated fairly by his fellow crewmen. While many boys did learn the sailing trade, sometimes with the help of a friendly sailor or even a kind captain that took him under his wing, the jobs they performed initially were of the basest kind. When Harry Sargent, Jr., first went to sea as a boy at the age of seventeen aboard the *Flying Fish* in 1851, his first task was "that of taking out contents of a barrel of salt junk, & transferring it to the harness cask, which was anything but agreeable at the outset" (Sargent, Jr., p. 3). The job which young Sargent was referring to involved the transfer of salted meat (called *junk*) from its storage barrel to a barrel located aboard ship from which the sailors were given their daily ration, a smelly and messy job. Boys were also sometimes referred to as cabin boys, as one of their jobs was to serve the captain, and many times they also served as the ship's cook.

Above the status of boy were the ordinary and able-bodied seamen. The ordinary seaman was still inexperienced at his trade, perhaps having made only a few voyages, enough to give him basic sailoring skills, but without the broad range of experience of an able-bodied seaman. The able-bodied seamen, on the other hand, were well-skilled seamen with many voyages to their credit; these men knew how to handle a ship's sails and rigging almost in their sleep and were well used to the dangers of the sea. In effect, they formed the backbone of the ship's crew. Other crewmen not of the officer rank included the ship's carpenter (traditionally nicknamed "chips"), whose job was to maintain the ship's smaller boats, to make or repair any number of wooden casks or kegs that held the ship's cargo and supplies, and, during times of duress, help with the repair or replacement of damaged spars and other ship's equipment; the ship's cook, who cooked the food for both the crew and captain; and the steward, who was often an African American during this time, and whose job was to serve the captain in a wide variety of personal duties. Some clippers also carried sailmakers; these men had special skills in the art of nautical sewing and usually had plenty to do aboard the heavily-canvassed clippers. All of these positions just described were paid positions from which a man could earn a decent, though hard-earned, living, assuming he was treated well by a fair and competent captain and his mates.

Above the crew and below the captain there were several officer positions, though not all of these were carried on every clipper ship. The lowest of these was the boatswain, or bosun; his position was generally similar to that, at least as regards pay, of a third mate, but was a highly skilled position. His job was to oversee deck operations and direct the seamen in their work, and a bosun by name had to be a good marlinspike sailor, that is one who was skilled in the art of knot tying and splicing that was so critical aboard a sailing ship. Many ships seem to have carried a bosun in place of a third mate. The mates on a sailing ship, having risen from the ranks, if they came through the forecastle and not the cabin window, were the officers that were the captain's eyes and ears on the ship. The first mate was the captain's right hand man and, ideally, would by the time he had gained his position, have become both a skillful sailor and navigator, ready to take over his own command in the near future or sooner if circumstances rendered a captain dead or too injured or ill to continue in command. Below the first mate were the second and third mates, most often younger and less experienced officers, but ideally ones that had shown enough promise to get them a position as a mate. In today's merchant marine, ship's officers climb the ladder to command based on their experience and learned skills, which they have to demonstrate by passing a formal exam. This was not the case in the age of sail, where a man was, or could be, promoted solely based on his skills and the reputation he built over many voyages, or sometimes, as was the case with Charles Low, only a few voyages. It was an informal system, if it can be called a system at all, that had been in use for years, but it was far from perfect. Indeed, during the clipper ship era there was a shortage of good mates because of both the lack of American-born seamen in general, as well as the large number of clippers that were being built from 1850 to 1855. On this matter the highly respected sailor and ship owner of Boston Robert Bennet Forbes commented in 1854, "When I speak of the absence of good seamen, I ought, perhaps, to include mates ... there are very few good mates to be found. Of course, where there are but few American seamen created, the supply of mates must be short of the demand, and where commanders are constantly wanted it is not surprising that good mates get speedily promoted" (Forbes, *An Appeal to Merchants and Ship Owners*, pg. 23). It should also be noted that mates had to have a number of unique qualities in order to command respect; they had to not only know the ins and outs of running a ship, but they also had to be tough enough to command the respect of the sailors beneath them and, all too many times, had to be tough enough to mete out discipline to an unruly sailor. Interestingly, when Harry Sargent, Jr., was at sea in 1851, one of his first impressions, not a good one, was of the *Flying Fish*'s third mate, he being "a young man of about 23 years of age, of very small stature.... He has hardly energy enough, and in my opinion is not capable of holding his office. He is laughed at (behind his back) by most of the old salts" (Sergeant, Jr., p. 4). However, this was not always the case and many officers, no matter what their physical stature, made a favorable impression on their men. While serving as third mate in the early clipper *Houqua* in 1844, Charles Low had this to say about the ship's first mate, Thomas Hunt, who "was a very short, stout man and was cross-eyed; you could not tell where he was looking. He said he was "born in the middle of the week, looking both ways for Sunday." He was every inch a sailor, a strict disciplinarian and yet full of fun and very kind to the men as long as they did their duty; and men who know their duty will always do it cheerfully if they are treated like men" (Low, p. 45). Whether or not Thomas Hunt ever rose to command a clipper is unknown (he may be the Captain Hunt that commanded the 868-ton clipper *Malay*), but it is unfortunate that not all first mates, as we will later discover, seemed to take his approach in the management of the sailors beneath him. In fact, while the captain was in overall command of the ship, the orders he gave were not usually given directly to the sailors, but to the first mate, whose job it would then be to make sure they were followed. A captain had very little direct contact with the sailors that ran his ship, except a speech that was often given to his men at the commencement of a voyage, and in cases of formal disciplinary action or emergencies. One exception to the rule of the aloof captain was Josiah Creesy of the *Flying*

Cloud; he had his own speaking horn, now a museum piece, which he used to give orders directly to his men, bypassing his first mate (in whose abilities, at least on the ship's maiden voyage, he had little confidence).

Having just read Robert B. Forbes' commentary on the lack of American sailors, it is here appropriate to give some account of the national origins of the clipper crews. American law dictated during the 1850s that two-thirds of an American ship's crew, not including officers, had to be American citizens, but this was seldom the case. Once again, Forbes, a recognized expert of the day on most every shipping matter, had much to say about this law, its lax enforcement, and the men that manned American ships: "We have heretofore depended mainly on foreigners ... the proof of American citizenship ... is in the 'protection,' which may truly be described as a small piece of paper procured from the Custom House, which makes out Yaen Schmidt, of Amsterdam, to be John Smith, of Bath, and Hans Andersen, of Copenhagen, to be Harry Anderson, of Wellfleet, and the cost of said paper being twenty-five cents at the Custom House, and from fifty cents to two dollars or more, according to the demand for American seamen ... every ship owner and every shipmaster who clears a ship, knows pretty well that in many cases, if not in all, the law is not complied with; many masters practically take a false oath when they swear" (Forbes, *An Appeal to Merchants and Ship Owners*, p. 8). In fact, as Forbes states, ship captains and owners alike were solely concerned with manning their clippers and, while they may have complained about the quality of the sailors shipped for a given voyage, were little inclined to do anything about it. Yes, there were some Americans, including African Americans, shipping out on the clippers, but they were in the minority. With America's great expansion westward, and the corresponding rise of railroads and manufacturing during the 1850s, fewer and fewer young man were seeking a professional life at sea. Thus, clippers commanders, and all merchant ship captains, relied on sailors from around the world to man American ships. Sailors from Scandinavian countries, Sweden, Norway, and Denmark were common, as were those from Canada, England, Holland, France, Belgium, the Netherlands, Spain, the Cape Verde Islands, and even Russia. For those ships involved in the Far East trade, natives from Hawaii, referred to as "Kanakas" (native sailors from any Pacific island and Australia also fell under this designation), were shipped as crewmen, as were those men called "Lascars" that hailed from the Indian subcontinent and had had a long history of serving in English ships, especially those of the British East India Company. In short, the American clipper ships represented one big melting pot and, considering the wide differences in language and culture among their crews, were manned quite capably in their speedy voyages. However, given the diverse nationality of the clipper crews, one has to question the long- and popularly-held notion that the events of the clipper ship era in America, the drive to get to California, were a uniquely American experience.

While those in the shipping business lamented the lack of American participation, their biggest problem lay in the system of crew procurement. During the 1850s, though sailor's rights were beginning to become more of a focal point, there were not yet any seamen's unions, or any fair labor practices yet established when it came to the methods in which sailors signed on for a voyage and how they were paid, not to mention shipboard conditions and disciplinary regulations. In the smaller seaports on the East Coast, places such as Thomaston, Maine, or Marblehead, Massachusetts, the prospect of getting a capable crew for a local ship that was ready to sail was largely a local affair; once word got around town or on the waterfront that a vessel would soon be sailing, the captain and his mates usually could hand-pick their crew from among the local population. This would include men that were already experienced sailors, as well as boys anxious to take up a life at sea, with or without their parents' permission. Whatever the case may have been, in the vast majority of cases these men signed on board of their own free will and had some expectation of how the voyage might go, what they would be paid, and how they would be treated. This was because of the simple fact that these hometown sailors knew the captain, as well as fellow crewmen, and in turn their officers very likely knew them, if not personally, at least by local or family reputation. This was the traditional method of employing a ship's crew that had worked since America's earliest seafaring days.

Despite the ideal described above, the systems in place for obtaining a crew were not so well functioning when it came to larger vessels sailing from the big ports like New York, Boston, Philadelphia, or Baltimore on the East Coast, and later on from San Francisco and Portland on the West Coast. At these places, there were a large number of ships ready to set sail for places such as California, China, India, or Europe on almost any given day and a captain looking to ship a crew had to deal with a great amount of competition. Early on in these large ports, decades before the clipper ship era had begun, a corrupt system of boarding house masters or, as they were more typically referred to, *crimps* had developed. Perhaps this system, in its very earliest form, was a fair and useful one, but if so, it did not last for long and devolved into one that was exploitative and abusive to the sailors involved, and often detrimental to the captains and ships that were forced to use their services. In fact, the boarding house system of obtaining labor was generally a lose-lose situation, with only the crimps themselves profiting. In short, here's how the system worked; a sailor in one of the big ports, whether arriving on foot (perhaps making his way to the big city to go to sea for the first time) or by ship, having just signed off on a voyage, needed a place to stay. This he would find, usually at one of the waterfront boarding houses for sailors. Knowing that a captain was ready to sail in the next day or two, and needed, let's say, twenty men, a boarding house master would begin his search. For providing the captain with a crew, the master would be paid a previously agreed upon price, generally ranging anywhere from $10 a man, to upwards of $50 a man during the height of the clipper ship era when sailors were at a premium. This money represented advance wages that were to be paid to the sailor he recruited for the voyage. In rare cases the price per man was greatly inflated, perhaps the best known case being that involving the notorious clipper *Challenge*; having just experienced a hellish passage from New York, when the ship was set to sail from San Francisco for Shanghai in late 1851 her commander had to pay $200 advance wages for each sailor. In the best case scenario, perhaps a *greenhorn* (the term for an inexperienced sailor) would willingly sign on with the boarding master, who might then kindly inquire if the sailor had all the gear he would need. If not, the master would provide, at a substantial cost of course, a sea-bag or outfit for him to take along with him on his voyage. This outfit might consist of used or inferior clothing or useless items altogether, but whatever the case, the crimp deducted this cost from the sailor's advance (future) wages even before he had shipped out. Thus, our new sailor already started out in the hole financially, and if the gear provided was inferior or useless, he had no recourse of action. This was how the boarding houses operated at their best. At its worst and most common form, sailors were plied with drink, or were drugged, while staying at one of these boarding houses until they were in such a stupor they were unable to function and make a rational decision on their own. Prostitutes and the sex trade were an integral part, and another exploitative aspect, of the boarding house system as well, which is why most waterfront areas were known as red light districts. Boarding house masters used these women to lure sailors to the boarding houses from which they operated. In their drunken and incompetent state, now left reduced in funds because of the alcohol they had consumed and the prostitution services they had availed themselves of, sailors were taken advantage of by signing unknowingly, or having their signatures forged, on the articles agreeing to make a voyage on a given vessel, and then, usually on the morning of a ship's departure, were literally dragged to the ship and dumped aboard. Many times a sailor shipping out was but little aware of where he was, what ship he was sailing on, or where it was bound. In many cases, sailors were virtually kidnapped and sent aboard a ship, this practice by the 1850s being referred to as *shanghaiing*, usually because the voyage was to be to a far-off place such as Shanghai, China. The boarding house system was further strengthened by the use of runners; these were strong armed men, perhaps accompanied by prostitutes, that would greet a ship as it was coming into port and in the operation of docking. Knowing that there were many sailors aboard anxious to get on dry land to let off some steam by drinking and carousing, the runner's job was to lure these sailors to their boarding house where they could soon be exploited. Many clipper captains tried to persuade their men, especially skilled sailors, to stay aboard the ship while in port, with the hopes they would stay on for another voyage, and even fought with the runners and crimps to keep them away from their men, but this usually had little or no effect. Many sailors, who as a class were traditionally viewed as simple and child-like and who had no impulse control once they set foot on land, succumbed to the temptations of the runners. As a result, it was quite common for such a recently arrived sailor, even if he had just been on a voyage lasting for months, to find himself within twenty-four hours dumped in a drunken state on the deck of an outbound clipper, bound to who knows where. Such was the life of a sailor, and even though many of these men had been through the boarding house cycle many times, they seemed powerless to resist and just accepted it as a part of their seafaring way of life. Captain Arthur Clark, himself an established mariner who knew the clippers and their commanders well and was seldom easy in his assessment of the character of sailors in general, had this to say about the whole crimping system: "The abuses from which sailors in those days suffered, were not when at sea or on board ship. It was the harpies of the land who lay in wait like vultures, to pollute and destroy their bodies and souls — male and female land-sharks, who would plunder and rob a sailor of his pay and his three months' advance, and then turn him adrift without money or clothes. It made no difference to these brazen hearted thieves ... whether a sailor was bound round the Horn in midwinter or to the East Indies in midsummer; they saw to it that he took nothing away with him but the ragged clothes he stood in, and perhaps a ramshackle old sea chest" (Clark, pg. 124–25). Sadly, these abuses, while the subject of much debate, would not even begin to be addressed until the 1860s, when laws protecting sailors began to be debated and enacted. However, the practice of crimping would, in effect, remain until the end of the days of sail in America. Lest it be thought that all on land were the enemy of the sailor, this was far from true. In most of the major ports, religious institutions, often more than one, were formed, such as the Seaman's Bethel in New Bedford, Massachusetts (established 1832), and Boston (established 1833), and the First Mariner's Baptist Church (established 1843) in New York, and the Ship Church (established in 1846, later called the Sailor's City Bethel and finally Sailors Union Bethel Methodist Church), constructed in Baltimore from the hulk of a ship. These institutions, the ministers that headed them and their congregations all had a mission to not only preach God's word, but also to better the plight of the sailor by providing sustenance and shelter and moral guidance, as well as advocating on their behalf.

Once a sailor was aboard his ship, ready for the voyage, whether it was a shorter one on a packet clipper bound from New York to Liverpool or a long-distance voyage, perhaps to California, out to China, or back to New York or Boston, this is when his work began. It was customary on departure for most captains to gather their new crews and, along with his mates, offer up a speech about his expectations. Harry Sergeant, Jr., shipping as a boy on the Boston clipper *Flying Fish* in November 1851, recalled that in his short speech to the crew gathered on the captain's quarterdeck, Captain Edward Nickels, a Boston commander of high repute and much experience, "gave us to understand, that we were embarked on a long voyage, that he would do his best to promote our comfort, that we were in a ship constructed to outsail every other ship that had been built heretofore, that we should have the best of food and plenty of it, and that any insult offered to any of his officers, he should consider as an insult to himself, and that he should punish it as such" (Sergeant, Jr., pgs. 3–4). On many clippers, especially those involved in the North Atlantic packet trade, while the captain was giving his speech, his officers were busy searching the crew's sea-bags for contraband weapons (brass knuckles and firearms) and alcohol and confiscating them. After his speech was over, a captain also took this opportunity to have all sailors present their knives (a part of any sailor's outfit) so that their sharp points could be broken off, thereby lessening the danger should an unruly sailor decide to attack an officer or fellow crewman. It was also at this time that the crew was gathered together by the mates and the ship's watch system would be established. Similar in nature to the shift system in a modern factory setting, the watch system was the method in which the crew was divided into the different working parties that operated the ship on an established timetable. These watches were divided into two or three different sections, with the two watch system being the most common. These watches were traditionally referred to as the starboard and larboard (sometimes called port) watch where two sections were used, and the foremast, mainmast, and mizzen watches when three sections were used. Each watch was commanded by one of the ship's officers, usually the first and second mates, and a man would generally remain in that watch the entire voyage unless some kind of difficulty arose. As for times of duty, the traditions of the sea and the watch system provided that each watch would alternate duty, generally four hours on and four hours off duty, with the first watch running from 8 P.M. to midnight, and subsequently from midnight to 4 A.M., 4 A.M. to 8 A.M., 8 A.M. to noon, noon to 4 P.M., followed by two shorter watches, called dog watches, that ran from 4 P.M. to 6 P.M. and 6 P.M. to 8 P.M. When it was time for each watch to come on duty, the ship's bell was rung to call the men, along with calls to duty by the mate of the watch whose duty was ending. The system, which was rotated so that sailors did not stand watch the same hours every day, was a time-honored one that worked well and is still in use today, with some modifications, on merchant and naval ships. The watch system was

Taking in a cargo. When in port, it was the stevedore's job to load a cargo, as is being done here, and discharge the cargo upon arrival. When cargos had to be handled at sea, often under difficult or dire weather conditions, then the crew was involved. This woodcut shows the loading of the McKay-built ship *Cornelius Grinnell* in 1850 (*The Illustrated London News*, August 31, 1850).

only varied in times of dire need, such as when extra hands were needed to work on deck during times of severe weather when extra sail handling was required, or when emergencies arose. During these exigent circumstances, it was, as the old saying goes, "all hands on deck" to man the ship. Though the men might grumble and curse when called to duty while off watch, all hands understood that, unless an incompetent captain or mate was the cause, such extra work was necessary to save the ship that would be, for a voyage lasting many months, both their workplace and home.

Once he had his crew, now a captain would soon find out what they were truly capable of, and this is where problems quickly arose during the clipper ship era. Having had most, perhaps all his seamen in some cases, supplied by the crimps, who really knew what they were capable of, or even if they *were* sailors by trade, and not just greenhorns? Robert Bennet Forbes in 1854 aptly describes a scenario whereby a clipper captain, while departing from Boston harbor, comes to the realization that his crew is not all that it should be:

> She passes Boston Light, and all hands are called to make sail. They appear slowly, and unwillingly lay aloft to loose the top sails. What a crew! Instead of the deep blue jacket, you find some clad in the remnants of the dress of marines or soldiers. Some of them look like they had been just taken off the wreck of the San Francisco, some are indelibly *blue* in another sense, and some know as little of the ropes as they know of Encke's comet.... At night the watch must be set, and now the captain realizes the want of good seamen.... It is found on examination that, out of a crew of forty men, all told only six *pretend* to know how to steer; of these, some are already "half-seas over." It is clear that some of them just graduated in the state prison, and that some have deserted from the army and navy. Instead of packing on studding sails and other light sails, the booms are sent down as useless lumber, and though the wind be fair and not over strong ... the top sails and main sail are reefed, as a precautionary measure. Bye-and-bye, a gale comes on, and the sails cannot be taken in; they blow away, sometimes taking away a top mast or two. Finally the ship is disabled, abandoned at sea on the first provocation, or she gets into some port on the coast, a mere wreck, *and mainly for want of good seamen*. This is no overwrought picture; it is of daily occurrence in most particulars [Forbes, *An Appeal*, pgs. 19–20].

No matter what their experience level may have been, once a sailor had shipped aboard, there was little recourse for either a captain with an incompetent crew, or the seamen himself; having signed the articles for a voyage, even if it was done while incapacitated, a sailor, by law, was required to make that voyage, and was subject to a fine or prison sentence should he not carry out his duty. Of course, by the time he may have come to the realization that he didn't want to serve, it was too late as the clipper was already headed out to sea and, except in rare cases, would not turn around. The captain, too, that had a poor crew was in a bit of a situation; to reject a seaman and attempt to find a replacement, with no guarantee that the results would be any better, meant a delay in sailing. Then as today, time meant money, and a captain had to get his cargo to sea and to its destination in as quick a time a possible for her owners, making continued delays unacceptable. Thus it was that a clipper ship sailed with the crew she had, the hand she was dealt, so to speak, and it was up to on the job training to fill the gap. According to Captain Arthur Clark, crewmen from Scandinavian countries were the best, being "splendid sailormen who could do any kind of rigging work or sail-making required on board of a ship at sea and took pride in doing it well, and who also had sufficient sense to know that discipline is necessary on shipboard" (Clark, p. 120). There were also the sailors that manned the North Atlantic packet ships, many of whom later served on California clippers to get to the gold fields out west. Of these *packet rats*, as these difficult sailors were usually nicknamed, Clark states that these "Liverpool Irishmen" were "splendid fellows to make or shorten sail in heavy weather on the Western Ocean ... the packet sailors showed up at their best when laying out a topsail yardarm, passing a weather reef-ear-ring ... a snow squall whistling about their ears, the rigging a mass of ice, and the old packet jumping into the big Atlantic seas," but that they were also "tough, roustabout sailormen and difficult to handle, so that it was sometimes a toss-up whether they or the captain would have charge of the ship" (Clark, p. 122).

No matter what the makeup of these clippers crews were, the fact is that most crews did their job and served well, allowing these ships to make numerous record passages.

The tasks performed by a sailor while on duty were many and varied. Since there are many published works on the subject, perhaps none better than Richard Henry Dana Jr.'s sea classic *Two Years Before the Mast*, published in 1840, I will give only a brief account of the work of a sailor. Interestingly, Dana's book, a bestseller, was sympathetic to the plight of the sailor and describes this Harvard graduate (and future lawyer's) voyage to California in the pre-gold rush days. In short, a sailor's work covered several main areas, including sail handling during all kinds of weather, good and bad, skilled deck duties, as well as regular shipboard maintenance while at sea and, if circumstances required, damage control work. Except in dire straits while at sea (say if a cargo had shifted in heavy seas and needed reworked), it was not the sailor's job to handle or load cargo while in port; this was usually the work of port stevedores.

Sail handling was by far the most skilled as well as the most difficult and dangerous part of sailor work. This required, whether in heavy seas or fair, night or day, climbing up into the ship's rigging and balancing on the ratlines or yard arms to bring in sail (called *reefing*) or unfurl the sails. During this work aloft, sailors, with the use of their knives and bare hands, also had to tend to the ships rigging, made of rope, and other technical details, directed by the ship's officer from the deck below. In effect, a sailor had not only to be skilled and quick at his work, but he also had to perform a balancing act while doing so. A landlubber can only imagine, and then probably an underestimation to be sure, how difficult these tasks could be with the rolling and heaving motion of a clipper speeding through heavy seas. When sail handling was required at night during harsh weather conditions, these difficulties were compounded, as there was no light (unless it be moonlight) to work by and a sailor had to know, both by feel and memorization, where each rope was and its function. In fact, thousands of sailors lost their lives during the age of sail in the performance of this work, plummeting from aloft to hit the deck, and such losses were an accepted part of the business. During her difficult California run in 1851, the big New York clipper *Challenge* (2,006 tons) lost three men who fell from the mizzen topsail yard while off Cape Horn, where many a sailor met his death. Regardless of their abilities or condition, a sailor was expected to perform duties aloft, even if he had to learn as he went along under difficult circumstances. Captain Clark gives us an example of the colorful and harsh commands a greenhorn or landlubber might be given when going aloft to handle sail by their first mate: "On the foretopsail yard there, if you cut that gasket, I'll split your damned skull; cast it adrift, you lubber," and "Here, some of you gentlemen's sons in disguise, get that fish davit out" (Clark, p. 115). Sadly, given the crews recruited by the crimps, not all men were capable of going aloft. On the New Hampshire clipper *Granite State* (1,108 tons) in 1855, one seaman, Edward McNulty, was badly beaten by second mate William Valentine for not going aloft at night when ordered. One of McNulty's hands, it turned out, was disabled, whereby he could not follow that old sailor dictum, "one hand for the ship, one hand for yourself," and to go aloft meant for him certain death. McNulty sought redress from the commander, but Captain Samuel Billings sided with his mate. The case was later brought to court, and while the captain was exonerated in a hearing, his mate was held over for trial (Brighton, p. 145).

The deck duties of a sailor were also rigorous, and perhaps only slightly less dangerous; a man would be expected to take his turn at the ship's wheel if he were experienced enough to do so, guiding the clipper along at the direction of a watchful mate, and also to man the ship's windlass when needed. This was a piece of standard shipboard equipment used to move the ship's heavy yardarms from one position to another, haul in the anchor, and other heavy lifting duties. The cylindrical drum of the windlass, around which heavy ropes were attached, was equipped with a number of iron spokes which a number of sailors at any one time grasped and moved in unison, often to a traditional sea chantey, to provide needed lifting power. This was backbreaking work, made even more difficult when a clipper was shipping heavy seas and her decks were filled with water, or when a clipper was taking a heavy weather beating and her deck was slanting on one side or another, making the footing very difficult. Another back-breaking job was that of manning the ship's pumps; while later vessels would have machine powered pumps to empty the ship's hold of water, it was manual work during the clipper ship era. It was not just old ships whose hulls leaked and took in water; even new clippers sometimes had their seams started by the hard driving and heavy weather they experienced. When the extreme Portsmouth-built clipper *Typhoon* made her maiden voyage from Portsmouth to Liverpool in March 1851, the ship's supercargo stated that even while in port "she leaks very badly, and has never been freed without one hour's pumping in each watch, which has completely disheartened some of our best men. One night I went out and six men were sitting down by the pumps and told me they were really beat out. So many have been on board today [visitors to the ship] that she has not been pumped out and Captain Salter did remark that she had three feet of water in her hold" (Brighton, pgs. 75–76). While manning the pumps was always difficult, its not hard to imagine the worst case scenario; when a clipper was taking in heavy amounts of water during a roaring gale, those manning the pumps were not only working to help prevent damage to the ship's valuable cargo, but also for the very lives of all aboard. Once a ship's pumps failed to keep up with the water entering her hold, it was only a matter of time before she became a waterlogged and unmanageable vessel in danger of sinking at any time.

Lookout duty, both alow and aloft, was also important duty, especially when a ship was in shoal seas near shore or known navigational hazards, or when inboard or out bound, typically in areas of heavy maritime traffic. As might be imagined, all deck duties were subject to the hazards of high seas, both during storms or even, sometimes, when a rogue wave hit the ship unexpectedly while the ship was speeding along. Severe injury or death could come from being washed overboard, as

Clipper scudding before the wind. This woodcut shows a clipper bowling along in high seas and heavy weather, perhaps off Cape Horn. It vividly illustrates the difficulties of operating a clipper when seas were continually washing over the weather deck. Notice in the foreground the floating wreckage of a ship that has already succumbed to the elements (*Ballou's Pictorial Drawing-Room Companion*, October 6, 1855).

often happened off Cape Horn, or being hit hard by heavy seas and slammed into the ship's side or some other deck fitting, or from being struck by a boom that came unrigged during heavy weather and was wildly swinging about. Later-day merchant sailing ships, especially Cape Horners, often carried safety nets to help prevent men from being washed overboard, but these were not used on the clippers of the 1850s. However, life-lines were often strung along the ship's side from fore to aft when heavy weather was expected so that men making their way from one part of the ship to another could get an extra handhold. Once a man was washed overboard, his chances of survival were small. Many, perhaps most, sailors were, paradoxically, unable to swim; as a matter of tradition, most had no interest in learning how to do so, preferring a quick death by drowning rather than the prolonged suffering from trying to stay afloat in an empty sea when there was little chance of rescue. Depending on the location and sea conditions at the time, if it was noticed right away that a man was washed overboard, a ship might stop her course and wear around to attempt a rescue. However, in stormy seas this was usually not possible and there was simply no chance of a rescue, it being difficult to stop a clipper quickly that was scudding along, whether under full sails or bare poles (without sail). Indeed, often it was not even noticed a man was washed overboard until way after the time for a possible rescue had passed and, in the lore of the sea (though no examples for clippers are documented), sailors often told yarns of a whole watch being washed overboard, their loss unknown until the next watch was due to come on duty.

Once a man died at sea, whether it be captain or crewman, there was little time to dwell over the circumstances. The clipper had to continue on her course and had to be managed. Whether a man died from crushing injuries suffered from a fall from aloft or of disease, his body was usually sewed up in a canvas or cloth bag, with weights placed at the feet. The body was then placed on a plank balanced on the ship's railing and, without much fanfare, was consigned to the sea by being slid overboard. If the captain was a religious man and circumstances allowed, he might give a brief sermon with some of the dead sailor's watch gathered around, as happened aboard the *Sea Serpent* while Captain William Howland was in command, while at other times it might just be a member of the crew who said a word or two. When George Harper, the African American cook aboard the clipper *Snow Squall*, died in November 1858, probably from the same disease that would later claim steward Alexander Brown and first mate Charles van Dolan, ship's boy Edmund Rice noted in his diary that "no one was near him when he died. As soon as it was found out he was sewn up in his blankets and hove overboard. No one thought anything of it.... The men simply took off their hats. The Captain didn't even come on deck" (Dean and Switzer, p. 150). Once a sailor was gone and buried at sea, his meager gear was usually auctioned off among the remaining crew or added to the ship's slop chest. In the case of the death of a mate or perhaps a ship's boy, if there were any personal effects such as letters, a photo, or some like item, a compassionate captain or passenger might make an effort to see that they were returned to remaining family once the clipper returned. In contrast to these burials at sea for a clipper's dead crewman or officer, it should be noted that dead captains were usually treated with a bit more reverence. While some captains did receive a burial at sea, others had their bodies kept aboard with the intent of burying them ashore. The *Young Mechanic*'s commander (and owner) Captain William McLoon died while the ship was at Calcutta, India, in 1865, his body subsequently brought home to Rockland, Maine, for burial, while the clipper *Eagle* in April 1857 "was reported as putting into Manila to bury her captain" while bound from Shanghai to London (Howe & Matthews, p. 147).

Having just described the basic skilled duties of the sailor, we must now describe the more mundane maintenance tasks of operating the ship. Then, as now in the modern navy and merchant marine, painting, scraping, and polishing duties to maintain the ship's condition and appearance were seemingly never ending. This was especially true for wooden ships in general, and extremely so for the clippers; noted for their beauty and ship-shape condition, no self-respecting captain would allow his ship to come into port after a voyage, no matter how long or how disastrous, without looking its best. Indeed, a captain was judged by his fellow captains, owners, and even his crew, on how well he kept up his command. Sailors might grumble about all this work, but they too took great pride in being part of the crew of a beautiful, top-notch clipper. Perhaps the classic sailor maintenance duty during the age of sail was that of holystoning the deck. This consisted of using a square piece of sandstone (the larger ones called bibles, the smaller ones prayerbooks) to scrub down the deck of a ship. To further complete the religious nature of this work, it was often done by the sailor while on his knees, as if he were in a prayer position (albeit for a considerably longer time!). Holystoning was generally done when fair weather permitted, and once done, finished after many man hours, would give the ship's wooden deck a shining white appearance. Charles P. Low, third mate on the clipper *Houqua*, tells of a humorous incident in this regard that occurred while on his ship.

> We had just finished holystoning the decks and the paint on the bulwarks was hardly dry. The second mate had a fifty pound keg of black paint in the paint locker on one side of the bowsprit, under the topgallant forecastle. Unfortunately, the sailors owned a large Borneo monkey or baboon, and he had been made fast on the bowsprit within reach of the paint ... he upset the bucket of paint, which ran down the scuppers as far as the mainmast over the clean white deck. The second mate, as soon as it was found out, caught the monkey and swabbed the paint up with him till he would hold no more, and then threw him overboard, but this made bad worse, for the monkey caught the side ladder hanging over the main rigging and came up, and before anyone could stop him, ran the whole length of the bulwarks, leaving black paint all over the fresh straw-colored paint, and making an awful mess. The man who owned him caught him and hurried him into the forecastle, but it was "All hands to clean ship"; for the decks had to be scraped and wiped off and then painted again, for Sunday must find the ship in perfect order ... the second mate was as mad a man as could be for a time, but he soon got over it after the ship was to rights again, and he never molested the monkey, who was a great pet [Low, pgs. 49–50].

In addition to this back-breaking work, sailors also had to scrape and paint the ship's deck areas and interior spaces, such as waterways and scuppers, and the deck cabins as needed, as well as the masts and yardarms and were also employed in polishing any of the ship's brass fittings and, a much dirtier job, tarring the ship's rigging to give it protection from the elements. Yet another dirty job was that of slushing the masts, which involved the periodic application of a greasy concoction, supplied from the cook's galley, to coat the ship's masts so that the yardarms could move more freely. To apply the slush further up the masts, a sailor was sent aloft in a sling supported by ropes called a bosun's chair. Sail making or repairs were another constant task to be performed, though not every sailor was skilled in this area. Yet another shipboard duty that is seldom mentioned, but was always required at various intervals was that of clearing the many rats that infested a ship by a process called smoking. This was done while a ship was in port prior to receiving her cargo, and consisted of sealing all the ship's open spaces and hatches, with holes drilled in the latter so that a crewman could stand watch, and making it as airtight as possible. Once this was done, fires were lit from charcoal and sulfur, surrounded by tubs of water under each hatch and left to burn for 24 hours, after which the hatches were unsealed and the ship aired out for a period of time. As one account notes, "Some ships will throw out a thousand dead rats" (Low, p. 29).

As to a sailor's downtime, this was traditionally spent in the forward part of the ship. In the old days sailors were quartered in the forecastle, a dark, dank, and wet area below decks at the forward most area of the ship beneath the bowsprit. However, the modern clipper crews were quartered in a cabin located just abaft (behind) the foremast, with a barrier down the center that separated the two watches into separate rooms. These cabins were drier and thus much better quarters than the traditional forecastle (mostly utilized on the clippers now as extra storage space). Compared to the captain's quarters, a sailor's home was simple indeed, no fancy wainscoting or decorative murals, but with just enough bunks around an open center space where the men could congregate in their off duty-time. Except when so ordered, a sailor never went aft to the quarterdeck as this was the domain of the captain and his officers. Occasionally, though how often is unclear, extremely sick sailors were taken to the captain's quarters to be cared for by his steward or the captain's wife. Most clippers carried no formally trained doctors, unless there happened to be one among their passengers. Robert Bennet Forbes, in addressing this subject, commented, "I was somewhat mortified to see the applause bestowed by the Christian Register, on the conduct of a captain who took a young man, who was ill, into the cabin, and carefully nursed him until he died there. I was mortified because this was mentioned as a rare case. I believe it is far from being a rare case ... there is no want of sympathy with good seamen. The master's best interest as well as his best feelings, dictate him to take the best care of his sick" (Forbes, *An Appeal*, pgs. 26–27). Back to the subject of crew quarters, a captain rarely, if ever, ventured into the sailors' quarters; if he did so it was usually only in the name of justice, perhaps a forced search for stolen property, or to apprehend a mutinous crewman. Otherwise, this was the domain of the sailor. Sailors off duty spent their time in typical activities, including sleeping, talking with one another and spinning yarns or telling tall tales, gambling, whittling, and reading or rereading letters from home. This would also be the time when he made repairs to his clothing and other sea gear; indeed, any sailor of consequence was a skilled sewer, as it was a necessity of his profession. When the weather was good, a sailor could be found on deck and, if circumstances allowed, might do some fishing or try to catch some seabirds. As to food and drink, it is often stated that clippers were good feeding ships, with owners and captains seldom scrimping on provisions. Fresh water was provided daily, about a gallon per man, placed in a deck-board container called a scuttlebutt from the ship's large water tank or tanks that carried thousands of gallons of water, enough to usually last an entire voyage unless it was prolonged due to storms or emergencies at sea. Wasting of water was not allowed (no such thing as showering in those days) and was policed by officers and fellow crewmen alike. Meals consisted of salted provisions, beef and pork, kept in the harness cask just abaft the mainmast, accompanied by biscuits or hardtack. Fresh meat was often provided on many clipper voyages from livestock that was carried aboard and penned in on the weather deck in an area known as the barnyard or farmyard, but these animals, mostly chickens, pigs, and the like that were tended to (and slaughtered by) the ship's cook, were not large in number and were soon used up early in a long distance voyage. Once gone, the animal pens on the weatherdeck were thrown overboard and the area scrubbed clean. One exception to this were the voyages of shorter duration made by the clipper packets in the North Atlantic passenger trade, where farmyard enclosures were almost a permanent fixture on the deck of immigrant ships that carried hundreds of passengers on each crossing.

As to sweets, desserts like we enjoy today were uncommon fare on clipper ships, but not totally unknown. The most popular was plum duff, a heavy pudding made of flour, water, molasses, and raisins. Rations were sometimes augmented, just for a change of pace, by the occasional fish (dolphin, shark, etc.) that was caught, but most sailors wanted their salt beef or pork. Sometimes a rare delicacy, the flying fish, ended up on deck; no doubt some of these were scarped up by a hungry sailor, but by tradition these were reserved for the captain's table. Daily meals were cooked by the ship's cook or steward, this person varying in popularity depending on his skill. As to beverages other than water, coffee was served in heavy quantities, especially during cold weather times and at night. Alcohol (called *grog*), in contrast to the British merchant marine, was not carried by American ships, including the clippers. While we may be sure that some sailors smuggled aboard their own supply or rum or whiskey, such drink was not provided as a matter of course by owners or commanders. However, former captain turned owner Robert B. Forbes advocated its controlled use not only for medicinal purposes, but also as a reward, stating, "During my experience at sea, I have often found that a glass of grog, judiciously administered at the right time, and in the right *spirit*, instilled into the men when called up at night, and as a reward for active exertion"

(Forbes, *An Appeal*, p. 17). How often this may have occurred aboard clipper can only be speculated upon, but Forbes' practice of reward was a commonsense one that, while never officially condoned, saw widespread use during the U.S. Navy during World War II.

Finally, the most controversial subject regarding the clipper crews is that of keeping discipline. It is difficult at this late date, with all our work-place regulations and recognized standards of fair labor practices that have evolved over many years, to fully comprehend the situations that took place daily on American clipper ships. I have attempted to not only describe what it was like to serve on these ships, but also the many difficulties and dangers that might arise during the course of raising a crew and operating a clipper. Humans being what they are, sometimes difficulties and disputes arose between a captain and his officers and his crew. Just how prevalent were these problems, and how were they handled? Sadly, they were quite common and on the rise during the clipper ship era. While minor disputes might be solved by talking or a reprimand or threat of action by an officer against a crewman, a clipper ship at sea might best be viewed in comparison with an army unit in a frontline battle situation. In order to fight nature's wildest elements on a daily basis and get his clipper to its destination as quickly as possible, a commander had to both maintain a strict discipline, but also, through his mates, promote a sense of teamwork, requiring a delicate balancing act. This act was upset when unduly harsh discipline was administered or when a crew failed to respond to the demands of the officers to do what was best for the survival of ship and crew. During the time of the clippers, indeed in all of the age of sail, there were captains who were unnecessarily harsh and unfair towards their crew, while at the same time there were those crewmen who refused to do their duty.

The practice of whipping, or flogging, a crewman as a disciplinary measure was once a common practice on American ships but was abolished by law in 1850. However, this recently-passed law was seldom enforced, if at all, until after the fact and flogging was still resorted to from time to time. Even when the whip was not used, threats of a flogging were still made, and beatings by fist or with a belaying pin, long wooden pegs used to secure rigging lines to the bulwark (side) of a ship, were all too common. Indeed, if a sailor did not jump to and execute an order given by a mate in quick time, he was likely to receive a blow or kick from him (remember Captain "Kicking Jack" Williams?). And woe to the sailor who refused an order altogether; he would be beaten until he did his duty, or might be beaten senseless and confined or thrown in the forecastle. Given the pressure that existed for clippers to make passages, the number of bully or bucko mates and captains proliferated, or at least became known to the wider public. Probably the most famous of these men was Captain Robert "Bully" Waterman, a hard-driving commander of the packet trade who later drove the clippers *Sea Witch* and *Challenge*. We will discuss more about him shortly. Once again, the practice of physical discipline was a controversial matter among not only commanders, but also ship owners and maritime experts alike. Even as forward thinking of a man as Robert Bennet Forbes, a former captain, clipper owner, and recognized expert on all things maritime, believed that the law prohibiting the whipping of a sailor, originally intended for the navy only but later amended to include the merchant service "*by an accident*" was incorrectly enacted: "The experiment has been tried long enough to prove that it does not work well.... Therefore, some further legislation is necessary in order to maintain subordination, without which no ship is safe upon the ocean. Some efficient substitute is demanded. I confess that whipping a man, next to hanging him, is the worst use you can put him to ... the effect of taking away the *power to flog*, is not simply that the sailor feels he cannot be whipped ... but the repeal of the *power* has been a signal to seamen, and especially the foreign seamen, to believe that the day has come when the law of the sea is to be dealt from the forecastle, and not from the quarter deck! It has induced them to believe that they can now do as they please, even to the taking in and making of sail, and in regard to the ordinary duties of the ship" (Forbes, *An*

Appeal, pgs. 14, 16). Sadly, though Forbes was correct in his assessment, the problem of shipboard discipline would never be fully solved.

Because of the special conditions prevailing aboard the clippers, crew difficulties and mutinies were seemingly on the rise in the 1850s. Historians Howe and Matthews record in their history at least sixteen instances of mutiny, crew difficulties, or murder (there were likely many more that they do not mention) that transpired between a crew and the ship's officers or captain from 1851 to 1861 aboard the following clippers: *Challenge* (1851), *N.B. Palmer* (1852), *Aurora, Sovereign of the Seas* and *Undaunted* (1854), *Atalanta* and *Ocean Express* (1855), *John Milton* and *Morning Star* (1857), *Black Prince, Tornado,* and *Adelaide* (1858), *Golden State* and *Messenger* (1859), *Stag Hound* (1860), and *Boston Light* (1861). Two other mutinies on record include the notable *White Swallow* case of 1865 and the *Dashing Wave* in 1869. To these we may also add another case of mutiny, documented by historian Nicholas Dean, that occurred aboard the *Snow Squall* in 1858. While these numbers, compared to the total number of clippers that were in operation during the clipper ship era, are seemingly small, they are nonetheless indicative of the working conditions aboard this type of ship. Of some of these mutinies, we have no details, but for those that we do, some are quite interesting. The Baltimore-built clipper *Atalanta* was outbound from Marseilles, France, having arriving there from Spain, when her Italian crew stabbed the mate and locked Captain Montell and his officers in his cabin and took command of the ship. The ship was initially sailed toward the eastern Mediterranean but ran low on provisions and eventually put back into Marseilles, where the mutinous crew was subsequently captured by the U.S. sloop of war *Constellation*. We know not why the Italian crew mutinied, but perhaps they had been shanghaied, or simply decided that they didn't want to voyage to America. The mutiny aboard the clipper *N.B. Palmer* was stopped solely by the actions of Captain Charles Low; after his mate was shot in the leg by a crewman, and his second mate beaten, Low came to the rescue wielding only an unloaded musket to subdue his unruly crew. With the troubles over, Low directed his remaining crew in sail handling, and then flogged the two mutinous sailors involved in the incident.

Captain Robert Waterman (1808–1884). This clipper commander was one of the most celebrated mariners of the 1840s and 1850, gaining a reputation as a driver in the China trade. He made a record run in the old packet *Natchez* and drove the new clipper *Sea Witch* home from China in then record time at the beginning of the clipper ship era. His reputation and career came to a sad end after a mutinous maiden voyage in the big New York clipper *Challenge* in 1851 (courtesy Peter Haley Family).

In 1861 the *Boston Light*, Captain Crowell, was bound from New York to California; the mate was stabbed to death by one of the crew for reasons unstated. Aboard the *Golden State* in 1859, while bound to Hong Kong, the crew refused to do their duty because of poor rations and subsequently beat the officers, from which beating the first mate died; the mutineers escaped via the ship's boat to Penang (Malaysia), where they were captured. The voyage of the

Messenger, Captain Benjamin Manton, is also an interesting case. In 1859 the ship had a difficult voyage from India to China. While the ship was subsequently at Hong Kong, Captain Manton was arrested and tried for cruelty to his sailors. He was convicted and sentenced to pay a fine and serve a three month jail term, but he was soon released after an appeal was made by British and American merchants there who had good proof that the ship's crew had been mutinous. Another overseas incident involved the Portsmouth-built clipper *Morning Star* in 1857; while at Callao, Peru, and getting ready to depart for France, the mate was stabbed by one crewmember while the rest of the crew stood by armed with knives and pistols. This mutiny was quelled by the crew of the British naval vessel *Monarch.* Likewise, the crew of the small Maine-built *Snow Squall* had difficulties when one man, after refusing an order from the second mate, was grabbed by the throat. The crewman retaliated by pulling his knife and threatening the mate. Luckily, Captain Thomas Loyd, who was "like a father" to some of the crew, came on the scene and had the sailor subdued and put in irons for the rest of the day (Dean and Switzer, p. 148). In yet another incident, the crew of the *Ocean Express* mutinied while off Rock Light, Liverpool, ready to sail for New York. They claimed that the mate had overworked them, but otherwise had no problem with the captain. Thirty of the men were eventually landed off the ship with nothing but the clothes on their backs, forced to leave everything else behind, but were not prosecuted by English authorities. Among other incidents about which there is little information, the *Undaunted*'s captain was injured during a mutiny while bound to St. Johns, Newfoundland, but survived, and aboard the *Tornado* in 1858 during a voyage from New York to Australia, her mate shot three crewmen, one of whom died, during the passage. Finally, we have the unusual case of the *Sovereign of the Seas* mutiny while the ship was bound from Australia to Liverpool, during which a fight broke out between a crewman and a ship's passenger; when the mate intervened and put the sailor in irons, a good part of the rest of the crew surrounded the mate and demanded he release the sailor or they would seize the ship. Eventually, the mutineers were dispersed by the ship's officers with the help of some armed passengers. One other account of mutiny, with no details as to names or dates and as yet unsubstantiated by any historic records, is also to be found in the history of the ships owned by the William F. Weld Company of Boston. Here it is mentioned that the company's second clipper named *Golden Fleece* (built 1855 — the first *Golden Fleece* was wrecked in 1854), had difficulties of some sort that led her captain to be hauled into a New Hampshire court because "there had been a mutiny aboard and several were killed and the captain was up for murder" (Anderson, p. 65). In this case, it is asserted that "because it was a matter of self-defence [*sic*] ... the captain was set free," but "the crew were sent to the New Hampshire state prison for three years, and one of them died there" (Anderson, p. 65). If this incident really occurred, it was an unusual one, as most clipper ship mutinies took place either on long foreign voyages or during the run from the East Coast to California. With the exception of ships involved in the North Atlantic packet trade, which *Golden Fleece* was not, only one other clipper mutiny, that of the *Undaunted* listed above, has been documented as having taken place in or around New England waters.

Despite the examples above, by far the most famous example of a clipper ship mutiny occurred early in the decade during the maiden voyage of the *Challenge* in 1851. In retrospect, this voyage seems to have been doomed from the start, with a variety of factors all coming into play at once that almost ensured a mutiny would take place. The expectations for the *Challenge* to make a record passage by her owners were present from the very day the ship was conceived; not only had her owners, N.L. & G. Griswold, paid William Webb $150,000 to build the biggest (2,006 tons) and best clipper afloat at the time, but they also desired a record passage, offering her captain a huge bonus for making the run to California in 90 days or less. The next aggravating factor in this disastrous voyage was the owner's choice of commander, Captain Robert "Bully" Waterman (born 1808 in New York). He was already a noted driver, having made a name for himself in both the

The New York clipper *Challenge*. This 2,006-ton ship built by William Webb in 1851 was one of the largest clippers ever launched at New York. No expense was spared in her building and her maiden voyage was expected to set the record on the California run, but she fell short of expectations due to contrary weather conditions and the struggle that developed between her crew and the hard driving Captain Waterman and his bucko mates (from a Currier & Ives lithograph, courtesy of the Library of Congress).

North Atlantic packet trade (where he gained his first command in 1836) first as a bully mate and then a driving captain, and the China trade, where he kept his reputation as a driver aboard the old packet *Natchez*, and later the early out-and-out clipper *Sea Witch*. That Waterman was a gifted captain is undisputed, but he was also harsher than many captains in his treatment of his crews, dating back to his days as a bucko mate. However, it must be said of him that, like most captains, he did have his supporters among sailors who regularly shipped under his command (Whipple, *The Challenge*, p. 102). The next prevailing factor was the crew shipped for the maiden voyage of the *Challenge* in July 1851. Waterman boarded his ship after it had already left the dock and found that his first mate had shipped a largely incompetent crew of about sixty men. So incensed was Waterman that he dismissed his chief officer nearly on the spot, with the intention of promoting the second mate, Alexander Coghill, and even considered putting back into port for a new crew. However, this was not Waterman's style and he resolved to continue the voyage without delay. It was at this time that fate of a darker kind intervened; as historian A.B.C. Whipple relates, "Waterman was considering whether or not to promote his second mate ... when he noticed a ship's boat putting out from the *Guy Mannering* ... the boat approached the *Challenge*, and the man sitting in the stern hailed the quarterdeck. Waterman recognized him as soon as he climbed over the rail. James Douglass was known on the transatlantic run and in every bar in New York and Liverpool as one of the toughest first mates in the packet trade" (Whipple, *The Challenge*, p. 150). Nicknamed "Black Douglass," this first mate was known for the beatings he gave to those serving under him and had left the *Mannering* before she even made port because he feared for his life after he had had a rough go with the packet rats that had brought the ship to New York. This combination of a bully captain and a bucko mate who enjoyed beating his crew was really the final straw that set the tone for the *Challenge*'s maiden voyage.

From the start, Captain Waterman was frustrated on the voyage, not just because of his inexperienced crew, but also because of the light winds that would not allow the clipper to reach her peak performance, thereby lessening his chance to earn the hefty bonus. Problems came to a head off the coast of Brazil when first mate Douglass was attacked by two crewmen and was stabbed in the leg; during the ensuing melee, Waterman quickly came to the mate's aid and in short time the mutiny was quelled. It was subsequently determined that nine of the crew were part of a plot to kill the *Challenge*'s captain and first mate and take the ship into Rio de Janeiro; one man even implicated the second mate, Coghill, later on, but he denied his involvement and remained in his position. While one of the nine was a sailor directly involved in the attack on Douglass, he had disappeared during the fight and it was thought he may have jumped overboard (he was discovered hiding on the ship a month later), the other eight conspirators were tied up and flogged by Douglass and were soon after back on duty. However, the tension on the clipper between officers and crew was palpable afterwards and the angry and sullen sailors did as little work as possible, enraging Waterman and Douglass even further. To complicate matters, the ship was now approaching Cape Horn and many men were sick from dysentery. While off the Cape, three men were killed in one day, falling from aloft while handling sails in a wild gale. The clipper took such a beating for nearly three weeks that at one point almost a third of the crew was in the sick bay. Two men would subsequently die due to the punishment meted out by Douglass during the remainder of the voyage; one man, who refused to go aloft because he had dysentery, was thrown down, his head held by the mate under the freezing water that was flowing on the clipper's deck. He was then tied to the side of the ship for an hour, fully exposed to the harsh elements, without shoes and only thinly clad. This man died less than two weeks later in the sick bay. Another man, an Italian who could speak little or no English and had come aboard with no sailoring skills and no shoes to wear, was also ordered aloft but would not comply due to his frozen feet and ran back to the forecastle. James Douglass followed him back and gave him such a severe beating that he died that same day.

In the end, the *Challenge* ended her hellish voyage by making San Francisco on October 29, 1851, 108 days out from New York. Waterman's race for his $10,000 bonus was lost, and so was any good that might have remained of his reputation. Soon after her arrival, the clipper's mutineers were handed over to the local authorities to be tried, but Waterman and Douglass were far from being in the clear. Fairly quickly, a waterfront mob had formed after hearing of the *Challenge*'s voyage, no doubt from one of her sailors. Soon enough, one or more of the crew hired a sea-lawyer and brought charges against Waterman and Douglass, and while they had escaped, at least thus far, mob justice, they did have warrants out for their arrest. Later, while Waterman was conducting the ship's business at a local office, a mob arrived, egged on in part by the local press, and attempted to capture Waterman. While he escaped the mob, old captain John Land, the former skipper of the *Rainbow* who also worked for the *Challenge*'s owners, was captured instead. The mob threatened to hang him but, luckily for Land, armed members of the Committee of Vigilance arrived on the scene and surrounded them, forcing them to release the captain. After this the mob dispersed, though there was talk of burning the *Challenge*; the following day, Waterman left town and went to his ranch, about fifty miles distant, in what is now Solano County, California, while James Douglass was captured by a local sheriff and thrown in jail to await trial.

During the series of *Challenge* mutiny trials that were subsequently held from November 1851 through February 1852, which Waterman is said to have insisted upon to prove his innocence, all of the clipper's officers, even Alexander Coghill, were tried on a number of charges ranging from cruelty, assault, and murder, while eight of the crew, as well as Coghill, were tried for mutiny. In the end, after much conflicting testimony, none of the crew was convicted of mutiny, the most powerful part of their defense being their description of the constant abuse heaped on them by Douglass and Waterman. As for Captain Waterman and his officers, they also underwent a series of trials and twice avoided convictions by hung juries. However, they were not so lucky on some of the other charges, with Douglass being found guilty for murdering the Italian crewman, Waterman found guilty of abusing a Finnish sailor, and Coghill found guilty for kicking a sailor. Despite the convictions, the sentences received by the clipper's officers were extremely lenient; Coghill served sixteen days in jail, Douglass was fined $250, and Waterman $400. The matter now closed, the parties went on with their lives; Waterman retired from the sea permanently, though he later served as a marine consultant, inspector, and wreck salvager in addition to expanding his California land holdings. Prior to his death in California in 1884, he never wavered in the belief that his actions were correct, at least not publicly. In fact, many in the captain's fraternity supported Waterman's actions. As for Douglass and Coghill's later lives, Douglass would never again serve on a merchant ship, but stayed in the San Francisco area and remained a close friend of Waterman. Alexander Coghill continued his seafaring for a number of years and apparently never got over his bucko ways; after serving as chief mate aboard the *Adelaide* on a voyage from New York to San Francisco in late 1858 and early 1859, he was subsequently fined fifty dollars by the U.S. Circuit Court in San Francisco "for cruel and unusual punishment of a sailor" (Dillon, p. 124) while serving under Captain Wakeman. As for the *Challenge*, the clipper gained a reputation as a hell ship, one that she would never shake. Indeed, on her next voyage out to Shanghai in late 1851, Captain John Land, her replacement commander, had to pay exorbitant advance money, at least four times the normally prevailing rates, to ship a crew, and even then the crew was mutinous and Land had to put in at Hong Kong for assistance. Worn out by his years of experience, and no doubt under duress from his dealings with the entire *Challenge* situation, Land died at Hong Kong and a new skipper had to be found. The big clipper continued under the American flag until being sold foreign in India in 1862; subsequently renamed *Golden City*, she sailed the seas for another fourteen years under the British flag before coming to an end in 1876, wrecked off the coast of France.

What conclusions can be drawn regarding the mutiny on the *Challenge*? At this late date, and with the benefit of hindsight, it may be easy for some to believe that the fault for the whole affair lay on Captain Waterman's head; in one way, this conclusion *is* correct. As commander of the clipper, all of the incidents that happened were under his control to either prevent or mitigate. He had the option of delaying his departure to ship a new crew, which might have prevented a mutiny altogether. Even though Waterman didn't take this course of action, he could have prevented the abuses and murder by Douglass, but, here too he seems to have done nothing to rein in his mate and stop his excesses. Given Waterman's hard driving reputation, it does not seem to have been in his nature to do any of these things. Of course, first mate James Douglass was undoubtedly the instigator of the whole affair if he even came close to living up to his reputation; had he not abused his sailors from the very start, it may be that the *Challenge*'s crew would never have plotted to take over the ship. And, finally, what about the actions of the crew? Plotting mutiny and murder, of course, was a crime and, perhaps, there were those in the crew that were shirking their duties even from the very beginning. In the end, the *Challenge* mutiny must be viewed as an indictment against the entire system then prevailing regarding the labor aspects (training, procurement, sailor's rights, etc.) of our merchant marine. If any good did come out of the whole affair, it lay in the fact that, first, the incident was brought to both the public's attention and, more importantly, that of our legal system, that trials were convened to hear the many cases, and that, ultimately, the sailors were released because a jury found merit in their arguments. This marked a big change, as had this case come to the courts maybe even five years before, it is likely that Captain Waterman and his officers would have been totally exonerated. Despite the fact that Waterman and Douglass received light sentences and essentially got off, the case was a step in the right direction.

Incidents of mutiny and sailor abuse such as happened aboard the *Challenge* are sometimes hard to accept when it comes to our sentimental notions about the clipper ships; on the one hand, we have in our mind's eye the white-winged wonder that was the American clipper ship, undoubtedly the most beautiful American ship ever built. On the other hand, we have the stark realities of the difficult life of the sailors that manned the clippers, as well as the bucko mates and bully captains that often drove them. It is hard to reconcile these two contrasting images and, notwithstanding the examples of the mutinies just described, it is difficult to think of these vessels as hell ships. However, the *Challenge* was not the only ship with such a reputation; the *Great Republic* made a hell voyage in 1864 under Captain Josiah Paul who, along with mates Walls and Coe, "practiced cruelty — too revolting to print" (Dillon, pg. 138). The *Herald of the Morning* also had difficult voyages with bucko mates George Field and William Brown in charge (ibid., p. 137), while *Charmer*'s commander, Captain J. Lewis, disciplined a sailor because he had kicked Lewis' pet dog, which had moments before bitten the sailor (ibid., pgs. 135–36). To balance the above incidents, several others of a more uplifting nature should also be recounted; Captain Charles Ranlett of the clipper *Surprise* apparently got so tired of seeing his bucko second mate in action that he finally yelled at his officer, "If you can't get along without swearing and knocking the men so, you may quit. I won't have it" (Dillon, p. 135). However, this admonition seemed to have little effect; the mate still continued in his bad ways, though one crewman noted that "the mate did not swear so much after that when he was beating up on the men" (ibid.). Captain Nathaniel Palmer, the noted clipper commander for the fleet of A.A. Low & Brothers, was known for his fair treatment of his crews, and so too was Captain Charles P. Low. In his recollections he tells of several interesting instances that give us an idea of the treatment crewmen in the Low fleet received; while in command of the *Samuel Russell,* Low once gave "a rap over the head" to a Hawaiian crewman slow in handling the sails, but was reprimanded by his mate who called to him, "Have patience, Captain Low, have patience ... he [the mate] enjoyed giving me some of my own medicine" (Low, p. 104). In yet another career incident, this time while Low was in command of *Houqua* in 1849, the captain was taking his ship to sea from New York with Captain Nathaniel Palmer and a number of visitors aboard who would be taken off by a pilot boat at Sandy Hook. Unfortunately, this crowd of spectators got to see first hand how the mate dealt with his new and unruly crew; they were so distressed at the first mate's brutal treatment of the sailmaker, who refused to work, that they remonstrated to old Captain Palmer. He subsequently took the unusual action of making young Captain Low, who was "very angry at his interference" (Low, p. 86), discharge the mate and accompany him back to New York via pilot boat in order to find a new mate, which he did. The new mate, as it turned out, was a much better man by Low's own admission, and the subsequent voyage to California was made without difficulty.

Interestingly, though many mutinies and crew difficulties would occur aboard the clippers throughout the 1850s, it would not be until fourteen years after the *Challenge* incident that another mutiny, a successful one this time on the clipper ship *White Swallow*, would capture the public's attention and also result in a trial. In this incident, the Medford-built clipper departed New York in September 1865 under Captain Elijah Knowles bound for San Francisco, but the *White Swallow* was said to be in poor condition, not uncommon for many of the old clippers, which were seldom kept up to their same condition as when they sailed during the 1850s. During the ensuing passage, not only was the crew brutalized, but they were also asked to perform particularly difficult maintenance duties during poor weather conditions which resulted in the deaths of two men who were washed overboard. Upset with this chain of events, the crew mutinied and took control of the ship, incredibly, without harming Captain Knowles and his mates. For three days the mutineers ran the ship, but allowed the captain out on deck to take navigational fixes and direct the crew in some matters. After this, an agreement was reached between the crew and the captain and all returned to their work as before, but without the brutal treatment and dangerous extra work. Despite the friendly agreement, once the ship reached San Francisco six of the mutineers were brought to trial and "prosecuted with vigor" (Howe & Matthews, p. 699) for the affair. Once again, as with the *Challenge* case, no sailors were convicted for their actions. Slowly, ever so slowly, the tide was turning in favor of sailors' rights and protections, but voyages by hell ships, clippers and non-clippers alike, would continue under the American flag until the end of the days of sail.

African American Crewmen

While there were few white American crewmen serving aboard the clippers of the 1850s, one oft-forgotten segment of men that did serve were black sailors. These men of color not only hailed from America, but also from the West Indies and the island of Cape Verde, off the coast of Africa. In fact, black seamen were an integral part of America's merchant marine dating back to colonial times, and though African Americans were seldom accorded fair rights and treatment ashore, they did serve at sea with a somewhat higher degree of equality. These "Black Jacks," as historian W. Jeffrey Bolster calls them, served in a wide variety of shipboard positions, ranging from steward and cook to ordinary and able-bodied seaman. While it is highly unlikely that any black sailor served as a mate on a clipper, and none served as captains, it may be that there were several instances where they served as bosuns. However, in other branches of the merchant marine, especially the whaling trade, there were many examples of black mates, while a number of African Americans served as captains of the ships or pilot boats that they themselves owned, mostly in the local coasting trade or, to a lesser extent, the West Indian trade.

While it is a near certainty that at least one black sailor served in every clipper ship, little has been documented about their careers and service to give historians much to work with. However, at least two well-known clippers, the packet *Dreadnought* and the *Adelaide*, both big ships, did have a regular crew, not including officers, that were all black. In 1857, Captain Edgar Wakeman of the New York–built *Adelaide* (1,831 tons) made a passage from New York to San Francisco and "all of her crew of 26 A.B.'s were negroes" (Howe & Matthews, p. 1). This passage took 127 days due to light winds throughout, including being stuck off the coast of California for a week, but seems to have been otherwise uneventful until the ship was coming into San Francisco on 29 September. During the docking maneuvers one of the mates knocked a man overboard and he was subsequently drowned. While the exact details of this incident are unknown, it was clearly no accident and the mate was arrested but was soon cleared of any wrongdoing. However, this incident surely remained a raw spot with the ship's black crew; six months later, while docked at Elide Island off the Mexican coast to take in a load of guano, the mate was murdered by one of his crew. The perpetrator was subsequently tried by a court convened from officers of the other ships then at Elide Island (certainly no trial by a jury of his peers in any sense of the word here) and he was quickly convicted and sentenced to death. He was soon afterward hanged aboard the *Adelaide*, as was the typical result for guilty mutineers in an earlier day, a vivid example to his fellow crewmen.

The only other known example, though there may have been others, of a clipper crewed entirely by black sailors is that of the Newburyport-built clipper packet *Dreadnought*, under the command of the legendary Captain Samuel Samuels (born 1823), in late 1862. On this voyage or series of voyages (how many is uncertain), Captain Samuels, perhaps tired of dealing with the typical "packet rat" seamen, had "resolved to ship a colored crew. They did very well during the summer months, but in cold, stormy weather they were worthless. It was difficult to keep them from freezing ... I was sorry for the poor wretches, but in order to keep their blood in circulation, and to prevent them from falling asleep and freezing while on duty, it was necessary for one of the officers to trot them around the decks and stimulate them" (Samuels, p. 292). Little is known about details of the voyages these black sailors made on the New York–Liverpool run, but the fact that the clipper's black sailors were not used to the cold weather leads one to believe that they may have been of West Indian or Cape Verde heritage, warm-weather places, but this is conjecture. Despite his hard driving reputation, Samuels seems to have been fair to his black sailors, and clearly showed compassion for their situation.

While black sailors served as regular seamen, the shipboard position in which they saw the greatest employment was that of the ship's cook or captain's steward. These positions used to be the lowest paid professions in the American merchant marine in the first decades of the 19th century, and were thus often relegated to African Americans. However, by the 1850s things had changed and the positions of steward and cook were actually high-paying ones, according to one historian equivalent to that of a second mate (Bolster, pg. 168). The job of cook on any merchant ship during the age of sail was a difficult one to be sure. Sailors were not always happy with the fare they were served, both in quality and quantity, and heaped their abuses in this regard on the ship's cook, even if the provisions shipped were of an inferior quality and short in supply, something that was usually not their fault. While sailors always complained about their rations, in fact the clipper ships were usually well provisioned compared to other merchant ships and, assuming the cooks didn't ruin the food during their preparation efforts, the crews were usually well served. When food was ill-prepared or, worse yet, wasted needlessly, cooks were often subject to severe discipline and ill-treatment from all sides, both captain and crew. Sailors always complained about their food but usually learned to live with it, but clipper ship passengers could be very critical, used to, as they were, a more varied fare, and perhaps a better prepared one, on land. Samuel Ferguson, a passenger on the doomed clipper *Hornet*, complained that cook Joseph Washington's pork was "not to his liking" and that his hog slaughtering was "sloppily done" (Jackson, p. 33), while passenger Hugh Gregory aboard the *Sea Serpent* stated, "The way we are fed is truly outrageous" (Whipple, *The Challenge*, p. 120), though he still ate what was served. However, just the opposite was true on many ships; the steward who did the cooking aboard the clipper *Whirlwind* must have been a good one, as the captain's wife stated that the man "cooks better than I do" (Hassell, p. 18). A smart clipper commander not only treated his cook well, but also did his best to keep him aboard and ship him on successive voyages. While there is some anecdotal evidence that suggests that cooks stayed aboard an individual ship for multiple voyages at higher rates than regular seamen, there were plenty of others who changed ships frequently just as regular seamen did.

The second shipboard position that was often filled by African Americans was that of steward. A steward was, in effect, the personal servant of the captain and his family, if they were also aboard, as well as any passengers the ship may have been carrying. This position was an outgrowth of the cabin boy position which dated back to the earliest days of sail in America, also a servant to the captain, but not always a paid one. Sometimes the cabin boy really was a boy or young man, perhaps going to sea for the first time, but this term was also applied to African Americans that also filled this position, no matter what their age may have been. By the 1850s, the steward was a paid position, while the position of boy was generally an unpaid one somewhat akin to that of an unpaid apprentice position, usually filled by a young white man going to sea for the first time. The steward, on the other hand, was usually a trusted servant to the captain of any clipper, and sometimes, perhaps often, was a friend or even a confidant, and the bond between captain and steward was a strong one. Of the steward named Essex (likely black, but uncertain) aboard his first command, Captain Charles Low had this to say; "He had been steward of the *Great Western*, the first steamer that crossed the Atlantic. He was lame in one arm, but he was the best steward out of

Burning of the California clipper *Hornet*. This dramatic woodcut shows the captain's lifeboat of the abandoned New York clipper *Hornet*, which caught fire on May 3, 1866, in the middle of the Pacific. At right is shown the remains of the burning clipper sinking beneath the waves, while Captain Josiah Mitchell is shown in the rear center of the lifeboat directing his crew. At far left in the background are the other two lifeboats that carried the remainder of the clipper's crew. While Mitchell's boat made landfall after a harrowing 43 days at sea, the other boats were never recovered (from *Harper's Weekly*, 1866).

New York and had been in the *Houqua* for two voyages and was ready to go with me in my first voyage as Master" (Low, p. 64). As this passage demonstrates, stewards were considered valuable crewmen and, like cooks, were often quite dedicated to their ships and served multiple voyages. However, not all stewards were so well treated; the notorious commander of the clipper *Sea Witch*, Captain Robert Waterman, supposedly "attacked his steward for some unrecorded offense and sliced his scalp with a carving knife" (Jackson, p. 64) in July 1851 while the ship was either at New York or coming to the end of a long voyage from China. Though details of the lives of most of the clipper crewmen have been lost to history, among the black stewards and cooks there are a few names that have been preserved. Aboard the Boston clipper *Challenger*, steward David Graves, "a mulatto from Philadelphia" (Shockley, p. 168), was well-regarded by Captain William Burgess. This steward was likely the same man that was listed in the 1850 Federal Census, born in Pennsylvania in 1831 and the son of Henry and Mary Graves, and living in Camden, New Jersey. Graves attended Captain Burgess during his final hours when he died aboard his clipper in 1856. How many voyages with the captain Graves made is unknown, but he was so well thought of that Burgess taught him how to take navigational fixes using the ship's chronometer. The *Challenger* was voyaging from the Chinchas Islands to Valparaiso, Chile, when Burgess died, and David Graves, a Freemason like his commander, followed his commander's dying wishes, among them that he help his wife, Rebecca, with navigation duties, which he did. He also would subsequently accompany the captain's wife on her homeward voyage, and later came to visit the memorial Hannah Rebecca Burgess had erected to her husband in Sandwich, Massachusetts, making the journey from Philadelphia. Graves later served aboard at least one other sailing ship, but almost nothing is known of his life. He might have gone undocumented entirely were if not for one strange occurrence. Following his time aboard the *Challenger*, Hannah Burgess presented Graves with an inscribed Bible in thanks for his service both to the captain and her in helping out in the difficult times after his death and accompanying her home. In 1864 Graves' Bible was recovered from a shipwreck of an unidentified American vessel off the coast of Formosa (Taiwan) and ended up in the hands of author turned U.S. consul, Richard Henry Dana, Jr. It was eventually returned to Mrs. Burgess in Sandwich and is now on display in the Sandwich Historical Society Museum. Graves' presentation Bible almost certainly was recovered from the wreck of the Medford-built clipper *Ringleader* (1,154 tons), aboard which Graves served Captain Matthews and, subsequently, the brothers Captain John and Otis White, as a steward beginning in 1858 until she was lost in a storm off the southwestern end of Formosa while bound from Hong Kong to San Francisco in May 1863 with several hundred Chinese coolies. Once the clipper was stranded off shore, it was soon surrounded by local pirates and plundered. All but two of the crew survived the wreck and its aftermath but lost all their personal possessions, some of which were later sold in local markets, which is where Grave's Bible was found. Unfortunately, David Graves does not appear in any census records after 1850, so the details of his fate remain a mystery, though Hannah Burgess' later account (which incorrectly states that he was shipwrecked while serving aboard *Invincible*) does record that he was working as a steward ashore in Shanghai and died there after contracting cholera.

Two other men that served as steward and cook, respectively, aboard the New York clipper *Hornet* (1,426 tons) were Henry Chisling and the previously mentioned Joseph A. Washington, both residents of New York. Little is known about these men, except that Chisling had previously served aboard the clipper packet *Dreadnought* under Captain Samuel Samuels and had been shipwrecked three times before. Chisling was termed by one of the ship's passengers, Samuel Ferguson, "an honest sort of fellow" (Jackson, p. 32). Their identities, like that of most clipper ship sailors, might have gone largely unrecorded except for unusual circumstances. They shipped aboard the *Hornet* in January 1866, bound from New York to San Francisco with a cargo of case oil and candles under the command of Maine skipper Josiah Mitchell. Though the ensuing passage was a slow one, it was uneventful; however, things aboard a clipper ship could change quite quickly. On the early morning of May 2 the ship was 111 days out in the Pacific, 2,500 miles southwest of Hawaii, when the mate accidentally caught the ship on fire when his lantern ignited some varnish. Very quickly the ship was entirely afire and the crew was forced to abandon ship before her cargo exploded. Being stationed in the ship's galley, Chisling and Washington quickly gathered food supplies on Captain Mitchell's orders while the sailors prepared three of the ship's boats. Captain Mitchell was in charge of one of the boats, while the other two were commanded by his mates; Chisling and Washington were in First Mate Samuel Hardy's boat with six other men. Mitchell's boat towed the other two boats and plotted a course for the Revilla Gegido Islands. For the next seventeen days the three boats sailed together, the men surviving on meager rations that were carefully doled out. Of Henry Chisling and Joseph Washington, one historian calls them "the hidden glue holding together morale" (Jackson, p. 62). Washington led the men in prayer services, while Chisling told stories of the previous shipwrecks he had survived, surely in an effort to persuade his fellow sailors that all hope was not lost. However, by May 19, many of the sailors, including Chisling and Washington, were beginning to look emaciated and the journey was slow for the three boats sailing together. On that day, Captain Mitchell, deciding that one of the three boats must separate and seek rescue on its own, divvied up the remaining rations and, after some difficulty with the second mate's boat, parted ways with his first mate's boat instead. Mitchell's boat would meet up with Hardy's boat three days later by accident, and their desperate situation was readily apparent; by this time "Washington and Chisling resembled stick figures, rags hanging from their bones, skin gray and ashen from sickness" (Jackson, p. 103) and its other occupants were also badly off. After a brief meeting, Hardy's boat continued on its way, while at the same time Captain Mitchell made the difficult decision to quit towing the other boat. Hardy and his men would never be seen again, and neither would the second mate's boat; only Captain Mitchell's boat made landfall, reaching Hawaii after a 4,300 mile journey that ended on June 15 after having spent 44 days at sea. The tragic story of the *Hornet*, her loss, and the epic struggle for survival may perhaps have been lost to history were it not for the fact that a previously unknown reporter for the *Sacramento Daily Union* by the name of Samuel Clemens (a.k.a. Mark Twain) was in Hawaii at the time and itching to become famous. He was the man on the spot when the *Hornet* survivors made land and was the first to tell their story, published on July 19, 1866, with all its horrifying details. The story was soon picked up by newspapers around the world, thereby not only giving Clemens the fame he desired, but also recording for posterity some personal details of the *Hornet*'s crew, including the two black men who were lost.

In the end, while we would like to know more about some of the other African Americans and their stories that served aboard American clippers, no such individual accounts have survived. Still, it is clear even from the few examples that are available that black sailors as a whole, whether serving as seaman, steward, or cook, were an integral part of the crews of these famed ships, carrying on in the same traditions set by earlier generations of black sailors.

The Female Presence on the Clippers

Another interesting group of individuals that sailed, and often effectively served, aboard the clippers during the voyages of the 1850s and 1860s were women, mostly captain's wives, but also captain's daughters and, in rare instances, as stewardesses. The tradition of women going to sea with their captain-husbands was well-established years before clipper ships came on the scene and was thus a widely accepted practice throughout the American merchant marine service on nearly every type of voyage, whether it was of the coasting variety or a long distance one to China and India. Just how many wives accompanied their husbands to sea aboard a clipper is unknown, but many examples abound. The *Boston Daily Evening Transcript* records fourteen such women (and one daughter) in their lists of passengers aboard clippers departing from Boston for two years running, including Reliance Paine (born 1829, husband Captain John Paine) on *Mountain Wave*, Jerusha Howes (born 1819, husband Captain Moses Howes, Jr.) on *Competitor*, Mrs. G.W. Elliot on *West Wind*, Lydia Hatch (born 1823, husband Captain Freeman Hatch) on *Northern Light*, Martha Miller (born 1818, husband Captain Lewis F. Miller) on *Witch of the Wave*, Mary Knight (born 1811, husband Captain Elias D. Knight) on *Morning Light*, and Mrs. William Knott on *Don Quixote*, all in 1853, followed by Sarah Chase (born 1824, husband Captain Josiah Chase) on *Starlight*, Lydia Hatch again on *Northern Light*, Clara Hatch (born 1818, husband Captain James Hatch) and her daughter Mabel (born 1849) on *Midnight*, Ruth Arey (born 1821 in Maine, husband Captain John Arey) on *Spitfire*, Mrs. J.S. Lucas on *Charmer*, Mrs. Harlow Kimball on *Telegraph*, and Mrs. Callaghan on *Boston Light*, all in 1854. Most of the passages for the ladies on these clippers were uneventful, though Lydia Hatch stands out for her consecutive voyages, while Mrs. Kimball aboard *Telegraph* had an unpleasant start (if this was her first voyage) when the clipper collided with another ship just three days out of Boston, causing her masts to come crashing down. Unfortunately, for these and most other sea-going clipper wives, personal accounts that give their point of view have seldom survived. It is interesting to note, though, that the owners of *Mountain Wave*, Alpheus Hardy & Company, "gladly paid a higher wage" to Captain John Paine "if he would take his wife with him" (*Some Merchants and Sea Captains of Old Boston*, pg. 26). The reasons for their enthusiasm for Reliance Paine are unknown; perhaps she was, as has been previously mentioned, a comforting presence to her captain-husband as many seafaring wives were, but the tenor of their comments suggest that this well-thought-of woman had more to offer (maybe some navigations skills or business acumen), for even the most generous of ship owners were usually not inclined to pay extra wages without getting something in return.

The reasons for these women going to sea were quite simple in nature; it was not for the sake of sheer adventure or sport, but rather to be with their husbands and to maintain their life as a couple or family. The clipper ship voyages came at the height of the Victorian era when such ideals were the standards of the day. Nothing illustrates this more than the words of clipper wife Hannah Rebecca Burgess, the spouse of Captain William Burgess. During a voyage from China to England aboard the *Challenger* in early 1856, Rebecca wrote in her journal, meant for her husband to read, "My Dear Husband, we have been together for 2 years and 6 months, with scarcely a week's separation, and even the thought of remaining alone is repulsive. I must allow there are pleasures on land which cannot be enjoyed at sea, but I have enjoyed luxuries with you William, that bereft of that companionship would bring no happiness. I know that I love the sea. But more I love to be with my Husband.... I enjoy going to sea because I am with my Husband. With him any place is home" (Hassell, p. 51).

That is not to say, of course, that some women were not excited by this change of pace from their normal town or city life. Indeed, many women enjoyed their time at sea, especially in the beginning when it was a new experience. Mary Matthews, the teenaged daughter of Captain George Matthews, commander of the clipper *National Eagle*, recalled during her first voyage, which commenced in December 1857, "That first night at sea! Shall I ever forget it! I lay quietly in my berth, watching the dim swaying light of the after cabins, into which our state rooms opened, and listening to the measured tread of the mates, as they paced back and forth on the upper deck. Sleep…was a belated visitor that night. Instead, I filled the hours with memories of the past; with hopes and plans for the future" (Bray, p. 13). It is interesting to note that aboard this same clipper just four years earlier, Ruth Pedrick (born 1815), the wife of Captain Knott Pedrick, had died, possibly in that same berth, due to an outbreak of yellow fever. Though many women, like their novice seagoing male counterparts, had to battle seasickness for a week or two on their first voyage, many soon came to love their new surroundings. Rebecca Burgess suffered from seasickness for two weeks when making her first sea voyage aboard the clipper *Whirlwind* beginning in February 1854, but she eventually got her sea legs and soon enough began to experience her new surroundings, exclaiming that "I love the sea…it fills the mind with a sense of majesty and greatness of the Ruler of the Universe to gaze upon this mighty expanse of water. I can say that it is pleasanter than any scene I have witnessed on land" (Hassell, p. 17). For those unrecorded women who were unable to overcome their seasickness in a short time (and there surely were some), it is a safe bet to say that their first voyage was probably their last and in the future they were forced to wait for the safe arrival home of their husbands.

However, even aboard the ship there were expectations and restrictions when it came to what women could and couldn't do. Even more so than the captain, his wife and children, if present, were restricted to the captain's quarterdeck at the aft end of the ship, as well as the captain's cabin and salon room, and passenger cabins if the occasion should arise. No woman was allowed to have the run of the entire ship, or even to converse with a sailor, as it was considered both improper etiquette and something that was beneath her station. In fact, except for the occasional interaction with the ship's mates, the only crewmen a woman would have regular contact with were the captain's steward and the cabin boy if there was one. The same was true for the captain's children, though it would not have been uncommon for a captain to sometimes overlook his son's interaction with the regular crew, and it was often the case that a lively lad became the favorite pet of off duty seamen. When she was not tending directly to her husband or children, a captain's wife spent her days with simple housekeeping duties, aided by the ship's steward, in cleaning the captain's cabin, reading, sewing, or perhaps writing in a journal. If passengers were aboard, this also provided added enjoyment and distractions. A female passenger might provide welcome and sympathetic company, and the children of passengers always provided some entertainment, though they also came with the typical worries for their health and safety on a long voyage. Male passengers, too, could be quite interesting, providing extra company and conversation (in a proper setting, of course) or, if they happened to be well-educated, perhaps even giving an improvised lecture on a topic of interest. On days when the weather was good, the captain's wife could go out on deck to sit or take a short stroll and enjoy the sea breeze or scenes of maritime life. Many women undoubtedly were interested in watching the sailors at their work, albeit at a distance, in handling the sails and perhaps enjoyed the chanteys they sang while doing so, even if some of these were a bit ribald in nature.

However, the position of captain's wife could also be a lonely and boring one, often fraught with worry over their husband's strenuous duty and, in times of peril, for the safety of all aboard. Indeed, when things were going well during a voyage and the captain's mood was good, so too, most likely, was his wife happy. On the other hand, when the passage was a difficult one, whether it be stormy seas or long periods of light winds, when the captain's mood sank, so too might his wife's. Perhaps the best record of the thoughts and feelings of a clipper ship captain's wife are to be found in the previously mentioned journals of Hannah Rebecca Burgess (born 1834) of Sandwich, Massachusetts. Her husband, Captain William Burgess, commanded the clippers *Whirlwind* and *Challenger* and, as has been previously mentioned, died aboard the latter ship. After their marriage in 1852, Rebecca (as she was usually called) first stayed at home while her husband went off on his first post-marriage voyage. Beginning in February 1854, however, she accompanied her husband on all his subsequent voyages for nearly three years until his untimely death. During her first voyage from New York to San Francisco, the novelty of accompanying her husband soon wore off and by late May 1854 she was "quite tired of it. I do wish we could be so favored as to have good winds and arrive in San Francisco all of a sudden.... The Sundays seem rather long now as William has nothing to occupy his mind and talks more of the long passage we are making. O I shall be glad when we get to California, and hear some other tune from this long one, 'Every ship is going to beat us'...after a good cry I always feel better and pursue the same even tenor again" (Shockley, p. 57).

It may seem strange to think about today, but family life aboard the clipper ships was not an uncommon occurrence, and many captain-husbands and their wives did their utmost to create a loving home away from home by bringing children into their restricted environment. Many children, in fact, were born while at sea, with captains playing the part as midwife during the birthing process, while at other times a nurse was brought along for this purpose. Charlotte Noyes Babcock (born 1826), the wife of Captain David Babcock, first went to sea with her husband aboard *Sword Fish*, and later, for six years on the *Young America*, turned that ship's cabins into the family home and is known at one time to have had a nurse aboard to help her out. Four of the Babcock's nine children were born aboard the clipper, including Lulu (born 1853 at Hawaii, died six months later in Connecticut), Edith (born April 1855 at Shanghai, China, died while the ship was in the Indian Ocean in October 1855), David (born 1856 while the ship was at Hong Kong), and Washington (born 1858 while the ship was bound from Singapore to New York via the Cape of Good Hope). And Charlotte Babcock was not the only wife to give birth at sea; Captain Charles Brown's wife gave birth while he was in command of the clipper *Black Prince,* while Mary Wakeman, the young wife of Captain Edgar Wakeman, commander of the *Adelaide*, gave birth to two children while accompanying her husband at sea, including their firstborn daughter, fittingly named Adelaide Seaborn Wakeman. However, the fate of this infant daughter of the Wakemans, as with several children of the Babcocks and many other seagoing couples, is a sad reminder that life at sea was not always easy; Adelaide was born when the clipper was just fifteen days out from San Francisco in April 1856, and died at that port in September, her body subsequently carried aboard the clipper, possibly for burial at home.

The cabins and staterooms where a clipper's passengers or captain's family spent their time indoors, either during heavy weather, times of illness, times of leisure or at night were often quite luxurious. Those of the Portsmouth-built *Witch of the Wave* were "finished in gothic panels of birdseye maple with frames of satin wood, relieved with zebra, mahogany and rosewood and surmounted with curiously carved capitals. The upholstery was rich velvet and speaking tubes connected the several cabins. There was a fine library of 100 volumes" (Howe & Matthews, p. 727). The McKay-built *Lightning* was even more sumptuously appointed, having "4 stern windows, and a large oblong square light in the after cabin, and similar skylights over the dining salon...the skylights are set in mahogany frames, and nearly all the windows are of stained glass...a more beautiful cabin or one more richly furnished we have never seen" (Howe & Matthews, p. 358). Even the little clipper *Whirlwind* aboard which Rebecca Burgess voyaged was finely finished, she noting during her first visit to her husband's new command in 1852 that the dining room "was beautifully ornamented with gilded work, which gave the room a very neat appearance...the floors of both Cabins, and all the State rooms are carpeted with nice velvet tapestry, to be taken up after getting to sea, there being cotton carpeting underneath. On the whole the Ship looked beautiful" (Shockley, p. 59). In fact, nearly all of the clippers had these fine appointments, their inside appearance just as important to their owners as that of their outward appearance. Finally, one might also wonder about the bathroom facilities, so to speak, aboard a clipper ship. In fact, all clippers were equipped with water closets, one located forward for the use of the crew, and one located at the aft end, usually along the side of the ship. In addition, though clipper plans are not always specific, it is thought that some facilities may have been located in the cabin areas themselves. Also located in the cabins for the captain and his family, as well as passengers, were separate washrooms. Showering facilities were rare on a clipper, or any sailing ship for that matter, so everyone had to make do as best as they could, often using rain water. Rebecca Burgess records her efforts at showering while her husband's clipper was in the tropical area around the equator, recounting that she "put on a loose frock and William dashed pails of water at me. Oh it gave me a tremendous shock and I gave vent to my feelings by screaming at the top of my voice. But it made me feel much better, and I think it is a very good plan to take a shower bath often in warm climates" (Hassell, p. 22). One can only wonder what the clipper's crew thought about these noisy proceedings! However, one clipper known to have had shower-bath facilities in the ladies cabin was the Portsmouth-built *Nightingale* (Crothers, p. 447). This is not a surprising feature when it is recalled that this lavishly built clipper was originally built to carry passengers to England for the World's Fair in 1851.

While these fancy cabins and staterooms were reserved for the captain and his family and paying passengers, there was one general exception to this rule. This occurred during those times when an extremely ill or injured sailor or passenger needed tending to, which job frequently fell to the captain's wife, especially when the captain had to tend to duties on deck. In fact, unless a clipper happened to have a doctor aboard as a passenger, no medical personnel were carried on most merchant ships and it was the captain's responsibility to medicate extremely ill sailors, set broken bones, and like procedures. One extreme example of a captain's wife attending to the sick occurred aboard the Maine-built clipper *Red Gauntlet* in the winter of 1855 and 1856 while the ship was bound from New York to San Francisco. Sarah Andrews (born 1828), the wife of Captain Thomas Andrews, "was unceasing in her efforts to increase the comforts of the crew by making hot tea, attending to the sick" when the ship had difficulty rounding Cape Horn, with her men suffering "terribly from cold and exposure" during the disastrous voyage (Howe & Matthews, p. 509). There are likely many more such instances of such medical duties being performed by captain's wives, even if these incidents have gone unrecorded.

Of course, many captain's wives took great interest in their husband's work and were often desirous of learning all that they could so that they could help out when possible. This was not only in keeping with that Victorian ideal of serving one's husband, but also reflected the keen intelligence of these women and their desire for education in all its varied forms. Rebecca Burgess, who stated early on that "I like to know about anything that concerns a ship" (Shockley, p. 75), assisted her husband by learning to keep the ship's log, which formally (and tersely) noted the daily course and position of the ship, weather conditions, and any notable incidents. To do this, she had to learn the difference between civilian time (measured from midnight to midnight) and nautical time (measured from noon to noon), which took some getting used to. At the same time, Burgess was also learning to use the ship's chronometer, a navigational device that was standard on all clippers and helped determine the ship's longitude and latitude. Her skills in figuring a ship's position would later be of use during what was undoubtedly the most stressful period in her young life. In December 1856 the clipper *Challenger*, with Captain William Burgess in command and his wife, Hannah Rebecca, with him, was bound from the Chinchas Islands, off the coast of Peru, for Valparaiso, Chile. The ship had a load of guano and was bound for Le Havre, France. However, Captain Burgess had been ill for most of the voyage and was not doing well. He subsequently died on 19 December 1856 while the ship was at sea some 250 miles from its destination, leaving *Challenger*'s command and overall navigation duties to his first mate, Henry Winsor. The first mate would not only guide the ship to Chile, arriving two days later, but also continued in command of the ship on all her subsequent voyages until she was sold to Peruvian interests in 1863.

This, seemingly, was the end of the story regarding the *Challenger*. Or was it? Once on Chilean soil, Rebecca Burgess oversaw the funeral arrangements for her husband at Valparaiso, and was thereafter accompanied home by the black steward David Graves on a voyage by steamship. She subsequently lived the remainder of her days in Sandwich, Massachusetts, as a captain's widow, an active and highly respected member of her church and community. However, by the 1880s she began to tell an enhanced version of the story of her final voyage on *Challenger*, first to children during her visits to local schools, explaining that the mate had problems with navigating the ship after her husband's death and that "the difference between Mr. Winsor's inefficiency, and my correct work, lay, in the foundations laid, in early life, & and have always enjoined on them [school children] to master their lessons" (Shockley, p. 167). In 1916, the year before her death, Rebecca Burgess wrote an explanatory letter giving the history of the *Challenger*'s log book, which she was donating to the Sandwich Historical Society. In this incredible document she greatly expands on the events surrounding the death of her husband, as well as her final voyage on the clipper from the Chincha Islands to Chile. She boldly states that her husband shipped Winsor as first mate, even knowing his navigational deficiencies, and that, despite the captain's urging, he refused to practice his navigation skills. When the clipper departed for Chile with her sick captain, she also states that all the captains of the ships then at the islands begged her husband to go to Callao, Peru, a short distance away to get a replacement captain and seek medical help, but this he refused to do. The day after the death of Captain Burgess, December 12, 1856, she further recounts that the ship's steward, David Graves, and mate Winsor worked the navigational fixes, but were having difficulties in making their calculations, Winsor apparently telling the ship's steward, "I wish you could tell Mrs. Burgess, 'I don't know where we are, and if she cares whether we all go to the bottom or not, I wish she would come and look over my work, and tell me what the trouble is.'...I did so, and found a mistake in figuring the result...I often say to myself, what would have happened, had I not had many month's experience, and felt capable of navigating the ship? Had confidence in my ability failed, where would the ship have gone" (Shockley, pg. 204–05). In this letter, Burgess goes on to say that mate Winsor, embarrassed by his lack of navigation skills, relinquished command of the ship at Valparaiso, but later in life became a worthy captain. As a result of this letter, latter-day historians, beginning with Henry Kittredge in 1935 in his work *The Shipmasters of Cape Cod*, in which he calls Burgess "mistress of the situation" in regards to the ship's navigation, have picked up the story of Hannah Rebecca Burgess and elevated her status to that of a heroine. Whether or not Burgess truly saved her husband's ship is open to question and historian Megan Taylor Shockley's close examination of her story and its evolution over the years leads us to the likely conclusion that the *Challenger* was probably not in danger and thus the idea that Mrs. Burgess saved the ship, something she hints at but never outright states, is in the end a great exaggeration. However, let us give the widow her due, for after all might there not be a grain of truth in her story? It may very well be that Winsor, in making his calculations, asked the captain's wife to check them out, and maybe she did even find a simple error that was quickly corrected. This may be the one grain of truth we are seeking, and in the end Hannah Rebecca Burgess is noteworthy just for the fact that she *was* one of those captain's wives who strove to learn the ways of the sea during the clipper ship era and bravely bore the trials and tribulations that came along with such a challenge.

While Hannah Rebecca Burgess may have slightly exaggerated her role as navigator aboard *Challenger* in her later years, there is another woman who, also in her later years, made some rather wild (and undocumented) claims about being in command of the *Gray Feather*. The story about a young Englishwoman, Mrs. Caroline Worrell Dubois of Sheepshead Bay, New York, that appeared in a Brooklyn newspaper over 125 years ago is a fascinating one. The ship on which she supposedly sailed in 1868 at the age of eighteen, the *Gray Feather*, was commanded by her uncle, Captain John Harford, and was said to be bound for the North Pole (presumably from a U.S. West Coast port) when he became ill; Ms. Worrell subsequently took command because "she knew if the mate took charge he would take the ship south, and to the captain, while in that condition, she knew it meant death. She then...kept the ship on its course. The second mate refused to obey her orders. Drawing a revolver from a belt around her waist she fired at a rope and shot it in two. She then told the mate that if he did not obey orders she would try her next experiment on him" (*Brooklyn Daily Eagle*, 1 April 1887, p. 1). She continued the ship's course toward the North Pole and here took on a cargo of ice, lumber, and fish from the Eskimos there in return for whiskey that was doled out to them three times a day, and then continued onward to Australia. Here it was that the crew mutinied and her hands were sliced up with a knife by the ship's black steward during the affair. Soon thereafter, Captain Harford recovered from his illness and apparently was the one to guide the ship to England. Mrs. Dubois would later visit America and while in Brooklyn she met and married her future husband. So what are we to make of this story? Well, there was a ship called the *Gray Feather*, a Maine clipper built in 1850, but she was sold to German owners in 1862 and renamed *Ida*. That clipper *did* make one voyage from San Francisco to Alaska for a cargo of ice, but this happened in 1859 and 1860 while she was still sailing under the American flag and commanded by Captain Daniel McLaughlin. One must also question why the captain would have been better served medically by heading toward some distant and frozen destination, rather than heading back to port, as the ship's mate apparently wanted to do. In the end, none of the details recounted by Mrs. Dubois have been substantiated, and her story does not seem to have received any contemporary notice. Since the later career of the *Ida* is unknown, it is possible, though again unlikely, that Dubois sailed aboard this vessel on an Arctic voyage late in that ship's career, but until further evidence comes to light, Mrs. Dubois's story must be viewed with a great deal of skepticism. Would that it was otherwise as this story, if true, would be quite an epic one!

Of all the women that sailed aboard the clippers, it is likely that none were as skilled as Eleanor Creesy, the wife of the *Flying Cloud*'s commander, Captain Josiah Creesy, when it came to the art of navigation. In fact, few today know of her quiet talents on their own account, but this is not giving Eleanor Creesy her just dues, for without her help it is possible that the *Flying Cloud* might not have made her two historic California runs. This remarkable woman, like her famed husband, was born in Marblehead, Massachusetts, in September 1814, the daughter of John and Eleanor Prentiss. It is said of her that her father, a master mariner, trained her in the arts of navigation and that she could plot a course as well as any ship's captain. Eleanor Prentiss married the up and coming Captain Josiah Creesy in 1841 and would subsequently be his life-long sailing companion, from his days commanding the China trader *Oneida* to his history making voyages on the *Flying Cloud*. However, Eleanor Creesy was not just a captain's wife, but she was also an officer in all but name only. The most important duty entrusted to her was that of ship's navigator, but she also helped in getting her husband's ship provisioned during the preparations for a long voyage, and made sure to obtain the most current nautical charts and sailing directions. As one historian states, "She found the art of fixing one's position every day exceedingly engaging and immensely satisfying, and she often missed it after too long a stay ashore" (Shaw, p. 7). Eleanor Creesy was no mere dabbler in the navigation arts; she was serious about her experience in this area and always sought to increase her knowledge, no doubt taking some sense of pride and accomplishment in an area usually dominated by men. Indeed, while her husband was a competent navigator in his own right, Josiah Creesy trusted his wife's advice and instincts in this area. Prior to the departure of the *Flying Cloud* on its maiden voyage in 1851, Eleanor Creesy read the newly published work of Matthew Fontaine Maury, soon to be known as "The Pathfinder of the Sea," which offered sailing directions for ship captains based on his exhaustive studies of the logs kept by naval and merchant ships. This monumental and groundbreaking work was not always accepted or trusted by old sea captains, who preferred to use their own knowledge and background, including Captain Creesy, but Eleanor Creesy was a believer and encouraged her husband to follow these directions (Shaw, p. 52). Whether the *Flying Cloud* would have made her record shattering 89 day, 21 hour maiden voyage to California without following Maury's directions, on Eleanor Creesy's forward thinking advice, may always be open to speculation, but the results speak for themselves. Eleanor Creesy was no lucky navigator, for she repeated her performance in 1854, shaving thirteen hours off the *Cloud*'s sailing time to make what many call the all-time record. With the *Flying Cloud* laid up due to poor business conditions in 1857, it is unknown if Eleanor Creesy ever went to sea again; she probably went to sea with her husband aboard the *Archer* after his Civil War service was ended, but by the mid–1860s the Creesys were retired from their seafaring days and lived together on a farm near Salem, Massachusetts, and later in a home in town. After her husband died in 1871, she survived alone (the couple had no children) until her death in 1900.

Despite the above notable women mentioned who sailed during the clipper ship era, however, there is one young woman who stands above them all when it came to the extreme circumstances she was able to withstand, and subsequently overcame, with a great deal of fortitude and courage. This woman is Mary Ann (Brown) Patten, the wife of Captain Joshua Patten. They were married at the State House in Boston on April 1, 1853, he a twenty-six-year-old up and coming shipmaster from Maine, and she the sixteen-year-old daughter of George and Elizabeth Brown, English immigrants who now lived in Boston. Mary Patten, later described as "a slender New England girl...a lady of medium height, with black hair, large, dark, lustrous eyes, and very pleasing features" (Northrop, p. 7), seems to have accompanied her husband at sea from the beginning of their marriage and, like Eleanor Creesy, became a valuable resource to her captain-husband. She may have had her first taste of sea life in early 1854, when her husband commanded the Maine-built *Flying Scud* on a roundtrip voyage between New York and England. In late 1854, Captain Patten took command of the big clipper *Neptune's Car* and drove her on her second California run, making San Francisco in 101 days; during this voyage Mary Patten perfected her navigational skills and tended to men injured when lightning hit the ship. Her husband said at the end of the voyage that

"Mrs. Patten is uncommonly handy about the ship, even in weather, and would doubtless be of service if a man" (Whipple, *The Challenge*, p. 110). The captain's last comment notwithstanding, which was typical for the day, he also proudly stated that his wife could gain a master's certificate if she had wanted to do so. During the clipper's subsequent voyage to China and home to New York via London, the captain's wife continued to study the ways of a ship and navigation. Master's certificate or not, the command of *Neptune's Car* would indeed fall to Mary Ann Patten on the clipper's next California run under extremely trying circumstances.

On July 1, 1856, *Neptune's Car* departed New York for San Francisco, racing two other famed clippers, the *Intrepid* and *Romance of the Seas*, to their destination. Interestingly, Mary Patten discovered during this voyage that she was pregnant; the expectation from her husband, if he even knew this fact, would probably have been that she should take things a bit easy and not overly exert herself. However, it was not to be and the situation aboard the *Car* quickly went from bad to worse. Within weeks, when it was discovered that the first mate was a poor one, insubordinate to Captain Patten and a bully mate toward the crew, he was taken off duty and confined to his cabin. Meanwhile, second mate Hare, while an excellent seaman, was a poor navigator. Thus it was that Mary Ann Patten helped with navigation duties while her husband did the work of both captain and first mate. However, soon after, Captain Patten came down with tuberculosis, what was then called a brain fever, and was incapacitated in his duties. Despite her pregnant condition, the captain's nineteen-year-old wife took command of the clipper, with Hare agreeing to serve as first mate. The first mate, confined to his cabin, warned her of the difficulty in getting round Cape Horn and offered to take command, but Mrs. Patten refused. Instead, she gathered the crew together and told them of the plight of her husband and asked for their help in getting to California. The crew responded with three cheers for their new female captain, and went about their work with great diligence. It took the big clipper some fifty days to round Cape Horn in one of the worst winters ever. Mary Ann Patten was charged with fixing the ship's position, but seldom had a clear sky to do so and had to rely on dead reckoning. Not only was Mary Patten tested mentally, dedicated to the task of caring for her often-delirious husband while commanding the clipper, but she also suffered physically. She never changed her clothes during the entire fifty days of stormy weather and slept but seldom, catching a few hours sleep here and there when time allowed. In between times, when Hare was running the clipper, Mary was busy reading the ship's medical guide to see what could be done for her husband. By the time the *Car* rounded the horn and was driving up the Pacific, Captain Patten was showing some signs of recovery. Noticing how worn out his wife was, he decided to give the imprisoned first mate another chance to do his job. However, within a few days, Mary Patten, in plotting the ship's course, discovered that the first mate was guiding the ship not toward California, but toward Valparaiso, Chile. She reported this to her husband, who eventually had the first mate confined again and trusted to his wife and second mate Hare to set the ship's course. Not long afterward, Captain Patten became blind and sank back into unconsciousness for most of the rest of the voyage. As for Mary Patten, she guided the ship to San Francisco under light weather conditions for the last two weeks, making port on November 15, 1856, and thus ending the clipper's 136 day voyage. Despite the dire circumstances of the voyage, and undoubtedly the furthest thing from Mary Patten's mind, the *Neptune's Car* even beat the big New York clipper *Invincible* by over a week.

Upon making San Francisco, the story of Mary Ann Patten and *Neptune's Car* quickly became a media sensation, she soon being called by the press the "Florence Nightingale of the Ocean" and her story was recounted in newspaper stories from coast to coast. However, Mary Patten cared but little for all this publicity. She tended to her husband and nursed him all the way back to Boston, taking one steamer to the Isthmus of Panama, making the overland journey to the Atlantic side, then taking another steamer back to New York. Once again, Captain Patten rallied for awhile during the voyage home, but eventually relapsed and had to be carried ashore when New York was reached. Joshua Patten was soon taken back to Boston, accompanied by his loving wife. His son, Joshua, Jr., was born on March 10, 1857, but his father would never know him. Captain Joshua Patten subsequently died at the McLean Asylum in Somerville, Massachusetts, on July 25, 1857.

Mary Ann Patten's actions were not just applauded by the press, but also by the clipper's insurance company and even a women's suffrage group in Boston. The latter group she rejected altogether; though the exact reasons for this are unclear, it seems likely that Mary Patten already had too much going on in her own life, being forced as she was to deal her husband's sickness and subsequent death, while at the same time caring for her newborn son. One also gets the sense that Mary Patten was a private person who had no interest in being held up as an example. Indeed, when the clipper's insurer, the New York Insurance Company, awarded her $1000 for saving the ship's $100,000 cargo (many thought she should have been awarded considerably more), she kindly replied that she was "grateful...for the kind expressions of sympathy...I have endeavored to perform that which seemed to me, under the circumstances, only the plain duty of a wife towards a good husband...I am seriously embarrassed by the fear that you may have overestimated the value of those services, because I feel that without the services of Mr. Hare...and of the hearty cooperation of the crew to aid our endeavors, the ship would not have arrived safely at her destined port" (Northrop, pg. 8).

The plight of Mary Patten and her gravely ill husband also caught the attention of East Coast newspapers, with one New York paper calling for some group to step forward with financial aid:

> The heroine whom we were so slow to recognize when she was in the midst of us is winning honors now from all the world.... The simple story of her bravery and her affection, of her true womanhood and her glorious wifehood, however, had gone before her, and it is echoing back to us now from the lips of eloquent orators at home, and from far foreign shores...a generous Briton has been moved by the tale to the production of an occasional poem...another has been impelled by it to the humbler but not less expressive homage of a handsome contribution in aid of the heroine, who, after all, can neither be fed with praises nor lodged in poems.... The Bostonians propose that the women of America shall at least be offered the opportunity of honoring their sex, in the person of this young wife. The proposition is most just.... Who will begin the good work? [*New York Times*, 27 July 1857].

The Bostonians indeed did respond, raising money to the tune of some $1,400 for Mary Patten, though it is, perhaps, an interesting commentary on the times that the public focus on Mary's deeds were evenly divided between her role in guiding the clipper to its destination and her wifely devotion to her husband.

Sadly, the story of the rest of Mary Patten's life has no happy ending as, while caring for her husband, she herself contracted tuberculosis. She and her young son would subsequently live with her widowed mother, Elizabeth Brown, in Boston, but she died on March 17, 1861, at the young age of twenty-four. As for her son, Joshua Patten, he too lived a tragic life. He grew up in Boston and lived with the Brown family, including his mother's brothers Edward and William and by the age of twenty-two was working as a carriage painter. Not long after 1880, he moved to Rockland, Maine, the town where his father was from, and worked as a common laborer, barely making a living. He was a resident of the town's poor house when he died an accidental death by drowning in September 1900 at the young age of forty-one.

Clearly, Captain Patten's wife was a humble young lady who had no desire for the limelight, and sought to downplay her role on the *Neptune's Car*. Despite this, the diminutive Mary Ann Patten looms large in the lore of the clipper ships, as she was, if even for a short time, the only woman ever to command one of these legendary vessels.

Finally, while we have talked about such women as Eleanor Creesy and Mary Ann Patten and their unofficial roles as crewmembers, some clippers actually did carry female crewmembers, signed officially on the ship's sailing list like any other sailor, who served as stewardesses. Like their male

Emigrants embarking at Liverpool. The immigrant passenger trade was a profitable one for many sailing ships, clippers included, during the 1850s and 1860s (from *The Illustrated London News*).

counterparts in this position, their job was to tend to the captain and his quarters, as well as those of the passengers. Unfortunately, little research has been done in this area, so the frequency in which women were shipped in this role is unknown. They were almost certainly more common aboard those clippers serving in the North Atlantic packet and immigration trade, where the number of paying passengers was greater in number, but some were also aboard the clippers that made voyages on the California and China routes. One interesting, and tragic, example of a clipper stewardess can be found in the person of Ann K. Flaherty, a native of St. John, New Brunswick. She signed on with the Portsmouth-built clipper *Cathedral*, commanded by Captain William Howard, and served for the ship's first North Atlantic runs sailing between Boston and Liverpool beginning in 1855. She continued aboard *Cathedral*, still serving Captain Howard, when she made what would be the clipper's final voyage from the East Coast to California in 1856 and 1857. By the time the ship was off Cape Horn in February 1857, the situation was already difficult; Captain Howard had been ill for a week and was unable to leave his berth, tended to by stewardess Flaherty. On 17 February a huge wave hit the ship during heavy weather, throwing the ship on its beam ends. First mate Andrew Clarke consulted with his captain and did all he could do to right the ship, including cutting away her masts, but it was a hopeless situation. Water was pouring into the ship and Clarke, knowing "the Vessel would go down in a very short time" (Brighton, p. 147), readied the lifeboats and tried to persuade Captain Howard to abandon ship. However, the captain refused, believing that the wild seas would destroy the lifeboats; as the ship began to rapidly settle with water, Clarke tried to persuade his sick captain to leave one more time, but once again Howard refused, telling Clarke to save himself. Clarke also tried to save Ann Flaherty, but she refused to leave her captain alone, as did a passenger doing duty as ship's doctor. Within minutes of abandoning ship, Clarke and the thirty-five other survivors witnessed *Cathedral* go down after being hit by another large wave. Gone were the captain, his stewardess, the passenger-doctor, and seven other men. As for the stewardess, one historian aptly states that "For sheer unequivocal guts Ann Flaherty rates heroic laurels" (Brighton, p. 149).

Clipper Ship Passengers

The final category of individuals that sailed aboard the clipper ships on their California and worldwide passages were paying passengers. There were two classes of passengers that sailed aboard these ships; the first, and greatest number, were those immigrant passengers sailing from ports in England and northern Europe to East Coast U.S. ports, primarily New York and Boston, on the transatlantic packet runs, those on the clippers sailing on the England–Australia run, and those Chinese immigrants sailing from Hong Kong and other ports in the Far East to San Francisco. These ships carried passengers in large numbers, up to 1,000 at one time and, except for those well-to-do passengers that could afford cabin accommodations, theirs was a group ordeal, experienced in below-deck accommodations that were crowded in nature. While the voyages to America, whether on the westward run in the North Atlantic or to San Francisco seldom lasted more than 60 days and were usually of much shorter duration, the stormy weather and resulting seasickness and other illnesses that broke out in these cramped conditions could be disastrous, sometimes resulting in many deaths. The steerage accommodations for immigrants sailing on the passenger clippers were not distinguishable from the immigrant ships of the 1840s and consisted of open bunks in the tween decks areas with no partitions for privacy. Bedding was not supplied, but rather consisted of what the immigrants brought with them. Bathing facilities were non-existent (as for the crew and most everyone else) and toilet facilities were crude, consisting simply of buckets placed below decks that had to be emptied overboard daily. Immigrant passengers were allowed on deck in good weather in limited numbers for a breath of fresh air, though they had to keep clear of sailors working the ship. Food and water was supplied to the immigrants and was of varying quality. Some ships were recognized as having a good reputation for passenger treatment, while others were noticeably lacking. As mentioned previously, fresh meat in the form of livestock was often a staple on immigrant ships, confined to a pen on the weather deck, with salted provisions also provided, while rice in bulk quantities was the norm for clippers carrying passengers from Asia. However, the longer a passage was prolonged, due to storm weather or damage to the ship, the greater a chance that provisions could run low. Like most immigrant voyages, passengers spent their waking hours tending to their children and tidying their space with the few personal belongings they carried with them, as well what leisure time they might spare playing games, and talking among themselves, surely anxious to start their new life in America or Australia. Because most immigrants were of a common heritage on a given voyage, coming from Ireland, Germany, or China, there were often family and local ties that offered familiarity and comfort to an otherwise drastic change in living. Shipwrecks of immigrant clippers were rare in contrast to the great number of passages made but were not unknown and there were several clippers wrecked, with attendant heavy loss of life, while carrying such passengers, including that of *Staffordshire* (1853) and *Driver* (1855).

The second category of passengers carried by the clippers were generally those that could afford private cabin accommodations costing anywhere from $100 to $300 per passage, much like flying first class on today's airlines. These passengers were usually small in number on a given voyage, ranging anywhere from one or two individuals up to as many as fifty. Usually they were men or women of standing, including shipping line owners and merchants, but also those seeking adventure and a new life in a new land, as well as those traveling to be reunited with their loved ones. A mother traveling with her child alone was not uncommon, perhaps to be with her husband who had already journeyed to California, and sometimes even the builder of the ship made a voyage; in early 1855 Donald McKay traveled on his namesake creation, the clipper *Donald McKay* on her maiden voyage from Boston to Liverpool, his ship designed with twelve large staterooms in the after cabin and 24 staterooms below "designed for gentleman passengers. All the cabins were profusely decorated according to the taste of the day" (Howe & Matthews, p. 135). On smaller clippers built before the gold rush, cabin accommodations, while certainly comfortable, were not lavish like the clippers of the 1850s as just described.

No matter who these paying passengers may have been, all dined at the captain's table and ate the best fare the ship had to offer and were tended to by the ship's steward. Interaction with the crew by tradition, if not outright order, was heavily discouraged, as passengers were restricted to the quarterdeck and away from the weather deck and forward areas where the sailors worked and lived. Passengers, including some missionaries, might spend their waking hours reading (some clippers carried large libraries for their cabin passengers) or conversing with other passengers and, when time on deck allowed, taking in the ocean view and noting their surroundings. Indeed, at this time individuals of wealth that were in poor health were often sent on sea voyages as the tropical climate was thought to be beneficial to their condition. One such passenger was Samuel Ferguson, son of a wealthy merchant from Stamford, Connecticut, who, after being diagnosed with tuberculosis, was told by his doctor that "Only an ocean voyage can save you" (Jackson, p. 3). He subsequently took passage on the clipper *Hornet*, along with his brother Henry, in early 1866 on her voyage from New York to San Francisco. When that clipper's cargo caught fire and the passengers and crew were forced to abandon ship, thousands of miles away from land in the open ocean, Samuel would subsequently die in a lifeboat, while his brother Henry survived to become an Episcopal minister. However, most passengers making a voyage for health reasons had better outcomes than this. In time of duress aboard the ship male passengers were often a great help; when the crew of the *Sovereign of the Seas* mutinied against Captain Warner and his officers during a voyage from Liverpool to Melbourne in early 1854, armed passengers (whether from steerage or cabin quarters is not stated) helped bring matters under control. Female passengers, too, could be of great help, usually in providing comfort and care to sick fellow passengers or injured and ill crewman. Among themselves, clipper passengers quickly formed a mini-society that was all their own during a passage that might last three or four months or more during a California run or passage to China or India. Male passengers of learning might, in due course to occupy their time, give lectures on a topic of interest, while passengers of both sexes might offer a reading from a popular literary work of the day, tell stories, or, if so talented, provide a musical performance. Missionary passengers often engaged themselves, and fellow passengers, in Bible study and readings. No matter what their standing, there were often complaints about the dullness or poor quality of the ship's fare over the course of a long voyage, and there were always periods of sheer boredom.

It is perhaps understandable that developing romances between passengers of the opposite sex were not uncommon on these long voyages, where close confinement with one another day in and day out was the norm, and sometimes these romances led to marriage vows. When the *Flying Cloud* made her maiden voyage out to San Francisco in 89 days in 1851, among her passengers were two sisters, Ellen and Sarah Lyon; the former was already betrothed and scheduled to be married in California after her arrival, while Sarah was her traveling companion. However, Sarah and fellow passenger Laban Coffin, a young gentleman from Nantucket, developed their own romance during the short voyage. As a result, both sisters were married aboard the *Flying Cloud* within weeks after making California on August 31, 1851, with the captain's wife, Eleanor Creesy, making the wedding cake for Sarah's small wedding. When the *Cloud* subsequently departed San Francisco for China, Laban Coffin had signed on as first mate and his wife, Sarah, accompanied him on their voyage around the world (Shaw, pg. 255). While this was certainly not the only clipper love story to result in marriage, it is hard to imagine a more romantic one.

Finally, just as with travel in any age, there were times when passengers could become unruly or otherwise make the captain's life miserable but these seem to have been few and far between, and sometimes were quite justified; when the small Baltimore clipper *Architect* departed New

Orleans in 1849 for San Francisco with 56 passengers aboard, troubles arose when a cholera outbreak resulted in several passenger deaths. Surely unhappy with the situation, it is said that "dissensions arose" and that Captain Adams Gray was forced to put in at Rio de Janeiro for assistance (Howe & Matthews, p. 20). While this may have been an extreme case, one part of any passenger ship commander's job was to soothe the minds of worried passengers during times of distress, although, to be sure, some captains handled these social duties better than others.

VI

Wild Rover
Clipper Ship Voyages and Trade

Having taken a look at how a clipper was built and manned, it is now time to take a close look at the business side of clipper ship operations. It is true that clipper ships today are best remembered for their speedy passages and graceful form, but we should not forget that these ships played a heavy role in the manufacturing and service sectors of the American economy during the 1850s and beyond, and the details behind their contributions in this regard are also of interest. The manufacturing or shipbuilding aspect we have already discussed, but what about the service side? Just what trade were they involved in and what kinds of cargos were these ships carrying all over the globe?

Most clipper owners employed their ships in carrying two categories of goods, general freight (a catch-all term) and bulk commodities, making their profits off the freight rates that they charged those brokers or merchants who had a need to get their goods from one destination to another in quick time. Some clipper owners employed their ships primarily on their own account for the goods that they themselves exported or imported. One such firm that operated in this manner was that of A.A. Low & Brothers of New York, who were heavily invested in the China trade. In yet other cases, clipper ship owners hired their vessels out on a charter basis for longer periods of use to other entities, including foreign governments and foreign based shipping lines, though they sometimes retained their American captains. The Crimean War (1853–1856), a conflict pitting the Russian empire against the French and British, was an important period when American clippers, including *Titan, Monarch of the Seas, Nonpareil, Ocean Herald, Gauntlet, Great Republic, Queen of Clippers, Rattler, White Falcon,* and *Golden Gate* (most of them sizeable ships), were chartered on a monthly basis by the French government to serve as troop transports. The last named of these clipper transports earned her owners $7,500 a month plus a bonus (Howe & Matthews, p. 237). Similarly, the clipper *Game Cock* was chartered by the British government at Hong Kong in 1860 for use during the second Opium War; her owners were paid twenty-two shillings per ton per month to transport horses and cattle for the troops. *Kingfisher* was also hired under charter for such service in 1860 but, interestingly, the clipper *Whirlwind*, offered for charter at Hong Kong during this same war, was rejected. This was perhaps because of her smaller size, registering but 960 tons versus the 1,392-ton *Game Cock* and the 1,296-ton *Kingfisher*. As for foreign shipping lines employing clippers, the most notable were the Black Ball Line and the White Star Line, both running from England to Australia, the former hiring *Sovereign of the Seas* and the later *Titan*. It was often the case, as happened with the *Queen of Clippers, Ocean Herald,* and *Monarch of the Seas* (all sold to French interests in 1856 after their Crimean War service), that once the charter had ended, the clipper was then sold outright to parties in the country that had hired them, surely an indicator of their satisfactory performance.

Of the different types of cargo carried by the clippers, and the trades they in which they were involved, the following is a breakdown of their varied aspects.

General Freight and the California Trade

This type of cargo, whether carried from the East Coast to California, or from abroad to America, consisted of all kinds of manufactured and handmade goods and products imaginable from shoes, pottery and crockery, and furniture to carriages, iron plows, hand tools, and nails, to name just a very few. Some agricultural-based products also fell into this category, mainly those such as milled flour, apples, tobacco, coffee, salted beef or pork, distilled liquor, or butter, again to name just a few, that were unlikely to comprise a majority of the cargo carried. To get an idea of the varied clipper cargos to California, especially early on, one need only look at the newspapers of the day; the advertisements in the *Daily Alta California* in the years 1851 to 1852 offer a partial list of items for several clippers;

Sea Nymph (Baltimore): 20 qtr. and 15 half pipes of Rochelle brandy, 20⅛ pipes of Leveque brandy, eight pipes Holland gin, Monongahela whisky, cherry brandy, 1000 dozen (bottles?) Byass ale and porter, advertised for sale on May 26, 1851. The ale and porter came from Robert Byass, a well known bottler in London, not to be confused with one of his competitors, the Bass Brewery. As to the quantities of these liquors, a pipe, typically used in the spirits business, measured on average about 108 gallons.

Sea Serpent: "Orange County" (New York) butter, "dress coats and pantaloons," and "a large and splendid assortment of a superior quality" of stationery, including onion skin paper, parchment envelopes, steel pens, sealing wax, and like items consigned to Cooke & LeCount and advertised for sale on May 26, 1851.

Stag Hound and *Sea Serpent*: "New York city cured hams," tobacco, "best brands" and " smoking and fine cut," raisins "fresh" from Malaga, harness and shoe leather, "Highlander playing cards," agricultural implements, including horse rakes and cultivators, all advertised for sale by Earl & Co. on May 26, 1851.

Clipper cargo advertisements. These ads show merchandise that arrived aboard the New England clippers *Sea Serpent* (top) and *Stag Hound* (bottom) in May 1851. The *Serpent*'s cargo, which included gold pens and silver pen holders, is illustrative of the fact that many items of luxury were carried to California, not just supplies for gold mine workers! (*Daily Alta California*, May 1851).

Witchcraft: Spanish chocolate, flannel shirts, "fancy dry goods," French cognac, "Genuine Westphalia hams," "Russian and hemp cordage, all sizes"; *Alert*: 20 barrels American brandy; *N.B. Palmer*: 50 boxes champagne, 10,000 "choice Regalia cigars," "a large assortment of drugs and medicines," including refined borax, 500 lbs. Tartaric acid, "Cooper's isinglass," "jujube paste," "Roussel's hair dye," prescription vials, and "oil bitter almond"; *Flying Cloud*: 500 kegs white lead, 100 cases imperial black paint, "lamp black in bulk," 100 cans turpentine, 130 dozen Brandy peaches, 100 dozen tomato and pepper sauces, 68 boxes candles. All these items were advertised by various merchants on September 5, 1851, just five days after the *Cloud* made the then fastest passage ever to California; as might be expected, the advertisements for goods from this clipper had the largest headlines, though none mentioned her fast passage.

Raven: 25 kegs sausage skins; *Eagle*, 300 cases "nailed" boots, 300 dozen colored shirts; *Syren*: 500 pounds harness leather, 200 kegs nails; *Sea Witch*: Havana cigars, 100 barrels "Dance brand" flour; *Telegraph*: boots, Jean Louis brandy, "Cassimere" pantaloons, "a few hundred pairs," and butter. All the commodities from these ships, not the only items they carried, were all advertised by various merchants on November 24, 1851.

Comet: "a large lot of lead pipe, leather hose with brass couplings, faucets, patent water closets "with all the fixtures complete," brass force pumps and common lifting pumps, all offered for sale by G. & W. Snooks, as well as 500 boxes "New Crop" Malaga raisins, 40 cases Myers Aromatic tobacco, "Extra Gallego flour in sealed barrels," ten pins and balls (bowling equipment), and 108 tons Lackawanna coal advertised by a number of other merchants, all on January 22, 1852.

It is interesting to note that the fact that a San Francisco merchant's goods were shipped by a clipper played an important part in the advertising and selling of these items, no matter what they may have been. While sailing ships and steamers of all sizes and types are also mentioned in local newspaper advertisements regarding recently arrived goods for sale, it was only the names of the glamorous clippers that were usually featured in the headlines of these ads during the early 1850s. Such bold headings as "Stationery, per Sea Serpent," "Ex Witchcraft & N.B. Palmer," "Received per Comet," "Received By The Flying Cloud," and many others were clearly an attempt by the merchant to link his goods, and the sale thereof, to the heralded ships that brought them.

Once a clipper was built and in operation, the fleet owner's biggest concern was the prevailing freight rates for general cargo, which fluctuated constantly based on a combination of factors, including the type of cargo to be carried, local and national market conditions, the availability of shipping at any one time, as well as a ship's anticipated sailing date. For those ships carrying cargos from the East Coast to California general freight was usually charged on a per cubic foot basis, with 40 cubic feet equaling about a ton of cargo. According to one economic historian, these cubic foot rates for clippers ranged anywhere from $1.00 to $2.00 per foot of cargo in 1850 and 1851, and thereafter went down to $0.50 to $0.80 per foot in 1852 and 1853, about $0.50 in 1854, $0.40 in 1855, and ranging from $0.27 to $0.35 in the years 1856 to 1860 (Evans, Jr., p. 39). Regular, non-clipper ships commanded freight rates that were anywhere from 20 percent to 50 percent less. These freight rates not only fluctuated based on demand, but also on the sailing times of a ship; it often took some time for a ship to fill up with cargo from many different sources until she was full enough to sail; it was not until late in the clipper ship era, when freights were difficult to come by, that a ship might often sail without being fully loaded. Those merchants who committed their cargos first, with the result that these goods not only stayed on the ship longer, but would also be the last to be unloaded (the first in, last out concept) once the clipper reached its final destination were usually charged at a lower rate. On the other hand, freight that was the last to load, perhaps mere days before a ship sailed and, once its destination was reached, would be the first unloaded and ready to hit their intended market were charged a higher rate. In addition, there seems to have been some commodities that were charged standard rates based on bulk or individual containers rather than weight; the New York–built and owned *Hornet* in 1860 charged $2.40 for a barrel of beef or pork, $3.25 for a barrel of whiskey, $0.50 for a keg of nails, and $0.20 for a box of candles (Evans, Jr., p. 33).

The California trade was important to all American ships, sail and steam, and especially the clipper ships, for two simple reasons: trade restrictions that dictated that goods shipped from one American port to another in what was considered the coastwise trade must be carried by American ships, and the simple concept of supply and demand. The trade restriction stated above, still in force to this day, meant that goods shipped from New York or Boston to San Francisco during the gold rush (or any other time, for that matter) had to be carried by American ships. Thus it was that the clippers had no foreign competition and virtually ruled the California market for several years until American steamships entered the trade in increasing numbers. And all this happened despite the fact that the California coastwise run was one of the longest of the then prevailing trade routes in the world, one that was thousands of miles in length, involving the dangerous passing of Cape Horn, far from American shores, and took anywhere from three to six months or more. Some coastal voyage! Were this coastal trade restriction have *not* been in place, one may question whether the clipper ship would have been developed at all or, if they were, what more economical hull form might have developed.

Of course, in the years from 1849 to 1850 demand was so high for goods of all kinds in California, and the number of goods manufactured there nearly non-existent, that no matter what cargos were shipped, they were usually profitable ones. Indeed, in the year 1848, only four ships had arrived in San Francisco from the East Coast, while during the first year of the gold rush, nearly 800 ships made their arrival. It is interesting to consider, however, that no matter what cargos were shipped, sometimes it was just a matter of luck as to which would prove profitable. It is difficult for us today, when the time for goods to reach their final retail destination from a manufacturer is measured in days or sometimes mere hours, to realize that the quickest goods might reach California from the East Coast was 90 days, though the average shipping time for clippers overall was probably closer to 130 days. Thus it was that, like a gambler playing a hunch, some cargos were golden and in high demand, while others never panned out, the market glutted by previous cargo arrivals whose timing was more fortunate. One historian tells the tale of two vastly different items that were once in high demand but soon fell out of favor in California: fabric tacks and cast-iron stoves. The former had been in high demand, used to hang the fabric partitions used in many of San Francisco's crudely constructed buildings in the first year of the gold rush, but by the time one New York shipment arrived a year later, the market was glutted and the tacks worthless; these were dumped overboard into San Francisco Bay, not being worth the warehouse charges that would be incurred storing them ashore. Similarly, a shipment of stoves that arrived was found to be useless, a previous shipment having filled the demand. The stoves were subsequently dumped like the unwanted junk they had become, with their iron lids used as stepping stones on the muddy, unpaved streets of San Francisco (Whipple, *The Challenge*, pgs. 219–20). However, after the initial excitement of the gold rush was over, freight that would prove profitable for sale in California was a much more risk filled situation. Too, competition from steamship companies also grew rapidly and in California, as elsewhere in the world, the steam-powered iron ships soon began to hasten the end of the wooden sailing ship era. For those clipper ship owners shipping goods on their own account, they would soon enough divert their ships to more profitable trades, but those owners that made their profits off the freight rates alone had to scramble to get a paying rate.

Foreign Trades

While serving as general freight carriers, most clippers, especially once the California run became more competitive and less profitable, were employed at one time or another in specific overseas markets or trades, with many clipper owners and merchants maintaining overseas trading or mercantile houses (called hongs in Asia) in such exotic Far Eastern locales as Canton, Shanghai, Hong Kong, and Foo Chow, not to mention those mercantile houses at London, Liverpool, Le Havre, and other locations in Europe, and at Calcutta and Bombay in India, where a great deal of business was conducted, cargos were bought and sold, and charters arranged. Interestingly, the early clipper *Houqua*, built at New York for A.A. Lowe in 1844 was named for Wu Bingjian (1769–1843), known to American and British merchants as Howqua, the most prominent and wealthiest Hong merchant of the day in Canton, China.

These foreign trades, along with a brief description of each, can be broken down as follows.

China

The China trade was one of the most lucrative for the clippers during the late 1840s and 1850s and consisted of two types of goods. The first of these was what may be termed general freight items, with no one item taking up a clipper's entire cargo hold, but rather a combination of all or some of them being carried at any one time. Chinese exports to America via the clippers included silk and nankeen fabric, some furs and animal hides, Chinese pottery, including the very popular blue and white porcelains for which that country was renowned, gall nuts (from which writing ink was made), ginger and cassia (Chinese cinnamon), both of which were used as both spices and medical remedies, incense sticks, decorative fans, rattan (used in the making of furniture and baskets), soy, and firecrackers (sometimes referred to as crackers). This last item was perhaps more widely used in Fourth of July celebrations in the 1850s in America then they are today; the *Intrepid* loaded a $660,000 cargo, including tea, silk, and a large amount of firecrackers, at Hong Kong for New York in early 1860, her consigners hoping to generate a big and fast profit by making port before the Fourth of July, but it was not to be. The Webb-built clipper went ashore early in the voyage in the Gaspar Straits and was subsequently plundered and her crew attacked by Malaysian pirates until being rescued by the French clipper *Gallileo*. Sadly, many ships in the China trade, both clipper and non-clipper alike, were the subjects of piratical attacks that emanated from the many inlets and small islands in the region, seeming to appear out of nowhere when a ship was in distress and at its most vulnerable.

Another item that factored in the China trade in this category was opium. This drug was often brought to China illegally (its importation banned altogether by that government) by British and American ships from India, though the trade was made legal at various times, its trade forced by Britain after defeating China in the First Opium War in 1843, and again in 1858 after the end of the Second Opium War. This drug was subsequently either clandestinely distributed in China or from here exported to America and other nations. While smaller clipper schooners and brigs, both American and foreign built, were predominant in the opium trade, American clipper ships were also involved in small numbers early on, including the pioneer clipper *Sea Witch*, and continued the trade into the 1860s, with the Cape Cod–built and -owned *Wild Hunter* bringing in 50 cases of the drug to San Francisco in 1860.

A second item, and one that was the most important, carried by many American clippers during the first half of the 1850s, was tea, which was loaded for both American and English ports. Americans consumed a great deal of tea, and in England they drank even more, it being their national beverage of choice. This tea was sent from the interior regions of China where it was grown and harvested every year to such port cities as Hong Kong, Canton (also called Whampoa), Foo Chow (modern day Fuzhou), and Shanghai beginning in April, from whence it was transported around the world. This tea was packed in wooden chests of varying size and was loaded into waiting ships by specially trained Chinese stevedores who packed the chests in a ship's hold in alternating rows, using a mallet to bang them into place. This loading proceeded at a quick pace, after which a clipper quickly made her departure for England or America. The size of these tea cargos depended both on how large a clipper might be, as well as what other cargo she already had aboard, but they could be sizeable; the Portsmouth-built *Witch of the Wave* loaded 19,000 chests of tea at Canton destined for England in January 1852 and subsequently made the trip in 90 days (Lubbock, p. 121). Indeed, a clipper ship was ideal for the tea trade, for this commodity was time sensitive because of both the freshness aspect of the product (the longer a tea cargo was at sea, the less fresh it became and at greater risk of spoilage), as well as the fact that the first teas to hit the market every year usually commanded the highest prices, and it therefore was the desire of all merchants to get their tea cargos to market as quick as possible. The clippers transporting tea to America in 1851 were the appropriately named, New York–built ships *Celestial* and *Mandarin,* followed by *Sea Witch, Houqua, Staghound, Sea Serpent, Panama, Gazelle,* and *Shooting Star,* all bound to New York, except the last named ship, which went to Boston. In 1852, even more clippers entered the tea trade, with some twenty-two of them making tea passages, with the big *Flying Cloud* making two such voyages within the year. While most American tea clippers were usually rated below 1,400 tons, a few of the bigger clippers also took cargos, including the 1,836-ton *Comet* and the 1,535-ton *Staghound.* In 1853, clippers in the American tea trade were reduced drastically, with only six such ships carrying the fragrant cargo; all were below 1,000 tons except for the 1,607-ton extreme clipper *Hurricane.* One unlucky tea clipper was the 985-ton *Sting Ray,* built in 1854 at Long Island by William Webb's brother Eckford Webb; this ship sailed from Hong Kong in late 1855 with a cargo valued at over $200,000, including 275,522 pounds of black tea and 18,000 pounds of green tea (an amount equivalent to over four million modern teabags), only to be wrecked at Fire Island during a storm in January 1856 just hours from making port. While the American trade in China tea would continue, for a few years, from 1850 to 1855, some American clippers also took part in the annual tea races to England. Because of the fact that English navigation laws and protective trade practices were abolished in 1849, the free trade that resulted thereby opened the English tea trade to American ships. The first American clipper to enter the tea trade and bring a cargo of tea to England was the aptly named 1,003-ton *Oriental* (built 1849) of the Low fleet of New York, which arrived at Hong Kong from New York on her second voyage in August 1850. Having made such a fast passage out, the clipper was subsequently coveted by the top British tea companies to carry their cargo homeward. The *Oriental,* commanded by Captain Theodore Palmer (Captain Nathaniel Palmer's brother), subsequently loaded 1,618 tons of tea for Russell & Company at an unprecedented rate that was double that received by British ships, thereby earning her owners $48,000 (more than half of the ship's original construction cost). The *Oriental* did not disappoint her British consignees, making the voyage to England in 97 days from Hong Kong, thereby "causing great excitement in English shipping circles, and all kinds of gloomy notices appeared in the papers, predicting the extinction of the British Mercantile Marine" (Lubbock, p. 108). The American clipper was such a novelty, in fact, since no ship like her had ever been seen before, that her lines and measurements were copied while she lay in the dry dock at Blackwall. The *Oriental* would not be the only American clipper to figure in the British tea trade; as mentioned previously, *Witch of the Wave* made quite the name for herself in 1852, as did the notorious New York clipper *Challenge,* which beat the British clipper *Challenger* (admittedly three times smaller than the American ship) on her tea trip from Shanghai to London, as well as the American clippers *Surprise* and *Nightingale* and the clipper bark *Race Horse.* Just as with *Oriental,* interest in the *Challenge* was intense and

VI. Wild Rover: *Clipper Ship Voyages and Trade*

The clipper *Lightning* off Otago Heads, New Zealand. This woodcut illustration shows the clipper taking her pilot from the pilot boat at right. The trade with Australia and New Zealand hit its stride in 1852 and 1853 after the discovery of gold in Australia in 1852. The *Lightning* was one of four ships built by Donald McKay at East Boston for Englishman James Baines' Black Ball Line of Australian packets (*Otago Witness* [New Zealand], February 20, 1864).

her lines, too, were taken off while the clipper was in drydock. The big clipper was subsequently hired to make another round-trip tea voyage, but her homeward bound passage was a disastrous one as she was forced to put into the Azore Islands leaking heavily and here discharged her damaged cargo. Subsequent American clippers notable in the China tea trade include the small Baltimore-built *Architect*, which in 1853 made London from Whampoa in 107 days and netted the ship a significantly higher freight rate on her next tea passage; the *Celestial* in 1854, which was beaten by one day on the passage by the British clipper *Chrysolite*; and *Nightingale* in 1855, making the run from Shanghai to London in 91 days.

While both aspects of the China trade would not fully end until decades later, by 1860 it was already in decline; demand for nankeen, for example, was replaced by American cotton fabric, while blue and white porcelain was soon being duplicated by American ceramic manufacturers. As for the tea trade, after 1855 fewer and fewer American ships were gaining cargos for England due to the rise of the British tea clippers, while in America tea consumption and demand began a long decline, due to its replacement with coffee as the national beverage of choice. Despite this decline, the Westervelt-built clipper *Golden State* brought a tea cargo to New York in 1867 that was sold for a million dollars, the largest such consignment on record (Howe & Matthews, p. 244). One other big hurdle that always existed in the China trade was the fact that American exports to the country in terms of actual goods was very low; our greatest commodity at that time was specie, either in gold or silver. Then as it is today, this was an unfavorable trade balance that could not last.

Australia–New Zealand

Clipper activities involving the land down under and its neighbor would probably have been similar to those of other lesser ports of call during the 1850s, with occasional stops made by ships carrying passengers, general freight, or bulk cargos such as lumber for this British colony, but this all changed in 1851 with the discovery of gold at Bendigo Creek and Ballarat, both in the state of Victoria. Like the California gold rush, there was suddenly a mad rush to get to Australia, with emigration rising from about 100,000 people a year to some 340,000 annually between the peak years of 1851 to 1854, most arriving at the port of Melbourne (Clark, p. 260). Prior to the gold discovery few American ships called here, so the fastest route to Australia was a bit uncertain for many masters, though British vessels, beginning with the convict ships in the late 1780s, had been making their way to the continent for over fifty years. Soon, the route to Australia would be filled with many ships, including some early British clippers, the famed Canadian-built clipper *Marco Polo*, as well as many American flyers. Outward bound cargos from Liverpool or London usually included general freight similar to that carried on the California run but also a large number of emigrants of varying status, including those headed for the gold fields, as well as British Crown officials and army personnel and merchant traders. Later on, by the late 1850s and early 1860s, once the gold rush had died down, lumber was a frequent cargo, coming from as far off as Puget Sound on the West Coast of America and Canada from the east (as well as the Baltic region in northern Europe) to provide valuable building material for the rapidly growing colony. As far as cargoes carried out of Australia for the journey homeward to the United Kingdom (which often included a stop at India), this at first primarily consisted of passengers making their return voyage, but also large amounts of gold dust and specie; the American clipper *Red Jacket* arrived in England in 1854 with a cargo consisting of 45,000 ounces of gold. Once again, after the gold rush was over, local goods would take over and the export of copper ore and other minerals, and, most importantly, wool from the massive sheep farming operations in Australia and New Zealand would be the mainstays, the latter product largely carried by the British wool clippers beginning in the 1860s. However, even in the sheep trade a number of American clippers were involved; *Sweepstakes* carried a cargo of live sheep from Melbourne to Rockhampton, East Australia in 1861, *Simoon* carried 1,000 "prime Leicester sheep, losing less than five percent on the voyage" (Howe & Matthews, p. 578) from Glasgow, Scotland, to Port Chalmers, New Zealand, in record time in early 1862, *Winged Arrow* carried sheep and emigrants from Glasgow to Otago, New Zealand, in 1861, while *Young America* also carried live sheep from Glasgow to Oamaru, New Zealand, in 1861 and 1862. Likewise, the clipper *Nor'Wester* was employed carrying cargo between Otago and Melbourne for a year in the early 1860s. The one aspect of the Australian trade that differed from the California trade, though also spurred on by an initial gold rush, was the fact that in the beginning sailing ships had a monopoly on the business. With Australia being far off the normal trade routes, coaling stations for steamers were few and far between and it would thus be some time before they began to be regularly employed. As for American clippers in the Australian trade, there were many, among them some of the largest and most renowned; the Maine-built *Red Jacket*, *Blue Jacket*, and the McKay-built *Chariot of Fame* were all chartered by the British White Star Line to make Australian passages, with the first two of these ships later being purchased by the line. However, the most important American-built clippers involved in the Australian trade were constructed by Donald McKay for the Black Ball Line of Liverpool–Australia packets, owned by James Baines. Baines commissioned four such ships for his line, each one bigger than the next, they being the 2083-ton *Lightning*, 2,447-ton *Champion of the Seas* and the 2,515-ton *James Baines*, all launched in 1854, and the 2,598-ton *Donald McKay*, launched in 1855.

Far East Asian Ports of Call

The port of Manila in the Philippines was a common stopping point on the voyage from San Francisco to China, with the most common cargos loaded being Manila hemp (often used to make the rope that became the rigging on the clippers and other American vessels), and sugar cane. Lesser commodities traded for here include spices and coconuts, of which there was an abundant supply. Among the many clippers that took part in the Manila trade were the Boston-owned ships

Winged Arrow, making three voyages from there in the years 1854 to 1856, and *Winged Racer*, which traded there in 1853 and 1854. The country of Siam (modern day Thailand) was also a destination for many clippers, rice being the primary cargo. Among the clippers employed in carrying cargos of rice were the Baltimore-built *Sea Nymph*, which was employed in the China-Siam trade for several years after her sale in the mid–1850s, *Reynard,* in 1857, from Bangkok to Shanghai, the *Wizard* in late 1860, *Storm King*, which carried two successive cargos from Bangkok to Hong Kong in 1861 and 1862 on her last voyages under the American flag, and *Panama*, also making her last American voyage, from Bangkok to Brazil in 1867. In the trade with Siam, as well as in Cambodia and Vietnam, Chinese and British merchants were heavily invested. The island of Formosa (modern day Taiwan) was also a source of rice and sugar, as well camphor oil, a pleasant smelling by-product of a specific type of Asian evergreen tree, used in medicinal preparations and food flavoring for many years. Likewise, Indonesia was also the source of cargos for rice, sugar, spices, and camphor. As in Siam and China, most of this Far East trade was controlled by British, Spanish, Dutch, and French colonial interests. Finally, the island nation of Japan would not be open to foreign trade until the clipper ship era was well under way, but nonetheless these fast ships made their appearance in Japanese ports. In late 1858, Robert Bennett Forbes' Boston clipper *Florence* was the first American ship to appear at Nagasaki. The clipper subsequently loaded a cargo of vegetable wax for England prior to her departure the day after Christmas.

American clipper ship making port. This woodcut shows a clipper entering an unknown foreign port, indicative of the worldwide voyages these ships made. Wherever these ships went, they attracted a great deal of attention for their beautiful form, "astonishing the natives of Japan" and exciting "as much attention in the waters of the Mersey as they do in the ports of Australia" (***Ballou's Pictorial Drawing Room Companion***, October 6, 1855).

India Trade

The trade with the Indian subcontinent, as well as other locales in the Indian Ocean was, like that with China, one that was multifaceted. Primary exports from India included such items as hand-crafted goods, silk, fine cotton, and indigo. Another raw material that saw an upswing in trade activity during the 1850s and beyond was jute. The fibers of this plant were used not only to make fabric (second only to cotton in terms of its versatility), but also rope and twine in British mills, and later was imported to California in large quantities to be turned into grain sacks for the wheat trade. As mentioned in connection with the China trade, opium was also produced in large quantities in India, and subsequently traded in China for tea, a valued commodity in this British colony. Like the China trade, clipper ships too numerous to mention made regular appearances at such ports as Bombay and Calcutta to buy and sell goods. Another important export to India by the late 1850s was that of iron rails, usually from England. This type of cargo came at a time when British companies were involved in railroad construction on a massive scale in India and American clippers, their fortunes declining and high-paying California freights now nothing but a distant memory, were open to any and all opportunities for a cargo. Many clippers, including *Panther, Bonita*, and the *Star of Hope*, were involved in this cumbersome trade. The shipping of rail iron was not an easy task; cargos often shifted in heavy weather with dire results; *Bonita* put into Algoa Bay, South Africa, in a sinking condition in 1857 while bound from London to Calcutta, while the *Star of Hope* was abandoned in a sinking condition off the Cape of Good Hope while transporting such materials from Liverpool in 1861. On the other hand, the newly-built *Panther* made three successful voyages from London to India with railroad iron from 1854 to 1856.

North Atlantic–Europe

This well-established trade between America and the Old World was a mainstay of the American mercantile trade, dating back to the colonial times, and emanated primarily from the port of New York, with Boston, Philadelphia, Baltimore and other East Coast ports running a collective distant second. The voyages to Europe across the stormy North Atlantic consisted of three different types of trade, those being the packet lines, whose ships had regularly scheduled sailings, the immigrant trade, and the bulk and general freight trade. The best known of the regular sailing packet lines ran from New York to Liverpool or London in England, with lesser lines running from New York to Le Havre, France, while Boston's only contribution in this area was Enoch Train's White Diamond Line to Liverpool. These shipping concerns, lines like the Black Ball, the Black X, and the Dramatic Line out of New York, ran on established schedules and carried a wide variety of cargos, including mail, general freight, and bulk cargos, as well as passengers and immigrants. Few clippers were actually involved in this trade, mainly because these lines were already heavily invested in their own sailing ships, many of which were built by the same builders that put over clippers in the 1850s, including Jacob Westervelt, Brown & Bell, and William Webb in New York, George Raynes in Portsmouth, and Donald McKay at both Newburyport and Boston. They simply had no urgent need for these fast and expensive vessels but, more importantly, the coming of the steamship in the North Atlantic trade by the 1840s soon made it apparent that the days of the sailing packets were numbered. Indeed, of all the major New York packet lines, only one, the Red Star Line to Liverpool, employed an out and out clipper, and even then only for several years. The Maine-built clipper *Phoenix* made two voyages for the Red Star Line after her launching in 1854 but was subsequently diverted to the California run and the Far East trade before again taking her place in the Red Star Line in 1857 and 1858. In the Whitlock Line of packets running from New York to Le Havre, the clipper *Rattler* was employed from 1854 to 1855, and again from 1856 to 1858, her owner, William Whitlock, Jr., also using her on the California run and elsewhere when opportunities were presented. The other clippers briefly involved in the packet trade include those built by Donald McKay in Boston for Enoch Train, which were the *Staffordshire* (1851), and the sister ships *Chariot of Fame* and *Star of Empire* (both 1853). These ships did sail in the White Diamond Line to Liverpool, the latter two only briefly before being diverted to the more lucrative California and Australian trades. The *Staffordshire* was lost in tragic circumstances off Cape Sable, Nova Scotia, when she hit Blond Rock in December 1853 while nearing the end of her voyage from Liverpool. The ship subsequently sank with the loss of 170 passengers and crew, including her injured commander, Captain Josiah Richardson, who refused rescue and went down with his ship, his last words being, "If I am to be lost, God's will be done" (Howe & Matthews, p. 614). The last of the Train ships that could be called a clipper was the Portsmouth-built *Cathedral* (1855), which sailed between Boston and Liverpool for about a year before being diverted to the Pacific, making one voyage out to Callao, Peru (presumably for a cargo of guano), and subsequently being wrecked while attempting her second passage around Cape Horn in 1857. The loss of these two ships, combined with the loss of several other vessels beginning in 1848, has led one historian to comment that the White Diamond Line "did a flourishing immigrant business for a while in splendid ships built by Donald McKay but met with several appalling disasters and finally disintegrated" (Albion, p. 47). One final vessel that may be mentioned is the 1851-built *Mercury*, put over by Westervelt & Mackey at New York for the Le Havre packet trade; little is known about her career, but she sailed in Boyd & Hincken's Second Line for sixteen years and is said to have been a medium clipper in model.

A second aspect of the North Atlantic trade to Europe, as alluded to above in reference to the Trains of Boston, was the transport of immigrants from Europe to America. Packet-type ships,

The deck of an immigrant ship. The crowded conditions of the immigrant trade between England and New York are here dramatically illustrated in this view that shows a vessel departing from the Waterloo Dock at Liverpool. While deaths on the westward passage were not uncommon, most immigrants would arrive safely to start a new life in America (*The Illustrated London News*).

including clippers, were involved in this booming business but with one main difference when compared to the established packet trade: the true packet ships sailed on regular timetables, while the immigrant packet ships sailed on a more irregular basis, usually basing their sailing times not on a set schedule but more generally when the ship was fully loaded. Like those ships sailing in the packet lines, the immigrant clippers were large and stoutly-built ships, sometimes constructed as triple-deckers so as to allow accommodations for the many steerage passengers they would carry. While historians debate whether some of these ships, such as the Bath-built *Emerald Isle* and the Newburyport-built *Driver,* were true clippers because of their less clipper-like hull forms, they are often categorized as such due to their lofty and heavily sparred sail plans. The outward bound, eastern passage to England, usually Liverpool, could be made in good time if a ship was of good form and well handled by her captain as the winds and the Gulf Stream current worked in their favor, as demonstrated by the twelve day passage of the *Mary Whitridge* from Baltimore in 1855. However, for the immigrants it was all about the westward passage to America, which cost the average man, woman, or child anywhere from $20 to $30 apiece for the cheapest accommodations. For wealthy travelers or immigrants who could afford cabin accommodations, the price was about five times that paid by steerage passengers. The voyage to America could be made in good time if the weather gods cooperated — the clipper *Andrew Jackson* made it in fifteen days in 1860 — but it was often the case that terrific headwinds and stormy seas prevailed and even some passages by normally fast ships could last thirty days or more in difficult circumstances. Seasickness was a privation suffered by many an immigrant, and deaths among immigrants were not uncommon on those ships carrying large numbers of passengers. Sanitary conditions were usually inadequate even in the best of times, and were made worse when passengers were confined below decks for extended periods, sometimes weeks on end, due to harsh weather. One of the best known of the immigrant lines that utilized clipper ships was the Red Cross Line of New York. This concern owned at least six ships, most built at Newburyport, including the clippers *Racer, Highflyer, Dreadnought,* and *Driver.* These Red Cross ships, all of which were ill-fated except the famed *Dreadnought,* carried thousands of Irish immigrants to New York from Liverpool during the first half of the 1850s. Other clippers employed as immigrant ships, often carrying anywhere from 300 to nearly 1,000 passengers on any given voyage to America at the height of their operations, include the William Webb–built *Invincible,* which "was designed for the Liverpool passenger business" (Howe & Matthews, p. 286), but it was not until 1860 that she was actually put to the use for which she was originally intended, having been diverted first to the California trade and subsequently to the Australian trade for the White Star Line of Britain; other ships were *Adelaide, Monarch of the Seas, Isaac Jeanes,* the aptly-named *Emerald Isle,* and the Mystic-built *Electric* (after her sale to German interests). These last four ships are interesting in that they were employed at several times during their careers in carrying Mormon immigrant saints from England and the Scandinavian countries to America. The *Monarch* was the largest carrier of Mormon immigrants to America, transporting nearly 2,000 such religious-minded passengers total in two voyages made in 1861 and 1864, while the *Emerald Isle* was also prominent, transporting 350 such passengers on an 1855 voyage and another 876 Mormons in 1868 (Sonne, pgs. 65–67, 81–83). The 1868 passage of the *Emerald Isle,* one of the last Mormon immigration voyages made under sail, was a rather disastrous one, with nearly forty deaths occurring due to unsanitary water, compounded by a captain and crew who treated the immigrants poorly. However, despite this late voyage the immigrant trade, like the clippers themselves, was a short-lived one for all sailing ships as by the 1850s steamships were largely taking over the trade.

The final portion of the North Atlantic trade was that involving general freight and, to a lesser extent, bulk cargos. All ships involved in the North Atlantic trade were involved in this activity, with immigrant ships and packet ships usually employed carrying large cargos destined for England or other European ports, while those clippers in the general trade carried European products such as coal, iron, and Russian hemp back to America and, like the California trade, a vast amount of both manufactured goods and agricultural products to Europe, including flour, tobacco, flaxseed, lumber, animal furs and hides, and many other items too numerous to list. However, the largest commodity carried overseas by far was cotton, which was picked and baled by enslaved African Americans on the plantations of the South and subsequently shipped either on the coastal run from such southern ports as New Orleans, Mobile, and Charleston to New York, or loaded directly for England, usually from New Orleans to England, in both cases bound across the Atlantic for the hungry textile mills of England and beyond. Indeed, just as textile manufacturers in the northern states were complicit by their business activities in helping to maintain the institution of slavery in the South for decades before the Civil War, so too were clipper and other ship owners of New York and New England also guilty of the same thing, making huge profits by shipping cotton overseas. Among the many clippers active in the cotton trade were the following: *National Eagle* in 1853; *Wild Rover,* whose cotton cargo caught fire in 1855 after lightning hit the ship; *Trade Wind,* which carried a load of nearly 4,700 bales of cotton from Mobile in 1854; *Titan,* which carried "the largest cargo of cotton ever carried in any ship previously, 6900 bales" (Howe & Matthews, p. 665) in 1857; *Reporter,* designed specifically for the cotton trade and said to be the first clipper to sail up the Mississippi River, doing so in 1853; the *Governor Morton,* also struck by lightning and burned on the Mississippi River while loading for England in July 1877; and the Portsmouth-built ships *Ocean Rover,* in 1854 and 1856, and *Express,* which carried a load of New England ice to New Orleans in 1854 on her maiden voyage, exchanging that cargo for a load of cotton (Brighton, p. 96). As far as return cargos from Europe go, these too were many in number; coal from the ports of Cardiff and Swansea in Wales, as well as that from England, was common, as was Russian hemp that was used in the manufacture of rope, and railroad iron. Two of the clippers that brought iron cargos from England to New York were *Starlight* in the early 1860s from Bristol and *Wild Hunter* from London in 1864. Of course, many of the large clippers made multi-legged trips that might, say, include a cargo of cotton destined for England from New York, subsequently loading perhaps railroad iron bound for India or Welsh coal bound for the rapidly expanding numbers of coaling stations for steamships that served the British navy and merchant service in the Mediterranean and on the Indian Ocean and Far East trade routes. After arrival and discharge in these ports, then the typical exports from these locales were often carried either directly back to America, or back to England, from whence additional freight or immigrants and passengers were then often carried to New York. Finally, in regard to the smaller clipper barks and other fast vessels, these vessels not only carried this same wide variety of general freight items, but were also quite active in the time sensitive Mediterranean fruit trade (and had been so for years), bringing back to America popular exotic fruits such as dates, figs, oranges and the like. Just as with the California trade, the first ships to make port with this produce every season in Boston, New York, and many other ports made large profits by capturing the initial market and setting the price.

South and Central America and Mexico

Clipper ship cargos from this area were important but more limited in number. From the Atlantic side, few clippers put into such ports as Montevideo, Rio de Janeiro, or Buenos Aires unless their ships were in distress and in need of repair. However, several commodities were traded for on the Atlantic side, mainly carried by smaller ships or clipper barks, but sometimes by larger clippers. These products include animal hides from Argentina, as well as fruit, coffee and exotic log and dye woods from Brazil to Mexico. The *National Eagle* was involved in the hardwood lumber trade in Central America during her later career in the 1870s The coffee industry in particular grew in importance during the 1850s and eventually replaced tea as America's premier non-alcoholic beverage. Like tea, coffee was a sensitive product that needed to get to market in quick time to command the greatest prices and be at its freshest. Thus it was that fast ships were employed in the coffee trade. It was in this trade that Donald McKay's first ship, the small but fast *Courier* (perhaps a proto-clipper) was employed with great success, while later on the Pennsylvania-built clipper *Grey Eagle* (the former S.S. *Bishop*) was employed as a Rio trader, making some fast passages between there and Baltimore beginning after her sale in 1856 and continuing into the 1880s.

The Pacific side of the Americas was well noted for its ports of call, primarily Valparaiso, Chile, Iquique (part of Peru, later ceded to Chile in the 1870s), and Callao, Peru, but also as far north as Mexico off the tip of the Baja peninsula. In this last mentioned country, the clipper *Eclipse* took in a cargo of Brazil wood at Ypala, near San Blas and Manzanilla, in October 1853, only to be driven ashore and wrecked by a hurricane, while the same fate here awaited the *Water Witch*, wrecked in June 1855 while loading dye woods. Other ships loading wood cargos in Mexico include *Rattler* in 1858, loading dye woods at Ypala for New York; *Ringleader* in 1861, loading dye woods at Ypala for England; *Southern Cross* in 1863 loaded a full cargo of logwood at Buena Vista in 1863; and *Fleetwing* a cargo of dye wood bound for Liverpool from Mazatlan and Altata in 1870 and 1871.

Much further to the south, Valparaiso, Chile, was traditionally a port of call for ships in distress after rounding Cape Horn, and thus not only had a great repair business for clippers and other vessels on the California run, but was also where the American consul was based. However, Chile was also known for its mineral resources and its exports in this area expanded greatly during the 1850s, with its development in great part spurred on by American business interests. One of the most common of Chilean mineral exports was copper ore, which was usually shipped to Europe or eastern U.S. ports; the Webb-built extreme clipper *Flying Dutchman* carried a load of copper ore from Copiapo in northern Chile to Baltimore in 1856. The area around Copiapo, still an important mining region today, was one terminal point for the first South American railroad ever constructed, built by the Pacific Steam Navigation Company, an American firm.

As for Callao, Peru, this city, close to Lima, was known the world over as the administrative port for the Chincha Islands guano trade. The three small, barren islands that comprise the Chinchas are located off the southwest coast of Peru and were known for their great deposits of sea-bird droppings that had built up for years on their granite surface. These droppings had high levels of nitrogen and phosphorus and were valuable for use both as a fertilizer and in the manufacture of gunpowder. Since the early 1800s, the guano trade, controlled by the Peruvian government, was a flourishing one and at one time, before the depletion of the deposits in the 1870s, comprised nearly two-thirds of Peru's income. During the 1850s, the carrying of this dry and powdery cargo was conducted by a great many vessels of foreign nationalities, including numerous American clipper ships of all sizes, from the 3.356-ton *Great Republic* to the 716-ton *Aramingo*, not to mention numerous other clipper barks and smaller craft. A load of guano was often loaded as a return cargo, destined either to the American East Coast or such European ports as London or Le Havre, France, after a voyage from New York or Boston to California. At other times, the Chinchas were a destination point for a clipper on one of its multiple legs of a foreign voyage, such as occurred when Captain William Burgess guided his clipper *Whirlwind* from England to pick up a load of guano at the Chinchas consigned to parties in France, having previously sailed from New York to San Francisco, and from thence to China and subsequently England. Guano, both from Peruvian deposits and, eventually, elsewhere in the Pacific would be a mainstay bulk cargo for clipper ships for many years to come and was an important source of revenue for their owners. More details about the guano trade will be discussed below.

Bulk Cargos

In conjunction with the various branches of global trade listed above, most clippers at one time or another in their career were involved in the transshipment of a single cargo, usually one that was either agricultural in nature or energy based. Most of these bulk cargos, with the exception of the guano and related coolie trade, did not become commonplace until the late 1850s, when clipper ship fortunes were in steep decline, or in the 1860s and beyond when the clipper ship era had already ended. Indeed, the involvement of the clipper ships in this kind of trade was in complete contrast to the California trade that spurred their creation, heralding the days when sailing ships in general were relegated to the unglamorous, yet economically important, role of a bulk cargo carrier as the age of sailing ships was coming to an end. With steamships rapidly taking control of the packet, passenger, and general freight trade on the coastal routes and the European trade, clipper owners had to seek whatever paying cargo opportunities that might arise, and many clippers at one time or another, especially those that were long-lived, carried one or perhaps all of these bulk cargos at different times throughout the course of their service.

Lumber

This commodity had been a mainstay of the American shipping economy since colonial times, but saw an increase by the late 1850s with the California trade and the subsequent economic development of shipping ports on the West Coast from San Francisco north to Portland, Oregon, and Tacoma and Seattle on Puget Sound in Washington. Here, great quantities of board lumber were produced from the prodigious forests of the Pacific Northwest and subsequently shipped both in the coastal trade to help build the towns and cities that were springing up all up and down the west coast of the Americas from Washington to Chile, as well as overseas to other boom locations such as Australia where a great amount of construction was taking place. Indeed, clipper ships participated in this trade from both ends of the era so to speak, from the beginning when board lumber from East Coast forests and even pre-fabricated house frames could be found on their cargo lists for California in the early days of the gold rush to the later days when they carried lumber all along the West Coast and beyond. While clippers were not specifically built for the lumber trade, many would be altered so as to be able to take in as cargo the long sticks of wood that comprised the bulk lumber trade, involving the cutting of openings or ports in either the stern quarter or along the side of the hull to enable its loading below deck. In some cases, such as happened with the *Elizabeth Kimball* in 1873 while bound from Puget Sound to Iquique, Chile, deck loads of lumber were also carried, which made a ship more unstable and difficult to handle in heavy weather or under other dire circumstances. This deck cargo was often jettisoned to save a struggling ship, as happened to the *Kimball*, albeit to no avail. Many clippers were involved in this trade later in their careers after being sold to West Coast owners, including *War Hawk*, *Grace Darling*, *Gem of the Ocean*, and *Dashing Wave*, this last clipper being one of the longest serving of the lumber clippers, operating from Tacoma for many years from the 1870s until after 1900. Among the clippers that saw activity in this trade early on include the Baltimore-built clippers *Sea Nymph* and *Cherubim*, the Donald McKay–built *Defender*, and the Maine-built *Wild Rover*. The first named ship loaded lumber at Puget Sound for Shanghai in 1859, while that same year *Cherubim* carried lumber from San Francisco to Valparaiso, Chile. The *Defender* was wrecked in the South Pacific in February 1859 while bound from Puget Sound to Sydney, Australia, while *Wild Rover* carried lumber from Puget Sound to Shanghai in 1863. One interesting west coast wood cargo was that carried by the *Messenger* in 1853 and 1854; the ship's only cargo from San Francisco to Philadelphia was "a few specimens of California products, among which was a ten foot long section from a giant redwood

The Quebec lumber trade, ca. 1860. This view shows the busy lumber docks in this Canadian city, which was vital to the North American timber trade. Many clippers, including the famed *Flying Cloud*, were employed in this trade between Canada and England and other European ports beginning in the 1860s, and while they were not designed for this trade, their large and well-built hulls were easily adaptable (*The Illustrated London News*).

tree, 92 feet in circumference at the ground and 66 feet at ten feet above. It had required 150 days labor to cut out the section" (Howe & Matthews, p. 391).

One other aspect of this type of bulk cargo was that of the Quebec and Nova Scotia lumber trade that was conducted on the east coast of North America from Canadian ports to Europe. This trade was conducted by Canadian and British-built ships for many years, but by the 1860s and 1870s a number of aged American clippers were purchased and converted into timber droghers, their days of glory now long gone. Clippers that operated in this trade, which we will discuss further on in detail, include *Flying Cloud*, *Red Jacket*, *Nightingale*, *Fearless*, and *Ocean Telegraph*.

Coal

This cargo was shipped from several locations in the United Kingdom by many clippers in the 1850s and beyond. The major ports were Swansea and Cardiff in Wales and Newcastle-upon-Tyne and the associated port of Shields (located eight miles to the east of Newcastle) in northeastern England. Coal shipments from the rich mines in these areas increased at a rapid rate beginning in the early 1800s with the advent of the Industrial Revolution and increased to an even higher level with the advent of the steamship in the 1840s. Coal was also shipped out of the ports of London and Liverpool, transported there from Newcastle and the other coal producing regions by small coal colliers working in the coastal trade. It is quite ironic that large sailing ships, including many clippers, were crucial in transporting this fossil fuel for the vessels that would ultimately replace them to coaling stations that were strategically located in increasing numbers around the world for the ships of the Royal and American navies as well as merchant steamships. English coal was also extensively exported to America, usually New York or San Francisco. Later on, with the fast-paced economic development of Australia, coal would also be shipped from that country from the vast coalfields of Newcastle, New South Wales, where coal was first mined beginning in the 1830s.

Much of the coal exported from here and carried by American clippers was destined for West Coast locations such as San Francisco. Similarly, with the development of coal fields in western Canada by the 1860s, ports in the province of British Columbia were also major shipping points for Canadian coal destined for San Francisco, carried by clippers in their twilight years. No matter where the coal came from or where it was bound, the cargo could sometimes be a tricky one, not to mention a dirty one. The slippery coals could shift during heavy seas or gale conditions and throw a ship on her beam ends, while spontaneous combustion or accidental fire was always a danger; the Medford-built *Hesperus*, which caught fire and burned at Woosung, China, in 1861 just after her arrival from Liverpool, was one such coal carrier lost due to fire, as was Donald McKay's *Stag Hound* that same year.

Among those clippers working in the coal trade, though by no means a complete list, to bring the black diamonds to America, before the extensive coalfields of Pennsylvania and Virginia were developed, and elsewhere around the globe were the following ships along with some interesting details of their voyages: *Hippogriffe*, from Cardiff for San Francisco in 1856; *Expounder*, on the return leg of her maiden voyage in 1856 and 1857 with a cargo from Cardiff bound for San Francisco; *Queen of the Pacific*, in 1857 from New York to San Juan del Sur, Nicaragua; the Pennsylvania-built *Morning Light*, in 1857 from Philadelphia to Panama on a U.S. government charter; *Gauntlet*, in 1860 from Cardiff to Shanghai, her last American voyage; *Challenger*, from Liverpool to New York in 1861; *Fair Wind*, in 1861 from New York for Acapulco, Mexico, for the Pacific Mail Steamship Company and in 1863, loading at Sunderland, England for Hong Kong; *Flying Dragon*, in 1861 on what would be her final voyage, from Australia to San Francisco with 1,000 tons of coal, subsequently wrecked on Arch Rock just off San Francisco and mere hours before reaching port; *John Stuart*, in 1861 from Cardiff to Callao, Peru; *Joseph Peabody*, in 1861, loaded coal cakes (made from coal oil and tar) for steamer use, Cardiff to Shanghai; *Stag Hound*, in 1861 from Sunderland, England, for San Francisco, subsequently lost off Brazil when her cargo caught fire; *Wizard*, in 1862 from New York bound for Acapulco but forced into Port Stanley, Falkland Islands, due to storm damage and there discharged her cargo; *Nabob*, wrecked in the Philippines in late 1862 while bound from Liverpool to Shanghai; *Minnehaha*, in 1862 New York to San Francisco for the Pacific Mail Steamship Company and in 1864, London to San Francisco; *North Wind*, in 1863 Cardiff to Singapore; *Frigate Bird*, in 1864, Shields, England, to San Francisco under the British flag; *Young Mechanic*, in late 1864 from New York to San Francisco but sprang a leak and was forced to put into St. Thomas, Virgin Islands, where the cargo was unloaded and sold; *Red Gauntlet*, captured by a Confederate raider in 1863 while bound with an assorted cargo including coal from Boston to Hong Kong; *Carrier Dove*, from Shields to New York in 1865 with the largest cargo, consisting of coal and general freight, to ever leave from there up to that time (Howe & Matthews, p. 51); *Elizabeth Kimball* from Australia to San Francisco in 1866; *Shooting Star* (the former New York–built *Ino*), from Alexandria, Virginia, to San Francisco in 1867; *Nor'Wester*, Port Stanley in the Falklands for San Francisco in 1867; *Flying Eagle*, in 1868, Nanaimo, British Columbia, to San Francisco; *Lookout*, 1871 until its loss in 1878, operated in coal and lumber trade, largely between Puget Sound and San Francisco; *Panther*, Nanaimo, British Columbia to San Francisco in 1874; *Orpheus*, in 1875, Puget Sound to San Francisco; *Syren*, in 1883, Seattle to San Francisco, and in 1888, Baltimore to San Francisco with 1,200 tons, but forced into Rio de Janeiro in a leaky condition, the cargo here discharged and the clipper condemned and sold.

Finally, it is also interesting to note that several large clippers were also used as coal storage hulks after their sailing days were over, including the *Donald McKay*, *Flying Childers*, and *Red Jacket*. These hulks were used at various ports around the world as storage facilities, either floating or beached on dry land, for bunker coal used as fuel for steamers or for coal exports awaiting shipment. Another famed clipper, the *David Crockett*, was cut down for use as a coal barge in 1890 after a long and profitable sailing career as was the *Mary Whitridge* sometime before 1886, being subsequently lost off the coast of New Jersey while being towed fully laden with coal in February 1902.

Whale Oil

This source of energy for illumination was also an important cargo, transported by some clippers based largely out of New England. Whale oil, which was America's primary source for lamp oil for decades, was traditionally extracted from the blubber of these great mammals harvested by American whaling ships and stored in barrels in their holds. These bluff-bowed factory ships and their greasy cargos, sometimes viewed with contempt by the clipper fraternity due to their workaday appearance, voyaged far and wide in all oceans of the world, with the Pacific being the main hunting ground. Once a ship was full up with whale oil and whalebone, a process that sometimes took two, three, or even four years or more, they then made their homeward voyage, usually to the great whaling port of New Bedford, Massachusetts, but also other ports from Boston to New York. However, by time of the arrival of the clipper ship, the port of Honolulu, Hawaii, in the Pacific, already a traditional port of call for whalers, was being used as a transshipment point for whale cargos of oil and bone (used to make such diverse items as ladies corsets and buggy whips) bound for New England. Later on, as the Alaskan whale fishery was being developed, ships also carried whale-related cargos from there back to New England, with San Francisco serving as an intermediary port for the voyage out from New England.

Sailing card for the clipper *Syren*. This attractive card is indicative of the most creative of the advertising methods shipping agents used to attract merchant cargos. Key phrases here include the fact that the clipper delivers her cargo "IN PERFECT ORDER" and that she was the "Smallest & Sharpest clipper loading" (author's collection).

Among the clippers employed in this trade were the following, all sailing on the Honolulu to New Bedford run unless otherwise noted: *Sovereign of the Seas*, 1852, Honolulu to New York with 8,000 barrels of oil and some whalebone for which was received $30,000 in freight, the passage being made in then record time; the *Charles Mallory*, wrecked off the coast of Brazil in 1853 while bound from Honolulu to New London with 4,500 barrels of oil, with some 3,000 barrels salvaged from the wreck; *John Land*, about 1857, with a cargo valued at $630,000; *John Gilpin*, 1857; *Anglo Saxon*, 1858 to 1859; *Golden Eagle* and *Skylark*,

1859; *Elizabeth F. Willets*, 1859, Honolulu to New London; *Raduga*, from 1859 to 1863 employed regularly in the Boston–Honolulu–New Bedford run, purchased by Charles Brewer & Co. of Honolulu and renamed *Iolani*, continued on same run until early 1870s; and *Dreadnought* and *Lookout*, 1864.

The clipper ship with the longest service in the whale oil trade was undoubtedly the *Syren*, built by John Taylor at Medford in 1851. She was put into the trade on the Boston–Honolulu–New Bedford route first from 1857 to 1861, and then again from 1866 to 1876. From 1877 to 1879 she continued in this line of work, but this time sailing between Alaska and Honolulu, with additional sailings between New Bedford (now owned by William Besse of that port) and San Francisco. After 1879, *Syren* continued to operate out of New Bedford but was largely employed as a coal carrier.

Case Oil, Kerosene, Crude Oil

The trade in this new form of energy, one that would replace whale oil, began after 1858, when the process for refining kerosene from the oil rock (coal) of western Pennsylvania was developed. Kerosene would quickly become a widely available source of fuel for illumination that revolutionized life in America and beyond; so cheap was this form of fuel that even those American households on the lowest rung of the economic ladder could now afford to stay up after dark, whether it be for work or social and entertainment reasons, no longer forced to go to bed at sunset. By the 1870s, America was also a major exporter of crude oil. For years kerosene was packed in five gallon tins, with two such tins shipped together in a wooden case, thus being termed the case oil trade, and was a staple cargo of American sailing ships for many years, while crude oil was shipped in barrels. Since the oil trade did not develop until the end of the clipper ship era, this cargo was not carried by the clippers in their heyday, but was instead a latter day cargo for a number of ships, what we might call the first oil tankers, seeking any freight opportunities that offered a profit. Many of the American-built clippers that operated in this trade had previously been sold to foreign interests. Outward bound cargos of case oil and barrels of crude oil, destined for European ports and those in the far east such as Yokohama, Japan, were usually loaded at New York and Philadelphia, with Baltimore and ports in Virginia also involved. As might be imagined, these petroleum products could be a dangerous cargo to carry due to their flammable nature, as is well illustrated by the loss of the clipper *Hornet* in 1866, which caught fire and quickly burned due to an accident while bound from New York to San Francisco with 45 barrels and 2,000 cases of kerosene. Other clippers involved in this trade later in their careers were the *N.B. Palmer*, from 1873 onward under foreign ownership and largely engaged in this trade between New York and the European ports of Antwerp and Hamburg with the cargo back to America consisting of empty oil barrels; *Surprise*, wrecked by the pilot while entering port on her last voyage in 1875 bound from New York to Yokohama with over 10,000 cases of kerosene, much of which was salvaged; *Shooting Star* (the former *Ino*), 1877, Philadelphia to Bremen, Germany; *Donald McKay* (while owned out of Liverpool), in 1878 at Philadelphia, the largest cargo of petroleum "ever loaded at that or any other port" (Howe & Matthews, p. 136); *Midnight*, in 1877 and 1878, New York for Yokohama, put into Amboyna (Indonesia) in a leaking condition and here condemned and sold; *Messenger*, in 1879, loaded at New York on what would be her final American voyage, in distress and jettisoned 300 cases of oil before putting into Mauritius where she was condemned and sold.

California Wheat

While the clipper ship era was born out of the California gold rush, wheat was another golden commodity in the west that would prove to be, beginning about 1854, perhaps even more profitable for sailing ships in the longer term. As late as 1839, "the geographic centre" of wheat production in America "was east of Wheeling, (West) Virginia" (Sharp, pg. 12), with little grown further west, but this would soon change with the influx of immigrants in the 1840s and the great migration westward. Indeed, before the gold rush in 1849, California's economy was largely agriculture based, with wheat having been grown there as far back as the 18th century by the Native American population, and even on the land where gold was first discovered, wheat was here being farmed by the Swiss immigrant John Sutter as his primary source of income. While Sutter's wheat crop was subsequently destroyed by the hordes of miners that descended on his land after the gold rush began, the crop would quickly also become yet another boom commodity that would help power the California economy for the next forty years or so. Wheat production and associated milling operations grew quickly after the gold rush, so much so that by 1852 local newspapers began to list price quotes for the commodity, and by 1854 the state was making its first exports (Gerber, p. 4). Yet another impetus to the California wheat trade and the involvement of clipper ships was the change in British trade laws. Even as far back as the days before the American Revolution, the island nation of Britain had always had problems feeding itself and relied heavily on American wheat exports. Except for periods of wartime, Britain's importation of American wheat continued at a high rate until the passage of the Corn Laws in 1815, which put heavy tariffs on the commodity and thus gave the advantage to British suppliers. However, there were sometimes years of bad harvests in Britain that necessitated the importation of American grain, even more spurred on by the Great Famine that began in Ireland in 1845. By this time, British advocates of free trade began to prevail and the Corn Laws were subsequently abolished with the enactment of the Importation Act of 1846, which gradually lowered the grain tariff for three years before its final elimination in early 1849. Within a decade American ships were transporting wheat to Britain in ever increasing quantities, and from 1860 to 1880 most of the American wheat that was exported there was shipped out of San Francisco, having been grown in the fertile Sacramento and San Joaquin valleys before making its final welcome destination after a 14,000 mile sea voyage. However, even before 1860, California wheat was an important export; with the growth of the Australian trade, spurred on by its own gold rush beginning in 1852, that country, along with New Zealand, "absorbed nearly ⅔ of California wheat exports, [and] almost ½ of its flour" (Gerber, p. 9). Other locales to which wheat were exported from California included the west coast of South America, as well as lesser amounts to American East Coast ports. That foreign involvement, and thus the use of sailing ships, was key to the California wheat trade is evidenced by the fact that at its height, "Of the ten or more leading banks in San Francisco that financed the trade, at least five were controlled by shareholders based in the United Kingdom and in Germany" (Rothstein, p. 88). This involvement is not really all that surprising when it is considered that, unlike the coastal voyages between East Coast ports and San Francisco, the grain export trade was open to ships of all nations, so American ships had a great deal of foreign competition.

American clippers were involved in the early years of the California grain trade to a small degree, and while no clipper made a voyage to Australia full up with wheat prior to 1855, within five years it would become a mainstay cargo. As to the specifics regarding wheat transport, the grain was packed in 100-pound bags before being loaded for shipment, packed into the holds of clippers and other ships by port stevedores. Interestingly, the bags in which the wheat was shipped were a separate business all their own: "The demand for grain sacks alone pumped $2 million per year into the local economy (growers paid 10–15 cents apiece for the bags that Chinese workers wove from Calcutta jute" (San Francisco Maritime National Historic Park, "Balclutha History—The Grain Trade"). As was previously mentioned, jute from India was a common cargo for British and American merchants alike and was carried by many clippers. In terms of quantity, wheat cargos were designated in either short-ton or long-ton figures, the former being a U.S. measurement that equaled 2,000 pounds, the latter a British (metric) measurement that equaled 2,240 pounds. Like any bulk cargo, a shipment of wheat could be difficult if it was stowed improperly, resulting in unstable conditions, or if a cargo shifted during heavy weather. While fire was not an issue with grain cargos, spoilage was always a factor as a leaking ship could have a part of her wheat cargo damaged in this way. When this happened, multiple problems could result that might further imperil a ship, for when a grain cargo becomes wet it can swell and burst out of the sacks in which it was stored, possibly clogging the pumps of a leaky ship, making the ship even more susceptible to foundering. While clipper involvement in the grain trade did not hit full stride until about 1860, the importance of the trade for these ships cannot be underestimated, as without this trade many clippers would have had difficulty finding employment after the end of the clipper ship era, likely being sold foreign even sooner or sent to the breaker's yard. Of course, the Civil War years, from 1862 to 1866, disrupted the grain trade, and by the time it had resumed many American clippers had been sold to foreign buyers. However, among those relatively few clippers that did remain, some continued in the trade.

The clippers listed below, a list by no means complete, are known to have made grain passages from San Francisco for the United Kingdom, Australia, or the west coast of South America from 1855 onward.

1855–57 sailings: Bark *Greenfield*, May 1855, 4,752 bags for New York, the first clipper to carry a wheat cargo; *Charmer*, 1855, 1,400 tons of wheat for New York at $28 per ton freight money (Clark, p. 254); *Flying Dutchman*, 1857, loaded a $150,000 cargo of wheat and animal hides for New York, subsequently wrecked on Brigantine Beach, New Jersey, in February 1858, only a short distance from port; *Ocean Express*, for Liverpool, date uncertain, possibly in 1855, 1857, or both.

1860 sailings: *Alarm*, 1,799 short tons for Liverpool; *David Brown*, for Liverpool with 1,854 short tons, chartered at a cost of 5,700 pounds sterling, subsequently sprang a leak and her pumps could not keep up and the ship was abandoned in a sinking condition in the Atlantic in early January 1861; *Golden State*, 1,195 short tons for Cork, Ireland; *Great Republic*, for Liverpool, arriving early 1862; *Winged Arrow*, also for Cork.

1861 sailings: *Flying Childers*, 1,355 short tons for Liverpool; *Grace Darling*, 27,264 sacks of wheat (100 pounds each) for London; *Herald of the Morning*, for London; *Lookout*, 1,471 short tons for Liverpool; *Nabob*, late 1861 for Queenstown (modern day Cobh), Ireland, arrived March 1862, grounded and damaged to the amount of $5,000 while entering port; *Spitfire*, 1,640 short tons of wheat and flour for Queenstown; *Webfoot*, 1,443 short tons for Liverpool; *Winged Racer*, original departure October 23 for Liverpool with 30,244 bags of wheat, along with a quantity of silver ore, hit a sunken rock off Alcatraz Island and Arch Rock, leaking badly was forced to return to port, cargo was subsequently unloaded and the ship repaired (cost $42,000) at Mare Island. The clipper was once again loaded and departed on December 10, arriving Liverpool March 1862.

1863 sailings: *David Crockett*, for Liverpool, arriving March 1864; *Grace Darling*, for Liverpool; *Hornet*, for Liverpool; *Osborne Howes*, for Liverpool.

Post–Civil War sailings; *David Crockett*, 1866, for Philadelphia with 1,980 tons of wheat and 110 tons of barley, 1869 for Liverpool, receiving three pounds per ton freight money, 1874 again for Liverpool; *Electric Spark*, for Liverpool, two voyages, 1867 and 1868; *Kingfisher*, 1869 for Queenstown, Ireland; *Messenger*, 1873 for Queenstown with 1,224 short tons, total freight valued at $26,000; *Ocean Express*, 1867, for Liverpool with 2,000 long tons, loading time 44 hours; *Swallow*, 1876 and 1877, for Antwerp, Belgium, with 1,569 short tons; *Young America*, during her long career, made six voyages from San Francisco to Liverpool and one to Antwerp, some of which cargos may have consisted of grain. In 1883 the old clipper sailed from Portland, Oregon, to San Francisco with a partial cargo of wheat.

Ice

This cargo is not one that we might normally think of for any ship, sailing or otherwise, but from 1806, in a time before refrigeration was invented, into the 1920s it was a commodity that was carried from New England and New York ports to locations in the southern U.S. the Caribbean, and overseas to Europe, India and the Mediterranean. When shipped to the southern U.S. to such ports as New Orleans and Mobile, ice was intertwined with the cotton trade, with northern ships bringing ice to the south and departing with baled cotton for the textile mills of the northeast, not a bad arrangement. No matter where it was shipped, in these warmer climates, ice to cool beverages (something we take for granted today!) was a highly sought after commodity for which a handsome price was paid. The "Ice King" of Boston, Frederic Tudor, started the business with his formation of the Tudor Ice Company in 1806 and began shipping ice harvested from a number of ponds around Boston and its suburbs, including those at Arlington, Wenham, and even Walden Pond in Concord, later known as the site of the cabin where philosopher and author Henry David Thoreau wrote his famed work. Tudor was nothing if not a daring businessman, for it was he who made the first ice shipments to India in 1833, which at the time was thought of as a joke or a publicity stunt. Tudor and his Boston-based shipping operations made nearly a quarter-million dollars worth of profit on shipments of ice to Calcutta, India, from its commencement through the 1850s and were the largest and best known ice dealers, but by the 1850s there were many competitors from New York to Maine, all doing the same thing. The state of Maine became a major supplier of ice, with dozens of ice houses to be found all along the Kennebec and Penobscot rivers. From 1856 to 1872 it is estimated that 2,768,000 tons of ice were shipped worldwide. As to its harvesting, ice was first cut or shaved by hand, but eventually came to be cut into blocks with saws; it was then stored in a large, well-insulated building called an ice house located near the location at which it was harvested, following which it was shipped by rail to such ports as Boston; New York; Portsmouth, New Hampshire; and Bath, Maine. Later on, with America's West Coast population booming, the demand for ice here was met by harvesting operations developed out of Alaska. While being loaded in a ship's cargo hold, the ice blocks were insulated with wood shavings, sawdust, or rice chaff, the former materials providing a profit for their suppliers who once considered these by-products of their lumber mill operations unwanted waste. Despite this insulation, a great deal of melting during a voyage occurred, entailing as much as a 33 percent loss on shipments to the southern U.S., and anywhere from 50 percent to 75 percent on voyages to India, Calcutta being the main port where ice was brought in. Interestingly, a loss of 50 percent to India was the norm and still made for a highly profitable voyage. Like any bulk cargo, an ice voyage could become difficult if it was either loaded improperly, or a ship's pumps malfunctioned and could not keep up with the melting that occurred throughout the voyage. Clipper involvement in the ice trade, as can be seen below, was varied; some carried the cargo in their heyday, while others were chartered in their twilight years. The following clippers, not a complete list, are known to have carried this frozen cargo: the Maine-built *Young Mechanic,* May 1865, Boston to Madras and Calcutta, India, under charter to the Tudor Ice Company; the second *Golden Fleece,* July 1871, loaded 1,902 tons at Boston for Bombay, India, but the wood sawdust insulation caught fire, probably due to port stevedores smoking, and the ship had to put into Halifax, Nova Scotia, where it was scuttled to put out the fire. Though the *Fleece* survived, the cargo was a total loss; *Coringa,* in 1874, Boston to Calcutta under charter to the Tudor Ice Company; *Gem of the Ocean,* 1867, Alaska to the Pacific Coast; *Elizabeth Kimball,* 1853, on her maiden voyage, Boston to Calcutta, her ice cargo filled in with barrels of apples, each apple fetching anywhere from fifty to seventy-five cents in India; *Queen of the Pacific,* 1853, maiden voyage Boston to San Francisco, made a long passage due to the melting ice which made the clipper difficult to handle; *Red Gauntlet,* 1863, left Boston with both coal and ice bound for Hong Kong, but was captured and destroyed by the Confederate raider *Florida*; *Reporter*, 1854, Boston to New Orleans, chartered by Gage, Hittenger, & Company; *Express*, 1854, maiden voyage Portsmouth to New Orleans, for the Portsmouth and South Berwick Ice Company (Brighton, p. 96); *Grey Feather*, 1859, Alaska to San Francisco (Matthews, p. 139).

Guano

This trade, of all the bulk cargos that clipper ships carried, was by far the most important. By the end of the 1850s, and well beyond, a large number of clippers, perhaps a majority of them, were carrying this cargo to the East Coast of America and Europe. Indeed, if there is any one cargo that serves to shatter the illusion that the clipper ship trade in general was glamorous, guano would be it. Simply put, guano, found on many small Pacific islands and also some in the Caribbean, was the by-product of hundreds of years of accumulated bird droppings that became sun-baked on these largely barren islands. On the islands where guano is found, the many layers are claylike in texture and appearance, but once mined turns into a fine powder that is yellow colored. Guano, which has high concentrations of ammonium phosphate and nitrates, was one of the most sought after commodities in the clipper ship era and beyond and was not only a key ingredient in the manufacture of gunpowder, but more importantly was used as a natural fertilizer for agricultural use. Pacific guano was particularly highly prized because the birds that produced the guano were largely fish-eaters, thus making their excrement even more soil-enriching than that produced by birds found on the mainland. Indeed, until the introduction of artificial fertilizers by the end of the 19th century, increased farming in America and Europe beginning in the 1840s made demand for guano grow to astonishing heights. So important was guano to the American economy that not only was Congress politically involved in its procurement, so too was the U.S. Navy involved to further the expansion of American holdings in the Pacific where the powdery substance could be found.

Beginning about 1840, the majority of the guano trade emanated from the Chincha Islands, which were owned by Peru and were located just off the west coast of South America. However, dealing with the Peruvian government and naval forces which administered the guano trade was both tedious and time consuming. Long delays in waiting for a load of guano were the norm, while departing ships were required to make their clearance from the port of Callao, wasting several days of sailing time. Disputes between Peruvian officials and foreign shipmasters, many of them American, were not uncommon and could sometimes boil over when tensions flared. In August 1853 the clipper *Defiance* was loading guano at the Chinchas and was nearly ready for departure when a crewman on leave

Guano advertisement, 1883. From the 1850s until the late 1890s guano from islands in the Pacific was king when it came to increasing the output of American farmers. The partnership of Glidden & Curtis highlighted in this ad included William T. Glidden, a well-known clipper owner and shipping agent at Boston in the 1850s (author's collection).

The northernmost Chincha (guano) Island. The rocky and steep guano islands that comprised the Chinchas, located off the coast of Peru, were the primary suppliers of guano to the world until their depletion in the 1870s. The administrative port for the islands was Callao, where ships were required to gain their clearance from Peruvian officials before departing with their powdery cargo (*The Illustrated London News*, August 17, 1850).

was arrested for having shot a pelican. Captain Robert McCerren asked the authorities to release his man, stipulating that he would also pay the one dollar fine that was proscribed for the offense, but Peruvian officials refused to release the man. A short time later, when the clipper was ready to sail, the crew fired one of the ship's guns to signal her departure as was the custom, but Peruvian naval officials, apparently looking for any reason to start a fight, quickly sent a boatload of men and boarded the clipper, demanding that her captain pay a $25 fine for this offense. A fight between the crew and the Peruvians subsequently ensued, during which several Americans, including Captain McCerren, were badly wounded before the Peruvians took control of the ship. Eventually, the *Defiance* was released to her rightful owners, with the national Peruvian government disavowing the actions of the local officials (Howe & Matthews, p. 131–32).

While serious disputes like the *Defiance* incident were not common (though minor ones were), it was yet another reason for American merchants to seek out other sources for guano. This they did throughout the Pacific, from Elide Island off the coast of Mexico to Baker, Howland, and many other small islands and atolls in the central Pacific. Interestingly, Congress formally sanctioned the search for more guano supplies with the passage of the Guano Islands Act in 1856, which allowed American merchants and shipmasters to claim United States ownership of any guano island, no matter where it was found, as long as it was previously unclaimed. Under the auspices of this act, over 100 such small islands and atolls were claimed by the U.S. government, most of them in the Pacific, beginning in 1857, thereby establishing an American presence in the region which was crucial later on during World War II and one that lasts to this day. Among the guano islands claimed, most less than a square mile in size, were Baker Island, Howland Island, McKean Island in the Phoenix Island group, Enderbury Island, Johnson Atoll, French Frigate Shoals, Midway Atoll, Bunker (now Jarvis) Island, Kingman Reef, and Clipperton Island (not named for American clippers, but for English pirate John Clipperton, who discovered them). Guano mining on these islands commenced as early as 1857 and was largely ended by American companies (the American Guano Company being dominant) by 1879, but it was very profitable in the intervening years, knocking down the price of guano to American farmers from $50 or more per ton (the going rate for Chincha Island guano) to $35 per ton (O'Donnell, p. 46–47). Most importantly, the guano trade from these islands was entirely under American control. Just as with the California run, guano voyages emanating from these islands were deemed coastal voyages and, as such, the guano could be carried only by American ships. In addition, U.S. naval squadrons in the Pacific not only provided protection for American traders, but also helped support the guano trade by making exploratory voyages and taking possession of some islands.

As to the details of taking in a cargo of guano, whether at the Chinchas or at one of the American owned islands, the operations for doing so were rather tricky. The powdery guano dug from the islands was typically transported to the loading place at a high spot on the edge of the island by carts on rail tracks and was then dumped into canvas chutes that funneled it into either launches (small boats) that then carried it to the ship moored further offshore, or often directly into the ship's hold below. If the seas were calm, the water was deep enough around most guano islands that a clipper (or any) ship could maneuver nearly right up to the cliff edge, its yardarms turned, cockbilled being the nautical term, so as to run parallel or nearly so in relation to the ship's hull so as not to scrape the cliff walls. This type of skilled ship-handling was required because most of the guano islands had no natural harbors and were ringed by steep cliffs and, as with some in the central Pacific, were sometimes surrounded by razor sharp coral reefs. Despite the hundreds of guano voyages made by many clippers, only a relatively few ships came to grief in the loading process: the *John Elliot Thayer* was burned while loading guano at the island of Patos in the Gulf of California in 1858, the Medford-built *Silver Star* was wrecked at Jarvis Island in November 1860 while loading; the unlucky *Kathay* had a partial load of 400 tons aboard at Howland Island in January 1867 when a sudden wind drove her onto the reef, causing to sink within an hour; while in April 1871 the former Baltimore clipper *Napier*, now British owned, had a load of over 1,300 tons of guano at Baker Island when she hit the surrounding reef and was stuck for several days before sliding off and sinking in deep water, a total loss. Two other clippers, both Medford-built ships, were lost at Baker Island while in the guano trade. The *Asterion* had taken on a full load of 1,600 tons at Howland Island but hit the reef while passing Baker Island, some fifty miles distant, and sank in September 1863. The crew made it ashore where they built huts from the ship's wreckage and here "dragged out a miserable existence, their principle food being snakes which they dig from their holes in the ground, and sea birds which they caught" (Gleason, p. 78). Three months later they were rescued by another Medford clipper, the *Herald of the Morning*. Another ship, *Robin Hood*, was burned by her crew at Baker Island in August 1869 while loading guano for Queenstown, Ireland, the captain being away from his ship at the time. Whether the crew was just mutinous in general or was fed up with loading guano is unknown, but several men were later jailed in Honolulu for the crime. For those ships that did survive the loading process, every square inch was covered in a fine yellow powder; as one passenger aboard a non-clipper observed, "When a ship or launch is loading she is in a complete smother, as if ashes were poured into her from a hundred and fifty feet overhead...all covered with guano, you would hardly recognize some of the finest clippers, that before they left New York or Boston were praised in the papers, visited by ladies, and, instead of guano, had their cabins perfumed by champagne. But, the dust is easily washed off; the sea birds smooth their plumage when they commence their homeward

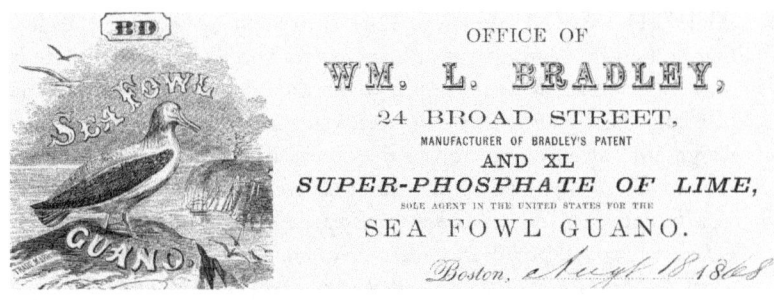

Sea Fowl Guano billhead, 1868. American clippers participated in this trade with the ships of all nations beginning in the early 1850s. Though not specifically designed for this unglamorous trade, it was a profitable one in which many clippers were engaged (author's collection).

flight" (Howe & Matthews, p. 324). In actuality, of course, the cleaning-up of the clipper ship on her homeward journey was no easy matter and likely caused some respiratory distress to crew and passengers alike, as breathing in guano dust is now considered a major health hazard.

While many clippers of all sizes, too numerous to mention in full, carried at least one guano cargo, and often more, during the course of their lifetime, the following is a partial list of some notable ships involved in the trade: *Boston Light, Champion of the Seas, Chariot of Fame, Charles Mallory, Comet, David Crockett, Empress of the Seas, Flying Dragon, Flying Mist, Golden Eagle, Morning Light, North Wind, Ocean Express, Osborne Howes, Phantom, Polynesia, Santa Claus, Sierra Nevada, Skylark, Spitfire, Storm King, Thatcher Magoun, Titan, Twilight, White Falcon, White Swallow,* and *Witchcraft.*

The Coolie Trade

At this point in the discussion of clipper ship cargos, it should by now be readily apparent that most of these items, though important, were everyday commodities that were without controversy. However, there was one trade in which clipper ships were involved in that was both controversial in its day and ran to the darker side of humanity, the coolie trade. The term coolie is a derogative one that was generally applied to manual laborers of Asian decent during the 19th and early 20th centuries, primarily those from China, but also those from India and the Philippines. These laborers were transported, often under slave-like circumstances, primarily to the Peruvian guano mines on the Chincha Islands, sugar plantations on the island of Cuba, and Australia, England, and California, where they labored in the gold fields and, later on, helped build the western railroads. Those individuals being transported to the U.S., England, and Australia, were more generally willing immigrants rather than forced laborers and the voyages to these locations were usually accomplished in typical immigrant fashion. Relatively few American flagged clippers took part in the coolie trade to England, though the Boston-built clipper *Blue Jacket* (by then under British ownership) arrived in London from Madras (modern day Chennai), India, in 1855 with 600 immigrants, receiving three pounds for each of them, it being stated that "immigration agents prefer American clippers because they make the shortest voyages and deliver the coolies in better condition than vessels of other nations" (Howe & Matthews, pgs. 45–46). Just how many clippers took part in the early Australian coolie trade, which was never as successful as the Cuban or Peruvian coolie trade, is uncertain, though the *Young America* transported 800 coolies, probably immigrants heading for the gold fields, from Hong Kong to Melbourne in late 1856.

The carrying of Chinese immigrants to California was very profitable early in the 1850s, but it soon declined due to California laws, and later federal laws, that were enacted in order to stop Chinese immigration altogether. Clippers involved in this branch of the trade include *Starr King, Ringleader, Viking,* and *Don Quixote*; the first of these ships arrived at San Francisco in 1856 from Hong Kong with 380 immigrants, while the activities of the other three ships, though separate at first, through force of circumstance became intertwined. The *Ringleader* departed Hong Kong in May 1863 with no cargo but several hundred immigrants, but when less than a week out was wrecked off Formosa, the immigrants and crew alike rescued. Meanwhile, about this same time in May 1863, the clipper *Viking* also departed Hong Kong, loaded with 400 Chinese passengers; less than a month out, the clipper was wrecked on Princess Island off Shimoda, Japan. The immigrants from this clipper were rescued and carried to Shimoda by a U.S. naval vessel. The *Don Quixote* subsequently sailed from Hong Kong empty in July 1863 and proceeded to Formosa to pick up *Ringleader's* passengers, and thence to Shimoda to pick up the *Viking's* passengers; all 600 coolies subsequently made it, finally, to San Francisco in September 1863. While most Chinese immigrant voyages to California were much less harrowing than those just detailed, it was once these immigrants arrived in California that trouble really began; prior to 1852, only several thousand Chinese immigrants arrived each year from 1849 to 1852. However, this figure had increased to over 20,000 arrivals by 1852, and they were generally unwelcome. In response, the State of California passed in 1852 a law that taxed foreign miners three dollars a month. This anti–Chinese and anti-coolie measure was followed up with a more restrictive one in 1855, entitled "An Act to Discourage the Immigration to this State of Persons who cannot become Citizens thereof." This act required either a ship's captain, owner, or the consignee of any vessel bringing in coolies to pay a head tax of $50 for each Chinese immigrant landed at San Francisco or any port in the state. The tax was to be paid within three days or else a suit could be brought against those who brought in the immigrants (*Statutes of California*, pgs. 194–95). From the subsequent anti-immigration laws that were passed, and the continued influx of Chinese immigrants during the 1850s, it does not seem that this law gained much traction and was probably largely ignored. In 1862 the Anti-Coolie Act was passed, which shifted the financial burden from ship owners, masters, and immigration agents to the immigrants themselves, charging anyone of Chinese origin applying for a miner's license a $250 tax. Due to these types of laws, followed up by the federal Naturalization Act of 1870 and the Chinese Exclusion Act of 1882 that denied Chinese immigrants any legal status, the coolie trade to California was largely ended by 1865.

By far the most despicable aspect of the coolie trade was that conducted which involved the Chincha Islands, owned by Peru, a former Spanish dependency, and the island of Cuba, still then a Spanish colony. Tens of thousands of coolies were transported to these locations in conditions that were similar to the African American slave experience in the Caribbean and the southern states. The guano mines of the former and the sugar plantations of the latter locale required huge amounts of labor to operate, and beginning in the late 1840s Chinese immigrant labor began to be utilized. The coolies came from mostly southern China, especially those regions where famine or war was prevalent and the promise of a better life elsewhere became hard to pass up. While the coolies were generally not recruited in the same manner in which enslaved Africans were, the methods used to entice them were largely fraudulent. Potential workers, most of them men, were recruited with promises of the great riches they might earn and some even paid up to fifty dollars for their passage. However, many were lied to and told they were going to the California gold fields and, in fact, few coolies were probably truly aware of the work that they would perform and the conditions they would have to endure. Many coolies, perhaps a majority, were also deceived about the length of their work contract, which typically lasted anywhere from five to eight years, being told that an American year was only half as long as a Chinese year (Narvaez, pg. 102). At periods of peak demand for labor, when deception and persuasion failed, many coolies were simply kidnapped and forced into servitude. However the coolies may have been recruited, they were subsequently brought in large numbers to southern Chinese port cities and were held, much like prisoners, in barracoons (guarded camps or fortresses) while awaiting transport overseas. Here they were often beaten or otherwise cowed into submission, many coolies by now aware that all that was promised to them was not to be. In Macao, where the bulk of the trade was conducted, the coolies were housed in a "large castellated building the courtyard of which was crowded with human beings dressed in white," while "at Whampoa they used a hulk" (Train, pgs. 147–48). The three major treaty ports open to foreign trade from which the coolie trade emanated, with American clippers being major carriers, were Swatow (modern day Shantou), Macao (controlled by the Portuguese), and Hong Kong (under British control), though coolies were also transported from a number of other ports as well. As the time for the commencement of a voyage approached, it was usually the custom that the coolies were sent aboard their transport ship and here formally signed their labor contract, sometimes in the presence of consular officials representing the countries involved in the trade; one Spanish consular official, in reporting on the process to high ranking government officials concerned with irregularities in the coolie trade, remarked in December 1855 about the proceedings on one clipper, "Yesterday I passed the whole day on board the 'Sea Witch' in order to be present at the signing of the contracts and I assure your Excellency that everything was carried out with greatest regularity. The coolies go very contented and completely satisfied with the treatment given them" (Narvaez, p. 197). However despite the above account, intimidation often played a part and few coolies, questioned by government officials about their willingness to enter into a contract, refused to go; doing so likely meant further abuse, if not death, at the hands of those who held them. Indeed, suicides were common among the coolies, either at the barracoons themselves while awaiting transport, or, once at sea, by jumping overboard into the sea. The truth of the coolie trade is succinctly explained in a letter written home by George Francis Train of Boston in 1855: "The days of the African slave trade are with the past...but the traffic in human life is not wholly abolished when we see English coal ships, Peruvian convict hulks, and American clippers all heading towards the west coast of South America, every square foot of space occupied by a poor devil of a Chinaman, who thinks, when he receives a dollar in hand, to be spent in clothing, and makes a contract to work five years at $8 per month — by paying $50 for a passage, with all the rice they want guaranteed — that he is leaving purgatory for paradise. But when his owner puts him to work on the guano deposits, under the burning sun of the Chinchas, he will find out how sadly he has been deceived" (Train, pgs. 76–77).

Once aboard the ship, coolies were held below decks in rather crowded and cramped conditions; one account of the fittings for a typical coolie ship states:

> Down the whole length of both lower decks were built tier on tier of berths, or rather large shelves — for they were without sides or dividing partitions. Large quantities of beef, pork, rice, etc., were stowed away. Hundreds of water-casks filled the holds, and on the upper or spar deck were erected galleys for cooking. Over every hatchway save one were set iron gratings to prevent too free access from below to the upper deck; that one, the main and nearly central one, was covered by the ordinary housing...the gratings were made of bars of iron...in addition to these preparations...a barricade was built, running athwart ship, from rail to rail, a short distance in front of the captain's cabin, twelve feet wide, ten feet high, and arranged so that a guard of armed men could, from their station on top, command the whole deck" [Howe & Matthews, p. 336].

The number of ships, clippers and others, departing from these south China ports loaded with coolies in the 1850s was heavy and the trade was a brisk one; among the clippers departing from Swatow in December 1855 alone were the McKay-built clipper *Westward Ho* with 800 coolies and *War Hawk* with 900, for Callao, Peru, while *Bald Eagle* and *Winged Racer* each departed with 700 coolies for Havana, Cuba. One American businessman in Swatow observed that "others have and are continually passing with their living freights" and that "the American shipmaster can but enter upon his voyage with the liveliest sense of danger" (Train, pgs. 76 and 80). Given this account, one must ask the question why were the coolie voyages considered dangerous? The answer is simple; because many of the coolies were unwilling passengers, it was often aboard ship that they saw their last chance to rebel, with the goal of taking control of the ship and gaining their freedom. One account states that "the most danger arises before they pass land" early in a voyage and that "afterwards, the boundless look of the ocean and their respect for navigation, under kind treatment, will usually keep them in their place" (Train, pg. 80). If a voyage were a peaceful one, coolies were allowed on deck in limited numbers to enjoy the sea air and scenery, and were otherwise engaged in activities among themselves, though always under the watchful eye of the crew. However, it was not uncommon for the interpreter, who was employed as both an intermediary between the coolie passengers and crew, and also to listen closely to his fellow countrymen, to report that a mutiny was brewing below decks. When a mutiny did arise, the consequences for both the ship and its crew and the coolies themselves could be deadly. When mutinous conduct, or the possibility of such became apparent, ship masters often took strong measures of repression to stop it; Captain Francis

Gorham of the clipper *Winged Racer*, "very much alarmed at the mutinous state of his cargo ... flogged some sixty passengers one morning" (Train, p. 79), while other masters also resorted to the same brutality. Among the other clippers that experienced mutinous coolie voyages were the *Challenge* (sometime before 1860), *Flora Temple* (1859), where a plan discovered before action was taken, and *Sea Witch* (1855), aboard which the coolies (as recounted above), seemed contented, but whose mutinous plans were discovered beforehand and not put into action. However, the most famous incident of a coolie mutiny on a clipper occurred aboard the *Kate Hooper*; while bound from Hong Kong to Havana, Cuba, in late 1857 with 600 coolies, a mutiny occurred and the passengers gained control of the ship's lower decks early in the voyage and set fires at three different locations. Eventually, the *Hooper*'s crew regained control of the ship, having killed four coolies in the process, and hanged the ringleader of the mutiny prior to making Cuba.

In addition to the ships detailed above, the following clippers also made coolie voyages: *Aurora* (1862); *Challenge* (prior to 1860), two voyages, one from Hong Kong to Melbourne with 800 passengers, another from Swatow to Cuba with 900 coolies on a voyage plagued by illness; *Competitor* (1858), a disastrous voyage from Swatow to Cuba with 380 coolies, of which 127 died; *Flora Temple* (October 1859), her final voyage Macao to Cuba with at least 850 coolies, all of whom drowned when the ship hit an uncharted rock and sank in the South China Sea; *Governor Morton* (1860), China to Cuba; *Live Yankee* (1859), 800 coolies loaded at Macao for Cuba, only twelve lost due to sickness; *Mary Whitridge* (1859), Swatow to Havana, Cuba; *Messenger* (1860), Macao to Havana, Cuba; *Queen of the Seas* (1857), Hong Kong to Melbourne, Australia; *Swallow* (1858), Macao to Havana, Cuba; *Wild Hunter* (1860), 58 coolies (more had been promised) Hong Kong to San Francisco. A number of other American-built clippers also took part in the coolie trade, but not until after they were sold foreign, all but one to Peruvian owners involved in the guano and coolie trade. These clippers, with their year of sale, were as follows: *Climax* (1855), *Challenger* (1863), *Gazelle* (1857 or 1858), *R.B. Forbes* (1862), sold at Hong Kong, *Starlight* (1864), *Telegraph* (1865), *Twilight* (1865), *Uncowah* (1865), *Westward Ho* (1857), following her last American voyage on which she also carried coolies, continued in the coolie trade until lost at Callao, Peru, in 1864, and *White Falcon* (1864). This last clipper, too, continued in the coolie trade until her loss in 1866. The *Falcon* was bound from China to Peru when her coolies mutinied and set fire to the ship. Unable to put out the fires, the clipper's crew abandoned the ship afire, leaving the coolies locked below deck. While the ship's crew was rescued by a passing boat, all the coolies, 650 in number, burned to death.

Despite the harshness of the coolie trade, which was controversial even in its own day, and the fact that many clippers had their white wings sullied by taking part in the business, there were some owners who had moral qualms about the trade and either refused to take part altogether, or curtailed their activities. The Boston firm of Sampson & Tappan, owners of *Westward Ho* and *Winged Racer*, apparently sent letters to their captains, after having investigated the trade and found it "perfectly legitimate, if properly conducted" (Howe & Matthews, p. 719), stating that they could not carry coolies to the Peruvian guano islands, but the two ships had already made contracts for just such a voyage. Though these two clippers did make their voyages, they were said to be Sampson & Tappan's last such coolie voyages. Whether or not one of the principles of this firm, Lewis Tappan, was related to the New York abolitionist family of the same name and also of Massachusetts origin is unknown, but if so this may have been the reason for their discontinuation of trafficking in human freight. Another Massachusetts clipper owner, Prince Crowell of East Dennis, prohibited his shipmasters from taking part in the coolie trade in no uncertain terms. When giving instructions to Captain Josiah Gorham, the new skipper of the *Kit Carson*, in 1860, he wrote,

> The Kit Carson is insured not to carry Coolies.... Besides, we have other than pecuniary reasons for not wishing any of our ships to engage in that trade. I thought I would mention this now, for should you find a

dull freight market in China, which I am a little afraid you will, a big offer of that kind might be a little tempting, and not wishing to subject you to too severe a test between moral obligation and a pecuniary gain, I would intimate the wishes of the owners in that respect [Kittredge, p. 243].

Finally, in regards to the coolie trade, the issue of mortality rates and the final fate of the coolies once they reached their working destinations must also be addressed. As to mortality rates on the voyages to Peru and Cuba, one historian has compiled comprehensive statistics. For the voyages to Peru, the overall mortality rate during the entire period from 1849 to the end of the trade in 1874 came in at 9.7 percent, but during the most intensive period from 1853 to 1862, when the clippers (and many other ships of all nations) were involved, "shot up dramatically" and ranged from 30 percent to 41.5 percent because "importers became less scrupulous trying to take advantage of the increase in demand for coolie labor" (Narvaez, pgs. 113–117). As for Cuba, the results here were even worse, with mortality rates on voyages made between 1847 and 1859 averaging over 15 percent (Narvaez, pg. 118). Though full statistics are lacking, American clippers probably delivered their live cargo in better shape than many other ships carrying coolies to Cuba, but ships with both disastrous and exceptional results show that their performances could be widely varied. This is well highlighted by the large loss of life (about 32 percent) on the *Competitor* in 1858, though the *Live Yankee*, with a mortality rate of less than 1.5 percent in 1859, showed that good voyages could also be made. To try and minimize these losses, the governments of both Cuba and Peru did pass shipping regulations to prevent overcrowding, proper provisioning, and fair treatment for the coolies, but these safeguards were often ignored by the agents, government officials, and ship owners and captains alike. While it is true that the coolie trade was not exactly on the same level as the African slave trade by virtue of both these protective laws regulating the voyages, and the fact that coolies, with some freedom of movement allowed during the passage, were not chained to one another and were allowed on deck for fresh air, the comparative statistics offer a harsh picture. From 1590 to 1699, the average mortality rate for the African slave trade was 20 percent, but after 1700 until its end in the mid–1800s had decreased to an average of 10–15 percent (Narvaez, pg. 119). No wonder the coolie trade, finally abolished in 1874, was viewed by many Americans as an abhorrent one. In regards to the coolies once they were landed in Peru or Cuba, those whose contracts hadn't already been purchased were sold at auctions that operated much as slave auctions did, with buyers examining the potential workers and their physical attributes. Once purchased, most were put to work under the most brutal conditions in the baking sun, in Peru to dig guano, and in Cuba to work on the sugar plantations. Worked by cruel overseers, a majority died before their service contract was fulfilled and, as has been starkly written, "Most of the coolies who went to Cuba and Peru died there. Few ever returned to China" (Narvaez, pg. 79).

VII

Titan

Clipper Ship Owners and Agents

The manufacturing or shipbuilding aspect of the clipper ship era we have already discussed, as has been the cargos they carried, but what about their owners? Just who was it that owned these fast ships and arranged their business affairs? First and foremost, the clipper ship owner was a businessman, and though he may have loved his ships and took great pride in having one or more of these white-winged wonders in his fleet, his greatest desire was for them to generate income. No matter how famous a clipper had become, or what kind of laurels she may have won that enriched both her owner's pocketbook and social standing, once that ship became unprofitable, a drag on company or personal finances, even the most renowned clippers were disposed of quickly, often being sold to foreign buyers or, if circumstances dictated, were sold as they were, whether damaged or worn out, or simply too big and expensive to operate in lean times. Even the *Flying Cloud*, the most famous of all the clippers, was sold by her owners, Grinnell & Minturn of New York, in 1859 after having previously laid the ship up for nearly three years. The famed flyer subsequently ended her days as a timber drogher, sailing between Canada and England. However, before the economic boom of the early 1850s ended, as many as 200 business firms, both in the form of partnerships and sole owners in the eastern states, couldn't resist the lure to add at least one clipper to their fleet.

The vast majority of clipper ship owners were located in the two primary East Coast shipping ports of New York and Boston, where many of these ships were also built. Secondary ports from which clippers were owned and operated include Salem and New Bedford in Massachusetts; Mystic, Connecticut; as well as Baltimore and Philadelphia. In addition, as has already been discussed, some clippers were locally owned, usually by multiple parties that included the builder, captain, and local businessmen. Among the facts that stand out among the clipper owners is first, that northern New England shipbuilders were patronized by prominent owners from the rival states of New York and Massachusetts alike, and secondly, that no matter where or by whom a ship was built, some owners returned time and again to the same builder or, on a secondary basis, those in the same city or immediate area.

Massachusetts Owners

Massachusetts not only led the way when it came to the number of clipper ships built in any given state, but also was the leader in clipper ship ownership. While most of these owners were based out of Boston, several other port cities and towns, including Salem, New Bedford, Marblehead, and East Dennis were also significant locations in terms of clipper ship ownership. Just as it was with shipbuilders, so it was with ship owners; a small number were all in for clippers and owned significant fleets, while other owners, more conservative in nature (and perhaps those with less capital) might only have several clippers in their fleet, or sometimes just one. Massachusetts clipper owners, if nothing else, were a bit more provincial in their ship purchasing habits. As the company profiles below show, few New York vessels were built for Massachusetts owners and, indeed, such a purchase would have raised an eyebrow among the Boston ship owning fraternity. On the other hand, once the decade of the 1850s was ended, it was not uncommon for Massachusetts owners to add a New York–built clipper, albeit a used one, to their fleets. Among the significant Boston-based owners that had a whole or part interest in at least four clipper ships (with launching dates noted) were the following firms or individuals;

Reed, Wade & Company (later Samuel G. Reed & Co.): This firm contracted for the building of thirteen clipper ships from 1851 to 1859 and also purchased another seven clippers in the years from the mid–1850s to 1868. Over their many years of operation they may have owned more clipper ships than any other American company. Samuel Reed was the financial man in this partnership, having been a provisions broker at the beginning of the 1850s, but clearly Captain John Wade was the ship expert in the beginning. He had been building ships in Boston since the 1820s and was also a ship owner. It was Wade who designed the company's first full sized clipper, the *Shooting Star*. The ships Reed & Wade had built on their own behalf were the clipper bark *George Webster* (1850) and the square-riggers *Shooting Star* (1851), *John Wade* (1851), *Onward, Sea Lark, Carrier Pigeon, Queen of the Pacific* (acquired soon after launching) and *Star of the Union*, all in 1852, *Flying Dragon* (1853), *Ocean Telegraph* (1854), *Ocean Express* (1854), *Silver Star* (1856), and the second *Shooting Star* in 1859, generally acknowledged as the last clipper ship ever built. Samuel Reed also later purchased the clippers *Vitula* in 1859, *Kingfisher* and *Challenger* in the 1860s, the McKay-built *Minnehaha* in 1862, *Ino* and *Guiding Star* in 1867 with their final clipper acquisition being the yacht-like beauty *Nightingale* in 1868. Though this company owned clippers built in Maine, New Hampshire, New York, and Massachusetts, they were regular customers of Medford shipbuilders James Curtis, who constructed six of their ships, and Hayden & Cudworth, who built the one bark and two ships for them. This company was heavily invested in the California and China trade early on, though its ships were later also employed carrying general freight, guano cargos from South America, and grain from California.

Baker & Morrill: This commission agent firm was headed by Cape Cod native Ezra H. Baker and Charles J. Morrill of Dorchester. Baker was a former ship's captain and ship owner who got his start in the Boston firm of Hardy & Baker before starting his own company, while Morrill was a merchant. The firm owned eight clippers, they being *Alarm, John Land, Radiant, Southern Cross, Starr King, Starlight, Winged Arrow,* and *Grace Darling*. With the exception of *Radiant* and *Starr King*, all these clippers were the product of the E. and H.O. Briggs shipyard of South Boston. These ships served as general freight carriers on the California run, but also frequently served in the trade to the Philippines, India, China, as well as the South American guano trade.

Sampson & Tappan: The owners of this firm, George Sampson and Lewis Tappan, were heavily involved not only in the early California trade, but also in the China and East Indies trade as well as the hemp trade from Manila. Smaller vessels were also employed in the South American coffee trade. Their clippers mostly came from East Boston shipyards, including *Flying Fish, Westward Ho, Stag Hound* and *Reindeer* from Donald McKay (the last two owned in conjunction with McKay supporter George Upton), the *Indiaman* from Hugh McKay, and *Winged Racer* from the yard of Robert Jackson. One of their other renowned ships was the Portsmouth-built *Nightingale*, which they acquired from a Boston ship broker in 1851 and put in the Australian trade. This firm also may have had an interest in the clipper *Telegraph*, which carried a sizeable cargo of Manila hemp for them in 1854.

Weld & Baker/William F. Weld & Company: This firm was founded by William Fletcher Weld

VII. Titan: *Clipper Ship Owners and Agents*   161

A clipper of the Weld fleet. William Weld owned a number of clippers, including the *Golden Fleece, Orpheus, Reporter,* and *Fearless*. The Weld clippers were distinguished not only by their hull color, but also by the black horse emblem that adorned both the fleet flag (note the flag flying from the main mast) and a larger version on the fore topsail (Isabel Anderson's *Under the Black Horse Flag,* 1926).

(born 1800), son of a ship owner and captain, and Richard Baker, Jr., in 1832 and for many years owned one of the largest fleet of sailing ships in America until its last vessel was sold in 1897. One prominent descendant of this firm is William F. Weld, a lawyer who was U.S. attorney for Massachusetts (1981–86), head of the Criminal Division, U.S. Justice Department (1986–1989), and governor of Massachusetts (1991–97). Getting back to the Weld fleet, their ships were easily recognized by their house flag that depicted a black racing horse and the distinctive dark green color of their hulls. Though the Weld fleet, employed in a wide variety of trades, included eleven clippers during various times, one historian states that "the Weld partners were not materially influenced by the speed craze associated with the California and Australia gold rushes" and "had no use for the type of big, sharp-modeled ships advocated by Donald McKay" (Fairburn, p. 3927). The clippers that were contracted for outright by this firm include the first *Golden Fleece* (1852), as well as the second ship by that name and by the same builder, Paul Curtis in 1855, *Peerless* (1852), *Competitor* (1853), *George Peabody* (1853), *Fearless* (1853), *Galatea* (1854), and *Orpheus* (1856). All these ships were built in the Boston area and all were regular or medium clippers, with the exception of *Fearless*, which is rated as an extreme model. The Weld fleet also purchased the clippers *Reporter, Asa Eldridge,* and *Beverly* on a second-hand basis between 1855 and 1868.

Bush & Wildes/Bush & Comstock: The principal in this firm was Massachusetts native Frederick T. Bush, a wealthy merchant who resided in Weston. He served as the first U.S. consul in Hong Kong beginning in 1844 and served until at least 1848. During this time he also maintained a commercial house in Hong Kong. Bush's first partner in his native state was Boston dry goods dealer M.B. Wildes, later replaced by New York native William O. Comstock, a merchant resident of Boston. Prior to his joining Bush, Comstock had worked in Canton, China, for Howland & Aspinwall of New York and traded with all the prominent firms there, including Bush & Co. Altogether, the two Bush partnerships owned seven clippers, *Hussar* (1852), *Whistler* (1853), *Charmer* (1854), *Daring* (1855), *War Hawk* (1855), *Reynard* (1856) and *Black Prince* (1856). All of these ships were built by George W. Jackman, Jr., at Newburyport and all were involved in the Cape Horn and Far East trade, though *Daring* and *Reynard* also worked in the guano trade, the latter of these ships additionally employed as a coal carrier, while *Charmer* worked in the Manila hemp trade. According to some surviving records, this firm kept a very tight control on its captains and was fairly rigid in its instructions, surely a reflection of Frederick Bush's vast amount of knowledge and experience.

Glidden & Williams: This firm was one of the most important in the clipper ship business operating in Boston during the 1850s, working not only as a ship owning concern, but also in the areas of ship management, commission merchants and agents, as well as partners in a number of shipping-related ventures. The principal owner was Newcastle, Maine, native William T. Glidden, who first worked as a sailor and later served as captain of the sailing packet *Stephen Baldwin* in Hand's Line sailing between Philadelphia and New Orleans during the 1840s. Also invested in the firm were his brother, John A. Glidden, as well as John M.S. Williams, a Virginia native and shipping commission merchant residing in Cambridge. In 1859 the firm even went into partnership with ship owner Captain Prince Crowell and the Shiverick family of shipbuilders in East Dennis to form the Pacific Guano Company. This company claimed islands off the coast of Honduras and even had processing facilities in South Carolina and at Woods Hole, Massachusetts, where the valuable guano could be processed into fertilizer. That this firm was a proponent of the extreme clipper ship models that prevailed at the start of the clipper ship era is well evident in the ships for which they contracted. Glidden & Williams had whole or part ownership in the following clippers, many of which sailed in their pioneer Glidden & Williams Line of packets running between Boston and San Francisco: the first extreme California clipper *John Bertram* (1850), *Witch of the Wave* (1851), *Golden West* (1852), *Belle of the West* (1852, managing owner), *Queen of the Seas* (1852), the Portsmouth-built *Morning Light* (1853), and *Sierra Nevada* (1854).

William Lincoln & Company: The head of this firm was a successful merchant whose residence was in Brookline. His trade appears to have been varied, ranging from general freight to San Francisco and the Far East, as well as the guano trade. The four clippers owned by this company were *Antelope* (Boston-built, 1851), *Gem of the Ocean* (1852), *Golden Eagle* (1852), *Kingfisher* (1853), and *White Swallow* (1853). All of these vessels were built at Medford, and all but *Antelope* were put over by Hayden & Cudworth.

Howes & Crowell: This prestigious Boston firm was started by two men hailing from Cape Cod, Osborne Howes of Dennis and Isaiah Crowell, Jr., of Yarmouth. At a young age, Osborne Howes moved with his family to Dedham, where they shared a house on Fort Hill with Captain Ezra Baker for some years. Howes subsequently gained experience in his father's ships, serving as supercargo and within a few short years as captain. While in command of the bark *Hebe* he is said to have been the first American captain to visit Turkey. In the late 1830s he formed a business partnership with his brother in law. When Isaiah Crowell, Jr., died at an early age in 1838, Crowell's half-brother Nathan Crowell took over his spot in the firm by 1842. The Howes and Crowell families were not just connected by business, but also by marriage as well, thereby combining the fortunes of two of the Cape's most notable seafaring dynasties. Their ships sailed the world over carrying cargos, including that of the California trade, as well as to South America in the guano trade, China, Australia, and Europe. The clippers they owned were all built at Medford by Hayden & Cudworth and include the following: *Climax* and *Ringleader* (both 1853), *Osborne Howes* and *Robin Hood* (both in 1854), and the ill-fated *Rival* (1855). The firm also purchased several used clippers over the years, including the *Fleetwing* (formerly owned by Crowell & Brooks of Boston) in the late 1850s, the *Ellen Foster* at an unknown date, and the *Swallow* in 1873. The first of these two later acquisitions were also Medford-built ships.

Enoch Train & Company: This well-documented firm was renowned in Boston for owning more ships than any other company at the height of its success, primarily in the packet business. Enoch

Train (1801–1868) got his start in business when he worked for his uncle, a dealer in leather goods, and later operated smaller vessels which imported animal hides from South America and Russia. However, in 1844 Train expanded his shipping operations and ambitions when he established his White Diamond Line of packets sailing between Boston and Liverpool. Very soon, as previously discussed, he persuaded ship builder Donald McKay to relocate to Boston from Newburyport and for years was one of his best customers. Train & Company commissioned six clippers for their fleet, these being *Flying Cloud* and *Staffordshire* (both in 1851), *Chariot of Fame* and *Star of Empire* (nearly identical ships, built 1853), *John E. Thayer* (1854), and *Cathedral* (1855). All but the last two ships were built by Donald McKay and, as previously detailed, the *Flying Cloud* was sold by Train while still under construction and never sailed under their flag. While under Train's ownership these clippers were largely involved in the packet trade between Boston and Liverpool, though several of them later made California runs and worked in the guano trade. The disastrous loss of several of their vessels, including the clippers *Staffordshire* and *Cathedral*, coupled with the financial panic of 1857, severely curtailed Train & Company's ship-owning operations. Their business subsequently shifted from packet operations to that of commission merchants. After Train's death, the company continued into the 20th century, operating first as Thayer & Warren, and later Warren & Company.

Enoch Train (1801–1868). This Boston merchant played a vital role in the coming of the clipper ships. Not only did he establish the sole packet line, Train's White Diamond Line, running between Boston and Liverpool, but he also put Donald McKay in the spotlight by financing his move to East Boston and becoming one of his greatest customers. The most notable clipper ever owned by Train was the one that never made a voyage under his flag; the *Flying Cloud* was commissioned by Train but sold to New York owners after they made an offer he couldn't resist. Though the deal was a profitable one, Enoch Train always regretted selling the *Cloud* (Richard McKay's *Some Famous Sailing Ships and Their Builder Donald McKay*, 1928).

Seccomb & Taylor: This firm was one of the most interesting of the clipper ship owners based out of Boston. The principals were Edward R. Seccomb and Captain Isaac Taylor, both wealthy merchants and commission agents who resided in Brookline and were near neighbors. Though they contracted for some of the best and most beautiful clippers ever built, all but one the product of Robert Jackson's East Boston shipyard, Seccomb & Taylor might best be regarded as clipper ship brokers rather than owner-operators. In fact, of their five clipper ships, only one, the *Swallow* (1854), did they own for any substantial period of time. The rest were all sold, probably at a great profit, within a year after taking delivery; *Winged Racer* (1852) was sold shortly after being launched, as was *Queen of Clippers* (1853), while the Maine-built *Red Jacket* (1853) was sold to English interests in late 1854, as was *Blue Jacket* (1854) after making her first voyage to England. The *Swallow*, however, was owned until her sale in 1862 and was largely employed in the China trade, sailing mostly from English ports. Finally, this firm also contracted for the clipper bark *Springbok* with builder George Thomas up in Rockland, Maine. They must have been satisfied with the deal, for they soon went back to Thomas for the much larger *Red Jacket*. Later on, Captain Taylor would build ships on his own and by the 1860s with Deacon George Thomas in Quincy.

Captain James Huckins & Sons: Many shipmasters turned ship owners and merchants loved their clipper ships, but perhaps none more so than this Barnstable native. After his sailing days were over, he started a mercantile house in Boston and took up residence in nearby Roxbury. Not content to just sit in his counting house at Commercial Wharf, he was also a presence in the shipyard where his clippers were built. Among the Huckins fleet were four clippers, *Northern Light* (1851), *Golden Light* (1852–53), *Bonita* (1853), and *Boston Light* (1854). These ships were all constructed by the Briggs brothers at South Boston, and all were superintended in their building by Captain Huckins personally, he also being the designer of *Bonita*. The Huckins clippers were mostly involved in the California trade, though *Golden Light* never got a chance to show what she was capable of, being hit by lightning and burned on her maiden voyage. *Bonita* was later condemned, in 1857, while bound to Calcutta, India, from London with a cargo of railroad iron. However, the most famous of Huckins' clippers was the fast *Northern Light* (designed by Samuel Pook); when that ship made its record passage from San Francisco to Boston in 1852, Captain Freeman Hatch went to Captain Huckins' home straight away to tell him the news, "shouting 'Here I am with the *Northern Light*, but I've strained her dreadfully getting here." An excited Huckins responded by asking if Hatch had beaten his New York rival, the *Contest*, and when Hatch replied that he had, Huckins declared, "Then I don't care a damn how much you've strained her!" (Kittredge, p. 169).

Alpheus Hardy & Co.: Bostonian Alpheus Hardy first went into business in the 1840s with Captain Ezra Baker, operating small vessels in the coastal trade. Their first international trader was the small, 150-ton brig *Otho*, but from there the company grew and came to comprise nearly twenty ships, barks, and brigs. The firm was particularly involved in the Mediterranean fruit trade, but with the addition to their fleet of five small (most under 900 tons) but fine clippers expanded their operations to the Far East and, on several occasions, in the California trade. Though Alpheus Hardy's namesake son would succeed his father in the family business, the company often shared ownership of their vessels with other Massachusetts parties, one of the most prominent being Joshua Sears of Dennis. In fact, Hardy & Company when at all possible chose Cape Cod men as their shipmasters, especially men from Chatham, because it was their founder's belief that it was the men that commanded his ships that made all the difference. The clippers owned by this firm were as follows: *Mountain Wave* (1852), *Ocean Pearl* and *Wild Rover* (both 1853), the bark *Bounding Billow* (1854), and the *Conquest* (1855). The first two clippers named were built by Joshua Magoun at his Charlestown shipyard, while the clipper bark was built at nearby Chelsea by Jotham Stetson. Little is known about 1,064-ton *Conquest*, which was built at Medford by James Curtis and was owned by the Hardys and Joshua Sears. The *Conquest* made at least one California run, later was a guano carrier, and was wrecked in 1865 while making a run from Boston to New Orleans, possibly in the cotton trade. The *Mountain Wave* was employed in a wide range of activities, including the California and Far East trade, as well as carrying railroad iron from New Orleans to New York on one occasion. The *Wild Rover* was one of Hardy's largest vessels, and was built at Damariscotta, Maine. It first served in the Boston and Liverpool trade, and was later put on the California run before going into the Far East trade. This clipper is notable for one of its illegal foreign passengers in 1865, an ex-samurai, Niijima Jo, who later became known as Joseph Hardy Neesima (1843–1890). Neesima had escaped from feudal Japan to Shanghai, China, aboard a Salem, Massachusetts, vessel in 1864, and in China was spirited aboard the *Wild Rover* for his voyage to the United States. Once in Massachusetts, Alpheus Hardy took Neesima under his wing and had him educated at Andover and subsequently Amherst College, from which he graduated in 1870. Neesima later returned to Japan in 1875, where he founded the Doshisha English School in Kyoto, now Doshisha University. To this day, Amherst College in Massachusetts retains close ties to the university, both considered sister schools, all made possible by a fortunate clipper ship voyage.

Daniel Bacon & Company: Captain Daniel C. Bacon (1787–1856) was yet another Cape Cod man, a native of Barnstable, who rose through the ranks from sailor to captain to ship owner. He gained his first command by 1807 in *Xenophon* and later commanded the vessels *Atahualpa Packet*, and *Vancouver*. After a China voyage in command of *Alert*, Bacon ended his seafaring days in 1820 and established his own mercantile firm after moving to Boston by 1832. He was later, by the late 1840s, joined by sons Daniel, Jr., and William in the business. The Bacon concern owned, either wholly or in part, five clippers, four of which were contracted for, while *Phantom* was purchased from a firm, Crocker & Sturgis, with which they had close ties. Daniel Bacon may have also had part ownership of the small clipper *Raduga* (1848), which was involved in the Far East trade (Sprague and Sprague, p. 14). The Bacon fleet, in addition to *Phantom* and *Raduga*, consisted of *Game Cock* (1851), *Hoogly* (1851), *Mystery* (1853), and *Titan* (1855). With the exception of *Mystery*, which was co-owned with Crocker & Sturgis, Daniel Bacon had only partial success with his clipper operations. *Game Cock* and *Hoogly* were both built by Samuel Hall; the former was a Samuel Pook–designed ship which held out great promise of speed but did not deliver such. Nevertheless, the ship had a long career trading in the Far East and involved in carrying such commodities as tea as well as coal at a later date. In contrast, the *Hoogly* was short lived, being wrecked on her first China voyage near Shanghai. As for the Bacons' other clippers, *Mystery* was sold to British interests after her first voyage, while *Titan* had but a short life. This large vessel, built at New York by Roosevelt & Joyce and one of the few Boston-owned clippers built in her rival city, was first used as a French troop transport during the Crimean War, after which she was sent to New Orleans to load the largest cotton cargo, nearly 7,000 bales, ever carried up to that time and bound for Liverpool. The ship was subsequently chartered by the White Star Line of Britain and carried over 1,000 passengers and a large cargo to Melbourne, following this up with a load of guano gathered at the Chincha Islands, only to be abandoned at sea after rounding Cape Horn in February 1858 when the leaks in her hull could not be stopped.

Cunningham Brothers/Cunningham & Sons/Dabney & Cunningham: The several firms under these family names provide yet another instance of those family shipping and mercantile firms which rose to prominence in Boston prior to the clipper ship era. Brothers Andrew and Charles Cunningham, Boston natives, were merchants and ship owners who founded their own trading firm in 1822. Their vessels were usually small ships, barks, or brigs and were largely employed bringing fruit home from the Mediterranean and hemp from Russia as well as trading in a variety of commodities in the West Indies and South America. Charles Cunningham, who retired in 1849, had a wife who was the daughter of the U.S. consul at Fayal in the Azore Islands, John B. Dabney; his son Frederic later formed a business partnership with his cousin, Charles Dabney, Jr., while Andrew Cunningham's sons James and Charles W. joined the original firm after their uncle retired. The four clipper ships of these family firms, most of them under 1,000 tons and largely employed in the China trade, were as follows: *Lotus* and *Flying Childers* (both 1852), and *Endeavor* and *Norseman* (both 1856).

In addition to those firms detailed above, the following Boston-based firms or individuals also owned multiple clippers: Samuel and Stephen Tilton (*Dashing Wave, Water Witch, East Indian*); Curtis & Peabody (*Cyclone, Meteor, Joseph Peabody*); Frederick Nickerson (*Criterion, Flying Eagle, Golden Rule*); Henry Hastings (*Charger, Midnight, Noonday*); David Snow, etc. (*Asterion, Reporter,*

Storm King); John Ellerton Lodge (*Argonaut, Don Quixote, Sancho Panza*); T.B. Waters (*Belle of the Sea, Morning Star*); William Appleton & Co. (*Living Age, Nabob*), Manning & Stanwood (*Flying Arrow, Spitfire*); Henry Hallet (*Asa Eldridge, Fair Wind*); Pierce & Hunnewell (*John Gilpin, Polynesia*); W. & F.H. Whittemore (*Challenger, Whirlwind*); Benjamin Bangs (*Cleopatra, Wild Wave*); W.N. Benjamin, and Nathaniel Goddard (*Dauntless, Matchless*); Thatcher Magoun & Sons (*Thatcher Magoun, Electric Spark*); J. & A. Tirrell (*Ellen Foster, West Wind*).

In regards to other clipper ship owners in Massachusetts outside of Boston, the seafaring town of Salem was the most prominent with eight clippers calling that port home, despite the fact that its harbor could not accommodate the large clippers, followed by the whaling town of New Bedford (owners or part owners of nine clippers), and East Dennis, which owned five clippers. The business partnership of Sillsbee, Stone, and Pickman (later on joined by Saunders and Allen) was established in Salem in 1798 and owned five clippers, including *Witchcraft, Syren, Malay, Aurora,* and *Derby*. All but the first of these clippers was built by John Taylor, with all except *Syren* being launched in Chelsea. This firm, which stayed in business until 1898, specialized in the China trade and often bought their cargos on a speculative basis, "not consigned to anyone, and the goods would be hawked around at oriental ports of call until sold at an acceptable profit. For a return cargo, the ship would wait until the owner could buy goods at a low price during a market sag" (Fairburn, p. 3020). Other Salem clipper owners include Edward Kimball, who had both the *Elizabeth Kimball* and *Mary* built for him at nearby Marblehead and later owned the Marblehead-built clipper *Belle of the Sea*. All of these ships were built by Benjamin Dutton and were usually employed in carrying general freight or the Far East trade; on its maiden run the *Elizabeth Kimball* carried an interesting cargo of ice and barrels of apples bound for Calcutta, India, but later was a coal carrier. A final Salem clipper owner of note was General Joseph Andrews, who commissioned the Portsmouth-built *Josephine*, the little known "ugly duckling" (though she was in fact termed a "handsome ship") sister ship of the *Nightingale*, also built by Samuel Hanscomb (Brighton, p. 134). This ship was utilized in the California trade first and later on in the Far East.

In New Bedford, George Hussey owned three clippers, including the Maine-built ships *Monsoon* and *Viking* (both built by Trufant & Drummond of Bath) and the *John Milton,* built at nearby Fairhaven, Massachusetts. These clippers not only carried general cargo, but also bulk cargos, the *Monsoon* being employed in the Manila sugar trade, while the *John Milton* was a guano carrier. Frank Hathaway (who operated in both New Bedford and New York), along with some junior partners, also counted several clippers in his fleet; the speedy *Hotspur* was built for him by Roosevelt & Joyce of New York and was employed almost exclusively in the New York–China trade, while he acquired the *Endeavor* second hand and utilized her in the Far East trade. Finally, Edward Mott Robinson was also a significant ship owner with ties to both New Bedford and New York. He owned the Maine-built clippers *Crystal Palace* and *Mary Robinson*, the Fairhaven-built *Sea Nymph*, and acquired second hand the Medford-built extreme clipper *Golden Eagle*, operating her until her loss during the Civil War. While the career of the *Crystal Palace* is unknown (she may have been sold foreign early on), all of his other ships carried general freight or worked in the guano trade. Finally, among Massachusetts owners the names of Captain Christopher Hall and Captain Prince S. Crowell of East Dennis must also be mentioned; both had full or part ownership of the five Cape Cod–built clippers constructed at East Dennis by the Shiverick Brothers. Hall was owner of *Belle of the West* and *Wild Hunter* (for a short time before selling her), Crowell the owner of *Kit Carson* and *Webfoot*, with both men sharing ownership of *Hippogriffe*. These ships were largely involved in the general freighting business, though the diminutive *Hippogriffe* was also employed in the Welsh coal trade. Both Hall and Crowell were successful ship captains turned ship owners and were well known and respected for giving their captains some latitude when it came to making business decisions.

New York Owners

Though Massachusetts was a leader in clipper ship building and the number of ships owned there, New York was nonetheless the epicenter of clipper ship activities during the 1850s. This is not surprising, given the fact that the port of New York (including neighboring New Jersey) was by the 1850s not only the largest in America, but also on the way to becoming one of the busiest worldwide. New York was not only a major destination for immigrant ships from Europe from the 1830s onward, but also grew rapidly with the completion of the Erie Canal in 1825. This later milestone soon made the already important port a key transshipment point for manufactured goods, as well as those from agriculture (cotton from the south) and mining (in the form of coal) operations coming from America's interior. Because of its maritime prominence, New York was also, naturally, a business center where many firms associated with the shipping industry either directly or indirectly were located. This included not only shipbuilders and related tradesmen, but also the offices of owners and shipping agents, many of which were located close to the waterfront area in the South Street Seaport district of lower Manhattan on the East River. Given that New York was such a beehive of merchant activity on the East Coast and thus a magnet for enterprising young merchants, it is not surprising to find out that many of the most influential clipper ship owners in New York were men with New England roots. Interestingly, unlike many Massachusetts clipper owners, there were fewer New York owners with actual seafaring experience in their background; many instead had learned the trade in the counting houses and offices of well-established overseas mercantile firms, usually rising up through the ranks after first serving long hours as a lowly clerk. As will also be seen below, New York owners, perhaps partly because of their New England roots, and partly due to simple, sound business decision making practices, had no qualms about patronizing New England builders for their ships and, unlike in Boston, such outside business was largely considered acceptable practice. The following is a list of the major New York shipping and mercantile firms that owned three or more clippers, and the ships they owned.

A.A. Low & Brothers: This large and very successful firm was started by Salem, Massachusetts, native Abiel Abbot Low (1811–1893) in 1840, whose father had moved the rest of the family to New York in 1834. The year before, A.A. Low, after having previously worked as a clerk for a Salem merchant, went to work as a clerk for Russell & Co. at Canton, China. This firm was the largest American trading house in China and here Low quickly made his mark, being made a member of the firm in 1837. Three years later, A.A. Low returned to New York, and with the capital he had saved, started his own mercantile firm. As one historical account notes, Low "immediately started on a large scale, built many vessels and added to his great fleet by buying others" (*Ships and Shipping of Old New York*, p. 60), and was successful from the start. Not only did Low subsequently bring members of his own family into the firm, including his younger brothers Josiah and Charles Porter Low (the future captain of several clippers in the Low fleet), but he also was fortunate in hiring as his premier ship captain and future advisor on all matters regarding ships, Captain Nathaniel B. Palmer. In all, A.A. Low owned eleven clippers from 1844 until well into the 1870s, of which seven were contracted for, and though the company was in the forefront when it came to clipper ownership, they did not get so caught up in the craze for extreme clippers and their investments were all sound ones. The clippers in the Low fleet of ships were as follows: *Houqua* (1844), *Samuel Russell* (1847), *Oriental* (1849), *Surprise* (1850), *N.B. Palmer* (1851), *Contest* (1852), *David Brown* (1853), all built for the company, and *Resolute* (1853), originally built for an English firm that could not pay for the ship upon completion, *Golden State* (built 1853, later acquired at an unknown date), *Great Republic* (built by McKay 1853, burned at New York prior to first voyage, sold as is to A.A. Low and rebuilt in 1854), and *Jacob Bell* (built 1852, acquired 1856). This firm, despite its New England roots, was a good customer of New York shipbuilders, especially Brown & Bell, and the successive firms of Jacob Bell and Roosevelt & Joyce, who built all but one of the ships they contracted for. The only ship they contracted for which came from New England was Samuel Hall's *Surprise*, built at East Boston. Two of the ships acquired by the firm were built by the Westervelt family, while the *Jacob Bell* was built by its namesake's son, Abraham Bell.

Crocker & Warren/Crocker & Sturgis: These firms, the first operating out of New York, the second out of Boston, were so closely related that the latter almost acted as a subsidiary of the former when it came to clipper operations. The New York firm of Crocker & Warren was headed by Massachusetts native Edwin B. Crocker (born 1812), with New York native George Warren (born 1810) as his partner. Out of their offices on Broadway Avenue, they had a very successful business as shipping merchants dealing in all manner of goods from around the world. Crocker had real estate holdings alone worth $15,000 in 1850 and in 1860 had a combined worth of $75,000 in real estate and personal holdings, a sure sign that the clipper ship decade had been a good one for him. Over in Boston, the related firm of Crocker & Sturgis was headed by Massachusetts native Henry H. Crocker (born 1820, possibly Edwin's brother) and with James Sturgis of Roxbury (born 1822) operated as commission merchants from the early 1840s into the 1860s. The Sturgis merchant family, including Russell Sturgis and his son Captain William Sturgis, had long been active in the China trade; the former had a close association with Russell & Co., the largest American firm operating overseas in the China trade, while the latter was first employed in the counting room of his father and later served as a shipmaster for Thomas Handasyd Perkins, the well-known Boston merchant. The New York branch of these combined merchant families contracted for five clippers on their own, all Massachusetts or Maine-built, and were as follows: *Alert* (1850), *Queen of the East* (1852), *Archer* (1852), *Skylark* (1853), and *Talisman* (1854). *Archer* and *Skylark* were both built by Captain James Hood at Somerset, Massachusetts, while the other three were built by Metcalf & Norris at Damariscotta, Maine. None of these clippers, except *Archer*, were of the extreme type and all gave good service for the company. In addition, Crocker & Warren owned several other clippers, they being the *Raven* (built 1851 by Hood), which was contracted for by Crocker & Sturgis, with ownership quickly transferred to Crocker & Warren and the William Webb–built *Swordfish*, bought by them in 1854 for $55,000 (Fairburn, p. 3776). One other clipper, the Medford-built *Phantom* (1852), was jointly owned by both companies, later sold to the Bacon firm of ship owners and merchants of Boston, while Crocker & Sturgis of Boston contracted for one clipper in partnership with the Bacons, the Samuel Hall–built *Mystery* (1853), which ship was sold to the British in 1854. More than any other clipper ship owners, perhaps, the Crocker companies are indicative of the close ties that existed between the rival states of New York and Massachusetts during the clipper ship era.

Bucklin & Crane: The principals in this firm were Thomas P. Bucklin (born 1805), a native of Massachusetts, and John J. Crane (born 1813), a native of New York. Bucklin got his start in business by working for the New York firm of Wetmore & Company, headed by William Wetmore and one that was active in the East India and China trade. For years Thomas Bucklin was the company's chief clerk before he left to start his own firm in the 1840s. Like other astute mercantile shipping firms, Bucklin & Crane had in their employ an experienced and knowledgeable ship master, Captain E.C. Gardner, who also was part owner of one of their fleet. The original clippers in the Bucklin & Crane fleet, all but one built by William Webb, were as follows: *Celestial* (1850), *Comet* (1851), *Haidee* (1854, built at Providence, Rhode Island, by Allen & Simpson), *Intrepid* (1856), and the second *Black Hawk* (1857). The first of these two clippers were extreme models, with *Comet* being one of the most renowned clippers of the era, while the last two were medium clippers, with Captain Gardner holding a part interest in *Intrepid*. The *Haidee,* which the firm owned in partnership with several Providence merchants, was a small but sharp clipper that could not carry a paying cargo; she was later sold and drifted into the illegal slave trade. In addition to these clippers, Bucklin & Crane bought two other clippers secondhand, the Mystic-built *Aspasia* in the late 1850s and the Medford-built *Asterion* in 1860. Both of these ships did not serve the firm for long, the former being sold foreign in 1863, while the latter was wrecked in September 1863 off Baker Island in the Pacific.

Olyphant & Co.: David W.C. Olyphant (1789–1851), a native of Newport, Rhode Island, founded this important China trading firm in 1828 and later his son Robert Morrison Olyphant (born 1824) would become his partner. In addition to their overseas operations at Canton, China, the Olyphants also had an office located right on the South Street waterfront. David Olyphant got his start after moving to New York after the death of his father in 1805, working for the China trading firm of King & Talbot. In 1820 Olyphant went to China for the firm and here stayed for three years. While in China, Olyphant met the Scottish missionary Robert Morrison and developed a close friendship with him, indeed so much so that he named his son after the missionary. Despite all his mercantile activities, the elder Olyphant was very active in Protestant missionary activity during his time in China (also spending time there from 1826 to 1827, 1834 to 1837, and 1850 to 1851) and is credited with bringing the first American missionaries to China in 1829. Olyphant would organize his own China trading firm in 1828, picking up the pieces after King & Talbot went bankrupt, and "was well-known for his opposition to the opium trade, and his was one of the only large trading firms not to engage in opium smuggling in China" (Scott, p. 2). David Olyphant would never return home from his last trip to China; forced by poor health to leave, he died in Egypt in June 1851 while making part of the trip overland. Despite their New York base, the Olyphants turned to New England for the four clippers they owned, all being built by George Raynes of Portsmouth, New Hampshire. David Olyphant, after the death of his father, was the one ordering the firm's ships, though another family member, George T. Olyphant, also became involved. The Olyphant clippers were as follows: *William E. Roman* (1850), "the third American ship to reach an English port with tea from China" (Fairburn, p. 3735) in January 1851 after changes to the Britain's Navigation Laws; *Wild Pigeon* (1851); *Tinqua* (1852); and *Wild Duck* (1852). Though these were fine ships, the Olyphants did not have the best of luck with them; while the good-luck *Pigeon* was under their ownership until her sale in 1863, the others were not so fortunate. The tea- and silk-laden *Roman* took a beating while rounding Cape Horn in late 1853 while bound from Canton to New York, and was abandoned in a sinking condition off Bermuda. The *Tinqua* was wrecked off Cape Hatteras in January 1855 while bound from Shanghai to New York, while *Wild Duck* was wrecked overseas, going ashore while sailing the River Min in October 1856, subsequently being condemned and sold at Foo Chow. Despite these losses, the Olyphants continued in business well into the 1860s.

James Bishop & Co.: This firm was headed by James Bishop (1816–1895), who was a native of New Jersey. He maintained an ornate residence (now on the National Register of Historic Places) in New Brunswick, New Jersey, and had real estate holdings in 1850 valued at nearly $16,000. His New York business was conducted out of offices on Beaver Street. Prior to the clipper ship era, Bishop had served in the New Jersey Assembly in 1849 and 1850, and later, from 1855 to 1857, in the U.S. House of Representatives from New Jersey's 3rd Congressional District. After his elected service ended, he continued in business in New York, heavily involved in the emerging rubber trade. The clippers owned by this firm, two of which were built at Mystic, Connecticut, were as follows: *Alboni* (1852), built at Mystic by Mason Hill on his own account, purchased by Bishop shortly after launching for $55,000, sold foreign 1863; *Rapid* (1852), built by Roosevelt & Joyce of New York, sold foreign in 1859; and *Pampero* (1853), built by Charles Mallory at Mystic, sold to the U.S. government in 1861 for use as a war transport. All of these ships made California runs first before being engaged primarily in the China and Far East trade.

Chambers, Heiser, & Co.: This firm was known to be a dealer in dry goods, but full information about its individual owners is lacking. The primary owners may have been brothers John (born ca. 1815) and William (born ca. 1810) Chambers, both listed as grocers in 1860, John being worth $27,000. One of the firm's clippers carried merchandise to California consigned to a J. Chambers in February 1852. The junior partner was possibly New York native Charles L. Heiser (born ca. 1824), a merchant in the city who, for a time, was also based in San Francisco and served as a shipping and commission merchant representing Chambers, Heiser, & Co. He may have been the son of wealthy businessman Christopher Heiser (born ca. 1793), who, with a partner, leased the former Castle Clinton fortifications in Manhattan beginning in 1822 and turned it into a famed entertainment hall known as Castle Garden. By 1850 Heiser's worth exceeded $50,000, but in 1855 his lease on the Castle Garden property was not renewed and the building was turned into an immigration center. This firm was active early on in the California trade, with Mr. Chambers (probably the J. Chambers that arrived in California aboard the company clipper *Golden State* in February 1852) arriving back in New York from California aboard the U.S. Mail steamer *Crescent City* in June 1852 with $41,000 in specie. This was just one of several steamers that brought back their company specie from California during the years 1852 and 1853. As can be seen, this firm went all in on the clipper ship craze early, building several golden ships and certainly made large amounts of money from their California voyages early on. The Chambers, Heiser, & Co. clippers, all built in New York by Jacob Westervelt or his sons, included *Eureka* (1851), a clipper of which much was expected, but little delivered. The ship was subsequently sold to the Griswolds for the bargain price of $25,000. *Golden Gate* (1851), a successful, but short-lived clipper, was set on fire and destroyed by one of her officers while being repaired at Brazil in May 1856; *Golden City* (1852), a successful ship, was sold at Boston about 1861; *Sweepstakes* (1853), built by Aaron and Daniel Westervelt, had an inauspicious start when her launching went bad, but she served the company well for almost ten years before hitting a reef in the Far East in 1862 and was subsequently sold as is at Batavia (modern-day Jakarta), Indonesia.

Foster & Nickerson: This partnership has proven elusive to identify with total certainty, but from available records it seems to have had New York native Frederick G. Foster (born ca. 1810) as principal, and Maine native and merchant Lorenzo Nickerson (born ca. 1820) as junior member. Alternative, though less likely, possibilities include Andrew Foster (born ca. 1800), active as a ship owner from the 1840s in the city, though his shipping activities are known to have been closely allied with the Ogden family and their Red Cross Line of packets, and master mariner Caleb (born ca. 1810) and merchant Elkanah (born 1808) Nickerson, both from Cape Cod (Dennis and Harwich, respectively) and who had an office in New York on Coenties Slip (the lower Manhattan waterfront) listed in 1859. However, Frederick Foster and Lorenzo Nickerson are our best candidates; the former was a known ship owner in New York, while the latter, who probably arrived in New York about 1850, was a native of the state of Maine where three of the firm's four clippers were built. The Foster & Nickerson clippers, none of which were built in New York, were as follows: *Empire* (1851), built at Thomaston, Maine, made one California run in 1852, otherwise employed in the transatlantic trade; the famed *Neptune's Car* (1853), built by Allen & Page at Portsmouth, Virginia, possibly designed by a New York builder. This big clipper's master was Maine native Captain Joshua Patten, who, after coming down with a deadly illness during a voyage, was replaced by his young wife Mary Patten as captain. Also, the Maine-built *Euterpe* (1854), put over by Horace Merriam at Rockland, with Maine native Captain John Arey in command from 1856 until ca. 1865, sold foreign 1867; and *Live Yankee* (1853), also built by Merriam, acquired from Captain George W. Brown (who commanded *Euterpe* on her maiden voyage for the company) of New York within a year of her building and sold to Lawrence, Giles & Co. about 1857.

Lawrence, Giles & Co.: The Lawrences were an old and distinguished mercantile family of New York City whose activities dated even before the 19th century. Principal John W. Lawrence (born ca. 1800) first served as a clerk before joining up with William Howland, another familiar surname in New York shipping circles, to become a junior partner in the shipping and commissioning agent firm of Howland & Lawrence. His activities in the business field were both varied and highly successful, his personal assets by 1870 amounting to at least $150,000. He served in the New York legislature in 1840 and 1841, was the director of the U.S. Bank in New York in 1846 and 1847, and was president of the 7th Ward Bank from 1847 to 1854. Business partner John L. Giles was also a native of New York and worked as a business agent. This firm owned three clippers, only one of which they contracted for; the big *Monarch of the Seas* (1854) was built to order by Roosevelt & Joyce and was subsequently sold overseas after serving as a troop transport during the Crimean War. The other two clippers owned by this firm were the *Live Yankee* and the famed *David Crockett*; the former, built in 1853, was acquired from Foster & Nickerson of New York about 1857, and was subsequently wrecked off the coast of Spain in 1861 while bound from Liverpool to India, while the *Crockett* was purchased from Handy & Everett of New York in 1857 and sailed as a New York–California packet until her subsequent sale, probably in the early 1860s.

Charles R. Green: Green (born 1810) was a native of Malden, Massachusetts, and got his start in business by serving as a clerk for Medford marine insurance businessman Peter Brooks. By the late 1830s, Charles Green was in New Orleans and a junior partner with his brother in the firm of George Green & Brother, involved in the Rio de Janeiro coffee trade. By 1847, with the death of his brother, Charles Green was sole proprietor and in 1849 he moved to New York, where he established an office on Wall Street. The ships he owned, large and small, were involved in a variety of trades, including the New Orleans cotton trade and the China trade. The three clippers owned by Green, sometimes in partnership with others, were the Maine-built *Snow Squall* (1851), of extreme model, purchased just after her launching and owned her entire career until 1864, when she put into the Falkland Islands after being damaged while bound from New York to San Francisco and was subsequently condemned; the Medford-built *Harry Bluff* (1855), which he owned until her loss off Nantucket while bound from Spain to Boston in early 1869; and the Maine-built *Dictator* (1855), which was captured by the Confederate raider *Georgia* in 1863 and burned. Though Green's ships were all lost while in service, two of the three had long and profitable careers, while the *Dictator* was well-insured at the time of her war loss. Green's estimated worth by the end of the Civil War, over half a million dollars, is a sure sign of his business acumen even if his name is not a prominent one among clipper owners of the period (Dean and Switzer, pgs. 41–48).

Grinnell, Minturn, & Co.: First established under the name Fish & Grinnell in the 1820s by two cousins hailing from New Bedford, Massachusetts (the former an ex-whaling captain), this firm later became involved in the New York–Liverpool packet trade with the creation of the Blue Swallowtail Line in 1822. The Grinnell family provided the shipbuilding experience and expertise early on and later control of the firm passed to brothers Moses and Henry Grinnell, as well as Henry's brother-in-law, Robert B. Minturn. By 1833 the firm's name was changed to Grinnell, Minturn, & Co., and for years it was the premiere New York firm in the packet trade, though they also were involved in the China trade as well as carrying general freight and bulk cargos. Because of their focus on packet operations even before the clipper ship era, Grinnell, Minturn, & Co. had built many big and, for their day, fast ships. Thus, when the day of the clipper arrived, while the company got involved, they did not do so to a great extent in terms of numbers. However, of the three clippers they did own, one was the most famous of all the clippers built, while another was also a noted flyer. The first clipper owned by Grinnell, Minturn, & Co. was the Portsmouth-built *Sea Serpent*, an extreme model put over by George Raynes; the owners "were so well pleased with her general appearance that they paid her builder a bonus and distributed a sum of money among the mechanics employed in her construction" (Howe & Matthews, p. 551). The company retained ownership of this clipper until her sale to Norway in 1874 for the price of $22,500, having made quite a bit of money off their original investment. No doubt because of this first success, the firm did, at least for a few years, become smitten with the clipper ship ideal, well evidenced by the fact that they purchased the Donald McKay–built *Flying Cloud* from her original owner, Enoch Train, while the ship was still under construction in 1851 for the whopping sum of $90,000. This ship made historically fast passages to California, but her large size proved a liability in the waning days of the clippers and the *Cloud* was laid up for nearly two years before being sold foreign in November 1859. The final clipper owned by Grinnell, Minturn, & Co. was the New York–built *North Wind*, from the yard of Abraham Bell in 1853. This extreme clipper was operated by the firm before being sold foreign sometime between 1861 and 1863 and shows evidence of having been a money-maker.

Harbeck & Co./Henry Harbeck: The Harbeck family of merchants and later-day stockbrokers and store owners included Henry S. (born ca. 1817, William H. Harbeck (born ca. 1814), and John H. Harbeck. Henry Harbeck, the youngest of the three brothers, was serving as a clerk in 1850 but soon had his own mercantile firm. He also was a partner in Harbeck & Company with his brothers, whose offices were located on Pearl Street in New York. The Harbecks owned three clippers, two of them of extreme models built by Perrine, Patterson, & Stack of New York: the *Eagle* (1851) and *Antelope* (1852). The third Harbeck clipper was the *Empress* (1856), built by Paul Curtis at East Boston; why they patronized a Massachusetts builder for their last clipper is unknown, but it was certainly occasioned by the fact that their old building concern was no longer in business. The clippers of this firm were primarily employed on the California run and in the China and Far East trade.

Howland & Aspinwall: This renowned mercantile firm was a pioneer when it came to the use of clipper ships and owned what many regard as the very first clipper, and by all accounts owned the first two clippers that led to the further development of the early California clippers. Two brothers, Connecticut natives Gardiner G. Howland (1787–1851) and Samuel S. Howland (1790–1853) went into the shipping business as partners in 1816, starting at first with small vessels which operated in the West Indian, South American, Mediterranean, and Chinese trade and even came to own several packet ships. Later on, by the 1830s, William H. Aspinwall (1807–1875), the son of John Aspinwall, Jr., and Susan Howland Aspinwall (the Howland brothers' sister), joined the firm. By the 1840s Howland & Aspinwall was one of the premiere shipping firms in New York and one

Edwin D. Morgan (1811–1883). While best known today as New York's twenty-first governor and U.S. senator from 1863 to 1869, this Massachusetts native got his start as a merchant and later as a broker and banker. In the 1850s he was among a group of owners that operated the Red Cross Line of packet ships, which included the famed Newburyport-built clipper *Dreadnought*. It is perhaps not coincidental that at the same time that his ships were carrying thousands of immigrants to America, Morgan served as the state commissioner of immigration (courtesy of the Library of Congress).

that was very active in the China and South American trades. A pioneer in the use of clippers in the China trade, commissioning two such vessels to be built by Smith & Dimon, the firm changed after 1851, with William Aspinwall going his own way and pioneering the use of steamships on the West Coast with the formation of his Pacific Railroad and Steamship Company. The three famed clippers owned by this firm included the *Ann McKim*, built in Baltimore by Kennard & Williamson for merchant Isaac McKim. While experts disagree as to whether or not this was the first modern clipper to be built, she was a noted and fast craft in her day. Built in 1833, she was acquired by Howland & Aspinwall after Isaac McKim's death in 1837 and was operated by them for ten years before being sold to Chilean interests. There were also *Rainbow* (1845), designed by John Griffith, a fast and noted ship in the China trade, but one whose career was cut short when the clipper went missing while bound from New York for China in early 1848; and *Sea Witch* (1846), also designed by Griffith and built by Smith & Dimon. This ship, commanded by Captain Robert Waterman, was a record breaker and very successful in the China trade, subsequently being lost on a coolie voyage in early 1856.

Benjamin A. Mumford: This native of Newport, Rhode Island, had a long and successful career as a New York merchant, though full details are lacking about how he may have gotten his start. Benjamin Mumford (1806–1864) was at one time the junior partner in the firm of Mumford & Murray but later served as the principle in his own firm or in conjunction with partner James Smith. Though all three of the Mumford owned clippers made at least one California run, they were more active in the guano trade, as well as the Indian and Australian trade. Mumford's three clippers, all New York–built, were the *John Stuart* (1851), the big and well-known *Tornado* (1852), and *Simoon* (1852). The first of these clippers was built by Perrine, Patterson, & Stack in partnership with James Smith, while the last two clippers were built by Jabez Williams at Williamsburg. The *Tornado* was co-owned with W.T. Frost & Co. but was commanded her entire career as an American ship by Captain Oliver Mumford, a relative and also a native of Rhode Island who "was accepted as an authority on matters of navigation" and commanded his first ship way back in 1833 (Howe & Matthews, p. 669). Benjamin Mumford retired from business before the clipper ship era was ended and shortly thereafter died at Catskill, New York, while Oliver Mumford (born ca. 1815) commanded the *Tornado* until her sale to British owners in 1863 and subsequently retired a wealthy man (worth $23,000) in Fairfield, Connecticut.

Ogden & Associates: This concern was a group of ship owners rather than a mercantile firm, with David and Joseph Ogden acting as trustees and primary operators. Along with the Ogdens, several other prominent businessmen from Connecticut and New York were co-owners of ten ships (not all of them clippers), all built at Newburyport, Massachusetts, by the shipbuilding firm of Currier & Townsend beginning as early as 1844 (Cheney, pg. 64). Most of the clippers sailed in the Red Cross Line of packets, which was managed by David Ogden (born ca. 1800) and his brother Joseph (born ca. 1804), both commissioning merchants of New York. Prominent associates included David Clark (born ca. 1807) of Hartford, Connecticut, worth over $25,000 by 1850 and a part owner in all the clippers listed below except *Highflyer*; Francis B. Cutting (1804–1870), a native of New York, a lawyer and noted politician serving at the state and local levels, and part owner of *Highflyer* and *Dreadnought*; and Edwin D. Morgan (1811–1883), born in Hartford and started out in business as a grocer's clerk before arriving in New York by 1830. He had a very successful business and political career, becoming a ship owner, railroad promoter, a state senator from 1850 to 1853, New York governor for two terms beginning in 1858, and later Republican U.S. senator for one term beginning in 1863. He was part owner of the *Highflyer, Dreadnought,* and *Driver*. Another associate was Dominick H. Lawrence (born ca. 1815), a native of Rhode Island and a wealthy gentleman of New York by 1850, part owner of *Racer* and *Driver*. The clippers owned by Ogden and his associates were as follows: *Racer* (1851), wrecked off the coast of Ireland in 1856;

Highflyer (1853), partly owned by her commander, Captain George B. Waterman of Hartford, intended for the packet trade but put on the California and Far East run, missing with all hands after departing San Francisco for Hong Kong in late 1855, thought to have been captured and destroyed by Chinese pirates off Formosa; *Dreadnought* (1853), nicknamed the "Wild Boat of the Atlantic" and commanded by Captain Samuel Samuels, one of the most famed of all the clippers, from 1853 to 1864 made thirty-one voyages as a Red Cross packet, sold to San Francisco parties about 1868; *Driver* (1854), went missing with all 372 passengers and crew in February 1856 in the North Atlantic (Cutler, p. 321); and *Victory* (1857), which cost $80,000, but nothing of her career is known. As can be seen, except for *Dreadnought* and the little-known *Victory*, the clippers of Ogden & Associates were rather ill-fated.

Robert L. Taylor/Taylor & Merrill: Shipping merchant Robert Taylor (born ca. 1808) was a native New Yorker and a longtime ship owner with an interest in fast ships. His partner was probably W. H. Merrill of New York, but I've been unable to find out much about his life. According to shipbuilder William Webb, both men were former sea captains, and Robert Taylor himself was quite involved in directing Webb while he was drawing up the plans for *Gazelle,* Taylor's first clipper, much to the detriment of that clipper's sailing abilities (Fairburn, p. 3802). The principals of this firm owned either individually or in partnership seven clippers from the early 1850s to about 1870, including *Gazelle* (1851), built by William Webb, arrived at Hong Kong from San Francisco in late 1854 in a sinking condition, subsequently condemned there and sold for $13,500; and *Red Rover* (1852), built at Portsmouth, New Hampshire. A speedy ship, the clipper was sold to James Baines & Co. of Liverpool in early 1861 for $25,000. *Mischief* (1853) was built by James Hood at Somerset, Massachusetts, for W.H. Merrill (with no involvement by Taylor), sold foreign in 1855; *Good Hope* (1855), built by James Curtis at Medford, but resold to New York parties within a short time; *Winged Racer*, a noted Boston-built ship acquired by Taylor secondhand about 1857 at a price of $35,000, later captured and burned by the Confederate raider *Alabama* in November 1863 off Indonesia in the Straits of Sunda; the famed Webb-built *Young America*, acquired in 1862 and operated to about 1870, possibly sold after being damaged; and the Boston-built *Gamecock*, acquired in 1864.

John A. McGaw: This clipper owner (born ca. 1801) was a native of Massachusetts who was living in Boston before coming to New York City after 1845 and established himself as a merchant. Previously he was the senior partner in the firm of McGaw & Lincoln in Boston. William Lincoln, like McGaw, would also become a clipper owner in the 1850s. As for McGaw, he owned five clippers, four of which he contracted for and was the sole owner of, and one which he co-owned with E.M. Robinson of New Bedford, Massachusetts. These ships were *Belle Wood* (1854), about which nothing is known; *Leah* (1855), lost on her maiden voyage; *Atmosphere* (1856); and *Prima Donna* (1858), all built by George Greenman at Mystic, Connecticut; and the Medford-built *Golden Eagle*, built in 1852, purchased by McGaw and Robinson about 1859, subsequently captured and destroyed by the Confederate raider *Alabama* in 1863.

N.L. & G.G. Griswold: This company was so successful in their business operations that their initials were said to stand for "No Loss and Great Gain"! Nathaniel L. (1773–1847) and George G. (1775–1858) Griswold came to New York in 1794 from Old Lyme, Connecticut. The Griswold family name was a prominent one both politically and socially in Connecticut and soon would come to be so in New York by these two brothers' efforts. They first operated a flour store on Front Street, but within several years got into the shipping business, shipping their flour to the West Indies, and soon branching out into the rum and sugar trade. With their shipping operations expanding rapidly, which eventually came to include a significant business in the China trade, the brothers in 1803 moved their offices to the South Street waterfront. Tall in stature, the brothers were also characterized as "six feet men in all their business operations" (Barrett, p. 333). The elder

Griswold largely kept to his own business and never sought outside business pursuits, but George Griswold was different; he served as an officer in a number of other prominent concerns, including the Columbia Insurance Co., the Franklin Fire Insurance Co., and as president of the Bank of the United States and the New York & Erie Railroad, to name just a few. Excellent businessmen though they may have been, the Griswolds were also believers in a bit of luck; one of their early ships was named the *Panama* and was so successful that they subsequently gave this name to three successive ships in their fleet. Of the three clippers owned by this firm, normally known for its judicious investments, only the extreme model *Panama* was a success. The other two Griswold clippers, one of which was contracted for, and the other purchased second-hand, were a bit more problematic. The clippers owned by the company included the notorious *Challenge* (1851), built by William Webb at a cost of $150,000 and commanded by Captain Robert Waterman on her maiden voyage, one filled with such crew troubles that the clipper's reputation was permanently damaged. The ship was sold at Hong Kong in 1861, having arrived badly damaged from San Francisco, for the small sum of $9,350. They also had the small clipper *Panama* (1853), built by Thomas Collyer of New York and well less than half the size of *Challenge*. This ship was owned by the Griswolds until she put into Brazil in a damaged condition in 1867 and was there condemned and sold. Finally, there was *Eureka*, built in 1851 for Chambers, Heiser, & Co. of New York, acquired by the Griswolds in 1859, and later sold to Canadian interests in 1863. This ship, according to some historians, "was very unfortunate and not successful and is said to have never been a popular vessel in any trade" (Howe & Matthews, p. 165).

In addition to the above listed companies, the following New York firms owned at least two clippers and are worthy of mention: John H. Brower & Co., *Harvey Birch* (1854) and the famed and fast *Andrew Jackson* (1855), both built at Mystic, Connecticut, by Irons & Grinnell; E. Buckley & Sons and G. Buckley, respectively, *Lookout* (1853) and *Mary Ogden* (1854), both built by Chase & Davis of Warren, Rhode Island; Chamberlain & Phelps, three Westervelt productions, the *Hornet* (1851), the little *Aramingo* (1851), and the small clipper bark *Zephyr* (1855); George B. Daniels, the Webb-built ship *Flying Dutchman* (1852), an ill-fated clipper, and the long-lived *Young America* (1853); Goodhue & Co., *Mandarin* (1850), built by Smith & Dimon, and *Kathay* (1853), built by Jacob Westervelt; Handy & Everett, *Governor Morton* (1851) and *David Crockett* (1853); Slade & Co., *Messenger* (1852), built by Jacob Bell, owned for only one voyage before being sold, and *Wizard* (1853), built by Samuel Hall at East Boston at a cost of $95,000; Wakeman & Dimon, *Stingray* (1854), built by Eckford Webb, and the *Arey* (1856), built at Frankfort, Maine, in 1856, and acquired after her launching; and Williams & Guion, the William Webb–built *Australia* (1852) and the packet clipper *Adelaide* (1854), built by Abraham Bell.

Notable Owners in Other Cities

Since a minority of the clippers were built outside of Massachusetts and New York, it is not surprising that relatively few multiple-clipper owners were also to be found in these locales. While Philadelphia, Baltimore, and Mystic, Connecticut, were important ports overall, in terms of clipper ship operations far fewer clipper voyages either emanated from or terminated at these first two cities, and none from the latter. Thus it was that there were only a small number of clipper owners based in these cities because of the simple fact that there were fewer readily available cargos to be had. Only four clippers, all of them Philadelphia owned, were even built by the only Pennsylvania shipbuilder, William Cramp of Kensington, that was building such ships, and while Baltimore and Mystic each launched over twenty clippers, many of these were built for outside interests. In regards to clipper ownership in northern New England locales, relatively few of these ships were even owned in New Hampshire or Maine, and a number of those that were involved the part, or sometimes entire, ownership of their builders, which circumstances have already been discussed. As will be evident below, the ports of Philadelphia and Baltimore in particular had a close relationship during the clipper ship era, with the later port providing a fair number of ships to Philadelphia merchants.

Philadelphia

In this city, only two firms had any substantial interest in clipper ships in terms of numbers. The most important was that of William Platt & Co., later William Platt & Son when William, Jr., entered the business. This firm owned three noted clippers, all built by Jacob Bell of New York, and all extreme in model. These included *White Squall* (1850), a ship that cost $90,000, but paid back her owners over $132,000 on her first round-trip voyage from New York to San Francisco, and from thence to China and home via London. She subsequently caught fire at New York in December 1853 during the port area fire that also gutted *Great Republic* and what remained was sold for $5,500. They also owned the big *Trade Wind* (1851), co-owned with Booth & Edgar of New York, a fast ship but ill-fated, lost after a collision in May 1854; and *Messenger* (1852), originally built for Slade & Co., but acquired after one voyage and had a long career.

The other multi-clipper firm in the City of Brotherly Love was that of Damon & Hancock and the later firm of Dawson & Hancock (also reported as Hancock & Dawson). The former partnership owned the Baltimore-built *Sirocco* (1852), operated until her sale foreign about 1862, while the later firm owned the Baltimore built ships *Euroclydon* (1853) and the big *Napier* (1854), which cost $140,000 and was sold foreign in 1862 for $55,000. Of these partners, Albert Damon was a commission merchant, as was Robert Hancock (born ca. 1814) and a native of Maryland. Though speculative, his state of origin, and the fact that all of the firm's ships came from Baltimore may lead to the conclusion that Hancock was the one in charge of procuring these clippers. The Dawson in the later partnership was likely Mordecai Dawson (born ca. 1799), a wealthy gentleman of Philadelphia worth over $100,000 by 1860. In addition to acting as commission merchants, Dawson & Hancock also were heavily involved in household goods, especially china and queensware, a cream-colored earthenware that was imported from the famed North Staffordshire region of England and was a standard item in American households.

Other clippers, three built at Philadelphia, three at Baltimore, and one each in Boston and New Jersey, that were owned and operated out of Philadelphia include the small ship *Grey Eagle* (1848), built for John McKeever (whether the sea captain or merchant of that name is uncertain) and others; *Eliza Mason* (1851), built at Baltimore, owner uncertain but possibly wine merchant William Mason, whose wife and daughter were both named Eliza; *Stilwell S. Bishop* (1851), built at Philadelphia for Henry Simons, Jr., a business partner in other ventures with the namesake of the ship, later sold to Baltimore parties and renamed *Grey Eagle*; *Frigate Bird* (1853), owned by grain dealer Charles H. Cummings & Co.; *Morning Light* (1853), built at Philadelphia and not to be confused with the much larger clipper of the same name built at Portsmouth, owned by Bucknor & McCammon, the senior partner in this firm being A.J. Bucknor, merchant and tobacco dealer, and the other being merchant David McCammon; and *Fanny McHenry* (1854), built at Boston for George McHenry & Co. McHenry was a young and successful merchant (born ca. 1825 in Philadelphia) who named the ship after his new wife, Francis "Fanny" McHenry (born ca. 1832). By 1860 he was worth nearly $100,000. Other Philadelphia clippers were the *Isaac Jeannes* (1854), built at Philadelphia for the Philadelphia fruit dealer of the same name (born 1810), involved in the Mediterranean trade; and the big *Manitou* (1855), built by Cramp at Petty's Island, New Jersey (across the river from Philadelphia), for merchant Stilwell S. Bishop (born ca. 1814). *Manitou* went missing with all aboard in 1859 while bound from New York to San Francisco.

Baltimore

In this sea-faring city, the traditional home of America's first fast sailing craft, there were at least four family firms that owned multiple clippers, most of them built by local builders, and possibly two others. The largest of these concerns was the commissioning agent firm of William Wilson & Sons. All were Maryland natives, the sons being Oswald, Thomas, David, and Henry. They got their start in clipper ownership in 1848 when David, Thomas, and Henry Wilson contracted locally for the fast early clipper *Andalusia*, the largest clipper built in the city up to that time. This ship made four California voyages. The next clippers this firm acquired, none of them built locally, were a major step up, they being the Maine-built *Black Warrior* (1853) and the Donald McKay-built *Empress of the Seas* (1853). The first of these ships was very successful and cost $90,000, eventually being sold to James Baines of Liverpool in 1862. As for the *Empress of the Seas*, this was a clipper McKay intended to operate on his own, but changed his mind when the Wilsons offered to buy the ship while she was still under construction. While they paid $125,000 for the ship, they soon paid her off as her first cargo netted $104,000 in receipts. The ship continued in service, later in the England-Australia trade until her loss by fire in late 1861 at Melbourne.

As for the more local clipper-owning concerns in Baltimore, Maine native and ship captain Adams Gray (born ca. 1791) owned the small clippers (each about 530 tons) *Architect* (1848), *Sea Nymph* (1850), and *Lady Suffolk* (1852). Not only did Gray own them, he also commanded the *Architect* and built the last two ships, perhaps operating them in a family way; his sons John and Horatio were also sea captains, while another son, Andrew, was a commission merchant, possibly handling the business end of things. The *Architect* was an early clipper and one of the first to carry the 49'ers to the gold fields of California under Captain Gray. He subsequently sold the ship for $20,000 after making a voyage to Hong Kong. The *Architect*'s builder was Virginia native Langley B. Culley (born ca. 1790), a veteran of the War of 1812; it is from him, we may surmise, that Gray learned the shipbuilding trade. The *Sea Nymph* was considered a beautiful ship, perhaps modeled by Captain Gray off the lines of his old command, and was ultimately sold by late 1853. The *Lady Suffolk*'s career was brief and involved the slave trade; of her we will learn more later on.

Another clipper-owning firm of Baltimore was that of Montell & Co., with principal Francis T. Montell (born ca. 1812 in New Brunswick, Canada). He operated as a commission merchant with offices on Smith's Wharf, and the commander for these ships at one time or another was Captain F. W. Montell. This firm went big, ordering the 1,289-ton *Atalanta* in 1852, the largest vessel ever built in Baltimore to that time, and followed up with the 1,694-ton *Carrier Dove* in 1855. The first of these ships was sold to Spanish parties by early 1857, while the latter was sold prior to 1863 when she went ashore on the Irish coast and, later that year, was subsequently sold at auction in New York for $67,000. Yet another clipper owning firm was that of James Hooper & Co. Hooper (born ca. 1801) had his hands in many business pies, serving as a shipping and commission merchant and also as a wholesale grocer, with an office on Spear's Wharf. Hooper owned the clippers *Kate Hooper* (1853) and *Pride of the Sea* (1854), both sizeable ships. The first of these was undoubtedly named after his wife, Caroline C. Hooper, and was involved in the California and Far East trade, including duty as a coolie ship, before being sold after having caught fire while at Melbourne, Australia, in December 1862. The *Pride of the Sea*'s career is largely unknown, but she was lost off Liverpool while bound there from New Orleans, likely with a cargo of cotton, prior to the Civil War. That Hooper's clippers did well for him is attested to by the fact that he was worth about $100,000 in 1860.

Another possible pairing of family firms to be discussed is that of Oelrichs & Lurman and S. Lurman & Co. The firms likely had related family members on the Lurman side, but this cannot be confirmed since I've been unable to discover anything about S. Lurman, who had built for his company the first Baltimore clipper to exceed a thousand tons in size, the 1,012-ton *Union*. This ship was a fast one that made one California run before entering the China trade, subsequently being sold to French interests in 1863. The principals of the later firm were Henry Oelrichs (born ca. 1811, a native of Germany) and Gustave Lurman, who both worked as commission and shipping merchants. This firm owned the small clipper *Canvasback* (1853), which was first employed in the Rio trade before going into the China trade and thereafter sold foreign in 1863. A final possible multi-clipper owner from Baltimore is Thomas J. Handy; while most clipper historians list Handy as being a New Yorker, he is not found in census records for that state, nor is he found in Maryland. However, one telling newspaper advertisement in the early 1850s in the *Daily Alta California* lists Thomas J. Handy as a commission merchant from Baltimore. This would seem to be supported by the fact that Handy purchased from the Baltimore builders Richard & Edward Bell the small and beautiful clipper *Seaman* (1850) and its obvious successor, *Seaman's Bride* (1851). The first of these clippers was struck by lightning and burned while voyaging from New Orleans to France in 1855, while the latter was sold that same year to German interests.

As to other Baltimore-owned clippers, the following firms are also known participants: M.R. Ludwig, the Maine-built *Crest of the Wave* (1854); commissioning merchants Thomas Whitridge & Co., the locally built *Mary Whitridge* (1855), named after partner Horatio Whitridge's ten-year-old daughter; and shipbuilders James Abrahams and Robert Ashcroft, who retained ownership of the 1,916-ton *Flora Temple* (1853), the largest of all the Baltimore clippers, which served as a guano and coolie carrier until her loss in 1859.

Mystic

This old seaport on the Connecticut coast is usually best remembered, when it comes to the clipper ship era, as a supplier of these ships for owners in New York, highlighted by the brilliant career of the *Andrew Jackson* (1855). However, this is only part of the story. While eleven of this port's clippers were indeed supplied to New York, the remaining number, nine in all, were in fact owned and operated locally. Interestingly, most of these Mystic-owned clippers were owned and operated by the men that built them, and the case can easily be made that these firms were, as a group, by far the most successful of any builders that attempted to operate their own creations in a business that was both fast-paced and ever-changing. Even the great Donald McKay's ventures in ship ownership, done so on a grand scale, fade in comparison to those of several Mystic builder-owners. What was the key to their success in Mystic? The answer is quite simple; not only did her builders construct solid, well-built ships that were of a medium model that combined both good sailing qualities and good loading capacity, but they also limited the size of their ships. There were no McKay-sized monster clippers ever built at Mystic, with no clipper built here exceeding 1,700 tons; of those clippers owned locally, they ranged from 632 tons to nothing higher than 1,482 tons, and only three of these exceeding 1,000 tons. This limited size meant that these clippers were more economically viable by having fewer problems in finding cargos to fill their holds and requiring fewer men to operate.

The most active and successful owner-builder in Mystic was Charles Mallory (born ca. 1796), who started out in his early years as a sailmaker, and by the early 1820s became a part ship owner as he started to build his fortune. Mallory eventually came to own his own shipyard and built a sizeable shipping business. The Mallory shipyard built eight clippers overall from 1851 to 1859, five of which Mallory retained and operated for long periods of time. These ships were the *Charles Mallory* (1852), a bad-luck ship that was wrecked off Brazil while carrying whale oil from Honolulu to New London, Connecticut, in early 1853; *Hound* (1853), a rather slow ship, sailed in Wells & Emmanuel's Empire Line to California from 1858 to 1859, sold by the Mallorys in 1863; *Elizabeth*

F. Willets (1854), a successful China trader into the 1860s, owned by Mallory to at least 1861, sold foreign at Shanghai in 1863; *Mary L. Sutton* (1856), a very successful ship owned by Mallory her entire career, wrecked at Baker Island in late 1864 while loading guano; and the *Haze* (1859), which served for a time in Comstock's Line of California clippers.

Another Mystic shipbuilding firm that operated in a similar manner to Charles Mallory, though not on as large of a scale, was that of Maxon, Fish, & Company; this firm had as its principals master carpenter and Rhode Island native William Maxon (born ca. 1811) and prominent merchant Nathan G. Fish (born ca. 1806). The firm built only two clippers, both of them owned by Fish, they being the *B.F. Hoxie* (1854), which served until her destruction by the Confederate raider *Florida* in 1862, and the small *Aspasia* (1856), which was sold to Bucklin & Crane of New York within a short time.

The other Mystic clipper ship owners were as follows: Captain Gurden Gates was both owner and commander of the Mallory-built clipper *Twilight* (1857) until her sale to New York owners in 1863; and Post, Smith, & Co., who owned the *Harriet Hoxie* (1851), named after the wife and daughter of prominent local merchant Benjamin F. Hoxie and built by Irons & Grinnell, later sold foreign to Belgium interests in 1859.

Shipping Agents

While many clipper ship owners carried cargos on their own account, many others did not and made their money instead by either chartering their ships out to shipping agents or hiring commission merchants to act as agents on their behalf. Under these circumstances ships then acted as carriers for other merchants and manufacturers seeking to get their goods, whether it was general freight items or bulk commodities, to market. The shipping agent was, in effect, the middleman in the entire shipping process and was the one who actively sought out the cargos for the ships whose owners he worked with. In return for his efforts, the shipping agent was generally paid anywhere from 2.5 percent to 5 percent of the total freight receipts he had generated. These commission rates, of course, varied with the economic times of the moment; in 1850 and 1851, for example, when competition was fierce for the space on any clipper loading for California, not only were the freight rates higher, but so too were the commission rates paid to the shipping agent. On the other hand, when there was a downturn in shipping, as occurred among clipper ships after 1854, not only were freight rates lower, but so too was an agent's rate. While records for most clipper voyages have not survived, some educated guesses can be made as to what the shipping agents were paid for loading; when the big *Challenge*, a ship of which much was expected, was loading at New York for her maiden voyage in late 1851, freight rates were high and she garnered a freight list valued at $60,000. Given the times, her agent probably received a 5 percent commission, garnering him a gross return of $3,000 ($66,100 in 2010 dollars). From this amount may be deducted a variety of expenses, including advertising, traveling, assisted labor costs, and, of course, an agent's own time and labor. Even with these expenses deducted, the return for the shipping agent in boon times was high and life was indeed very good. And this was just for one ship; shipping agents, when times were good often had multiple clippers loading at any given time. Consignees were falling over themselves to get their goods loaded on a clipper and the shipping agent's task was a much simpler one in some aspects. On the other hand, once the clipper craze began to die down after 1854, freight rates dropped, and so too did a shipping agent's commission. In fact, the shipping agent took a double hit, for not only did the freight rates go down (which his commission was based on), but so too did the percentage paid for his services. The last New York to San Francisco voyage of another Webb-built clipper, the *Flying Dutchman*, in 1857 provides a stark contrast. The ship had a freight list valued at only $18,275, and with the boom times long gone, we can safely assume that her shipping agent, again if one was so used, was commissioned at a lower rate, as low as 2.5 percent. However, if we presume a generous 3 percent, the agent's return would have amounted to only $548.25 ($10,700 in modern figures), once again a gross amount not including his own business expenses and time involved. To make this much lower rate of return a shipping agent had to work much more diligently to drum up a cargo to fill the clipper he was in charge of because times were hard and cargos scarce. Because of this, many clipper voyages were delayed in the wait for a ship to fill up, and some big clippers, such as the *Flying Cloud* and *Hurricane*, were laid up entirely in the years 1857 and 1858 because they simply could not find enough cargo to fill their holds or could not be operated on a profitable basis sailing with their holds only partially filled.

Though he did not usually own the clippers he was loading, a shipping agent was generally styled as the operator of a line of clippers, such as Coleman's California Line or Sutton & Co.'s Dispatch Line, and, from what we do know of these agents, many had multiple business interests both on the East Coast and in California. However, not all of these so-called lines were big or long lasting. Some lines might consist of but one or two ships and have only a fleeting existence, and some did not survive either the general downturn in shipping that occurred in the mid–1850s, or the financial panic of 1857. While many lines had agents for the same company at both New York and San Francisco, at least one major line operated under two names, having two agents involved in its operation; the Sutton & Co. Dispatch Line was based out of New York, while the George Howes & Co. Dispatch Line was based out of San Francisco and handled the West Coast loading business. Interestingly, some clippers served in more than one line during the 1850s and 1860s, different agents working with the same owner (or sometimes new owners) at varying times during a ship's life. The South Boston–built *Winged Arrow* served in both Glidden & William's Line, a Boston-based enterprise, but also later served in Sutton's Dispatch Line out of New York. Likewise, the Rhode-Island built *Lookout* served early on, about 1853, in the Shipper's Line, and later in Sutton's Dispatch Line, both from New York. While most of the clipper lines established concerned the New York to San Francisco run, there were other lines that ran from Boston to San Francisco, from San Francisco to the Far East, and even one from the East Coast to Valparaiso, Chile and Callao, Peru, though whether this last line actually employed clippers is uncertain.

Perhaps even more so than the ship's owner, an agent had to build an image for his line and the clippers he worked on loading. To that end, shipping agents utilized all the publicity and advertising of the day, including newspaper accounts publicizing new clippers coming on line and information provided to reporters writing up the marine intelligence columns that appeared daily in New York and Boston papers, regular paid newspaper advertising, as well as posters and, later on, personally distributed clipper ship sailing cards. The earliest form of advertising for clipper voyages outside that found in local newspapers were posters in public places made of rather flimsy paper; while few of these artifacts have survived, that for the South Boston–built *Fair Wind* sailing in Cooley's Merchant Express Line measures about 20 inches wide by 14 inches high and boldly proclaims below an image of its house flag that "None But First-Class Clippers Loaded In This Line." However, it is the most artistic surviving remnants of the clipper ship era, the highly collectible and sought after sailing cards, that really give us a sense of the hype and promotion that surrounded a clipper ship in the process of loading for California; on them we read such lavish descriptions as "The Splendid and Favorite A-1 First-Class Clipper Ship" (for the Medford-built *Ocean Express*), "The Extreme Out-And-Out Clipper Ship" (the Portsmouth-built *Sea Serpent*), "The Popular A-1 Extreme Clipper Ship" (the Medford-built *Star of the Union*), "The Well-Known and Celebrated New-York Clipper Ship" (the *Hornet*), "The Fastest Ship in the World! The Renowned Clipper Ship" (the Mystic-built *Andrew Jackson*), and "The Magnificent Out-And-Out Clipper Ship" (the Medford-built *White Swallow*). These sailing cards were not in widespread use until the mid–1850s and later, when competition for freight was high. Not only were the descriptions of the clippers on these sailing cards designed to catch the public notice and that of potential consignees, but so too were the exciting illustrations they featured; on the sailing card for the big Bath-built immigrant clipper *Emerald Isle* may be seen an armor-clad warrior perched on a rock in the sea, bearing a sword in one hand and the Irish flag in another, while in the background there is a magnificent ship under full sail; on that for the Newburyport-built *Black Prince*, a knight on horseback is charging into battle, the foot soldiers behind him bearing the beehive flag of the Sutton Dispatch Line; that for the *Comet* depicts a blazing comet across the night sky, with Uncle Sam riding the forward part and carrying the house flag of the Coleman Line, while in the background are two clippers under full sail; and that for the *Syren* depicts a woman in the dress of the day standing on a rock by the ocean with one hand to her brow and looking landward, with a clipper under full sail behind her. These images and many others equally striking were all created for one purpose: to fill a clipper's cargo hold, which in turn would also fill a shipping agent's cashbox. Just as the ship descriptions and illustrations on these sailing cards are sometimes over the top, so too are the advertised sailing times and these must be taken with a grain of salt, so to speak. Despite such claims as "Sailing regularly on advertised days," "She will have quick dispatch," "Is now rapidly loading," "Another small and sharp clipper now loading," and "Will promptly sail as above," many voyages commenced at later times than those advertised as verified by contemporary records.

The following shipping agents were known line operators that employed true clipper ships built during the 1850s (many ships built in the 1860s that served in these lines were advertised as clippers, but are not classified as such), and were in operation in the 1850s to 1870 time-frame, though this list should not be considered a complete one.

The Pioneer Line

New York merchant John Ogden started this line that ran from New York to San Francisco as early as 1852, and possibly even earlier. He had previously been a junior partner with E.B. Sutton, operating the Dispatch Line out of New York beginning in the late 1840s. As its name implies, the Pioneer Line was one of the earliest such clipper lines and was established at a time when freight rates were high and there was plenty of business to go around. Thus it was that printed advertisements for this firm are rare. Among the clippers that sailed in the Pioneer Line, many of them famed flyers of extreme model that were built at the beginning of the clipper ship era, were the following: *Atalanta, Shooting Star, Wings of the Morning, Tinqua, Flying Fish, Wild Pigeon, Wild Duck,* and *Antelope*. How long this line lasted is uncertain; while it may have been out of business by 1855 or thereabouts after the clipper craze had died out, John Ogden himself was still involved with clippers, purchasing the Massachusetts-built *Onward* in 1857 for $32,000 and operating the ship until her sale in 1861.

Australian Pioneer Line

This line was established by Canadian Roderick W. Cameron (1823–1900) in 1852 and was based out of New York. Not only was his line, which was also called the Pioneer Line of Monthly Packets, one of the most successful ones to employ clipper ships (as well as non-clippers) in general, it was the most celebrated Australian line and was also the longest lived of all the clipper lines

☞ The new clipper *Nightingale*, built expressly for exhibition at the World's Fair in London, will be dispatched from this port on the 20th inst. for Melbourne, Australia, in CAMERON's Pioneer Line of Monthly Packets. She will carry the United States mail to Australia, by order of the Post-Office Department. The *Nightingale* arrived on Saturday from Boston.

Nightingale notice. This Portsmouth-built ship was the first clipper employed by the Cameron Line and made a fine run of 75 days out to Australia, carrying 125 passengers in luxurious style, on the passage here noted (***New York Times***, May 1854).

established; long after the age of sail was over, R.W. Cameron & Co. was still in the shipping business as late as 1930. Cameron himself, interestingly enough, had no nautical experience; he was born in Glengarry County, Upper Canada, and was educated at several schools in Williamstown, Cornwall, and Kingston. He started his business career at the age of sixteen, working as a clerk in a dry-goods store and came to America with little money to his name in 1849 to work as a lobbyist in Washington, D.C., working in support of a U.S.–Canada reciprocity treaty. Among his financial backers at this time was Boston merchant Samuel Lawrence, and within a few short years Cameron migrated to New York. With the Australian gold rush of 1851, and its resultant publicity in the U.S., Cameron established his line in early 1852 and in July 1852 chartered his first ship (a non-clipper) to take passengers and goods from New York to Australia. He followed this venture with twenty-two other voyages undertaken between 1852 and March 1855. The first known American-built clipper to serve in the Australian Pioneer Line was the *Nightingale* in May 1854, which made the passage out in a record 75 days. Another clipper serving in this line was the Maine-built *Windward* in December 1854, while Cameron also bought another clipper, the renowned *Flying Scud*, also Maine-built, for $100,000 in early 1854. This ship was subsequently sent to Australia in September 1854, thereby earning $30,000 on one trip. Other clippers employed in Cameron's line include the McKay-built *Minnehaha* and the Maine-built *Sportsman*. From the ships employed in his line, it is clear that Cameron had great confidence in Maine shipbuilders. As for R.W. Cameron, his business acumen resulted in large personal wealth and the establishment of a personal estate on Staten Island. He was an avid horse-breeder and racer, yachtsman, and though living in America, always remained a British subject. His Australian business interests led him to represent New South Wales, Australia, at the Centennial Exhibition in Philadelphia in 1876 and at the Paris Exhibition in 1878, as well as acting as the honorary Canadian representative to later exhibitions held in Sydney and Melbourne. For this service, Cameron was awarded the honor of knighthood in 1883 and was thereafter known as Sir R.W. Cameron. Cameron's business continued to flourish, even though he was involved in all these far-ranging activities, being closely involved in Canadian and American diplomatic affairs. At about the time of Cameron's death the firm he had established (taking in William Street as a partner in 1870) gave up owning ships, though it still operated them under charter (MacGillivray, R.C., *Dictionary of Canadian Biography*). The Australian Pioneer Line has the unique distinction of being the only major clipper line to be owned by a foreign national.

Coleman's California Line for San Francisco

This line was established by William Tell Coleman (1824–1893) in New York about the year 1854 and, though not the first or the longest-lived line, it was the most renowned of all the clipper lines. Coleman himself had no nautical experience; born in Cynthiana, Kentucky, he later went to college at St. Louis University and subsequently served as a plantation overseer in Louisiana and in the lumber industry in Wisconsin before heading overland with his brother to California in 1849. He came to California, however, not to be a gold miner, but instead he speculated in real-estate and began a mercantile business. Though his business was burned out by a fire in San Francisco in 1851, he quickly rebuilt and soon was the largest commission merchant in the city. He was also largely involved in the politics of the city and was a prominent member of the city's Committee of Vigilance, which served to keep crime under control in the raucous city. In 1852, Coleman went east to Boston, where he was wed, and soon thereafter established his shipping line, with offices first at 88 Wall Street in the Tontine Building and later at 161 Pearl Street in New York. From about 1857 to 1870 Coleman resided in New York, though he made many trips to California to check on his business operations there. Many prominent clippers, including *Anglo-Saxon*,

VII. Titan: *Clipper Ship Owners and Agents*

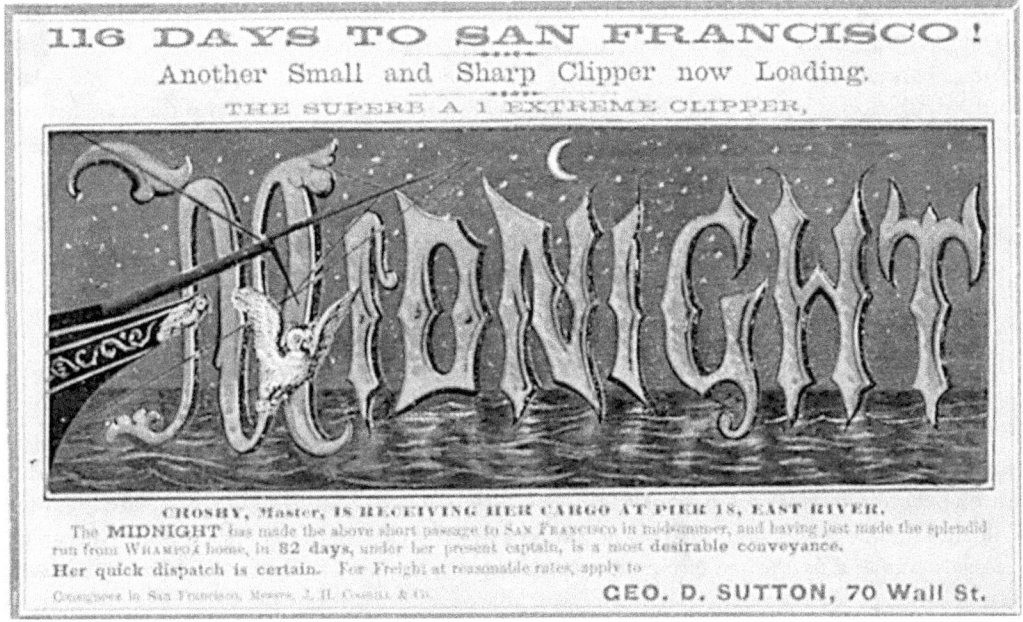

Sailing card for the clipper *Midnight*. This card advertises a California voyage made by this Portsmouth clipper under the Sutton flag in 1865, eleven years after the 116 day run touted at top. This voyage was the only one made under Captain Crosby, the passage taking a tedious 142 days (author's collection).

Asterion, Challenger, Cyclone, Comet, Carrier Dove, Derby, Emerald Isle, Flora Temple, Flying Scud, George Peabody, Governor Morton, Hornet, Mary Robinson, Neptune's Favorite, Osborn Howes, Spitfire, Starlight, Syren, Twilight, Young America, Sea Nymph, Wizard King, and *David Crockett*, to name just a few, served in this line, which continued for many years. By 1860, Coleman's personal holdings amounted to over $525,000 and later he would go into the steamship business. Politically, Coleman was an active Democrat in New York during the Civil War, even helping to subdue the draft riots

Eclipse Line

This line was operated by William T. Coleman and may have been the original name for his California Line. The only sailing card I've seen for this line advertises the Maine-built *Euterpe*, probably dating from 1856.

Timothy Davis & Company Line

This Boston-based agency was better known as ship brokers, involved in the business of buying and selling ships, including the famed Portsmouth-built clipper *Nightingale* in 1851. However, they also served as shipping agents for the Medford-built *Kingfisher*, chartering that ship for a voyage or two, and the McKay-built *Romance of the Sea*.

Sutton & Co./George Howes & Co. Dispatch Line

This New York line was one of the premier clipper lines of the 1850s and 1860s and continued in operation to the 1890s. Its primary operator was merchant E.B. Sutton, who originally partnered with John Ogden. They advertised the clipper *John Q. Adams* (not a clipper at all) sailing in their line for San Francisco in 1849 (Cutler, p. 146). George D. Sutton would later take over the firm by the 1860s, while early on Ogden went to California to establish his own line. In San Francisco, Sutton's partner was George Howes & Co., while the firm of Sutton & Beebe handled business in Portland, Oregon. These firms together operated a large number of clippers over the years between New York and San Francisco and other Pacific Coast ports, including the following: *Aurora* (early 1856), *Phantom* (1856), *Black Hawk, Black Prince, Comet, Eureka, Galatea, Hornet, John Gilpin, Lookout, Manitou, Midnight, Napier, Ocean Express, Orpheus, Panama, Prima Donna, Radiant, Sea Serpent, Skylark, Thatcher Magoun, Winged Arrow,* and *Young America.*

Glidden & Williams Line of San Francisco Clippers

Just as William T. Coleman was the major player among New York shipping agents, in Boston that role was filled by the agents and owners William T. Glidden (born ca. 1810) and John M.S. Williams (born ca. 1818). While I have already discussed some aspects of their business as Massachusetts-based clipper ship owners above, their line of California clippers was the largest operating out of Boston and rivaled Coleman's in scope. Prior to going into the business side of things, William Glidden had first gone to sea at the age of twelve on one of his uncle's ships, and gained his first command by the age of twenty-one (Eastman and Forbes, *Yankee Ship Sailing Cards,* p. 68). In short, he knew the shipping business in all its varied aspects by the time he began to invest in clipper ships and established his line. In all, William Glidden was in the shipping business for about forty years, and from their offices on Lewis Wharf, ran their clipper line well into the 1860s. Among the clippers operating in this line, with those owned by Glidden & Williams denoted with an *, were the following: *Grace Darling, Thatcher Magoun, Westward Ho, Archer, California, Charger, Fearless, Flying Eagle, R.B. Forbes, Herald of the Morning, Robin Hood, Santa Claus, Sierra Nevada*, Starlight, Witchcraft, Radiant, Asa Eldridge, Harry of the West, King Philip, Queen of the Seas*, Morning Light*, Golden West*, Belle of the West*, Witch of the Wave*, Volunteer, John Bertram*, Winged Arrow, War Hawk,* and *Conquest.*

Merchant's Express Line of Clippers

This New York line was operated primarily by shipping agent and commercial broker Randolph M. Cooley, who for a time served as a junior partner in the shipping concern of Babcock & Cooley (with offices on the corner of Water and Wall streets in New York), which loaded the clippers *Contest* and *Wizard.* Prior to establishing his California line, Cooley was doing business on the West Coast in San Francisco. Here he not only worked at the California mercantile exchange but was also a member of the Committee of Public Vigilance, which was active in controlling crime in San Francisco. Cooley would later have his New York operations based out of the Tontine building on Wall Street, his representatives in San Francisco being DeWitt, Kittle, & Co. Among the clippers that loaded in Cooley's line, which lasted well into the 1860s, were *Polynesia, Robin Hood, Boston Light, Don Quixote, Eagle Wing, Ocean Express, Panther, Sea Serpent, White Swallow, Undaunted, Andrew Jackson,* and *Galatea.*

Celestial Line

This San Francisco concern was operated by Ogden & Haynes, the principal partner being John Ogden, who also established the Pioneer Line of clippers from New York, described above. As its name implies, this was a line of San Francisco to China (and other Far East ports) vessels. The first ship in this line, also called the Oriental Line, was the fast clipper bark *Pathfinder,* which departed for China in October 1852. Prior to the inaugural sailing, a party was held on board the *Pathfinder,* with one news account stating, "It is the first step towards establishing a regular line of packets to the antipodean world...the line...is one of immediate importance to our commercial community" (*Daily Alta California, Supplemental,* October 1, 1852). Two other clippers that operated in the Celestial Line were the ships *Mischief* and *Whistler*. Because this line, whose history is uncertain, was operated by John Ogden, it may be that ships from the East Coast that sailed in his Pioneer Line to San Francisco and continued on to the Far East did so in the Celestial Line.

Wells & Emanuel's Empire Line

Commission merchants Amos Wells and Michael Emanuel were partners in this concern, which was a major line in New York and remained in operation into the 1860s. The company operated a number of clippers, including the *Empress of the Seas,* the Mystic-built *Harvey Birch* and *Hound,* the latter in 1858, and the New York–built *Kathay* in early 1859.

Empire Line

There is one sailing card for the Boston-built clipper *Game Cock* which lists this New York line from ca. 1851, with James Smith as agent. This line may have been a predecessor to the Wells & Emanuel Empire Line.

The Race Horse Line

Information about this line is largely lacking and it is doubtful that it was ever formally established. It is usually referenced in regards to the Newburyport-built clipper *Dreadnought,* launched in October 1853, which was said to have been intended for use in the Race Horse Line of California clippers. However, this clipper was employed on the New York–Liverpool run in the Red Cross Line of packets for its first ten years or so. It is possible that the ship's New York owners, David Ogden being the managing partner, did intend to start a California line, but were perhaps deterred from doing so when all their Red Cross ships, excepting *Dreadnought,* were lost at sea by 1857.

The Eagle Line

This New York line was operated by merchant William C. Annan & Co., with offices at 94 Wall Street. Among the clippers operated under its auspices were *Archer* and *Lookout*. Annan was still in business by the early 1860s, but whether he was still in the shipping business is unknown. The striking house flag for this line depicted an eagle in flight holding a capital letter "A" in its beak.

Bingham & Reynolds

This was another partnership of two merchants, James W. Bingham being the principal. The Reynolds part of this firm is uncertain, probably one of two New York merchants, John N. (a resident of the West Indies) or Odell Reynolds. Like many other shipping merchants and agents, this concern had offices at 88 Wall Street in the famed Tontine Building but also operated in San Francisco. They loaded at least one known clipper, the *Sancho Panza,* from New York to San Francisco, and also advertised the *Queen of Clippers* loading at San Francisco direct for Callao, Peru, in November 1853.

Winsor's Regular Line

This line out of Boston was one of two major clipper concerns operating out of that port and was in operation for twenty-three years beginning in the 1850s. Merchant Nathaniel Winsor, Jr. (1806–1890), of an old Boston mercantile family, was one of the first to establish a California line and during its years of operations is said to have loaded more than 350 ships, many of them clippers, for San Francisco. Indeed, by 1860 Winsor had done so well that his personal holdings were valued at the sizeable sum of $146,000. Nathaniel's son Justin, who worked as a merchant with his father before becoming a noted scholar, librarian and historian, once said of him, "He generally comes home at night, gets a cigar, sits and thinks, thinks and thinks of his business without relaxation, and allows it even to disturb his nights; 'tis business, business, business" (Forbes and Eastman, *Yankee Ship Sailing Cards*, p. 76. Among the many clippers that loaded in Winsor's Line from India Wharf were *Ocean Rover, Seaman's Bride, Expounder, Nightingale,* and *Dashing Wave*.

Fowler's Line of New York–San Francisco Packets

This shipping company was operated by New York merchants DeGrasse (born ca. 1824) and Francis Fowler, who in May 1853 advertised the East Boston–built *Queen of Clippers* as sailing in their line (*Daily Alta California*, May 21, 1853). What other ships they may have chartered or loaded is unknown. Like many agents, the Fowlers were active early on in San Francisco business affairs, but how long-lived their line may have been is uncertain. By the 1860s DeGrasse Fowler was a merchant residing just outside New York in Paterson, New Jersey.

Charles Brewer & Co.'s Line of Boston and Honolulu Packets

This company, whose owners were natives of Boston, had its beginnings as far back as the 1820s, when mariner turned businessman James Hunnewell started a small trading outfit in Honolulu, taking in as partners Bostonians Henry Pierce and Thomas Hinckley. Captain Charles Brewer of Boston joined the firm in 1845, the firm subsequently known as Pierce & Brewer, and later was controlled entirely by Brewer. This company traded in a variety of whaling products, as well as sugar and dyewoods, and by the late 1850s was also acting as shipping and commission merchants (Forbes and Eastman, *Other Yankee Ship Sailing Cards*, pgs. 68–69). While this firm primarily employed smaller ships and barks in their line, they owned the Medford-built clipper *Syren* for many years and later purchased the small clipper *Raduga*, operating her in their line for about ten years beginning in 1863.

Hawaiian Packet Line

Like Brewer's line, this line operated between Boston and Honolulu, but to what extent is unknown. Its agent in Boston was Charles Brooks, while at Honolulu its agents were Aldrich, Walker & Co. The line employed at least one clipper, *Onward*, probably in the mid–1850s.

Shipper's Line of San Francisco Packets

This New York line was in operation from at least 1853, if not earlier, and well into the 1860s. Its agents at first were Earle & Weed, including merchant John I. Earle and probably the merchant William Weed, with offices on Wall Street, as well as George Bulkley, whose office was located on the South Street waterfront. Later on, Earle seems to have been the sole proprietor of this line.

The clippers in this line included the *Flying Cloud, Mastiff, Ocean Telegraph, Queen of the Pacific, Contest* and *Lookout* in 1853 and 1854, and later *Wild Rover* and *Morning Star*.

New York and California Line

This line was operated by merchant Stephen B. Babcock and Co. of New York and operated at least one known clipper, the Maine-built *Dashaway*, built by Johnson Rideout of Hallowell in 1854, and owned by Read, Page, & Co. of the same town. Stephen Babcock also worked in partnership with Randolph M. Cooley, the latter establishing his own Merchant's Express Line of clipper ships (see above).

Comstock's California Line of Clippers

This line was in operation beginning about 1860 in New York, and in January 1864 was incorporated as a partnership between Cornelius Comstock (born ca. 1825) and Robert Simonson. Though this line came along after the reign of the clipper ships had nearly ended, it provided employment for many of these ships for nearly ten years until its dissolution in early 1873. Comstock was a merchant of New York and the younger brother of two other prosperous merchants with ties to the trade of the day in both New York and Boston; the eldest, Samuel, was a partner in the firm of Howland & Aspinwall from 1848 until his death in 1867, while William Comstock served as a merchant in China representing Howland & Aspinwall, and later was junior partner in the Boston firm of Bush & Comstock and heavily involved in the China trade. As for Cornelius Comstock's partner, Robert Simonson, he was surely the ship expert in the firm, having commanded the Newburyport-built clipper *Daring* from 1859 to 1863 (which was owned by Bush & Comstock), before going into business with Cornelius Comstock. The long-time agent for Comstock in San Francisco was Albert Dibblee. As might be expected, the Comstock Line employed many of the clippers owned in Boston by his brother's firm, as well as many other vessels (including non-clippers), and though the line was based out of New York, most of the clippers it managed were Massachusetts-built ships. Among the clippers sailing in the Comstock Line at one time or another were *Charmer, Daring, Harry Bluff, Wild Hunter, War Hawk, Reynard, Kingfisher, Aurora, Belle of the Sea, Carrier Dove, Celestial Empire, Comet, Conquest, Criterion, David Crockett, Galatea, Emily Farnum, George Peabody, Goddess, Golden Fleece, Governor Morton, Great Republic, Haze, Intrepid, King Philip, Lookout, Malay, Messenger, Monsoon, Nightingale, Panther, Prima Donna, Queen of the East, Quickstep, Radiant, Rattler, Red Gauntlet, Ringleader, Sea Serpent, Sierra Nevada, Snow Squall, Twilight, White Swallow, Wild Hunter, Wild Pigeon, Witch of the Wave,* and *Young America*. These ships and many others made voyages not just to California, to which they shipped such varied goods as candles, tobacco, coal, animal hides, and whiskey, stationery, printing ink, butter, lard, bacon, and iron, but also to and from Europe and the Far East. At least one of Comstock's ships even carried naval stores from the New York Navy Yard to the Mare Island Navy Yard in 1869. On one of their vessels shipping coal from Cardiff, Wales to Manilla, the *Reynard* in 1862, Comstock & Co. paid ⅛ of the freight proceeds to the clipper's owner, Bush & Comstock. After the Comstock and Simonson partnership was dissolved, Cornelius Comstock continued in the shipping business into the 1880s, including a short-lived partnership lasting from 1876 to 1879. He later, in the 1890s, was president of a Massachusetts lumber company.

Clipper Ship Insurance and Surveys

While financial and business laws and regulations in the 1850s were certainly more free-wheeling and much less restrictive than they are in modern times, that does not mean that there weren't self-imposed practices that were conducted in the marine trade of the day to protect both a shipowner and his backers, as well as the merchants who shipped their goods aboard the clippers. Indeed, by the 1850s the marine insurance business in America, though not well-regulated, was well established and the vast majority, if not all, of the clippers and the voyages they made were protected by at least several insurance policies.

Prior to the 1800s marine insurance was primarily underwritten by private individuals, but by 1820s many insurance companies had been formed and by the time the clipper ships appeared on the scene there were many established companies that specialized in maritime matters. Among these were the Atlantic Insurance Co. (later Atlantic Mutual), Great Western Insurance Co., Columbian Insurance Co., Orient Mutual Insurance Co., Mercantile Mutual Insurance Co., Sun Insurance Co., New York Insurance Co., Union Insurance Co., Ocean Insurance Co., Pacific Insurance Co., Neptune Insurance Co., Commercial Insurance Co., Boston Marine Insurance Co., India Fire and Marine Insurance Co., Commerce Insurance Co., and the Phoenix Insurance Co. The largest of these companies was the Atlantic Insurance Co., which was established in 1838 before the clippers came on the scene (and lasted until it went defunct in 2010). Likewise, the Boston Marine Insurance Company had a long history, having been established in 1799.

The voyages of clipper ships involved three kinds of insurance. The first under discussion is that covering the ship itself which could be purchased by shipowners on either a time basis (usually one year) or on a per voyage basis (Evans, Jr., p 38). A second type of insurance that was also underwritten was that covering a ship's cargo and was purchased by the owner of that cargo. Premiums paid for this kind of protection covered not only the entire loss of a cargo, say if a ship was lost at sea or went ashore and the cargo was rendered a total loss, but also if a cargo was damaged during the voyage, perhaps due to shifting during a violent storm or damage that resulted from sea water getting into a ship's hold. As clippers often shipped cargos for many different consignees, the loss of an entire clipper cargo could affect many different insurance companies and resulted in a tangled financial mess (and much paperwork) for the clipper ship owner. Additionally, some cargos were

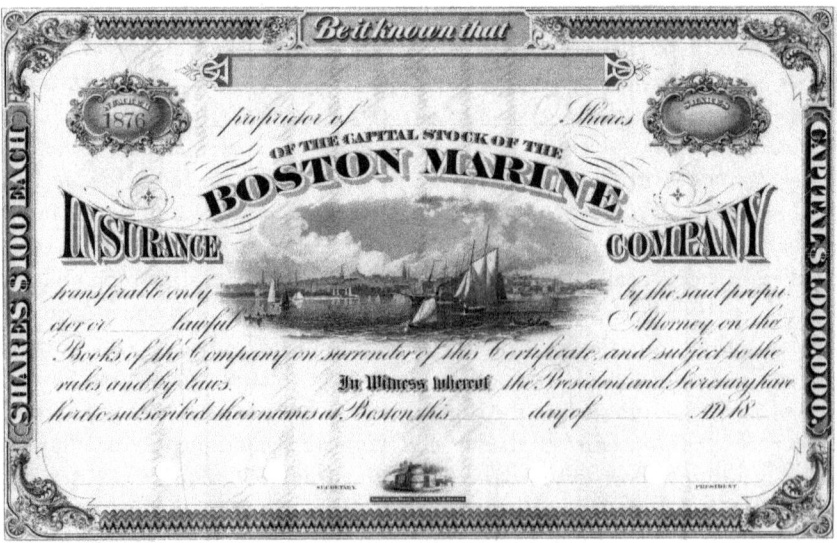

Boston Marine Insurance Company stock certificate. Companies like this one were active during the clipper ship era, insuring voyages to all parts of the globe. Times were good when successful voyages were made, but insurance companies often suffered large business losses with such clipper disasters as the burning of the *Great Republic* and the wreck of the *San Francisco* (author's collection).

VII. Titan: *Clipper Ship Owners and Agents* 189

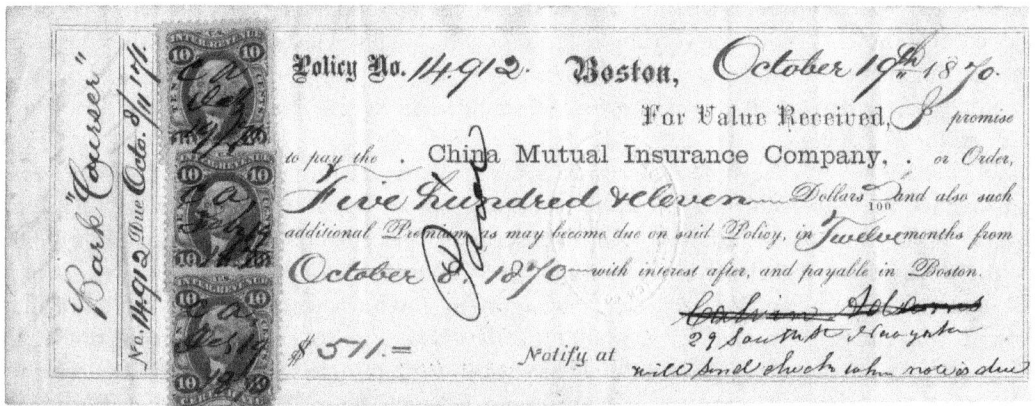

China Mutual Insurance Company receipt, 1870. Merchant ship voyages, clippers included, were insured for the duration of a voyage or for a specific time period. The Maine-built bark *Courser* (not a clipper), for which this receipt was issued, was insured for one year at a substantial cost (author's collection).

insured at higher rates, including such bulk commodities as guano or grain, because they were either more difficult to load and transport or, in the event a ship was in distress, the probability of salvaging even a portion of such cargos was unlikely. A third type of insurance purchased was that covering the freight money earned (generally not paid until the freight was successfully delivered) by the owner or the shipping agent operating the clipper. Of course, even with these types of insurance there were many variables to take into account that also affected insurance rates; some of these were intangibles, such as the reputation of a ship and whether or not she had a record for delivering cargos in sound condition, or was known as a ship that made fast passages. Among those clippers that were a favorite among shippers because they consistently delivered their cargos in good order were the *David Crockett, Young America, Prima Donna,* and *Golden State,* while those that had less than stellar reputations include *Eureka* and perhaps *Sword Fish.* Of these ships mentioned above, the *Crockett* was so successful in delivering her cargos that she "is said never to have cost the underwriters one dollar" (Howe & Matthews, p. 125), while *Sword Fish,* though a fast ship, was very sharp and took on so much water that she gained the nickname "Diving Bell." This clipper was not only despised by the sailors that manned her, but was sold by her original owners within three years of her building, though the reasons for the sale are unknown. Yet anther variable in determining insurance rates was the time of the year a voyage was being made; those ships that had to round Cape Horn in wintertime were subject to higher rates, as were those Far Eastern voyages that might be made during the monsoon season. Finally, man-made conditions also affected a clipper ship's insurance rates, including the possibility of piratical attacks on voyages to China and Indonesia, and the dangers to northern shipping that resulted from the American Civil War beginning in 1861. As to total insurance costs for any given clipper voyage, one economic historian has concluded that during the 1850s, "The cost of insurance was 6 percent of the value in the early years and 7–8 percent just before the Civil War" (Evans, Jr., p. 38). During the Civil War, Confederate raiders caused insurance rates to skyrocket prohibitively, thereby helping in the continued selling-off of American merchant ships. Sadly, these high insurance premiums were not based on reality, as relatively few merchant ships, just over 200 in all, were actually destroyed by enemy raiders, including fourteen clippers.

In regards to insurance company losses, historians Howe and Matthews list many examples of what insurance companies paid out when a clipper suffered damage or came to grief and, as might be expected based on the construction costs of these fine ships and the high freight rates they often earned, these amounts could be very high. The following are just a few examples of these losses by year during the 1850s.

1852: *Hoogly,* August 20, on maiden voyage, stranded on river at Shanghai, China, a total loss, insured for $74,000.

1853: A bad year for the underwriters with losses involving the following clippers: *Flying Arrow,* January and February, damaged in a storm while bound from Boston to San Francisco, picked up by a steamship and towed into the Virgin Islands; the steamer's owners subsequently paid $10,000 by the underwriters for their salvage efforts, another $5,000 spent on repairs; *Golden Light,* February 22, bound Boston to San Francisco, struck by lightning and burned only ten days out on maiden voyage, ship and cargo insured for $288,000; *Carrier Pigeon,* June 6, ashore at Pigeon Point, California, while nearing completion of maiden voyage, total insurance payout $195,000 on ship (valued alone at $54,000), cargo, and freight receipts; *Eclipse,* October 11, ashore at Ypala Roadstead, Mexico, valued at $90,000, "well insured"; *Great Republic,* December 26, burned at dockside New York while loading for maiden voyage, ship a total constructive loss and abandoned by owner and builder Donald McKay to the underwriters, insurance $180,000 on ship, $275,000 on cargo, despite which this was still a financial blow to McKay. This was one of the greatest insurance losses ever suffered during the clipper ship era and the largest up to that time, and does not even include the other clipper lost during this same fire, the *White Squall,* which was also burned to the water's edge and subsequently sold as is for $5,500, though her insurance losses are unknown. Both ships were soon thereafter raised and rebuilt, though smaller.

1854: *San Francisco,* February 8, bound from New York to San Francisco, ashore off the Golden Gate while entering San Francisco at end of maiden voyage, ship insured for $103,000, cargo at $365,000 (though valued at $400,000), and freight receipts $50,000, wreck subsequently sold as is by underwriters for $12,000; *Trade Wind,* June 26, bound from Mobile, Alabama, to New York with a load of cotton, collided with another ship and subsequently sank, ship valued and fully insured at $100,000, cargo $250,000, and freight receipts $50,000.

1855: *Water Witch,* June 1, wrecked at Ypala Roadstead, Mexico, while loading dyewood during her second voyage, ship valued and insured at $68,000, wreck sold for $500; *Cleopatra,* August 15, sank two days after hitting a submerged wreck while bound from Callao, Peru, to New York with guano, ship insured for $90,000.

1856: *Sting Ray,* January 9, bound from Hong Kong to New York, ashore at Fire Island while being piloted into New York Harbor, ship insured in New York for $40,000 and freight receipts for $20,000, the valuable tea cargo itself was consigned to Boston parties and insured in that city; *Sea Witch,* March 28, hit a coral reef off Havana, Cuba, and sank while carrying a load of coolies, ship (now ten years old) insured for $40,000; *Wild Duck*, October 1, bound from Foo Chow, China, for New York, went ashore on the River Min, insurance on ship and cargo $250,000; *Neptune's Car*, August to November, bound from New York to San Francisco, Captain Joshua Patten taken ill, ship subsequently commanded by his wife, Mary, and brought to San Francisco successfully with the help of the second mate; for her efforts the ship's insurers, the New York Insurance Co., paid her $1,000, and while many believed she deserved much more for her heroic efforts, the company "pleaded poverty; it had been a bad year for the insurance companies" (Whipple, *The Challenge,* p. 113).

Insurance losses like those listed above continued into the 1860s and 1870s for those few clippers that remained under the American flag, but with one difference. Now aged, some of these ships were underinsured, their owners making such a business gamble in return for lower insurance premiums. Among the clippers that were underinsured at the time of their loss in later years were the following: *Polynesia,* 1862, set on fire by crew at San Francisco, ship valued at $50,000, insured for $47,000, burned out hulk sold by underwriters for $2,300; *Charger,* 1873, ashore at Manila, Philippines, insured for only $25,000, wreck there sold for $7,595; *Orpheus,* 1875, off Victoria, British Columbia, hit by a steamship (which sank with heavy loss of life), made repairs and was trying to make port when she went ashore a total loss, ship valued at $30,000, insured for $20,000.

As can be seen from some of the above examples, one of the ways in which insurance companies recouped their losses was by selling what remained of a shipwreck, usually by auction, to salvage companies or individuals who then tried to salvage what they could from the wreck, including remaining cargo, supplies, and ship components, with the intent of realizing a quick profit by reselling these items. Of course, the salvagers were taking a gamble as they had to fight nature's elements, not only risking their own lives, but also with the possibility that a wreck could shift position or a sudden storm could come up that would complete its destruction before everything of value was removed. With such risks involved, it only made sense that some of these salvagers were former captains who well knew the ways (and value) of a ship and how and what they could salvage and resell. Two ex-clipper captains, Edgar Wakeman and Robert Waterman, were among those that did salvage work on the West Coast; Wakeman, formerly commander of the *Adelaide,* bought what remained of the New Bedford–built clipper *Sea Nymph* after she went ashore near Point Reyes, north of San Francisco, in early 1861 and made several thousand dollars in profit for his efforts, while the notorious (and very smart) Waterman, his seafaring days over after bringing the *Challenge* out on her maiden voyage, bought the wreck of the ill-fated *San Francisco* in 1854 for $12,000, but removed from her $20,000 worth of cargo.

Armed with the knowledge of what insurance companies were paying out when losses occurred on a clipper voyage, it is now left to explain by what process insurers determined a given risk when it came to the ships involved. While the insurance values for any given cargo were fairly easy to set based on valuations current at the time, the value of a clipper ship (or any vessel for that matter) was more subjective in nature and varied, depending on the age of the ship, its prevailing physical condition, as well as size and construction features, both original and those added later on. In the 1850s there were no regulations regarding the seaworthiness and overall safety of a sailing ship, and the issues regarding such were, as a matter of course, left up to the owner and a ship's commanding officer. This same was true regarding the accommodations for passengers on immigrant and packet ships. Then, as it is now in many transportation-related businesses, we can speculate that decisions regarding safety and seaworthiness were balanced between doing what was absolutely necessary to keep a ship in top condition versus those expenditures that might be viewed as less critical and perhaps possible to put off for the time being. However, in order to be insured a ship usually underwent periodic surveys to ensure that it was in sound condition. In all of the major ports these surveys were conducted by outside parties and their representatives, being men, often former captains, with seafaring experience who had no financial interest in the ship or the voyage at hand. One of the earliest surveyors at the port of New York for American Lloyd's in the late 1850s was Jabez Williams, a shipbuilder of Williamsburg and Greenpoint, New York, who built the clippers *Tornado, Simoon,* and *Eclipse.* The results of these surveys were then presented to the insurance companies, and based on a ship's sound hull condition inside and out and proper provisioning, a determination was made as to the ship's overall fitness as a risk for a given cargo and voyage. Until the late 1850s there was no formal American agency to perform these surveys, but there were two major European firms that did; these were the famed Lloyd's of London and the Bureau Veritas of Antwerp, Belgium (later Paris, France). Lloyd's was a well-known marine insurance group that first began surveying ships in the 1760s (where the terms "good," "middling," and "bad" were used), but it was not until 1834 that the firm established permanent survey standards and procedures. American clipper ships were not regularly surveyed by these agencies however, unless a special survey was required in a foreign port, or they were making voyages on behalf of British or European consignees originating from overseas ports, or in later years when they came under foreign ownership. However, in 1857 the American Lloyd's agency was established with the backing of many of the insurance companies listed above so that American ships could be surveyed for seaworthiness on a more standard basis, with the results then published in book form, just as Lloyd's of London did for British shipping, in a shipping registry that listed each ship (generally only those 100 tons or more), her builder, place of building, and the classification assigned based on the most recent survey, and the number of years that classification remained valid. Ships that were in first class condition were given an A-1 rating, this implying "confidence for the transportation of perishable cargos on long voyages" (*American Lloyd's Registry*, 1859, p. xxii), while ships with a second class rating of A-1 ½ were also deemed suitable for long voyages, while those ships of the third and fourth classes, rated A-2 and A-2 ½, were only suitable risks for voyages of shorter durations. Ships rated in fifth class condition, A-3, were liable to have trouble gaining any insurance, or paid much higher premiums if they did, as this rating implied that a cargo was almost certainly subject to sea damage. While these surveys by American Lloyd's and other agencies were primarily done for insurance purposes, not for the safety of passengers or crew, they nonetheless spoke to the seaworthiness and ultimate safety of a given vessel, and A-1 ratings were often highlighted on the clipper ship sailing cards previously discussed. However, it would not be until the 1870s that actual safety conditions regulations would begin to be established, long after most clipper ships had gone to a watery grave or to the breaker's yard.

While most clippers were given an A-1 rating, a testament to their well-built nature, many had to have special surveys done when they reached a port in distress and repairs were required. When a ship was in such bad shape after making port, most often due to storm damage, often the ship was condemned by surveyors and thereby deemed unseaworthy. A captain on the spot then had to make a decision, often in consultation with the owners, as to whether or not to undertake such repairs, or simply sell the ship as it was. This happened to many clippers, especially those that made foreign ports in distress where repair costs were very high; the Medford-built *Syren*, launched in 1851, was the longest-lived of all the clippers but was condemned in 1888 after putting into Rio de Janeiro in distress with a cargo of coal. No doubt deemed to be too old to be worth the repair bill, the clipper was sold to local interests and eventually repaired, sailing under the Argentine flag into the 1920s. Likewise, another Medford-built clipper, *Kingfisher*, put into Montevideo, Uruguay, in 1871 in a leaking condition and was condemned after survey, subsequently sold as is for $6,150 to a local ship owning family and repaired. This repaired clipper sailed for another nineteen years until being scrapped at Montevideo in 1890. Other clippers that were so condemned at foreign ports and then resurrected for more years of service include *Daring, Defiance, Webfoot,* and *Undaunted*. As can be seen from these examples, while condemnation in a foreign port was not necessarily the end of a clipper's career, it did end its time as an American merchant vessel and, though this was just a normal part of the maritime trade, served further to reduce our merchant marine. Of course, not all condemned clippers had such positive outcomes, and many a clipper's bones were left to rot on a foreign shore or were sold as scrap after making their final fated voyage. The most unusual example of a ship condemned in a foreign port and then resurrected, so to speak, was the Maine-built *Snow Squall*; she put into the Falkland Islands in distress in 1864 and was subsequently there abandoned because of the prohibitive cost of repairs, costing the insurance company some $65,000. The clipper, which we will discuss in detail further on, would not make another voyage until 1986.

VIII

Sweepstakes

Fast Passages and
Record Setting Voyages

    Though famed for their beauty, the clipper ship's place in history is today secured in large part due to their record making passages. While passages between American and Far Eastern ports, as well as those between America and Europe, were being made at an ever-faster clip by larger and better designed ships from the 1820s onward, the passages made by the clippers in the 1850s were the crowning achievement in this field for American merchant sailing vessels. Indeed, in some cases the records set by American clippers have never been eclipsed, while in other cases they have only been broken by modern sailing vessels carrying no cargo, a one or two man crew, and a multiple hull form made of modern materials (metal alloys and fiberglass), thus giving rise to that old adage that comparing these historic and modern day voyages is like comparing apples to oranges. Other than the route involved, and the stormy seas that go along with it, the only comparable aspect of such voyages widely separated in time is the bravery, skill, and endurance qualities of the men involved.

    One of the most interesting aspects of the clipper ship era were the many races that took place among those ships departing from Boston and New York, as well as other ports all around the world. These, of course, were not formally organized sailing races as we know them today, but were informal races held among clippers that were loaded and ready to go at or near the same time. During the early 1850s in particular departures were so numerous that it was possible that at any given time two, three, or even four or more clippers might be ready to depart for California. When these occasions arose, then not only was the race on, but so also did heavy bets take place between rival ship owners, merchants, and anyone involved in the shipping trade as to which ship might make the fastest passages. The Tontine Coffee House in New York, located on the corner of Wall and Water streets, was not only the early home of the New York Stock Exchange, but also was where many shipping merchants and agents had their offices, and it was here that thousands of dollars were bet and changed hands, all riding on the outcome of the clipper ship races. And these bets were not just made between merchants in New York, but also were especially heavy between New York and Boston mercantile and shipping interests. Indeed, while most everyone today with any sporting knowledge is aware of the baseball rivalry between the Boston Red Sox and the New York Yankees, few realize that the sporting competition between these two shipping cities dates even further back, not to the time when that famed baseball player "Babe" Ruth was sold by the Red Sox to the Yankees in 1919 (thereby kindling a permanent baseball rivalry), but even earlier to the days of the clippers when the rivalry was, at least for a time, equally intense. The bets about which city's clippers were the fastest even carried over into back and forth exchanges in the newspapers of the day, where partisans for each city, or even a particular ship, would often write letters to the editors of local papers detailing their support. These media-related accounts are also found out west in the pages of California papers and can be quite humorous at times; in an exchange between readers calling themselves "Yankee" and "Challenge" in the *Daily Alta California,* "Yankee," certainly a native of Massachusetts, wrote to his rival that "His *challenge* ship has arrived...but her performance did not, I think, equal New Yorker's expectations," and goes on to say that "all Bostonians...are content to wait till perchance some *flying cloud* passes over born in a New York Ship Yard" (January 21, 1852). The New Yorker calling himself "Challenge" responded soon after that his rival "should not be surprised at anything which goes to show the superiority of New York clippers," further stating, "The Flying Cloud was built at Boston by a man who learned his trade in New York, on New York capital, and after a model approved by New York merchants simply because materials and labor, as well as wooden nutmegs and hams, are cheaper in Yankee land than in New York, and who knows but that 'New York' on the Flying Cloud's stern helps her along a knot or two an hour" (January 23, 1852). Given such spirited exchanges as this in print, is it any wonder that the betting was fierce early on between the clipper partisans of New York and Boston!

American ship owners, however, did not confine their rivalry to our country, but were also brash enough to bet their clippers against ships of any nation and sometimes did so in a big way; the American Navigation Club, with clipper owner Daniel Bacon of Boston as its president, made a ten thousand pound challenge in September 1852 to the "ship-builders of Great Britain to a ship-race, with cargo on board, from a port in England to a port in China and back" (Clark, p. 202). When no response to the challenge was received by the Americans, they even offered to give any English challenger a head start of two weeks, allowed the ship to have a hand-picked crew of experienced China trade sailors of any nationality, and upped the ante to 20,000 pounds. Even with these terms, no English ship dared to match the challenge. Interestingly, while the American Navigation Club challenge was still open, the owners of the Portsmouth-built *Nightingale*, Sampson & Tappan of Boston, also offered up a bet of ten thousand pounds sterling in late 1852 to anyone interested in a race to China and back, but no takers were found, either among the British clipper owners or their fellow Americans. This bet, it should be noted, was offered up despite the fact that *Nightingale*, due mostly to her sailing at a time of unfavorable weather, finished second to last among the seven clippers of both nations making tea passages home that year, her 110-day passage being bested by another Portsmouth-built clipper, the *Witch of the Wave* (90 days), as well as *Challenge* (105 days), *Surprise* and the British-built *Chrysolite* (106 days), and the British-built *Stornoway* (109 days).

Before discussing some of the record voyages of the clippers, it will also be of interest to highlight some of the early clipper ship races to California that took place in the early 1850s. One of the earliest and most interesting of these contests was that that involved the experienced New York–built *Sea Witch* (907 tons), the Massachusetts-built *Raven* (711 tons), and the New Hampshire–built *Typhoon* (1,611 tons) in late 1851. The last two of these clippers were newly-built and were of extreme model, while the *Sea Witch* was not quite as sharply built and was by this time five years old and had experienced some hard driving in her early days in the China trade. The race began in early August, with the *Witch* and *Typhoon* departing from New York on August 1 and 4, respectively, while *Raven* departed from Boston on August 6. The *Raven* led the three ships at first, but by the time they were off the coast of Brazil, the *Witch* was neck and neck with *Raven*, while *Typhoon*, despite her size advantage, trailed just a bit. The race continued in this fashion around Cape Horn and into the Pacific, but as the ships headed toward the equator, *Typhoon* gained heavily on her rivals and led all three ships into San Francisco. However, her lead was not quite big enough to gain her the victory. From the equator to San Francisco, the *Witch* lagged just a bit while the *Raven* continued her speedy ways and ended up the winner, making San Francisco in 105 days versus the 106 day passage of *Typhoon* and the 110 day voyage of the *Witch*. This victory by the *Raven*, built by Captain James Hood at Somerset, was even more remarkable given her small size and the fact that no other ship of her size had ever before bested the famed *Sea Witch* (Clark, p. 192). To gain the full impact of this three-way contest, however, the reader must use his imagination due to the lack of specific details; that the weather, except for that around Cape Horn, was fine sailing weather is known, but otherwise we can well imagine the hard driving captains, George Fraser of the *Witch*, Charles Salter of *Typhoon*, and William Henry of the *Raven*, setting all sail to gain every bit of air they could while lookouts kept an anxious watch for their rivals. We can imagine, too, on the final stretch of the course from the equator to the Golden Gate, that all three commanders pushed their men hard and worked for every bit of wind they could gain to carry their clippers along. Captain Salter, in the lead, perhaps was hopeful that he had left his rivals far enough behind to carry the day, while Captain Fraser, the hard-driving Scotsman who had first served as mate on the *Witch* under Robert Waterman and was later murdered by one of his own officers (Howe & Matthews, pgs. 570–71), was probably in a foul mood as his ship faded to third place. Finally, we can also picture Captain Henry and the tired crew of the *Raven* when they made port, inquiring of the pilot the status of the other ships, and the subsequent joyous mood aboard the ship when it became known that they had bested the passage of two clippers that, in the mind of most nautical experts, they had no business beating. Such were the joys and disappointments of the clipper ship races.

Of course, this 1851 race was just one of many such contests that took place in the years between 1851 and 1854. Several other notable races on the run out to California include that between the William Webb–built *Sword Fish* and the Donald McKay–built *Flying Fish* in 1852, and that between the *Flying Fish* and the *John Gilpin* in 1852 and 1853, while on the run from California back to the East Coast the most famous race by far was that in 1853 between the New York–built *Contest* and the Boston-built *Northern Light*. The first of these races is important because it pitted two of the finest of the clippers ever built by the two most renowned of all the clipper ship builders. Though McKay's *Flying Cloud* was undoubtedly the fastest clipper ever built, in this contest Webb's *Sword Fish*, commanded by Captain David Babcock, made the fourth fastest passage on record (90 days, 16 hours), beating *Flying Fish* by almost ten days. However, the *Flying Fish*, one of McKay's best clippers, redeemed herself the following year when racing against the *John Gilpin*, another Boston-built clipper crafted by McKay's main Boston rival, Samuel Hall. The McKay clipper won the race, making the Golden Gate in just a few hours over 92 days, but the *Gilpin*, a medium clipper that measured some 500 tons less than her rival, also made a fine run of several hours short of 94 days. Finally, the race homeward between the *Northern Light* and *Contest*, a Boston versus New York contest, was an interesting and historic run; the *Light* (117 days) was beaten on the passage out to California by *Contest* (100 days), but the tables were turned when the *Light* made a record passage home in 76 days, 6 hours, besting the 80 day, 8 hour passage of *Contest*. With this record passage, Boston newspapers crowed about the victory, while the backers of the New York clipper whined in response that in the round trip passage overall their ship was the victor (which was true) and the subsequent challenge was made that "if the owners of the *Northern Light* feel inclined to bet on a race with the *Contest*, we will accommodate them" (Howe & Matthews, p. 105). As far as is known, the offer of a race was never accepted by the *Light*'s owner, Captain James Huckins, probably because his clipper had been badly strained on the record voyage.

Finally, of the many ocean routes on which the American clippers made historic runs, I have listed below some of the most important of these along with a discussion of the clipper that set the record, as well as those rival ships that were close runners-up. As with anything that has to with record-setting events, these voyages in some cases have engendered great controversy. Perhaps the greatest debates of all are those involving the determination as to when a particular voyage had begun and at what point it had ended. Records, which include surviving ship's logs kept by the captain (usually considered definitive proof), data from marine intelligence reports in local newspapers (not always reliable), and other personal accounts are sometimes vague, for example, as to what time, either the day or down to the hour, when a ship left port under escort of a pilot boat, while at the arrival port the debates often center around both when the ship gained a pilot (or if a delay was incurred in doing so), versus when the ship actually arrived in port. Sometimes a clipper commander could not obtain a pilot to bring him into port because the pilot was busy with another ship, or perhaps the weather conditions were poor and no pilot was in the offing. These differences are usually measured in mere hours but, as we will see in regards to the California run, these few hours were sometimes the difference in determining whether a record was set or not. Thus it is that records or fast passages are often qualified as having been made from either port to port, or pilot to pilot.

While there have been some disagreements on a few of these records among the major clipper historians (Carl Cutler, Octavius Howe and Frederick Matthews and Captain Arthur Clark), I have largely followed the judgments of Carl Cutler, as published in his *Five Hundred Sailing Records of American Built Ships* (1952). Though published over sixty years ago, Cutler's work is still definitive in this area of clipper ship activities.

New York to the Far East

The direct run on this route was primarily performed by those clippers directly built for the China trade and it is thus of interest to note that the record holders were not the large clippers of the 1850s but the pioneer clippers of the 1840s. The all-time record to any Far East port is held by the appropriately named *Oriental*, which made an 80 day, 10 hour passage from New York to Hong Kong in mid–1850. So fast was this passage that the 1,003-ton *Oriental* was subsequently chartered by British merchants at a price that was double the going rate. The runners-up on this route were the 1,246-ton *Nabob* (84 days) in 1857 and the *Houqua* (85 days, 17 hours) in 1846, this last passage notable because the 583-ton *Houqua* was considerably smaller. One other passage of note on this run was that of the *Samuel Russell* out to Canton, under the command of Captain Joseph Limeburner (later commander of the *Great Republic*), made in 93 days in 1851 and 1852. This passage was made against the prevailing monsoon season and was said to be the "best run for season ever known" (Cutler, *Five Hundred Sailing Records*, p. 82).

The Far East to New York and Boston

The record on this run was set in March 1849, just at the time the gold rush was underway in California, when the *Sea Witch* arrived at New York after a passage of 74 days, 14 hours from Hong Kong under Captain Robert Waterman. He also made the second and third fastest passages on record, both from Canton, China; commanded the *Sea Witch* on a 77 day passage in 1847 and 1848, and set the initial record when he drove the old packet *Natchez* home in 78 days in April 1845. Interestingly, no clipper built in the decade of the 1850s would beat these passages, and only one, the Portsmouth-built *Sea Serpent*, would join these ships in breaking the 80 day barrier, arriving from Canton in 79 days in March 1856. One other clipper that broke the 80 day mark was the *Rainbow* (built 1845) under skipper John Land, who also made a 79 day passage from Canton to New York in 1846. In regards to voyages made from Shanghai to New York, the *Swordfish* set the mark of 81 days in 1859 and 1860, breaking the old record of 82 days shared by the *Surprise* (1857) and the *N.B. Palmer* (1858 and 1859). While the run sailing from Canton direct to Boston was not as common among clippers (most big cargos were landed in New York), the record holder on this run is the Medford-built *Shooting Star*, which made her arrival in 84 days in 1851 and 1852.

Clipper ship *Red Jacket*. This Currier & Ives print from 1855 shows the clipper in the ice off Cape Horn while voyaging from Australia to Liverpool in mid–1854. This Pook-designed clipper, built by Deacon George Thomas in 1853 at Rockland, Maine, made the record run on the New York–Liverpool run during her maiden voyage under Captain Asa Eldridge (courtesy Library of Congress).

New York to India

This record is held by the *Sweepstakes*, the extreme clipper built by Daniel and Aaron Westervelt, the young sons of renowned New York builder Jacob Westervelt. This ship arrived at Bombay in July 1857 under the command of George Lane (a relative of the famed marine painter Fitz Henry Lane) after a 74 day passage. The only other ship to crack the 80-day barrier on this run was another New York–built clipper, the *Jacob Bell*, which arrived at Bombay in June 1856 in a passage of 77 days.

India to Boston and New York

A Portsmouth-built clipper owns the record on this route. The record 81-day run to the United States from India by the *Witch of the Wave*, which arrived at Boston from Calcutta in July 1851, has stood for all time, though several other clippers came close. The Donald McKay–built *Staffordshire* arrived at Boston from Calcutta in 82 days in March 1852, while the Portsmouth-built *Charger* made the same voyage in 82 days in March 1859, though local news reports credited her with an 81-day run. The fastest run to New York was performed by the *Whirlwind* in 83 days in 1855 and 1856 from Calcutta, while the medium clipper *Webfoot*, built at Cape Cod arrived at New York from Calcutta in a passage of 85 days in March 1859.

San Francisco to the Far East

This route was typically the second leg on a voyage that originated at New York, Boston, or another East Coast port. The most common destination ports in the Far East were Shanghai, China, Hong Kong, and Manila in the Philippines. In regards to the first named port, the William Webb–built extreme clipper *Sword Fish* holds the palm on this voyage (which measures over 7,000 miles), arriving in July 1853 in 32 days, 9 hours. The runner up on this route was the 34 day, 4 hour passage made by Donald McKay's *Romance of the Sea* in December 1856. For those clippers making the run to Hong Kong, the Connecticut-built *Pampero* holds the record, making a passage of 31 days in early 1854, followed by the 35 day passage of the *Challenge* in 1858 and 1859. For the run to Manila, two Boston-built clippers share the record passage of 36 days, the Samuel Pook–designed *Fearless* (1856) and the *Winged Arrow* (1854).

East Coast U.S. to the United Kingdom

The records on this run can be a rather confusing lot when looked at on an individual basis as a number of major ports, including New York, Boston, Portsmouth, and Baltimore each have their own record holder. Even when the actual distance between these ports is taken into account, an exact accounting of the overall record holder cannot be made without some speculation. The longest of these common routes were that from New York to London (3,442 miles), followed by New York to Liverpool (3,332 miles), and Boston to Liverpool (3,058 miles). The fastest passage given this information is probably the fastest from New York; the big clipper *Red Jacket* under the command of the old packet captain Asa Eldridge arrived at Liverpool in January 1854 after a passage of 13 days, 1 hour, 25 minutes, dock to dock. Not far behind is the passage made from Boston to Liverpool by the *James Baines* on her maiden voyage in September 1854, taking 12 days, 6 hours from Boston Light to Rock Light and 12 days, 12 hours port to port. However, if we look at the record on the longest of the routes listed above, the run of the *Simoon* from New York to London in 14 days in early 1855 also compares favorably, especially considering her size disadvantage in comparison to the *Baines* and *Red Jacket*. Yet another notable and fast passage occurred in May 1851 when the *Typhoon* made the run from her port of building, Portsmouth, to Liverpool (a 3,038 mile voyage) in 13 ½ days port to port, and would have arrived in under 13 days but was delayed by fog. Other notable clipper passages to the UK include the following:

Clipper ship *Dreadnought*. This Currier & Ives print from 1854 shows the "Wild Boat of the Atlantic" off Sandy Hook, New York, on February 23, 1854, after her nineteen day passage from Liverpool. This Red Cross Line packet, commanded by Captain Samuel Samuels, was the fastest and longest lived of the Red Cross ships.

Sierra Nevada, arrived at Liverpool from Hampton Roads, Virginia (3,246 miles), in April 1855 in 15 days, passage reported as having been made in less than 14 days, but without documentation.

Dreadnought, 13 days, 8 hours from Sandy Hook to Rock Light, Liverpool, arrived June 1859. The *Illustrated London News* in its July 9, 1859, issue erroneously claimed that the famed Red Cross packet clipper had made the voyage in 9 days, arriving off Cape Clear, Ireland, on June 27, and the ship subsequently arrived at Queenstown in a total time of 9 days, 17 hours, but abstracts of the log disprove this entirely. That this clipper was one of the fastest on this run, however, is without dispute, for in late 1854 she made the same passage pilot to pilot to pilot in 13 days, 11 hours.

Ino, 12 days land to land, 13 days, 13 hours port to port, from Boston to Cadiz, Spain (3,392 miles sailed), this achieved in February 1862 while a U.S. Navy cruiser under the command of former *Flying Cloud* commander Josiah Cressy, and possibly the land to land record from the U.S. to Europe.

Racer, 14 days, from New York to Liverpool in January 1852 under Captain Henry Steele, a land to land passage of 12 days, but subsequently detained by fog.

United Kingdom to New York or Boston

The difficult westward passage from the British Isles to the United States is an interesting one in that its shared record-holders, with one exception, were not the clipper ships of the 1850s. Instead, as might be expected, the route was dominated by the packet ships that had sailed the route, month in and month out, ever since the 1820s. The fastest clipper passage was made by the medium clipper *Andrew Jackson*, which arrived at New York from Liverpool in November 1860 after a passage of 15 days. The packet ships that share the glory on this route are the William Webb–built *Yorkshire*, which made New York from Liverpool in November 1846 in less than 16 days; the 490-ton Black Ball Line packet *Columbia* in April 1830 from Portsmouth, England, in 15 days, 23 hours; and the 15 day, 14 hour passage from Liverpool to Boston made by the 352-ton packet ship *Emerald* in March 1824. All things considered, including distance (the Liverpool–Boston route was about 200 miles shorter than that to New York), the small size of this ship (half the size of *Yorkshire* and less than a third of the size of the *Jackson*), the *Columbia*'s passage is the most remarkable. It is perhaps fitting that, of all the clippers to sail this route, the *Jackson* would be the fastest; as previously discussed, not only was her commander, Captain John Williams, an experienced packet commander who knew the route well, but the flat-floored hull form of his clipper was ideal for the sailing conditions in the North Atlantic.

New York to Melbourne, Australia

The record holder on this run is held by another Webb-built clipper of extreme model, the *Mandarin* under Captain J.W.C. Parritt, arriving in December 1855 in 69 days, 14 hours. The following year, the extreme clipper *Panama*, built at New York by Thomas Collyer for the Griswolds, arrived in July after a passage lasting 74 days, 8 hours. Two other clippers, the *Whirlwind* (1855) and the Maine-built *Snow Squall* (1862 and 1863) made this run in 75 days.

Liverpool to Melbourne, Australia

The top passages on this route were made by American-built clippers, almost all of them while under British management. The record is held by the *James Baines*, one of the quartet of large clippers built by Donald McKay for James Baines' Australian Black Ball Line of packets. The *Baines* anchored at Hobson's Bay in February 1855 under Captain Charles McDonnell (formerly commander of the Canadian-built clipper *Marco Polo*) after a passage of 63 days, carrying with her 700 passengers and 1,400 tons of cargo. The second fastest passage on record, which is rather a forgotten achievement, was the 66 day run made by the New York–built *North Wind* in 1859 and 1860 while owned by Grinnell, Minturn, & Co. This passage is notable in that this clipper, built by Jacob and Abraham Bell, was only 1,041 tons in size, less than half the size of the big and powerful *James Baines*. Other runners-up on this route were the following: *Empress of the Seas* (66 days, 12 hours), arriving in August 1861 but subsequently lost to fire at Port Phillip; *Red Jacket* (67 days, 13 hours) in 1854 while under charter to the White Star Line; *Ocean Chief* (71 days) in 1854, built in Maine for the Australian Black Ball Line; William Webb's *Young America* (71 days) under Captain David Babcock in 1858; and the *Lightning* (73 days) in 1855, another of the famed Black Ball liners built by Donald McKay.

San Francisco to New York or Boston

This homeward run, when made directly without a stop for a cargo of guano or logwood off the west coast of South America, was not as prevalent in the early days as many clippers continued their voyaging from San Francisco to ports in the Far East, and the early clippers came home rather light in the way of cargo. The record holder on this run is the previously mentioned Boston-built *Northern Light*, built by the Briggs brothers of South Boston and commanded by Freeman Hatch; he drove his ship home hard in competition against the New York–built *Contest*, arriving at Boston in May 1853 after a 76 day, 6 hour passage. It was the crowning achievement of Captain Hatch's career, as evidenced by the fact that the event was later inscribed on his gravestone! Only two other clippers broke the 80 day barrier on this run, both coming close to the record. The famed *Comet*, one of William Webb's masterpieces, made the pilot grounds off New York at Sandy Hook in March 1854 in 76 days, 7 hours, while Donald McKay's fast but ill-fated *Bald Eagle* arrived in New York in May 1854 after a passage of 78 days. The record on this run by a sailing vessel would stand until April 1993, when the 53 foot trimaran *Great American II* arrived in Boston after a 69 day, 19 hour voyage. This triple-hulled vessel was manned by a crew of two and, at just six tons in size, carried no cargo, while the *Northern Light* carried home, among other things, ten tons of copper, over 1,000 animal hides, and a number of boxes and trunks of miscellaneous items. Regarding the remarkable achievement of this small craft, crewman Rich Wilson would later state that the clippers "were the most technologically advanced boats of their days, as we are.... But there's no way to compare the two. If anything, we have a much greater respect for the sailors on those boats and what they accomplished. They had it much rougher than we did" (Chamberlain, *Record 'round the Horn is eclipsed*).

New York to San Francisco

This route, the one that was virtually created by the clipper ships and dominated by them for the entire decade of the 1850s, is also the one that has, understandably, been the subject of the most debate and discussion by maritime historians and ship lovers alike for over 150 years now. And this is all because of the arguments over the few hours that separate the record holder and near record holders on this run, both of them making the run in under 90 days. But first, let's take a look at some of the clippers that also had notable voyages, those making the run in 100 days or under, which was also very fast sailing and something achieved by only a handful of ships among the hundreds of passages made out to California between the years 1849 and 1860. The voyages are here listed chronologically with the month and year of arrival and reflect the actual length of

VIII. Sweepstakes: *Fast Passages and Record Setting Voyages* 201

Clipper ship *Great Republic*. The biggest of Donald McKay's clipper creations, this giant four-masted ship was the only clipper of her type ever built. Though she made no records runs, the *Great Republic* was undoubtedly fast; her 92 day passage from New York to San Francisco in 1857 was beaten by only three other clippers. Courtesy the Library of Congress.

the voyage and do not include any net passages, whereby times spent in a port along the way (usually due to storm damage) for a given vessel are deducted. The initials refer to the shipbuilder.

Ship	Passage
Sea Witch (July 1850)	97 days, the first record holder (S & D)
Surprise (March 1851)	96 days, 15 hours, a record at the time (SH)
Flying Cloud (August 1851)	89 days, 21 hours, third fastest on record (DM)
Sword Fish (February 1852)	91 days (WW)
Flying Fish (January 1853)	92 days, 4 hours (DM)
John Gilpin (February 1853)	93 days, 20 hours (SH)
Contest (February 1853)	100 days (Westervelts)
David Brown (March 1854)	99 days (R & J)
Romance of the Seas (March 1854)	96 days (DM)
Witchcraft (August 1854)	98 days (PC)
Antelope (March 1856)	97 days (P, P & S)
Great Republic (March 1857)	92 days (DM)
Sweepstakes (May 1857)	93 days (Westervelts)
Twilight (April 1858)	100 days (CM)
Sierra Nevada (March 1860)	98 days (T & L).

It is interesting to note that of the above passages, some of the great New York clipper builders (WW) William Webb, the Westervelts, (S & D) Smith & Dimon, (P, P & S) Perrine, Patterson, & Stack, and (R & J) Roosevelt & Joyce are represented, as are those from Massachusetts (DM) Donald McKay, (SH) Samuel Hall, and (PC) Paul Curtis. Outside of these two states, there is also one Connecticut builder (CM) Charles Mallory and one New Hampshire builder (T & L) Tobey & Littlefield on the list of fast California passages. Noticeably absent are any Maine-built clippers, though several runs were made by clippers launched in the state that came close to the 100 day mark.

As can be seen from the above passages accomplished in under 100 days, only one ship cracked

Clipper ship *Flying Cloud*. This famed flyer was the best known of all of the McKay-built clippers, and was one of the fastest. Under Captain Josiah Creesy, ably assisted by his navigator-wife Eleanor, the *Cloud* is the only ship ever to make two passages of under 90 days on the New York–San Francisco run. The clipper is here depicted from a Currier & Ives print issued in 1852 after she made her then record setting passage in 1851. Courtesy the Library of Congress.

the 90 day barrier, Donald McKay's *Flying Cloud,* prior to 1860. Incredibly, after the record passage of 1851, one that set the bar high for all the subsequent California voyages of the 1850s, the *Cloud* did it yet again in 1854, arriving at San Francisco after a passage of 89 days, 8 hours in April 1854, thereby shaving 13 hours off her record mark. This record was broken, and the all-time best mark for a wooden sailing ship thereby set, on March 23, 1860, when the medium clipper *Andrew Jackson* arrived at San Francisco after an 89 day, 4 hour passage. The historic and speedy passage of this ship, built by Irons & Grinnell at Mystic, Connecticut, is measured from pilot to pilot, not port to port, and would much later on be the subject of a bit of controversy. Partisans on the side of the *Flying Cloud* would later claim that the *Jackson* departed from the pilot grounds at New York on December 25, 1859, and did not take her pilot off the Farallon Islands at San Francisco until 8 A.M. on March 24, 1860, thus making her pilot to pilot passage 89 days, 20 hours. It is interesting to note that the *Jackson*'s record passage was not disputed at first for many years, and that even the *Cloud*'s owners, Grinnell & Minturn, would later acknowledge the fact that their ship's record was beaten in a letter written in 1892 (Cutler, p. 364). However, at an unknown point after this time, the *Jackson*'s passage began to be questioned, so much so that the normally reliable historians Howe & Matthews would later tersely claim in their 1926 work that "the *Jackson* broke no records" and that any record run claimed by the ship was "mythical" in nature (Howe & Matthews, p. 8). After making this statement, the historians go on to churlishly state that "the fast passages of the *Jackson* were due to hard driving and also to a succession of winds favorable to her running near to a direct course, rather than to her ability to move through the water rapidly" (Howe & Matthews, p. 9). These authors, however, were only kidding themselves and, being true experts in their field, surely knew better at heart; true it was that the *Jackson*'s commander, Jack Williams, was a hard driving captain, but certainly no more so than the *Cloud*'s Josiah Cressy, while the claim that the *Jackson* had better weather is simply ridiculous. While weather is and always will be a deciding factor in any ocean voyage, record runs are not handicapped based on this factor and the victor is and always has been the ship that arrives at its destination first, come hell or high water. The academic debate over the *Jackson*'s fast passage was, by 1930, solved once and for all after Captain Williams' log for the voyage came to light. This important document settles the matter, clearly stating that the *Jackson* departed the New York pilot grounds at or near 1 P.M. on December 26, 1859, and arrived at the pilot grounds off San Francisco and took her pilot on March 23, 1860, at 7 A.M., making her run 89 days and 4 hours. It is interesting to note that Captain Jack Williams, as his fast voyage neared its end, was acutely aware that he might have the chance to best the record of the *Flying Cloud*; on March 16, one week from reaching San Francisco, he writes in his log, "I am in hopes yeat [*sic*] to Do as well as the Flying Clouds time" and the day before taking a pilot, while experiencing "Squalley" weather, writes that "we are good for the Flying Cloud yeat [*sic*]" (Cutler, pgs. 538–39). The *Andrew Jackson* was, indeed, good enough, if only by a few short hours, to beat the *Flying Cloud*. The *Cloud*'s second place status on this route, it should be noted, takes nothing away from the fame of the ship, as the *Jackson* herself was a notable ship that made consistently fast voyages.

As with some other clipper records of old, the New York to San Francisco run has also been bested by modern day sailing craft; in February 1989 the 60 foot American racing yacht *Thursday's Child* made the Golden Gate, manned by a crew of three, in 80 days, 20 hours. Since that time the record has been broken twice, the current mark being held by the French racing craft *Gitana 13*, a 110-foot catamaran with a crew of ten (no cargo), which made the run in 43 days, 38 minutes in February 2008.

The Fastest of the Clipper Ships

Finally, perhaps one reason why the debate about the record on the California run continues to be discussed to this day is the simple fact that it is tied up, mistakenly so, perhaps, among Americans with the overall question of which clipper ship was the fastest of them all. While the *Andrew Jackson*

Clipper ship *Sovereign of the Seas*. This Donald McKay–built clipper, which was commanded by his brother, Captain Lauchlan McKay, may have been the fastest of his clippers in terms of pure speed (*The Illustrated London News*, 1853).

is *the* record holder on the famed New York to San Francisco run, there can be little doubt given the available data that McKay's *Flying Cloud* was one of the fastest of all the clippers ever built, paradoxically proven by the fact that the ship made not just one passage under 90 days to California, but performed the feat twice. However, fast individual passages aside, which are a test of a clipper's performance over a long period of time, there are two other yardsticks used by historians to measure the speed records of the era in shorter bursts of time. The first of these under consideration is the top speed attainment, measured in knots per hour. Claims for these records come from several sources, including the log of a given vessel kept by her officers, abstracts of such logs, or various news accounts (which include newspapers published aboard several clippers). Four clippers are recorded as having achieved speeds in excess of 19 knots per hour, including the *Sovereign of the Seas* (22 knots), *James Baines* (21 knots), *Champion of the Seas* (20 knots), and *Defiance* (20 knots). All of these claims are fairly firmly established with the exception of that of the last named ship, and all with the exception of the latter were built by Donald McKay. The 1,600-ton *Defiance*, built by Deacon George Thomas at Rockland, Maine, and designed by Samuel Pook, was no doubt fast and probably *did* reach such a speed (accomplished on her maiden run while empty), though there is only a news account to back up this claim. In regards to other fast clippers, two others are recognized as having achieved speeds of 19 knots per hour, these being the *Lightning* and the *Great Republic*, both also built by Donald McKay, while three others have been recognized as having achieved speeds in excess of 17 knots per hour, the *Flying Cloud* (18.5 knots), *Donald McKay* (18 knots) and the *Sweepstakes* (18 knots), this last vessel a product of the Westervelt yard in New York. What is clearly evident from these lists is the dominance of Donald McKay's clippers when it came to the attainment of pure speed, due to their long length and overall size (the *Flying Cloud* being the smallest of the McKay ships on the list) and huge sail plans.

One final yardstick that has been used in measuring the speed of the clippers is that of the single-day's run, or how many miles were made on a given nautical day (running from noon on one day to noon the next day) during a given voyage. This method of measuring speed has the advantage in that it takes into account performance over a longer sustained period than the shorter bursts of speed measured in knots per hour. While a number of clippers made day's runs of 300 miles or more, the gold standard in this record category is that of 400 miles or more, which has been accomplished by only seven (and possibly two other) American-built clippers. The record holder is the aptly-named *Champion of the Sea*, which traveled 465 miles on December 11 and 12, 1854, during her run from Liverpool to Melbourne, Australia, though the total passage time of 75 days was said to have been "not quite up to expectations" (Howe & Matthews, p, 73). The runner-up in this list is the *Lightning*, which made 436 miles on her maiden voyage to Australia while fully loaded in March 1854, came close to this mark yet again, making 430 miles on March 19 and 20, 1857, and also made 420 miles on one day during yet another run in late 1854. All of these day's runs were made on the Liverpool to Melbourne route while sailing in the Australian Black Ball Line, and while the *Lightning* was not then considered the beau ideal among the crop of Donald McKay–built clippers, her performance tells another story. Finally, after the *Lightning*, five other clippers, all but one built by McKay, have day's runs to their credit of 400 miles or greater, these being the following: *James Baines* (423 miles, 407 miles, both on the same voyage in 1855, and 404 miles in 1856), *Donald McKay* (421 miles, Boston to Liverpool, 1855), *Red Jacket* (417 miles, maiden voyage New York to Liverpool January 1854, and 400 miles, July 1854, Liverpool to Melbourne), *Great Republic* (413 miles, December 1856, New York to San Francisco), and *Sovereign of the Seas* (411 miles, March 1853, Honolulu to New York). Two other American clippers may also have day's runs of 400 miles or better to their credit, though neither are documented; the Maine-built *Flying Scud* was said by her ship's surgeon to have made 449 miles in November 1854 while bound for Melbourne, but his calculations (he being no navigator) were likely off, while the *Blue*

Jacket, a fast clipper built at East Boston by Robert Jackson, may have made more than 450 miles (and attained speeds of anywhere from 20 to 23 knots) while outward bound from Australia toward Cape Horn, but this is based purely on "personal recollections" and while "within the range of reasonable possibility" (Cutler, *Five Hundred Sailing Records*, p. 12) has no other corroborating evidence. Once again, as with the records in regards to knots per hour, the McKay-built clippers, including all of his clippers designed for the Australian Black Ball Line, dominate in this category. In the end, while the debate will always continue over which among the clipper fleet of the 1850s was the fastest overall, there can be no doubt that whatever ship may be chosen, Donald McKay must have been her builder.

IX

Hurricane
Shipwrecks and Other Noteworthy Clipper Events

The life of every ship is filled with many different events, from the day of her launching to the day she is either lost or sent to the breaker's yard. These events can be classified broadly as those that were positive, which for the clippers meant fast passages of a historic nature, or those that were negative, usually incidents that either resulted in damage to a ship or the loss of the ship entirely. When compiling ship histories in general, the negative events have always been the most publicized due to the simple fact that they are the most dramatic and newsworthy. Indeed, beyond the fast, record-making passage, the voyages of the clippers, barring any calamitous events, make for rather mundane reading. For example, when we read that the clipper *Skylark*, to take one random example, made the passage from San Francisco to New York in 1861 in 93 days, and experienced light winds throughout the entire voyage and never had to reef her topsails, there is not much of interest to contemplate. At best, we can perhaps imagine the captain's frustration at his inability to get his ship going at a consistently fast clip, but otherwise there is little to command our attention. In contrast, here is a brief account of the loss of the Donald McKay–built *Mastiff*, which caught fire while on a voyage from San Francisco to Hong Kong in September 1859:

> Captain Johnson, "Here Mr. Bailey, fire in the ship!"... Call all hands aft. Rig hose to pump. Mates jump down the hatch aft ... smoke pours up in volumes.... Captain Johnson immediately gives up all hopes of saving ship, and stops pumps, and all hands go to work in clearing boats for lowering.... A British ship has been in sight the last two days, sailing with us.... Set our ensign union down, and half mast.... Captain Johnson asks me to see his wife safely in boat. She goes over the side on rope. Chief mate and I help her in. Chinese rush for the boat, beaten back.... Five boats now employed [in rescuing crew and passengers].... These boats all flying to and fro.... Captain last to leave. Flames burst out through deck at mainmast. Now nearly dark, and flames glow over the ocean.... The poor, noble *Mastiff* is abandoned. Flames mount the rigging, catch the sails, and all a mass of fire. Main and mizzen mast fall. Foremast stands long, then drops, and only a burning hull. Captain Hart of the *Achilles*, a generous, frank British sailor, takes Captain Johnson by hand. Now the excitement is over, and his duty done, the magnitude of the loss comes over him, and he says over and over, "My ship *Mastiff*! My ship *Mastiff*! Is it possible she is gone!" [McKay, pgs 315–16].

Tragic though it was, the powerful emotion in this detailed account (which came from the diary of passenger and author Richard Henry Dana) makes for interesting reading, as most such events usually do, about a clipper that otherwise was not particularly notable. These are the small bits of clipper ship history that today remain compelling, and though most of us today have never undergone such experiences as this, and others described below, perhaps we can still well imagine (or at least try!) what it may have been like to have been there. Despite the overall negative result (the loss of the ship and human life) in these kinds of events, there are nonetheless many instances of uplifting examples of heroism and herculean efforts by the commander and crews involved (win or lose) which is what has always, ever since man has gone to sea, been symbolic of man's attempts to defy or tame the elements of nature. At its heart, this is the essence of much that has been written in the field of shipwreck and maritime disaster related literature.

What follows are some of these varying life events, some common, some not so common, with examples of some of the clippers that experienced them. I have not included the previously discussed incidents relating to crew mutinies or cargo-related losses.

Gone Missing

These very words describing a vessel missing at sea were once commonly heard at one time or another in most seaport villages, towns, and cities in America and beyond during the age of sail. When a vessel goes missing in our modern world, which is a very rare occasion due to the great advances in communication and weather forecasting, there is often at least some idea of that vessel's last known position or even a mayday call. However, the circumstances surrounding a ship gone missing in the days of sail were much more uncertain; maybe a ship in peril, perhaps while rounding Cape Horn, was spotted by another vessel and her situation reported, sometimes named, often not, when she made port. Other times, there was simply no news to be had; a ship's general departure time was known from whatever port she was bound from, but she never made her intended destination, leaving her owners, as well as the captain's and crew's families to wonder what may have become of them. Indeed, the outdoor balcony located high up on many a New England seaport home, known as the widow's walk, was not so named just for quaintness, for it was here that many a captain's wife would wait in vain for her husband's ship to appear on the horizon.

Eighteen clipper ships are known to have gone missing over the years from 1848 to 1886, including one in the 1840s, five in the 1850s, nine in the 1860s, two in the 1870s, and one in the 1880s. Of course, while the cause for these losses cannot be ascertained with certainty, there are those instances where reported storm activity in the area in which a ship was voyaging is deemed the likely culprit. Those ships that went missing after the clipper ship era had come to an end, eleven in all, are perhaps not as surprising as many of these clippers still at work in the 1860s, 1870s, and 1880s were now aged and had been subject to much heavy driving earlier in their careers, making the possibility of their foundering at sea a greater possibility. The fact that only a handful of clippers went missing in the 1850s is remarkable considering the fact that the hundreds of clippers that were launched were driven all out on their incredibly long and dangerous voyages. It is also of interest to note, though certainly no negative commentary on Massachusetts shipbuilding, that with the exception of two New York ships and one Pennsylvania-built ship, all the other clippers that went missing were built in the Bay State.

The first clipper ship to go missing, rather ironically, is one of the first clippers ever built, the John Griffiths–designed *Rainbow*. Launched at New York in 1845, the famed ship was lost on her fourth voyage to the Far East when she departed New York in March 1848, bound to China via Valparaiso, Chile. The *Rainbow* was never again seen after her departure and it is speculated that she was lost off Cape Horn. The next clipper to sail into the unknown on the Cape Horn route was the Medford-built *Dauntless*, launched in 1852. She departed Boston under the command of Captain James Miller in October 1853, bound for Valparaiso, Chile, but never made her destination and was probably also lost off Cape Horn. Another clipper lost on the Cape Horn route was the Samuel Hall–built *Lantao*, built in 1849, sailed from Chile bound for Boston in October 1856. The two other clippers lost on the Cape Horn route were the Philadelphia-built *Manitou*, lost while bound from New York to San Francisco in 1859, and the Newburyport-built *Black Prince*.

This clipper was bound from San Francisco to Boston with a partial cargo of copper ore when she ran into trouble off Cape Horn. After rounding the cape, the *Prince* made contact with a British vessel off Argentina on February 15, 1865, requesting provisions and reporting water in her hold and the fact that she had been forced to jettison 80 tons of cargo. The next day a severe storm was experienced by the British vessel, and while she survived, the *Black Prince* was never again seen.

Cape Horn, however, was not the only graveyard of missing ships, as the waters of the Far East also had their perils. The Boston-built *Edwin Forrest*, while bound from New York to Hong Kong, departing August 1860, was never seen again. The *Queen of the Seas* was loaded with coal at Liverpool in 1860 bound for Shanghai, China. In September she experienced gale-force conditions while traveling in company with another ship in the Formosa channel for eight days, was missing after the gale had ended and is supposed to have been lost on the night of September 21, though no trace of the ship was ever found. The McKay-built *Bald Eagle*, which sailed from Hong Kong in October 1861 bound for San Francisco, was fully loaded with tea, rice, and $100,000 in treasure. No trace of her was ever seen after departure and though the loss is thought to have been due to a typhoon in the China Sea, piracy cannot be ruled out due to the nature of her cargo. The McKay-built *Romance of the Seas* was bound from Hong Kong for San Francisco in December 1862 and was officially posted as missing in April 1863 with a crew of 35. The *Houqua,* built in 1844, was posted missing 20 years later while bound from Yokohama, Japan, to New York in August 1864, likely lost during a typhoon. And the Medford-built *Rival* disappeared on a voyage from Rangoon, Burma (modern day Myanmar), to Falmouth, England, commencing in March 1872.

As to other clippers gone missing, two were lost in the India trade: the small *Waverly*, built by Joshua Magoun at Charlestown, Massachusetts, going missing while bound from Coringa in southeast India to Calcutta in September 1862, the possible victim of a cyclone; and the Medford-built *Eagle Wing*, which sailed from Boston for Bombay in February 1865 and was never reported. The large clipper *Monarch of the Seas*, built at New York and sold to British interests in 1865, also went

Clipper ship *Young America*. This famed clipper, built in 1853 at New York, was William Webb's masterpiece. Her long-lived career and relative good fortune made her, perhaps, the most profitable of all the clippers. She met her end in 1886 under the Austrian flag, going missing in the Atlantic due to causes unknown (Currier & Ives lithograph dated 1853).

missing on a voyage after departing from Liverpool in March 1866, but what her destination may have been is uncertain. Finally, two other clippers were lost almost certainly due to storm activity, the Newburyport-built *Driver*, a Red Cross Line packet with 372 crew and passengers aboard bound from Ireland to New York in the North Atlantic in February 1856, and the Boston-built *Grace Darling*, lost after 24 years of service while bound from Nanaimo, British Columbia, to San Francisco in January 1878. She was spotted by a passing vessel when 15 days out, hove to during a heavy storm, but never made port and is supposed to have foundered with her heavy cargo of coal and all 18 aboard. The last of the clippers known to have gone missing was the famed ex–*Young America*. This clipper was sold to Austrian in-

The clipper *Golden Light*. This Boston-built ship, depicted in dramatic fashion in this Currier & Ives print from 1853, was lost to fire on her maiden voyage shortly after her departure for San Francisco. This print is one of Currier & Ives' more unusual, and now rare, prints in their clipper ship series; instead of showing a glorious American clipper under full sail, a clipper in her death throes is here shown, thus providing the public a view of one of the many dangers encountered by these fast-sailing ships (author's collection).

terests in 1884 and renamed *Miroslav*, subsequently involved in the transatlantic trade; she departed the Delaware Breakwater February 17, 1886, for Europe and was never again seen, having likely foundered at sea after a career that lasted thirty-three years.

Maiden Voyage Losses

Shipwrecks are just a fact of life in the maritime business, but those that occur when a vessel is brand new and in the course of making its first voyage are particularly unfortunate. Sometimes, as was the case with the famed liner *Titanic* in 1912, such losses are of epic proportions. While none of the five clippers lost on their maiden voyages of the 1850s rise to this level of drama, the financial losses, as previously discussed, incurred by the owners and insurance companies were substantial. The earliest and most catastrophic of these losses was that of the Boston-built clipper *Golden Light*. Launched by the Briggs brothers of South Boston on January 8, 1853, for Captain James Huckins, her career lasted just 46 days. The fully loaded clipper subsequently departed Boston for San Francisco on February 12 under the command of Captain Charles Winsor, but it was struck by lightning and set on fire at midnight on February 22 in mid-ocean. The crew of the clipper tried to save their ship, but the newly tarred rigging carried the fire to every part of the ship and by the evening of the 23rd the battle was a losing one. The crew of 35 subsequently abandoned ship in five lifeboats and watched as, one by one, the ship's masts were toppled and the entire ship was ablaze. The five lifeboats, with that commanded by Captain Winsor in the lead, subsequently set a course to the southwest for land. Four made it to safety, three picked up by a British ship, and one made the island of Antigua, while the fifth, with eight people aboard, was never recovered.

Interestingly, another clipper that commenced her maiden voyage from Boston in early 1853 also came to grief; the Maine-built *Carrier Pigeon*, owned by Reed, Wade, & Co. of Boston, sailed for San Francisco on January 28, just fifteen days ahead of the *Golden Light*. While this ship, commanded by Azariah Doane and carrying 1,300 tons of cargo, nearly made her destination, she encountered heavy fog while approaching the California coast in the first week of June and after losing her way went ashore 50 miles south of San Francisco near Point Ano Nuevo. No lives were lost, but the ship and cargo were a total loss, subsequently sold by her insurers for just $1,500. The point of land where the clipper went ashore was subsequently named Pigeon Point and a tall lighthouse, now a historic park, was erected here beginning in 1871.

Perhaps the most publicized of these maiden voyage losses was that of the 1,307-ton *San Francisco* in February 1854. Not only had this extreme clipper, built by Abraham Bell at New York, shown promise of a great future by making a fast passage of 106 days, but her very name was symbolic of the great port city of the gold rush era that had grown to prominence virtually overnight. Captain Isaac Sitzer had made a masterful passage, beating the clippers *Ringleader, Golden City,* and *Morning Light*. However, upon entering the Golden Gate passage while under a pilot's control, the ship went ashore on the rocks at Rialto Cove. News of the wreck within the harbor spread quickly and soon many locals, including soldiers stationed at the Presidio across the Golden Gate, were on the scene plundering the wreck.

The final clippers under discussion that were lost on their maiden voyages were the *Hoogly* and *Leah*. The *Hoogly*, built by Samuel Hall at East Boston for Daniel Bacon, made a successful, if unspectacular, 127 day voyage from Boston to San Francisco in 1852, and thence went to Hawaii before departing for China on the second leg of her maiden voyage. The clipper did make Shanghai, China, in August 1852 but was stranded while bound up the Huangpu River (a tributary of the Yangtze River) and deemed a total loss to her insurers and owners, though no lives were lost in the accident. The 1,428-ton *Leah* was a clipper whose career was also short lived; built by George Greenman & Co. in Mystic in 1855 for John McGaw of New York, the ship went missing on her first voyage with no clue as to what happened or where she went down.

THE GREAT CONFLAGRATION.

THREE CLIPPER-SHIPS DESTROYED.

TOTAL LOSS OF THE 'GREAT REPUBLIC.'

Burning of the 'White Squall,' and 'Joseph Walker.'

NINE BUIDINGS DESTROYED ON FRONT-ST.

LOSS, $1,500,000.

INSURANCE, $500.000 to $700,000.

Newspaper headline, the burning of the *Great Republic* and *White Squall*. The loss by fire of the brand new clipper at her dock in New York was big news. Having been previously open to the public, thousands had come to view McKay's giant creation (*New York Times*, December 28, 1853).

Fire and Lightning Damages and Losses

Losses of this type were some of the most common in the age of sail and the clippers experienced their share. As has previously been discussed, fire could be caused internally from a variety of sources, including flammable cargos like coal that could spontaneously combust, crew accidents in handling hazardous materials, as with that that caused the loss of the *Hornet* in 1866, as well as cases of outright arson, as occurred aboard the *Telegraph* in 1857 just prior to her setting sail from Savannah, Georgia. Dockside fires, like that in New York that gutted the new *Great Republic* and the *White Squall* in December 1853, were sometimes a source of danger, as were those fire incidents caused by careless stevedores, as happened aboard the second *Golden Fleece* in 1871, while in the loading process. On the other hand, fires due to lightning strikes at sea, as described above regarding the loss of the *Golden Light*, were always a hazard, especially during

IX. Hurricane: *Shipwrecks and Other Noteworthy Clipper Events*   211

The loss of the *James Baines*. This McKay-built clipper was destroyed at the Liverpool docks after a fire broke out in her hold during unloading on April 28, 1858. This view shows her still on fire, burned to the lower deck with her masts toppled (*Illustrated Times*, May 8, 1858).

storms. The possibility of a ship being lost at sea due to fire must have been, for many sailors and passengers alike, a terrifying prospect. Not only can a wooden ship burn quickly, aided by prevailing winds that fanned the flames and fueled by most any cargo, but the chances of saving such a ship in peril were often slim. If a ship was in a position close to land, a captain and crew at least had the hope of making landfall in the ship's lifeboat, or being rescued by a passing vessel. However, when a ship was far from land and in the middle of the ocean, the chances of the ship's lifeboats being picked up or making landfall on their own were considerably dimmed, something Captain Josiah Mitchell and the survivors of the *Hornet* found out first hand under the harshest of conditions.

At least sixteen clippers, not including those lost during the Civil War, were casualties due to fire and lightning, while many others suffered damage due to these same causes. Among those clippers lost to fire while still in port were the *Invincible, James Baines, Lightning,* and *Governor Morton.* The *Invincible*, built by William Webb, was docked near Montague Street in Brooklyn on the night of September 11, 1867, when a night watchman discovered the ship on fire. While fireboats tried to put out the fire so the ship could be towed to deeper water and scuttled, the effort failed. The *Governor Morton,* built by Captain James Hood at Somerset, Massachusetts, had finished loading over a thousand bales of cotton and was at anchor above New Orleans at South West Pass on the Mississippi River when she was struck by lightning on July 2, 1877. The ship was subsequently scuttled in twenty feet of water but was burned beyond saving; 800 bales of cotton were subsequently salvaged and the remains of the ship raised and towed to New Orleans. Two of the four big clippers built by Donald McKay for James Baines' Australia Black Ball Line also succumbed to fire; the first to go was the namesake of the fleet and the ship considered by some historians to be the fastest of all the clippers, the 2,515-ton *James Baines*. In April 1858, when less than four years old, the clipper had just arrived at Liverpool from India and part of her cargo was soon unloaded. However before the rest could be discharged, including bagged rice, animal hides, and over 2,000 bales of jute, the ship caught fire and was destroyed along with much of the remaining cargo because there was not enough water to scuttle the ship. The combined insurance value of the loss was put at $170,000. In opposite fashion, the *Lightning* was partially loaded with wool and copper ore at Melbourne, Australia, in October 1869, and due to complete her loading the next day, when she caught fire in the middle of the night. While the ship was scuttled in deeper water, she was soon thereafter destroyed as a hazard to navigation. Though uncertain, the loss of both these McKay-built ships during the unloading or loading process may have been due to stevedore or crew carelessness, perhaps improper disposal of smoldering cigarettes.

Among those ships lost or damaged due to fire and lightning while at sea were the *Blue Jacket*, *Stag Hound*, *Comet*, *Typhoon*, and *Alboni*. The *Blue Jacket*, a fast clipper built by Robert Jackson at East Boston in 1854, was later sold to Australian interests and sailed in the Fox Line of packets running between Australia and New Zealand and London. The *Jacket* met her end after leaving New Zealand in February 1869; after rounding Cape Horn and near the Falkland Islands, the ship was discovered to be on fire and was subsequently abandoned on March 5. The 71 crew and passengers spent eleven days in lifeboats until they were rescued by a passing German vessel. Similarly, the crew of the McKay-built *Stag Hound* was also lucky in their ordeal by fire; the coal-carrying clipper was found to be on fire on October 12, 1861 while off the coast of Brazil. The crew fought the blaze for over twelve hours, but to no avail and the ship was subsequently abandoned in the afternoon hours. Once again, all hands were saved when landfall was made the following day. The former clipper *Comet*, built in 1851 by William Webb and a premier ship of the decade, was sold foreign in 1863 and was subsequently renamed *Fiery Cross*, an unintended portent of her future fate. The clipper was subsequently employed as an Australian packet ship and departed on her last voyage from Moreton Bay, Queensland, Australia, in April 1865 bound for London. When three weeks out the ship was discovered to be on fire and, despite efforts to control the blaze, the decision to abandon ship was made. However, of the 98 crew and passengers aboard, the lifeboats

Clipper ship *Comet*. This dramatic Currier & Ives print from 1855 shows the New York clipper, built by William Webb in 1851, caught in a hurricane off Bermuda during her second California run in October 1852. As this picture shows, the *Comet* lost her fore topmast and main royalmast and had her topsails shredded by the heavy blow. Once the weather calmed, repairs were made and the clipper made San Francisco in the respectable time of 112 days (courtesy the Library of Congress).

could only hold 80 people. Left aboard the ship were the first mate and seventeen other crewmen. Ironically, just as the *Fiery Cross* was about to sink, a passing ship arrived on the scene and was able to rescue the remaining crew. However, none of those that took to the lifeboats were ever rescued, all no doubt lost due to either heavy weather that may have capsized their boats, or due to exposure or lack of provisions once their fresh water and food had run out. More fortunate in surviving their lightning ordeals were the clippers *Alboni, Typhoon,* and *Radiant*; the former was hit by lightning during a thunderstorm while voyaging from Bremen to New York in June 1861, and though the ship was not damaged, "the smell of sulphur was so strong between decks that the passengers were in a panic" (Howe & Matthews, p. 6), while the *Typhoon*, whose racehorse figurehead was surrounded by clouds and lightning bolt emblems, was twice hit by lightning on her speedy maiden voyage from Portsmouth to Liverpool in March 1851, suffering damage to her deck cabin and one burned crewman. The last named clipper truly lived up to her name during a voyage from New York to San Francisco in July 1855, the *Radiant* being lit up when her foremast was struck by lightning, her topgallant and royal masts damaged, and the topgallant sail burned as the lightning bolt traveled downward. It is interesting to note that while there is little documentation as to what type of fittings the clippers may have carried to protect them from lightning strikes, there were systems that had been invented for the purpose and perhaps some clippers employed one of the following systems. One clipper that carried no such protection was the Portsmouth-built *Water Witch*, put over in 1853 by Fernald & Pettigrew. It is striking that one Boston writer, in discussing the fact, blamed the insurance companies for this lack of protection, stating that "like all our other fine ships, she has no lightning conductors. For this omission we hold the underwriters alone responsible" (McLean, *Boston Daily Atlas*, July 11, 1853). One of the earliest and most popular lightning conductor systems involved long lengths of chain attached to a small rod mounted on the mainmast (the tallest part of the ship) which led downward into the sea, while another, the Harris system, devised by English inventor William Harris in 1830, employed copper conductors that ran down the mast and through the deck, ending at the base of the mast. A third system was patented by Robert Forbes in 1854 and followed the old chain system in principal by conducting electricity from a lightning strike through a series of tubes down to the sea. Forbes was an innovative and highly respected authority on all matters maritime-related, but whether his system was used among clippers built after 1854 is uncertain.

Reefs, Shoals and Other Offshore Navigational Hazards

By the 1850s the world's oceans were becoming more accurately mapped and better understood, but uncharted coral reefs, shoals, mudflats, and sandbars were constantly being discovered and rediscovered and inaccuracies still abounded. These hazards were found not just in the far reaches of the Pacific, where many reefs, shoals, and atolls lurked to snare wayward mariners, but even closer to home in the waters of the Americas and off the major ports. In the Pacific especially the underwater landscape was (and still is) constantly changing due to underwater volcanic activity and sometimes new hazards appeared virtually overnight. Woe then, to the ship that was the first to encounter such a hazard, and even when a captain plotted the location of this newfound hazard (usually after striking it), it was not often done with pinpoint accuracy, thus resulting in further incidents until its precise location eventually became mapped and widely known. Earthquake activity, too, could sometimes be a concern, even if no known clipper losses are associated with such an event. The poet Bayard Taylor was voyaging homeward from China to New York aboard the clipper *Sea Serpent* in October 1853 "when the ship suddenly stopped and shook so violently from stem to stern that every timber vibrated. This motion was accompanied by a dull rumbling, or rather humming noise, which seemed to come from under the stern.... Captain Howland...came on deck just in time to feel a second shock, nearly as violent as the first. Those who were below heard a strong hissing noise at the vessel's side.... The length of time which elapsed, from first to last, was about a minute and a half. The breeze fell immediately afterwards, and we had barely steerage way until morning" (Taylor, p. 514).

Elsewhere on the ocean's highways, other known hazards remained as such, like the shoals of Cape Hatteras off the coast of North Carolina or Goodwin Sands in the English Channel, even when marked accurately on the maps, mainly due to faulty navigation or storms that drove a vessel onto such hazards that she would normally avoid at all costs. In addition to these unmoving navigational hazards, numerous others abounded that were sometimes impossible to predict in the seemingly vast and empty ocean, including icebergs, submerged wrecks, and whales; to hit any of these floating objects while bowling along under full sail could result in a ship being severely damaged or sunk.

Over 30 clipper ships were lost, and many others damaged, over the years due to the navigational hazards listed above (not including those previously discussed clippers that went missing or were lost off the guano islands). European waters were the kindest to the clippers in this regard, mainly because the hazards were well known to American mariners and the area was well mapped and surveyed, having been subject to ocean navigation for hundreds of years. Only one known clipper, the Red Cross Line packet *Racer*, was lost by such hazards in this area. Built at Newburyport by Currier & Townsend in 1851, the 1,669-ton clipper departed Liverpool for New York in May 1856 and when only a day out struck the Arklow Bank, near Wicklow on the east coast of Ireland. The ship's passengers and crew were saved, but the ship was a total loss, her destruction hastened by the local population who plundered the wreck. Other clippers, to be sure, suffered mishaps in United Kingdom waters due to like causes, including the *Sparkling Wave*, which grounded on the Goodwin Sands, a ten-mile long sandbank off the Kentish coast near Deal, in April 1862. Fortunately, the ship was able to get off and make it to London for repairs.

The waters of the North Atlantic from Canada to the Caribbean also had its share of dangers and claimed at least four clippers as victims, including the *Staffordshire, Roebuck, Witchcraft,* and *Tinqua,* while several others, including *Atalanta* and *Simoon*, were more fortunate. The first named clipper, built by Donald McKay, was lost under tragic circumstances in December 1853 while bound from Liverpool to Boston with over 200 crew and passengers aboard. While approaching the Canadian coast the clipper endured heavy gales that caused great damage and injured her captain. Near midnight on Christmas Day *Staffordshire* struck Blonde Rock, four miles from Seal Island, near Cape Sable and quickly sank in deep water, taking down 170 of those aboard with her, including her injured captain. Farther south, the rocky coast of Massachusetts was also a constant danger to mariners; in January 1859 the Maine-built clipper *Roebuck*, loaded with cotton and bound from Boston to Philadelphia, crashed into the West Willies, a series of rocks along the Eastern Channel entrance to Cohasset Harbor. While stranded there and in the process of unloading her cargo, a storm came up that grounded the ship and her cotton cargo on the rocks, following which the beaches were strewn with cotton while 100 whole bales of cotton washed ashore. The waters off New York and New Jersey near the entrance to New York Harbor also posed many hazards, including Romer's Shoals, which had been charted by 1700 and had a beacon marking the spot since 1838. Despite this, the Baltimore-built clipper *Atalanta* ran aground here in March 1853 while nearing the end of her voyage from China to New York. The clipper was subsequently stuck on the shoals for nine days, but was eventually gotten off with only minor damage after some of her cargo was discharged. Likewise, the clipper *Simoon* struck a shoal of water only twenty-four feet deep near Cape Henry while inbound to Baltimore in March 1861, but the seas carried her right over the shallow water without any damage. Farther south, on the North Carolina coast in an area historically known as the "Graveyard of the Atlantic," the Portsmouth-built clipper *Tinqua*,

IX. Hurricane: *Shipwrecks and Other Noteworthy Clipper Events*   215

Clipper-packet *Racer*. This Newburyport-built ship, launched by Currier & Townsend in 1851, served in the Red Cross Line but was lost in 1856 when she hit Arklow Bank, off the coast of Ireland. The *Racer* was the second of the Red Cross Line clippers to be lost that year (*The Illustrated London News*, October 18, 1851).

a little beauty of only 668 tons put over by George Raynes in 1852, left her bones. Driving home from Shanghai with a cargo valued at $300,000, the clipper struck on the outer shoals of Cape Hatteras in January 1855 and within a day, pounded by the surf, had her stern destroyed and bottom knocked out, beyond all hope of saving. No lives were lost in this incident, but not so lucky was the Chelsea-built *Witchcraft*, which was bound from Callao, Peru, to Hampton Roads, Virginia, in April 1861. She struck somewhere between the lights at Cape Hatteras and Bodie Island in the early morning hours and the heavy seas subsequently pounded the doomed clipper, and fifteen of the crew and passengers were drowned. Lost were the chief mate and second mate, as well as passenger Captain John Hayes, formerly commander of the clipper *Flying Eagle*, and his wife and child. Finally, farther south in waters near the American coast two other clippers were lost. In March 1876 the Baltimore clipper *Carrier Dove* was bound from Liverpool to Savannah, Georgia, but got caught up on Stone Horse Shoal near Tybee Island and was a complete wreck, while the *Sea Witch* ended her storied career in March 1856 while bound with a cargo of coolies from Amoy, China, to Havana, Cuba, by hitting a coral reef when close to her destination. While the ship was a total loss, her crew was saved and, presumably, the coolies, though no specific mention of them is made in U.S. news accounts.

The waters of the South Atlantic were yet another area where many navigation hazards lurked. Among the clippers so lost here were the *Fleetwood*, *Cleopatra*, and *John Gilpin*, while the *Herald of the Morning* was severely damaged in most unusual circumstances. The *Cleopatra*, built at East Boston by Paul Curtis in 1853, had just rounded Cape Horn in September 1855 when she struck a submerged wreck (identity unknown) while going under full sail at a good clip; severely damaged by the collision, the clipper foundered two days later, her 26-man crew taking to the lifeboats and making Rio de Janeiro nine days later. Two other clippers also came to grief around Cape Horn after striking icebergs; the *John Gilpin* was bound from Honolulu to New Bedford with 7,500 barrels of whale oil and had just rounded the horn in late January 1858 when the clipper was heavily jarred after striking what was later determined to be a submerged iceberg. The ship began to steadily take on water and was abandoned by Captain John Ropes when there was fifteen feet of water in the hold. To make matters worse, during the process of abandoning the clipper it caught fire and quickly burned. While the *Gilpin*'s crew were soon rescued by a passing British vessel, Captain Ropes' problems were compounded upon his return to New York when some of her crew sued for lost wages, claiming the ship could have been saved by making the Falkland Islands and accusing him of not paying attention to the ship after the collision and that he even deliberately set the fire. Though it is unknown if these crewmen gained their lost wages (their pay stopped the minute they abandoned ship), the sensational charges against Ropes were "not substantiated" (Howe & Matthews, p. 306). The other clipper to go down after striking an iceberg was the Portsmouth-built *Fleetwood*; she was bound from Boston to Honolulu in early May 1859 when she struck and immediately began taking on water. The ship was quickly abandoned, with the mate and four seamen in one lifeboat and Captain Frank Dale, his wife and son, one passenger and the remainder of the crew (17 people in all) in the other. Sadly, while the mate's boat was rescued by a passing vessel, the captain's boat was never seen again. Much more fortunate was the Samuel Pook–designed *Herald of the Morning*; the Medford-built clipper was off Cape Horn during an 1859 voyage from Peru to Hampton Roads, Virginia, when she collided with a large sperm whale. Both whale and ship were considerably jarred, and though the fate of the former is unknown, the *Herald*'s bow was damaged and leaked heavily during the remainder of the voyage, thereby requiring her weary crew to man the pumps continuously until making port. Seven years later in 1866 the *Herald* was bound from Boston to San Francisco when she encountered numerous large icebergs, over fifty in number, while rounding Cape Horn but managed to dodge them all. Cape Horn could be like this and at times still is; in some years icebergs can invade the narrow and storm-tossed waters, while in other years the Horn is relatively free from ice hazards.

In regards to navigational hazards on the West Coast, a number have already been discussed in relation to pilot-related errors. Several other clipper losses, separated in time by fifty-seven years, worthy of notice involving ocean navigational hazards are those involving two Portsmouth-built clippers that were launched by Fernald & Pettigrew, the *Noonday* and *Dashing Wave*. The former clipper, built in 1855, was voyaging from Boston to San Francisco on New Year's Day 1863 and was just miles from making harbor when she brushed over some rocks and quickly began to take on water, her bottom ripped open. The clipper was quickly abandoned and her crew was picked up by a local pilot boat; the ship subsequently sank in over 200 feet of water a few hours later, a total loss. The rock formation which doomed the clipper, lying just eighteen feet below water, had been known to local pilots but had not yet been charted. Thereafter, the underwater hazard was named Noonday Rock; interestingly, some years later, in 1934, a local fisherman brought up the clipper's bell in his net (Brighton, p. 105). The 1853-built *Dashing Wave* came to grief under much less dramatic circumstances after having been afloat for sixty-seven years. The long-lived clipper was last under sail sometime between 1902 and 1910, but by 1920 had been cut down to a barge, having shortened masts, and was utilized in the Alaskan fishing industry, operating out of Tacoma, Washington. Just weeks after being surveyed, her hull found to still be in A-1 condition, the clipper barge was subsequently stranded on the mudflats at Seymour Narrows near Vancouver Island while loaded with over 1,000 tons of cannery supplies destined for Alaska. Though the Narrows, part of Discovery Passage, are just three miles in length, even today the strong currents make them extremely difficult waters to navigate.

Despite all the losses described above, these are nothing compared to those that took place in the Pacific and Indian ocean waters of the Far East, where over a dozen clippers were lost due to offshore hazards, including *Lookout, Alarm, Charger, Andrew Jackson, Radiant, John Wade, Hotspur,*

Antelope, Phantom, Mandarin, Sovereign of the Seas, Sweepstakes, Wild Wave, Samuel Russell, and *Reindeer,* while numerous others, including *Lightning, Hippogriffe,* and the *N.B. Palmer* suffered damage yet survived to sail another day. Perhaps one of the earliest, and surely one of the most interesting accounts of this type of loss and its harrowing aftermath, was that involving the Maine-built clipper *Wild Wave,* built by George Ferrin at Richmond on the Kennebec River in 1854. While bound from San Francisco to Valparaiso, Chile, in March 1858, carrying ten passengers and $18,000 in gold coin, the clipper hit a coral reef of the atoll surrounding Oeno Island (one of the Pitcairn Island group) in the South Pacific. The clipper hit the reef while making 13 knots and soon after striking was filled with water. The passengers and crew made it to Oeno Island and here salvaged what they could from the wreck, including the livestock they were carrying, and were able to dig for water on the island. Captain Josiah Knowles soon decided that one of the ship's boats, manned by him and six other men, and carrying with them the gold coin, would try to make Pitcairn Island, which was less than 100 miles away and thought to be inhabited. After a harrowing voyage to the island, it was found to be deserted, the population having moved over 3,000 miles distant to Norfolk Island. With their boat damaged, Knowles decided to build a new boat and did so within three months, thereafter setting a course for Tahiti. Along the way, storm winds developed so Knowles changed course and decided to try for the Marquesas Islands with a planned stop at Oeno to check on the rest of the *Wild Wave*'s complement. While the latter goal could not be achieved due to prevailing winds, the 30-foot-long boat did make the Marquesas, but finding none but the local native population, who appeared very hostile, Knowles decided to continue on his way, making the island of Nukahiva in early August, where a U.S. Navy sloop was at anchor. Captain Knowles promptly sold his boat to a local missionary and took passage on the U.S.S. *Vandalia* to Tahiti with his other men. The remaining survivors (one of whom had died) on Oeno Island, who had also built their own boat but were unsuccessful in getting her launched, were also soon after rescued. It was later said that when Captain Knowles, who subsequently commanded Donald McKay's last creation, the *Glory of the Seas,* returned to San Francisco in September 1858 he "was greeted by his friends as one risen from the dead" (Howe & Matthews, p. 713).

Other, less dramatic losses in the Far East include, in early 1859, the Medford-built *John Wade,* which hit an uncharted rock in the Gulf of Siam and was lost while bound from Bangkok to Hong Kong, while about the same time the McKay-built clipper *Reindeer* was wrecked after hitting a coral reef off the Philippines. Yet other McKay-built clippers suffered like incidents around this same time, albeit with different results; the *Sovereign of the Seas,* now sailing under the British flag, ran onto the Pyramid Shoals in the Straits of Malacca, between the Malaysian peninsula and the island of Sumatra, in 1859 while bound from Germany to China and was a total loss, while the famed *Lightning* also hit some uncharted rocks, known afterward as the Lightning Rocks, off Melbourne, Australia, in late 1862, but was more fortunate and kept right on course having experienced little or no damage. Earlier that same year, while bound from San Francisco to Hong Kong and experiencing heavy weather, the Medford-built *Phantom* went to pieces after hitting Pilot Reef, near Pratas Shoal in the South China Sea, just a short distance from her final destination; her young captain, twenty-eight-year-old Henry Sargent, Jr., would later write home to tell his parents, "I have lost the *Phantom* on the Pratas Shoal — but have fortunately saved my life" (Sargent, p. 58). Captain Sargent's luck may have held out in this incident, but not for long; late in 1862 he took command of the bark *Emily C. Starr,* but that ship went missing on his first voyage while bound from Shanghai to Japan in early 1863. Yet another clipper lost in 1862 was the famed *Sweepstakes*; she hit a reef in the Sunda Strait between the Indonesian islands of Java and Sumatra, and though she was eventually freed, a survey at the navy yard dock in Batavia (modern-day Jakarta) showed she was badly damaged and the clipper was soon thereafter sold to the ship-breakers. Also freed from her predicament was the *Alarm*, which struck Preparis Reef off the coast of Burma (modern-day Myanmar) in the Indian Ocean in late 1863 and though she eventually slid off into deeper water and stayed afloat after her crew abandoned ship, she was deemed too damaged to be worth saving. The following year the William Webb–built *Mandarin* came to grief in the China Sea after striking an uncharted reef just north of the Thousand Islands. Yet another danger area was the Gaspar Strait, connecting the Java Sea to the South China Sea among several islands of Indonesia; the famed *Andrew Jackson*, now under the British flag, was bound from Shanghai to Europe but was lost after hitting a reef while transiting this strait in December 1868, while two years later the experienced China clipper *Samuel Russell* was also lost after hitting a coral reef. Later losses in the Pacific and Indian oceans include *Radiant*, which sank after hitting Crocodile Reef off Singapore in 1871 at the beginning of her voyage to Boston; the Portsmouth-built *Charger* hit a reef off Cebu in the Philippines in 1873 and was beyond saving, while the famed and long-lived Rhode Island–built clipper *Lookout* was bound from Shanghai to Washington state in 1878 when she was damaged in a typhoon and driven on the reef off the Japanese island of Kutsunoshima, all but three of her crew being rescued by local fishermen.

Finally, there are two interesting cases of near shipwrecks due to these causes that had both happy and extremely lucky outcomes. The *N.B. Palmer*, a clipper "singularly fortunate as to mishaps" (Howe & Matthews, p. 415), was bound from China to New York in February 1853 when she hit Broussa Shoal off North Watcher Island in the Java Sea. The ship had to be kedged to get off the reef and leaked heavily as a result, thus forcing her to put into Batavia to discharge her cargo and make repairs at the navy yard. During this process, a large chunk of coral fell out of her hull which, had it come out while the *N.B. Palmer* was at sea, would have likely caused the ship to sink before making port safely. Similarly, the Cape Cod–built *Hippogriffe* was bound from Boston to Hong Kong in May 1858 when she struck an uncharted rock in the Java Sea. The clipper eventually got off the rocks and made port, where she was put into dry dock for repair. Here it was discovered that a large chunk of coral was solidly imbedded in the *Hippogriffe*'s hull; had it been dislodged while still at sea, the clipper likely would have gone down. This underwater obstruction, a coral encrusted boulder 150 feet in diameter covered by only three feet of water, was charted in 1867 by a British survey ship, being named Hippogriffe Shoal.

Pirates in the Far East

With the exception of the dangerous Cape Horn passage, the hazards of the Far East were surely the most dangerous for the world's merchant shipping. The hazards in this area were made even more harrowing by the fact that not only were wrecked vessels in this area, more than anywhere else, quickly plundered, but survivors were sometimes taken prisoner by unsavory elements, many described as pirates, among local native populations and were held until ransom money was paid to secure their release. Even beyond incidences of shipwreck, shipmasters working their clippers through the narrow waters in the Java and China seas had to be extremely vigilant of approaching native craft to avoid pirates, while the same was true for those ships that might become becalmed due to light winds and thus unable to proceed at a quick pace. As a result of these very real possibilities, many clippers working in the Far East trade carried firearms and even were armed with cannon to fight off would-be attackers. The early clipper *Houqua*, originally built as a warship for the Chinese government, had sixteen gun ports, eight on each side, and carried at least several cannon, the clipper *N.B. Palmer* was equipped with a pair of brass cannons, the New Jersey–built *Gravina* carried two deck guns (and used them to successfully fight off pirates), while the clipper bark *Racehorse* was pierced for six guns. In addition, the following clippers are all known to have been well armed: *Bald Eagle* and *Whirlwind* (both with two long six-pound cannons), and *Intrepid* and *Staffordshire* (both with two nine-pound cannons). There were probably many more clippers armed in like fashion prior to the Civil War that have gone undocumented.

Just how many clippers were lost directly due to acts of piracy is unknown, perhaps just one; the Newburyport-built *Highflyer*, originally built for the Red Cross Line of packets, went missing after departing San Francisco in October 1855 bound for Hong Kong. The prevailing opinion at the time of her loss was that the ship was captured and destroyed and her crew murdered by pirates off Formosa. A search of the area did turn up a ship that was stranded and destroyed, and though the ship could not be identified, a spyglass was found that was thought to have been owned by the *Highflyer*'s commander, Captain Gordon Waterman.

Despite the uncertainty around the loss of *Highflyer* a number of other ships were subject to attacks after getting in trouble. In addition to the loss and subsequent plundering of the previously discussed *Ringleader* off Formosa in 1863, five other clippers were lost under similar circumstances. The Medford-built *Courser* was lost in April 1858 while bound from Foo Chow to New York. She ran onto Pratas Shoal in the South China Sea and soon began to sink. The crew quickly got off in three boats and while making for Hong Kong encountered what was thought to be Chinese fishing junks. However, they were not fisherman, but would-be pirates and they soon began to fire on the *Courser*'s boats. Two of the boats made it to safety and eventually landed at Macao, while the third, manned by the chief mate, confronted the attackers, with the result that their boat was capsized and two men drowned. The ten surviving crewmen were subsequently able to right their boat and made Hong Kong the next day. It was later reported that Captain Cole was so distressed by the clipper's loss that "anxiety and vexation...brought on a fever from which he died" (Howe & Matthews, p. 110). Another Medford-built clipper, the *Antelope,* was bound from Bangkok to China in August of that same year when she struck on Discovery Shoal, Paracels Reef, and quickly sank. Her crew and ten Chinese passengers got off in two boats, the captain's boat later making contact with a Chinese fishing junk, making a deal that they would be provided with fresh water and given a tow to land for twenty dollars. However, when it was discovered that the fishermen had other plans, the captain cut the tow line and tried to make his escape; attacked by stones, and having no weapons of their own, the captain had to surrender, following which his boat was plundered. The tables were quickly turned when the would-be pirates were distracted and two of the American crewmen jumped aboard the fishing junk and killed the Chinese crew. The captain and crew of the *Antelope* subsequently made the port of Hong Kong, but there is no mention of the other lifeboat ever being recovered. This incident is clearly one in which native fisherman, not well-established pirates, were at work trying to take advantage of an opportunity, and the happy results are indicative of such. In a similar ordeal, the New York–built *Hotspur* was also, in February 1863, wrecked on Paracels Reef while carrying a cargo valued at a million dollars. The crew and passengers got off in three boats; the captain's longboat was picked up by a Chinese junk and carried to Bangkok without incident, while the chief mate's boat eventually made shore, with the loss of one female passenger. The second mate's boat made landfall at Cape Patterman, but those aboard were taken prisoner by local natives. They were held in captivity for a week before making their escape, eventually gaining safety aboard a British vessel bound for Saigon. A more successful ransom scheme than those described above involved the previously mentioned *Phantom*; while all her passengers and crew eventually made it to safety, two lifeboats were picked up by pirates off the Chinese coast at Swatow and the occupants held until Chinese merchants paid a ransom of $25 per person. A final notable accident that came to involve piracy involved the New York clipper *Intrepid* in March 1860 after she piled up on Belvidere Reef in the Gaspar Strait. The captain and crew subsequently tried to get their ship off the reef by dumping part of the cargo overboard and even cut the ship's masts away so that she would not be visible from a distance. However, these efforts failed and the following morning a large number of native craft manned by Malaysian pirates converged on the scene intent on plundering the wreck. A tremendous battle ensued with the pirates trying to make the deck of the stranded clipper, while her crew fought valiantly using small arms, pikes, the ship's cannons, and even boiling water to repel them. While one crewman was killed in the battle, many more pirates were killed and the battle might have continued had not the French clipper *Gallilei* arrived on the scene. The *Intrepid* crew was subsequently carried to Anjer, Indonesia, and while a salvage attempt was later made, the clipper was found to be completely in the control of the pirates. They were later driven off by two Dutch warships, but only $2,000 worth of her $660,000 cargo could be recovered.

Pilot Related Losses

Whenever a merchant sailing vessel was operating on the open seas, it was her captain that was in charge. However, when approaching her port of arrival, a pilot was usually hired to guide a vessel in as he was a mariner who well knew the local waters, including prevailing currents, wind conditions, and navigational hazards. In all major ports in the U.S. pilots were on call at most times and cruised the sailing grounds off port in small and sharp-built pilot schooners ready to be taken aboard a vessel. In most ports ships were required to pay pilotage fees even if they chose not to hire a pilot directly, the fee based on the size of the ship, but in many, perhaps most cases, a pilot was hired after a fee was negotiated between a captain and the pilot. Once taken aboard a ship, the pilot became the one in charge of the ship and directed the crew in sail handling operations, though the captain was still legally in command. In the vast majority of cases, a ship was guided into port successfully without incident, but in a few cases a clipper was wrecked while under the pilot's charge. Sometimes this was due to direct pilot error, other times it was due to the crew of a clipper not following a pilot's orders to the letter, or being delayed in doing so. As for pilot losses in foreign waters, these are much more difficult to identify. All major ports in the Far East and Europe also had traditionally employed pilots in one form or another; the pilotage system had been in use in Europe for centuries, while pilots had also been in use for a century in such Far East ports as Macao, Shanghai, and Hong Kong. In these ports, prior to the Opium Wars of the 1840s, pilots were controlled directly by the Hong merchants themselves.

Six clippers are known to have been lost due to errors while under control of a pilot, these being the previously discussed *San Francisco* on her maiden voyage, as well as the *Oriental, Electric Spark, Golden Fleece, Flying Dragon,* and *Surprise,* while the *Archer* suffered damage due to pilot error. Five other clippers, the *Hoogly, Swordfish, Golden Racer, Wild Duck,* and *Flying Fish* may also been lost due to pilot error. The early clipper *Oriental* in late 1853 is said to have been the first foreign ship to sail up the river Min after the port of Foo Chow was opened to western traders, but while sailing down the river in preparation for her departure in February 1854 she was guided by a pilot who was assisted by native boats. However, these native boats did not follow the orders of the pilot, causing the clipper to hit a point of rocks and slide off into deep water. While the ship's crew and passengers were saved, the ship and cargo were a total loss. Another unusual clipper loss that occurred in oriental waters due to pilot error was that of the *Surprise* in 1876. Bound from New York to Yokohama, Japan, with a cargo of case oil, the ship took a pilot at the entrance to Yeddo Bay in early February 1876 during a storm, but subsequently sought shelter and while trying to make Kaneda Bay came too close to the Plymouth Rocks and struck. Thrown on her beam ends, the ship quickly took on water. Luckily, all the ship's crew, as well as the pilot, were able to get off in lifeboats and make it ashore. Though some of the cargo was saved, the *Surprise* was a total loss. As for the pilot in charge, it was later found out that he was no pilot at all, but a mere beachcomber, and a drunk one at that; he never was found and prosecuted for his actions. Interestingly, the Japanese pilot system at this time was left entirely to the private sector, with various individuals competing for pilot opportunities. However, in the same year, 1876, that *Surprise* was lost the Japanese government took steps to control pilot operations more closely by passing that country's first pilot regulations, modeled after those of Great Britain. Luckily, not all pilot errors resulted in a clipper being lost; the *Archer* hit a sandbar while under control of a Chinese pilot while dropping down the river Min in 1865 and though damaged was soon repaired and fit to sail again.

Closer to home, the first *Golden Fleece*, built at Medford in 1852 by Paul Curtis, was ready to depart San Francisco for the Philippines in April 1854 after making her second California run. While under the pilot's control, the clipper did not make the proper tack (in nautical terminology, *missed stays*) and got caught in the swirling current and subsequently drifted broadside, crashing on the rocks near Fort Point, Golden Gate, with her masts toppling over. Though tugs tried to pull the clipper free, the effort was to no avail as the ship was holed and had taken on water. The hull would be pounded by the surf for months afterward, but stayed intact until it broke up the following October, the wreck having previously been sold for $3,180. The pilot blamed the loss on the ship's crew who failed to follow his orders. The *Golden Fleece* and *San Francisco* were not the only clippers lost off the Golden Gate; in late January 1862 the *Flying Dragon,* carrying a thousand tons of Australian coal, was entering the port late at night during rainy and squally weather and was near Fort Point when she tried to anchor but a defect in her windlass caused problems and before the anchor chains were let out she drifted onto the reef at Arch Rock and quickly took on water. Though tugs were sent to assist in rescue operations and soldiers from Alcatraz Island were brought aboard to man the *Dragon*'s pumps, the effort failed and the following day the clipper slid off the reef and sank, with nothing being saved. The pilot was investigated for possible incompetence but was found not to be in error.

Clipper losses in European waters are generally rare, and those caused by pilot error even more so. However, the Medford-built *Electric Spark* fell victim to just such a mishap in late September 1869. After loading a cargo at Liverpool for the U.S. West Coast, the clipper was subsequently stranded at night on Blackwater Head off Wexford, Ireland. Her pilot had made a mistake in identifying the local lights. As was often the case, the passengers and crew survived the ordeal, and while some cargo was salvaged, the ship was a total loss, with the insurance companies paying out some $100,000.

One other incident that involved damage to an American clipper took place in British waters while under a pilot's guidance, although under very unusual circumstances, that is also of interest. The big Portsmouth-built *Sierra Nevada*, launched by Tobey & Littlefield in 1854, made her second voyage in March 1855 from Hampton Roads, Virginia, to Liverpool, but collided with a British ship en route; it was subsequently decided that she would put into the Wellington Dock at Liverpool for repairs. While being guided into a dock by a Mersey River pilot, the 1,942-ton clipper only made it part way into the dock when she got hung up on the sill and was stranded for over a week. Originally scheduled for only minor repairs, once the clipper was eased into the dock it was found that her back had been broken and that serious and expensive repairs would be required. Because of this, the clipper's original owners, Glidden & Williams of Boston, sold their ship for the low price of $43,750 and subsequently sued the dock company for damages (Brighton, pg. 116). While the pilot in charge suggested the ship and her crew were at fault for the accident, nobody bought this argument and, after four years of litigation, the British courts found in favor of Glidden & Williams, ruling that the dock company had been negligent in allowing mud to accumulate at the dock entrance which caused the *Sierra Nevada* to become damaged. Interestingly, while the clipper would be repaired and sail the seas for another twenty-two years until being lost off the coast of Chile in 1877, she would suffer a number of other serious accidents, including going ashore at San Francisco near Fort Point, Golden Gate, probably also while under control of a pilot.

Illustrated News **masthead, 1853. The masthead of this New York paper well illustrates the crowded sea conditions of such large ports as New York, San Francisco, Liverpool, and many others worldwide (*Illustrated News*, New York, March 26, 1853).**

Finally, while a number of clipper losses have been identified in this category, there are also a number of others for which the exact cause of their loss has gone undocumented, especially among those clippers lost in Chinese waters. Five possibilities of pilot-related losses include the previously discussed *Hoogly*, lost while bound up the river to Shanghai in 1852; the William Webb–built *Sword Fish*, also lost near Shanghai on the north bank of the Yangtze River while departing with a load of cotton for Amoy (Xiamen), Fujian province, southeast China, in July 1862 after her anchors became fouled; the Portsmouth-built *Wild Duck*, lost when only three years old in October 1856 when departing Foo Chow for New York fully loaded, went ashore on the bank of the river Min and was deemed a total loss; the Maine-built *Golden Racer,* launched at Thomaston by Joshua Morton in 1852, was also lost on the river Min, becoming stranded and a total loss while empty in mid–1856; and the McKay-built *Flying Fish*, lost in November 1858 sailing down the river Min while fully loaded with tea, bound from Foo Chow to New York. The ship failed to make tack while being brought into the wind and her captain was forced to use her anchor to bring the ship around but the operation failed and the clipper subsequently drifted onto a sand bank and began taking on water. The ship was eventually got off and was taken into port where a survey showed she was considerably damaged, with the result that the *Flying Fish* was subsequently sold to owners in the Philippines. The famed clipper, renamed the *El Bueno Suceso*, was soon thereafter repaired in China and sailed on the trade route between Spain and Manila for some years. All of these clippers were lost in circumstances in which a pilot was likely aboard, though it is possible that the *Flying Fish* had no pilot as she was near the river's mouth and may have already discharged the pilot. If these losses were due to pilot errors, it is unclear whether this is a reflection of the pilotage system then in force in Chinese ports, simply an indicator of the overall difficult conditions on the rivers involved, or, as is most likely the case, a combination of both factors.

Collision Incidents

While it is true that the oceans of the world are vast and there are many places where the rolling waves are all that can be spied as far as the eye can see, it is also true that the shipping lanes in the days of sail were often crowded places, especially in the coastal waters close to any major port. These coastal shipping lanes were not just filled with sailing vessels of all types, including clippers, packet ships, ordinary merchant ships and barks, coastal schooners, barges, ferry boats, pilot boats, and pleasure craft but also by an increasing number of steamships of all sizes that were also engaged in the same trades. Because of these conditions collisions between vessels of all different sizes was a fairly commonplace event, and while many clippers were involved in these incidents, only a few went to the bottom of the ocean as a result. Among the contributing factors in these collision events was, first, poor weather conditions that reduced visibility, but also the fact that the rules of the road, so to speak, in ocean navigation between sailing and steam vessels were not yet fully established. Eventually, maritime laws would be drafted that gave sailing ships the right of way, primarily because they were subject to the vagaries of the wind in their maneuvers, but this would not be the case until the 1890s. Prior to such laws being formed, sailing and steamship captains alike sometimes misjudged either the intentions or course of a vessel in their vicinity, and with no set rules to follow a collision often resulted. Another factor in these collisions was probably the lack of running lights that clearly identified a vessel either at night or in poor visibility weather conditions. As far back as the 1830s, steamships were required to carry a signal light while running from sunset to sunrise, but the nature, number, and placement of such was not regulated. By 1850 sailing ships were also required to follow this same vague requirement. Today, almost all vessels, even pleasure craft, have such lights mounted forward so that they are clearly visible to approaching vessels, with a red light mounted on the port (left) side and a green light on the starboard (right) side of a vessel. Today, established maritime laws dictate which vessel has the right of way and on which side they should pass based on the visibility of these lights. Generally speaking, if the captain of a vessel sees the red (port) light of an approaching vessel, than he must yield to that vessel, but if he sees green, than he has the right of way.

Six clipper ships are known to have been lost due to collisions, they being the *Trade Wind, Wild Ranger, Northern Light, Star of the Union, Atmosphere,* and *Coeur De Lion*. The earliest of these losses was that of the big New York clipper *Trade Wind*, built by Jacob Bell in 1851 and, measuring 2,051 tons, the largest sailing ship ever built in the U.S. up to that time. When less than three years old, on June 26, 1854, just an hour before midnight, she was bound from Mobile, Alabama, to Liverpool carrying a cargo of over 4,500 bales of cotton when she collided with the sailing ship *Olympia*, bound from Liverpool to Boston. The two had crossed paths and not discovered each other until it was too late; the latter ship was cut down all the way to her main mast and after scraping down the side of the clipper for a short time drifted off on her own and slowly began to settle. In the meantime, the bow of the *Trade Wind* was totally stove in while what remained of the bow topsides to the stern was also heavily damaged. While the two ships were tangled up together, several crewmen from the *Olympia*, including her captain, jumped aboard the clipper, thinking that she had a better chance of staying afloat. Some hours later, as daybreak came, both ships were still afloat and the captain of *Olympic* decided to take a boat back to his vessel. However, soon after it was discovered that the clipper was slowly sinking; Captain Smith attempted to launch two lifeboats; one with the passengers, about thirty in all, was successfully got off, but the other boat was damaged in the process, leaving the captain and 25 of his crew left aboard the sinking clipper. When *Trade Wind* finally sank, she took down with her Captain Smith, 15 of his men, and a $250,000 cargo, while some men survived by holding on to bits of wreckage before being picked up by a Belgian ship that came on the scene. In the meantime, the *Olympia* had also sunk, she losing eight of her crew and a cargo valued at $200,000. There is no mention in this incident whether either of these ships had any running lights.

Two other clippers lost in the 1860s due to collisions were the famed *Northern Light* and the Medford-built *Star of the Union*. The former clipper, which set the record for a passage from San Francisco to the East Coast in 1852, was sold to her record-setting captain, Seth Doane, for $60,000 in 1854, but was never again quite as speedy. Under the command of Captain Lovell on the night of January 2, 1862, the clipper was bound empty from Le Havre, France, to New York when she collided with the French brig *Nouveau St. Jacques*, a much smaller vessel. The French ship quickly foundered but her crew got off in time and made it aboard *Northern Light*. However, the clipper too was fatally damaged and taking on water and had to be abandoned several hours later; both crews were saved by two vessels which landed them in England. The *Star of the Union* also likely met her ultimate end by collision, but under much different circumstances; she was bound from Honolulu via Baker's Island for New York in late 1866 with a cargo of guano when she collided with the British bark *Simon Habley* off Cape Horn, a dangerous but also at times a crowded shipping lane. While the British ship went down, the *Star* survived and continued on her voyage but was forced to put into Rio de Janeiro due to heavy damage. The clipper's fate after this is unknown, but there are indications she was condemned at Rio and subsequently sold, possibly having her name changed or being scrapped altogether. While collisions that happened anywhere were usually harrowing events for a sailing ship, those that occurred in the waters off Cape Horn (they were not uncommon) had the added dangers of stormy seas and the always attendant difficulties in this area of rescuing a crew in distress.

In regards to the final three clippers lost due to collision, these all occurred when they were long past their prime; the Medford-built *Wild Ranger* was lost after nineteen years of service in 1872 after having been sold foreign and renamed *Ocean Chief*. She was sunk off Rio de Janeiro after colliding with a steamship. The Mystic-built *Atmosphere* was lost after a twenty-six-year career in 1882 while sailing under the British flag. The old clipper was bound from Liverpool to Valparaiso when she collided with a British ship off the coast of Brazil. Finally, the last clipper lost to collision was one of the longest-lived clippers of them all. The Portsmouth-built *Coeur de Lion* was launched in 1854 by George Raynes and by 1860 had been sold to Russian interests and renamed *Zaritza*. The old clipper was later sold to Swedish interests without a change in name and was sailing under that flag still in August 1915 when she sank in the Baltic Sea off the Skagerrak after a collision, thus ending her career after sixty-one years.

In addition to the losses above, many collisions both minor and major were suffered by a number of clippers, including *Gazelle* (1852), *Houqua* (1853), *Chariot of Fame* and *Phoenix* (1854), *Red Rover* (1858), *David Brown* (1859), *Robin Hood* (1861), *Sierra Nevada* (1862), *North Wind* (1863), and *Orpheus* (1875). Among the more interesting incidents among these ships that survived to sail again, the *David Brown* collided with a bark while changing her berth at the busy port of Shanghai, causing the clipper to drift ashore. She had to discharge some of her cargo before she was gotten off. The William Webb–built *Gazelle* collided with a Spanish ship off Cape Horn and suffered considerable damage forward; though leaking at the rate of ten inches of water, the clipper was able to complete her voyage from New York to San Francisco without putting into another port for repairs. The small clipper *Houqua* was struck by the ferryboat *Tonowanda* in New York Harbor during foggy weather, forcing her to undergo repairs before departing for San Francisco. The Maine-built *Phoenix* had an inauspicious start to her career when she ran down the schooner *William E. Baird* and cut it in two during a heavy snow squall while bound from Portland to New York on her maiden voyage. All but one of the schooner's crew was saved and the clipper suffered only minor damage, she being a much larger vessel. The Portsmouth-built clipper *Red Rover* had the distinction of having suffered several collisions in the first two years of her career; at her launching in 1852 she collided with an inbound Canadian schooner, and two years later while at London she was run down by a German steamer and forced to go into dry dock there for major repairs. Another Portsmouth-built clipper, the big *Sierra Nevada*, also had a bit of bad luck; she was damaged by going ashore at Fort Point upon arriving at San Francisco and subsequently was repaired at the Mare Island Navy Yard. When she was getting ready for sea, her anchor failed to hold and she drifted into the clipper *Phantom* that was anchored nearby. The *Sierra Nevada* suffered several thousand dollars worth of damage to her spars and rigging and had her departure delayed yet again.

However, of all these types of accidents, that involving the 1,272-ton *Orpheus* was the most deadly; the old clipper, launched at Chelsea, Massachusetts, in 1856 by Rice & Mitchell, was carrying a cargo of coal from San Francisco to Puget Sound on the night of November 4, 1875, when she collided with the 876-ton sidewheel steamship *Pacific*, also an aged vessel having been built in 1851, off Cape Flattery, Washington. This steamer had left Victoria, British Columbia, just hours before in a badly overloaded condition and quickly sank after the collision, taking down with her many of those aboard, while many more died in the cold waters; overall, 273 of an estimated 275 crew and passengers died in the sinking and its aftermath. A Canadian inquiry into the accident determined that the clipper's commander, Captain Charles Sawyer, who tried to avoid the collision, was guilty of manslaughter (nothing came of this sentence) for failing to offer assistance; the *Orpheus* after the collision continued on her way without helping the *Pacific*, apparently either unaware of her dire circumstances, or more worried about their own ship. Their investigation also revealed that the steamer had a rotten and leaky hull and should not been certified as being seaworthy by the U.S. Steamboat Inspection Service, and that the *Pacific* should not have sunk after the relatively light-impact collision. Interestingly, the inspector that certified the *Pacific* as being sound was the former commander of the infamous clipper *Challenge*, Robert Waterman, who was the inspector of hulls in the San Francisco area after his seagoing career ended. However, a separate American inquiry by the Steamboat Inspection Service cleared the clipper's captain of any misdeeds for failing to offer assistance, but did blame him for causing the collision, a somewhat dubious finding in the light of the conflicting evidence. As a result of the collision the *Orpheus* lost several portions of her fore and main masts and all her starboard rigging and was able to make repairs and continue on her way. Just two days after this collision the clipper was lost when she went ashore due to a navigational error, though some claimed that Sawyer was trying to wreck his ship to destroy evidence concerning the collision. This accusation was unfounded when it was discovered that Sawyer did not have updated charts for the area in which he was sailing, causing him to misidentify one of the two navigational beacons in the area.

Going Ashore

Whether due to stormy weather, faulty navigation, or just plain bad luck, going ashore or piling up on some island was one of the most common happenings in the life of a clipper ship and caused the loss of many of them. These incidents happened all around the world and account for at least 10 percent of all known clipper ship losses, including the following, which does not include those previously discussed: *Whistler* and *Lightfoot* (1855, China waters), *John Milton* (1858, Montauk Point, NY), *Flying Mist* (1862, New Zealand), *Starr King* (1862, South Pacific), *Ocean Pearl* (1864, Portugal), *Euroclydon* (1864, Ireland), *Granite State* (1868, United Kingdom), *Dreadnought* (1869, near Tierra del Fuego), *Crest of the Wave* (1870, Virginia), *Wild Rover* (1871, Long Island, NY), *Flying Cloud* (1874, Nova Scotia), *Windward* (1875, Puget Sound, WA), *Golden City* (1879, South Pacific), *Gem of the Ocean* (1879, Vancouver, B.C.), *Messenger* (1879, New Zealand), *Good Hope* (1881, Quebec), *National Eagle* (1884, Adriatic Sea, off Pola, Croatia), and *Golden State* (1886, Cape Elizabeth, ME).

Just reading the simple accounts, usually described in a sentence or two, of these ships that were lost going ashore in some news accounts and books, however, does not convey the true nature of these losses. One must first imagine the captain and crew in peril, perhaps during a storm, and that one terrifying moment when land is sighted, and then the frantic attempts to wear the ship around to avoid going ashore. However, it is too late, and the inevitable occurs, the fateful crash comes with such force, with the result that the ship's bottom is torn out and she fills up fast with water. Then imagine the feverish attempts to launch the lifeboats by the crew, hard enough in shoal water even in good conditions in daylight, but trying to do so in a gale, or at night, or under both conditions requires almost superhuman efforts, and yet, it was often done for seamen are a hardy breed. However, what about those crewmen or passengers that didn't or couldn't make the lifeboats? We can only imagine what it must have been like to flounder about in the water, looking for some piece of wreckage, grabbing something, anything which you could cling to. Many do not make it, perhaps because they can't swim, are injured, or are just exhausted by the ordeal, their heavy and wet clothes dragging them down to suffer a death by drowning. This, in many cases, is what it meant for a clipper to be lost by going ashore. Among the most interesting of these incidents, the *Flying Mist* was bound from Glasgow, Scotland, to New Zealand with a cargo that included 1,760 sheep and eighteen shepherds to watch over them. After her arrival at Bluff Harbor, the clipper was subsequently blown ashore at night, causing the loss of over half of the sheep aboard, but all the crew and shepherds were saved. Less fortunate were the crews of the Thomaston, Maine–built *Crest of the Wave* and the New Bedford–built *John Milton*; the former was bound from Liverpool to Boston, manned by a crew of twenty and carried a cargo of salt and general merchandise. During a gale in early April 1870 she struck Wreck Island, some miles north of Cape Henry, Virginia, and went to pieces. Two boats probably got off the wreck, but, sadly, dead men tell no details, and what exactly transpired is unknown. One boat washed ashore with three dead crew members, the other with the lifeless body of Captain Jones. Nearby on the wreck strewn beach was discovered the ship's flag and part of her name board. The end of the literary-named clipper *John Milton* is surely a horrific example of paradise lost on the high seas if ever there was one; like *Crest of the Wave*, the *Milton* was just miles from her journey's end when she came to

Clipper ship *Tornado*. Heavy weather was the constant danger to any ship during the course of her voyaging life. Even in seemingly calm conditions, things could change in just an instant. This woodcut shows the big New York clipper, launched by Jabez Williams in 1852, after she was hit by a sudden whirlwind in the Pacific on September 11, 1852, while bound San Francisco to New York. The clipper lost her bowsprit and her foremast in the blow, but Captain Oliver Mumford and his crew were able to make repairs and re-rig the ship at sea and subsequently made the passage in 100 days, of which a week was spent making repairs (***Gleason's Pictorial Drawing-Room Companion,*** January 29, 1853).

grief. The clipper was bound from Hampton Roads, Virginia, to New York in ballast in late February 1858, manned by a crew of twenty-six, when she encountered a heavy winter gale that sent her on the rocks off Montauk, Long Island. The clipper was subsequently pounded to pieces, and though some of the crew made it ashore alive, including one African American, all perished in the wreck, probably due to exposure. One individual who was the first to arrive on the scene later stated, "The shore looked like a wrecked shipyard. But for the breakers you could have walked for yards on broken masts, spars and timbers.... Only a part of the bow was left crunching on the rock where she struck...the bodies of the crew, all frozen stiff, were on the beach, some covered with snow" (Howe & Matthews, p. 316). Twenty-one of the crew were subsequently buried close to where they met their end at the churchyard in Easthampton.

Foundering at Sea

This category of clipper ship losses was also one of the most commonly experienced by any wooden vessel during the age of sail. To founder at sea, simply put, means that a ship is taking on water faster than it can be pumped out, resulting in the ship's sinking. In many cases this is due, at least in part, to the age of the vessel, sometimes due to storm or cargo-related damage, and often a combination of several of these factors. As wooden sailing ships aged, their seams, the small gaps between each individual hull plank, sometimes opened up even though they were sealed with oakum and let in water. This could happen due to heavy weather which battered a ship's hull, or shifting cargos that put a heavy strain on the hull. Either way, once the water-tight integrity of the hull was breached, it was up to the ship's pumps and the crew that manned them to keep the ship afloat. Many times the pumps did the job and a ship could be kept afloat until she made port for repairs, but when the battle against rising water in the ship's hold was clearly a losing one, then a

American clipper ship on her beam ends. This woodcut view shows a ship in distress in heavy seas, her mizzen and main masts cut away in an attempt to right the ship, while it appears as if her foremast was damaged. A ship in this condition was virtually helpless, wallowing like a log. The only thing that can save her now is calm weather or the hope of a passing ship to offer assistance (*Ballou's Pictorial Drawing-Room Companion*, October 6, 1855).

Clipper ship *Great Republic*. This, the largest of all the clippers ever built, had a much longer career than most expected from such an expensive vessel to operate. She met her end off Bermuda in 1872 when her pumps, and the crew that manned them, could not keep up with the water entering her cavernous hold during a strong gale (*The Illustrated London News*, 1855).

ship's commander had a decision to make. If he was voyaging in a busy shipping lane or traveling in close proximity to another ship, he could signal for assistance or, if no such help was available, the only other option was to abandon ship and have the passengers and crew take to the lifeboats with the hopes that they could make landfall or be rescued by a passing vessel. As we have seen in a number of cases regarding clipper ship losses, while many of these lifeboats *did* make landfall or were rescued in some manner, many others were never seen again.

Among those clippers which were lost by foundering are the following, along with the year lost and age of the ship at the time: *Tam O Shanter* (1853, 4 years), *Black Hawk I* (1854, 1 year), *Titan* (1858, 3 years), *David Brown* (1861, 8 years), *Belle of the West* (1862, 10 years), *Santa Claus* (1863, 9 years), *John Land* (1864, 11 years), *Mary* (1869, 15 years), *White Swallow* (1870, 17 years), *Euterpe* (1871, 17 years), *Nonpareil* (1871, 18 years), *Great Republic* (1872, 19 years), *White Squall* (1877, 27 years), *Celestial Empire* (1878, 26 years), *Archer* (1880, 28 years), *Pride of America* (1883, 29 years), *Swallow* (1885, 31 years), *Ocean Express* (1890, 36 years), *N.B. Palmer* (1892, 41 years), *Wild Pigeon* (1892, 41 years), and *Nightingale* (1893, 42 years).

As can be seen from the above, many of the clippers were indeed staunchly built and long lived, and few of them foundered in their early years. In reality, however, this is as it should have been as most clippers were rated A-1 by survey, meaning that their hulls were certified to be sound for ten or twelve years. Indeed, it was usually only after many years of hard driving and hard service that these ships, like any aging wooden vessel, finally succumbed to the ocean elements. More surprising, then, are the losses of several of the above listed clippers in their early years; little is known about the *Black Hawk*, the first of two clippers to bear this name. She was built by Hall & Teague at Black Rock, Fairfield (now part of Bridgeport), Connecticut, and launched with the name *Chief of Clippers*, but this was changed early on. She apparently foundered in a storm after becoming dismasted, but the full details of this loss are unknown. Likewise, the 1,985 ton, New York–built clipper *Titan* had troubles that led to her early demise. This ship was in a serious collision at Malta in 1855 during her first year of service while under lease to the French government during the

IX. Hurricane: *Shipwrecks and Other Noteworthy Clipper Events* 229

American clipper ship righted-masts cut away. This woodcut shows the aftermath of a storm-damaged clipper, with the crew in the process of setting up a jury rig (*Ballou's Pictorial Drawing-Room Companion*, October 6, 1855).

Crimean War and was never the same again. In 1857 she arrived at Liverpool with a load of American cotton in a badly leaking condition and was subsequently repaired, but apparently not well enough. The clipper later foundered in early 1858 while bound from Peru to Queenstown, being abandoned in a sinking condition after barely making it around Cape Horn. Her crew of 49 men all took to the lifeboats and survived a week at sea before being rescued by a passing vessel. One must question either the quality of construction or whether properly seasoned timber was used in the building of the *Titan*, as many clippers endured much greater trials without coming to a bad end so early in their career. Finally, among the short-lived clippers that foundered at sea, it is interesting that the *David Brown* is also on this list. This fast and well-regarded clipper was launched in 1853, being the first production of the New York shipbuilders Roosevelt & Joyce, who took over the yard of Jacob Bell. This same concern would put over the *Titan* several years later. The *Brown* did have a fine career, but was battered by a heavy gale while bound from San Francisco to Liverpool and subsequently leaked so heavily her pumps could not keep up. The ship was abandoned and all her crew eventually picked up. Of the other clippers that foundered at sea, several may be mentioned as representative occurrences; the Marblehead-built *Mary* was bound from the Chincha Islands to Cork, Ireland, with a load of guano when she began to take on water during a storm; the clipper was abandoned with fourteen feet of water in the hold, all her crew subsequently rescued after enduring cold weather and a lack of water; the *John Land* was abandoned without loss on a voyage from Britain to New York after simply springing a leak and getting eight feet of water in the hold, her pumps unable to save the ship; similarly, the *Euterpe* sprang a leak while bound from Callao, Peru, to Falmouth and had to be abandoned, but her crew was not as lucky, as one boat with nine men was lost; and finally, the famed *Great Republic* met her end while bound from Brazil to England in ballast. After enduring a strong gale, the big clipper's pumps could not keep up with a leak that developed and the ship was subsequently abandoned, all her crew being saved, with twelve feet of water in the hold.

Shipboard Epidemics

This final category of events in the life of a clipper is one that is seldom considered, but one that was an ever-present danger nonetheless for any vessel. Many ships during the age of sail suffered epidemics among their crew and passengers, especially those making long distance voyages to and from foreign ports. The biggest problem aboard the clippers that led to such outbreaks was not necessarily due to outright unsanitary conditions but was more related to the close conditions that prevailed. While the captain and his family had their own private cabins, the greater part of the crew all slept, ate, and bunked together in very close quarters, thereby creating the perfect setting for the spread of communicable diseases. It is almost certain that these diseases were brought aboard the ship while in a tropical port, carried unknowingly by some sailor who had there signed on for a voyage or by an existing crewman who, after having a bit of liberty, brought back aboard with him an unpleasant souvenir of his time ashore. Of the diseases that afflicted clipper ship crews and passengers, the most common were cholera and yellow fever. The former is a bacterial infection that was usually contracted from unsanitary drinking water, while yellow fever is a viral disease that is transmitted via the bite of the mosquito. Given the causes of these diseases, it is thus not very surprising to learn that of the seven clippers known to have suffered such epidemics (though the true number is likely much greater), all of their voyages began at such warm weather ports as New Orleans, Acapulco, the Virgin Islands, Shanghai, Calcutta, and Havana. Gaining suitable drinking water in particular was always a potential problem because clippers often had to fill their iron tanks with fresh water prior to departure from a foreign port, and places such as Calcutta and Shanghai were busy places teeming with people where waste was disposed of by dumping it into the local waters. While modern science has identified the cause and treatments for both these diseases, this was not the case in the days of the clippers and resultant deaths were not uncommon, exacerbated by the fact that merchant ships carried no trained medical personnel.

The clippers which are known to have suffered from these epidemics are *Architect* (1849), *Flying Arrow* and *National Eagle* (1853), *Nor'Wester* (1856), *Swallow* (1858), *Sovereign of the Seas* (late 1850s), and *Crest of the Wave* (1864). The Baltimore-built *Architect* was one of the first clippers to make the California run during the gold rush era, departing New Orleans for San Francisco in January 1849. On the way, a cholera epidemic broke out among her 56 passengers, resulting in several deaths and making for a long and stressful voyage that lasted 160 days. The Maine-built *Flying Arrow*, an unlucky ship her entire career, was bound from Boston to San Francisco in February 1853 when she suffered severe storm damage and was subsequently towed into St. Thomas, Virgin Islands, for repairs. While undergoing repairs, "Yellow fever broke out and nearly all on board were stricken; the fatalities among passengers and crew were very large" (Howe & Matthews, p. 183). That same year, in July, the Medford-built *National Eagle* was bound from New Orleans to Liverpool when she suffered an outbreak of yellow fever which caused the deaths of several crewmen, the first mate, and the captain's wife, forcing the ship to put in at Boston for assistance. Two other clippers that suffered from outbreaks of cholera were *Nor'Wester*, when bound from Calcutta, India, to Boston and *Sovereign of the Seas* during a voyage from Shanghai to Liverpool, while the *Swallow*'s entire crew suffered from yellow fever, with one reported death, while bound from Havana, Cuba, where she had just delivered a cargo of coolies from Macao to New York. A final clipper which suffered greatly from a yellow fever epidemic was the unlucky *Crest of the Wave*. This ship was bound from Acapulco, Mexico, to Valparaiso, Chile, in late 1864 when the entire crew, about twenty men altogether, were stricken; fourteen of the crew subsequently died, including the first mate, as well as the captain's wife. How closely these deaths followed one another and at what point they occurred in the voyage is unknown, but they surely resulted in the ship being severely short-handed even for this relatively short passage.

Several final notes of interest on this subject include the fact that in America and Great Britain there were, respectively, local and national quarantine regulations in effect for incoming ships that suffered from epidemics. New York had a quarantine station on Bedloe's Island, while Philadelphia had the oldest quarantine hospital in the U.S., established in 1799, but I've found no evidence that any of the clippers were subject to such quarantines. Finally, it is also noted that cholera in particular continued to be a problematic shipboard epidemic for years after the clipper ship era had ended; in 1892 the disease was rampant in New York Harbor, brought there by steamships carrying large numbers of European immigrants.

X

Twilight
The End of the American Clipper Ship Era

The year 1853 burned brightly in the history of the clipper ships and was, in many ways, the height of the age of sail in America. After the discovery of gold in California in 1848, and by the time the news became public on the East Coast, the building of clipper ships expanded at a rapid rate. While just twenty-two of these ships, most of them of extreme models, were built in 1850, 54 were added to the fleet in 1851, 75 in 1852, and a whopping 120 in 1853. Among the most notable of the clippers to be launched this year, just a small sampling to be sure, were the *Young America, David Crockett, Flying Dragon, Great Republic, Lookout, Neptune's Car, Red Jacket,* and *Morning Light.* Not only that, but it was a year in which many fast passages were made and it seemed like the sky was the limit. However, this would not be the case; thereafter, the building of clippers quickly subsided, with only 102 being built in the last five years of the 1850s combined. The year 1853, too, was also the last great one on the California runs in terms of high freight rates and extremely profitable voyages, and many extreme clippers were still being built to take advantage of the need for speed.

However, hindsight shows that there were also signs that the clipper ship bubble was about to burst; the California economy was growing at a rapid pace and no longer needed anything and everything exported from the East Coast at exorbitant prices. Some ship owners and commanders, perhaps mindful of the future, began to look elsewhere for cargos, whether it was bulk commodities, the lowly guano trade, or even the coolie trade. This was also a year in which ever increasing numbers of steamships were being built, both in America and Great Britain. While steamships at that time still had a difficult time competing with the clippers, it was becoming quite evident that they would, soon enough, start siphoning off the trade formerly conducted by sailing ships. Luckily for the clipper owners, American steamships were not yet that advanced, most of them being side-wheel steamers that were not always durable and, because they required huge amounts of coal, were still expensive to operate. Thus, at least for now, the long-distance clipper routes were still safe although, as previously discussed, within ten years it would be the clippers carrying the coal for their rivals to all parts of the globe.

In regards to steamship competition, just as the packet service between New York and Europe saw some of the first great developments in the speed of sailing ships, so too did this service become the first to gravitate toward the steamships; not only did the steamers tend to make faster western passages, but their passenger accommodations, albeit expensive, were also much better than the cramped conditions of the wooden sailing packets. Finally, this was also a run that saw the use of the much more advanced British steamships, whose vessels in this class were far and away much better developed during the 1850s than their brethren in America, especially with the development of the propeller driven ships.

The years 1854 through 1856 saw a mixed bag, but by and large the bad outweighed the good when it came to the clipper ships and the overall health of the shipping industry. On the plus side, the trend for extreme clippers was almost over by 1854 and the new half or medium clippers were taking over. While it is true that Donald McKay was still building clippers to the extreme, including the big and fast *James Baines*, other builders were becoming more realistic; in New York Abraham Bell put over the medium clipper *Adelaide*, in New Hampshire George Raynes launched the *Coeur de Lion*, while John Taylor in Chelsea built the medium clipper *Nabob*; again, this is just a sampling of some of the 71 clippers that came out in 1854.

Clippers cigar advertisement, 1858. Though the clipper's days were numbered after 1854, the ships still captured the American imagination, and their commercial appeal was very high (courtesy of the Library of Congress).

As previously discussed, these ships combined speed with carrying capacity, being a little bit more fully built, and many had reduced sailing plans, which in turn not only lowered operating costs, but also lowered the manpower needs to run them. Also on the positive side for the clippers was the Crimean War, pitting France and Britain against the Russian empire; as previously mentioned, a number of large clippers were chartered by France and Britain to serve as troop transports, which service was ended by early 1856. This opportunity came at just the right time, as the shipping industry was becoming stagnant in America by late 1854, with hundred of ships being laid up at New York alone due to a lack of business. Not only was the California run, and prevailing freight rates, on a large downward turn, but by 1855 the Australian gold rush had also subsided. While it is true that Australia's growth did create a permanent demand for regular freight and passenger service from both England and America, many of the American clippers put on this run, such as *Lightning, James Baines, Blue Jacket,* and *Red Jacket,* had been, or soon would be, sold to British interests and thus America's shipping industry did not reap the rewards. One bright spot in the Australian trade, however, was the establishment of R.W. Cameron's line of Australian packets operating out of New York, which employed some clippers in the mid to late 1850s but also many full-built non-clipper ships. In reality, about the only trade that remained consistently high from 1850 to 1856 was the China and India trade. Ironically, this slow-down period for the clipper ships was also a time when the American merchant marine as a whole had reached a high-water mark; according to historian Carl Cutler, United States "shipping (5,212,000 tons, less than 15 percent of which was in the form of steamers) was greater than ever before and relatively greater than at any time since...no other nation shared so largely in the most desirable and profitable commerce in the world" (Cutler, *Greyhounds of the Sea*, p. 307). However, this was also a time, which continued to the end of the decade, when fewer and fewer ships of all kinds were being built and, as Cutler succinctly states, "The story of the clipper ship is the record of a losing fight" (ibid., p. 310). Such were the ups and downs of the clipper ship era in a nutshell.

Despite the shipping slowdown that began in 1854, the end of the clipper ship era for good stemmed from one financial event, the Panic of 1857, which was spurred on by a number of factors, including the failure of a large bank based at an inland city in the Midwest which had nothing to do with clipper ships directly, at least at first. This event, which is said to be the first such worldwide financial event, was caused by a number of business factors that primarily affected the newly occupied western territories of the United States. The main problem was that western expansion and migration was beginning to slow down considerably as compared to the past seven years, thus affecting the revenues in both the shipping and the railroad industry. We have already seen that the freight rates on the California run had already began to fall four years earlier for the clipper ship operators, but this in and of itself was not enough to cause a full-blown financial panic. However, the railroads were a different story altogether; when their passenger and freight receipts began a downward trend by early 1857, this had a ripple effect among the many eastern banks that had financed their rapid expansion as their railroad securities also fell in value. Land prices and assessed values were also falling in 1857 due to the slower migration rate. All of these factors together not only caused a number of large regional railroad networks to go bankrupt, but it also spooked merchants, bankers, and investors alike, resulting in a tightening of the commercial credit market that further led to decreased merchant purchases and, in turn, decreased profits for northeastern merchants.

Clipper ship *Hurricane*. This Currier & Ives print from 1852, one of the rarest of their clipper prints, depicts a New Jersey–built ship that was perhaps the sharpest clipper, with 40 inches of deadrise, ever built. Though fast and well-built, the big ship could not carry a big enough paying cargo by the late 1850s and was laid up by her owners for several years.

Two other negative impacts, one direct, the other indirect, on the American economy in 1857 were the end of the Crimean War and the Dred Scott decision issued by the U.S. Supreme Court. During the two years of the Crimean War from 1854 to 1856 American farmers had profited greatly, their grain being shipped in great quantities to Europe, as production there had decreased due to the many men required for the war against Russia. Grain profits were so large that many farmers who had previously bought tracts of land in the west to start a new life during these years bought even more land (secured by bank loans) to increase their grain production. Once the Crimean War had ended, however, the bottom soon fell out of the grain market, resulting in many western farmers being unable to repay their land loans (and property taxes), resulting in even more financial woes for the banks as well as the railroads that shipped their produce. The Dred Scott Decision, on the other hand, was a ruling that had far-ranging implications going beyond the central question of slavery. In this case, the court ruled that not only were individuals held as slaves *not* protected by the Constitution and thus not citizens, but also that they had no legal standing to sue in court, nor could they be taken from their owners without due process. This decision, which was among the many causes that helped propel America toward the Civil War, initially led to a great amount of uncertainty in the western territories and whether slavery would be allowed there or not. This political uncertainty just added to the merchant fears and uncertainties that already existed, further hindering the market.

As if all the preceding factors weren't enough, the Panic of 1857 did not really hit full stride until the failure of the Ohio Life Insurance and Trust Company, a large bank which also had offices in New York, in August of that year. While this bank failed primarily due to fraudulent internal management and its liabilities were eventually covered, the failure nonetheless drew a wider public scrutiny of both the railroad industry and western land markets.

As a result of the Panic of 1857, America suffered a financial depression that lasted until well into 1859, and during much of this time many clipper ships lay idle in port, unable to find a paying freight; in New York alone many clippers were laid up for a long period, including the *Flying Cloud* and *Hurricane*. However, despite this depression, smaller clippers continued to survive on the California run, while a dozen or so American clippers were employed overseas in the British–China tea trade as late as 1859, including the Portsmouth-built *Sea Serpent*, *Bald Eagle*, and *Ringleader*. Regarding the California run, it is interesting that on many of the sailing card advertisements for these vessels from the period we see the claim made that such-and-such ship is the "smallest & sharpest clipper loading." Indeed, while merchants still wanted their goods to get to California in quick time, they also did not want their merchandise sitting aboard a big clipper waiting weeks or months for her hold to be filled. While forty-two medium clippers were built in 1855 and forty in 1856, only ten were built in 1857, followed by six in 1858, and but three in 1859. While maritime historians still debate when the last true clipper ship was built, the year 1857 effectively marks the end of the era. It is perhaps not a coincidence that one of the clippers launched in that year was the famed Mystic-built *Twilight*.

In ending this discussion of the clip-

The Case of the Sunken Slaver Haidee.

INTERESTING AFFIDAVIT.

Near 1,200 Negroes on Board.

Two Hundred Die on the Passage—The Remainder Landed on Cuba, and the Vessel Scuttled and Sunk off Montauk.

The slave ship *Haidee*. This dramatic headline tells the story of a Rhode Island–built clipper that was later converted to a slave ship and participated in the illegal trade of transporting African captives from their native land to Cuba (*New York Times*, October 6, 1858).

per ship era of the 1850s, it is perhaps ironic to note that just as the decade began on a high note and brought forth the dominance of the clipper ship, epitomized by such great ships as the *Flying Cloud* and *Comet*, so too did the decade end on a correspondingly low note, both for the nation and the clipper fleet. Not only had the economy slowed down considerably, but the nation was also spiraling toward a civil war and the slavery question pervaded nearly every aspect of American life. Even clipper ship operations were not immune to the greatest issue of the day; as has been previously discussed, many clippers were forced to drift into other, less glamorous, but paying nonetheless, trades, such as hauling guano, iron, and wheat. However, at least five clippers, the Baltimore-built *Lady Suffolk*, the Rhode Island–built *Haidee*, the bark *Wildfire*, the ironically named *Sunny South*, and the famed *Nightingale*, fell even further in status, becoming involved in the illegal and morally reprehensible slave trade. While four of these vessels became involved in the trade later in their careers at the end of the decade, the *Lady Suffolk* was an early participant and may have even been built expressly for the trade. She was built at Baltimore in 1852 and commanded by her builder and owner, Captain Adams Gray. By late November 1852 the ship was at Havana, Cuba, having been detained there by a British naval squadron, along with her crew, on suspicion of having been outfitted as a slave ship. In this case the American consul intervened, claiming that the ship had been sold to Spanish parties, resulting in the release of Captain Gray and his crew, much to the outrage of British residents of Havana. As for the *Lady Suffolk*, she apparently remained in Cuba, and though her later operations are unknown, she may still have been used in the slave trade, with one press report stating, "It is to be hoped that the *Lady Suffolk* may be captured on the coast of Africa by some of our cruisers; though glancing in that direction, we are at a loss to reconcile the account from time to time sent home, of the breaking up of slave depots, with this recent information of the activity of the trade in Cuba" (*New York Times*, "The Cuban Slave Trade and the English Squadron," December 16, 1852). In fact, it is unknown for certain how many smaller so-called clipper ships and barks may have been involved in the illegal slave trade early in the 1850s, but the trade was an active one and both American and British naval squadrons, working

The Africans of the slave bark *Wildfire*. This woodcut is based on the real life photographs taken aboard this Massachusetts-built clipper turned slave ship after her capture off Cuba by U.S. Navy warships in May 1860. As with many other slave ships since the trade began, many of the ship's original captives died during the passage. Though often flying foreign flags, many of these slave ships were outfitted in America at such ports as New York and Newport, Rhode Island, and were in fact owned by Americans participating in this illicit trade (*Harper's Weekly*, June 9, 1860).

X. Twilight: *The End of the American Clipper Ship Era*

The slaver *Sunny South* captured by a British warship. This New York–built clipper was supposedly sold to Cuban interests in 1859 and was renamed *Emanuela*. However, contemporary accounts make it clear that she was fitted out as a slave ship in New York and sailed then under the American flag. Though fast, her career in the flesh trade was a short one; this woodcut view shows the *Emanuela* being captured by the HMS *Brisk* (at left) in the Mozambique Channel (*Illustrated Times*, 1860).

both independently and in combined efforts, continually worked to interdict the trade around Cuba and on the coast of Africa.

Of those clippers found to be working in the slave trade late in the decade was the *Haidee*, a small ship built by Allen & Simpson at Providence, Rhode Island in 1854 and measuring but 395 tons. Purported to be a fast and sharp built ship and said to have been originally intended as a pleasure yacht, the *Haidee* was first owned by the well known shipping merchants Bucklin & Crane of New York along with several Providence merchants. Her career in the traditional clipper trades, however, was brief, she making but two voyages, one to China and one to the Mediterranean, due to her small size and inability to carry a paying cargo. In February 1857 the clipper was sold in New York, and this is where her story, a largely forgotten one, gets really interesting; the *Haidee* was sold to one Senora Georgia De Abranches (herself a Kentucky native) in New York, perhaps the only woman ever to own an American clipper ship, though one reporter stated that she probably purchased the ship on behalf of her husband, who was likely a native of Portugal, J.W. Abranches. In any event, the *Haidee*, which is said to have "sailed at about the same expense as a ship of twice her tonnage" (*New York Times*, October 5, 1858), was transferred later that same year in December to one Emilio Sanchez (born ca. 1822) of New York, a native of Cuba who had immigrated to New York in 1828 as a young boy and later made a living as a ship broker. Sanchez seems to have purchased the ship on the behalf of a Portuguese man named Boutelle. Soon after changing hands the *Haidee* was loaded with a cargo of rum, flour, tobacco, beef, cloth, and even one box of toys, bound for Gibraltar via Cadiz, Spain, and, commanded by Captain F.G. Whitney. The combination of her Portuguese and Cuban owners, destination, as well as her cargo all made locals suspect that the *Haidee* was fitting out as a slave ship, and though this was communicated to local authorities, nothing came of it and the clipper cleared port on January 7, 1858. She subsequently voyaged to Cadiz for repairs, then proceeded to Gibraltar to discharge her cargo, and then went back to Cadiz where she loaded a cargo of beans, flour, and rice and probably had her lower decks outfitted for carrying slaves. The crew was subsequently told that from here they were going to the West Indies, but instead the clipper made for the west coast of Africa, where 1,134 slaves were crammed in her hold, destined for the sugar plantations of Cuba. During the *Haidee*'s subsequent voyage, about 200 Africans died in the middle passage, the remainder being unloaded and sold at the slave markets at the port of Cardenas. Afterwards, the clipper cleared Cuba, with the American first mate, Macomber, a resident of New Bedford, Massachusetts, telling the crew they were bound for New Orleans, but once at sea the mate told his crew the truth, namely that the ship had no legal papers. The crew, which had been paid for their services in Cuba and included sailors from Portugal and the U.S. including the African American cook, William Jack, and another black man known only as Baltimore, likely the clipper's steward, did not know what to do so they followed the mate's advice. He advised that their only option was to sail the ship northward to New York and scuttle her off Long Island. This the crew agreed to do, subsequently sailing northward. Once they were off Montauk, a canvas sheet painted with the fake ship's name of *Elizabeth* and a hailing port of New Orleans was mounted on the ship's stern and in the early morning hours of September 16, 1858, holes that had previously been drilled in the hull of the *Haidee* and plugged were unplugged and the ship slowly began to sink. The crew all got off in two boats and subsequently walked calmly ashore at Montauk, where one group of them hired the light-keeper's son to carry them in a wagon to Sag Harbor. Here, the crew freely spent their Spanish doubloons on new clothing (and probably much food and drink) which, along with their appearance, created quite a stir in the small town. While it was eventually decided that these sailors were up to no good, by the time authorities decided to arrest them, they had made their escape. Eventually, in the following days, a number of these sailors were arrested, including First Mate Macomber, and were tried in federal court for taking part in the slave trade, and as the details of the *Haidee*'s final voyage came to light the "Montauk Point Mystery" (*New York Times*, "The Montauk Point Mystery Explained," October 5, 1858) was finally explained. The whole affair was not only a tragic one and a sad end for a ship, but also one of those many events that just goes to show that truth really is stranger than fiction.

The next clipper known to have seen service as a blackbirder was the bark *Wildfire*, built at Amesbury, Massachusetts, by Simon McKay. This vessel, which holds the record for the fastest voyage from Boston to Gibraltar, was captured by the U.S.S. *Mohawk* off the Florida Keys in May 1860 with a cargo of 514 African slaves, 100 of them women. Though the captives were said to have been landed in good condition, it was later reported that 51 had died on the passage, about a 10 percent casualty rate, and a woodcut illustration of these captives on the deck of the *Wildfire*, published in *Harper's Weekly* and based on actual photographs that were taken to document the scene, is one of the most iconic slavery images to appear in print before the Civil War. Among the captives there was a young mother with her six-month-old baby who was ill when the *Wildfire* was captured and soon after died, as well as a middle-aged mother with several children who was happily reunited at the slave camp on Key West with four daughters, all brought in as part of the cargo of another slave ship that had been captured around the same time. In September 1860 the clipper, referred to as the "American slave bark" ("Naval Intelligence," *New York Times*, May 19, 1860), was stolen by a Captain Patten while she was moored at Key West, but was quickly re-captured by a party of wreckers armed with rifles. Though the captain and crew, many of them either Cubans or Spaniards, of the *Wildfire* were brought to trial for their slaving activities, all were eventually acquitted by a Florida court and by late January 1861 the clipper again set sail from New York, bound for who knows where, under Captain Philip Stanhope, who had been her commander during her slaving days. What became of the captives of the *Wildfire* is unknown for certain, but they were likely returned to Africa.

Yet another slaver, one perhaps destined to become one given her name, was the 776-ton extreme clipper *Sunny South*, which also has an interesting history. She was built at Williamsburg, New

York, in 1854 by George Steers, the famed designer of the yacht *America,* and her model was said to have been based, at least in part, on that vessel. Though she was a pretty little clipper, built at a cost of $70,000, the *Sunny South* never lived up to expectations and broke no speed records. The clipper made one long California passage but was later primarily engaged in the South American trade before she ended her service under the American flag in 1859. Once again, as with *Haidee,* this ship's final ownership was under suspicion when she last cleared the port of New York in November 1859, the general consensus being that she had been fitted out there as a slaver. While Howe & Matthews state that the clipper was subsequently sold at Havana, Cuba, for $18,000 and renamed *Emanuela,* one contemporary reporter was convinced that this sale only came later "because I have a perfect recollection of the sailing of the Sunny South from this port, and remember my regret at the desecration of the glorious Stars and Stripes, knowing as I did at the time her destination was the coast of Africa" (*New York Times,* "Affairs in Havana," December 25, 1860). Whatever the case may have been, the ex–*Sunny South* made at least several slaving voyages and had gained a reputation as the fastest ship operating out of Cuba, but her slaving career was a short one. On August 10, 1860, while becalmed in the Mozambique Channel off southeast Africa and loaded with 800 Africans she was captured by the British sloop-of-war *Brisk* and sent into Mauritius. Here, the former American clipper was condemned for her illegal activity and subsequently renamed *Enchantress* with the intent that she would be taken into the British Navy as a cruiser. However, this was not to be as the clipper was wrecked in the Mozambique Channel in February 1861.

The final clipper to end the decade and begin the next by taking part in the slave trade was the famed Portsmouth-built *Nightingale.* Though slightly larger than the *Sunny South,* measuring in at 1,060 tons, and over twice the size of *Wildfire* and *Haidee,* this clipper shared the same yacht-like lines and was the fastest of the quartet. She had just completed a voyage from China to New York in January 1860 when she subsequently changed ownership under mysterious circumstances; though it was rumored that *Nightingale* was sold to a Brazilian merchant for use in the slave trade, the reality is that she was purchased by Captain Francis Bowen of New York, called the "Prince of Slavers," and hailed from that port and flew the American flag when she became a slave ship. Bowen had previously been engaged in the slave trade and knew the business all too well so within months of her purchase the clipper, once fitted out for the World's Fair in London, was converted in America to a slave carrier and then made for the west coast of Africa. Here she loaded a cargo of 2,000 Africans at Kabenda, Angola, a Portuguese colony. Just where these slaves were delivered is uncertain, but by the summer of 1860 the clipper was back in New York, where she later took on a cargo of grain for England, arriving at Liverpool in November. From here, the *Nightingale* carried a cargo of cloth and guns bound for St. Thomas on the west coast of Africa; while flitting about the coast in this area, no doubt seeking an opportune time to sneak into port to gather a load of human cargo, the *Nightingale* was in January 1861 boarded by a combined American and British naval task force but, her papers being in order, she was released. Captain Bowen's luck ran out, at least monetarily, on April 21, 1861, when she was boarded on the night of the 20th while in port at Kabenda and was found to have 961 slaves aboard, with more due to be loaded. The clipper was subsequently seized and was manned by a prize crew of 29 men commanded by Lt. John Guthrie. The first job of the crew was to liberate the slaves onboard; they subsequently sailed from Kabenda for Monrovia, Liberia, on April 23, 1861, but a yellow fever epidemic broke out which killed 160 of the African captives as well as two of the prize crew by the time port was made on May 7. Likely many more captives died once they were landed at Monrovia, but their full story is not known. As for the slaving crew of the *Nightingale,* in the end only the three mates were brought back to the United States for prosecution. Bowen was allowed to escape, along with one other man, even before the ship departed Kabenda, almost certainly because the prize crew of the *Nightingale,* all of them southerners, were sympathetic to his plight; Lt. Guthrie himself was a slaveholder back home in

North Carolina. The *Nightingale* subsequently departed Monrovia for New York with a sickly prize crew on May 13, 1861, and in late June was condemned by the courts and in July was sold at a U.S. marshal's sale to government agents, destined to become a U.S. naval vessel during the Civil War.

Finally, to end the discussion of the clippers and their involvement as slave ships, it should be mentioned that at least one clipper was put to commendable work in this area, and possibly others as well. The Medford-built *Star of the Union* was chartered by the U.S. government at New York in 1859 to carry African passengers, all of whom had been recovered from captured slave ships, back to their homeland in Africa. Likely destined for Monrovia, we can only hope that the return voyage of these former captives was a speedy and uneventful one. It is interesting to note that these returned captives, and others like them, were supported by the U.S. government, based on previously passed anti-slave trade laws, once they were landed at Liberia, receiving a lump sum $100 payment and being provisioned for a year, which arrangement was not to the liking of southern representatives in Congress

The Civil War's Impact on the Clipper

While the time of the clipper ships had passed by 1860, many still were operating under the Stars and Stripes as a regular component of the American merchant marine fleet. Some were still employed in the old clipper trades, while many others were operating in less glamorous lines of

The destruction of the *Harvey Birch*. This Mystic-built clipper was burned by the Confederate raider *Nashville* on November 19, 1861, while bound in ballast from Le Havre, France, to New York. She was one of fifteen clippers sunk by Confederate raiders during the Civil War (*The Illustrated London Times*, November 30, 1861).

X. Twilight: *The End of the American Clipper Ship Era*

Destruction of the clipper ship *Jacob Bell*. This dramatic woodcut shows the burning of this New York clipper by the Confederate raider *Florida*, called a "British pirate" in some accounts. This clipper was captured and destroyed on February 13, 1863, in the Atlantic while bound homeward from Foo Chow in late 1860 with 9,000 chests of tea. Many in the north considered the Confederate raiders nothing but pirates, as most were built in England and never put in at any U.S. port during the course of their wartime careers (*Harper's Weekly*, March 21, 1863).

work. However, the coming of the Civil War in 1861 would have a dramatic impact on these ships, as well as the entire American fleet. The operations of the clippers were affected in several distinct ways, some having immediate consequences, while others had more long-lasting implications.

When war broke out between the North and South in April 1861, within two months the small Confederate Navy began to put steam-powered raiders to work. Their goal, quite simply, was to capture and destroy Northern shipping whenever and wherever it could be found, thereby disrupting commerce. These Confederate raiders were small in number and reflective of the size of the Confederate Navy as a whole, but they did some real damage and truly did disrupt the North, albeit not to any great degree that impacted the war effort. Overall, less than ten of these raiders made it to sea to wreak their havoc, capturing or destroying just over 200 merchant ships of all sizes and types, while the rest were either captured or destroyed by Union forces while trying to get to sea, were interned in foreign ports, or came along too late in the war. A number of these raiders, including the most famed of them, the *Alabama* and *Shenandoah*, were built in England and initially crewed by British sailors. Their building and delivery to the Confederate Navy was all done with a high degree of secrecy, but word soon got out and these raiders were not viewed by the North as men-of-war, but as mere pirates. Indeed, though taken into the Confederate Navy, a number of these ships never once put into a Southern port, or any other American port for that matter. As a result of these shenanigans, the British government in 1872, after a series of negotiations, paid the U.S. government $15.5 million to cover the losses that occurred as a result of these British-built raiders. Of these raiders, the CSS *Tallahassee* sank 33 ships, many of them small barks or schooners, but also the 1,000-ton packet ship *Adriatic*, but no clippers. Likewise, the large CSS *Shenandoah* made it to sea in 1864 and though she sank no clippers, she did score 38 prizes, including many New England whaling vessels. Indeed, of all the branches of the merchant marine, the New England whaling fleet by far suffered the most at the hands of the Southern raiders.

However, eight other raiders did impact the clipper fleet, sinking fifteen of them. The CSS *Sumter* destroyed the Maine-built *Golden Rocket*, the CSS *Nashville* the Mystic-built *Harvey Birch*, the CSS *Georgia* the Maine-built *Dictator*, while the CSS *Chickamauga* destroyed the Portsmouth-built *Shooting Star* (II). The most successful raiders were the CSS *Florida* and the famed CSS *Alabama*; the former, commanded by Lt. John Newland Maffitt, destroyed the Boston-built *Southern Cross*, the New York–built *Jacob Bell*, the Maine-built *Red Gauntlet* and *Anglo Saxon*, the Newburyport-built *Star of Peace*, and the Mystic-built *B.F. Hoxie*, while the *Alabama*, commanded by the dashing Raphael Semmes, destroyed the New York–built *Contest*, the Medford-built *Golden Eagle*, the Maine-built *Talisman* and *Sea Lark*, and the Boston-built *Winged Racer*. Interestingly, Semmes was also in command of the first Confederate raider, the *Sumter*, when she destroyed the *Golden Rocket* in July 1861, the first clipper destroyed in the Civil War. The capture was made while the *Rocket* was sailing in ballast off the coast of Cuba on July 13, 1861, under command of Captain Bailey. Soon enough, the ship was put to the torch and was no more, though, as Semmes later recalled, "the ghastly glare thrown upon the dark sea as far as the eye could reach and then the deathlike stillness of the scene — all these combined to place the *Golden Rocket* on the tablet of our memories forever" (Fairburn, pg. 3547). In fact, the burning of this Maine clipper was the same fate suffered by nearly all the clippers that were captured. Usually the ships captured by the raiders were burned within a day, and often within mere hours, after they were plundered of supplies that the raider or her crew could use. The *Winged Racer* which, along with the *Contest*, was captured in the Straits of Sunda, far from the American conflict, in November 1863 was particularly useful; the *Alabama*'s commander would later write, "She had sundry provisions aboard, particularly sugar and coffee, of which we stood in need. She had besides a large supply of Manila tobacco and my sailor's pipes were beginning to want replenishing" (Semmes, p. 691). Once the *Winged Racer* was stripped of these things, she was put to the torch, though we can imagine that it certainly pained the sailor in Captain Semmes to do so, he calling this clipper "a perfect beauty; one of those ships of superb model" (ibid.). Of course, supplies were not always the only things stripped from the clippers; the *Talisman*, captured by the *Alabama* five months before in the Atlantic, carried four brass 12-pound guns and the powder and shot used by them which Semmes gladly took as his own, two of which were later used to arm another Confederate raider. Again, while most captured ships were burned quickly, this was not always the case. The clipper *Red Gauntlet*, captured by the CSS *Florida* in June 1863 while bound for Hong Kong loaded with coal, sailed in company with the coal-powered raider for many days, effectively serving as a traveling coal bunker. Once the coal had all been transferred to the *Florida*, the *Red Gauntlet* too was set on fire. Despite all these harrowing adventures, and the ill-will

Clipper ship *Ocean Express*. This drawing shows this Medford-built clipper during her time as a naval transport during the Civil War in the winter of 1861 and 1862. Like other clippers, this clipper probably set little or no sail during the course of her service and was actually towed by a steamship (courtesy of the Library of Congress).

that developed between many a clipper captain and their raider counterparts, it must be said that the captured crews and passengers alike were usually treated with the utmost respect, not as prisoners of war, and were often put ashore at neutral ports in Europe as circumstances allowed. Finally, there were several very rare occasions when a clipper gained a reprieve from the torch; the Portsmouth-built *Morning Star* was captured by the *Alabama* in March 1863 while bound from India to London, but since her cargo was owned by British interests, she was released and allowed to continue her voyage. The Maine-built *Snow Squall,* however, had a quite different experience; she was commanded by Captain James Dillingham, Jr., in late 1863 when bound from Malaysia to New York and came into close contact with the raider *Tuscaloosa*, a 350-ton bark that was a former northern merchant vessel recently captured and converted to a cruiser and armed with the guns captured from the clipper *Talisman*. Captain Dillingham acted like he was going to submit to the raider, but as the Confederates were gathering men to board his ship, he maneuvered his fast, 742-ton clipper forward and into the wind and quickly made his getaway. Though the *Tuscaloosa* fired on her potential prize, her shots were off the mark and after a chase lasting several hours the *Snow Squall* had made good her escape, leaving the raider empty handed. For this daring escape Captain Dillingham was amply rewarded by the ship's insurance agents in New York.

Admiral Raphael Semmes (1809–1877). This former American naval officer joined the Confederate Navy with the outbreak of the Civil War, and subsequently had a brilliant career commanding the commerce raiders *Sumter* and *Alabama*, During his wide-ranging depredations on the high seas he became the champion clipper killer during the war, sinking six of them (Semmes' ***Memoirs of Service Afloat***, 1869).

Several other interesting facts regarding the clippers and their losses in the Civil War include the fact that one clipper built in 1856, the only such ship built in the Deep South, the Key West, Florida–built *Stephen R. Mallory,* was named after the man, formerly a Florida senator, who would become the Confederacy's secretary of the navy, while the last clipper to be destroyed during the war was also one of the very last clippers to ever be built, this being the *Shooting Star* (II). Her loss occurred in October 1864 while she was bound from New York to Panama. Finally, of all the clippers to fall victim to the Confederate raiders, only two were built by the same builder; the Maine clippers *Dictator* and *Red Gauntlet* were both built at Robbinston by James W. Cox, his only clipper productions. Their destruction within several months of each other between April and June, respectively, of 1863 gives Cox the dubious distinction, if only through sheer bad luck and circumstance, of being the only clipper builder with multiple ships to his credit to have all of them destroyed by Confederate raiders.

Another interesting aspect of clipper ship operations during the Civil War is the fact that some of them, at least twelve in number, served the U.S. Navy and Army by performing duty as transports, store ships, hospital ships, and even warships. Some of these clippers were chartered by the army for a short period of time, usually a voyage or two, while others were purchased outright by the navy and served for the duration of the conflict. Among those clippers chartered were the Maine-built *Euterpe*, which served as an army hospital ship in 1861 and 1862 and was towed from location to location; the Medford-built *Golden Eagle* in 1861 and 1862 served as a transport making a voyage to Port Royal, South Carolina, but also has the distinction of being the only clipper that saw military service that was later destroyed by a Confederate raider, this happening in February 1863 while bound with a cargo of guano from Howland's Island to New Orleans after returning to her regular merchant duties; the McKay-built *Great Republic*, which served as a transport ship in 1861 and 1862 and twice went ashore during her brief service; the Medford-built *Kingfisher*, which made one round-trip voyage as a troop transport from Boston to Mississippi in 1861 and 1862; the Maine-built *Nonpareil* served as an army transport making one round-trip voyage from New York to New Orleans in 1862 and 1863; the Medford-built *Ocean Express* served as an army transport in 1861 and 1862, making a voyage from New York to Port Royal, South Carolina, in one of the war's first amphibious operations; and yet another Maine clipper, the *Undaunted*, which served as an army transport in 1862 and 1863 and was employed carrying horses. How many of these clippers actually worked under sail is uncertain; the *Great Republic*, for instance, is depicted as working at the end of a towline and probably carried little sail during her brief service simply due to her large size, while the *Ocean Express* was employed in a like fashion, being towed by the steamship *Illinois* during her transport duty.

Of those clippers that were purchased outright by the government, all were acquired in 1861 by local agents and most served during the duration of the war and sometimes beyond. The most prominent and successful of all the clippers in military service was the New York–built *Ino*. This small and fast clipper was purchased for $40,000 and armed with eight 32-pound cannons and one 20-pound Parrott rifle (whose barrel alone weighed 1,800 pounds), manned by a crew of nearly 150 men and commanded by volunteer Lt. Josiah Creesy, the former commander of the famed *Flying Cloud*. The U.S.S. *Ino* embarked on her first cruise in September 1861 and was subsequently involved in hunting down the Confederate raiders as well as protecting fishing vessels on the Newfoundland Banks in the North Atlantic and performing coastal blockading duties. The *Ino* returned to civilian service in 1867 when she was sold to Boston interests. The Mystic-built extreme clipper *Pampero*, purchased at a cost of $29,000, was probably also acquired with an eye towards using her as a cruiser; she was indeed rated as a fourth-class cruiser but was instead assigned to the West Gulf Blockading Squadron and spent most of her time at the mouth of the Mississippi River. Though armed with four 32-pound cannons, a 20-pound Parrott rifle, and a 12-pound rifle, she served mostly as a store ship. Two years after the war ended the *Pampero* was sold at auction in New York for $6,000 and disappeared from history. In contrast, the clipper warships *Onward* and *Morning Light* (II) saw some real battle action during the war; the former, a Medford-built vessel, was purchased for $27,000 and was heavily armed with eight 32-pound cannons and a large 30-pound Parrott rifle. Manned by a crew of 103 men, this clipper cruised in search of the Confederate raiders, escorted American merchant vessels homeward off the coast of Brazil, and even captured a British vessel trying to run the Union blockade. Unlike most clippers, after the war ended the *Onward* was retained by the Navy, but was soon relegated to duty as a store ship at Callao, Peru. Here the former clipper languished until the navy sold her in 1884 for a paltry sum. On the other hand, the Pennsylvania-built clipper *Morning Light* (II) would be lost in the course of her naval service. Purchased at a price of $37,500, the 938-ton clipper was armed with eight cannons and first employed as a cruiser but later, in 1862, was assigned to the West Gulf Blockading Squadron. In late 1862 the U.S.S. *Morning Light* took part in an expedition to destroy some Confederate salt works off the coast of Texas. The following year, on January 21, 1863, the clipper, commanded by Acting Master John Dillingham, was on blockade duty off Sabine Pass near the border of Texas and Louisiana when she was attacked by a combined force of Confederate naval vessels and Texas infantry who were trying to bust the Union blockade off Galveston. Due to light winds, the clipper could not make sail to escape and suffered such heavy fire that she was forced to surrender. Since the clipper had been riddled with gunfire from stem to stern she proved to be unsalvageable and was subsequently burned two days after being captured, giving her the distinction of being the only clipper to be lost due to direct battle conditions. One final clipper-turned-warship that must be mentioned is the famed Portsmouth-built *Nightingale*. As previously related, this clipper was sold in 1860 and was soon employed in the most vile branch of commerce, that of the slave trade. After being captured by the U.S. Navy in April 1861 while taking part in this illegal trade, the *Nightingale* later returned to New York where she was condemned in June 1861 and the following month was sold to the U.S. government for the small sum of $13,000. The clipper was subsequently armed with four cannons and sent south to join the Gulf Blockading Squadron at Key West, Florida, but was largely used as a store ship and was never employed as a cruiser. She was almost lost in October 1861 when she went ashore on a sandbar on the Mississippi River and plans were made to set her on fire to prevent her capture by the Confederates, but she was eventually got off, albeit with major damage. In May 1864 the *Nightingale* was sent north to Boston carrying a group of men due to be discharged from the navy because their time was up, but also because the ship was thought to be infected with yellow fever. The following year, in February 1865, the *Nightingale* ended her undistinguished naval career at Boston when she was sold to Chelsea resident and master mariner Captain David E. Mayo for $11,000.

Despite the clipper losses during the Civil War, many continued to make their voyages; to combat the possibility of being captured by a raider, it is interesting to note that a number of clipper owners took measures to provide for their own protection by arming their ships with cannons. One newspaper reported to this effect in August 1861, noting that Captain Harriman of the Mystic-built *Prima Donna*, sailing in Sutton's Dispatch Line, had a "fine rifled cannon on board" to "make good use of it if any pirate of the Jeff. Davis stripe should interfere with him" (*New York Times*, "California Ships Arming," August 5, 1861). The paper also reported that the Wiard type of steel rifled gun was popular among ship owners; these light artillery pieces were manufactured in New York City, but their popularity seems to have been fleeting as only sixty of them were cast in 1861 and 1862. Such drastic measures aside, many owners took an altogether different approach when it came to their clippers; because of the depredations of the Confederate raiders, by 1863 insurance rates for cargos and voyages had risen to such astronomical heights that most ships were simply uninsurable. These rates added so greatly to the already razor-thin profit margins of American ship owners that many simply gave up and sold their vessels to foreign owners. Indeed, the sell-off was so drastic among all owners, and not just those with an interest in clippers, that by the end of the Civil War some 1,600 ships aggregating about 800,000 tons had been sold off, thereby decreasing the overall American merchant marine fleet by about a third. It was a blow from which the merchant marine would never really recover and whatever commercial supremacy the U.S. had on the world's oceans faded considerably. This sell-off of American ships is one of the great tragedies of the war from a business standpoint and was all out of proportion in comparison to the losses actually inflicted by the handful of raiders that were out there. Fear and uncertainty, as it were, among owners, underwriters, and agents caused the loss of the many ships sold foreign, including about a third of the clipper fleet, just as surely as if they had been burned at sea. What's more, the vast majority of the ships sold went to British interests, thereby increasing that maritime power's commercial presence on the high seas at the same time that her shipbuilders were aiding the Confederate cause. Other buyers included Peru, primarily for the guano trade, and a relatively few to the Germans, French, Spanish, and Norwegians. The sell-off of the clipper fleet, as with other merchant vessels in general, started slowly at first, with only thirteen such ships being sold to foreign interests in 1861 and 1862, among them being the famed *Flying Cloud*, *Challenge*, and

Wizard. However, the year 1863 saw the most panic in the shipping market, again coinciding with the depredations of the *Alabama,* and nearly sixty clippers were sold foreign in that year alone, among them such renowned vessels as the *Andrew Jackson, Comet, Flying Scud, Flying Childers, Morning Light, Neptune's Car, Ocean Telegraph, R.B. Forbes, Sierra Nevada, Spitfire, Tornado, Typhoon,* and *Wild Pigeon.* In the last two years of the war, the sell-off of the clippers slowed somewhat, totaling nineteen ships, including the *Mountain Wave, Sparkling Wave, Morning Glory,* and *Starlight.* However, the damage was done, and once sold and registered under a foreign country, these ships could not return to American registry. In all, during the years 1861 to 1865, about 140 clippers were sold to foreign interests; in contrast, for the years 1850 to 1860 inclusive fewer than forty clippers were sold foreign, while after 1865, of what clippers remained under the American flag another fourteen would be disposed of over the years.

American Versus the British and Canadian Clippers

It is common among the public at large and maritime enthusiasts in general to lump the clippers of America, Canada, and Great Britain together, which is perhaps understandable as many maritime historians have also done so. Aside from their common designation of being clippers, these ships did indeed have a few other things that tied them together; the foreign clippers, like the Americans, were fast, beautiful, and were also the most famed sailing ships of their day. However, while it is convenient to tell the histories of these clippers together, the fact of the matter is that the American-built clippers had but a slight influence over their British and Canadian cousins. First of all, the need for speed among British merchant sailing ships was not as great for a variety of reasons, though it cannot be disputed that the British had the ability and did build some fast vessels well

The British clipper *Chrysolite*. This 570-ton extreme clipper was built at Aberdeen by Alexander Hall in 1851, and though much smaller in size than the American clippers being launched at this time, her building was directly influenced by the appearance of the American clipper in England the previous year (*The Illustrated London Times*, March 1851).

The British clipper *Schomberg*. This large clipper, put over by Alexander Hall in 1855, was also built in direct response to the American clippers, namely the four clippers ordered from Donald McKay by James Baines for employment in his Black Ball Line of Australian packets. Hall was the most noted builder in the British Isles, and the *Schomberg* might have proved herself to be a fast clipper, but she never got the chance after being wrecked on her maiden passage out to Australia in December 1855 (*Illustrated Times*, April 12, 1856).

before the 1850s. Just as America had her Baltimore clippers and the clipper pioneer *Ann McKim*, so too did localized trade in the British Isles, especially that on the run from Aberdeen to London, produce some early vessels of clipper form, the 150-ton *Scottish Maid*, built in 1839 by Alexander Hall, being recognized as the first such vessel built in the United Kingdom. However, in regards to long distance voyages, commerce to the British Isles and her colonies was greatly controlled, with no outside ships from other nations taking any great part until the 1850s. The vaunted English tea trade, for which British clippers would later be built, was initially monopolized by the East India Company by way of government charter, and while some of their Indiamen, usually called "tea wagons" due to their slow sailing, would make fast passages, there was no competitive need to do so. After the expiration of the East India's charter in 1834, British ships did make tea voyages, but these were mostly smaller ships, well under 500 tons. As to other areas where speed might be used, the British, of course, had no gold rush of their own and were unable to take part in the American California trade. British vessels also took part in the opium trade in Far Eastern waters from the 1820s onward, which did employ fast vessels, but most of these were small and schooner rigged. By 1850 the mercantile situation in Britain was changing; the nation's restrictive trade policies had been phased out and maritime commerce by ships of other countries could now participate. The two major trades that would be impacted by these legal changes were the tea trade and the grain trade. I have already discussed the latter, and speed was never a real factor in the grain trade. However, just as with the California trade, the China tea trade was becoming more and more speed driven and would soon become the hallmark for the British clippers. The Australian trade, after the discovery of gold there in 1852, also brought about a need for speed, but it was largely American-built clippers and many from Canada that were either chartered or purchased for this burgeoning trade.

The shipbuilders of Aberdeen, Scotland, were the pioneers in building clippers in the British Isles and, just as John Griffiths in New York was proposing the long and sharp bow, so too was shipbuilder Alexander Hall the pioneer in that town in the early 1840s. However, few of these sharp ships were built until the 1850s, and they came about directly as a result of the appearance of the New York–built clipper *Oriental* at London in December 1850. Not only had this clipper made a fine tea passage, but she was the first American ship to load directly with a tea cargo for Britain as a result of the new trade laws. Her performance, and the fact that she garnered the highest freight rates on subsequent voyages really was a wake-up call to British merchants and ship owners, resulting in the building of the first two British tea clippers, both built by Hall at Aberdeen, the *Stornoway* and the *Chrysolite*. Both these clippers were small, about 500 tons, and in fact, while a number of British tea clippers were built that measured close to 1,000 tons most of them came in at 700 or 800 tons, including the latter-day famed flyers *Cutty Sark* and *Titania*. This was one of the major differences between the American and British clippers, their size, but also the number that were built; in the twenty-year period from 1850 to 1870 fewer than 90 British tea clippers were built, and only sixteen of these in the years 1850 to 1860. The largest number of British clippers built in any one year was in 1863, when thirteen such ships were built. While there clearly was a desire for speed in the tea trade, it was always tempered by economic factors, and British owners never went all out in the clipper trade along the lines of what Donald McKay was doing in Boston. As for the Australian trade, there was a bit of competition in this area, but it was rather short-lived. There was one clipper, the big 2,600-ton *Schomberg*, that was built almost certainly based on American influence. Not only was this clipper, built specifically for the Australian trade, the largest ship ever built in the United Kingdom up to that time, but her launching in July 1855 at the Alexander Hall shipyard in Aberdeen for the James Baines & Co. Black Ball Line was surely the British response to the earlier purchase by Baines of the four big American clippers, *Lightning, James Baines, Champion of the Seas,* and *Donald McKay,* the last of which was delivered in early 1855. British shipbuilders were eager to prove that they were the equals of their American counterparts, and many of them, including Hall and Walter Hood in Aberdeen, William Pile in Sunderland, Robert Steele in Greenock, and Charles Connell in Glasgow, certainly were. However, while the *Schomberg* showed great promise, she was an ill-fated vessel, being wrecked on her maiden voyage while off Cape Otway, about 100 miles from her final destination on December 27, 1855. Though the loss of this ship was through no fault of her builder or the ship itself, by the time such a large wooden clipper would again be built the clipper ship era in America had ended.

The construction details of British clippers were also somewhat different from their American counterparts; not only did British shipbuilders build smaller clippers, their vessels were also not as heavily sparred and thus were not usually subject to the same serious dismasting events and loss of top-hamper on their voyages. Few British clippers carried skysails and moonsails, though a few did carry the former. However, the greatest difference, which came about in 1863, was the use of composite construction methods. The British clippers were vastly lighter than similarly sized American clippers because of this construction, which meant a ship so built had an iron skeleton and ribs that were covered by wooden planking. The iron frame of the British clippers meant that these clippers could be driven hard and still withstand the pounding of the ocean's waves, and as a result, several of them have survived to this day, including the famed museum ship *Cutty Sark* (built in 1869), as well as the *City of Adelaide* (built in 1864), the oldest surviving intact clipper hull in the world. As to which clippers were the faster, the American or the British, the larger and longer American ships were, without a doubt, the faster of the two classes, especially in heavy weather. However, the narrow breadth of the British clippers meant that they were generally more maneuverable, and it is interesting to note that one experienced shipmaster, and the first clipper historian, does make the case the case that in perfect weather, and all things being equal in terms of size, "they were, perhaps, as fast as the American clippers of the same class" and that "it may again be said that they probably combined the good qualities of a merchant ship in a higher degree than any other vessels that have ever been built" (Clark, pgs. 337–338). Like the American clipper ships, the reign of the tea clippers was also a relatively short one; while the tea races homeward from China to the United Kingdom would continue well into the 1870s, the trade was doomed for sailing ships beginning in November 1869 with the opening of the Suez Canal, which connects the Mediterranean and Red seas. Once this shortcut was available, steamships could now make it to the Far East in much quicker time, while sailing ships were forced to make the longer voyage around the Cape of Good Hope, the southern tip of Africa, because the prevailing winds in the Suez area were detrimental to sailing ships.

Finally, our neighbor to the north, Canada, also built a number of clippers, perhaps as many as two dozen. These, like their American counterparts, were all built in the 1850s and were of standard wooden make, as opposed to composite construction. However, like the British clippers, the Canadian ships were prohibited from taking part in the California trade, which must have been a hard pill to swallow for builders and owners alike in Quebec and the Maritime Provinces, as just to the south of them the shipyards in Maine were reaping the benefits of a trade they could only dream of. The discovery of gold in Australia, however, gave a huge boost to Canadian shipbuilders and their ships made a name for themselves in that trade. The Canadian clippers were not extreme models like the early California clippers, nor were they as heavily sparred, and instead were close in model to the later-day half or medium clippers and could carry a great deal of cargo. Only one

The Canadian clipper *Marco Polo*. Though not as sleek and pleasant to the eye as the typical American clipper, this Canadian cousin, built at Saint John, New Brunswick, in 1851 and originally employed as a timber ship, was nevertheless a well-built and fast ship that could stand hard driving. She made a name both for herself and Canadian builders during the course of her service in the Australian trade in the Black Ball Line of Australian packets (*The Illustrated London Times*, 1852).

Canadian shipbuilder, Thomas Conrad Lee of Quebec, seems to have been directly influenced by the Americans, he going so far as to travel to New York in 1852 and hiring William Power, presumably previously employed in one of the many New York shipyards, as his designer and yard superintendent, their first production together being the 1,602-ton clipper *Arthur the Great* (Wallace, pg. 67). Though the clipper is said to have made some fast passages and is known to have served as troop transport under charter to the British government, her career is largely unknown. The size of this Canadian clipper, designed by an American, does point to the fact that American clipper building practices were more influential perhaps in North America than Great Britain in terms of ship size, as several of the Canadian clippers rivaled the productions of Donald McKay in dimensions, including the 2,337-ton *Morning Light* (not to be confused with the Portsmouth- and Pennsylvania-built clippers of the same name), the 1,887-ton *Ocean Monarch*, as well as the 2,339-ton *White Star*.

Though they were certainly well built, only one of the Canadian clippers rivaled the American clippers in terms of speed, that being the famed *Marco Polo*. This clipper was built by James Smith at Saint John, New Brunswick, in 1851 and was a three-decked ship measuring 1,625 tons. This ship was probably originally intended for the Canadian lumber trade, but after carrying her first cargo to Britain she was sold there in 1852, first to a shipbroker, and soon thereafter to James Baines & Co., who put her into their Black Ball Line of Australian packets, on which runs she made some fast passages. The *Marco Polo*, which was stoutly built and more resembled a packet ship or a naval frigate than a traditional clipper, continued as a favorite in the Australian trade for many years until being relegated to general cargo carrying duties in 1867, and in 1871 was sold and put in the coal and lumber trade. Like many American clippers, the *Marco Polo* was later re-rigged as a bark and was sold to Norwegian interests in 1882; she ended her days the following year, in July 1883 when she began to take on water while traveling down the St. Lawrence River after departing Quebec with a load of deals and was subsequently beached on Prince Edward Island, where the wreck was subsequently auctioned off. A gilded bust of Marco Polo that decorated the stern of the clipper was salvaged and is housed in the New Brunswick Museum. Among the other notable Canadian-built clippers was the 1,321-ton *Mermaid*, built in 1853 by John McDonald at St. John's, Nova Scotia, soon thereafter sold to Pilkington & Wilson and put into their White Star Line of Australian clippers; later, in the 1860s, she went into the New Zealand trade, was subsequently sold foreign in 1872, put in the coal and lumber trade, went ashore off Southport, England, during a storm and was lost in December 1883. The 1,195-ton *Conway*, built at St. John, New Brunswick, in 1851 by Owens & Duncan, was originally built as an immigrant ship; she was purchased by James Baines & Co. in 1853 and put into the Australian trade, and was later abandoned at sea in 1875. The 2,012-ton *Guiding Star*, built by the Wrights at St. John, New Brunswick, in 1853, was built specifically as an Australian clipper, chartered by the Golden Line of packets; she went missing with all hands and 480 passengers on her second run after departing Liverpool in January 1855. The 1,219 ton *Star of the East*, also built in 1853 by the Wrights in New Brunswick, was purchased by the Golden Line of Australian packets. There was also the previously mentioned *White Star*, built at New Brunswick by the Wrights in 1854 to the order of Pilkington & Wilson as the flagship in their White Star Line of Australian packets. Other known or reputed Canadian clippers include the *Golden Age, Indian Queen, Goldfinder, Arabian, Star of the South, Golden Era, Prince of the Seas, Shooting Star, Boomerang, Rock City, Shalimar, Morning Star,* and the small clipper bark *Stag*. As can be seen, many of these clippers carried names that were similar or identical to American built clippers, and almost all were built as a result of the Australian trade, many of them serving in one of a number of packet lines, including the White Star Line, the Black Ball Line, the Golden Line, or the Fernie Brothers' Red Cross Line. Just as the craze for American clippers began to fade in the mid–1850s, so too was this the case for

Canada, and once the Australian boom was over and that trade settled into more normal patterns by 1856, no more clippers were being built.

Survivors in Sail: the Last of the Clippers

Though the American clipper fleet was drastically reduced in the aftermath of the Civil War, the entire American merchant marine, which included some of the smaller clippers remaining under the Stars and Stripes, saw an upturn in their fortunes. Not only was this due in part to the normal resumption of trade and commerce, but also because of the renewed growth and expansion of America from 1865 to the 1880s. West Coast exports in particular were huge, especially in grain and timber, but other resurgent trades that led to this revival which we have already discussed include the petroleum industry, and a resumption of the tobacco and cotton trades in the South. Yet another trade that kept the merchant fleet going was that of imported iron; after the Civil War there was so much demand for iron, especially in the renewed expansion of the railroads, but also due to rebuilding efforts in the South, that many ships were employed bringing iron into the United States. No matter what the trade, there was a brief revival in wooden shipbuilding. The vast majority of this wooden tonnage built from 1860 to 1880 came in the form of the so-called downeasters and would hail from the state of Maine. The downeaster was really a slightly fuller model of the half or medium clippers that succeeded the extreme clippers in 1854, and like the medium clippers, these well-built Maine vessels carried a large paying cargo yet did so with reduced manpower requirements. Though the lofty sail plans of the 1850s built clippers were largely abandoned, the downeasters could still make some fast passages. As far as the building of large wooden merchant ships of the downeaster type in other locales goes, it was a much different story. Such large cities as New York, Boston, Baltimore, and Philadelphia were largely done with building wooden ships, with the exception of East Boston. Not only did the timber have to be imported to these areas for building needs at great cost, the local supply long since exhausted, but labor costs were simply too prohibitive. Other areas outside Maine, including Mystic, Portsmouth, and Newburyport, did continue to build square-rigged sailing ships in small numbers, but it was the Pine Tree State that would remain the last bastion of large-scale wooden shipbuilding in America down to the 1890s. By this time, the much more labor-intensive ship rig was replaced by the handy fore and aft schooner rig, and the era of the wooden square-rigger as a whole was over.

Of course, despite the decline of the sailing ship, the clippers still roamed the world's oceans and made their occasional appearances at ports in America and elsewhere. Even before the end of the 1850s many of the heavily sparred clippers had their sail plans reduced in size by eliminating skysail yards, this being done not just for economy's sake, but also because the aging clipper hulls could no longer withstand the heavy strain their use entailed. Many clippers, such as *Ino*, *Nightingale*, *Syren*, and *Houqua*, had their sailing plans reduced even further and were re-rigged as barks, that is, having only square-rigged sails on her fore and main masts, and a fore-and-aft sail on her mizzen mast. While such measures certainly reduced the appearance and beauty of the ship, they did prolong the useful working lives of these aging clippers in some cases. As to the later careers of the clippers of the 1850s, many of their fates have already been discussed, but several others are here worthy of highlight. The *Flying Cloud*, after her sale to British interests in 1862, was put on the Australian run and made some fast passages. However, no doubt worn out, the *Cloud* was later operated in the timber trade between Canada and London, usually sailing between St. Johns and London. We can only imagine what a thrill it must have been for her later-day captains to have gained command of this ship due to her reputation, and perhaps it is appropriate that her last commander, probably an Englishman, was known locally as the "Wild Goose." The *Cloud* would, late in 1874, end her days after becoming stranded on Beacon Island Bar just off St.

Johns after trying to return to port during a storm. While her timber cargo was being discharged in an attempt to free up the old clipper, her back was broken, and she was subsequently condemned and sold for scrap. Some months later, in June 1875, the *Flying Cloud* met her end by fire, being burned so that her metal fittings could be salvaged from the ashes. Whether the *Cloud*'s figurehead of an angel blowing a trumpet, which once led her into port to herald one of the fastest sailing ship voyages ever made, was saved from her funeral pyre is unknown but unlikely, as owners and ship-breakers alike didn't seem to have much sentimentality in this regard. Another Donald McKay–built clipper, indeed his namesake vessel, to end its days in relative obscurity was the *Donald McKay*; sold to the Germans in 1879, she became a coal hulk at the island of Madeira, just off the coast of Portugal. Likewise, the Maine-built *Red Jacket* ended her days as coal hulk at Cape Verde, while the Medford-built *Ocean Telegraph*, after being sold to James Baines & Co. at London, was renamed the *Light Brigade*, was later cut down to a bark, and after 1883 was sent to Gibraltar and converted into a coal hulk, becoming a familiar sight on the waterfront there for several decades. The extreme clippers like those mentioned above were too large to operate, but their cavernous and stoutly built hulls were perfect to serve as storage ships. However, many of the smaller clippers continued in service; the Norwegians in particular kept many of them in paying condition for many years. The Portsmouth-built *Sea Serpent* was sold by Grinnell & Minturn of New York to go under their flag in 1874 and, renamed *Progress*, was still in operation after 1890, the same being true of the more obscure clipper *Brewster,* built at Newburyport by Currier & Townsend in 1855. This ship was sold to Norway by the 1880s and, renamed *Fama*, was last reported in 1890. Similarly, another Portsmouth-built clipper, the famed *Nightingale,* also ended up in Norwegian hands, being sold for $15,000 and put into the Canadian lumber trade. Hailing from the port of Krageroe, she was abandoned at sea in 1893 during a voyage from Liverpool to Halifax, Nova Scotia, thereby ending a 42-year career that was probably more varied and adventure filled than that of any other clipper. Yet another long-lived clipper, one of the longest ever to continue under sail, was the New York–built *Simoon*; launched by Jabez Williams in 1852, she was sold to British interests in 1863, and thereafter to Norwegian owners in 1874. Renamed *Hovding* and re-rigged as a bark, the old clipper was still in operation in 1912, though her final fate is unknown.

Among the other long-lived clippers not previously mentioned are the *Malay, Competitor*, and *Syren*. The former ship, measuring 868 tons and built by John Taylor at Chelsea, Massachusetts, was launched in 1852 and had a long and profitable career entirely under the American flag. In her later years she was re-rigged as a barkentine and operated as a packet ship between San Francisco and Hong Kong, and still later as a lumber carrier. Her end came at Tahiti in late 1891, where she was condemned after making port in distress while carrying a cargo of railroad ties. The *Malay* was unusual in her conversion to the barkentine rig, where only the foremast is square-rigged, the main and mizzen mast being fore and aft rigged, as few, if any other clippers were so converted. It was her economical rig that probably contributed to the clipper's prolonged life; among the Tall Ship sailing vessels in operation today, a number of them are barkentines. The Medford-built *Competitor*, put over by James Curtis in 1853, had an active later life; sold by Weld & Co. of Boston to the Germans in 1863 for $31,000, a few years later she was sold to British interests, and sold yet again to the Germans and soon thereafter Swedish interests. The *Competitor* was no doubt highly thought of even if she did change hands many times; in 1899 the forty-six-year-old ship was completely overhauled and though she made some trans–Atlantic voyages, was largely operated in the Baltic lumber trade. In 1901, after suffering a collision, the old clipper was sold to Finnish interests and was subsequently re-rigged as a bark and renamed *Edward*. While her final fate is uncertain after this time, it would not be surprising if the old *Competitor* was still afloat twenty years later. Finally, to end this account of clipper ship operations, it is fitting that the last word be given to the longest lived ship of them all, the medium clipper *Syren*. Like the *Malay*, this small clipper, measuring 1,064 tons, was built by John Taylor at Chelsea for the Salem, Massachusetts, mercantile firm of Silsbee & Pickman and was launched in 1851. She sailed as an American vessel for thirty-seven years, including a long period in the Boston–Honolulu–New Bedford triangular whale oil trade route, but in 1888 she put into Rio de Janeiro in distress. Though condemned, the *Syren* was subsequently sold to South American parties, repaired, and re-rigged as a bark. In 1920 she was still afloat, now named the *Margarida*, and was owned by one J. Hurley with a homeport of Buenos Aires, Argentina. This gave the old *Syren* the distinction of being the longest serving clipper, her career spanning over six decades.

Today, the clipper ships of the 1850s are all gone, none being left afloat to serve as a museum ship, though remnants of them, including some figureheads, can be viewed at some of our nation's best maritime museums. Over the years there has been talk of building a replica of the American clipper ship and organizations have been formed to raise funds for such an undertaking; while there is much surviving documentary evidence, in the form of contemporary plans and models, to ensure the accuracy of such a project, the factors of old, finances and skilled manpower, have made all such efforts fall short. To just build a wooden clipper ship today would cost tens of millions, if the needed skilled workers could even be found for such a venture. Too, once built, the massive costs associated with operating, maintaining, and finding a permanent home for such a unique and historic vessel would be astronomical. Probably the last attempt to build such a replica was in the 1990s, when retired shipmaster Charles Quinlan, Jr., established the Shining Sea Foundation. His goal was to raise $21 million to build a clipper for the East Boston waterfront which would be adorned with a figurehead depicting clipper heroine Mary Ann Patten. One of Captain Quinlan's motivating ideals was his sincere belief that "America should not have a flagship that was a war prize from Nazi Germany" (Lawrence, J.M.), a reference to the our nation's most famed Tall Ship, the United States Coast Guard training ship *Eagle*. Unfortunately, Quinlan's efforts failed and his foundation was dissolved within ten years.

All the clippers of old may be gone, but that does not mean that they don't make an appearance on the American coast from time to time; as previously mentioned, the remains of the New York–built *War Hawk* can be viewed by recreational divers in person at Discovery Bay, Washington, or even online in a You Tube video, while the remains of the wrecked clipper *King Philip*, built at Alna, Maine, in 1856, make their appearance in the sands of Ocean Beach at San Francisco from time to time. The wreck was left in place when the clipper was lost in 1878, and periodically has emerged from the sands over the years, doing so in the early 1900s,

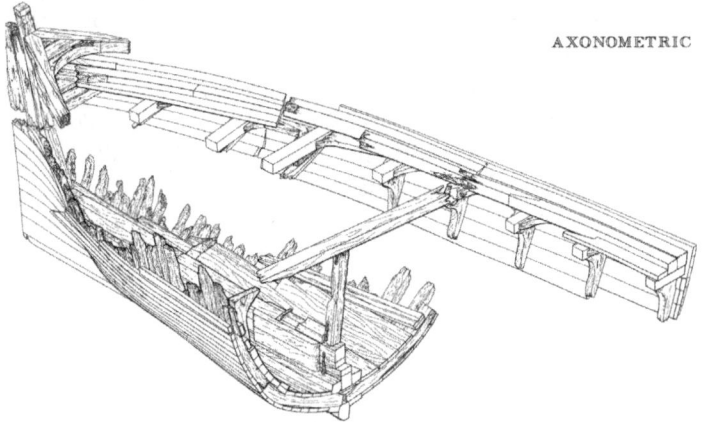

Bow section of the *Snow Squall*. This drawing shows the recovered bow portion of the Maine-built clipper *Snow Squall*. She was a fast vessel that put into the Falkland Islands in 1864 in a leaking condition, and was subsequently condemned and abandoned along the waterfront at Port Stanley. Remarkably well preserved, as have been a number of other Port Stanley wrecks, the bow of the clipper was surveyed and salvaged by a Maine museum team, eventually being brought back to Maine after an absence of more than 120 years. From Historic American Engineering Record (HAER), 1992, delineation by Karl Bodensiek (courtesy of the Library of Congress).

then again at various times from 1982 to 1984, and recently in 2007, 2010, and 2011. After a historical survey of the wreck was made it was determined that about 45 percent of the hull is intact, the "most complete remains of an American medium clipper of the mid–19th century" (Delgado, p. 223).

Despite the historic clipper sites just described, the most interesting and the oldest clipper that can be seen, at least in part, today is the Maine-built *Snow Squall*. After suffering damage while attempting to round Cape Horn in late February 1864, the clipper, commanded by Captain James Dillingham, Jr., reversed course, arriving at Port Stanley, Falkland Islands, in distress in March 1864 with water in her hold and a damaged rudder. Though Captain Dillingham made attempts to salvage the ship, the high expense of such a venture, combined with the age of the ship and the fact that the Civil War was still ongoing meant that the *Snow Squall*'s fate was sealed; the clipper was eventually abandoned at the Falklands and left to rot among the other hulks along the Port Stanley waterfront. In a bit of irony, Captain Dillingham took passage home in late 1864 in a Baltimore bark which was captured along the way by the Confederate raider *Florida*, thereby being robbed of some of his tools of his trade, including charts and directories, two chronometers, a spyglass, a sextant, and a number of other items (Dean & Switzer, p. 198). Just the year before Captain Dillingham had outwitted a Confederate raider and prevented the *Snow Squall* from being captured, but this time his luck had run out. However, the fortunes of the *Snow Squall* would, eventually, rise again; left along the waterfront for over a hundred years, the clipper and other significant hulks in Port Stanley eventually came to the attention of marine archeologists in America, and indeed worldwide, for here at the Falklands, frozen in time, was an outdoor museum, or graveyard if you prefer, of ships from all around the world, many of which arrived under similar circumstances. It would not be until the late 1970s that what remained of the *Snow Squall* came to the attention of maritime historian Nicholas Dean, who subsequently founded the *Snow Squall* Project in an effort to recover a portion of the clipper and bring her back home to Maine. After several years of hard work and an interruption by the Falklands War in 1981, the project got under full way in 1983 and culminated in the recovery of a 30-foot bow section of the clipper's hull in 1987, which was subsequently transported back to Maine and is now on display at the Maine Maritime Museum in Bath. When the bow of the *Snow Squall* arrived in Portland Harbor on March 11, 1987, aboard a container ship, not far from where she was originally launched at Cape Elizabeth in 1851, the last American clipper had made her final voyage, and a significant piece of American history had finally made port.

PART TWO: CLIPPER BUILDERS AND THEIR SHIPS BY STATE

This section is organized geographically by both state and town locations within each state where clipper ships were built, beginning with those built in northernmost New England at Robbinston, Maine, moving south and ending with the only clipper built in the state of Florida.

The clipper ship was built in eleven states along the East Coast between Florida and Maine. This section will cover their builders, with brief details of their careers where known and a list of their clippers, detailing their tonnage, year built, and the year, where known, of their demise. I have paid particular attention in offering details about some of the lesser known builders listed herein, while some of the major builders, such as Donald McKay and William Webb, have already received a great deal of attention in these pages and other works and need not be fully detailed here. Likewise, additional details about many of these ships, their career details and voyages and, in some cases, construction details, can be found in some of the sources consulted for this work. I have offered only select interesting details about their passages, various career events and, where known, their final fate. About the clippers listed for each builder: While, as has been discussed previously, there has been some debate about which ships built during the era were really clippers and which were reputed clippers that just made fortunate passages under ideal weather conditions or hard-driving commanders, I have elected to take the inclusive approach here even though some are certainly borderline candidates, while a few may not have been clippers at all. With this in mind, some 480 clipper ships, barks, and one brig are listed in this chapter; of many of them quite a bit is known, but of some of these vessels little is known but their name and tonnage. However, this listing includes no ships built after 1859, when the clipper ship era had ended. There were a number of ships built at East Boston, Mystic, and several other ports in the 1860s and 1870s that have been termed clippers, but, if clipper at all, were half or medium clippers at best; while some had clipper-like speed at times and many were loftily sparred, all of them were built first and foremost for cargo carrying capacity. A number of these ships, such as the Long Island–built *Blue Jacket* (1865), carried the names of original clippers, while other ships, such as the *Great Admiral* (1869), *Glory of the Seas* (1869), and *Seminole* (1865), were built by men (respectively, Robert Jackson, Donald McKay, and Maxon and Fish) who were clipper builders in the 1850s. Additionally, there were many other ships built in the 1860s that were designated as clippers and so immortalized in the clipper ship sailing cards put out by shipping lines in the 1860s and 1870s; once again, while some of these ships made fast passages, these vessels, including the *Cremorne* (1862) and *Sunrise* (1860) were not clippers in the original sense of the word.

Finally, in this state by state recap I have highlighted the most significant of the clippers, representing approximately the top 10 to 15 percent at most, built in each of them in terms of their performance, eventful career, and durability. While this list is somewhat subjective, I believe it represents a worthy selection of some of the most outstanding ships built during the clipper ship era. If nothing else, such a compilation continues the debate concerning which ships might be considered the most outstanding clippers, a debate that has taken place among nautical enthusiasts and historians alike ever since the time of the clippers passed into history. For this chapter I have largely relied for information on the two-volume work *American Clipper Ships 1833–1858* by Octavius Howe and Frederick Matthews (1926–27), Carl Cutler's *Greyhounds of the Sea*, and William Armstrong Fairburn's *Merchant Sail* (1945–1955), as well as some very detailed regional histories that can be found in the bibliography and the American and Lloyd's of London shipping registers.

Maine

Maine was second only to Massachusetts when it came to clipper ship production, building 90 such vessels that can be classified as clippers to varying degrees. Interestingly, clipper ships were built in twenty-eight different cities or towns, more than in any other state. However, this is not surprising given the fact that Maine has just over 3,400 miles of tidal coastline; in other words, there were plenty of places from which clippers could be set afloat. While most clippers were built fairly close to the Atlantic Coast, no matter the state in which they were constructed, Maine is one of only three states (the others are Pennsylvania and Maryland) in which a number of clippers were built well inland, some distance away from the ocean, on major rivers or bays. These include the *Golden Rocket* at Brewer on the Penobscot River, some thirty miles from the ocean, and the *Dashaway* at Hallowell on the Kennebec River. Of the builders of the Maine clippers, thirty-eight of them are known; Trufant & Drummond of Bath, the "City of Ships," led the way in building six clippers, closely followed by Metcalf & Norris in Damariscotta, who built five clippers, and George Thomas in Rockland, who built four. The large number of clippers built in the state of Maine is not surprising and is well in line with the fact that the state was, well before the clipper ship era and as early as 1820, the national leader in the tonnage of merchant sailing vessels built (Fairburn, pg. 3100). However, when maritime historian (and Maine resident) William A. Fairburn boldly states that "In the 1850s Maine Alone Resists the Demand to Sacrifice Other Qualities of Ship Design for Speed" (*ibid.*, pg. 3198), he is quite blinded by the fact that Maine *was* a major producer of the clipper type (the numbers of them built alone bears this out), even if they weren't generally as sharp as the extreme clippers built by Donald McKay and others. In reality, Maine shipyards were happy to have the business and were more than willing to build sharp ships to a prospective owner's tastes, while many mercantile firms were surely happy to do such long distance business, sometimes at a price per ton that was cheaper, say, than in New York or Boston. Surely indicative of the idea that Maine, like her fellow maritime states to the south, was swept up by the clipper craze is the fact that even in the northernmost part of the state, far from the larger and more influential shipbuilding seaports like Bath and Thomaston, clippers too were built, and not just for out of state interests. The very first Maine-built clipper by all accounts was the small but fast *Grey Feather*, launched at Eastport in 1850 for a local merchant.

The largest clipper ship built in Maine was the 2,305-ton *Red Jacket*, the smallest being the 345-ton clipper bark *Grapeshot*. As for Maine's most significant clipper ships, there are many to choose from; the nine vessels listed below are

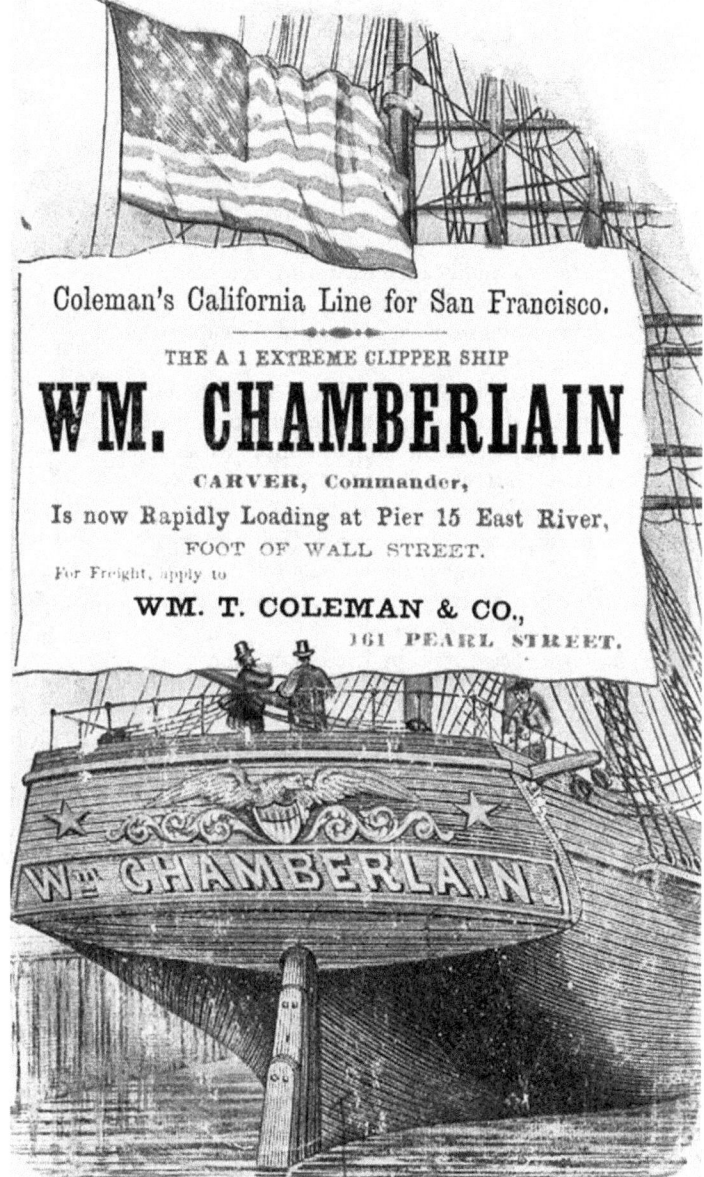

Sailing card for the *William Chamberlain*. Like many of the ships that were designated a clipper serving the shipping lines of the 1860s and 1870s, this ship was probably no extreme clipper, if clipper at all, though little is known of this vessel (author's collection).

representative of the fine clippers, big and small, produced in the aptly nicknamed "Pine Tree State."

1. *Red Jacket*, built by George Thomas at Rockland, designed by Samuel Pook. This

was not only the largest clipper built in Maine, but also the fastest and one of the most beautiful.
2. *Snow Squall*, built by Cornelius and Alford Butler at Cape Elizabeth. This clipper was small as most clippers went but had a good record for speed. Over 120 years after her career ended, a piece of the clipper was salvaged and brought back to Maine, where it is now a significant museum artifact, being the only physical remnant of the primary object, the ships themselves, of the clipper ship era.
3. *Spitfire*, built by Captain James Arey & Sons at Frankfurt, designed by Samuel Pook. One of the few extreme clippers built in Maine.
4. *Grey Feather*, built in Eastport, this early clipper has been described by one maritime historian as "a historic vessel" (Fairburn, pg. 3557). Though small in size, it was not only the first Maine clipper, but also a speedy and long serving vessel.
5. *Flying Scud*, built by Metcalf & Norris at Damariscotta. This ship was big and well-known in shipping circles, noted for its speed.
6. *Flying Dragon*, built by Trufant & Drummond of Bath, this flyer was the fastest of the Maine clippers, making the passage out from the East Coast to California in runs of 97 (just eight days off the all-time record), 114, 116, 119, and 126 days between 1855 and 1861. The *Dragon* was one of just a small number of clippers to ever beat the 100 day mark.
7. *Phoenix*, built by Thomas Knight and Nathaniel Blanchard at Cape Elizabeth, this ship was one of the most loftily sparred of all the Maine clippers, carrying both skysails and moon sails. Not only were the circumstances of the building of this ship, rising from the ashes as its name implies, most interesting, but it was one of the few of the clipper fleet overall that saw duty as a transatlantic packet.
8. *Grapeshot*, built by David Spear, Jr., at Cumberland. This little clipper bark was probably the most famous of this type of clipper and was also well known for her speed. Many incidents attended this bark's career, including the apprehension of a noted criminal overseas and one that resulted in a case being brought before the U.S. Supreme Court.
9. *Emerald Isle*, built by Trufant & Drummond at Bath. This ship's hull may have been designed more on the lines of a true packet ship, but her spar plan made her a clipper. Not only did this clipper carry thousands of immigrant passengers over the years, but she was also one of the longest lived of all the Maine-built clippers.

Robbinston

James Madison Balkans (born 1810), a merchant trader, and later a deputy customs collector, built one clipper:

- *Francis Palmer,* 1852, a 302-ton clipper bark sold to New York interests in 1858 for $14,000, later owned at San Francisco from 1868 to 1886 and served as a Hawaiian packet, had a great reputation for speed.

James W. Cox (born 1819), a merchant trader turned shipbuilder who later, by 1870, was a local hotel keeper. He built two clipper ships:

- *Red Gauntlet,* 1852, 1,038 tons, built for F. Boyd & Co. of Boston, first put on the Boston–Liverpool route, in 1854 put in the California–Far East trade, 118 days to San Francisco, in 1855 and 1856 a disastrous California run, passage time 194 days, forced into Valparaiso due to storm damage, in early 1863 chartered by the U.S. government as a troop transport to New Orleans, final voyage Boston to Hong Kong with coal and ice in 1863, subsequently destroyed by the Confederate raider *Florida* in late June 1863.
- *Dictator,* 1855, 1,293 tons, built for Samuel Train of Boston, later sold to Charles Green of New York, employed as a general trader, lost in April 1863, captured and burned by the Confederate raider *Georgia*.

The Vose family built one reputed clipper, but which member is uncertain; some sources list Thomas Vose, but he seems to have been a farmer, not a shipbuilder. The most likely builder of this ship is Peter L. Vose (born 1797).

- *Virginia*, 1854, 959 tons, for George Hunter of Boston, her first captain being Freeman Sparks. Nothing is known about this clipper.

Gilbert Spears (born 1813 in Ireland), a mechanic according to the 1850 Federal Census, or Oliver Dow (born 1802), a millwright living in nearby Calais in 1850, built this clipper (Kinney, p. 126). Spears probably was the shipwright, with Dow surely providing the timbers, in this partnership.

- *Juniper*, 1852, 514 tons, owned by Oliver Dow and Boston parties, subsequently sold to New York interests, wrecked after hitting a reef off Pernambuco on the coast of Brazil on November 12, 1857.

Pembroke

Isaac Ewell (born 1807), a Medford, Massachusetts, shipwright, built one clipper:

- *Queen of the Pacific*, 1852, 1,357 tons, of medium model, built for Reed, Wade & Co. of Boston, a bad luck ship employed in the California and Far East trades, carried ice on her maiden voyage for Boston to San Francisco and became unmanageable due to melting and also developed a leak, forcing her to put into Valparaiso; later in the guano and coal trades, dismasted and severely damaged in a hurricane early 1857 while bound from New York for San Juan del Sur, Mexico, with a cargo of coal, forced to put into St. Thomas, Virgin Islands, in distress, here condemned and sold to American owners; subsequently repaired; final voyage from New York to San Francisco in mid–1859, hit a reef off the coast of Brazil and subsequently broke in two, a total loss.

S.C. Foster (born 1800), a successful merchant trader by 1850 with an estate worth at least $16,000:

- *Western Continent*, 1853, 1,272 tons, built for John Mayo of Boston, employed in the transatlantic trade, last surveyed at New York in 1868, out of registry after 1873.

Either Isaac Ewell (see above) or Charles V. Minott (born 1826), which one is uncertain, was the builder of the below listed clipper in the yard of S.C. Foster (Kinney, p. 58). If built by Minott, this would be one of his first vessels, as by 1860 his Phippsburg shipyard built a fleet of large sailing vessels, including the last wooden sailing ship-rigged merchant vessel ever built in the U.S., the 2,124-ton *Aryan*, launched in 1893.

- *Comet,* 1852, 536-ton bark, designed by George Fountain, built for Edward Bates of Boston and made an impressive maiden voyage to San Francisco in 1852, making the run in 116 days and beating the bigger and more famous clippers *Syren* and the Bath, Maine–built *Monsoon*. The following year, the *Comet* was involved in a race home from Indonesia to New York or Boston; though she did not finish first, her total sailing time was within a day of the larger clippers *N.B. Palmer* and *Wild Pigeon* and three days off the pace of the victor, the *Samuel Russell*, a fine showing. This clipper was sold to West Coast interests, and then to Hawaiian owners and renamed *Hokulele*, out of registry after 1891. This bark should not be confused with the larger, and more famous, New York–built extreme clipper ship *Comet*.

Eastport

Caleb S. Huston (born 1814), learned the shipbuilding trade from his father, Robert Huston, who was building ships at Eastport as early as the 1820s, continued building ships well into the 1860s; of this shipbuilding family it is said that "they were the builders of the principal part of the fine sailing craft which gave our frontier town its wide commercial celebrity" (Kilby, pg. 284). In 1850, at the beginning of the clipper ship era, the Huston shipyard employed 35 workers, paying some $1,600 in workers' wages a month, with real estate assets worth $10,000 and 2,500 tons of lumber and 140 tons of iron materials on hand worth $18,000. It was also a busy year for the yard, as they had four vessels totaling 1,200 tons and worth $36,000 either on the ways or in the pipeline.

- *Grey Feather*, 1850, 586 tons, the first Maine-built clipper, named after a chief of the Passamaquoddy tribe, for merchant John W. Bass (born 1813 in Massachusetts) of Eastport who subsequently sold her to Smith & Boynton of New York in 1852. The clipper was later owned by the L.H. Sampson Company of New York, sold foreign 1862 to Germany, renamed *Ida*, and her further history unknown. This small clipper made three fast California runs, averaging just over 130 days, to begin her sailing days and was first commanded by Captain Daniel McLaughlin.

- *Aetos,* 1854, 1,430 tons, for John Bass, launched as the *Aquilla* but was quickly changed because of a Bath-built ship of the same name, first master was Captain John Bean, and by 1855 Daniel McLaughlin; employed in the West Indian and Indian and Australian trade as well as the cotton trade between New Orleans and Liverpool; sold foreign to British interests at North Shields in 1860, renamed *Lancastrian,* subsequently lost during a storm near her homeport while loaded with coal for Australia about 1873. This ship, while commanded by Captain McLaughlin, made the second fastest passage on record between Liverpool and Bombay, India, 77½ days, in 1856, just a half day off the record run.

George E. Fountain (born 1823, New Brunswick, Canada) was previously employed as a ship's carpenter in Pembroke at the yard of Nova Scotia native Abraham Livingston along with his older brother Stephen Fountain (born 1815). They soon thereafter came to Eastport and established Fountain & Co. shipbuilders, with George as the master builder, building ships here at least into the 1860s. While still working in Pembroke, Fountain is credited with designing the fast clipper bark *Comet* in 1852 (Kinney, p. 58). The local newspaper at the time of this clipper's launching erroneously credited Stephen Fountain as being the builder "and had to 'eat crow' for some time after" (Kinney, p. 86).

- *Crystal Palace,* 1854, 653 tons, built on consignment, later sold to E.M. Robinson of New Bedford, Massachusetts, in 1854 and first commanded by Captain Benjamin Simmons and sailed in China trade; made a fast passage from Macao to London of sixty days in 1859; sold at North Shields, England, in 1866 and renamed *Victoria,* final fate unknown.

Trescott

John W. Balch (born ca. 1804), merchant, shipbuilder, and sea captain worth $15,000 by 1850 was first involved in the lumber trade before becoming a shipbuilder in 1851; by 1860 he was a resident of Roxbury, Massachusetts, where he died in February 1861. He was primarily a builder and owner of smaller craft, including a number of brigs and schooners (none greater than 250 tons). He built two clippers:

- *Kate Hayes* (also given as *Cate Hayes*), 1851, 700 tons, built on own account. According to local records Balch had a three-fourths share of the clipper that was valued at $8,400, though he later sold her to Stephen W. Dana of Boston. First commanded by Captain Miner York of Trescott, career details unknown. Not in American registry by 1859.
- *Sea Lark,* 1852, 973 tons, built for Samuel Reed of Boston and E.M. Robinson of New Bedford. First commander was twenty-six-year-old Massachusetts sea captain Charles L. Willcomb, a native of France, career details unknown. Lost in May 1863 when she was captured and burned by the Confederate raider *Alabama.*

Brewer

Unknown builder:

- *Golden Rocket,* 1858, 608 tons, built at this inland location on the Penobscot River, next to Bangor, for merchants Moses Giddings and E.S. Dole; said to be "rather heavily sparred" (Fairburn, pg. 3547), a half-clipper at best. Maiden voyage on the California run in 158 days, returned eastward with guano via Valparaiso, Chile. Captured and burned in July 1861 while sailing in Cuban waters, the first ship destroyed by Captain Rafael Semmes of the *Sumter.* As for the clipper's owners, Giddings fared quite well after his brief venture into clipper ships, perhaps having sold his ship, for he was a lumber dealer with an estate valued at $32,000 by 1860, and over $65,000 by 1870.

Frankfort

Isaac (born 1808) and George (born 1812) Dunham established their two Penobscot River shipyards on Dean Street, one above the wharf, one below, in 1849. Both brothers were active in the shipbuilding trade before coming here, with George Dunham said to have been a "foreman shipwright at Yarmouth" (Fairburn, pg. 3532). They were quite active builders during the 1850s, launching at least nine vessels in addition to their clippers, and continued in the trade into the 1860s. Their clippers were as follows:

- *Ocean Spray*, 1852, 1,089 tons, attributed to George Dunham, built for Veasie & Co. of Bangor, Maine, career details unknown, abandoned at sea during a voyage from London to India in 1857.
- *Flying Yankee,* 1852, 1,092 tons, attributed to Isaac Dunham, likely built off the same model as *Ocean Spray*, built for Captain James Arey of Frankfort, soon thereafter sold to Boston interests, name changed to *Flying Arrow*. Subsequently sold foreign to London interests in January 1856 while in a damaged condition at Melbourne, Australia, for the sum of $15,000; here rebuilt and rechristened *Wings of the Wind*. Subsequent career details unknown.
- *Nonpareil,* 1853, 1,431 tons, attributed to both brothers, in business as Dunham & Company, with George as master builder, of medium model. Built on speculation and sold by Boston shipbrokers to New York owners, employed in the transatlantic trade. Maiden voyage Boston to New Orleans, in 1855 made passage between Philadelphia and Liverpool in fast time of 16 days; later that year chartered by the French government for use during the Crimean War, while at Constantinople collided with a steamship, towed to Toulon, France, for repair. Made one California passage of 115 days in 1858 and 1859. In early 1863 employed as an army transport making a round-trip voyage New York to New Orleans; thereafter sold foreign to British interests in May 1863 without a name change and employed in the England–Far East and Indian trades. Foundered at sea in October 1871 after departing Bombay, India, with twenty-three crew members lost. This ship is probably the same clipper that was originally referred to as *Flying Dragon* and was also attributed to the Dunhams, not to be confused with the Bath-built clipper of the same name, as her tonnage was identical to that of *Nonpareil*.

Captain James Arey (born 1805) was the original owner of the Dunham-built *Live Yankee*, but he quickly sold her, surely making a tidy profit. He followed up this venture by building several clippers, the second in partnership with ship carpenter Daniel Williams (born 1810). Like many other builders, Arey was provided plans for his first clipper from the owners that contracted for her; the fact that Pook designed this fast clipper was not known until her builder's model came to light and was put up for sale by private owners in 2010 and, fittingly, was acquired by the Penobscot Marine Museum.

- *Spitfire*, 1853, 1,520 tons, of extreme model, designed by Samuel Pook, built for Manning & Stanwood of Boston. Immediately put in the California trade, maiden voyage from Boston to San Francisco made in just over 100 days in 1853 and 1854, two subsequent California runs of 118 days in 1854 and 1855 and 107 days in 1861, later put in the China tea trade. Subsequently sold foreign to British interests without a name change in 1863 after arriving at London in a damaged condition; in service into the early 1870s, out of registry after 1871.
- *Arey*, 1854, 1,137 tons, built by Williams & Arey for New York owners, sold to British interests in the early 1860s and renamed *Caroline*; still operating into the 1870s as the British ship *Nautilus*.

Belfast

John David and Hiram Pierce (born 1819) are the reputed builders of this clipper (Rowe, p. 313). Nothing is known of David, while Pierce was a local merchant. The ship's figurehead, carved by Rufus Emery of Bucksport, depicted a "handsome figure of a western hunter" (Fairburn, pg. 3472).

- *Sportsman*, 1856, 626 tons, of medium model, originally owned by William Thompson of Boston, was soon sold to New York interests, including R.W. Cameron, for $31,250, and may have thus sailed in Cameron's Australian line of packet ships; later sold foreign to Chilean interests and renamed *Baronese*. By 1878 sold to Nicaraguan parties in 1878 and re-rigged as a bark, sailing under the name *Enrique Wilbert*, out of registry after 1885.

Carter & Company shipbuilders was headed by master shipwright Columbus Carter, this firm being one of the largest and long-lasting shipbuilding firms in Belfast. By 1876 Columbus Carter had built his 100th ship after getting his start in the 1840s, and built his last vessel, an 858-ton schooner, in 1899. In 1850, the Carter shipyard, with assets valued at $15,000 and 400 tons of timber, as well as iron, copper, and additional lumber valued at $10,000, employed sixty men and had five vessels either completed or under construction valued at $50,000, sure signs of a booming shipyard.

- *Moses Kimball*, 1853, 499-ton bark, built for Moses Kimball, later owned by Kimball & Co., homeport Belfast, Maine, designated a half-clipper in some contemporary accounts. Primarily employed in the New York–Liverpool transatlantic trade; out of American registry after 1859, likely sold foreign with a change of name.
- *Seaman's Bride,* 1856, 758 tons, of medium model, built for Boston interests. Little is known of this ship's career and she is sometimes confused with the clipper of the same name built at Baltimore in 1851, lost while loading guano at Baker's Island in 1865.

Warren

The Burgess & Clark shipyard was located at the tidal head of the St. George River, the head of this firm being Thomas Burgess (born 1812), a shipwright who lived in Warren and made a steady living as a local builder for over twenty years and earned a considerable fortune in doing so, having an estate valued at $11,700 by 1870.

- *Stephen Crowell*, 1855, 936 tons, built for Snow & Burgess in New York; Captain Burgess was her first commander. Nothing is known of the ship's career. Owned by original owners her whole career under American flag, out of registry after 1869.

Orland

Samuel B. Keyes (born 1773), a farmer by trade, is listed as the builder of one clipper in Orland by one noted historian (Rowe, p. 313). Whether this is an error or not is unknown, but it is interesting to note that all of the known shipbuilding families in town active in the 1850s, in particular George Partridge (born 1797) and his son Joseph (born 1821), as well as merchant and master-builder John Buck (born 1795), all had significant farm holdings which are listed in census records, unlike their shipbuilding activities.

- *Stornaway*, 1853, 750 tons, built for Welles & Gowan of Boston, probably named after the first of the British tea clippers to come out. Nothing of her career is known, not in registry under original name after 1858. The company that bought this clipper was very involved in the development of diving apparatus for the salvage business; employed in 1854 on the Great Lakes to raise the wreck of the steamboat *Erie*.

Rockland

George Thomas (born ca. 1794) established his shipyard in Rockland by 1851 and had a sizeable estate valued at $3,000 by 1850. Though not fully documented, most of his earlier vessels, as with most other pre-clipper shipbuilders in Maine, were smaller ships. After building the clippers listed below, he subsequently relocated his shipyard to Quincy, Massachusetts, where he built several others, though none nearly as notable. His Maine clippers were as follows:

- *Springbok* (also listed in registers as *Springbock*), 1851, 370-ton bark, built for the Boston firm of Seccomb & Taylor, career details uncertain. Surveyed at New York in 1860, later sold foreign by 1864, homeport Cape Town, South Africa, out of registry after 1866.
- *Defiance,* 1852, 1,691 ton (one account states 1,900 tons), of extreme model, designed by Samuel Pook, building supervised by Captain Isaac Taylor of Chelsea, Massachusetts, acting for New York owner William Dugan. Maiden voyage Rockland to New York at speeds up to 20 knots, then put on the California run, passage time 136 days in 1852. Bound from the UK to India in late 1856, battered by a storm, her first and second officers badly wounded, put into the Canary Islands badly leaking and was subsequently condemned and sold foreign to Spanish interests. Later repaired and renamed *Teide*, homeport Cadiz, Spain, disappears from registry after 1869.
- *Rattler*, 1852, 1,121 tons, of extreme model and said to be a smaller version of the *Defiance*, built on speculation but soon after launching sold to William Whitlock for service in his packet line between New York and Le Havre, France, price $66,000. From 1853

to 1868 made eight California passages, maiden passage in 1853 made in 121 days, best time 114 days in 1866. In 1855 and 1856 chartered by the French government for service as a transport during the Crimean War. In 1867 departed San Francisco for Hong Kong with $800,000 in gold, was subsequently caught in a typhoon and went ashore, but got off, later repaired at New York. In 1870 carried coal from Australia to Hong Kong. Sold foreign in 1873 to Nicaraguan interests, later to Costa Rican parties, and still later under the British flag and renamed *Martha*, re-rigged as a bark. Final voyage Hong Kong to San Francisco in November 1889, arrived in a sinking condition and subsequently was sold to the shipbreakers and scrapped in 1890.

- *Red Jacket*, 1853, 2,305 tons, of extreme model, designed by Samuel Pook for her owners, Seccomb & Taylor of Boston, and first commanded by veteran packet commander Captain Asa Eldridge. Sent on her maiden voyage by her owners to Liverpool, hoping to sell their new ship at a tidy profit, and though manned by a poor crew, the ship made a record run, just over thirteen days, that stunned the marine fraternity both at home and abroad; in fact, many in England refused to believe Eldridge's claim, so he kindly offered the ship's log book to confirm the feat. Subsequently chartered by the British White Star Line in their Australian packet business between Liverpool and Australia and made another fast passage in record time. Departed Melbourne, Australia, for Liverpool in August 1854 with gold dust valued at 200,000 pounds sterling, after arrival in 73 days sold foreign to British interests in late 1854 and continued service in the White Star Line, price 30,000 pounds sterling. Later employed in the Indian trade and then the Canadian lumber trade between Quebec and London, in the early 1880s owned at Newcastle, England, and employed in the coal trade. Out of registry after 1884, sold in the Cape Verde Islands and turned into a coal hulk.

Francis W. Rhoades (also spelled Rhodes, born 1804) built three clipper ships:

- *Anglo-Saxon*, 1853, 868 tons, of medium model, built on speculation, soon sold her to New York interests, probably E.M. Robinson, for the reported price of $50,000 (Fairburn, pg. 3416). Made six California runs, best time 121 days in 1855 and 1856. Lost off the coast of England while bound from Liverpool to New York on August 21, 1863, when captured by the Confederate raider *Florida* and destroyed.
- *Progressive*, 1853, 1,119 tons. Nothing is known about this ship, likely sold foreign soon after building with a change in name.
- *Young Mechanic*, 1855, 1,375 tons, of medium model, the only Rockland clipper built for local interests, her owner being Captain William McLoon of Rockland. Named by the builder for one of his sons, whose whittled model inspired his father. At the time of her building, Rhoades and his wife, Nancy, had eight children, including their younger sons Galen (age 11), Daniel (age 9), and Ellis (age 6); any of these boys may have been the inspiration for this clipper. Employed as a general trader, maiden voyage Rockland to Savannah, Georgia, and from there to Liverpool in the fast time of 17 days; made one California run, passage time 127 days, in 1862. Later employed in the guano and Indian trades. Her owner and commander, Captain McLoon, died at Calcutta, India, in 1865. Final voyage departed Boston for Hong Kong in March 1866 with a cargo of ice, pitch, and kerosene; cargo caught fire off Brazil and ship was abandoned, crew saved.

Horace Merriam (born 1815) a successful shipbuilder by 1850 with an estate valued at about $2,000, built two clippers.

- *Live Yankee*, 1853, 1,637 tons, of extreme model, built on speculation, design possibly based on a copy of Pook's model (Fairburn, pg. 3415); soon after her building, sold to Foster & Nickerson of New York. First voyage a round trip between New York and Liverpool; in mid–1854 departed New York for San Francisco, passage time 113 days, subsequent voyages to India, late 1857 London for Australia, in 1858 continued on to Hong Kong via Batavia. Made two voyages as a coolie ship carrying nearly 800 Chinese to Havana, Cuba, in 1859 and 1860. Final voyage Liverpool for Kurrachee, India; wrecked on the Galician coast on 26 June 1861 with the loss of seven crewmen.

- *Euterpe*, 1854, 1,985 tons, of medium model, built for Foster & Nickerson of New York. Maiden voyage New York to India in 90 days, return voyage Calcutta to London in 85 days, the all-time record on this route. First California passage in mid–1856, passage time 115 days; later loaded guano at the Chinchas Islands for Hampton Roads, Virginia, in 1860 arrived at San Francisco from New York in 118 days, subsequently put aground by her pilot and damaged, repair cost $24,000. From 1862 to 1863 under charter to U.S. government and employed as a hospital ship, afterward returned to merchant service and employed as a general trader. By 1868, sold foreign, abandoned in a sinking condition in the south Atlantic on June 4, 1871, while bound Peru for Falmouth, England, nine crewmen lost.

Robert Trowbridge (born 1824), a Maine native who was a sparmaker according to the 1850 Census and possibly worked in the shipyard of one of the men listed above. After building one clipper, he later became a local customs inspector and had an estate valued at nearly $2,000 in 1860.

- *Yankee Ranger*, 1854, 708 tons, built for Abbott, Kimball & Co. of New York, career details unknown, sailed out of New York, out of American registry after 1859, reported sold to German interests with a change in name.

Thomaston

George Thorndike (born ca. 1814) built one clipper here, though Captain Ebenezer Thorndike (born 1827) is often credited as the builder. George Thorndike was a merchant in Thomaston, worth $4,000 by 1850, and was active in the both the lime and shipbuilding trades. His relationship to Ebenezer Thorndike is uncertain, perhaps an older brother, and George was probably the principal in the building of this clipper. Ebenezer Thorndike was but a youngster compared to most clipper ship builders, being but twenty-four years old when he collaborated on the building of this clipper. Captain Thorndike did quite well during the 1850s, the master mariner having amassed a fortune worth $20,000 by 1860. George Thorndike was an active shipbuilder in the 1850s; his later productions included the 848-ton *Alice Thorndike* and the 47-ton bark *William A. Banks*, both built in 1854.

- *Empire*, 1851, 1,272 tons, for A. Zerega of New York. Made one California run in 128 days, otherwise employed in the Z Line of transatlantic packets carrying passengers between New York and Liverpool. Sold foreign to British interests, M. Wilson of Liverpool, in 1864 and continued in same trade; out of registry under original name after 1867.

Joshua Morton (born 1789) was one of Thomaston's older builders, being well established by the time the clipper craze arrived. In partnership with his son Charles C. Morton, he built two clippers. The Mortons did well with their clipper ship activities during the decade. Shipbuilder Charles Morton increased his wealth substantially by 1860, having assets valued at $19,400, though his father, Joshua Morton, had died by this time and the Morton shipyard was closed. The only Morton active in shipbuilding by 1860 was shipsmith James C. Morton.

- *Hyperion*, 1852, 837 tons, of medium model, built on speculation and soon sold her to Boston parties, where her name was changed to *Golden Racer*; thereafter sold at auction to New York interests for $45,000 in 1855. Maiden passage on the California run in 1853, passage time 130 days, returned eastward with guano. Second California run, Baltimore to San Francisco in 135 days, lost mainyard off Cape Horn. Third and final voyage New York to San Francisco in 1855 and 1856, 117 days, from then to Shanghai, China, in May 1856; lost when she ran aground in the River Min, Formosa Strait, near Foo Chow, China, and was a total loss.
- *Ocean Chief*, 1854, 1,228 tons, designed by Samuel Pook, built on speculation, sold foreign soon after launching to James Baines & Company of Liverpool, England, for use in their Black Ball Line of Australian packet ships. Maiden voyage Liverpool to Hobart, Tasmania, in the then record time of 72 days; made two other outward bound passages to Australia in 80 and 75 days. Lost ca. 1856 or 1857, destroyed by a fire set by one of her own crew while at Bluff Harbor, New Zealand.

The shipbuilding firm of Chapman & Flint consisted of Isaac Chapman (born ca. 1814) and William Flint (born ca. 1814), both well-to-do shipping merchants in Thomaston. They built one known clipper,

- *Oracle*, 1853, 1,196 tons, built for own interests. Maiden voyage on the California run made in 109 days, then employed in the China-England tea trade. Subsequently sold foreign to James Baines & Co. at Liverpool in late 1862 and renamed *Young England*, employed in the Australian trade, last surveyed at Liverpool in December 1867. Out of registry after 1873.

Joshua Patterson (born 1801), probably with help from his son Edwin, who was also a shipwright, built Thomaston's last clipper,

- *Crest of the Wave*, 1854, 942 tons, of medium model, sold to Baltimore interests early in her career and is termed by one historian "an unfortunate ship" (Fairburn, pg. 3388). First employed in the transatlantic trade, said to have made a run from East Coast U.S. to New Orleans in quick time of several hours under 9 days, made on California run in 1859, passage time 163 days; later employed in the guano and Puget Sound lumber trades. In late 1864 arrived at Valparaiso, Chile, from Acapulco, Mexico, with an outbreak of yellow fever, fifteen crew and passengers dead. Final voyage departed Liverpool for Baltimore with a cargo of salt and general merchandise, in early April experienced stormy weather and went ashore on Wreck Island off Cape Charles, entire 20-man crew lost.

Waldoboro

Edwin Achorn (born 1809) built two clippers, one on his own, and a second in partnership with ship carpenter George Gleason (born 1805). His first clipper is perhaps best known for its association with commentary on the naming practice of clipper ships in general by merchant George Francis Train of Boston. Achorn continued building in the area, putting over the 1,286-ton *Cavalier* at Rockland in 1854 as the principal in the partnership of Achorn & Dyer.

- *Wings of the Morning*, 1852, 916 tons, built for New York owners and her first commander, Captain H.A. Lovell. Maiden voyage in 1853 on the California run, passage time 183 days; partially dismasted when five days out and battered by strong gales, put into Rio de Janeiro for repairs, hit by storms again off the Platte River and suffered damaged sails and rigging, damaged again by heavy weather off Cape Horn. Second voyage New York to Melbourne, Australia, in mid–1854, then to the Chinchas Islands to load guano for Hampton Roads. In 1856 voyaged Callao, Peru, with guano for Le Havre, France, passage time 106 days; here sold foreign and renamed *Surate*, homeport Toulon. Last surveyed at homeport in 1867, out of registry after 1872.
- *Woodcock*, 1853, 1,091 tons, built by Achorn & Gleason for Dunham & Dimon of New York. Career details unknown, likely employed in the transatlantic trade; lost prior to 1859, ashore off Dungeness, County Kent, UK, a total loss.

The builder of the following clipper is unknown.

- *Spark of the Ocean*, 1853, 895 tons, for Boston owners, including Arthur Blanchard and William Greely; for final ten years of career owned by Comery & Storer of Waldoboro. Employed in the New Orleans and transatlantic trade, last surveyed at Boston in August 1864, out of registry under original name after 1869.

Bristol

One clipper was built here at the shipyard of Enos B. Richards (born ca. 1811). By 1850 the Richards' yard employed seven hands and built mostly smaller vessels under 300 tons. Richards was more active as a merchant in the cod fishery, being the owner of seven fishing vessels employing 28 men, and he likely built most of his own vessels. While his yard was only invested to the amount of less than $1,500, the Richards' cod fishing activities had assets of some $2,000 in 1850.

- 893-ton *Sparkling Sea,* 1854, 893 tons, owned by Blanchard & Sherman of Boston. Employed in the transatlantic trade with Liverpool, here surveyed in October 1861. Out of registry under original name after 1862, likely sold foreign.

Damariscotta

The firm of Metcalf & Norris was the most prolific of the clipper builders in this town, its principals being Benjamin Metcalf (born 1802) and Elbridge Norris (born 1816). This firm sold all its clippers to New York owners and continued to build vessels into the 1870s and was very profitable. In 1850 the Metcalf & Norris shipyard was one of the largest in Damariscotta, with assets valued at $15,000, employing anywhere from eighteen to thirty-five men, having in stock in their yard about $30,000 worth of timber, iron, copper, rigging, anchors, and other items, and with one 500-ton ship on the stocks valued at $35,000.

- *Alert*, 1850, 764 tons, built for Crocker & Warren of New York. Made two California runs from 1850 to 1853, passage times 148 and 150 days. Sold foreign at Calcutta, India, in 1857; lost off Formosa in October 1858, with loss of half her crew.
- *Levanter*, 1852, 868 tons, built for New York interests, later owned in Boston. Made no California runs, career details uncertain. Sold foreign to British interests in 1865, homeport Cowes, Isle of Wight, thereafter employed in the transatlantic trade, out of registry after 1870.
- *Queen of the East*, 1852, 1,275 tons, built for Crocker & Warren of New York, late in career owned by D.G. Bacon of Boston. Made one California passage, arriving via Callao, Peru, in September 1852. In 1854 employed in the China-England tea trade; after 1856 put in Australia and transpacific trade, lost on a reef in the South Pacific while bound San Francisco to Newcastle, New South Wales, Australia, in 1872.
- *Flying Scud*, 1853, 1,713 tons, of extreme model, sold after launching to Roderick W. Cameron of New York for use in his Australian packet line, price $100,000. Maiden voyage New York to Melbourne, Australia, in 1854, overloaded with a full hold and deck cargo, passage time 76 days, twice struck by lightning during a storm which affected her compass. Continued in the Australian and Indian trades. In early 1862 departed New York for San Francisco, passage time 118 days. Sold foreign at London in early 1863 and renamed *Cestrian*; after 1865 owned at Liverpool, out of registry after 1874.
- *Talisman*, 1854, 1,238 tons, of medium model, built for Crocker & Warren of New York. First put in California trade, arrived at San Francisco in 1857, 140 days, later made four additional passages, fastest time 112 days in late 1861; in 1862 loaded guano at the Chinchas Islands for England. Final voyage departed New York for Shanghai, China, in May 1863, subsequently captured and burned by the Confederate raider *Alabama* on June 5; prior to her destruction four brass guns and powder that were part of her cargo were offloaded, later used to arm another Confederate raider.

Austin & Hall, and its successor Austin & Co., was a new shipbuilding firm, established after 1850, that built two clippers at Damariscotta. The principal in both firms was merchant turned shipbuilder Nathaniel Austin (born 1803), who had an estate valued at $6,000 in 1850 and $15,000 by 1860. His partner in building his first clipper is uncertain, possibly boatbuilder James Hall, who had a yard in 1850 valued at $1,200 which employed eleven men in 1850 building small craft. Austin's partner may also have been ship carpenter David Hall of nearby Nobleboro.

- *Wild Rover*, 1853, 1,100 tons, of medium model, built for Alpheus Hardy & Co. of Boston. Intended for the transatlantic trade and first employed there; in January 1855 hit by lightning and her cotton cargo set afire while bound New York to Liverpool, ship saved by jettisoning burning bales. In 1855 and 1856 made her first California passage, time 136 days. Later employed in the Indian trade, fastest California passage in 1862 and 1863 made in 126 days. In early 1863 departed Puget Sound with lumber for Shanghai, China, returning to Boston with a Japanese passenger, an ex-samurai and "the first Japanese to come to the United States in search of learning" (Howe & Matthews, p. 710). Subsequently lost after going ashore on Long Island, New York, in 1871.
- *Black Warrior*, 1853, 1,828 tons, of medium model, built on speculation, sold for $90,000 to William Wilson & Son of Baltimore. First employed on the transatlantic run from New York to London and then to

Melbourne, Australia, in 76 days. By 1855 back at New York via Peru with guano for Hampton Roads. First California passage in late 1855, time 124 days, in late 1860 loaded dyewood in the Gulf of California for the UK; upon arrival at Queenstown, Ireland, in January 1861 collided with a British ship while inbound. Sold foreign to James Baines & Co. in 1862 and renamed *City of Melbourne*, employed in the Australian trade. Caught fire while loading at Port Philip in February 1868 and scuttled, later raised and repaired, by 1877 out of service, cut down to a storage hulk at Melbourne.

Col. Cyrus Cotter (born 1807) was a wealthy merchant in Damariscotta, worth over $7,500 in 1850, who built one clipper, probably on speculation. In 1850 his small yard had $1,500 in assets and employed three men and primarily built schooners of under 100 tons.

- *Ocean Herald*, 1853, 1,658 tons, soon after launching purchased by Everett & Brown of New York. Employed as a transport during the Crimean War by the French government and by late 1856 sold to French interests and renamed *Malabar*, homeport Marseilles. Out of registry under original name after 1869, possibly sold with a name change.

William Hitchcock (born 1792) was a shipbuilder and merchant who built ships on both sides of the river that separated Newcastle and Damariscotta. He had been a shipbuilder for some years before the 1850s, by which time he had amassed an estate valued at $9,000. The clippers below, all built for Frederick Nickerson & Co. of Boston, were his last such productions, Hitchcock having previously built one clipper (see below) on the Newcastle side.

- *Golden Rule*, 1854, 1,185 tons, built for Frederick Nickerson & Co. of Boston. Made one California run in 1857 of 132 days (reported as 114 days). Sold foreign to Quebec interests, D. & J. Maguire, April 1881, possibly employed in the Canadian lumber trade; last surveyed at St. Johns in 1891, in service as late as 1900, register expired.
- *Criterion*, 1855, 1,387 tons, built for Frederick Nickerson & Co. of Boston, later owned by Vernon H. Brown & Co. of New York. Employed in the transatlantic trade and cotton trade with Liverpool. Sold foreign to British interests in 1881, homeport London, later owned at Monrovia, Liberia; out of registry under original name after 1883.

Abner Stetson (born 1800) was a very successful shipwright, his shipyard being one of the largest in Damariscotta in 1850, employing 34 men, and at peak times as many as 69, and holding assets worth $22,000. In 1850 the yard had one ship on the stocks of 900 tons, valued at $58,000.

- *Western Empire*, 1852, 1,398 tons, built for William Sprague and others at Boston, later owned at New York by George Howes & Co. Employed in the transatlantic trade with Liverpool; lost in February 1882, abandoned at sea.

Newcastle

Two clippers that have been traditionally attributed to this town were actually built at neighboring Damariscotta and are listed above.

William Hitchcock built the one clipper launched on this side of the river, his first such production, also for Frederick Nickerson of Boston.

- *Flying Eagle*, 1852, 1,093 tons, owned by Frederick Nickerson & Co. of Boston, a full-built clipper with 15 inches of deadrise, a good cargo carrier, employed in the California trade. Maiden passage to San Francisco from Boston made in 169 days, partially dismasted when only five days out and forced into Rio de Janeiro for repairs that took 25 days; later made eleven other California runs, the fastest being her last in 1869 and 1870, passage 112 days, sometimes returned eastward with guano or the mails. In 1868 and 1869 made a voyage San Francisco to Cork, Ireland, in fast time of 102 days; in 1873 carried coal from Newcastle, New South Wales, Australia, for Hong Kong. Final passage from San Francisco in early 1872. On final voyage put into Mauritius in August 1879 in distress, here condemned and sold, further career, if repaired at all, unknown, out of registry after 1882.

Alna

Dennett Weymouth (born 1798) built the largest ship and only clipper ever launched at this small town located at Head Tide, over 20 miles north of the ocean coast. This was quite an accomplishment as most of the other vessels built here averaged under 300 tons. Weymouth is listed in the 1850 census as a trader with holdings valued at $3,000, but nothing is known of his other building activities.

- *King Philip*, 1856, 1,194 tons, built for Glidden & Williams of Boston, a full built ship that one historian calls an "early Down Easter, with good cargo carrying capacity ... and fair speed" (Fairburn, p. 3355). Set on fire by her crew while at Honolulu in early 1869, subsequently condemned and sold to West Coast interests, repaired at a cost of $20,000, then employed as a wheat carrier operating out of the West Coast. In May 1874 set on fire by her mutinous crew while anchored in Chesapeake Bay, the ship then made Annapolis and was taken charge of by a squad of marines. Final voyage in late January 1878 while bound San Francisco for Port Gamble, Washington, went ashore a total loss just south of the Golden Gate, her wreckage still visible on the beach today at varying times.

Wiscasset

Clark & Wood built this seafaring town's sole clipper, one of the medium type, in 1854. The principals in this firm were merchant Henry Clark (born 1800 and worth over $72,000 by 1860), and master mariner George H. Wood (born 1824).

- *Golden Horn*, 1854, 1,193 tons, owned locally by Henry Clark and others, sold foreign in 1863. Later re-rigged as a bark and owned in Norway, homeport Christiania, possibly employed in the Welsh coal trade and the Baltic lumber trade. Surveyed at Cardiff in February 1888, re-caulked in 1899, still afloat after 1900.

WE WILL SELL

FOR ACCOUNT OF WHOM IT MAY CONCERN

WRECK OF THE BARK

"KING PHILIP,"

As she now lies stranded on the beach below the Cliff House. The "Philip" is a 1200-ton bark, coppered and well found in sails, anchors, chains, spars and provisions. She will be sold in one lot entire, as she now lies.

Terms Cash in U. S. Gold Coin, at time of sale.

Advertisement for the sale of the wreck of the *King Philip*. The day after this old Maine-built clipper, now re-rigged as a bark, went ashore at Ocean Beach, California, her wreck was advertised for auction. It was sold for $1,050, and later three attempts were made to get rid of the wreckage by blowing it up. These evidently failed as a large part of her hull is still visible from time to time in the shifting sands (*Daily Alta California*, January 26, 1878).

Hallowell

Johnson Rideout (born 1795) has one clipper to his credit among the many vessels he built at several shipyards in the area during the years. In Bath, Maine, alone he built over 70 vessels from 1823 until his death in 1865, making him one of the most prolific shipbuilders of his time. Though Rideout worked at yards throughout the area, his yard in Bath was substantial; in 1850 it had assets worth $25,000 and nearly $47,000 worth of timber, iron, oakum, and other materials on hand and employed 60 men in the building of 2,100 tons worth of shipping that year, including three ships and two steamers valued at a total of $84,000.

- *Dashaway*, 1854, 1,012 tons, for Reed, Page, & Co. of Hallowell, sold foreign in 1863 and renamed *Mauritius Merchant*; career details unknown but employed in the Indian trade. Last surveyed at Calcutta, India, in 1865, out of registry after 1871.

Farmingdale

George Pierce built several ships here on the west bank of the Kennebec River from 1853 to 1856, including one reputed clipper. He was likely related to the shipowning family of the same last name in Boston, as well as to fellow Farmingdale shipbuilder E.G. Pierce, who not only built ships here, but also one clipper further south at Portsmouth, New Hampshire.

- *Miss Mag*, 1853, 727 tons, built for Samuel Grant of Farmingdale and Pierce & Bacon of Boston; name later changed to *Beaver* and owned by H.P. Sturges & Co. of Boston. Last surveyed at New York in July 1860, disappears from registry after 1862, likely sold foreign with a change in name.

Pittston

William and Franklin Stevens (born 1801) built a number of ships at their shipyard, including one fine clipper, here on the east bank of the Kennebec River. This clipper was the largest vessel ever built at Pittston. The Stevens shipyard was likely a family affair, as many family members were employed in the shipbuilding and other related trades.

- *White Falcon*, 1853, 1,372 tons, a sharp ship built for M.O. Roberts of New York. Employed in China and South American trade and never made a California voyage. In 1856 and 1857 chartered by the French government for use during the Crimean War, sailing from Marseilles. Later employed in the guano trade in 1859; in early 1862 went ashore at Foo Chow, China, and damaged, repaired at Hong Kong. Later that year sailed from Manila to New York, partially dismasted off the Cape of Good Hope and arrived in a leaking condition. In 1862 seized at New York by the U.S. government because of her southern ownership and sold. Late 1862 carried coal from New York for San Juan del Sur, Nicaragua, put into Rio de Janeiro in a leaking condition and repaired. Final American voyage Acapulco, Mexico, to San Francisco empty, subsequently sold foreign there to Peruvian interests in 1864 for $28,000 in gold, renamed *Napoleon Canavero* and put in the coolie trade; lost by fire in 1866 when her coolies rebelled and set fire to the ship. The crew got off safely, but the coolies, 650 in number, were left confined below and either burned to death or drowned.

Richmond

Thomas J. Southard (born 1809) was a very successful shipbuilder, commencing his career in 1846, with the last vessel at the Southard yard being launched in 1890. Southard, both a shipping merchant and shipbuilder, was worth a respectable $15,000 in 1850 but by 1860 had assets totaling over $194,000. His shipyard alone in 1860 had assets worth $50,000, material on hand worth another $72,000, and employed 82 men. Southard's two clippers are classed as half clippers, being more akin to the Down Easters that supplanted them.

- *Gauntlet*, 1853, 1,854 tons, built for Stephenson & Thurston of New York, the largest ship built in Maine up to that time. First employed in the cotton trade between Mobile, Alabama, and Liverpool, later chartered for use as a transport in the Crimean War by the French government in 1855. In 1856 departed Malta for Le Havre, France, in heavy weather, then to New York; made one guano voyage in 1857, loaded coal at Cardiff, Wales, for Shanghai in early 1860, later that year sold foreign to British interests at Hong Kong, renamed *Sunda* and put in the Australian service. In 1863 made the then record run London to Brisbane in 76 days, on another run passed the famed *Flying Cloud* after sailing in company with her for four days. Final voyage in 1878, lost by fire at sea while bound from Norfolk to Liverpool.
- *Wizard King*, 1854, 1,398 tons, built for own interests and so operated until her sale foreign in 1863 at Moulmein, Burma, to British interests, subsequently renamed *Munsoory*, last seen at Calcutta, India, in 1870, out of register after 1876.

Patton & Sturtevant built two clippers at Richmond, the primary partner being master builder and merchant William Patten (born 1794), worth $25,000 in 1850, while William Sturtevant (born 1814), a man of much less capital (though erroneously listed in some sources as being the firm's financial provider) was also a shipbuilder. Like many Maine clippers, their ships were of the medium or half-clipper design.

- *Peerless*, 1852, 633 tons, built for Boston and Gloucester owners, sold foreign 1864 to Cuban interests, homeport Havana, renamed *Aurora* and re-rigged as a bark, out of registry after 1891.
- *Pride of America*, 1853, 1,826 tons, built on speculation, soon after launching sold foreign in March 1854 to British interests and renamed *Pride of the Ocean*. Employed in the transatlantic trade, homeport London. Foundered at sea in 1883, at the time homeport Gibraltar.

The partnership of Allen & McFarland built one clipper here (Baker, p. 381). Daniel Allen (born 1823) was a ship carpenter from Litchfield, Maine, who came to Richmond after 1850 and here built several vessels, including a schooner, a brig, and the 1,079-ton square-rigger *Walter Lord* in 1854. His partner was probably ship carpenter John McFarland (born 1815) and working in Bath by 1860.

- *Strelna*, 1853, 714 tons, built for William Ropes of Boston, career details unknown, wrecked in 1854. Most sources credit this vessel to Patten & Sturtevant, but recent research has proved otherwise.

George H. Ferrin (born 1822) was the most modest of the clipper builders in Richmond, building one such vessel, possibly with his brother James Ferrin (born 1828), who was also a shipbuilder. George Ferrin built several other vessels in Richmond between 1854 and 1863, but none as large as his clipper.

- *Wild Wave*, 1853, 1,547 tons, of medium model, built for Benjamin Bangs of Boston. First put in the transatlantic trade, in August 1855 departed the UK for the Chinchas Islands, Peru, to load guano for Genoa, Italy. In 1857 and 1858 made her only California run, time 140 days. Final voyage departed San Francisco for Valparaiso, Chile, with ten passengers and $18,000 in gold coins in February 1858, subsequently wrecked on a coral reef at Oeno in the Pitcairn Islands on March 5; crew made shore safely, eventually all but one rescued after her captain and part of the crew sailed in one of the ship's boats to the Marquesas Islands via Pitcairn Island, an incredible long distance open-boat voyage.

Brunswick

George Skolfield (born 1776) was one of this noted family of shipbuilders in Brunswick which built its first vessels as early as 1805. At his death in 1866 at the age of 90, he is said to have averaged one ship a year during his career. Though he became one of the richest men in town, the story goes that Skolfield had to borrow a dollar to buy the axe which he used to cut down the timber to build his first vessel (Fairburn, p. 3305). It is also interesting to note that Skolfield was a native of the neighboring town of Harpswell but moved his operations to Brunswick when he felt he was being taxed unfairly for a vessel he was building at Harpswell.

- *Rising Sun*, 1855, 1,319 tons, for the builder's interest, commanded by Captain Samuel Skolfield. Nearly lost at sea on her maiden voyage Mobile, Alabama, to Le Havre, France, with 4,291 bales of cotton (Baker, p. 381). In service and owned by Skolfield her whole career. Put into St. Thomas in 1869, here condemned, circumstances unknown.

Bath

Trufant & Drummond were the most prolific of the clipper ship builders in all of Maine, launching six such ships between 1851 and 1854, and possibly a seventh (see below). The senior partner was Gilbert Trufant (born 1782), a wealthy merchant of Bath, while William Drummond (born 1801) was also a wealthy merchant. However, both men were active and accomplished shipbuilders well before the clippers came along, and each descended from a long line of shipbuilders, the Trufants first building ships in Maine in 1791, while the earliest recorded Drummond vessel dates to 1803. Indeed, Gilbert Trufant was first a shipbuilder, launching his first vessel at Bath in 1820. The first ship built by Trufant & Drummond was the 342-ton *Sarah Boyd* in 1846, but it is unclear if this partnership was with William Drummond, or possibly his brother James Drummond, as the Drummonds in 1849 teamed up to build a sizeable ship of their own, the 1,200-ton *Saratoga*, and a reputed clipper the following year (listed below). By 1850 the Trufant & Drummond yard employed 60 men with assets worth $45,000, had stockpiled over $35,000 worth of shipbuilding supplies and in that year alone had two ships totaling 1,662 tons on the ways valued at $66,480.

- *Monsoon*, 1851, 773 tons, built for George Hussey of New Bedford, Massachusetts. Put in California trade and later the Far East trade, maiden passage to San Francisco made in 130 days, fastest passage 120 days in 1854. In late 1864 made a voyage Manila, Philippines, to San Francisco with 1,000 tons of sugar. Sold to German interests in 1865 for $23,000, subsequently sold to Norwegian interests in 1870, homeport Krageroe, employed in European trade. Surveyed at Lisbon, Portugal, in October 1872, out of register after 1876.
- *Flying Dragon*, 1853, 1,127 tons, built on speculation, soon after sold to Reed, Wade & Co. of Boston and first commanded by Captain Judah Baker. Employed in the California and Indian trades, maiden passage to San Francisco in 148 days in heavy weather conditions; in 1857 made a 101 day California run, the fastest of any Maine-built clipper. In 1860 while bound Baker's Island for Hampton Roads, Virginia, loaded with guano began to leak and forced into Tongataboo to discharge of part of cargo, subsequently made Sydney, Australia, for repairs. Final voyage departed Australia with coal for San Francisco, lost off the Golden Gate, San Francisco, in January 1862 after striking Arch Rock while entering port, a total loss.
- *Mary Robinson*, 1854, 1,371 tons, of medium model, built for Edwin Mott Robinson of New Bedford, Massachusetts, put in California trade. Maiden voyage to San Francisco 139 days, made five other passages through 1864, fastest passage 115 days in that year, made three returns eastward in the guano trade. In 1858 went from San Francisco to Australia, lost off Howland's Island in June 1864, blown on a reef during a sudden squall and subsequently sank, all hands saved.
- *Viking*, 1853, 1,350 tons, built on model of the *Mary Robinson* for George Hussey of New Bedford, Massachusetts. First employed in the California trade, made six runs on that route, fastest 108 days in 1858, later employed in the guano trade. Final voyage bound Hong Kong for San Francisco with 400 Chinese passengers in June 1863; lost after going ashore on Princess Island off Shimoda, Japan, a total loss, crew and passengers rescued.
- *Emerald Isle*, 1853, 1,736 tons, a heavily sparred ship though full modeled, built for the Tapscott Line of Liverpool packets operating out of New York and called a clipper packet; later was an immigrant ship operating between Europe and the British Isles and the U.S. Sold to Grinnell & Minturn of New York by 1877, sold foreign to Dutch interests by 1882 and renamed *Barendina Oriria*, sailing out of Batavia, Indonesia.
- *Windward*, 1854, 818 tons, built for New York interests, a full modeled ship and a good carrier for her size. Later sold to West Coast parties. Wrecked on Whidbey Island, Puget Sound, December 1875, while bound Seattle to San Francisco.

James Drummond (born 1811) in partnership with William Drummond, built this early clipper, though not all experts agree as to whether she really was a clipper. This vessel was typical of Bath ships of the day, "primarily good carriers and fast sailers" (Fairburn, p. 3199). Shipping registers list this vessel as being built by Trufant & Co. or Trufant & Drummond.

- *Continent*, 1850, 1,008 tons, said to have been built as a California clipper, owned by George Hussey of New Bedford, Massachusetts, by 1858, possibly employed in the whale oil trade. Sold to New York interests in early 1865 and employed in the transatlantic trade. Final survey at Liverpool in 1866, out of registry after 1867.

Hall, Snow & Co. built two half-clippers at Bath, both for Boston owners. Willard Hall (born 1818) was an established shipbuilder in Bath by 1850 that employed some 37 men and though one of the smaller yards in the City of Ships, he did have $14,000 in assets and over $20,000 worth of materials on hand. The second man in this partnership, clearly the financial backer, was Joseph Snow (born 1821), the local deputy sheriff and, later, postmaster.

- *Carrier Pigeon*, 1852, 844 tons, of medium model, built for Reed, Wade & Co. of Boston. Wrecked near end of maiden voyage some fifty miles off San Francisco at a point of land now called Pigeon Point in June 1853.
- *Undaunted*, 1853, 1,371 tons, of medium model, built for W.H. Foster & Co. of Boston. First put in the cotton trade running between New Orleans and Liverpool, later employed in the West Coast South America trade. Made one California run in 1857, passage time 132 days; in 1858 made a passage Liverpool to India. Later chartered by U.S. government during the Civil War in 1862 and 1863 for use as a troop and horse transport between New York and New Orleans. In late 1863 departed New York for San Francisco, put into Rio de Janeiro in distress, there condemned and sold foreign to British interests, renamed *Caprice*; subsequently sold to Norway 1867 and renamed *Halden*, engaged in the transatlantic trade. Surveyed at Liverpool in 1870, final survey in New York 1880, out of registry after 1881.

Charles (born 1799) and William (born 1805) Crooker were part of a shipbuilding and mercantile family that built twenty-three ships in Bath from 1803 to 1854, with both men described as merchants by 1860 with personal assets worth $50,000. The possible clipper below is recognized by few marine historians, and if she can indeed be classed as such, was likely of medium model.

The Lost Ship Carrier Pigeon.
BOSTON, Monday, July 11.
The clipper-ship *Carrier Pigeon* was a new vessel, built at Bath, Me., in December, 1852. The vessel, cargo and freight money, were insured in this city as follows: The Neptune office, $22,915; Boyleston, $1,750; Suffolk, $4,800; United States, $1,848; Equitable Safety, $13,000; Hope, $10,700; Manufacturer's Mutual, $17,000; New-England Mutual, $36,000; Merchant's, $5,500; American, $1,070; Boston, $17,000; National, $700; Commercial, 15,000; City Mutual, $23,000; Alliance Mutual, $25,000. Total, $195,283.

Clipper *Carrier Pigeon* newspaper notice. This Maine-built clipper was lost on her maiden voyage, with resulting large insurance losses, as noted in this published notice (*New York Times*, July 11, 1853).

- *Mermaid*, 1853, 1,221 tons, nothing further known, likely sold foreign with a change in name after launching, not to be confused with the bark of the same name built by Samuel Hall at Boston.

The Houghton family was one of the premier shipbuilders in Bath, launching some 45 ships from the years 1819 to 1891. Levi W. Houghton (born 1815) learned the family trade and also was a successful shipping merchant by 1850. At this same time his shipyard had assets totaling $8,000 and employed 25 men. As usual, experts disagree on the inclusion of this ship, one stating that Bath shipbuilder Johnson Rideout considered this ship a clipper (Baker, p. 374), while another states in rather contradictory fashion that "not one of the Houghton ships was a clipper," but concedes, "It was only in the design of the *Pocahontas* ... that the Houghtons made any concession to the tendency of the fifties to sacrifice cargo capacity for speed" and that "speed was given more consideration than was customary by contemporary Bath shipowners" (Fairburn, p. 3264–65). Based on this evidence, the inclusion of the ship below as a clipper seems appropriate.

- *Pocahontas*, 1855, 1,087 tons, built on own account, Levi Houghton & Sons. Employed in the transatlantic cotton trade between New Orleans and Liverpool; sold foreign to British interests in 1873, homeport Liverpool, out of registry after 1879.

The builder of the clipper below, almost certainly of the medium model, is disputed. Perhaps the most likely possibility is Thomas Simpson (born 1815), a master carpenter who built a handful of ships in Bath from 1846 to 1859 but was more likely usually employed in one of the city's many larger shipyards. This clipper is attributed to an M. Simpson in custom house records, but this is almost certainly an error as no man by this name can be found in Bath or the area at this time. Other local sources credit Henry W. Owen (born 1803) and others as the builder, but it is more likely that he was the financial backer in the construction of this clipper, he being a wealthy merchant in town (Fairburn,

p. 3201). The clipper below is, in fact, similar in size to some of Thomas Simpson's known productions, including the 521-ton *Rio Grande* (1846) and the 672-ton *William D. Sewall* (1848). To further confuse matters, the maritime historian William Avery Baker records this vessel's builder as Stephen Larrabee (born 1807), a ship's carpenter who built some 32 ships ranging in size from 200 to 1,200 tons, either alone or in partnership with others, between the years 1835 and 1865.

- *Maid of the Sea*, 1859, 661 tons, for Jacob Stanwood and others of Boston, one of the last of the clippers to be built in the U.S., but nothing is known of her career; out of registry after 1868, possibly sold foreign with a change in name.

Cumberland

David Spear, Jr. (born 1818), was the son of David Spear, who began building ships here at Broad Cove just after the end of the War of 1812 and continued until his death in 1842. His son took over the business and continued in his father's footsteps, building mostly small barks and schooners, but he also built three large ships in the years 1849 through 1851. Activities ceased at the Spear yard by 1858 after the Panic of 1857 resulted in the loss of "something over twenty thousand dollars" (Fairburn, p. 3150) for the last three barks he built. Spear built at least one clipper bark, and though his last barks (*Storm King, Arizona,* and *Liberty*), built in 1856 and 1857, are not recognized as clippers it seems likely that at least two others built from 1854 to 1855 were possibly built on a similar model to *Grapeshot* and are thus here included. It is also possible that the 301-ton *Peacock* (1852) or the 316-ton *Star of the East* (1853), both also barks, were of a clipper model that brought Spear to the attention of a wider audience.

- *Grapeshot*, 1853, 345-ton bark, built for merchant Sebastian Lawrence of New London, Connecticut, sank at her mooring in shallow water in the East River, Brooklyn, New York, on January 30, 1854, due to the movement of ice that gouged two holes in her bow below the waterline while loaded with a cargo of flour and due to depart the

Clipper bark *Grapeshot*. This Maine-built bark, launched at Cumberland by David Spear, Jr., in 1853, had a lively career, and though little remembered today, she was so famous in her day that the printmakers Currier & Ives saw fit to issue this lithograph.

next day; subsequently raised, repaired and sold to George Law, Esquire, of New York. In 1855 the fast clipper bark became famous when in March she was loaned by Law to New York officials and, manned by four New York policemen and sixteen volunteers, was sent in pursuit of a brig (some stories cite the vessel as a steamship) carrying a notorious murder suspect named Lew Baker. Though the local press would complain that the bark had "about as much prospect of securing Baker, as of capturing the Sea Serpent or the Flying Dutchman" (*Brooklyn Eagle*, "The Death of Bully Poole," March 20, 1855, p. 3), the bark, despite sailing a day after its prey, made fast time and arrived at its scheduled stop in the Azores before the brig did, thereby securing the surprised suspect upon his arrival and bringing Baker back to New York for trial (he was tried three times but never convicted!). This clipper later made a voyage to Constantinople in early 1857 and two subsequent voyages carrying salt from the Cape Verde Islands to Rio de Janeiro. Later seized for legal reasons at New Orleans in June 1858 and sold to pay off debts in September 1858. By 1862 owned by Trowbridge & Sons of New Haven, Connecticut, out of American registry by 1864, likely sold foreign, final fate uncertain.

- *Pointer*, 1854, 506-ton bark, owned by a Captain Steutwant and others of New York in 1857; name does not subsequently appear in American registry, indicating a possible name change or foreign sale, and nothing further is known of her career.
- *Uncle Sam*, 1855, 336-ton bark, nearly identical in size to *Grapeshot* and possibly built on the same model, owned by Coby & Co. of Charleston, South Carolina, in 1859; nothing further is known of her career.

Portland–Cape Elizabeth

Alford (born 1822) and Cornelius (born 1823) Butler were brothers and natives of Portland who bought their shipyard from ship carpenter Samuel Dyer in December 1848 and built their first vessel by early 1850. Interestingly, Alford Butler also owned a clothing factory in Portland and is said by one historian to have been "a complex and slightly shady character" (Dean & Switzer, p. 20). The brothers, with Cornelius the apparent designer and head man, built four ships in all before closing up shop and selling their yard. While Cornelius worked for a time locally as a ship carpenter afterward, Alford Butler moved to Boston and continued his career in the clothing business.

- *Black Squall*, 1850, 420-ton bark, built for Captain John Codman of Boston. Made possibly one California run, and also employed in the South American trade. In May 1852 tied for the fastest passage ever on the Rio de Janeiro to New York route, 26 days, and some hours less than fifteen days from the equator to New York, the all-time record. Sold foreign in 1853, later career unknown.
- *Snow Squall*, 1851, 742 tons, of extreme model, possibly built on plans drawn up for sale by Donald McKay (Dean & Switzer, p. 27), built for Charles Green of New York. Employed mostly in the China trade in which she made some fast passages. Went ashore in the Straits of Le Maire while trying to round Cape Horn, subsequently put into the Falkland Islands in distress and here condemned and abandoned in March 1864 where she lay until her bow section was detached and raised and sent back to Portland, Maine, in 1987 for display as a museum artifact; now housed at the Maine Maritime Museum in Bath.
- *Warner*, 1852, 500-ton bark, built on speculation, sold to William Merritt of New York and put into European trade; lost ca. 1854 while bound New York to Dunkirk, France.

Shipwright Thomas E. Knight (born 1817) and trader Nathaniel Blanchard (born 1817) worked together in 1852 to build a clipper, but, sadly, as it was nearing completion at the Blanchard shipyard it caught fire and burned. Undaunted, Blanchard furnished the capital to build another clipper, which was done the following year.

- *Phoenix*, 1853, 1,458 tons, built on speculation as a transatlantic packet for Nathaniel Blanchard; sold at New York in early 1854 to Charles Carow to sail in the Red Star Line, sailing between New York and Liverpool in 1854 and 1855 before being put on the California and Far East run in 1856, in 1857 and 1858 again employed as a transatlantic packet. In 1859 voyaged from Savannah, Georgia, to Queenstown, Ireland, and subsequently to Australia, where she was destroyed by fire at Melbourne in February 1860.

Joseph W. Dyer (born 1814), whose shipyard was located on Clay Cove at Cape Elizabeth and was active during the 1850s, learned the trade from his father, Lemuel Dyer, who was an active shipbuilder for years on the Portland waterfront before the city's development forced the closure of his yard there.

- *Portland*, 1853, 958 tons, built for Nathaniel F. Deering (an IRS agent), builder's interest, and others of Portland. Employed in the transatlantic trade, surveyed at London in August 1862, out of registry after 1869.

Freeport

Captain Enos C. Soule (born 1793) and his firm of Soule Brothers was the most prominent shipbuilding firm in Freeport. Its founder was himself a mariner who sailed during the War of 1812, during which he was captured and imprisoned in England. Soule continued to build ships until his death in 1869, after which his son, also Captain Enos C. Soule, took over the business until ceasing shipbuilding activities in 1879.

- *Tam O'Shanter*, 1849, 777 tons, built for the owner's interests and commanded by his son, Captain Enos Soule, foundered off Cape Cod while bound from India to Boston in December 1853. A second ship by this name was built by Soule in 1875 and was a fast ship of the Down Easter type.
- *Quickstep*, 1853, 836 tons, built for Dunham & Dimon of New York, career details unknown, sold foreign in 1863.

Kennebunk

Bourne & Kingsbury built one clipper here during the first years of the clipper ship era. The senior partner was George Bourne (born 1801), probably the ship expert in the firm and possibly a descendant of shipbuilder Aaron Bourne of nearby Wells, who was active as early as 1819, while Henry Kingsbury (born 1801) was a well-to-do merchant.

- *Roebuck*, 1851, 815 tons, a medium clipper, built for Boston owners, made one California run, one voyage to China; subsequently wrecked off entrance to harbor at Cohasset, Massachusetts, in January 1859 while carrying a load of cotton bales.

New Hampshire

When it comes to the history of shipbuilding in New England, New Hampshire does not readily come to mind for many, perhaps understandable given the fact that the state has only seventeen miles of ocean coastline. Only landlocked Vermont has less in New England, and yet New Hampshire has had a long history of shipbuilding dating far back into the colonial days over one hundred years before the American Revolution. In fact, the forests of New Hampshire were a prime source of timber for the British Navy for years, providing the masts for many of their warships, and after the Revolution wooden shipbuilding continued to be an important industry for the state. It is thus highly appropriate that the state seal of New Hampshire depicts a ship (the Revolutionary War frigate *Raleigh*) on the stocks with a rising sun in the background. All of this state's clipper ships, twenty-eight in number, were built on the Piscataqua River at or near the city of Portsmouth within several miles of each other, which locale has always been the center of shipbuilding in the state. Most of these clippers were built on the Portsmouth side of the river, though several clippers, including the famed *Nightingale*, were built on the Maine side of the river. However, with the exception of several Maine historians, most authorities credit these clippers to Portsmouth as all were registered in the Portsmouth customs district and were built under similar circumstances and influences by shipyard workers who often worked at several of these yards during the course of any given year as work became available. While few outside the region recognize Portsmouth for its maritime history, for many years this port was one of the most important in America, even surpassing such better known ports as Baltimore in maritime economic activity. In fact, other than the greater Boston area,

Medford, and New York, Portsmouth built more clippers than any other city or town in America.

Seven builders put over clipper ships in Portsmouth, all except one of which built two or more clippers. The leader by far in building these ships was George Raynes and, after his death, his son George Raynes, Jr.; their yard built ten clippers between 1850 and 1859, including the city's first clipper, the little known *William E. Roman* in 1850 and the last (also one of the last of all the clippers built anywhere) in 1859, the *Shooting Star* (II). Next in prominence was the shipyard of Fernald & Petigrew, builder of seven clippers, followed by Tobey & Littlefield, the builders of three clippers, including the largest ever launched on the Piscataqua, the 1,942-ton *Sierra Nevada*.

As to the characteristics of the New Hampshire–built ships, they were, like their neighbors to the north, constructed largely of locally obtained timber and were solidly-built by men who had a large amount of experience; both the Raynes and Fernald & Petigrew yards had been building packet ships for New York owners well before the clippers arrived on the scene. In addition, E. G. Pierce (builder of the *Charger*) had previously worked in Maine for nearly thirty years, while the Hanscom family had been building ships on the Piscataqua River since at least 1697! In no way are the qualities of the Portsmouth-built clippers demonstrated better than their long careers. Among those ships that had careers lasting in excess of twenty-five years are included the *Dashing Wave, Nightingale, Sea Serpent, Coeur de Lion,* and *Wild Pigeon*, all of which sailed the seas into the 1890s and beyond. As to the types of clippers built here, a number of them were of the extreme model, though some good carrying medium clippers were also built. In regards to speed, the Portsmouth clippers also compare well with those built in New York and Boston, with four of them averaging 120 days or less on their California runs, while another four averaged less than 124 days. Determining which of the state's clippers were the fastest is largely a toss-up, with perhaps the *Typhoon* edging out the big *Sierra Nevada*, though several other flyers, most notably *Nightingale* and *Witch of the Wave,* certainly could hold their own.

That there were many notable clippers built at Portsmouth is very evident, but the following five ships represent the finest and most interesting that were launched here:

- *Typhoon*: This ship, the first production of Fernald & Petigrew, made one of the fastest sailing ship passages ever between America and Great Britain, making the trip on her maiden voyage in the speedy time of 13 1/2 days from Portsmouth to Liverpool.
- *Sierra Nevada*: The life of this clipper may have been one that was accident prone, but this ship, the largest clipper built at Portsmouth, not only made a fast, 98-day California run, but also made a quick passage from Hampton Roads, Virginia, to Liverpool in 15 days.
- *Sea Serpent*: This clipper built by George Raynes was the first extreme clipper built at Portsmouth. She did quite well in the British tea trade and made a near record run from Hong Kong to New York.
- *Nightingale*: Built by Samuel Hanscomb, this yacht-like clipper had a more varied career than any other ship of the clipper fleet. Originally built for the World's Fair in London in 1851 and subsequently put in the Australia and China tea trade, the clipper also saw duty as a slave ship and U.S. naval vessel and had a long life lasting over forty years.
- *Witch of the Wave*: This clipper was one of the most beautiful and long-lived of the Portsmouth clippers and also a fast ship, making a record run from India to the U.S.

Portsmouth

Seven builders put over clippers at their Piscataqua River shipyards.

George Raynes (born 1799 in southern Maine) was the dean of Portsmouth builders by 1850, having built his first ship here in 1828 after apparently having learned the shipbuilding trade in one of the Canadian Maritime provinces. In 1832 Raynes, with the financial backing of shipmaster William Neal, bought the estate of the old colonial shipbuilder George Boyd, which included his mansion and the shipyard which had launched ships as far back as the 1750s. By 1838 Raynes bought out Neal entirely and was the sole proprietor of his yard, called one of the most beautiful in America, and here built some 28 ships before 1850. In partnership with his son George Jr., Raynes built eight clippers from 1850 until his death in 1855, after which his son built two more, one in 1856 and one in 1859. By 1860 the Raynes yard was closed, his heirs no longer interested in shipbuilding, though several ships were built here afterward by another builder.

- *William E. Roman*, 1850, 774 tons, of medium model, built for Joseph Taylor and the Olyphant family of New York, put into the China tea trade. Lost late 1853 off Bermuda while bound from Canton to New York, abandoned after being set on fire to prevent her from becoming a navigational hazard, entire eighteen man crew rescued.
- *Sea Serpent*, 1850, 1,337 tons, an extreme clipper built for Grinnell & Minturn of New York who would later tell Raynes that "we do not own a ship that has given us more satisfaction" and that "there is not a clipper afloat that can rank higher than she" (Brighton, p. 28). Put into California–Far East trade, active in the China–England tea trade, maiden voyage to San Francisco in 125 days, forced into Valparaiso, Chile, for repairs, another passage of 110 days in 1853, in 1856 departed Whampoa, China, for New York, passage time 79 days, one of the fastest on record. Sold foreign to Norwegian interests in 1874, renamed *Progress* in 1883, lost in 1891 while bound from Quebec to Dublin with a load of lumber.
- *Wild Pigeon*, 1851, 996 tons, built for the Olyphants of New York. Her maiden voyage on the California run was an impressive 106 days in length. Sold foreign in 1863 to British interests and worked in the China trade; sold to Spanish interests in 1865 and renamed *Bella Juana,* subsequently named *Voladora* after 1868 and re-rigged as a bark, abandoned in a sinking condition off Bermuda February 17, 1892.
- *Witch of the Wave,* 1851, 1,498 tons, an extreme clipper built for Glidden & Williams and others at a cost of $90,000. Put on the combined California–China run, made a very quick tea passage from China to Britain in 1852, later made the record voyage from Calcutta, India, to Boston in 81 days. Subsequently sold to Dutch interests in 1856 and renamed *Electra*; subsequently sold to Norwegian interests in 1882 and renamed *Ruth*, later career unknown.
- *Tinqua*, 1852, 668 tons, of extreme model, built for the Olyphants of New York and

Clipper *Witch of the Wave*. This Portsmouth-built ship, put over by George Raynes in 1851, was one of the fastest of the early clippers employed in the California and Far East trades(*Gleason's Pictorial Drawing Room Companion*, June 14, 1851).

named after a hong merchant in Canton, China. Put on California–China run, maiden voyage in 1852 and 1853 115 days, and made some fast passages. Lost off Cape Hatteras, North Carolina, coast January 1855 while bound Shanghai to New York.

- *Wild Duck*, 1853, 860 tons, of extreme model, similar to *Wild Pigeon*, built for the Olyphants of New York; originally to be named *Stranger*, but name changed before launching. Put on California–China route, went ashore on the River Min at Foo Chow while departing for New York in March 1856, a total loss.
- *Coeur de Lion*, 1854, 1,098 tons, built for Boston and Portsmouth interests. Put on the California–China route, maiden voyage to San Francisco made in 133 days, fastest California run 119 days in 1855; in 1856 chartered at Hong Kong to carry British troops to Calcutta, India, in 1857 idle at Singapore due to a slowdown in commerce. Sold to German interests by 1860, soon after sold to the Russian-American Fur Company under the Russian flag and renamed *Zaritza*, subsequently sold to Sweden 1874 and re-rigged as a bark; lost after a collision in the Baltic Sea in 1915.
- *Emily Farnum*, 1854, 1,119 tons, a medium clipper built for W. Jones & Co. of Portsmouth. First put in the guano trade, later the Indian trade, captured by the Confederate raider *Alabama* in October 1862 but released because she carried British owned goods. Subsequently sold out of Portsmouth in 1872 to West Coast interests and re-rigged as a bark, wrecked with a cargo of railroad iron while bound San Francisco to Washington in November 1875.
- *Witch of the Wave* (II), 1856, 1,020 tons, built by George Raynes, Jr., for Newburyport interests. Put into the cotton trade and in 1856 carried the most valuable cargo of cotton ever loaded for Le Havre, France, at Charleston, South Carolina, valued in excess of $223,000; later put in the guano and Indian trades, later owned at Boston. Surveyed at Calcutta, India, in 1873, out of registry after 1874.
- *Shooting Star* (II), 1859, 947 tons, a medium or half-clipper, built for Massachusetts interests including Samuel Reed of Boston,

later owned by Reed, Wade & Co. Named after the early extreme clipper built at Medford in 1850. Destroyed by Confederate raider *Chickamauga* in October 1863.

The firm of Fernald & Petigrew built seven clippers at their yard on Badger's Island. This yard was acquired by Frederick Fernald (born 1811) in 1837, where he subsequently built several ships in partnership with another builder and some on his own until 1844. In that year William Petigrew (born 1812 in Maine) joined Fernald, thereby establishing the successful firm that was George Raynes' greatest rival. It is interesting to note that Petigrew had formerly been employed by George Raynes as a master shipbuilder. This shipbuilding partnership lasted until the death of Frederick Fernald in 1855 at the young age of forty-four.

- *Typhoon*, 1850, 1,612 tons, of extreme model, for D. & A. Kingsland of New York. Nicknamed the "Portsmouth Flyer" after her maiden voyage from Portsmouth to Liverpool in 13½ days, subsequently put on the California–China route, fastest passage 108 days in 1851. Sold foreign to British interests in 1863 while at Singapore, later renamed *Indomitable* and lost in 1871 in a typhoon in the China Sea.
- *Red Rover*, 1852, 1,021 tons, of extreme model, built for Robert Taylor & Co. of New York. Put on California–China route, her four California passages averaged under 117 days, the best of any Portsmouth clipper; damaged in the fire that burned the clipper *Great Republic* at New York in December 1853 but repaired, later put in the guano trade, sold foreign to James Baines & Co. in 1860 and renamed *Young Australia*. Subsequently wrecked off Moreton Bay, Brisbane, Australia, in May 1872.
- *Water Witch*, 1853, 1,204 tons, built for Boston interests, damaged during maiden voyage from Boston to San Francisco and put in Rio de Janeiro, completed voyage in 228 days, made one guano voyage. Subsequently wrecked while loading at Mazatlan, Mexico, early 1855.
- *Dashing Wave*, 1853, 1,230 tons, of medium model, built for Boston interests. Put on California–Far East route, her 1858 California passage of 107 days the second best ever by a Portsmouth clipper; beginning

about 1870 operated on the West Coast at Puget Sound hauling lumber for many years. In 1900 sold to Tacoma, Washington, interests and in 1902 was sold to a canning company for $6,000 and converted to a barge. Her hull surveyed in 1920 and still rated A-1; later in 1920 lost due to stranding at Seymour Narrows.

- *Express,* 1854, 1,050 tons, built for local interests. Maiden voyage from Piscataqua to New Orleans with a cargo of ice, subsequently put in the transatlantic cotton trade and later employed carrying guano. Captured and destroyed by the Confederate raider *Alabama* in April 1863 while bound from Callao, Peru, to Antwerp, Belgium
- *Midnight,* 1854, 962 tons, rated a half-clipper, built for Henry Hastings of Boston. Put in the Boston–India trade for many years; early 1878 put into Java in distress while carrying a cargo of case oil, condemned and sold.
- *Noonday,* 1855, 1,189 tons, of medium model, launched after the death of Frederick Fernald for Henry Hastings of Boston. Put into Boston–India trade via San Francisco and later the guano trade. Struck an uncharted rock in the Banda Sea ca. 1857 and put into Batavia, Indonesia, for repairs. Wrecked in January 1863 while bound Boston to San Francisco after striking an uncharted rock off San Francisco that was subsequently named Noonday Rock.

The firm of Tobey & Littlefield was the third most active in Portsmouth in terms of the number of clippers they built, but they nonetheless built on a big scale and put over two of the finest ships of the American clipper fleet. Stephen Tobey (born 1809 in Maine) came from a family of shipbuilders and got his professional start by apprenticing under George Raynes, later rising to the position of foreman at the Raynes shipyard (Brighton, p. 107). Tobey's partner in the shipbuilding trade was Daniel Littlefield (born 1822 in Maine); he was a newcomer to Portsmouth, arriving here in the early 1850s. The Tobey & Littlefield shipyard on Noble's Island was in operation for thirty years beginning with their first clipper in 1853.

- *Morning Light,* 1853, 1,713 tons, of extreme model, built for Glidden & Williams of Boston, cost $117,000, the largest vessel ever launched at Portsmouth up to that time. Put on the California run for the first part of her career, fastest passage 112 days in 1854 and 1855, later a coal and guano carrier. Sold foreign to James Baines & Co. for service in their Black Ball Line of Australian packets, re-named *Queen of the South,* out of registry after 1869.
- *Sierra Nevada,* 1854, 1,942 tons, of extreme model, built for Glidden & Williams of Boston and put in the California trade, making a 98-day passage in 1859 and 1860; made at least one Australian voyage in 1861. Subsequently sold foreign in 1863 to McKay & Baines Co. of Britain, renamed *Royal Dane* and put in their Black Ball Line of Australian packets until the line's dissolution in 1866; later put in the guano trade, wrecked on the coast of Chile in 1877.
- *Ocean Rover,* 1854, 777 tons, of extreme model, built for local interests, part of which included the builders. Served as a transatlantic packet carrying cotton from southern ports to Liverpool, ashore near that port in 1856 and severely damaged but repaired. Purchased by Salem, Massachusetts, parties in 1863 and possibly re-rigged as a bark. Later lost in River Jeganna, Brazil, in July 1870 while bound from Hamburg, Germany, to Baker's Island.

Samuel Badger (born 1794) probably learned the shipbuilding trade from his uncle, the famed local shipbuilder William Badger, at his Badger's Island yard and began building ships on his own after the elder Badger's death in 1830. It is interesting to note that one tale surrounding the death of William Badger tells of Samuel Badger paying someone to sit by his uncle's deathbed to take notes should he have anything to say about shipbuilding (Brighton, p. 140). By 1832 Samuel Badger had moved to the Maine side of the Piscataqua River at Kittery Foreside where he established his own shipyard just opposite the Portsmouth Navy Yard. Here he built 27 vessels, including three clippers, until his death in 1857.

- *Fleetwood,* 1852, 663 tons, of medium model, built for Boston interests and her first commander, Captain Frank Dale. Put on the California–China route initially, later made at least one voyage to India, lost in May 1859 after colliding with an iceberg off Cape Horn, ship abandoned by all hands, but lifeboat carrying Captain Dale, his wife and son, and fourteen others was never recovered. This clipper's construction is erroneously credited to George Raynes by Howe & Matthews.

- *Granite State*, 1853, 1,108 tons, built for Portsmouth and Kittery, Maine, interests; first commanded by part-owner Captain Samuel Billings and put in the transatlantic cotton trade and later in the India trade. Later career uncertain, lost in 1875, details unknown. This ship should not be confused with a later sailing ship of the same name wrecked on the coast of Cornwall, England, at Porthcurno in 1895.
- *Cathedral*, 1855, 1,650 tons, a half-clipper and the largest vessel ever built by Badger, built for Enoch Train of Boston at a cost of $125,000. Employed as a transatlantic packet ship carrying passengers between Boston and Liverpool, lost February 17, 1857, during second voyage while bound from the East Coast to San Francisco with a cargo of coal off Cape Horn when damaged in a gale and subsequently abandoned, 36 crew rescued but the clipper's ill captain, his stewardess, a passenger-doctor, and one sailor went down with the ship.

Samuel Hanscom, Jr., (born 1805 in Maine) came from a long line of shipbuilders, his father, John, having worked at the trade, as did his brother William Hanscom, who worked at the yards in Bath, Maine, before returning to Portsmouth in the 1850s to become the foreman at the Portsmouth Navy Yard. Little is known about Samuel's prior building career, but he undoubtedly gained some measure of skill and experience at the family shipyard on the Maine side of the Piscataqua River at Elliot before 1849. Samuel Hanscom's nephew, Isaiah Hanscom, is generally credited as being the designer of the Hanscom clippers; he worked at the Portsmouth Navy Yard from 1845 to 1849 and may have even obtained the idea for a clipper design indirectly from Samuel Pook, whose father worked at the Portsmouth Navy Yard.

- *Nightingale*, 1851, 1,060 tons, of extreme model, originally to be named *Sarah Cowles* and intended both as a transatlantic packet and an exhibit for the World's Fair in London; subsequently sold at auction and acquired by Sampson & Tappan of Boston. First employed in the Australian packet service and China trade, subsequently sold in 1855 and again shortly thereafter New York to Francis Bowen and turned into a slave ship, captured by U.S. naval forces off the coast of Africa in 1861, subsequently condemned and sold to the U.S. government for use as naval vessel; resold to Captain David Mayo of Boston in 1865 and employed in a variety of trades being again sold to other American interests. Later sold foreign to Norwegian interests in 1876 for $15,000 and put in timber trade with a homeport of Krageroe, later re-rigged as a bark. Abandoned at sea in April 1891 while bound Liverpool to Halifax, Nova Scotia.
- *Josephine*, 1852, 947 tons, built for Joseph Andrews of Salem, Massachusetts, first employed on the California run in the Empire Line, caught fire and burned in the harbor at St. Louis, Mauritius, in June 1859, a total loss.

Daniel Moulton (born 1815 in Maine) was the head of the Mechanics Shipbuilding Company, a joint stock company established in late 1853 at Portsmouth that was "composed of 40 industrious and enterprising mechanics of the various trades and occupations in building vessels" (Brighton, p. 150). This concern established their shipyard on Noble's Island and built five ships between 1854 and 1858, two of which were clippers. Moulton must have done well in this short term venture; he was listed as a carpenter worth $2,200 in the 1850 census but by 1860 was listed as a shipbuilder worth $5,500. After ending this venture, Daniel Moulton later went to work for the Portsmouth Navy Yard.

- *Morning Glory*, 1854, 1,119 tons, built for Portsmouth and Boston interests, the first ship from this new shipbuilding company. Put in the transatlantic cotton trade where she traded between southern U.S. ports and Liverpool and Le Havre. Sold foreign to British interests in 1864 and renamed *British Crown*, later employed in the coal trade, homeport North Shields, UK, out of registry after 1875.
- *Star of Hope*, 1855, 1,198 tons, built for northern Massachusetts interests; originally named *Saint Paul* but changed after launching. First voyage carried naval supplies from New York to California in 1856 but put into

Montevideo, Uruguay, on fire, repaired and resumed voyage to California which took eleven months. Later abandoned at sea off the Cape of Good Hope in June 1861 while bound from Liverpool to India loaded with railroad iron.

Elbridge G. Pierce (born 1802 in Maine) built one clipper at Portsmouth soon after his arrival in town about 1855. He had previously learned the trade in Maine from his shipbuilding father and built a number of small vessels, all under 450 tons in size, on the Kennebec River while a resident of Farmingdale. What caused Pierce to come to Portsmouth to build a clipper is unknown for certain, but one factor was surely the thriving shipbuilding business in the city overall. Pierce established his shipyard on Pierce Island, which he leased from the Pierce family of Boston and Portsmouth, thus giving some credence to the idea that Elbridge Pierce may have been related to that branch of the Pierce family. Whatever the case regarding his family ties, Elbridge Pierce and his son Elbridge Pierce, Jr., built two ships at their shipyard including one clipper, before ceasing operations in 1858. Like many Piscataqua area shipwrights, the elder Pierce afterward worked at the navy yard and retired in 1873, though he worked as a pattern maker as late as 1880.

- *Charger*, 1856, 1,169 tons, of medium model, built for Henry Hastings of Boston. Immediately put in the California trade in early 1857, later operated in the China tea and Far Eastern trade. Lost December 1873, wrecked on a coral reef while in the Philippines sailing to Cebu to complete the loading of a cargo of hemp for Boston.

Massachusetts

This state was the most important of all when it came to the number of clippers produced, 233 in all being built here from 1844 to 1859. These clippers were built in sixteen communities from Amesbury, Newburyport, and Marblehead north of Boston on the Merrimack River and in the Cape Ann region, south to Medford and the greater Boston area at Charlestown, Chelsea, East Boston, Boston, Quincy, and South Boston, on the South Shore at Kingston, further south at East Dennis on Cape Cod, and into southern Massachusetts at Fairhaven, Mattapoisett, Swansea, and Somerset. Not only did Massachusetts build the most clippers, the state also built the largest, Donald McKay's *Great Republic*, as well as the fastest by almost every measure, including the *Lightning*, *James Baines*, and *Flying Cloud*, all of which were also the work of McKay. As might be expected, Donald McKay put over the most ships of any clipper builder anywhere in the world, twenty-eight in number, and his production also was greater than the combined efforts of any other entire state with the exception of Massachusetts, Maine, and New York. However, while McKay was the most prominent of the clipper builders, there were many other builders that were also producing excellent clippers. The most forgotten of these yards is that of J. Edwin and Harrison Briggs of South Boston; they built twenty clippers, while Samuel Hall of East Boston built fourteen. Rivaling Boston was the nearby city of Medford, located on the Mystic River; among the builders active here was the partnership of Hayden & Cudworth (19 clippers), J.O. Curtis (17 clippers), Joshua Foster (6 clippers), and Samuel Lapham (4 clippers), as well as those from the yards of Paul Curtis, Jotham Stetson, and Benjamin Delano. While most of the Massachusetts clippers were produced in the greater Boston area, there were other important locales where these ships were being produced; Newburyport to the north was a notable clipper producer, with Currier & Townsend building fourteen such ships, George Jackman eight, three by John Currier, Jr., along with one by Benjamin Dutton, while in southern Massachusetts the Shiverick brothers built five clippers at East Dennis on Cape Cod, Captain James Hood launched nine at his Somerset yard, and two others were built at Fairhaven. Notably absent on the list of towns in which clippers were built in the state are Salem and New Bedford, both of which had a long maritime history by 1850. The former port was generally too shallow to support the bigger clippers, and while several clippers were owned here by local merchants, it may be that the Salem builders were a bit more conservative in their building practices. While a number of fine barks were built here into the 1870s, none were produced in the 1850s that were of clipper model. Likewise, the port of New Bedford, though also the homeport for several clippers, was best known for its whaling activities and fine fleet of whalers and had no local builders willing to dive into the clipper ship business. However, there are listed below several whaling ships that were identified by a contemporary authoritative source as clippers, two of which were built at nearby Mattapoissett. The prime newspaper of the whaling trade, the *Whalemen's Shipping List and Merchant's Transcript*, comments on two whaling clippers launched in 1852 in this town (and one in Newburyport), but does not designate other vessels added to the fleet as clippers, which gives rise to the possibility that these ships were somehow different in model. While these whaling clippers were certainly not in the same class as the California clippers, or even the later medium and half-clippers, it can be speculated that they may have been more heavily sparred and perhaps adopted to some degree the flat-floored hull principals of the clippers and are thus included herein.

Finally, in regards to Massachusetts builders, there were two very important areas in the state where these men received their early training: the North River region in the South Shore coastal area between Boston and Cape Cod, and the city of Medford on the Mystic River. While but two small clipper barks were built in the South Shore area, a number of important builders hailed from here, many of them the sons of local shipbuilders in such towns as Scituate and Marshfield, and together they account for over half of all the clippers built in Massachusetts. Among these notable builders were such men as Samuel Hall, the Briggs brothers, Elisha Hayden and William Cudworth, James Curtis, Paul Curtis, John Taylor, Joshua Magoun, and Jotham Stetson. Furthermore, many of these North River builders made their way early on to Medford, the state's most important shipbuilding center prior to the clipper ship era, where they served their apprenticeships and received technical training from Medford builders. However, the North River–Medford connection began with the state's most important builder prior to the 1840s, Thatcher Magoun. From the early 1800s to the late 1830s Magoun launched (and owned) many notable merchant sailing ships; because of his importance, Magoun is one of the few pre-clipper era builders to have a clipper ship named in his honor

Just why Massachusetts came to be the largest producer of clipper ships is an interesting question to ponder; while the state had a long history of shipbuilding and maritime commerce dating back to the 1620s, until the 1840s the state built mostly smaller merchant ships under 600 tons for the coasting trade, as well as the China and European trade. In contrast, the larger transatlantic packets were being built at New York and Maine and, to a lesser extent, in New Hampshire. This began to gradually change in the 1830s when a number of future clipper builders, including Paul and James Curtis and Samuel Hall, were getting their start in the shipbuilding business, and continued in a big way in the 1840s when Donald McKay moved his shipyard from Newburyport to East Boston and began building, first, some large packet ships, and later on the clippers that gained him undying fame. While historian William Armstrong Fairburn credits the rise in Massachusetts shipbuilding in the clipper ship era to the fact that her builders could deliver a ship on time and on demand, unlike the severely overtaxed New York shipyards of the early 1850s, this was only one part of the equation, the other part being that established builders like Hall, the Curtises, Hayden & Cudworth, and McKay, as well as newly established builders like Robert Jackson, James Hood, and the Briggs brothers were now becoming known to a larger audience. It was soon discovered by New York merchants and those elsewhere that Massachusetts shipbuilders were every bit the equal of those outside the state.

As to the most significant of the Massachusetts clippers, there are many to choose from, but the following thirty ships represent the best of the many such vessels produced here. While builders from all areas of the state are represented here, Donald McKay leads the way with nine vessels on the list.

- *Flying Cloud*: with two California passages to her credit of under 90 days, this clipper was one of the fastest ever built and to this day is the face, the name that everyone knows, of this class of ships.
- *Lightning*: this ship attained some of the highest rates of speed of any sailing ship in history and made her mark on the Australian run.
- *Champion of the Seas*: this clipper sailed the greatest number of miles in a single 24-hour period than any other clipper.
- *James Baines*: this clipper may have been the fastest of all the McKay clippers, making a record passage between Boston and Liverpool on her maiden voyage.

- *Sovereign of the Seas*: yet another McKay clipper, and one of his best known for her speed, including a maiden California run of 103 days.
- *Flying Fish*: considered by some contemporaries a faster ship than the *Flying Cloud*, this McKay clipper *averaged* under 106 days on her seven California runs.
- *Northern Light*: the first ship on this list not built by McKay, this Briggs brothers production set the record for the San Francisco to New York run.
- *Surprise*: built by Samuel Hall, this clipper, a long-lived one, was the first such ship built at East Boston and on her maiden California passage made San Francisco in under 97 days.
- *Great Republic*: this McKay-built giant, the only four-masted clipper ever launched, was the largest merchant sailing ship in the world at her launch, and later made a 92 day passage, one of the best ever, on the California run.
- *Dreadnought*: one of the few clippers specifically built as a transatlantic packet, this ship built at Newburyport by Currier & Townsend made two of the fastest passages ever on the New York–Liverpool route.
- *Romance of the Seas*: this McKay clipper was yet another fast vessel and the record holder in terms of sustained speed, achieving 22 knots during one Australian run.
- *Staffordshire*: though a short-lived clipper, this McKay ship was fast and one of the first built for the transatlantic packet service.
- *Stag Hound*: the first of the extreme clippers, this McKay-built vessel was the largest and longest American merchant ship when launched.
- *Witchcraft*: another fast ship, this extreme clipper built by Paul Curtis at Chelsea made a California run in 98 days.
- *Shooting Star*: this small clipper, built by James Curtis, was the first true clipper built at Medford and was a fast and well-known ship.
- *Blue Jacket*: a fast clipper built at East Boston by Robert Jackson, showing that Donald McKay was not the only one in town who knew how to build a flyer.
- *John Gilpin*: this Samuel Hall-built clipper made her maiden voyage on the California route, arriving in several hours under 94 days, one of the best ever.
- *John Bertram*: the first of the California clippers, she was built by Jackson & Ewell in quick time, 61 days from keel laying to launching, and made some fast California runs of 105, 108, and 115 days.
- *Herald of the Morning*: one of the most beautiful of the clipper fleet, this fast ship built by Hayden & Cudworth at Medford made her mark on the California run with a maiden passage of just over 100 days.
- *Governor Morton*: a consistently fast and reliable ship on the California run for many years, the best to come from Captain James Hood's yard in Somerset.
- *Winged Racer*: another beautiful and fast clipper designed by Samuel Pook and built by Robert Jackson, this ship made some very creditable California runs.
- *Syren*: this clipper, built by John Taylor at Medford, truly demonstrates how well built this class of ships often were, still sailing the high seas as late as 1920 after sixty-nine years of hard service.
- *Swallow*: another well-built clipper by Robert Jackson that saw some thirty years of service and made consistently above average passages on the California run.
- *Wild Fire*: this Amesbury-built bark, the smallest of the Massachusetts clippers, made the record run from Boston to Gibraltar.
- *Phantom*: yet another fine example of Medford shipbuilding and built by Samuel Lapham, this fast vessel has two fine California runs (102 days, 9 hours and 105 days) to her credit.
- *Raven*: though small, under 800 tons, this fast clipper built by Captain Hood at Somerset has several fine California runs to her credit, including a 106 day passage on her maiden voyage in a race in which she beat two larger and well known record-setters, including the famed *Sea Witch*.
- *Malay*: another fine little clipper from an under-appreciated builder, John Taylor of Chelsea. She sailed the seas for 39 years, all under the American flag.
- *Don Quixote*: this clipper, one of the most notable to come from the yard of Samuel Lapham at Medford, was one of the best of the medium clippers and was not only able to carry a large cargo, but was also fast, making three California runs of 111 days and under.

- *Ocean Telegraph*: one of the best clippers produced by James Curtis, this vessel averaged under 117 days on seven California runs, and made five runs from San Francisco to New York with an average of just under 97 days.
- *Wild Hunter*: though not the best known of the Cape Cod clippers, this ship was the fastest of the five built by the Shiverick brothers.

Amesbury

Simon McKay (born 1821 in Nova Scotia, Canada) built two small clippers here at this town, just upriver from where the Powwow River flows into the Merrimack River. He originally was the junior partner in the firm of Osgood & McKay, Timothy Osgood said to be a former supervisor in Donald McKay's East Boston shipyard, and was active from about 1842 to 1850 building small ships and barks. However, by late 1852 Simon McKay was on his own, a competent designer and builder, and would build two small clippers, one of them noted for its speed. Later on, McKay continued his building activities, launching small barks and schooner, but also proposed a 1,000-ton schooner, which apparently was never built. McKay later worked with Newburyport builder Benjamin Dutton, who was down in Virginia cutting timber for their use in early 1861 (Cheney, p. 180); they later opened a yard in Charlestown, Massachusetts, and were employed building some larger ships and barks here in 1863. Though uncertain, it is very probable that Simon McKay, given his place of origin and his very name, was related to the famed Boston clipper builder Donald McKay, perhaps a younger brother or cousin.

- *Wildfire*, 1853, 338-ton bark, built for Peter Hargous of New York and intended for the Mediterranean trade, the vessel claimed by her builder to be a fast one, so much so that "they will challenge the whole fleet of sailing vessels in New England to a trial of speed" (*Amesbury Villager*, March 31, 1853). Maiden voyage Boston to Malta May 1853, passed Gibraltar when fourteen days out, the fastest such passage ever on record, later endured heavy weather while bound from Gibraltar to Malta; said by her commander, Captain Mosman, to be "not only an excellent sea boat, but the swiftest vessel he ever saw ... no vessel in the Mediterranean trade can begin to approach her in speed" (*Boston Daily Atlas*, July 9, 1853). Later employed in the South American trade sailing between New York and Vera Cruz, Mexico, until her sale in late 1859 to Pierre L. Pierce (born 1829 in Louisiana) who was both a ship carpenter in New York with assets approaching $20,000 and a known slave trader; departed New York under command of Captain Philip Stanhope for St. Thomas, West Indies, within days of her sale in December 1859, then sailed for the west coast of Africa to load a cargo of slaves, further outfitted as a slave ship on the Congo River, departed there March 1860 bound for Cuba with over 500 captives, boarded by the USS *Mohawk* off Cuba April 26, 1860, and subsequently detained along with her crew, one of whom committed suicide, ship and captives subsequently landed at Key West, Florida. Ship condemned in June 1860, subsequently sold at auction to Gomez & Willis of New York for $6,454 and refitted in January 1861, later career unknown.
- *Alma*, 1854, bark, launched December 5, 1854, tonnage and owners unknown, described as a "beautiful half-clipper bark" (Cheney, p. 180), no further details known.

Newburyport

William Currier (born 1807) and James Townsend (born 1815 in New York) formed the partnership of Currier & Townsend in 1843 and would build 14 clipper ships and barks from 1850 to 1857 at their yard located in the North End at the foot of Ashland Street, the most prolific in this regard of all the Newburyport builders. Currier had formerly been the partner of Donald McKay beginning in 1841 and together they built three ships together before parting ways in late 1842. Townsend, too, had his McKay connections; he was a native of New York and had served his apprenticeship as a shipwright with McKay under Isaac Webb and arrived in Newburyport with McKay in 1839. While McKay found employment here, Townsend did not and so returned to New York to work as a foreman in one of the major yards there. Of his abilities, one historian states that Townsend was "a man of science and one of the greatest naval architects of his day" (Cheney, p. 60). How Townsend came to return to Newburyport is unknown for sure, but we can be sure that he and Currier had previously known one another, likely through their connections to McKay. In their fourteen years of business, Currier & Townsend would build over 50 ships and barks of all sizes, the largest being the ill-fated *Racer*. After their partnership was dissolved due to financial difficulties, James Townsend built one clipper at their old yard and would continue building ships at another site in town through 1864, but by 1870 he had moved to East Boston and was working building sailing ships of the downeaster type into the early 1880s as part of the firm of Smith & Townsend, the former man being Silvanus Smith, a shipbuilder from the North River area of Massachusetts. As for William Currier, he would build another ten ships on his own, none of them clippers, until ceasing operations in 1865.

- *Raduga*, 1848, 587 tons, of medium model, built for H. Prince and others of Boston, sold in 1851 for $32,500. Employed in the Far East trade, beginning in 1857 employed in the Boston–Honolulu trade carrying whale oil home to New Bedford, sold foreign to Hawaiian interests in 1863 to Charles Brewer & Co. and renamed *Iolani*, kept in same trade; early 1870s sold again, this time to parties in Barbados, renamed *Modesta* and re-rigged as a bark, lost after a collision in 1890.
- *Dragon*, 1850, 290-ton bark, built for commission merchants Williams & Deland of Boston; nothing is known of this vessel's career.
- *Racer*, 1851, 1,699 tons, built for the Red Cross Line of New York, Ogden, Morgan, and others owners, cost reported to be over $120,000. First employed as a transatlantic packet but made one California run in late 1852, subsequently employed in the European–Far East trade. Lost in May 1856 after departing Liverpool for New York, struck Arklow Bank off Wicklow, Ireland, and soon settled with water, subsequently abandoned by crew and passengers, and then plundered by local population during cargo salvage attempt.
- *Memnon*, 1852, 430 tons, whaling ship built for E. Field and F.C. Sanford of Nantucket, Massachusetts, launched August 14, 1852, intended for use in the sperm whale fishery (*Whalemen's Shipping List*, August 24, 1852), departed Nantucket August 2, 1852, bound for the South Pacific and sent home 442 barrels of sperm oil, subsequently burned at Payta, Peru, October 1854 (Starbuck, pgs. 498–99).
- *Dreadnought*, 1853, 1,414 tons, of medium model, built for the Red Cross Line, Ogden, et al., construction superintended by Captain Samuel Samuels. Employed on the New York–Liverpool run, made 31 round trip voyages from 1853 to 1864, nine of which were under sixteen days on the eastward run, her best time being 13 days, 11 hours in November 1854, fastest westward passage 19 days in February 1854 on her maiden round-trip voyage. In January 1863 while bound for New York experienced a heavy storm which damaged the ship and injured her captain, forcing the ship into Fayal for relief; on a subsequent westward voyage was dismasted and Captain Lytle injured (later died) in December 1863 and forced to put into Fayal for repairs. Mid-1864 put in the California trade for several voyages, departed Liverpool for San Francisco April 1869, subsequently went ashore in July 1869 off Tierra del Fuego and was a total loss, crew saved.
- *Highflyer*, 1853, 1,195 tons, of medium model, built for the Red Cross Line of New York. First put in the California trade, maiden voyage out taking 143 days after ship forced to put into Rio de Janeiro due to a leak. Made a second California run in 1855, thereafter departing San Francisco for Hong Kong in October 1855; subsequently went missing, possibly captured by pirates off Formosa and destroyed, her crew murdered.
- *Eloisa de Valparaiso*, 1854, 725-ton trading yacht, purchased by Samuel Crane of Boston for Valparaiso, Chile, interests. Career largely unknown but was involved in salvage efforts on the wreck of the clipper *Sovereign of the Seas* which was lost on Malacca Reef, Malaysia, in 1859.
- *Troubadour*, 1854, 1,199 tons, built for William Hammond of Marblehead and Fisher & Co. of Boston, career details unknown.

"An American Ship Rescuing the Officers and Crew of a British Man of War." This Currier & Ives print from 1863 shows the Newburyport-built *Dreadnought* giving assistance to a vessel in distress, though where and when this event took place is not stated.

- *Driver,* 1854, 1,594 tons, a clipper packet built for the Red Cross Line. Went missing in February 1856 with all 372 crew and passengers aboard while bound Liverpool to New York, likely due to storm.
- *Brewster,* 1855, 984 tons, built for interests from Brewster, Massachusetts, Boston, Cotuit, Massachusetts, and New Orleans, Louisiana, later sold to New York interests. Made one California run of 126 days in 1855, further career details uncertain; subsequently sold foreign, by 1886 was owned in Norway and named *Fama,* out of registry after 1890.
- *Courier,* 1855, 554 tons, built for Foster, Elliot & Co. of New York. First employed in the South American trade, later career details unknown.
- *East Indian,* 1856, 897 tons, built for Stephen Tilton & Co. of Boston and others. No career details known, sold foreign at Calcutta, India, in 1864.
- *Eddystone,* 1856, 949 tons, built for local interests, later owned by Bucksport, Maine, interests. Largely employed in the Indian trade, made one California run in 1870, sold foreign to British interests in 1874. In 1875 departed Mexico for Liverpool with guano, put into Tahiti in a leaking condition, there repaired and continued her voyage only to return in a short time; then condemned and sold to San Francisco parties and sent to Sydney, Australia, to be sold, no takers found so loaded coal for San Francisco, again forced into Tahiti in a leaking condition, again sold, this time to sail under the Costa Rican flag, renamed *Don Nicolas* and re-rigged as a bark and put in the west coast coal and lumber trades. Final voyage departed Newcastle, New South Wales, Australia, with coal for San Francisco, subsequently began to founder after encountering severe storm weather and was abandoned on March 13, 1891, off New Zealand, entire crew saved.
- *Victory,* 1857, 1,799 tons, a packet-type clipper, built by James Townsend for the Red Cross Line of New York, the second clipper built here to bear this name, career details unknown.

The Jackman family had a long history of shipbuilding in this seaport town dating back to 1790, with George W. Jackman, Jr., (born 1804) carrying on the tradition during the clipper ship era. He got his start after purchasing the shipyard of his brother Stephen after his death in early 1849, launching his first vessel that same year, a 525-ton bark in the North End area of town next to the yard of Currier & Townsend. George Jackman would subsequently build his first clipper in 1850 and his last in 1856, launching nine in all that were mostly of medium model. After 1856 Jackman continued his building career in a big way, launching U.S. Navy gunboats and steamships in the 1860s. These included several large, 3,000-ton steamers designed by Samuel Pook, and a number of ships and barks. Jackman launched his last ship, the 1,419-ton *Landseer*, in December 1874, after which his yard closed down. Two ships that do not make the Jackman list of clippers and did not sail under the American flag for long, though their lines were likely similar to those of his last clippers and were very close in tonnage, are the 1857-built *Reina del Seano*, a 1,040-ton vessel built for Boston and West Indies owners, and the 1860-built *Fear Not*, a 1,000-ton ship that was sold foreign upon arriving in England after her first voyage (Cheney, p. 77).

- *Falcon*, 1851, 510-ton bark (not a ship as listed by Cutler), built for John E. Lodge of Boston and part Jackman interest. Likely employed in the Far East trade, later owned by Tuckerman & Townsend of Boston, likely continued in the Far East trade, also possibly made voyages to India or the Mediterranean, areas in which its owners were active. In 1863 sold foreign to British interests, homeport Port Elizabeth, South Africa, out of registry after 1872.
- *Hussar*, 1852, 721 tons, built for Bush & Wilds of Boston, later sold to G. Hussey of New Bedford. Possibly involved in the whale oil or the Far East trade but career details uncertain, sold foreign at Singapore in late 1864.
- *Whistler*, 1853, 820 tons, of extreme model, built for Bush & Wilds of Boston with Jackman retaining a part interest. Put in the California–Far East trade, made one California passage of 130 days in 1853. Lost on second round-trip voyage while bound Melbourne, Australia, to Singapore, going ashore on King's Island in the Bass Straits in late May 1855, two crewmen lost.
- *Starr King*, 1854, 1,170 tons, of medium model, built for Bates & Thaxter of Boston. Put in the California–Far East trade, maiden voyage to California made in 118 days, early 1856 sailed from Melbourne, Australia, to Hong Kong in the then record time of 34 days, made one guano voyage Callao, Peru, to Hampton Roads, Virginia, in 1858; in early 1860 carried cargo and almost 400 Chinese passengers from Hong Kong to San Francisco in a quick 40 day passage. On final voyage departed Hong Kong in ballast for Singapore in June 1862, went ashore on Point Romania, a total loss, entire crew saved.
- *Charmer*, 1854, 1,055 tons, of medium model, built for Bush & Wilds of Boston. First put in the California–Far East trade, maiden voyage Boston to San Francisco made in 114 days; in late 1860 while bound Manila to New York with a cargo of hemp went ashore but got off with little damage. Sold foreign at Liverpool in January 1863, still afloat with original name, homeport Glasgow, Scotland, in 1875.
- *Daring*, 1855, 1,097 tons, of medium model, built for Bush & Comstock of Boston. Put in the California–Far East trade, maiden voyage out to San Francisco made in 112 days, made one guano voyage in 1860, 1863 and 1864 employed in the transatlantic trade; late 1864 made another guano voyage Baker's Island to Liverpool but was dismasted during a storm and forced to put into Valparaiso, Chile, condemned and subsequently sold foreign to British interests for $1,090 without a name change and repaired, disappears from registry after 1873.
- *War Hawk*, 1856, 1,067 tons, of medium model and a sister ship to *Daring*, built for Bush & Comstock. Put in the California–Far East trade, making ten California runs from Boston and New York, fastest passage 128 days in 1856. Employed in the coolie trade in 1856, carrying 900 coolies from Swatow to Havana, Cuba, also carried whale oil Honolulu to New Bedford in 1858 and coal from Liverpool to New York in 1861, sold at San Francisco in late 1871 after arriving there from Liverpool after a passage of 440 days, being forced to put into Rio de Janeiro in distress en route. Subsequently employed in the West Coast lumber trade between San Francisco and Puget Sound,

carrying a large cargo of 750,000 feet of board lumber in early 1872 from San Francisco to Fort Discovery in the record time of 25 days. Lost to fire while in port at Fort Discovery in April 1883.
- *Black Prince*, 1856, 1,061 tons, of medium model, built for Bush & Wilds. Made three California passages, all under unfavorable conditions including a crew mutiny in 1858 that forced her to put into Rio de Janeiro. Went ashore at Woosung, China, in 1862 and damaged. Final voyage departed San Francisco for Boston late 1864, damaged in a storm, reported low on provisions and water in her hold to a British ship that rendered aid; thereafter lost with all hands in a severe gale on or about February 16, 1865.
- *Reynard*, 1856, 1,051 tons, of medium model, built for Bush & Comstock. Put in the California–Far East trade, made one guano voyage in 1858, in 1860 put in the transatlantic trade and the England–China trade, carried coal Cardiff to Hong Kong in 1861 and from Cardiff to Calcutta, India, in 1863. By 1864 back in the California trade, made another guano voyage in 1871, thereafter sold to Boston shipbuilder Daniel D. Kelly and re-rigged as a bark, subsequently sold foreign to British interests at Quebec in 1877 after a San Francisco to Cork, Ireland, passage; still operating in the transatlantic trade, possibly as a lumber carrier, in 1886.

John Currier, Jr., (born 1801) was Newburyport's most important shipbuilder in the nineteenth century, building nearly 100 vessels between the years 1831 and 1884 at his large yard at Moggridge Point. Perhaps because he was so well established, Currier did not get heavily involved in the clipper business, unlike his younger competitors, and did not suffer in any way financially for this decision, he having assets worth $155,000 by 1860. All three of his clippers were of medium model and their similar tonnage may indicate that they were built off the same model.

- *Guiding Star*, 1853, 904 tons, built for Moses Davenport and others of Newburyport. Career details uncertain; sold to Samuel Reed & Co. of Boston in 1867, subsequently condemned and scrapped at Hong Kong in 1870.
- *Black Hawk*, 1857, 941 tons, built for local interests, including the builder. Not to be confused with two other clippers of the same name built at Connecticut and New York; career details uncertain.
- *Star of Peace*, 1858, 941 tons, built for Moses Davenport, Charles Hill of Boston, Captain Lambert of Portsmouth, New Hampshire, and the builder. Career details uncertain; captured and burned by the Confederate raider *Florida* in May 1863 while bound Calcutta, India, to Boston.

Benjamin Dutton (born 1814) was a ship carpenter from nearby Newbury, the son of a ship carpenter, who got his start in Newburyport before later moving to Marblehead (see below).

- *Victory*, 1851, 671 tons, built for Benjamin Gould and others of Boston, later owned by New York interests. Lost off Cape Henry, Virginia, while bound Callao, Peru, to Hampton Roads with a cargo of guano in February 1861.

Marblehead

Only seven ships were ever built at Marblehead, three of them clippers by Benjamin Dutton, who moved his shipbuilding operations here from Newburyport by 1851 and built his last clipper in 1857. Dutton likely moved his yard to Marblehead due to the heavy competition and resulting lack of yard space in Newburyport in the early 1850s. All of the Dutton clippers were owned by Edward Kimball, a lumber dealer of Newburyport, though one of these was first owned by Boston interests, and all were commanded by local captains, for which the seaport was noted. Dutton's last clipper was built in partnership with ship carpenter Henry T. Ewell (born 1808), who was a native of Marshfield and trained in Medford, building at least one clipper in partnership with East Boston builder Robert Jackson (see below).

- *Elizabeth Kimball*, 1853, 998 tons, of medium model, built for Edward Kimball and named after his wife (born 1815). Intended for the Indian and Far East trades, maiden voyage Boston to Calcutta, India, with a cargo of ice, while bound from India homeward to Boston experienced a submarine earthquake that stopped the ship in its tracks and caused her to leak, forcing her to put in at Mauritius, after continuing voyage struck on Nantucket Shoals while near port but escaped without damage. In June 1863 sold to West Coast interests and put in the lumber trade. Final voyage departed Port Gamble, Puget Sound, bound for Iquique, Chile, in early 1873, subsequently began to leak and was beached at remote Easter Island; part of the crew subsequently built a schooner from material salvaged from the wreck and sailed to Tahiti for rescue, while others remained on the island and were later rescued by a French vessel.

- *Mary*, 1854, 1,148 tons, of medium model, built for Edward Kimball and named after his daughter (born 1842). Employed as a general trader, first in the transatlantic trade, then put on the California route in 1856, making a 152 day passage and one of 112 days in 1857. In 1858 went ashore on a reef in the Bahamas, the crew got the ship off safely despite attempts by local wreckers to the contrary. Final American voyage commenced at New York in January 1867 for San Francisco, subsequently began leaking after rounding Cape Horn and put into Callao, Peru, in distress, condemned and sold to British interests. Later repaired and sailed under her original name in the guano trade. Lost December 1869 while bound Callao, Peru, to Cork, Ireland, sprang a leak after a gale and was abandoned after her hold filled with water, crew got off in two lifeboats, both of which were rescued.
- *Belle of the Sea*, 1857, 1,255 tons, of medium model, built by Ewell & Dutton, originally owned by T.B. Waters & Co. of Boston, later by Edward Kimball. First employed in the California–Far East trade, maiden voyage on the California route accomplished in 126 days; early 1864 sold foreign at Liverpool for $45,000 and renamed *Strathpeffer*. In 1871 employed in the guano trade, put into Valparaiso in distress while bound Callao, Peru, to Liverpool, condemned and sold, still afloat in 1874.

Charlestown

Joshua Magoun (1794–1856) was an active builder here for many years. He was a native of Pembroke, Massachusetts, (another North River town) who first went to Brookline, Massachusetts, in 1832 to build ships in partnership with Francis Turner (from Scituate) at their shipyard on the Charles River. Here, the firm of Magoun & Turner built about ten ships, the largest the 406-ton bark *Burlington*, until 1836, when they moved to Charlestown Neck. Over the next twenty years, the firm would build some fifty ships, including four clippers built by Magoun after the death of Turner in 1851 and one clipper built by Joseph Magoun, Joshua's son.

- *Mountain Wave*, 1852, 633 tons, of medium model, built for Alpheus Hardy & Co. of Boston. Maiden voyage out to California in 130 days, a second run in 1855 took 154 days, forced into Rio de Janeiro in distress, later put in the Boston–Honolulu–New Bedford trade 1858 to 1863, then in the Far East trade. Final American voyage Boston to Calcutta, India, in early 1865, forced to put into Rio with sail and spar damage, sold to local interests and renamed *Maria del Gloria*; repaired and re-rigged as a bark, further career unknown.
- *Ocean Pearl*, 1853, 847 tons, of medium model, built for Hardy & Sears of Boston. Employed in the California–Far East trade, maiden voyage out to San Francisco made in 135 days. Employed as an army troop and supply transport for the Butler expedition in July 1862, making a round-trip voyage New York to New Orleans. Lost in October 1864 while bound New York to Lisbon, Portugal, went ashore at Terragona while in charge of the pilot, crew saved by boats from a British ship.
- *Waverly*, 1853, 749 tons, built for Curtis & Nichols of Boston. Career details uncertain, employed in the Indian trade in part; went missing while bound Coringa to Calcutta, India, in late September 1862.
- *Galatea*, 1854, 1,041 tons, of medium model, built by Joseph Magoun for William F. Weld & Co. of Boston. Employed first in the California–Far East trade, making thirteen passages out to San Francisco from 1854 to 1871, the fastest being her maiden voyage of 115 days, in 1873 and 1874 employed in the Indian trade. Sold by her original owners in 1875 for $18,000; later in 1882 sold to foreign interests in Norway, out of registry by 1887.

- *Expounder*, 1856, 1,176 tons, of medium model, built for Paul Sears of Boston. First put in the transatlantic and UK–San Francisco trade, carrying coal from Cardiff, Wales, to San Francisco in 1856 and 1857. In 1863 served as navy transport and was stranded at Stone Inlet, South Carolina, in May 1863, sold in 1881 and converted into a barge. Later listed as a two-masted schooner owned by the Philadelphia & Reading Railroad in 1888, out of American registry by 1906.

Chelsea

John Taylor (born 1808) was the most important builder in this small city located on the Mystic River, across from the city of Boston. He built nine clippers in all from the years 1851 to 1859, several of them having long-lived careers and eight of which were built here. Prior to building in Chelsea, Taylor was living in nearby Medford in 1850 and working as a shipbuilder with $1,800 in personal wealth. He had come here in his youth from his native town of Marshfield on the North River, the son of shipbuilder William Taylor. Where Taylor served his apprenticeship in Medford is uncertain, but given the fact that he built his first ships here at the foot of Foster's Court off Riverside Avenue in the old yard of Sprague & James, it may have been with that firm, or perhaps from the most noted shipbuilder in the Boston area of the day, Thatcher Magoun. Taylor first operated as a shipbuilder as the junior partner in the firm of Foster & Taylor, his compatriot being Joshua T. Foster, and they built their first vessel, the 195-ton bark *Pearl*, in 1838. They would continue their partnership and built a number of ships before Taylor went solo in 1846. However, Taylor would build his first clipper, the famed *Witchcraft*, in late 1850 in partnership with Paul Curtis, returning to Medford to build his most famous vessel, the long-lived *Syren*, in 1851, but by the next year Taylor had moved to Chelsea and, as that town's most noted shipbuilder, had over $50,000 in assets by 1860. After the end of the clipper ship era, John Taylor would move his operations yet again, this time to East Boston by 1861, where he would build sailing ships with his son Justin (who later took over his father's yard) into the 1870s.

- *Witchcraft*, 1850, 1,310 tons, of extreme model, built by Curtis & Taylor for Rogers & Pickman of Salem, Massachusetts; see career details below under builder Paul Curtis.
- *Malay*, 1852, 868 tons, built for Silsbee & Pickman of Salem. Engaged for the first twenty years of her career in the California, Far East, and Australian trades, best California run was 116 days on her maiden voyage. Also a fast ship in the Far East trade, 1872–75 was employed as a San Francisco and Hong Kong packet. Arrived at San Francisco from Hong Kong in March 1875 in a damaged condition due to a severe storm, subsequently sold to West Coast interests, repaired and re-rigged as a barkentine and employed in the lumber and coal trade between Australia and the U.S. Final voyage in August 1891 while bound San Francisco for Mollendo, Peru, with a cargo of railroad ties, put into Tahiti in a sinking condition after suffering storm damage, there condemned and scrapped.
- *Lotus*, 1852, 660 tons, built for Dabney & Cunningham of Boston. Intended for the Far East trade, maiden voyage Boston to China in 1852 and 1853, then made four California runs 1853 to 1859, her best time being 121 days on her first run; after 1859 employed as a San Francisco–Hong Kong packet. Final American voyage in May 1863 San Francisco to New York in 107 days, thereafter sold upon arrival to French interests and subsequently employed in the Mediterranean trade under her original name, homeport Marseilles; disappears from registry after 1871.
- *Storm King*, 1853, 1,289 tons, of medium model, built for Snow & Rich of Boston. Suffered severe weather off Cape Horn on her maiden passage to San Francisco from Boston and forced to put into Callao, Peru, for repairs; had another storm-wracked passage New York to San Francisco in 1859, passage time 139 days, best California run was 118 days, Boston to San Francisco in 1861. Last American voyage departed San Francisco for the Far East in mid–1862, made two voyages between Thailand and Hong Kong with cargos of rice; by 1863 idle at Hong Kong and subsequently sold to British interests, still afloat in 1875, homeport North Shields, England.

- *Aurora*, 1853, 1,396 tons, of extreme model, built for Silsbee & Pickman. Maiden voyage to California forced into Rio de Janeiro due to a mutinous crew. In 1856 made her fastest California run, 112 days. During 1857 California run forced to put into Rio again after suffering a broken rudder near the Falkland Islands; in 1862 collided with a bark at sea while bound San Francisco to Hong Kong. In early 1863 sold to British interests at Boston, thereafter departed New York for Australia and India, later employed in the England–India trade. About 1870 deliberately burned near Bombay, India, by her captain and mates who were later tried and convicted.
- *Nabob*, 1854, 1,246 tons, of medium model, built for William Appleton & Co. Said to be designed for the Far East trade but first put in the transatlantic trade from New Orleans to Liverpool; by 1862 employed in the grain and coal trades. Final voyage departed Liverpool for Shanghai, China, with a load of coal in June 1862, subsequently hit by a typhoon off the Philippines in November 1862 and severely damaged; with her masts cut away and her hold full of water the ship was deliberately beached on the coast of Luzon, many of the crew, at least twelve in number, were subsequently drowned while trying to reach shore in the ship's boats.
- *Derby*, 1855, 1,062 tons, of medium model, built for Silsbee & Pickman. Employed in the California–Far East trade, maiden voyage Boston to San Francisco made in 120 days, fastest California run was made in 1870, 117 days. Sold to George Howes & Co. at San Francisco in 1865 for $30,000; in 1876 sold foreign to German interests without a name change and employed in the transatlantic trade between Bremen and New York. Later sold yet again to Norway and still afloat in 1890 under her original name.
- *Sumatra*, 1856, 1,073 tons, of medium model and called a sister ship to *Derby*, built for B.W. Stone & Brothers of Salem. Employed for most of her career in the Far East trade, made four California runs in her career, best time 121 days. In 1870 and 1871 put into Yokohama, Japan, while bound Hong Kong to San Francisco in a leaking condition, there repaired, thence to Puget Sound, loading coal for San Francisco, struck a rock off Vancouver Island and sank. Subsequently raised and repaired at San Francisco, caught in a typhoon at Hong Kong in 1874 and crew deliberately cut her masts away to prevent her from being blown ashore; repairs took two years, with new spars sent out from Boston. In final years employed in the Puget Sound lumber and coal trade up to 1891, then mothballed at San Francisco before being sent to Honolulu for use as a storage ship. Finally sold for scrap and broken up in 1895.
- *Autocrat*, 1859, 1,130 tons, of medium model, likely built on speculation and first owned by her builder, later by Thomas Howe of Boston. Full career details uncertain; final voyage departed Baltimore for San Francisco with a cargo of coal in late 1867, subsequently lost on April 6, 1868, after striking Arch Rock while entering San Francisco Harbor while in charge of the pilot. Later towed ashore but filled with water and was a total loss.

Jotham Stetson (born 1794) was another important Chelsea builder who also got his start at Medford after moving there from Scituate; by 1850 he was an experienced ship carpenter with $10,000 in assets. His independent career as a builder in Medford began in 1833 when he built the bark *Ruble*, going on to build another 31 vessels here, including his first clipper in 1851 (see below), at his yard on South Street, just above the Winthrop Street bridge before moving on. In 1852 he built one clipper at South Boston, but either could not secure the property for a shipyard, or did not find the locale to his liking, and subsequently settled in Chelsea in 1853. He would build seven clipper ships in all, five of them at his Chelsea yard.

- *Young Brander*, 1853, 1,467 tons, built for Brander, Williams & Co. of Boston. Employed in the transatlantic trade, sold foreign in 1855 to British interests and renamed *Timour*; later sold to Liverpool interests and renamed *Golden Dream*. Final voyage in September 1873, abandoned at sea while bound Pensacola, Florida, to Liverpool.
- *Neptune's Favorite*, 1854, 1,347 tons, of medium model, built for H.A. Kelly & Co.

of Boston. Employed in the transatlantic trade, maiden voyage Boston to Liverpool via St. George, New Brunswick; made three California runs, quickest time 115 days Philadelphia to San Francisco in 1856. Loaded guano at Callao, Peru, for England in 1859, subsequently put into St. Thomas, Virgin Islands, in a leaking condition, discharged cargo before proceeding to New York for repairs. Final American voyage in early 1862, departed New York for San Francisco, passage 146 days, thence to Callao for a cargo of guano, departed there August 1862 for Queenstown, Ireland; after arrival went to London and there sold in early 1863 for a high price, renamed *Mataura*, homeport Glasgow, Scotland, still afloat in 1874.

- *Bounding Billow*, 1854, 354-ton bark, built for Lombard & Conant and others of Boston. Employed first in the Mediterranean trade, made the fastest passage on record, 28 days, Boston to Smyrna, Turkey, in October to November 1859. Suffered storm damage off Bermuda in December 1864 while bound Lisbon, Portugal, to U.S. By 1876 sold to Gifford & Cummings of New Bedford and put in the whaling trade; later sold to West Coast interests and from 1886 to 1891 sailed in the whaling trade out of San Francisco, many of her crew for these voyages being shanghaied. Last surveyed in 1885, still in service after 1900, no further details known.
- *Beacon Light*, 1855, 1,376 tons, built for own interests and possibly sold foreign; nothing of this ship's career is known.
- *Harry Bluff*, 1855, 1,244 tons, built for Charles Green of New York. Career details uncertain; lost on South Shoal, Nantucket, while bound from Cadiz, Spain, to Boston in late February 1869, four crewmen lost.

Captain Isaac Taylor (born 1818) was active in maritime affairs during the clipper ship era. A commission merchant of Boston, with a residence in Brookline, in 1852 he supervised the building of the *Defiance* at the yard of George Thomas in Rockland, Maine, in 1852, and in 1853 he was co-owner of the famed Maine clipper *Red Jacket* in 1853 as the junior partner in the firm of Seccomb & Taylor. That same year he also built one clipper at Chelsea on his own. Taylor was active prior to and during the 1850s in the Cape of Good Hope trade involving goods from southern Africa and India. His sons Isaac and Alphonse were involved in the same trade by the 1860s, while his daughter Alecia was born at the Cape of Good Hope in 1852. Later, by the 1860s, Taylor was working building ships with George Thomas at his Quincy yard, continuing a relationship that dated back to Thomas' shipbuilding days in Maine.

- *Matchless*, 1853, 1,053 tons, built for Nathaniel and Benjamin Goddard of Boston. Maiden voyage to California made in 111 days net time in 1854 after being forced to return to Boston after being partially dismasted during a hurricane when two days out. Later sailed in the Far East and Indian trade. Departed New York for the Philippines mid–1857, subsequently lost, no details given, in the Java Sea off Anjer, Indonesia, in October 1857.

Abner Stetson built one clipper in Chelsea in 1854, though which man by that name was the builder is uncertain. One man by this name (see above) had a fully established and sizeable shipyard at Damariscotta, Maine, where he built one clipper in 1852. Another candidate may be the Abner Stetson that worked as a shipbuilder on the North River at Hanover, Massachusetts, and was likely a relative of shipbuilder Jotham Stetson; if he is our man, he probably built this clipper in the shipyard of Jotham Stetson. However, this Stetson does not seem to have any large scale building experience on his own, one of his known products being a 99-ton schooner built in 1838.

- *Asterion*, 1854, 1,135 tons, of medium model, built for David Snow and others of Boston at a cost of $67,000. Originally chartered for the transatlantic trade, later worked as a guano and coal carrier. Made one California run in 1863, a passage of 151 days due to very poor weather. Subsequently sailed to Howland's Island to load guano, departed there September 1863 and lost soon after, hitting a reef off Baker's Island; some of the crew survived alone on the island for three months, while others sailed for help in one of the ship's lifeboats, entire crew eventually rescued.

Paul Curtis built one clipper here in partnership with John Taylor, which was Chelsea's first and, perhaps, most famous clipper of all. As detailed below, Curtis got his start in shipbuilding at nearby Medford well before 1850. After building his first clipper here, Curtis would go on to build sixteen other clippers at Medford and East Boston.

- *Witchcraft*, 1850, 1,310 tons, of extreme model with 35 inches of deadrise, built by Curtis & Taylor for Rogers & Pickman of Salem. Put in the California–Far East trade, maiden voyage New York to San Francisco in early 1851 took 107 net sailing days; put into Rio de Janeiro to repair spar damage, subsequently sailed for Hong Kong and lost all three topmasts in a storm, repairs at Hong Kong costing almost $29,000. Second California run in mid–1854 resulted in a passage of 98 days. Final voyage loaded guano and departed Callao, Peru, early 1861 bound for Hampton Roads, Virginia; subsequently lost on April 8, 1861, went ashore at Chickamaconic off Cape Hatteras, North Carolina, and went to pieces very quickly, fourteen crew and three passengers lost.

The firm of Rice & Mitchell built one clipper at Chelsea. The principals of this firm are unknown for certain but were possibly carpenter John Rice (born 1793), a resident of Chelsea with $7,000 to his name by 1850, and Nahum Mitchell (born 1813 at Marshfield, Massachusetts), a ship-joiner who worked in East Boston and the surrounding area but lived in Medford, his assets by 1860 totaling $10,000.

- *Orpheus*, 1856, 1,057 tons, of medium model, built for William F. Weld & Co. of Boston. Maiden California passage a long one, 180 days, made ten other California runs, best time 112 days in 1868; employed in the wheat trade 1867. Sold in the early 1870s to C. L. Taylor & Co. of San Francisco and employed in the coal and lumber trade, in late 1875 departed Victoria, British Columbia, loaded with coal and on the night of November 4 collided with the passenger steamer *Pacific*, which quickly sank with the loss of 273 crew and passengers. The clipper was damaged and continued on her way, did not render aid at the disaster scene, subsequently went ashore off Cape Beale the following morning due to a navigation error and was a total loss.

Medford

The firm of Hayden & Cudworth was the leader in clipper ship building in Medford, putting over nineteen such ships between the years 1850 and 1856. Both of the principals of this concern came from the North River area of Massachusetts, Elisha Hayden (born 1806) being from South Scituate, and William Cudworth (1814–1877) being from the Sea View area of Marshfield. Cudworth had a love for ships from an early age and first served as a sailor at the insistence of his sea captain father before learning the shipbuilding trade; later, in the first home he owned, he would draw ships and carve pictures of them with varying sail plans on the wooden paneling of some of its rooms (Wooley, p. 95). Hayden & Cudworth began their partnership in 1846 at the old yard of Thatcher Magoun on Riverside Avenue near Park Street, which had previously been occupied by the company of James and Paul Curtis and the firm of Waterman & Ewell, for whom both Hayden and Cudworth may have been working. Both men were identified as carpenters in the 1850 Federal Census, and by 1860 Cudworth had an estate valued at $28,000, while Hayden was worth but $5,000. The firm of Hayden & Cudworth continued building sailing ships at Medford into the late 1860s, their 39th and last vessel being their largest, the 1,500 ton *Henry Hastings,* before finally ceasing operations in 1866.

- *George E. Webster*, 1850, 354-ton bark, built for Reed, Wade & Co. of Boston. Maiden voyage to California made in 112 days, arriving in January 1851, second California run made in 142 days; further career details unknown.
- *John Wade*, 1851, 639 tons, of medium model, built for Reed, Wade & Co. of Boston. Employed in the California–Far East trade 1851 to 1854, fastest passage 117 days, later purchased for use in the Heard Line of packets sailing between New York, China, and London. In late 1859 departed Bangkok, Thailand, for Hong Kong and hit an uncharted rock in the Gulf of Siam, a total loss, entire crew saved.
- *Golden Eagle*, 1852, 1,121 tons, of extreme

model, built for William Lincoln & Co. of Boston, construction supervised by her first commander, Captain Samuel Fabens. Employed in the California run, maiden voyage to San Francisco made in 110 total sailing days but ship suffered severe damage en route due to heavy seas and forced to put into Rio de Janeiro for repairs that took a month, returned eastward with guano for Hampton Roads. Second voyage out to San Francisco in 124 days, then to Swatow via Hong Kong to load coolies for Havana, Cuba, in 1855, made another guano voyage in 1857, carried whale oil from Honolulu to New Bedford in 1859, in early 1862 employed as a military transport vessel to Port Royal. Final voyage departed New York for San Francisco, arriving there in mid–1862 in 117 days, from there to Howland's Island to load guano for Cork, Ireland, subsequently captured and burned by the Confederate raider *Alabama* February 21, 1863.

- *Alexander*, 1852, 596 tons, built for J. Baxter & Co. of Boston. Employed in the European–Far East trade; sold foreign to British interests in 1861. Lost in February 1864 while bound Liverpool to Singapore with a cargo of coal, hit Frederick Rock in the Straits of Rhio near Malaya and subsequently beached, a total loss.

- *Gem of the Ocean*, 1852, 702 tons, of medium model, built for William Lincoln & Co. Launched at midnight due to the prevailing tides, the proceedings witnessed by builder William Cudworth's mother, the first time she had ever seen one of her son's creations take to the water. One California run on her maiden voyage, a 120 day passage, then put in the Australian, Indian, and Far East trades; sailed from Hong Kong to San Francisco in early 1867, from there went to Alaska for a cargo of ice. Subsequently sold to West Coast interests for $18,000 in gold and employed in the South American lumber trade; later in 1867 repaired and re-rigged as a bark. In August 1879 was lost while bound Seattle for San Francisco, went ashore on Vancouver Island, a total loss.

- *Herald of the Morning*, 1853, 1,294 tons, of medium model, designed by Samuel Pook and one of the fastest clippers afloat, built for Thatcher Magoun & Son of Boston. Maiden voyage Boston to San Francisco in early 1854 made in 106 days, subsequently made seventeen other California runs, a 116 day passage in 1859, 108 days in 1860, 118 days in 1868; on eastward runs often carried guano to East Coast U.S. ports or the UK. Sold foreign to Norwegian interests after 1875 and was re-rigged as a bark, still afloat in 1890, British owned.

- *Kingfisher*, 1853, 1,286 tons, of extreme model, built for William Lincoln & Co. Employed in the California–Far East trade, maiden voyage Boston to San Francisco made in 114 days, the fastest of her four California runs; in June 1855 departed San Francisco for Honolulu, arriving in just under ten days, the fastest passage up to that time. Employed as a transport by the British government in China in 1860. In April 1861 ran ashore by her pilot off Yokohama, Japan, finally got off and sailed for San Francisco, making a fast passage of 22 days, a near record. Employed in late 1861 and 1862 as an army transport, sailing Boston to Ship Island, Mississippi. Subsequently went ashore in a driving snowstorm off Provincetown, Massachusetts, in February 1862 on her return voyage but got off with little damage. Later employed in the Far East trade, in 1871 departed New York for San Francisco, put into Montevideo, Uruguay, in a leaking condition after suffering heavy weather, condemned and sold to local interests; repaired and renamed *Jaime Cibils*, operating in the South American trade. In 1890 sold at auction and scrapped at Montevideo.

- *White Swallow*, 1853, 1,192 tons, of extreme model, built for William Lincoln & Co. Employed in the California and Far East trade, made nine California runs from 1853 to 1868, fastest passage 110 days in 1860, slowest her maiden voyage out in 150 days. On 1865 California run the ship's crew mutinied due to poor treatment and took over control of the ship, allowing the captain to direct operation and perform navigation duties, crew subsequently exonerated in a court of law. After 1858 made a number of eastward runs carrying guano; in early 1871 departed Boston for Hong Kong with 1,015 tons of ice, ship subsequently abandoned off Fayal in a foundering condition, entire crew saved.

- *Ringleader*, 1853, 1,157 tons, built for Howes & Crowell of Boston. Employed in the California–Far East trade, the fastest of her six California runs was her maiden voyage of 110 days. In late 1860 passage from Boston battered by a hurricane, arrived at San Francisco in 115 days. Final voyage departed Hong Kong for San Francisco May 1863 with several hundred coolies, went ashore off Formosa and quickly attacked and surrounded by Chinese pirates, all but two of crew saved, coolies driven ashore by pirates and saved, later transported to San Francisco aboard the clipper *Don Quixote*.
- *Climax*, 1853, 1,051 tons, built for Howes & Crowell, building supervised by Captain William Howes, her first commander and inventor of the Howes topsail rig, first installed on this clipper. First employed in the California and guano trades, maiden California run 115 days, manned by a crew of 16 due to her improved rig. In early 1855 loaded guano at the Chincha Islands and subsequently departed Callao, Peru, but began to leak when just hours out and put back into port with eight feet of water in the hold, subsequently sank at her moorings with only part of her cargo discharged and sold as she lay to local parties for $13,000. Thereafter raised and repaired and renamed *Antonio Terry* and employed in the coolie trade supplying the guano islands; later sold at Hong Kong in 1864 for $19,000, later fate unknown.
- *Edith Rose*, 1853, 510 tons, built for Crowell & Brooks of Boston; career details unknown, last reported in 1886.
- *Robin Hood*, 1854, 1,182 tons, of extreme model, built for Howes & Crowell. Employed in the California–Far East trade, made twelve California runs, two of them in 107 days, one in 108 days. In August 1869 was loading guano at Baker's Island for Hampton Roads, Virginia, when she caught fire and was destroyed; some of crew later charged with arson and imprisoned at Honolulu.
- *Rambler*, 1854, 1,119 tons, built for Baxter Brothers of Yarmouth, Massachusetts, and others. Career details uncertain; sold foreign to German interests in 1863 and renamed *Fanny*, final fate unknown.
- *Osborne Howes*, 1854, 1,119 tons, of medium model, built for Howes & Crowell. Employed in the California trade 1854 to 1860, fastest passage 124 days in 1856, eastward voyages carried guano. In 1861 while bound McKean's Island for New London, Connecticut, forced to put into Rio de Janeiro due to a severe leak, here re-caulked and repaired. Sold foreign at Calcutta, India, in June 1864 to British interests without a name change, disappears from shipping registry after 1870.
- *Fleetwing*, 1854, 896 tons, of medium model, built Crowell, Brooks & Co. of Boston, possibly originally named *Director* according to Cutler. Employed in the California trade from 1854 to 1873, fourteen voyages departed Boston or New York, fastest passage 113 days, slowest 158 days. Eastward voyages carried guano from Peru and Baker's Island in 1864, in 1873 and 1874 voyaged New York to Melbourne, Australia, then loaded coal at Newcastle, New South Wales, for Hong Kong, after 1875 made another New York–Australia run. Subsequently sold foreign upon arrival to British interests and re-rigged as a bark without a name change, thereafter employed in the British Columbia lumber trade. In October 1884 departed Victoria, British Columbia, for Melbourne, began to leak after enduring two weeks of heavy storms and put back into port. Final voyage again departed Victoria for Melbourne in late 1884, condemned and scrapped after arrival in March 1885.
- *Electric Spark*, 1855, 1,216 tons, of medium model, built for Thatcher Magoun & Sons. Largely employed in the California trade, making eight runs, her best being her maiden passage of 106 days in 1855 and 1856, all other passages vexed by bad weather; eastward voyages returned with guano on several runs. In 1857 while bound from San Francisco to Callao, Peru, the crew mutinied and took control for the ship for two weeks. In early 1865 sailed from Shields, England, for Portland, Maine, went ashore at Hog's Island off Portland but got off with little damage. In September 1869 departed Liverpool for San Francisco but stranded at Blackwater Head off Wexford, Ireland, just four days out due to a pilot error, crew saved by coastal lifeboats, ship a total loss.

- *Goddess*, 1855, 1,126 tons, a half-clipper at best, built for Baxter Brothers of Boston. Made two California runs, her best 129 days on her maiden voyage, also employed in the transatlantic and Indian trades. Sold foreign at London in late 1864 to Norwegian interests and renamed *Nordens-Dronning*, subsequently employed as a general cargo carrier. Loaded coal at Newcastle-upon-Tyne for San Francisco in early 1870, arrived after a disastrous 201 day passage after suffering a collision in the English Channel and forced to put back into port for repairs. Was loading at Pensacola, Florida, in 1886 and still afloat in 1887, no further details known.
- *Rival*, 1855, 984 tons, built for Howes & Crowell. Employed largely in the Far East trade, made one California passage of 143 days. Sailed from Rangoon, Burma, early 1872 for Falmouth, England, and went missing.
- *Thatcher Magoun*, 1856, 1,248 tons, of medium model, built for Thatcher Magoun & Sons, named after the firm's founder who died that same year. Made twelve California runs from 1856 to 1873, the fastest being 113 days in 1864, her maiden voyage out was 121 days. In 1869 while bound San Francisco to New York grounded on the East Bank off Sandy Hook after a passage of 96 days. Also involved in the guano trade and the coal trade between San Francisco and Australia. Sold foreign to Norwegian interests about 1874 and renamed *Hercules*; later lost off the coast of Africa in the early 1880s.

James O. Curtis (1804–1890) was one of Medford's most prolific shipbuilders for three decades and ranks with fellow Massachusetts builders Donald McKay and Samuel Hall as one of the most important clipper builders. Curtis was born in Scituate and, like many other young men from the North River area of Massachusetts aspiring to be shipbuilders, he moved to Medford, arriving there in 1820 to serve his apprenticeship in the yard of Thatcher Magoun. After completing his training, Curtis stayed on as a shipwright in Medford for some years before forming his own company, Curtis & Co., in 1834 with fellow shipbuilder Paul Curtis, with whom he had no close family connection. This company lasted for five years, building nine vessels, including several at Magoun's old yard beginning in 1836, after his mentor had retired. James Curtis's clippers were some of the best known of all the American clippers, his career subsequently continuing until his retirement in 1869. Overall, Curtis built seventy-eight vessels at Medford during a thirty-year span, with the clippers he built from 1851 to 1858 comprising over 20 percent of his total production.

- *Telegraph*, 1851, 1,069 tons, of extreme model, designed by Samuel Pook, cost $70,000, built for Sprague & Co. of Boston. Maiden voyage to California in 125 days, departed Boston for San Francisco December 1854, collided with another ship when three days out but continued and repaired damaged spars and rigging at sea, made San Francisco in 109 days; 1855 sailed from Archangel, Russia, for London, having been detained at the former port by blockade during the Crimean War. In 1856 sold at Boston for $36,000 then departed for Australia but forced into Savannah, Georgia, in a leaking condition, repaired and when about ready to sail caught fire, likely set by crew, and subsequently sold for $6,200. Later raised and repaired, renamed *Harry Brigham*. Final passage as an American ship in 1865, thereafter sold to Peruvian interests at San Francisco and renamed *Compania Maritima del Peru, No. 2*, put into the coolie trade. Sold to Italian interests in 1866 and renamed *Galileo*, still employed in coolie trade with Peru; dismasted during voyages from San Francisco to Hong Kong in 1866 and 1867, lost, burned at sea, in 1868.
- *Shooting Star*, 1851, 903 tons, of extreme model, built for Reed, Wade & Co. of Boston. Intended for the California–Far East trade, maiden passage out to California made in 124 sailing days; forced into Rio de Janeiro after being partially dismasted. Second California run made in 105 days; in 1855 and 1856 while bound Honolulu to New York put into Brazil due to short provisions, subsequently hit some uncharted rocks after departing there and damaged. After mid–1856 employed in trade on the Asian coast between Hong Kong and Thailand, subsequently damaged by a typhoon and forced to put into Singapore for repairs

in 1862, sold to Thai interests, sold for $40,000. Later wrecked on the coast of Formosa in 1867.
- *Antelope*, 1851, 587 tons, of medium model, built for William Lincoln & Co. of Boston. Put in the California trade, maiden passage a slow 149 days; later put in the South American and Far East trades. Lost in July 1858 while bound Bangkok, Thailand, for China, struck on Discovery Shoal, Paracels Reef, and quickly filled, abandoned by crew in two boats, of which the captain's boat was attacked by Chinese fishermen, who were successfully fought off.
- *Star of the Union*, 1852, 1,057 tons, of extreme model, built for Reed, Wade & Co., in 1854 sold to Bartlett & Son of New Bedford, Maine. Made eight California runs, fastest 121 days in 1855 and 1856. In mid–1859 chartered by the U.S. government at New York to carry African captives from captured slave ships back to Africa. In 1866 put into Rio de Janeiro in distress after colliding with a British bark while bound Honolulu to New York, condemned and sold, possibly for scrap, out of registers after 1868.
- *Whirlwind*, 1852, 961 tons, of extreme model, built for W. & F.H. Whittemore of Boston. Employed in the California, Far East, Australian, and Indian trades, maiden voyage to San Francisco made in 119 days. In 1860 voyaged from Hong Kong to Bangkok, and then to Calcutta and Bombay, India. Owned in New York in 1862 but disappears from the registry after this time, fate uncertain.
- *Onward*, 1852, 874 tons, of medium model, built for Reed, Wade & Co. Employed in the California and Far East trades, maiden run to San Francisco made in 125 days. Sold to John Ogden of New York in 1857 for $32,000. Final voyage as a merchant ship Shanghai to New York, 115 days, in mid–1861, there sold to the U.S. government for $27,000 in late 1861 for use as a fourth class warship, operated during the Civil War in search of Confederate cruisers and blockade duties. After the war used as a navy store ship at Callao, Peru, sold there in 1884.
- *George Peabody*, 1853, 1,397 tons, built for William F. Weld & Co. of Boston; career details uncertain. Final voyage departed New York for San Francisco in early 1881, subsequently put into Valparaiso, Chile, May 1881 in a leaking condition, condemned and sold.
- *Eagle Wing*, 1853, 1,174 tons, of medium model, built for Chase & Tappan of Boston, employed in the California–Far East trade, maiden voyage to San Francisco made in 105 days during which a hurricane washed two men overboard and caused minor damage, made five other California runs, passages of 118 days in 1856, 122 days in 1861, 119 days in 1862. During 1864 passage, 140 days, Captain Eben Linnell died after being thrown against the ship's wheel in heavy seas encountered off the River Platte, South American coast, mate brought the ship into San Francisco. Final voyage in early 1865, departed Boston for Bombay, India, and went missing.
- *Wild Ranger*, 1853, 1,044 tons, built for Sears & Thatcher of Boston. Damaged off Cape Horn on her maiden voyage to California, arrived in 125 days, made two other California runs. Later in the Australian and Indian trade. Collided with a British ship while bound London to Boston in January 1862 and badly damaged, put back into Falmouth, judged to be in fault for the accident and sold at auction under libel. Subsequently renamed *Ocean Chief* and owned at Liverpool, lost in 1872 while bound Liverpool to Rio de Janeiro, foundered after colliding with a steamship.
- *Competitor*, 1853, 871 tons, built for William F. Weld & Co. First employed in the California–Far East trade, maiden voyage Boston to San Francisco made in 115 days. In early 1858 made a disastrous voyage, Swatow for Havana, Cuba, with 380 coolies, 127 of whom died. Final American voyage Manila to New York in mid–1863, thereafter sold to German interests for $31,100 and renamed *Lorely*; later sold to British interests by 1869 and sailing under original name, making a voyage Baltimore to Hong Kong. From 1869 to 1873 involved in trade between New York and Far East and Australia. Late 1873 sold to German interests again, and later sold yet again, this time to Swedish interests. In 1899 sailed London to West Indies and also employed in the Baltic lumber trade. Involved in a

collision in 1900 and subsequently libeled and sold to Finnish interests, renamed *Edward*, final fate unknown.
- *Ocean Express*, 1854, 1,697 tons, of medium model, built for Reed, Wade & Co. Employed extensively in the guano and grain trades, maiden voyage Boston to Callao, Peru, in 99 days, made seven U.S. East Coast–San Francisco runs, best time 125 days in 1858. In 1861 and 1862 chartered for use as a U.S. Army transport between New York and Port Royal; in mid–1870 departed Brazil for San Francisco, put into Montevideo, Uruguay, in distress, temporarily repaired, later sent home to be rebuilt, cost $60,000. Sold foreign at Peru in early 1872, by late 1872 was sailing under the flag of El Salvador, and was subsequently under the Costa Rican flag before going back to Peruvian interests, operating in West Coast lumber trade. By 1876 sold to German interests with name change to *Friedrich*, thereafter sold to Norwegian interests, lost, abandoned in a sinking condition in the North Atlantic in 1890.
- *Ocean Telegraph*, 1854, 1,495 tons, of extreme model, built for Reed, Wade & Co. A consistently fast ship, made eight California runs, best time 106 days, in late 1861 departed New York for San Francisco, 112 day passage; thereafter in 1861 and 1862 voyaged from San Francisco via the Chincha Islands, Peru, to Queenstown, Ireland. In 1863 sold foreign at London to James Baines & Co., renamed *Light Brigade*, and employed in the Black Ball Line of Australian packets. By the early 1880s was employed in the Quebec lumber trade. Final known voyage New York to Queenstown, Ireland, arriving in February 1883 in a leaking condition, shortly thereafter cut down and employed as a coal hulk at Gibraltar.
- *Good Hope*, 1855, 1,295 tons, built for R.L. Taylor of New York. Made four California passages over the years, maiden voyage to San Francisco made in 144 days. Later employed in the Indian trade between England and Calcutta. Condemned at Bahia, Brazil, in June 1873, subsequently sold to Swedish interests, repaired, and renamed *Solide* and, later, *Frederick Hasselman*. Lost near Quebec in 1881, likely while employed in the timber trade.
- *Silver Star*, 1856, 1,195 tons, built for Reed, Wade & Co. Made two California passages, fastest time 140 days, later career uncertain. Wrecked in November 1860 while loading guano at Jarvis Island.
- *Flying Mist*, 1856, 1,183 tons, of medium model, built for Theodore & George Chase of Boston. Maiden passage Boston to San Francisco made in 115 days, involved in the guano trade, sailing Baker's Island to New York via Hampton Roads in late 1860. On final voyage in March 1862 departed Glasgow, Scotland, for Bluff Harbor, New Zealand, with a cargo of sheep, upon arrival in late August 1862 was blown ashore while at her anchorage and was a total loss, crew and eighteen shepherds aboard were saved, 940 of the 1,760 sheep aboard were lost.
- *Wild Gazelle*, 1857, 490-ton bark, built for Alpheus Hardy, Joshua Davis and others of Boston, later sold to Baltimore interests. Employed in the South American trade for part of career, full details uncertain. Abandoned at sea in a sinking condition September 1872 while bound Baltimore to Uruguay.
- *Industry*, 1858, 1,106 tons, built for Theodore Chase of Boston. Made one California run of 146 days, later career details uncertain. Changed ownership several times, last known in late 1870, disappears from registry after 1881.

Joshua Turner Foster (born 1810) was yet another prolific builder in Medford who also turned to the business of building clippers, though not to a large extent, and none being of the extreme type. His yard was located off Riverside Avenue near Foster's Court and was originally the site of the Sprague & James shipyard, where he served his apprenticeship after coming here from Scituate, Massachusetts, at the age of sixteen. J.T. Foster (as he was often referred to) first began his independent building career in 1831 after he finished his training, returning to his hometown to build four vessels in partnership with Joseph Clapp. He returned to Medford to work as a foreman in the Sprague & James yard in 1835 (marrying Miss Ellen Sprague soon after) but by 1838 had gone into partnership with John Taylor, with whom he would work until Taylor removed to Chelsea in 1852. In 1850 Foster is described as a simple carpenter, with an estate valued at $1,800, but by 1860 was described as shipbuilder, with assets of $23,000, which had increased to $60,000 by 1870. All of the Foster clippers were of medium model, with *National Eagle* and *West Wind* being built off the same model. Foster would continue his shipbuilding activities at Medford into the 1870s and has the distinction of building the last ship ever built there, the 956-ton *Pilgrim*, in 1873, his sixty-fourth vessel built at Medford. At his death he was esteemed as one of the city's finest citizens.

- *National Eagle*, 1852, 1,095 tons, built for Fisher & Co. of Boston. First employed in the Boston–New Orleans–Liverpool trade up to about late 1854, thereafter sailed in the Indian trade, usually carrying ice outward bound from Boston for many years; also employed in the hardwood lumber trade in Central America for a time, later in the 1870s was New York owned and was converted to a bark. Lost in 1884, ashore off Pola in the Adriatic Sea while bound U.S. to Trieste, a total loss.
- *Ellen Foster*, 1852, 996 tons, built for J. & A. Tirrell of Boston. First employed in the Indian trade between Boston and Calcutta; made three California runs, best time 147 days. In mid–1867 departed Callao, Peru, with guano bound for Hampton Roads but forced to put back in distress, subsequently condemned and sold at Callao, then repaired and sailed for Puget Sound to pick up a cargo of lumber but went ashore at Neah Bay in December 1867 while close to destination.
- *Morning Star*, 1853, 1,105 tons, built for T.B. Wales & Co. of Boston, incorrectly attributed to Portsmouth, New Hampshire, builders by Howe & Matthews. Maiden voyage Boston to New Orleans and from there to Liverpool in 1853 and 1854, then made six California runs, best passage 102 days in 1857. That same year loaded at Callao, Peru, for Le Havre, France, and had just made her departure when the crew mutinied, stabbing the first mate, mutiny subsequently put down with assistance from a British warship. In early 1863 when bound Calcutta, India, to London was intercepted by the Confederate raider *Alabama* but released after examination as her cargo was owned by neutral parties. Subsequently sold after arrival at London and renamed *Landsborough*, later employed in the Black Ball Line of Australian packets. Lost in 1890, details unknown.
- *West Wind*, 1853, 1,071 tons, built for J. & A. Tirrell. First employed in the California trade, made six passages to San Francisco, all but one from Boston, best time 129 days in 1855; eastward passages back home were via the Far East and India, later in 1859, via Honolulu, and in 1861 via the Chincha Islands with guano. Sold foreign to British interests at New York for $40,000 in 1863 after arriving there from Calcutta, India, name changed to *Lord Clyde*, homeport Calcutta, no further career details known.
- *Hesperus*, 1856, 1,020 tons, built for T.B. Wales & Co. Made no California passages, employed as a general cargo carrier, career details unknown; lost by fire in January 1861 after arriving at Woosung, China, with a load of coal from Liverpool.
- *Templar*, 1858, 946 tons, built for T.B. Wales & Co. Employed in the Indian and Far East trades, later made two California runs, sold at New York to West Coast interests in 1878. Subsequent California run in 1878 and 1879 taking 320 days, forced into Rio de Janeiro due to storm damage, after departure hit by a yellow fever epidemic that caused three deaths, then battered by storms off Cape Horn. Later employed in the coal and lumber trade and re-rigged as a bark, in 1894 sold to Peruvian interests and renamed *Los Tres Amigos*, then in the guano trade; blown ashore and lost while loading guano in April 1895.

Paul Curtis (born 1800, no relation to James Curtis) got his start early on at Medford, moving there from South Scituate, Massachusetts, in 1819 to serve his apprenticeship under Thatcher Magoun. During his training period and subsequent employment in Magoun's yard, Paul Curtis was called "Honest Paul" (Wooley, p. 94). In 1834 Curtis joined with James Curtis to form Curtis & Company; in their five year partnership the two Curtises built nine vessels, working in the old Magoun yard after that pioneer's retirement in 1836. After going their separate ways in 1839, Paul Curtis would build another twenty-seven vessels at Medford; though Curtis subsequently moved his operations to East Boston in

1852, he did return to Medford to build a ship from time to time, possibly including one clipper in 1854. Because Curtis worked at multiple locations, just where all of his clippers were built is sometimes open to question. Howe & Matthews credit the *Panther* to Medford, but Medford historian Hall Gleason does not list this clipper as being Medford-built. In addition, Curtis built his first clipper ship in 1850 at Chelsea in partnership with John Taylor, perhaps on the site that would later be occupied by John Taylor, though why this partnership was of such a brief nature is unknown.

- *Kremlin*, 1850, 504-ton bark, built for Craft & Co. of Boston, later owned by James Hunnewell and Charles Brewer of Boston, thereafter by John E. Lodge of Boston, John Emery & Co. and, by 1869, E.P. Emerson. Career details uncertain; wrecked in March 1870 at Saranac Keys while bound Aspinwall, Panama, to Cuba.
- *Courser*, 1851, 1,024 tons, of medium model, built for Richardson & Co. of Boston. Mainly employed in the California–Far East trade, maiden passage Boston to San Francisco in 1851, 108 days, the fastest of her four California runs. In 1854 loaded guano and departed Callao, Peru, for Liverpool. Lost in April 1858 while bound Foo Chow, China, for New York, went on Pratas Shoal when just two days out and quickly filled with water, crew got off in three lifeboats but one was attacked by native fishermen, two crewmen drowned when their boat capsized, rest of crew later made Hong Kong or Macao safely.
- *Queen of the Seas*, 1852, 1,356 tons, built for Glidden & Williams of Boston. Employed in the California–Far East trade initially, maiden voyage to California in 131 days, forced to put into Valparaiso, Chile, for three plus days due to being in bad trim, probably from shifting cargo. In 1857 loaded coolies at Hong Kong for Melbourne, Australia; in early 1860 loaded coal at Liverpool for Shanghai. Lost in Formosa Strait on or about September 21, 1860, during a severe storm, sailed in company with another American vessel, but is supposed to have foundered and been lost with her entire crew as she was never seen again.
- *Beverly*, 1852, 676 tons, of medium model, built for Whitney & Perkins of Boston. Her maiden and only California run made in 144 days, later employed in the Indian and Australian trades. In 1864 was pursued by the Confederate raider *Florida* but evaded capture, that same year sold foreign at Batavia, Indonesia, and renamed *Alexander*, owners said to be American. In 1867 operating under the name *Argonaut*, homeport Port Louis, Mauritius, in 1868 purchased by William F. Weld & Co. of Boston, later in late 1872 sold to Yarmouth, Nova Scotia interests. Disappears from the registry after 1873.
- *Panther*, 1854, 1,278 tons, of medium model, built for R.C. McKay & Sons of Boston. First employed in the Indian trade, carrying three successive cargos of railroad iron from England to Calcutta. From 1857 to 1868 made six California passages, her best time being 139 days in 1859 and 1860; in 1868 sold to West Coast interests and employed in the Puget Sound lumber and the Australian coal trades, after 1871 almost entirely in the coastal lumber and coal trade. Final voyage departed Nanaimo, British Columbia, for San Francisco loaded with coal and went ashore on Vancouver Island in January 1874, salvage efforts subsequently failed.

Samuel Lapham, Jr. (born 1808), was a longtime Medford shipbuilder, having been born there, though his namesake father originally came from Marshfield in the North River area. The younger Lapham apprenticed with Thatcher Magoun and soon afterward began his independent career in 1830 when he built the 309-ton brig *Nabob* at his yard on Riverside Avenue near Cross Street. By 1850 he had already done quite well for himself, having assets to the value of at least $10,000. Lapham retired from shipbuilding in 1856 after building his twenty-third and last vessel, the 705-ton *Magnet*, of which he was half owner. By 1880 he was listed in the Federal Census as a retired marine architect, a true testament to his shipbuilding prowess. While Lapham did not build all that many clippers, those he did build were noted for their good carrying capacity, turn of speed, and quality of craftsmanship.

- *Phantom*, 1852, 1,174 tons, of medium model, built for Crocker, Warren & Sturgis of Boston and New York. Maiden voyage out to California in 1853 made in 105 days despite being damaged in a strong gale, returned eastward with guano, then a roundtrip on the transatlantic run between New York and London; made a California–Far East roundtrip in 1855 to 1857. Final voyage departed San Francisco for Hong Kong in early 1862, subsequently ran on Pilot Reef, near Pratas Shoal, July 13, 1862, and began to take on water, ship subsequently abandoned by crew and passengers in five lifeboats, two of which were subsequently captured by pirates and eventually ransomed and saved.

- *Don Quixote*, 1853, 1,429 tons, of medium model, built for John E. Lodge of Boston. Employed in the California–Far East trade, making seven runs to San Francisco and from there to Hong Kong up to about 1863, best California passage 107 days. In 1863 sailed from Hong Kong for San Francisco via Formosa and Shimoda, Japan, picking up Chinese coolies from the wrecked clippers *Ringleader* and *Viking*. In 1864 sold at Boston to French interests and renamed *St. Aubin* and employed in the Quebec lumber trade, homeport Le Havre, still afloat in 1874.
- *Nor'Wester*, 1854, 1,267 tons, built for J.T. Coolidge & Co. of Boston. Maiden passage on the California run in 122 days, thereafter employed in a variety of trades, including Boston to Calcutta, India; Cardiff, Wales, to Singapore, and the trade between New Zealand and Australia. In 1865 while bound from New York to San Francisco forced to put back into Portland, Maine, because of hull damage from her anchor. In 1867 went from New York to Port Stanley, Falkland Islands, to pick up a cargo of coal from a condemned ship; 1868 and 1869 employed in the guano and West Coast lumber trades. In 1869 sailed Callao, Peru, with guano for Hamburg, Germany, forced into St. Barts in a sinking condition, repaired. Final voyage early 1873 departed New Orleans with a cargo of cotton for Liverpool, forced into Key West, Florida, because of a fire in her lower hold, beached, a total loss, about half of her cargo of nearly 3,000 bales of cotton was salvaged.
- *Sancho Panza*, 1855, 876 tons, of medium model, built for John E. Lodge. Called a "very neat and pretty little ship" (Howe & Matthews, p. 540), but after her maiden voyage out to California in 147 days, her captain wrote in the ship's log, "The devil take *Sancho Panza*; she is as bad as her namesake" (ibid.). Employed largely in the California–Far East trade, in 1861 arrived at New York from Foo Chow, China, after a 102 day passage and enduring a typhoon that damaged the ship when only three days out and a strong gale that battered the ship just days before making port. After a voyage from Foo Chow to London in 1862 and 1863, sold foreign to London interests and renamed *Nimrod*; in 1874 re-rigged as a bark, by 1890 under German ownership, final fate uncertain.

Jotham Stetson (born 1794) built his first clipper here and thirty-one other vessels, as previously noted, until his move to Chelsea in 1853. He originally came from Scituate, Massachusetts, as did many Medford builders, and his family had a long tradition of shipbuilding dating back to 1730 on the North River. He likely apprenticed under Thatcher Magoun at Medford and worked at his yard before going solo. About 1818 he lived in a house on Ship Street with apprentice and fellow future clipper builder Paul Curtis.

- *Coringa*, 1851, 777 tons, a full-built ship, built for Godard & Co. of Boston. Intended for the Boston–Far East trade, made three passages on the California route from 1852 to 1855, fastest 132 days. In August 1852 collided with a schooner off Cape Ann while bound Boston to San Francisco, sinking the schooner and suffering damage that forced her to return to Boston for repairs; in 1857 went aground while bound from Manila to Boston and had to return for repairs. Later put in the guano trade to Europe by 1873, and in 1874 was re-rigged as a bark and put in the ice trade under charter to the Tudor Co. of Boston, voyaging to India and China. Subsequently lost in November 1889, wrecked off the coast of Patani, Malaysia, while bound Singapore for Bangkok, Thailand, three crewmen lost.

Benjamin F. Delano (born 1812) was a shipwright from Scituate who built one clipper ship and one clipper bark at Medford, as well as one clipper bark at Kingston (see below). His career was quite an interesting one; he served his apprenticeship in New York at the Brooklyn Navy Yard and then returned to his hometown to build some small vessels. He would also work in Brookline for the firm of Magoun & Turner sometime between 1832 and 1835. In 1833 he was sent to Grand Island on the Niagara River in New York to clear timber, taking a number of men from his hometown with him, and subsequently built seven vessels from the harvested timber. By 1847 he was a naval constructor working at Portsmouth, New Hampshire, and in the 1850s went back to the Brooklyn Navy Yard, where he built 21 warships during the Civil War and retired as chief builder there in 1873 (Briggs, pgs 226–27). At Medford Delano, who came from a shipbuilding family, built one clipper, and one pilot boat in 1854.

- *Rocket*, 1851, 391-ton bark, of extreme model, designed and modeled by her owner, W.N. Goddard, 15 inches of deadrise. Intended for use as a trader in the Pacific, first employed in the South American trade, making a voyage from Boston to Valparaiso, Chile, in early 1852; made a California passage in late 1852, arriving at San Francisco in January 1853 after a 150 day passage. In 1853 arrived at San Francisco from Rio de Janeiro, passage time 127 days. By 1858 owned by W.F. Weld of Boston, rig overhauled in 1868, in 1875 sold to New York interests, out of registry after 1886.
- *Dauntless*, 1852, 791 tons, of extreme model, designed and modeled by her owner, W.N. Goddard of Boston, who also superintended her building, a larger version of the bark *Rocket*, said to be the most expensive ship for her size ever built in Boston up to that time. First put on the California run, making a 116 day passage on her maiden voyage; subsequently sailed back to Boston via Callao, Peru, departed Boston October 1853 for Valparaiso, Chile, and subsequently went missing without a trace.

East Boston

Donald McKay (1810–1880) was this city's greatest shipbuilder after his arrival here in 1845 and the most prolific of all American clipper builders, building twenty-eight such ships between 1849 and 1859. While his career has previously been discussed at length, this builder, who was born in Nova Scotia and made his way to America in his early manhood, launched the fastest and most celebrated clippers of his time, including the *Flying Cloud*, *Great Republic*, *Lightning*, and *Champion of the Seas*. Furthermore, McKay was noted for his big ships, as he launched the largest sailing ships of the day. McKay's reputation as a shipbuilder was not just confined to America but was known the world over. He was the only clipper builder to contract with foreign companies for more than one clipper, and while the building of even one such ship for overseas interests was a rarity (William Webb had one such contract, but the deal fell through before the ship was launched), McKay built four great clippers for James Baines & Co. of England as well as a later medium clipper for another British concern. While many of his earlier clippers were of extreme model and were built expressly for the California trade, by 1855 McKay's star was beginning to wane; he launched few large clippers after 1854 due mostly to reasons of economy and the financial fallout from the loss he took on the burning of the *Great Republic*, and most of these later clippers were rather undistinguished ships. However, McKay never did give up his dream of building more clippers even after the era had ended; he launched a second *Sovereign of the Seas* (not of clipper model) in 1868, which was inexplicably slow, but rebounded in 1869 to build his last great ship, the long-lived *Glory of the Seas*. Though whether or not this ship was a medium clipper has been greatly debated and came along a decade after the end of the great clipper ship days, it may nonetheless be considered, if not in form then at least symbolically, as the last of the clippers. Following the building of this ship, Donald McKay retired from shipbuilding, surely sensing that the day of the sailing ship was nearly over; though he did build one iron steamship, his heart clearly was not in the building of such modern vessels. Perhaps more so than any other clipper builder, there is some debate as to just how many of the ships built by Donald McKay were truly clippers; of the thirty-one ships he built between December 1850 (beginning with *Stag Hound*) and 1858, historian (and relative) Richard McKay, perhaps not surprisingly, classifies all of them as clippers, while marine architect turned historian William Fairburn identifies twenty-nine as clippers. On the other hand, the noted Massachusetts clipper historians Howe & Matthews list only nineteen of these ships as clippers, while Captain Arthur H. Clark gives clipper status to twenty-three of them. Finally, according to one historian (McKay, p. 372), Donald McKay launched a clipper named the *Zephyr* in 1855, but this is incorrect, as this ship was the product of Daniel Kelly's East Boston shipyard.

- *Reindeer*, 1849, 800 tons, built for George Upton of Boston. Intended for the California–Far East trade, maiden voyage out to San Francisco in 1850 in 130 days; lost in February 1859, wrecked on a reef off Zambales, Philippines.
- *Stag Hound*, 1850, 1,534 tons, of extreme model, built for Sampson & Tappan and George Upton of Boston; said to be the first of the extreme clippers, having 40 inches of deadrise. Intended for the California–Far East trade, maiden passage out to San Francisco made in 113 days, the fastest of her six California runs. Forced into Valparaiso, Chile, partially dismasted. Later carried tea home from Whampoa, China. In August 1861 departed Sunderland, England, with coal for San Francisco, later found to be on fire when off the coast of Brazil, ship subsequently abandoned on October 12, crew landed safely at Pernambuco.
- *Flying Cloud*, 1851, 1,782 tons, of extreme model, built for Train & Co. of Boston, sold while still on the stocks to Grinnell, Minturn & Co. of New York for $95,000. Intended for the California–Far East trade, maiden voyage to San Francisco made in the then record time of 89 days, 21 hours, the first ship to ever break the 90 day barrier on this route. On third California run in early 1853 had her rudder head damaged during heavy weather, passage time 92 days; early 1854 departed New York on her fourth California passage, arrived out in 89 days, 8 hours, breaking her own record and the second fastest passage ever on this run, the only ship to ever make the voyage in under 90 days twice. From San Francisco proceeded to Hong Kong and then to Canton, China, to load tea, departed there in mid-1854 but soon ran on a coral reef, got off without major damage. In 1856 completed sixth and final California run, 113 days, subsequently laid up at New York due to slow business conditions from the fall of 1857 to late 1859. Once back in operation sailed to London to load for Hong Kong, in 1861 departed London for Melbourne, Australia, returning with British troops from Hong Kong. In mid-1862 sold foreign to British interests without a name change and put in the Australian trade; in 1870 arrived in Australia from Liverpool, passage time 87 days. Shortly thereafter put in the Canadian lumber trade sailing between London and St. Johns. In 1874 went ashore off St. Johns at Beacon Island Bar, subsequently condemned and sold, in June 1875 burned for her metal fittings.
- *Staffordshire*, 1851, 1,817 tons, of extreme model, built for Train & Co., employed in the Train Line of Liverpool packets. Maiden voyage Boston to Liverpool made in 14 days, 18 hours full up with cargo and 200 passengers. In 1852 made first California passage, arriving out in 102 days, from there to the Far East. Final voyage departed Liverpool for Boston in late 1853, suffered a damaged rudder and partially dismasted during stormy weather on December 24, 1853, after passing Grand Bank, Captain Josiah Richardson injured by falling spars, that same evening went ashore on Blonde Rock, near Cape Sable Island, Nova Scotia, 170 crew and passengers, including Captain Richardson, went down with the ship.
- *Flying Fish*, 1851, 1,505 tons, of extreme model, built for Sampson & Tappan and George Upton. Employed in the California–Far East trade, maiden voyage Boston to San Francisco 1851 and 1852 made in several hours over 100 days; second California run in 1852 and 1853 made in 92 days, 4 hours, a near record run. Later made five other California passages, slowest time on these runs being 114 days. In November 1858 loaded tea at Foo Chow, China, for New York, subsequently went ashore on departure at the mouth of the River Min, later got off and condemned and sold foreign, name changed to *El Bueno Suceso*, homeport Manila, employed in the trade between that port and Spain, later said to

Clipper ship *Staffordshire*. This early clipper was built for Enoch Train & Co.'s White Diamond Line of Boston–Liverpool packets in 1851. Note the Train flag on her main mast, while flying on the fore and mizzen masts are the Union Jack and Stars and Stripes, indicative of the nations this clipper would be serving (*Gleason's Pictorial Drawing-Room Companion,* July 12, 1851).

have foundered in the China Sea, details unknown.

- *Sovereign of the Seas*, 1852, 2,421 tons, of extreme model, built on own account, shortly after launching sold to New York shipbrokers, commanded by Captain Lauchlan McKay. Maiden passage on the California route in late 1852 made in 103 days, then went to Honolulu to load 8,000 barrels of whale oil eastward for New York, the first ship engaged in this trade. In mid-1853 chartered by Baines' Black Ball Line of Australian packets; on her return voyage in 1854 crew mutinied, uprising put down with help of passengers. Upon return to UK sold foreign to German interests, homeport Hamburg, employed in the Australian and Far East trade. Lost in 1859 while bound Germany to China, going ashore on Pyramid Shoal, Straits of Malacca.
- *Westward Ho!*, 1852, 1,650 tons, of extreme model, built for Sampson & Tappan. Employed in the California, Far East, and Indian trades, maiden voyage out to California made in 107 days, then to Manila in the fast time of 39 days; in early 1855 made a 102 day passage Boston to San Francisco, her fastest run on the California route. In 1855 and 1856 carried 800 coolies from Swatow to Callao, Peru, thereafter withdrawn from this trade by her owners. In 1857 voyaged from San Francisco to Callao, here sold foreign to Peruvian interests without a name change, thereafter put back in the coolie trade between China and Peru. Lost by fire in early 1864 while preparing to depart Callao for China.
- *Bald Eagle*, 1852, 1,704 tons, of extreme model, built for George Upton. Employed in the California–Far East trade, maiden passage to San Francisco made in 107 days; second passage out in 1853 and 1854 made in 115 days, returned eastward to New York in just under 79 days, the second fastest passage ever on this route. In 1855 employed in the coolie trade, carrying 700 coolies from Swatow to Callao, Peru. In 1860 carried coal and naval stores from Liverpool to Foo Chow, China. Final voyage departed Hong Kong in October 1861 for San Francisco with a cargo of rice, sugar, tea, and $100,000 in treasure, subsequently went missing with all hands, later speculated that she was lost in a typhoon in the China Sea.
- *Empress of the Seas*, 1853, 2,200 tons, of

Clipper ship *Empress of the Seas*. Builder Donald McKay intended to operate this ship on his own account but sold her to Baltimore interests while she was still on the stocks, having received an offer he couldn't pass up (*Illustrated News*, March 5, 1853).

extreme model, built for own account but sold on the stocks to Wilson & Sons, Baltimore, Maryland, price $125,000. First employed in the Oakford Line of California clippers, maiden passage to San Francisco made in 121 days, back eastward to New York with guano from Callao, Peru, subsequently voyaged to Bombay, India, via Quebec and London; 1856 California passage in 115 days. Later put in the Australian trade, making a 66 day, 12 hour passage between Liverpool and Melbourne in 1861. Subsequently lost in December 1861, burned at Port Phillip, Melbourne.

- *Star of Empire*, 1853, 2,050 tons, of medium model, built for Train & Co., employed in the Train Line of Boston-Liverpool packets. Maiden voyage out in 19 days, in August 1853 returned to Boston with over 830 immigrant passengers; in January 1854 passage Boston to Liverpool in 14 days, 15 hours. Later employed in the Indian and Far East trade. Final voyage in 1856, Rangoon, Burma, to Falmouth, England, put into Alagoa Bay, Azore Islands, in a sinking condition, probably due to storm damage, condemned and scrapped.
- *Chariot of Fame*, 1853, 2,050 tons, of medium model, sister ship to *Star of Empire*, built for Train & Co. First employed in the Train Line of Boston–Liverpool packets making seven roundtrips in 1853 and 1854. In January 1854 departed Liverpool for Boston with the most valuable cargo ever to leave there for the U.S., value 100,000 pounds sterling, collided with another vessel outbound, experienced stormy weather the whole passage with damage to sails and rigging, subsequently put into Provincetown, Massachusetts, in a snowstorm, from here towed to Boston to unload cargo and repair. Subsequently employed as a general trader including guano voyages in 1856, 1858, and 1859 to 1860; in mid–1861 roundtrip voyage UK to Australia, return to London via New Zealand. Late 1863 sold foreign at London to Wilson & Chambers and employed in the White Star Line of Australian packets. Registry expired in 1874, likely sold again, said to have been lost in January 1876, abandoned at sea in a sinking condition while bound Callao, Peru, to Cork, Ireland, with guano (McKay, p. 109).
- *Great Republic*, 1853, 4,555 tons, of extreme model, built for owners account and commanded by Captain Lauchlan McKay. Launched October 4, 1853, subsequently towed to New York to load for her maiden voyage, there opened to public view for paying visitors, of which proceeds in the

amount of $1,000 were donated to a local sailor's charity; ship subsequently damaged on the night of December 26, 1853, due to a warehouse fire on shore and burned to the water's edge, later abandoned to the underwriters as a total loss. Hull later sold to A.A. Low & Brothers of New York, raised, cut down in size, and repaired at the yard of Sneden & Whitlock at Green Point, Brooklyn, New York; in February 1855 first sailed on her own. See below in New York section for career details of the rebuilt clipper.

- *Romance of the Seas*, 1853, 1,782 tons, of extreme model, built for George Upton. Put in the California–Far East trade, maiden passage Boston to San Francisco in just under 97 days. In late 1856 departed San Francisco for Shanghai, China, passage just over 34 days, a near record run. In May 1861 departed San Francisco for Queenstown, Ireland, passage of 93 days also a near record run. Final voyage departed December 31, 1862, bound Hong Kong for San Francisco, subsequently went missing with all hands.
- *Lightning*, 1854, 2,083 tons, of extreme model, built for James Baines & Co. of Liverpool, England and employed in the Black Ball Line of Australian packet ships, the first of four clippers Donald McKay built for this line. Maiden voyage Boston to Liverpool in then record time of 13 days, 20 hours, second fastest all time; from Liverpool out to Melbourne, Australia, in 77 days, return to UK in 64 days with gold dust valued at a million pounds. In 1857 departed Liverpool for Melbourne, passage made in some hours over 69 days. Later carried British troops and supplies to India. In late 1862 while outward bound from Melbourne hit uncharted shoals but continued undamaged, these shoals later named Lightning Rocks. In October 1869 caught fire while loading at Melbourne, ship towed out of harbor and scuttled to put out the fire, part of cargo salvaged but ship a total loss, thereafter destroyed as a navigational hazard.
- *Champion of the Seas*, 1854, 2,447 tons, of extreme model, built for James Baines & Co., one of the four Black Ball Line Australian packets built by McKay. Maiden voyage New York to Liverpool, then to Melbourne, Australia. In 1857 chartered by British government to carry troops to India, later continued in the Black Ball Line. By 1869 sold and employed as a general trader in the Canadian lumber trade; by 1873 sold again and repaired and put in the guano trade. Final voyage in late 1875 bound Callao, Peru, for Cork, Ireland, abandoned in a sinking condition off Cape Horn in January 1876, all hands rescued by a passing British vessel.
- *James Baines*, 1854, 2,525, of extreme model, built for James Baines & Co. for service in their Black Ball Line of Australian packets, the third of four ships McKay built for Baines and the fastest of all the clippers built by him. Maiden voyage Boston to Liverpool in record time of 12 days, 6 hours, then to Melbourne, Australia, in 1854 to 1855 with 700 passengers in record time of 63 days. In 1857 chartered by the British government to carry troops to India, thereafter departed Calcutta for Liverpool, arriving in April 1858, passage time 77 days. The day after arrival while unloading was discovered to be on fire below deck and was subsequently destroyed at dockside.
- *Blanche Moore*, 1854, 1,787 tons, of extreme model, built for Charles Moore & Co. of Liverpool, England. Full career details unknown but built for the England–India trade in which her owners were heavily involved; later sold to Wilson, Cunningham & Co. of Liverpool, Wilson having formerly co-founded the White Star Line of Australian packets. Ship lost May 24, 1867, while bound Liverpool for Calcutta, India, with a cargo of salt, struck Long Bank off Wexford, Ireland, in the Irish Channel and quickly filled with water, a total loss, crew rescued through use of own boats with assistance of Carnesore Point lifeboat.
- *Santa Claus*, 1854, 1,286 tons, of medium model, built for Joseph Nickerson & Co. of Boston. First employed in the Indian trade making a round-trip voyage between Boston and Calcutta; in 1856 made a California passage of 146 days. Later employed in the guano and coolie trades. Final voyage departed Callao, Peru, with guano for Hamburg, Germany, subsequently sprang a leak and was abandoned in a sinking condition in August 1863 in the Caribbean Sea; all hands reached land safely at Cayenne, French Guiana.

- *Donald McKay*, 1855, 2,594 tons, of medium model, built for James Baines & Co., the last of the four Black Ball Line of Australian packet ships built by McKay and the second largest ship in the world for some time (after *Great Republic*). Maiden voyage Boston to Liverpool in 17 days with Donald McKay aboard as a passenger, then out to Melbourne, Australia, in 81 days; continued as a popular ship in the Black Ball Line up to 1867, thereafter sold for employment as a general trader. In 1875 carried British troops to India, later carried troops to Mauritius. In 1878 carried the largest oil cargo from any U.S. port to Europe. In 1879 sold to German interests, homeport Bremerhaven, employed in the transatlantic trade between that port and New York. Last surveyed at New York in 1882, out of registry after 1883, sent to Madeira and cut down for use as a coal storeship.
- *Defender*, 1855, 1,413 tons, of medium model, built for Kendall & Plympton of Boston. Made three California passages in her short career, best time 136 days. Final voyage in 1859 while bound from Puget Sound to Sydney, Australia, with a cargo of lumber, lost after going ashore on Elizabeth Reef in the Tasman Sea, several hundred miles off the coast of Australia.
- *Henry Hill*, 1856, 568-ton bark, built for Boston parties, later owned at New York. Career details uncertain; disappears from registry after 1863, likely sold foreign with a change in name.
- *Mastiff*, 1856, 1,030 tons, of medium model, built for George Upton of Boston, later owned at New York. Made two California passages, best time 133 days. Also engaged in the Far East trade, departed San Francisco for Hong Kong in September 1859 with 175 Chinese passengers and $76,000 in gold, and caught fire when only a few days out, crew tried to fight fire without success, ship subsequently abandoned, all crew and passengers saved by a British vessel.
- *Minnehaha*, 1856, 1,695 tons, of medium model, built for Kendall & Plympton of Boston, later sold to Samuel Reed & Co. for $62,500 in 1862. Employed in the Australian and Far East trade. In mid–1862 departed New York for San Francisco with a load of coal, stormy weather caused her

Clipper ship *Donald McKay*. This woodcut shows the namesake vessel of her prolific builder taking a pilot at Liverpool after her arrival from Melbourne, Australia, in December 1855. The clipper was built for James Baines' Black Ball Line and served in the Australian trade for over a decade after her launching in 1854 and was said to be a popular ship (*Illustrated Times*, January 12, 1856).

to develop a leak forcing her to put into Rio de Janeiro for over a month, total passage time over 200 days. In late 1864 departed London for San Francisco with coal, battered off Cape Horn and arrived after a 189 day passage. In late November 1867 arrived at Baker's Island from Honolulu to load a cargo of guano, lost on December 3 after stormy weather put her on a reef.

- *Amos Lawrence*, 1856, 1,396 tons, of medium model, built for Emmons & Parsons of Boston. Made one California passage prior to 1860, time 141 days; also employed in the Far East or Indian trade, career details uncertain. Out of American registry after 1863, likely sold foreign with a change in name
- *Abbott Lawrence*, 1856, 1,497 tons, of medium model, built for George Upton of Boston, by the late 1860s owned at Newburyport. Employed in the Far East and European trades, full career details unknown. Last survey at Plymouth, England, in 1867, sold foreign 1868 to Spanish interests without a name change, homeport Manila, Philippines, disappears from registers after 1873.
- *Baltic*, 1856, 1,372 tons, of medium model, built for A. Zerega & Co. of New York. Intended for the Z Line of packets, career details uncertain, out of American registry by 1861.
- *Adriatic*, 1856, 1,327 tons, of medium model, built for A. Zerega. Intended for the Z Line of packets, nothing is known of this ship's career; out of American registry by 1859, likely sold foreign with a change in name.
- *Alhambra*, 1859, 1,097 tons, of medium model, built for William Thwing & Co. of Boston, sold foreign at Liverpool in 1863 without a name change. Employed in the transatlantic trade, about 1875 sold back to American interests, owned by Snow & Burgess at New York; in 1882 sold foreign again to Bremen, Germany, interests, disappears from registry after 1884.

Samuel Hall (1800–1870) may not have built the most clippers in East Boston, but he is important not only for the clippers he built, but also because he was the first builder of note in East Boston. Hall was born in Marshfield, the son of a local shipbuilder, who served his apprenticeship at the shipyard of Elijah Barstow in nearby Hanover and afterwards, "with twenty five cents in his pocket and a broad-axe on his shoulder he went to Medford and from there to Camden, Maine, from which later place he returned to Marshfield" (Briggs, pgs. 356–57). Samuel Hall would subsequently build some vessels with his brothers at Marshfield from 1825 to 1827, thereafter moving to Duxbury, where he built both in partnership and on his own for over a decade. In 1839 Samuel Hall moved to East Boston to establish his own yard, building his first ship there, the 642-ton *Akbar*, for a group of some of Boston's best known merchants, including R.B. Forbes, Daniel Bacon, and John E. Lodge. Hall would later employ marine architect Samuel Pook at his own yard for a short period and put over his first true clipper in 1850 for New York owners. It is interesting to note that historian William A. Fairburn has treated Samuel Hall rather harshly, claiming (without citing his sources) that Hall was "hard to get along with" and was "ambitious for credit as a designer as well as a builder" (Fairburn, p. 2955), and lays the design for all of Hall's noted clippers as being from designer Samuel Pook's plans after the two had parted ways. While there seems to be no doubt that Hall and Pook parted company in a decidedly cool fashion, Hall's great skill as a designer and builder cannot be denied. The clipper status of Hall's below listed pre–1850 clippers may be debated, but all of them were fast ships, and though a bit fuller in model than the clippers that followed these vessels were sparred in the fashion of the California clippers that would soon arrive on the scene. After his clipper building days were over, Hall would continue to build ships almost up to the time of his death, launching some 110 vessels at his East Boston yard in almost thirty years. Hall was also active in many other maritime and community affairs and was the driving force of the East Boston Drydock Company, the East Boston Ferry Company, and the Maverick National Bank (Hall's shipyard was located at the foot of Maverick Street), all of which he served as president.

- *Coquette*, 1844, 457-ton bark, built for the Russel & Co. of Boston. Employed in the China tea trade, in December 1844 made the all-time record passage from Macao to Calcutta, India, arriving via Singapore in the net sailing time of 20 days, 13 hours

under Captain Oliver Eldridge; out of American registry by 1859.
- *Lantao*, 1849, 593 tons, built for Daniel Spooner of Boston. Employed in the Far East and California trade, arrived at San Francisco from New York in 121 days in mid–1853. In October 1856 departed Caldera, Chile, for Boston and went missing with all hands.
- *Hazard*, 1849, 404-ton bark, a heavily sparred ship with a 130 foot long mainmast, built for Henry Gardner, Salem, Massachusetts, interests, later owned at Boston by Mansfield & Roberts. Employed in the South American coffee trade, from 1849 to 1852 made six passages to Rio de Janeiro, average time from Boston to the equator being 26 days, "a truly remarkable record" (Cutler, p. 145); major repairs in 1864 and 1869, disappears from registry after 1881.
- *Surprise*, 1850, 1,262 tons, designed by Samuel Pook, built for A.A. Low & Brothers of New York, the first true clipper built at East Boston. Intended for the Far East trade but first put on the California run, maiden passage 1850 to 1851 in 96 days, 15 hours, the record up to that time; made two more such runs, both in 118 days, in 1853 and 1854, thereafter put in the Far East trade. Rebuilt at New York in 1867 after many years of hard driving. Final voyage departed New York September 1875 for Yokohama, Japan, with case oil, subsequently put ashore in Kaneda Bay while under control of a man claiming to be a pilot (he in fact was not), crew rescued and most of cargo salvaged but ship was a total loss.
- *Race Horse*, 1850, 514-ton bark, built for John Forbes of Boston, later owned by Goddard & Co. of Boston, first commanded by Captain David Babcock. Maiden passage on the California run made in 109 days, only 94 days, 14 hours land to land. In 1851 carried missionaries for Armenia from Boston to Smyrna, Turkey. Out of registry after 1870, rating expired and likely scrapped.
- *Game Cock*, 1851, 1,392 tons, of extreme model, built for Daniel Bacon & Co. of Boston and was owned by them her entire career. First employed in the Far East trade, passage New York to Batavia, Dutch East Indies, in 78 days, return home via Sri Lanka and Mauritius; in 1854 made a California run of 114 days. Later continued in the Far East and Indian trade. In 1863 loaded coal at Newcastle, New South Wales, Australia, for San Francisco. Career ended in early 1880 when condemned at the Cape of Good Hope.
- *Hoogly*, 1851, 1,304 tons, of medium model, built for Daniel Bacon & Sons. Maiden voyage to California in early 1852, 127 net sailing days, partially dismasted when only a few days out and forced into Rio de Janeiro for repairs. From San Francisco sailed for Shanghai via Honolulu, subsequently lost August 1851 after going ashore while making port.
- *R.B. Forbes*, 1851, 756 tons, of extreme model, built for Hunnewell, Pierce, & Brewer of Boston. Employed in a variety of trades including to California and the Far East, as well as that with Hawaii and South America; maiden voyage Boston to Honolulu in 1851 to 1852 in record time of 99 days. In late 1863 sold foreign at Hong Kong to Macao interests for $17,000 and employed as a coolie ship. Condemned at Hong Kong in August 1864 after being dismasted, later sold and repaired, operating as the ship *Donna Maria Pia*, out of registry after 1872.
- *Mermaid*, 1851, 540-ton bark, of extreme model with 24 inches of deadrise, figurehead a mermaid with a comb and spyglass in hand, built for Edward Gassett and others. Intended for the California and Far East trade with China; maiden voyage on the California run took 160 days, forced into port at Pernambuco, Brazil, for repairs, made one final California passage prior to 1860 in 108 days. In 1852 sailed from China to Boston in the fine time of 87 days; in 1853 sailed from Batavia, Dutch East Indies, to San Francisco in the then record time of 50 days. Out of American registry by 1859, likely sold foreign, final fate uncertain,
- *Flying Childers*, 1852, 1,150 tons, of medium model, built for John Forbes and the Cunningham Brothers of Boston. Employed in the California–Far East trade, maiden voyage on the California run 113 days in 1852 and 1853. In 1858 sold to New York parties

for $53,000. In 1859 117 day passage Boston to San Francisco, in 1861 carried wheat from San Francisco to Liverpool, in 1862 loaded at Manila for London, arriving in late 1862. Subsequently sold foreign in early 1863 to McKay, Baines & Co. and renamed *Golden South*, later employed in the Australian trade. Out of shipping register after 1867, later becoming a coal hulk at Port Jackson, Sydney, Australia, and destroyed by fire after many years of service.

- *John Gilpin*, 1852, 1,089 tons, of medium model, built for Hunnewell & Pierce of Boston. Employed in the California–Far East trade, made several eastward return voyages with whale oil; maiden voyage Boston to San Francisco made in near record time, several hours under 94 days, second California run in 1854 made in 114 days. Final voyage commenced in late 1857, bound Honolulu for New Bedford, Massachusetts, with 7,500 barrels of whale oil, subsequently lost, abandoned while slowly foundering on January 30, 1858, after hitting a submerged iceberg the previous day; while crew left the ship in a hurry she accidentally caught fire, entire crew saved by a passing British ship.
- *Polynesia*, 1852, 1,075 tons, of medium model, built for Hunnewell, Pierce & Brewer. Employed in the California–Far East trade, returning eastward with whale oil from Honolulu. Generally considered an unfortunate ship due to her many mishaps. Maiden run out to San Francisco made in a disappointing 140 days; second California run in 1854 made in 104 days. In September 1858 departed Boston for California but voyage terminated, forced back due to heavy leaking; voyage resumed but ship battered by heavy storm on the approach to Cape Horn, arrived in March 1859 after a 152 day passage. In 1860 collided with another vessel while approaching San Francisco on her seventh California run. In March 1862 loaded at San Francisco for Hong Kong but set on fire by her crew on evening before departure, ship subsequently beached, a total loss.
- *Mystery*, 1853, 1,155 tons, built for Crocker & Sturgis and the Bacons of Boston. Made only one American voyage, maiden passage Boston to San Francisco in 139 days, then to Shanghai; subsequently made a 116 day passage from Woosung to London, arriving in early 1854, there sold foreign in March 1854 without a name change, later employed in the UK–India trade. Last surveyed at London in 1865, out of registry after 1871.
- *Wizard*, 1853, 1,601 tons, of extreme model, built on speculation, sold to Oliver Slate & Co. of New York, price $95,000. Employed in the California–Far East trade, maiden voyage on the California run made in 104 sailing days, 127 days total, forced into Rio de Janeiro with damaged spars and rigging, repairs taking 23 days. In early 1859 made a difficult 144 day passage New York to San Francisco, partially dismasted and damaged during a heavy gale. Later made a coal voyage New York to Acapulco in 1862, heavily damaged during stormy weather and forced into Port Stanley, Falkland Islands, twice to effect repairs. Sold foreign at London in November 1863 to McKay, Baines & Co. and renamed *Queen of the Colonies* and put in the Australian trade. Wrecked in 1874 while bound Java to Falmouth, UK.
- *Amphitrite*, 1853, 1,687 tons, built for Boston parties, sold foreign in 1855 to Richard Green of London and renamed *Result*, out of register after 1872.
- *Quick Step*, 1855, 523-ton bark, built for Ephraim Lombard and others of Boston. Not to be confused with the Maine clipper ship of the same name. Later owned by Captain Osworthy, who was also her commander. Career details uncertain, last surveyed at New York in 1866, out of register by 1873.
- *Florence*, 1856, 1,065 tons, of medium model, built for the Forbes brothers of Boston and Captain Philip Dumaresq. First employed in the Far East trade, maiden voyage Boston to Hong Kong in 91 days in 1856. In 1858 was the first American ship to put in at Nagasaki, Japan, voyaging there from Shanghai. In late 1862 made a passage New York to Liverpool, sold foreign and renamed *Hypathia*; still afloat under Norwegian ownership in 1887 and employed in the Canadian lumber trade. Lost in 1888 after going ashore, crew saved.

Robert E. Jackson (born 1814) was one of the most important East Boston builders of the

1850s (and beyond), and though his achievements are often overshadowed by those of Donald McKay and Samuel Hall, Jackson built some of the finest clippers ever to be launched there. Where Jackson got his start in shipbuilding is uncertain, but it was probably at Medford, possibly in the yard of Waterman & Ewell in the 1830s and 1840s. This seems most likely as Jackson built his first clipper in 1850 as the junior partner in the firm of Ewell & Jackson, the senior partner probably being Henry Ewell of Medford. No matter how he got his start in shipbuilding, the decade of the 1850s was a good one for Jackson, he having assets totaling some $44,000 by 1860. Robert Jackson would continue to build notable sailing ships into the 1870s, his most famous later-day production being the 1869-built *Great Admiral*, which had the lines approaching those of a medium clipper.

- *John Bertram*, 1850, 1,080 tons, of extreme model and the first clipper designed for the California–Far East trade, built by Ewell & Jackson for Glidden & Williams of Boston. Maiden voyage out to San Francisco in 1851 in 126 sailing days, forced into Valparaiso, Chile, en route due to spar problems. Second passage in 1851 and 1852 made in 105 days, after voyaging from Manila to Boston in 1854 and 1855, sold foreign at Boston to German interests for $45,000, homeport Hamburg, subsequently employed in the transatlantic trade; in 1863 sold to Norwegian interests and employed in the Quebec lumber trade. Final voyage in early 1883, departing New York for Rotterdam, Holland, abandoned in a sinking condition, crew rescued.
- *Winged Racer*, 1852, 1,767 tons, designed by Samuel Pook, built for Seccomb & Taylor of Boston but quickly sold to Sampson & Tappan. Employed in the California–Far East trade, maiden voyage to San Francisco in 108 days. In late 1855 departed Swatow, China, with 700 coolies for the Chinchas Islands, coolies mutinied but were put down by force. In 1857 loaded wheat at Baltimore but began leaking while off Annapolis and was beached with 18 feet of water in her hold; subsequently repaired and sold, employed in the wheat trade between California and the UK. Late October 1861 departed San Francisco for Liverpool with over 30,000 bags of wheat, subsequently hit a submerged rock off Alcatraz Island while in charge of a pilot and was repaired at Mare Island. Final voyage departed Manila for New York and subsequently captured and destroyed by the Confederate raider *Alabama* on November 10, 1863, while in the Straits of Sunda.
- *Queen of Clippers*, 1853, 2,361 tons, built for Seccomb & Taylor, but sold soon after launching to Zerega & Co. of New York for $135,000. Maiden voyage New York to San Francisco in 118 days. In 1854 voyaged New York to Liverpool, there chartered for service as a transport in the Crimean War by the French government; in 1856 sold foreign to French interests at Marseilles and renamed *Reina des Clippers*. Later career details and fate unknown.
- *Challenger*, 1853, 1,354 tons, of extreme model, designed by Samuel Pook, built for W. & F.H. Whittemore of Boston. Maiden voyage on the California run in 111 days, the fastest of her five passages prior to 1860. In early 1856 loaded a tea and silk cargo at Shanghai, value $2 million, bound for New York. Carried guano from 1858 to 1860 to U.S. and Europe. Collided with a vessel at Bremerhaven, Germany, in October 1862 but only small damage. After her final California passage in 1863 sold foreign at San Francisco to the Peruvian government for use in the coolie-guano trade, price $41,000, renamed *Camille Cavour*. Later employed in the Puget Sound lumber trade, lost in October 1875 while bound Port Discovery to Peru, damaged during a storm and abandoned by her crew off Manzillo, Mexico, where the ship drifted ashore and was wrecked.
- *Lightfoot*, 1853, 1,996 tons, of extreme model, built by Jackson & Ewell for Howes & Co. of Boston, cost $140,000. Intended for the California–Far East trade, maiden voyage to San Francisco 1853 and 1854 made in 114 days and from there continued to Hong Kong via Honolulu, later from Canton, China, to London; departed London for Calcutta on her final voyage, subsequently wrecked late June 1855 at the mouth of the Hooghly River near Sagar Island.

- *King Lear*, 1854, 1,936 tons, built for Seccomb & Taylor, likely sold foreign soon after her building. By 1858 owned by the Somes Brothers of London and employed in the Far East and Australian trades. Arrived at San Francisco from Hong Kong in late April 1863 with a cargo valued at over $28,000; out of registry after 1874.
- *Blue Jacket*, 1854, 1,790 tons, built for Seccomb & Taylor. Maiden voyage Boston to Liverpool, there sold to John J. Frost's Fox Line of Australian packets; subsequent passage out to Melbourne, Australia, made in 68 days. Later carried 600 coolies from Madras, India, to London, continued in Australian trade and later owned by the White Star Line of packets. Final voyage departed Lytleton, New Zealand, for the UK, was found to be on fire below deck while off the Falkland Islands and abandoned on March 16, 1869, entire crew got off and later saved by a passing vessel.
- *Swallow*, 1854, 1,435 tons, built for Dugan & Leeland of New York and Seccomb & Taylor of Boston. Employed in the Far East trade, making no California passages until 1862; from that time to 1873 made nine runs to San Francisco, five of them from New York, best time 109 days. Most early China voyages originated from the UK. Maiden voyage New York to London and thence to Melbourne, Australia, by charter. In 1857 employed in the coolie trade, sailing from Macao to Havana, Cuba. Final West Coast voyage in 1876, departing San Francisco for Antwerp, Belgium, with 1,569 short tons of wheat; in 1885 departed London for Sydney, Australia, but foundered en route, all hands saved.
- *Harry of the West*, 1855, 1,050 tons, built for Calvin Adams of New York and employed in the transatlantic cotton trade; lost to fire at Southwest Pass, mouth of the Mississippi River, after loading cotton at New Orleans for Liverpool in November 1865.
- *Endeavor*, 1856, 1,137 tons, of medium model, built for Cunningham Brothers of Boston; first employed in the California–Far East trade. Maiden voyage to San Francisco from New York made in 131 days, made seven other runs from 1857 to 1869, best time 122 days in 1858. Later sold to New Bedford, Massachusetts, and New York interests and employed in trade with Japan, there destroyed by fire in 1875.
- *Norseman*, 1856, 812 tons, built for the Cunningham Brothers. Made one California passage prior to 1860, time 144 days. Sold foreign at Thailand in 1863, homeport Shanghai, disappears from shipping registers after 1864, likely due to a name change.
- *Gemsbok*, 1857, 622-ton bark, built for Boston parties, merchant career details uncertain. Sold to the Federal government in September 1861 at Boston for Civil War service and first employed in the South Atlantic Blockading Squadron, capturing five vessels off the coast of North Carolina. By February 1863 employed with the West Indies Squadron as a coal collier and storeship. Decommissioned at New York in July 1865 and sold to New York owners; later owned there by Roberts & Mansfield. Wrecked in April 1886 while owned by N.B. Mansfield of Boston.

Paul Curtis (see Medford and Chelsea above for career details) began building ships at East Boston in 1852 after getting his start in Medford and would continue to build in East Boston into the 1870s, both on his own and in the partnerships of Curtis & Smith and, later, Curtis, Smith & Cushman.

- *Golden West*, 1852, 1,441 tons, of extreme model, built for Glidden & Williams of Boston, intended for the California–Far East trade. Maiden passage in 1852 and 1853 made in 124 days. In early 1855 went ashore on a reef in the Gaspar Straits while bound Manila to New York but got off safely after discharging part of her hemp cargo. In May 1856 departed Japan for San Francisco, arriving in 22 days, the second fastest passage on record. In early 1863 sold foreign at Liverpool and was by 1866 employed in the coolie trade with Peru; out of registry after 1876.
- *Cleopatra*, 1853, 1,562 tons, of medium model, built for Benjamin Bangs of Boston, first employed in the California trade. Maiden voyage to San Francisco made in 131 days, returned eastward with guano from the Chincha Islands. Second voyage on the California run 110 days in 1854 and 1855, subsequently loaded guano at the Chinchas for New York; lost on September

25, 1855, after striking a submerged wreck two days earlier, crew abandoned ship in two boats, both making Rio de Janeiro safely nine days later.
- *Reporter*, 1853, 1,474 tons, of medium model, built for David Snow of Boston; intended for the cotton trade with New Orleans, cost $80,750. Maiden voyage New York to New Orleans and then to Liverpool in early 1854 with 3,000 barrels of flour and over 3,000 bales of cotton, passage time 30 days; upon arrival was offered for sale but found no takers due to business conditions then prevailing. Later that year chartered by the Train Line of packets and continued in same trade. In 1855 sold to William F. Weld & Co. and put in the California trade; first voyage out in 1855 and 1856 made in 107 days, fastest time on the run was 103 days in 1861. Final voyage departed New York for San Francisco, subsequently battered by a severe storm while rounding Cape Horn and began to founder on August 17, 1862; the clipper was that day abandoned by her crew on two rafts, one of which was never seen again while the other only had four survivors, total crew lost was 34 men.
- *Radiant*, 1853, 1,318 tons, of medium model, built for Baker & Morrill of Boston. Maiden voyage out to California in 134 days, second voyage New York to Australia in 1855. In 1861 carried wheat from San Francisco to Queenstown, Ireland, from there to London and then to Cardiff, Wales. In 1863 departed London for Mauritius and then to Calcutta, India, final fate uncertain. Howe & Matthews claim she was sold foreign without a name change, homeport Calcutta in 1863, but shipping registers show American ownership up to 1871 or 1872, thereafter disappears from registry.
- *John Elliot Thayer*, 1854, 1,918 tons, built for Enoch Train & Co. First employed as a transatlantic packet in the Train Line; made one California passage of 130 days. Lost after catching fire while loading guano at Patos Island in the Gulf of California in September 1858.
- *Golden Fleece* (II), 1855, 1,535 tons, of medium model, built for Weld & Baker of Boston, regarded as Paul Curtis' "finest production" (Howe & Matthews, p. 232). Employed in the California trade making fifteen passages between 1856 and 1876, three from Boston, and twelve from New York, best time 111 days in 1870. In 1857 struck Four Fathom Bank while entering San Francisco in charge of a pilot and beached with fourteen feet of water in her hold but was repaired. In 1871 departed Boston for Bombay, India, with a cargo of ice but was found to be on fire below when just a few days out and forced into Halifax, Nova Scotia, where she was scuttled to put out the fire, subsequently pumped out and returned to Boston where she was repaired. Final voyage in late 1877 while bound New York to San Francisco, put into Montevideo after grounding off the Rio de la Plata and found to be badly damaged, condemned and sold for scrap in 1878.
- *Empress*, 1856, 1,294 tons, built for Henry Harbeck & Co. of New York. Made no California passages prior to 1860, career details uncertain. Sold foreign to British interests, homeport London, in 1864, likely involved in the Quebec lumber trade, surveyed there in 1876. By 1881 sold to German interests and renamed *Elisabeth*, homeport Bremen, employed in the transatlantic trade. Surveyed at Baltimore in 1886, out of registry after 1887.
- *Mary Bangs*, 1856, 958 tons, built for W. Bangs & Co. of Boston, commission merchants. Made no California runs prior to 1860, still homeported at East Boston. Howes & Matthews report vessel wrecked off Altata, Mexico, in 1874, this either inaccurate or the vessel was repaired, still listed in the registers under original owners until 1880.
- *Belvedere*, 1857, 1,322 tons, built for Weld & Baker, later William F. Weld & Co. Employed first in the California trade, made two passages to San Francisco prior to 1860, best time 127 days. Later sold to West Coast interests, homeport San Francisco beginning in the late 1870s and employed in the coal trade. Final voyage departed San Pedro, California, for British Columbia and subsequently went ashore at Bonilla Point near Cape Flattery in November 1886, was gotten off but filled with water and sank while being towed to Port Townsend.

Ship-building at East Boston. It is unknown which shipyard this woodcut may have been intended to portray, but it is nevertheless indicative of the great building activity that was taking place in this concentrated area at the shipyards of such master builders as Donald McKay, Samuel Hall, Robert Jackson, Paul Curtis, Daniel Kelly, and several others (author's collection, likely from *Gleason's Pictorial and Drawing Room Companion*, ca. 1852).

- *Fortuna*, 1857, 659 tons, built for Israel Lombard & Co. of Boston, and later the commission merchants Lombard and Charles Whitney. Made no California voyages, likely employed as a general trader. Sold foreign to British interests at Singapore in 1864 and there homeported, employed in the San Francisco–Far East trade; out of foreign registry after 1873.

The brothers Augustus (born 1806) and George T. (born 1819) Sampson built three clippers at East Boston. While they were primarily involved in building smaller craft (and repair work) from 1849 into the late 1860s, their clippers averaged three times the size of the vessels they normally launched. One intriguing product from this yard is the 1857-built *Voyageur de la Mer*, a 1,221-ton ship built for the viceroy of Egypt. Her size, very close to that of the clippers they built, may indicate that this foreign-built vessel was also of a clipper model. G.T. Sampson is listed in the 1860 Federal Census as a shipbuilder with $5,000 in assets, while Augustus was worth $5,300 an amount on the low end of the scale compared to their better known East Boston rivals. In addition to their shipbuilding activities, the Sampsons were also shipping merchants and shipowners.

- *Fearless*, 1853, 1,184 tons, of extreme model, designed by Samuel Pook, built for William F. Weld & Co. of Boston. Employed in the California–Far East trade, made twelve voyages to San Francisco from Boston or New York by 1868, best time 114 days. In October 1878 sold at Hamburg, Germany, to Norwegian interests, price $6,500, name changed to *Johanne* and re-rigged as a bark, subsequently employed in the Nova Scotia lumber trade; disappears from registry after 1892.
- *Peerless*, 1853, 1,100 tons, built for William F. Weld & Co. Made one California passage of 210 days; career details unknown, out of American registry by 1858.
- *Fanny McHenry*, 1,237 tons, built for G. McHenry & Co. of Philadelphia. Career details uncertain, sold foreign to British interests in 1863 and renamed *Sanspareil*, homeport Liverpool, owned by Globe Navigation Co. By 1873 owned at North Shields, England, likely involved in the coal trade. Last survey at New Orleans in early

1875, wrecked October 1875, details of loss unknown.

Daniel D. Kelly (born 1818) built three clippers here and was active as a shipbuilder and ship owner in the area for a number of years beginning in 1848. By 1860 his assets totaled some $45,000, three times that of Donald McKay, a sure indicator of a thriving business. Many of his non-clipper vessels were small brigs, schooners, or barks.

- *Edwin Forrest*, 1853, 1,141 tons, of medium model, built for Crosby, Crocker & Co. of New York. First employed in the transatlantic and Indian trades; made first California voyage in 1856, arriving out in 132 days, and a second in 1857 of 133 days, carried guano from the Chincha Islands to Hampton Roads, Virginia, in 1858. Final voyage departed New York for Hong Kong August 1860, subsequently went missing with all hands.
- *Zephyr*, 1854, 1,184 tons, built for Wales & Emmons of Boston, this ship is sometimes incorrectly attributed to Donald McKay. Employed at least in part in the transatlantic trade between Liverpool and New Orleans; surveyed at Liverpool in 1877, New Orleans in 1879, and New York in 1881. In 1884 sold foreign to the Adelaide Steamship Co., homeport Port Adelaide, Australia; out of registry after 1891.
- *Bostonian*, 1854, 1,099 tons, built for Henry Brookman and others of Boston, figurehead a full sized likeness of Benjamin Franklin; by 1858 owned by George Callender of Boston. First employed in Allen & Welch's line of New Orleans packet ships, full career details unknown. Made two slow California passages, 140 and 142 days; later commanded by Captain Burnham. Disappears from register after 1859, likely sold foreign with a change in name.

Hugh R. McKay (born 1818 in New Hampshire) built two clippers here. Given his last name, it is possible that he was related to Donald McKay, but there is no evidence of this and his New Hampshire origins make this unlikely. He should not be confused with Donald McKay's father, Hugh McKay, who lived in East Boston but was not a shipbuilder by trade. McKay built six ships here from 1854 to 1858, all but one over 1,000 tons, but he disappears from the records after 1860.

- *Indiaman*, 1854, 1,165 tons, built for Sampson & Tappan of Boston. Career details uncertain; made two California passages, shortest 124 days, later likely employed in the Indian and Far East trades. Sold foreign to British interests in 1862 without a change in name, homeport London. Last surveyed at Rangoon, Burma in 1867, disappears from register after 1873. Probably not the same 1857-built Boston ship that was renamed *Indian Merchant*, as reported by Howe & Matthews.
- *Ganges*, 1855, 1,254 tons, built for W.S. Bullard of Boston. Career details uncertain but likely employed in the Indian and Far East trade and made no California voyages. Sold foreign to British interests in May 1863, owned by the Merchants Trading Co., homeport Liverpool; disappears from register after 1874.

William Hall (born 1799) and his son William Hall, Jr., (born 1831) formed the firm of William Hall & Co. in the early 1850s and from 1854 to 1857 built four ships at East Boston. Their first ship was their only clipper. Like his brother Samuel Hall, William Hall was first a shipbuilder in Marshfield on the North River before coming to Boston.

- *Fatherland*, 1854, 1,180 tons, owned by Richard Green of London that same year, but unknown if he was original buyer or whether ship may have been built on speculation and then sold foreign; disappears from the registers after 1861, career details of ship uncertain.

Jairus Pratt (1795–1870) built one clipper among the five vessels he launched at East Boston from 1850 through 1858, the last three built in partnership with Edward Osgood under the firm name of Pratt & Osgood. His yard was well established by 1850, with $12,000 in capitol invested in the business, nearly $9,000 worth of lumber on site, and twelve hands employed.

- *Lady Franklin*, 1852, 464 tons, first owned by her commander, Captain Nagle, later sold to William Ropes of Boston. Career details unknown, may have been employed in R.W. Cameron's Pioneer Line of Australian packets in 1853, though the ship by this name so employed was listed as being of 900 tons burthen. Lost in October 1856, abandoned at sea while bound New York to Trieste, Italy

Shipwright Andrew Burnham (born 1824) built one clipper here but little is known about this builder. Interestingly, he was a close neighbor of Hugh McKay, the father of famed clipper builder Donald McKay, and may very well have been previously employed in the McKay shipyard. By 1855 Burnham was employed as a U.S. steamboat inspector, with an office on Long Wharf, a position he would hold for over twenty years.

- *Northern Eagle*, 1854, 655 tons, built for Tirrell & Dellaway of Boston. Made a California passage of 168 days in 1856, and one of 190 days in 1859; forced to put into Rio de Janeiro en route for repairs. By the late 1850s owned at Newburyport by A. & W. Currier. Disappears from American registry after 1859, likely sold foreign.

The firm of Brown & Lovell built one small clipper bark here in 1853. The senior partner was shipwright and caulker George W. Brown (born ca. 1815), while the junior partner in this firm was shipwright Josiah Lovell (born ca. 1835). The Brown & Lovell Wharf was located opposite London Street, where the firm also had under construction a 1,000-ton vessel ready for launching in early 1854.

- *Eringo*, 1853, 327-ton bark, partly owned by her first commander, Captain Lewin, with a gilded sea-crow as her figurehead, deadrise 15 inches, rigged with Russian hemp, yellow metal bottom, hull painted black. Intended for the Mediterranean trade, career details uncertain; not in American registry after 1857, possibly sold foreign with a change in name.

Boston

Paul Curtis (see Medford and East Boston above for full career details) built one clipper in Boston proper.

- *Golden Fleece*, 1852, 968 tons, of medium model, built for Weld & Baker of Boston, the first clipper to bear this name. Maiden voyage on the California run in 1852 and 1853 made in 140 days, from there voyaged to Manila and back to Boston. Made second California run in 1854, passage time 128 days from New York; subsequently loaded at San Francisco for Manila but while leaving port on April 21, 1854, missed stays and drifted ashore off Fort Point, Golden Gate, while in charge of the pilot, a total loss.

South Boston

The firm of E. & H.O. Briggs built twenty clippers here from 1851 to 1858, their output among all clipper builders being topped only by that of Donald McKay. The principals of this firm were two brothers from Scituate, on the North River, James Edwin (1821–1880) and Harrison Otis Briggs (1824–1881). They both learned the trade and apprenticed under their father, Cushing O. Briggs, with Harrison serving somewhat less time, his apprenticeship ending early when his older brother had completed his time. Together, the brothers sought their fortunes in Boston in the early 1840s, working as "journeyman shipbuilders" (Briggs, p. 324) for a time before going into partnership with Captain Noah Brooks. This partnership was subsequently ended in 1847 when the Briggs brothers went off on their own and established a shipyard at South Boston. Here they would build ships, including some of the finest and fastest of the clipper fleet, from 1848 until their retirement by 1865. By 1860 the Briggs brothers were wealthy men indeed; James was worth some $83,000, while Harrison was worth $79,000. Upon their retirement, James E. Briggs never worked again, while Harrison managed a steamship line and also served as a local bank president. Interestingly, two of the Briggs brothers' clippers, *Southern Cross* and *Starlight*, have had their likeness preserved for posterity in the marine paintings of the luminist artist Fitz Henry Lane (formerly known as Fitz Hugh Lane), who worked out of Boston from 1840 onward. These works are among the most accurate, and beautiful, contemporary portrayals of the American clipper ship.

- *Northern Light*, 1851, 1,021 tons, of medium model, designed by Samuel Pook and built for Captain James Huckins of Boston. First employed in the California trade, maiden passage made in 109 days after being partially dismasted, returned eastward via Acapulco, Mexico; second voyage out in 117 days, subsequently departed San Francisco for Boston, making the passage in 76 days, 8 hours, the all-time record on this run. Later made one Indian voyage, after which she was sold at Boston in early 1854 to Captain Seth Doane for $60,000 and employed in the Far East trade. In 1856 departed Boston for Manila, arriving in 89 days, a record or close to record run. Final voyage in late December 1861 departed Le Havre, France, in ballast for New York, subsequently collided with a French vessel on the night of January 2, 1862, and was subsequently abandoned in a damaged and sinking condition, the crews of both sunken vessels being rescued and landed at Cowes, Isle of Wight.

- *Southern Cross*, 1851, 938 tons, of medium model, built for Baker & Morrill of Boston. Employed in the California–Far East trade, departed on maiden voyage Boston to San Francisco in May 1851, partially dismasted in a storm while just a week out and again in a pampero off the River Platte, South America, arrived after a 136 day passage. Subsequently made nine more California runs, fastest 119 days in 1854 and 1855. In late 1862 damaged while bound Hong Kong to San Francisco, repairs performed at the Mare Island Navy Yard, cost $20,000. Final voyage loaded logwood at Buena Vista, Mexico, subsequently captured and burned by the Confederate raider *Florida* on June 6, 1863, while in the Atlantic, ship valued at $55,000 at time of loss.
- *Meteor*, 1852, 1,068 tons, of medium model and said to be similar in design to *Northern Light*, built for Curtis & Peabody of Boston. Employed in the California, Far East, and Indian trades; maiden voyage to San Francisco in 113 days, fastest passage 110 days in 1855. In 1862 employed in the Far East trading between Hong Kong, Bangkok, and Singapore. Sold foreign after 1864, final fate unknown.
- *Winged Arrow*, 1852, 1,052 tons, of medium model, built for Baker & Morrill. First put in the California–India trade, maiden voyage out to San Francisco made in 113 days, the best of her nine California runs; on her third California voyage arrived out in 115 days. In mid–1860 departed Boston for San Francisco, hit by a squall off the River Plate, South America, and partially dismasted, subsequently jury-rigged as a bark at sea, took 26 days to round Cape Horn due to heavy weather, finally arrived after a passage of 150 days, then went from San Francisco to Cork, Ireland, with wheat and thereafter Glasgow, Scotland, to Otago, New Zealand, with a cargo of sheep; 1864 passage Boston to San Francisco in 141 days almost totally dismasted after rounding Cape Horn, damages repaired at San Francisco to tune of $8,900. Final American voyage arrived San Francisco from Boston in 120 days, thereafter sold to the Russian-American Fur Company (later the American Fur Company) without a name change, homeport San Francisco; later voyaged San Francisco to Sitka, Alaska, later from Sitka to Kronstadt, Russia. Disappears from registry after 1874.
- *Boston Light*, 1853 (Howe & Matthews incorrectly list as 1854), 1,154 tons, of medium model, built for Captain James Huckins & Sons. Early career details unknown, likely involved in direct trade with Far East or India. First passage out to California made in 1854 and 1855 in 103 days; second passage made in 1861, departing Boston, 163 days, battered off Cape Horn, hove to for eight days and forced back eastward with sails blown away and rudder damaged, again passed the cape but experienced violent weather that washed away her figurehead and forced her to jettison cargo, also experienced mutinous behavior by crew, mate stabbed to death, finally arrived November 1861. Later carried guano from McKean's Island to Mauritius arriving May 1862, then to India, Hong Kong, and back to India. Sold foreign at Bombay in January 1863 and renamed *Tulga*, continued in coastal Indian trade. Out of registry after 1870.
- *Golden Light*, 1854, 1,140 tons, of medium model, built for Captain James Huckins & Sons. Departed Boston for San Francisco on her maiden voyage February 12, 1853, subsequently struck by lightning at midnight on February 22 and set on fire; the crew worked to save their ship but aban-

doned the clipper at 6 P.M. The crew got off in five lifeboats, one boat with eight men was never seen again, all other hands saved; insurance loss on clipper and cargo was $288,000.
- *Bonita*, 1853, 1,127 tons, of medium model, designed by and built for Captain James Huckins. Made two California passages, her maiden voyage taking 141 days, her second in 1854 124 days. In 1856 arrived at London from Shanghai, from here sailed for Calcutta, India, with a cargo of railroad iron in early 1857. Subsequently put into Algoa Bay on the South African coast near Port Elizabeth in a sinking condition in June 1857, condemned and scrapped.
- *Cyclone*, 1853, 1,109 tons, of medium model, built for Curtis & Peabody. Employed in the California–Far East trade, maiden voyage out to San Francisco made in 114 days, her fastest passage, made two other California runs. In July 1863 sold foreign at Boston to British interests for $24,000, but with her original owners still listed, renamed *Avon*, now homeported at Hong Kong; subsequently owned by London interests after 1866, out of registry by 1874.
- *John Land*, 1853, 1,054 tons, of medium model, a sister ship of the *Winged Arrow*, built for Baker & Morrill. Employed in the California–Far East trade, maiden voyage to San Francisco made in 126 days, thereafter made three other California runs, her fastest being 102 days in 1858. Her second voyage to California was a disaster, departed July 1854 but forced into Valparaiso, Chile, in a leaking condition, subsequently repaired but leak continued, fell in with an American whaling ship which offered assistance only if the clipper crew would abandon their ship; this being refused the *Land* went to Tahiti via Nukahiva for repairs accompanied by the whaler, here repaired from December 1854 to April 1855 before proceeding to San Francisco, total passage 310 days; costs in salvage paid to the whaling ship owner and crew about $63,000. Yet another disastrous passage in 1859 and 1860 Boston to San Francisco, began to leak off Cape Horn and put into Valparaiso for repairs, which took about five months, subsequently arrived at San Francisco 270 days after leaving Boston. Later employed in the transatlantic and Far East trades. In early 1864 departed Newport, England, for New York but began to leak, subsequently abandoned at sea in March 1864 with eight feet of water in her hold and rising, crew rescued by a British bark.
- *Saracen*, 1854, 1,266 tons, built for Curtis & Peabody. Career details uncertain, made one California passage in 1854 or 1855, 147 days. Sold to San Francisco interests about 1862, disappears from American register after 1865; likely sold foreign with a change in name.
- *Grace Darling*, 1854, 1,197 tons, of medium model, built for Charles Fessendon of Boston, bought by Baker & Morrill of Boston in 1858 for $37,000. Maiden voyage out to California made in 143 days, subsequent fastest such run was 125 days. Also employed in the Far East and Indian trades. Made two wheat voyages to the UK, the first in 1861 for London, the next in 1863 for Liverpool. In 1868 sold to West Coast interests and employed in the Puget Sound lumber and coal trade. Final voyage departed Nanaimo, British Columbia, for San Francisco January 1878, sighted by a passing vessel during a heavy gale on January 18, thereafter went missing, thought to have foundered in the gale.
- *Starlight*, 1854, 1,153 tons, of medium model, built for Baker & Morrill. First employed in the California–Far East trade, made nine runs to San Francisco, fastest being 117 days, maiden voyage there in 118 days. In late 1861 sailed Puget Sound to Adelaide, Australia, while in port blown ashore during a heavy storm but got off without serious damage. From there loaded a cargo of horses in 1862 for Calcutta, India. In December 1864 sold at San Francisco for $34,000 to Peruvian interests and renamed *R. Protolongo*, subsequently employed in the coolie trade between China and Peru. Last visit to San Francisco made in early 1865, departed in ballast but loaded with $180,000 in treasure. Later career and fate unknown.
- *Cossack*, 1854, 586-ton bark, built for Curtis & Peabody. First employed in Lincoln's Line of Australian packets, career details uncertain. By 1858 owned by John Ellerton Lodge of Boston, likely employed in the Far

East trade like many of Lodge's other vessels. Last reported in 1863, possibly sold foreign and name changed.
- *Mameluke*, 1855, 1,303 tons, of medium model, built for Curtis & Peabody. Employed first in the California–Far East trade, maiden voyage to San Francisco with 76 passengers and 2,400 tons of cargo made in 139 days; later made four other California runs, best time 137 days in 1862 and 1863. Subsequently loaded guano at Callao, Peru, for the UK, there sold foreign to British interests and renamed *Milton*, employed in the transatlantic and Quebec lumber trade. Surveyed at Quebec in 1877, Hamburg, Germany, in 1878, disappears from register after 1879.
- *Fair Wind*, 1855, 1,299 tons, of medium model and a sister ship of *Mameluke*, built for Henry Hallett & Co. of Boston. Employed in the California–Far East trade, maiden voyage to San Francisco made in 138 days. Original commander, Captain Allen, subsequently died at Calcutta, India, in late 1856. Departed Boston for San Francisco in April 1857, forced into Rio de Janeiro due to her captain's illness, later made California in 146 sailing days. Later made several guano voyages. In January 1861 departed San Francisco for Baker's Island via Honolulu, arrived at the latter port in 8 days, 18 hours, the fourth best time ever, missing record by but 16 hours. Subsequently loaded guano for Hampton Roads, went ashore on Hog Island off the Chesapeake, got off and towed to New York for repairs. Thereafter put in the coal trade until being sold foreign at New York to British interests in 1866, continued on without a change in name. Last reported in 1875.
- *Vitula*, 1855, 1,188 tons, built for Williams & Daland of Boston. Made two California passages, best time 128 days. In 1859 sold to Samuel Reed of Boston. Final American voyage mid–1867, when bound New York to San Francisco put into Rio de Janeiro in distress, condemned and sold to British interests, subsequently repaired and renamed *Bessie & Annie*, later renamed *James Rowan*. Last reported in 1876.
- *Asa Eldridge*, 1856, 1,324 tons, of medium model, built for Henry Hallett & Co. Employed in the California–Far East trade, maiden voyage on the California run made in a 123 day passage in 1857, the fastest of her ten California runs. Made four guano voyages. In 1865 sold to W.F. Weld & Co. of Boston, sold foreign in 1873 to British interests in 1873 and renamed *Norfolk*, still afloat in 1880.
- *Joseph Peabody*, 1856, 1,198 tons, of medium model, built for Curtis & Peabody. Maiden passage to California in 145 days, subsequently involved in the guano, coal, and Far East trades. In early 1862 arrived at San Francisco in a leaking condition; later that same year loaded guano at the Chincha Islands for London, upon arrival was sold foreign to British interests and renamed *Dagmar*. By 1874 had been re-rigged as a bark, thereafter disappears from the register.
- *Alarm*, 1856, 1,184 tons, of medium model, built for Baker & Morrill. Maiden passage out to California in 130 days, carried guano back eastward. In mid–1860 made a long 182 day passage Boston to San Francisco, taking five attempts to clear Cape Horn, then loaded almost 1,800 tons of wheat for Liverpool. Thereafter in the English-Indian trade. In late 1863 departed Akyab, Burma, for Singapore, subsequently struck Preparis Reef on November 15, 1863, crew made it off the ship, which was abandoned, a total loss.
- *Memnon*, 1858, 789 tons, built for own interest and that of Hallett and Eldridge of Boston, the third clipper of this name (the first built at New York by Smith & Dimon). Sailed in Randolph Cooley's Merchant Express Line of San Francisco clippers in the 1860s, made one California passage prior to 1860, 159 days. Later owned by J. Henry Sears of Boston, by 1886 sold to West Coast interests, homeport San Francisco; out of registry after 1897.

Jotham Stetson (see Chelsea builders above) built one clipper at South Boston before his move to Chelsea in 1853.

- *Celestial Empire*, 1852, 1,630 tons, built for C. H. Parsons & Co. of New York. Made one California run of 146 days before 1860 and four more thereafter, last one in 1875, largely employed in the transatlantic trade throughout most of her career. Abandoned at sea February 1878 while bound Bremen, Germany, to New York.

Quincy

Deacon George Thomas, the Maine shipbuilder who launched the famed *Red Jacket* and other clippers at Rockland, Maine, before relocating to Quincy, built one medium clipper here. While this ship was not as notable as his Maine clippers, Thomas continued to build quality ships well into the 1870s. He first built on his own but by the mid–1870s partnered with Captain Isaac Taylor in the firm of Taylor & Thomas, with whom he had first worked up in Maine way back when he first began to build clipper ships. Several of his later productions are regarded as some of the finest sailing ships built in the post-clipper era, including *Red Cloud* (1877), *America* (1874) and *Triumphant* (1874).

- *King Philip*, 1854, 1,486 tons, American shipping registers credit Seccomb & Taylor as the builders, this ship not to be confused with the Maine-built clipper of the same name; this ship was also owned by Seccomb & Taylor and was early in her career, by 1858, sold foreign to British interests, homeport London. Later career details unknown, out of registry after 1868.

John Taylor (see above) apparently built one clipper at Quincy in 1856, though why he did so is unknown as he was firmly established at his Chelsea yard north of Boston. George Thomas is traditionally credited as this clipper's builder, but shipping registers clearly and consistently identify this clipper as being built at Quincy by J. Taylor. It may be that this vessel was really built by Captain Isaac Taylor and that John Taylor was mistakenly credited. Isaac Taylor would later become a partner of George Thomas at Quincy, which may be the basis for some of the confusion surrounding this ship's builder.

- *Logan*, 1856, 1,541 tons, built for William Whitlock, Jr., of New York. Employed in the California trade in the late 1850s, sailing in Sutton & Co.'s Dispatch Line between New York and San Francisco. From about 1859 to the end of her career employed in Whitlock's Havre line of packet ships; out of register after 1865.

Emery Sawyer built one small clipper here at his Quincy Point yard.

- *Richard Busteed*, 1857, 662 tons, built for Jacob Stanwood of Boston. Employed in the California trade during the 1860s and 1870s. Later owned at New York and put in the transatlantic trade between Hamburg, Germany, and other European ports and New York and Philadelphia; disappears from registry after 1879.

Kingston

Scituate native and itinerant shipbuilder Benjamin F. Delano built two clippers up in Medford (see above), but also built one clipper bark here for outside interests in 1852. This clipper is little known and even historian Carl Cutler mistakenly lists her as a Maine clipper. However, shipping registers clearly indicate that Delano was her builder and Kingston, Massachusetts, as her place of building. This bark is one of only two clippers to have been built between Boston and Cape Cod.

- *White Wing*, 1852, 293-ton bark, built for Thomas and John Dallett of Philadelphia. Employed in the Dallet's Red D Line of packets sailing between Venezuela and Philadelphia carrying soap, flour and other commodities outward bound, bringing back animal hides and coffee. Continued under same ownership until the mid–1860s, though by 1863 was registered under British flag at Turks Island by her original owners. Made three or four round trips yearly from 1861–1867 between Philadelphia and South American ports; disappears from registry after 1871.

Shipwright Nathaniel Drew (born ca. 1785) was likely the builder of this clipper bark, but her builder may also have been Nathaniel D. Drew (born ca. 1810), also a shipwright and presumably the elder Drew's son. The elder Drew had an estate valued at over $2,000 by 1850, a goodly sum for a builder of small vessels (mostly schooners), while the younger Drew's estate by this time was valued at $600. This bark has also often been incorrectly attributed to New York builders and the town of Kingston, New York, on the Hudson River. However, shipping registers clearly identify this bark as being built at

Kingston, Massachusetts. The Drew family was active in Kingston for many years, building ships here by 1713, including the brigantine *Independence*, which was built in 1776 and served in the Massachusetts State Navy during the American Revolution, and as late as 1874. The clipper bark below was one of the largest vessels ever built at Kingston, with only nine vessels exceeding her size, none of them measuring above 611 tons (Fairburn, p. 2885).

- *Messenger Bird*, 1852, 419-ton bark, built for Francis Danielson of Boston, by 1858 owned by her commanders, Captain Delee, and, later, Captain Russell, early on managed by Holmes, probably Alexander Holmes, a wealthy merchant of that town; disappears from register after 1863, career details uncertain, likely employed in the South American or Mediterranean trade.

East Dennis

The Shiverick brothers, David, Paul (born ca. 1813), and Asa, Jr. (born 1816), are important as the only builders of clipper ships on Cape Cod, putting over five such vessels from 1852 to 1856, and building twelve vessels overall from 1849 to 1863. Their original yard, located on Sesuit Creek, was established by their father, Asa Shiverick, after his arrival here from Falmouth during the War of 1812 and he built many small vessels beginning in 1815. Upon their coming of age, Asa, Jr., and David served their apprenticeships in Boston area shipyards, with the former going even farther afield to Maine to gain experience, while Paul learned the trade from his father. All three brothers would later continue to build small vessels in their father's yard, but after his retirement they moved the shipyard farther down the creek so that the larger vessels they wanted to build could more easily be launched. The building of their clipper ships was truly a community affair as all were financed and their sales arranged by Captain Christopher Hall of East Dennis, who also was part owner in several of the clippers. Another local man involved with these clippers was Prince Crowell, a noted captain turned merchant and ship owner. The timber for the Shiverick clippers, and their other vessels no doubt, was harvested by the brothers in Maine and other locales to the south. Though some of the smaller Shiverick-built vessels were rigged at East Dennis, all of the clippers were towed to Boston under temporary jury rig for complete rigging and final outfitting before heading off on their maiden voyages. After the clipper ship era had ended, the brothers would build at least one other ship that has nominally been rated a clipper, the 960-ton *Ellen Sears*, in 1862 before going their own separate ways in the maritime business; David Shiverick was a ship captain (retired by 1870), while Asa and Paul by the early 1860s had moved to Barnstable, both employed at the guano works located nearby at Woods Hole.

- *Hippogriffe*, 1852, 671 tons, built for Christopher Hall, Prince Crowell, and other local parties. Maiden voyage out to California made in 155 days, returning eastward with guano; later employed in the Indian and Cardiff, Wales, coal trade. In 1858 departed Boston for China, subsequently struck an uncharted rock in the China Sea, thereafter called Hippogriffe Rock, and proceeded to Hong Kong, here placed in drydock for repairs. Final American voyage late 1862 departed Cardiff for Hong Kong, and from there went to Calcutta, India, sold foreign to British interests in December 1863. Disappears from the registers after 1869.
- *Belle of the West*, 1853, 936 tons, of extreme model, designed by Samuel Pook, built for Christopher Hall and Glidden & Williams of Boston. Maiden voyage on the California run made in 132 days, in late 1854 voyaged London to Melbourne, Australia, later involved in the Indian trade. In 1864 sold foreign to Indian interests at Calcutta and renamed *Fiery Cross*, employed as a general trader on the coast of India. Lost in mid–1868, foundered in the Bay of Bengal while bound Calcutta to Muscat with a cargo of rice.
- *Kit Carson*, 1855, 997 tons, built for Prince Crowell and other local parties, employed in the California trade for two passages, best time 129 days, as well as that with India, the Far East, and made at least one guano voyage. By the early 1860s sold to New York interests. Said to have been sunk off Rio de Janeiro as a block ship during the War of the Triple Alliance fought between Paraguay, Brazil, and Argentina sometime

between 1865 and 1870 but this is either incorrect, or she was raised and repaired as shipping registers indicate the ship was sold to Captain J.W. Spencer in 1874 without a name change, homeport Port Gamble, Washington, likely here involved in the coal or lumber trade; out of American registry after 1882.

- *Wild Hunter*, 1855, 1,081 tons, built for Christopher Hall but soon sold to Bush & Wildes of Boston. First put in the California trade, maiden voyage to San Francisco in 112 days, then proceeding to Calcutta, India. In 1858 loaded coal at Cardiff, Wales, for Ceylon, from there went to Hong Kong via Burma and Singapore. In late 1859 and into 1860 departed Hong Kong for San Francisco, experienced heavy weather en route off Formosa and lost three men overboard. In early 1861 sailed New York to Liverpool, damaged while entering dock at the end of her voyage, was subsequently beached and repaired, most of her cargo being damaged. In late 1863 carried guano from Phoenix Island in the Pacific to England; in 1873 re-rigged as a bark, still Boston-owned. Disappears from the register after 1883.
- *Webfoot*, 1856, 1,091 tons, of medium model, built for Prince Crowell. Her maiden voyage to San Francisco in 1857, 119 days, was the fastest of her five California runs; also employed in the Indian and Australian trade. In April 1864 was voyaging London to Dunkirk, France, when she was stranded on a bank and badly damaged, subsequently towed to London and sold to British interests without a change in name; later re-rigged as a bark and homeported in Belfast, Ireland. In November 1886 departed Puget Sound with a cargo of lumber for Callao, Peru, subsequently began leaking off Cape Flattery and returned to port in distress and found to be afire below and beached, a total loss.

Fairhaven

Reuben Fish (born ca. 1801) is most noted for the whaling ships he built at this seafaring town just across the way from New Bedford, but he also built two clippers for interests in New Bedford. No matter what kind of ships he was building, Fish was generally considered to be one of "the finest ship designers and builders along this part of the coast" (Mendell, Jr., p. 23). By 1850 the Fish shipyard employed thirty men and had stockpiled some $8,000 worth of timber and other building supplies.

- *Sea Nymph*, 1853, 1,215 tons, of medium model, built for Edgar Mott Robinson of New Bedford. Maiden voyage New Bedford to New Orleans leaked badly due to a hole bored in her bottom; 1854 and 1855 made first California passage, arrived out in 145 days after being forced into Valparaiso for repairs, made the return eastward with a cargo of guano; another California passage in 1856 of 113 days. Final voyage in 1861 departed New York for San Francisco, subsequently went ashore near Point Reyes, just north of the Golden Gate on May 4, one man lost while ship was being abandoned; wreck and cargo subsequently sold for salvage rights and a portion of the latter recovered.
- *John Milton*, 1855, 1,445 tons, of medium model, built for George Hussey of New Bedford. Maiden voyage to California made in 136 days, delayed by heavy weather off Cape Horn, returned eastward with guano for Hampton Roads, Virginia; second California passage in early 1857 made in 149 days, upon arrival thirteen of the crew released for mutinous behavior. Thereafter proceeded to the Chincha Islands to load guano for Hampton Roads, there discharged her cargo and departed February 1858 for New York, when one day out was caught in a snowstorm that continued for several days, during which the clipper was driven ashore at Montauk Point, New York, the ship being quickly ground to pieces on impact, entire 26 man crew was lost, 21 of them buried close by at the Easthampton churchyard.

Mattapoisett

The Barstow shipyard here was one of the oldest in this seafaring town, established by Gideon Barstow after his arrival in town about 1765 from Hanover. By the 1820s, one of Gideon's grandsons, Captain Wilson Barstow (born ca. 1798), began building ships, first with the family firm of Gideon Barstow & Son, and by 1844 was operating his own shipyard on the original site. He built his last ship in 1866 before retiring from shipbuilding. Of Wilson Barstow, one historian has commented, "He was no businessman — he failed three times — but he hired the finest master builders available" (Mendell, Jr., p. 16). One of his ships built in 1852 was called "a beautiful clipper ship" by the *Whalemen's Shipping List* (August 3, 1852). The true clipper ship *John Milton*, built by Reuben Fish at Fairhaven, has sometimes been attributed incorrectly to Barstow.

- *Gay Head*, 1852, 389 tons, built for J.B. Wood & Co. of New Bedford. Intended for the sperm whale fishery, departed New Bedford September 1852 on maiden whaling voyage, returned home late June 1856 with over 1,500 barrels of sperm oil. Second voyage 1856 and 1860, during which second mate was killed. Lost on fifth whaling voyage, departed New Bedford late October 1870, trapped in the Arctic ice in 1871 and abandoned, later burned by native Eskimos.

The Holmes shipyard was one of the most important shipyards in Mattapoisett and was first established about 1814 by Josiah Holmes (1779–1859). From 1816 to 1823 Holmes built ships in partnership with the Barstow family (see above), but then the two went their separate ways. In 1841 Holmes' sons, Josiah, Jr., (born ca. 1812) and, after 1850, Jonathan (born ca. 1824), entered the business, and when the elder Josiah retired, the firm name changed to Josiah Holmes, Jr., & Brother. The firm built some 17 vessels from 1846 to 1867, when Josiah Jr. got out of the shipbuilding business (he was still active as a shipping agent). Jonathan continued his building career, launching five vessels, including the town's last whaler, the bark *Wanderer*, in 1878. Interestingly, Jonathan Holmes was employed by Reuben Fish at Fairhaven in 1850 and may have served his apprenticeship there. The Holmes yard launched one ship in 1852 that was called a medium clipper by local authorities.

- *Polar Star*, 1852, 475 tons, built for Charles R. Tucker & Co. of New Bedford.

SEA AND SHIP NEWS.

Latest from the Wreck John Milton—Eleven Bodies Found.

There have been found drifted up on the beach three more bodies, making the whole number thus far found of the wrecked with the ship *John Milton*, eleven. The bodies were all taken to East Hampton, where the Coroner has been holding inquests

Wreck of the *John Milton*, newspaper article. This Fairhaven-built clipper came to a bad end, being wrecked in a snow storm off Montauk, Long Island, on February 20, 1858, with the loss of her entire crew (*New York Times*, February 1858).

Departed on maiden whaling voyage for the Arctic in October 1852, returning home June 1856. Departed on third and final whaling voyage September 1860, subsequently lost on the Kamchatka Peninsula May 1861, some of the crew being drowned while trying to make shore in the first mate's boat.

Somerset

Captain James Madison Hood (1815–1871) built nine clipper ships and barks at his shipyard here located on Narragansett Bay. While these vessels were generally smaller in size, averaging less than 900 tons in size, several were noted for their speed and all were noted for their quality of construction. Hood had previously been a mariner and merchant ship captain (his commands including the sloops *Rose Bud* and *Independence*) involved in the coastal and West Indies trade, as were his father and brother, and also supplied transport services to the army during the Mexican-American War. In 1848 Hood turned to shipbuilding and would build some thirty vessels, including some small revenue cutters and lightships in addition to his clippers, before his shipyard caught fire in September 1854 and was totally destroyed. Captain Hood would subsequently move to Illinois by 1860 and made a living far from the sea as a farmer. While in Illinois, Hood became such a solid supporter of Abraham Lincoln that, after his election to a second term as president, Hood was appointed to the position of U.S. consul overseas in Siam, serving from 1865 to 1868 and subsequently returning stateside to live in Sycamore, Illinois. James Hood is not only noted for the fine ships he built, but also for the fact that he was the only Massachusetts clipper builder to sell all of his ships to out of state interests, all of them from New York. Of Hood's character, he was certainly an interesting one; one historian has said that he liked to make a fast buck, which his clipper creations certainly accomplished, and that he also seems to have been an avowed bachelor that liked younger women, evidence of which, perhaps, is the fact that his only companion in 1870 was a 26-year-old live-in housekeeper named Sarah.

- *Rosario*, 1850, 499-ton bark, built for A. & M. Howes of New York. Employed in the Mediterranean trade, homeport Malaga, Spain, by 1858, under original owners; subsequently sold foreign to Spanish interests by 1861. Out of registry prior to 1871.
- *Greenfield*, 1851, 560-ton bark, built for Wakeman & Dimon of New York. Full career details uncertain, employed in the California trade for four voyages New York to San Francisco; first voyage arrived out in October 1852 after a 122 day passage, second passage 130 days in 1853 and 1854, third passage 113 days in 1855, and final passage 1855–56 111 days. Was the first clipper to carry a California wheat cargo, loading 4,752 bags for New York in May 1855. By 1857 homeport was Southport, Connecticut, same owner; disappears from American registry after 1859.
- *Governor Morton*, 1851, 1,430 tons, of medium model, built for Handy & Everett of New York, intended for the Handy & Everett Line of packets running between New York and Liverpool, however first put in the California trade. Maiden voyage out in 125 days, later made twelve other California runs, best time 104 days in 1855. Engaged in a variety of trades during her long career and was a well-regarded ship. Made one coolie voyage, China to Havana in 1859 and 1860. In 1861 collided with another vessel while bound London for New York. In 1862 while bound New York to San Francisco forced to put into Montevideo, Uruguay, due to a severe leak, was repaired and continued the voyage but damaged off Cape Horn and lost two men overboard, total passage time 279 days, damage repairs cost over $27,000. In 1863 rebuilt at New Bedford, Massachusetts, at a cost of $30,000; on her 1868 California run also damaged and forced to put into Rio de Janeiro, repaired at a cost of $7,000. In July 1877 loaded cotton for the UK and was anchored at South West Pass on the Mississippi River when struck by lightning and burned to the water's edge, only a small part of the cargo salvaged. Remains of ship raised and towed to New Orleans, there subsequently libeled by the tugs that had helped in salvage efforts and sold for scrap.
- *Raven*, 1851, 712 tons, of extreme model, built for Crocker & Warren of New York. Employed in the California–Far East trade, arrived at San Francisco on her maiden voyage in November 1851 after a passage of 106 days, beating the larger clippers *Typhoon* and *Sea Witch*; made three other California runs 1852 through 1855 in 122, 119, and 124 days. Thereafter employed in the direct Far East trade with voyages out to Singapore, Batavia, and Hong Kong. In 1863 sailed New York for San Francisco but put into Rio de Janeiro in a leaking condition, condemned and sold. Subsequently re-rigged as a bark and renamed *Bessie*, homeport Rio; later owned by Lisbon, Portugal, interests. In 1875 registered as the bark *Mondego*, after this date disappears from the registers.
- *Rip Van Winkle*, 1851, 1,095 tons, built for Eagle & Hazard of New York. Career details uncertain, probably sailed in the Eagle Line of packets in the cotton trade between New York and Mobile, Alabama, and the transatlantic trade between New York and Liverpool. Made at least one voyage Liverpool to Australia in 1852, arriving at Melbourne in October 1852 after a passage of 70 days, the fourth fastest on record. Possibly sold foreign before 1857 with a change in name.
- *Archer*, 1852, 1,096 tons, built for Crocker & Warren. Employed in the California and Far East trades, made eleven voyages to San Francisco from 1853 to 1872, best time 106 days, accomplished twice, the first time in 1854. Rebuilt in Boston in 1862, cost $25,000. In 1865 after arriving China from New York put aground on a sandbar by the pilot while going up the River Min. In 1865 while bound New York to San Francisco

damaged off Cape Horn and struck by lightning, passage 144 days. In 1866 battered by a severe storm after departing New York, put into Boston, damage to ship and cargo $12,000. Later re-rigged as a bark, foundered at sea February 1880 while bound New York to Le Havre, France, crew rescued by a passing steamer.

- *Pathfinder*, 1852, 373-ton bark, built for Ogden & Haynes of San Francisco. Made one California passage of 151 days on maiden voyage, thereafter employed as the inaugural ship in the Ogden & Haynes Line of Hong Kong packets up to 1859. Later career uncertain, sold to German interests by 1861, homeport Hamburg; disappears from registry after 1869.
- *Mischief*, 1853, 561 tons, of extreme model, built for Merrill & Townsend of New York. Maiden voyage on the California run 133 days, forced into Valparaiso, Chile, in a leaking condition, upon arrival at San Francisco sold for $22,000. Subsequently employed in the Far East trade; while bound Foo Chow, China, to New York in 1854 crew mutinied while transiting the Straits of Sunda. In early 1855 voyaged New York to Bremen, Germany, there sold foreign to Danish interests and renamed *Sleipner*, homeport Copenhagen; disappears from registry after 1877.
- *Skylark*, 1853, 1,209 tons, of extreme model, built for Crocker & Warren. Employed in the California and Far East trades, made six California runs, best time her maiden passage in 1853 and 1854, 117 days. Final American voyage departed San Francisco for Baker's Island to load guano for Falmouth, England, in 1864. Thereafter sold to German interests, homeport Hamburg, renamed *Albertine* by 1867; out of registry after 1874.

Swansea

The experienced shipbuilder Mason Barney (ca. 1784–1868) built ships here on the Palmer River for many years beginning about 1802. Prior to his coming of age, the yard was operated by his father, Peleg Barney, and primarily built fishing boats and other small river craft. However, Mason Barney had bigger plans and built vessels not just for local waters, but bigger ships for ocean commerce. His operations in the Barneyville section of Swansea (the first Barneys arrived here in the late 1690s) were large in scope, employing many of his fellow townsmen in shipbuilding and its allied trades, and by 1850 he had amassed a solid personal wealth to the tune of at least $30,000. Overall, Barney would build some 137 ships big and small, including one clipper, before finally retiring from the business, likely because of the financial panic, in 1859.

- *Sparkling Wave*, 1853, 665 tons, of medium model, built for Eben Balch of Boston but quickly sold to New Orleans interests in early 1854 for $50,000. Made two California runs, both times forced to put into ports en route, first in 1855 bound Philadelphia to San Francisco, put in at Montevideo, Uruguay, for reasons unstated, total sea time 122 days, but only 61 days from Montevideo, an all-time record; in 1860 sailed New York to San Francisco in total of 324 days, forced to put into Rio de Janeiro in distress, cargo discharged and repairs made, thereafter a long 162 day run from Rio. Afterwards largely employed in the transatlantic and Indian trade. In June 1864 sold foreign at London and continued under same name; out of registry after 1871.

Rhode Island

Like the other coastal New England states, Rhode Island has a long history of shipbuilding, dating back to the days before the American Revolution when the great commercial city of Newport was also one of our nation's busiest ports. By the 1840s, however, most of the ships built in the state were small trading or fishing vessels, though a few more sizeable ships, all under 700 tons, were built before the clippers came along. When the demand for clippers exploded in the early 1850s, several Rhode Island builders at Warren and one at Providence were able to gain some business, with most of their ships going to New York and other outside interests. It is interesting to note that all of this state's clippers were built in less than a two year span from 1853 to 1854 and none were of the extreme type. The best of the five Rhode Island clippers by far was the *Lookout*; this clipper was a good carrier and a well-built ship that had a long life. The ship, though built for the Australian trade, was used extensively in the California trade and was a popular ship, making sixteen such passages, her fastest being a very respectable 108 days.

Providence

The firm of Allen & Stimson (also given as Simpson) in this city built several vessels in the 1850s, including one clipper. The principles in this enterprise were shipbuilder Francis Allen, and his partner was Charles Stimson. The yard was probably located at the foot of East Street, based on period city directory information, but little is known about these builders.

- *Haidee*, 1854, 396 tons, built for Bucklin & Crane of New York and local interests. Put in the China trade but said to be a very expensive ship to operate. Later used as a South American trader, sold to New York–based parties of Portuguese nationality and converted to a slave ship by 1857 and made several slave voyages in 1857 and 1858; departed Cuba in September 1858 after last such voyage empty and without clearance papers, subsequently scuttled off Montauk Point, New York, by her captain and crew with a false name painted on her stern. Crew escaped and made shore at Montauk in two lifeboats, later on some were captured and brought to trial for their slaving activities.

Warren

Chase & Davis were the state's most experienced clipper builders, putting over three such vessels at this well established maritime port on Narragansett Bay. The Chase portion of the partnership consisted of master mariner Phillip Chase (born 1810 in Massachusetts) and worth $10,000 by 1860, along with his son Hiram (born 1836 in Massachusetts), a shipwright by 1860. Shipwright Benjamin Davis (born 1827 in Massachusetts), a new arrival in Warren by 1850, may have been the junior partner.

- *Gem of the Sea*, 1853, 372-ton bark, likely built on speculation, soon sold to New York interests for the Australian trade, possibly in Cameron's Dispatch Line. Made a record passage of 35 days Port Phillip, Australia, to Callao, Peru, in 1854. Later owned by Samuel Reed & Co. of Boston and thereafter by Lewis & Folger of same; repaired at New Bedford in 1868, out of register after 1870.
- *Lookout*, 1853, 1,291 tons, built for E. Buckley & Sons of New York, said to have been designed for the Australia trade but used extensively in the California trade making sixteen such voyages. In October 1870 on her last California voyage severely damaged and had to put back in at the Falkland Islands for repairs; upon arrival at San Francisco subsequently sold for use in the coal and lumber trade. Wrecked September 1872 while bound from Shanghai to Puget Sound during a storm.
- *Mary Ogden*, 1854, 969 tons, a ship not a bark as some sources report, built for G. Buckley of New York. Full career details unknown, employed in the California trade; surveyed at San Francisco in 1866. Also employed in the transatlantic trade with Liverpool; out of registry after 1876.

Shipwright Daniel Foster (born 1826 in Massachusetts) built Rhode Island's largest clipper, but little is known of his career.

- *Pride of the Ocean*, 1853, 1,525 tons, built for Cady, Aldrich, & Reid of Providence; sold to British interests in April 1854 and renamed *Belgravia*, homeport Liverpool. Later career details unknown, out of register after 1878.

Westerly

Silas Greenman, Jr. (born 1797), and his son George (born 1826) built one clipper here on the Pawcatuck River. Silas Greenman got his start here in his father's shipyard, which began building in the 1780s, but in the 1820s moved to Mystic, Connecticut, to build ships, but returned to Westerly in 1833 to run his father's old yard, leaving the Mystic yard in the hands of his younger brothers George and Clark Greenman (see below). Master ship carpenter Silas Greenman built many ships at Westerly until his death in 1881.

- *Island City*, 1852, 700 tons, built for Stanton & Thompson of New York; nothing is known of this vessel's career.

Connecticut

While the great ports of New York and Boston received more than their fair share of patronage when it came to the building of clipper ships, the larger state sandwiched between them was also an important producer of ships. The maritime history of the Nutmeg State in fact dates back to colonial times, and even into the 1830s the state was second only to New York in the building of sailing ships for the packet trade (Fairburn, p. 2843). Additionally, the state was also famed for its whaling ships operating out of such ports as Stonington, the home of famed clipper captain and designer Nathaniel B. Palmer, New London, and others. While the Connecticut River area produced many of the pre–1840s packets, the place where most of the large scale building took place after this time was the more easterly area around Mystic and New London. It was here, at Groton that the largest ship ever built in America up to that time was launched, a 720-ton ship built for the Royal Navy in 1723. The area was also known for building at least one fast packet; the 337-ton *Crisis* was put over in 1819 at Norwich for the London Black X Line. However, the greatest producer of clipper ships was the fine port of Mystic, several miles from the ocean coast on the Mystic River. Here was where twenty clippers were launched by five builders, the most prominent being Charles Mallory, who launched eight clippers, followed by George Greenman & Co., with five clippers to their credit. In fact, all but two of Connecticut's twenty-two clippers were built at Mystic, with the others being built farther west on or near the Connecticut River, neither of them significant vessels. As discussed previously, the clippers produced in Connecticut were a bit unusual in that while ten of them went to New York interests, the others were owned and operated by local interests, a higher percentage than those clippers built in any other state excepting Massachusetts and New York. A question of interest posed by one maritime historian involves two Connecticut builders who built the most important of the flyers produced here, the *David Crockett*, built by George Greenman, and the famed *Andrew Jackson*, built by Irons & Grinnell. Historian William A. Fairburn states that "it is surprising" that these builders "should turn out extraordinarily fast and successful clipper ships considering their very limited experience in this line and their lack of technical knowledge in the realm of naval architecture" (Fairburn, p. 2857). Fairburn goes on to assert that these ships were probably designed in some form by Samuel Pook based on plans provided by him to New York owners that did not wish to contract with Boston builders. This assertion may or may not be true, but there seems to be no documentary evidence to back this up, other than the fact that both ships were of identical tonnage. As to the qualifications of the builders mentioned in this connection, Greenman learned his trade from his father, who had been building ships at his own yard in Rhode Island since the time of the American Revolution and had himself been a shipbuilder since the 1830s, as had Dexter Irons. Given this background, and viewed in comparison with the training of clipper builders in other states, there seems to be no reason to dismiss the qualification of these builders that produced two of the most significant ships launched in the clipper ship era. Another interesting note in this regard is the fact that noted clipper builder Charles Mallory himself bought one of the Greenman-built clippers later on in the ship's career, perhaps the only instance where one clipper builder invested in a ship built by his main rival!

The following are the most important of the Connecticut clippers;

- *Andrew Jackson*: built by Irons & Grinnell, this clipper was a good carrier *and* a fast ship, beating the *Flying Cloud*'s record on the California run to set the all time record for any wooden sailing ship.
- *David Crockett*: built by George Greenman, this clipper was well-built (not bad for a builder with "very limited experience," as discussed above), sailing into the 1890s, and a good carrier that made many California voyages, her fastest being a 103 day passage when she was seventeen years old.
- *Twilight*: one of the last true clippers to be built, this Charles Mallory production was indicative of the good ships that came from his yard. She made a California passage in under 101 days on her maiden voyage and had a long life.

Mystic

Charles Mallory got his start her early on working as a sailmaker in 1817, but soon turned to the business of owning and managing ships in the early 1820s, and by the early 1840s he had given up the sailmaking trade and was heavily invested in the whaling trade. Mallory built his first substantial vessel in 1849 and would soon enter the clipper building business in a big way. In 1853 Mallory bought the Forsyth & Morgan shipyard on Appleman's Point to expand his operations. While Mallory certainly knew the shipping business inside and out and was one of the most astute businessmen in the shipping industry of his time, he did have some help on the building end of things; both John and Peter Forsyth served as master builders for him in the construction of his clippers. After the end of the clipper ship era, the Mallory yard continued for many years and turned to building steamships when the age of sail was coming to an end.

- *Eliza Mallory*, 1851, 649 tons, built for New York interests. Found to be unsuitable due to her small size for the California trade, likely employed as a general trader. Out of American registry after 1859, likely sold foreign with a change in name.
- *Charles Mallory*, 1852, 698 tons, built for own account. Made one California passage of 115 days in 1852 and 1853. Wrecked on the coast of Brazil in June 1853 while bound from Honolulu to New London with a cargo of whale oil, crew saved, part of cargo salvaged.
- *Hound*, 1853, 714 tons, built for own account. Early career uncertain, later sailed in Wells & Emanuel's Dispatch Line on the California run, made a slow voyage of 343 days from New York to San Francisco in 1857 and 1858 after putting into Rio de Janeiro for repairs. Sold foreign by Mallory in October 1863 at Liverpool, out of registry after 1871.
- *Pampero*, 1853, 1,375 tons, of extreme model, built for J. Bishop of New York. Employed on the California–Far East trade routes, maiden voyage to San Francisco in 109 days. In 1861 sold to the U.S. government and converted to a 4th class warship, said to be out of naval service by late 1866 and sold at New York in 1867 for $6,000, but still appears in shipping registers through 1871 as being government owned, afterwards disappears from register.
- *Elizabeth F. Willets*, 1854, 825 tons, built for own account. Put on the California–Far East trade routes, maiden voyage to California a very creditable 118 day passage. In 1858 carried gold miners to Fraser River, British Columbia. In 1859 made another fast California run of 111 days. Final U.S. voyage New York to Shanghai in early 1863, sold there, later career unknown.
- *Mary L. Sutton*, 1856, 1,448 tons, of medium model, built for own account. Employed largely in the California trade; maiden voyage to California made in 111 days, with a record run of 17 days from the South Pacific to the equator. Also made a 106 day California run in 1860 and 1861 and a 114 day run in 1863. Ashore at Baker's Island while loading guano due to storm in November 1864, a total loss.
- *Twilight*, 1857, 1,482 tons, of medium model, built for her commander, Captain Gurdon Gates. Put in the California trade and made a maiden passage out in several hours under 101 days in 1858, followed by a 114 day passage in 1859 and 109 days in 1861. Sold at San Francisco in 1863 to Peruvian parties, subsequently renamed *Compania Maritima del Peru, No. 1*, and put in the coolie trade; soon after sold at Macao to Portuguese parties and renamed *Dom Pedro 1st*. Later, by 1877, sailed under the Costa Rican flag as the *Hermann*. Suffered severe storm damage in February 1877 while bound Callao, Peru, to San Francisco, subsequently sold for scrap in May 1877 for $4,575, later towed to Sausalito and broken up and burned for her metal fittings.
- *Haze*, 1859, 862 tons, built for own account. Sailed in Comstock's Clipper Line for California in the 1860s, later employed as a general trader, still owned by Mallory in 1880, re-rigged as a bark by 1881. Sold foreign to German interests in 1884, last surveyed at Boston in early 1886. Subsequently lost at sea, circumstances uncertain, in December 1886.

George Greenman (born 1806) & Co. was formed in 1833, but really began in 1824 when Silas Greenman, Jr., moved from Westerly, Rhode Island, to establish a second family yard here. When Silas returned to Westerly in 1833 to continue his father's business, his younger brothers George and Clark, and by 1838

Thomas, took over the business. Here, the Greenmans, with George the controlling partner, built 66 sailing vessels and 28 steamships from 1833 to 1878, including five clippers. The Greenmans built at several yards on the Mystic River, finally ending up some miles downstream at Adams Point where they could build more sizeable ships. Their most famous production, the *David Crockett*, was the largest sailing ship ever built in Connecticut up to that time, and all the Greenman clippers went to New York owners, including one company that bought four of them.

- *David Crockett*, 1853, 1,679 tons, built for Handy & Everett of New York. Originally intended as a New York–Liverpool packet ship with continued service to India, later employed in the California trade from 1857 to 1883. Maiden voyage to Liverpool; first California voyage in 1857, passage time 122 days, subsequently made 24 more California runs through 1883, fastest passage 103 days in 1871 and 1872, this after nineteen years of hard driving service. In 1889 cut down and re-rigged as a bark and operated in Atlantic waters. In 1890 was sold and sent to Philadelphia to be cut down into a barge, employed carrying coal between Massachusetts and Maine ports. Out of registry after 1898.
- *Belle Wood*, 1854, 1,399 tons, built for John McGaw of New York. Likely employed first as a general trader. Sold foreign at Liverpool in 1862 to Williams & Guion for service in their Black Star Line of packets operating between New York, Liverpool, and Queenstown, Ireland. Out of registry after 1875.
- *Leah*, 1855, 1,428 tons, built for John McGaw of New York. Departed for San Francisco early January 1856 on maiden voyage, subsequently went missing with all hands en route.
- *Atmosphere*, 1856, 1,486 tons, of medium model, built for John McGaw of New York. After a maiden round-trip to England put on the California run in 1857 and made one long passage. By 1859 put in the India trade, went ashore late 1860 but got off; in 1861 at Calcutta collided with another vessel and lost her figurehead. Sold foreign to British interests without a name change in 1863. Lost off Brazil in 1882 while bound Liverpool for Valparaiso, Chile, after colliding with another British ship.
- *Prima Donna*, 1858, 1,529 tons, of medium model, built for John McGaw of New York. From 1858 to 1877 made 14 California runs, the shortest being 118 days. By 1875 owned by Charles Mallory of Mystic; by 1878 in the Far East trade. In 1883 sold foreign without a name change to Austrian interests and hailing from Trieste; out of registry after 1888.

The firm of Irons & Grinnell was yet another well-established ship builder in this town that produced some fine clippers, among them one of the fastest of all, the *Andrew Jackson*. Ship joiner Dexter Irons (born 1810 in Rhode Island) may have apprenticed in the Greenman yard, given his origin, while shipwright Amos Grinnell (born 1812) was a native of Connecticut. Irons himself began building on his own in the 1830s but in the 1840s partnered with Grinnell, who was also a shipowner. They later moved their operations to a larger yard located at Pistol Point, thus enabling them to build their big clippers. Dexter Irons subsequently died at the beginning of the Civil War, but Grinnell continued to build ships into the 1870s in partnership with others. The site of the Irons & Grinnell shipyard would continue to build ships until the close of World War I.

- *Harriet Hoxie*, 1851, 678 tons, built for Post, Smith & Co. of Mystic. Made three California runs from 1852 to 1855; sold foreign to Belgium interests at Antwerp in 1859.
- *Electric*, 1853, 1,274 tons, of medium model, built for G. Adams of New York, later sold to the Gerry family of New York. First operated in the transatlantic trade, made her first California run in 1854 and 1855, arriving in 116 days. Sold to German interests at Hamburg in 1860 without a name change and thereafter traded between that city and New York. Went ashore at Egg Harbor, New Jersey, with 350 passengers in December 1868 but got off and repaired at New York. Abandoned at sea in a leaking condition November 1872 while bound Hamburg to New York.
- *Harvey Birch*, 1854, 1,482 tons, built for J.H. Brower & Co. of New York. Generally employed in the transatlantic trade but made three California passages, her best

being 123 days. Captured and burned by the Confederate raider *Nashville* in November 1862 while bound Le Havre, France, to New York.
- *Andrew Jackson,* 1855, 1,679 tons, of medium model, originally named *Belle Hoxie* and perhaps built on speculation, but soon sold to J.H. Brower & Co. of New York and her name changed. Put in the California trade and made seven runs, including the record of 89 days, 4 hours, and ones of 105, 101, 103, and 114 days, also made one very fast transatlantic passage from Liverpool to New York in 15 days. Commanded by Captain John "Jack" Williams from her launching until 1860. Sold to British interests in 1863 without a name change and employed in the Far East trade. Lost December 1868 after hitting a reef in the Gaspar Straits while bound from Shanghai to the United Kingdom.

The firm of Maxson, Fish & Co. built two clippers at their yard in West Mystic. William Maxson (born 1816 at Westerly, Rhode Island) was a master shipbuilder who may have apprenticed at the Greenman yard (or even worked for them as a master builder) before establishing his yard in partnership with Captain Nathan G. Fish (born 1804) by 1854. Both of their clippers were built for N.G. Fish & Co., prominent shipowners in Mystic. The yard continued in operation into the 1860s, building a number of steamships and some notable sailing ships of the downeaster type. By 1860, both men had done quite well for themselves; William Maxson had some $10,000 in assets, while Captain Fish had holdings worth $35,000.

- *B.F. Hoxie,* 1854, 1,387 tons. Made four California runs, employed at least in part in the whale oil trade between Hawaii and Connecticut; full career details uncertain. Destroyed by the Confederate raider *Florida* in June 1862.
- *Aspasia,* 1856, 632 tons. Made two California runs from 1856 to 1858 in slow time. Full career details uncertain, later sold to Bucklin & Crane of New York and possibly put in the China trade in which they were invested. Sold foreign to British interests in 1863, out of registry after 1865.

Mason C. Hill (born ca. 1820) was another builder active at Mystic early on in his career. He constructed one clipper here; though this is sometimes credited to Charles Mallory, it was probably built for him by Hill at the Mallory yard. By 1860, Hill had moved from his native state to Jersey City, New Jersey, where he continued his career as a shipbuilder, having assets of $6,000 in 1860.

- *Alboni,* 1852, 917 tons, designed by Hill, soon after launching was sold to James Bishop & Co. of New York. Largely employed in the California–Far East trade, maiden voyage on the California run made in 131 days. Her 1855 passage to San Francisco was a difficult one taking 165 days, with several men lost overboard and much of the rest of the crew incapacitated. By the early 1860s engaged in the European trade and sold foreign in 1863 to German interests, renamed *Elsie Ruger,* and employed in the same trades. Out of registry by 1874, final fate unknown.

Fairfield

The firm of Hall & Teague built one clipper here in the Black Point part of town (now a part of Bridgeport). I've been unable to ascertain the principals of this firm with certainty, but possible candidates include Henry Hall (born 1812), a wealthy grocer and merchant, and shipmaster John Teague (born 1821 in England).

- *Black Hawk,* 1853, 1,100 tons, built for the builder's interest, the first clipper to bear this name, originally named *Chief of Clippers.* Dismasted during a storm and foundered in 1854. Not to be confused with the William Webb–built New York clipper of the same name.

New Haven

The firm of Lane & Jacobs built one reputed clipper here. Ebenezer Lane (born 1802) was the principal in this firm which put over their vessels near Union Wharf. His partner may have been oysterman John Jacobs (born 1819), but this is not certain.

- *Gazelle,* 1852, 253-ton bark, 108 feet long, 10.3 feet depth, 25.3 feet beam, built for local owners H. Trowbridge & Sons of New Haven. Possibly used in the West Indies trade, this "shapely, fast craft" (Fairburn, p.

2847) owned by the Trowbridges its entire career. Out of registry after 1883.

New York

The Empire State was true to her name during the clipper ship era, being the center for much of the trade that was conducted by the clippers and was both a starting point from which many cargos were shipped, as well as a final destination for many clipper voyages emanating from elsewhere, both in the United States as well as from all over the world. For reasons and circumstances previously discussed, the first true clippers were built at New York, the state's shipyards acknowledged as being the best in the nation, and many clippers were built here at the height of the California gold rush. Indeed, by the year 1850 the number of shipyard workers was close to 3,000 and by 1852 was even higher. Interestingly, the business of building ships in New York wasn't always so large; prior to 1790 few shipyards were located here and, despite its advantageous location, shipbuilding simply was not an important industry. However, this all changed with the growing European and China trade in the late 18th century and, with the establishment of regularly scheduled sailings in the packet trade, exploded by the 1820s. Not only would New York's tonnage output increase dramatically (being the center of ship production for the packet and transatlantic trade), but so would her leadership in the field of building fast ships also greatly increase by the 1830s and by the 1840s was indisputable. While Boston-built clippers would soon wrest the speed crown away from New York, it was New York's pioneer clippers that set a high bar early on for performance.

Early on, New York builders led the way in clipper production, but this would change drastically by 1854; while the demand for the clippers was great, New York builders were so busy that they could not always deliver the clippers that the city's merchants were clamoring for, thus resulting in contracts being signed for ships built elsewhere in Massachusetts, Maine, and New Hampshire. In fact, as one historian writes, New York yards were so busy "during this boom period" that in order to "make room for the laying of another keel" they launched "what was complete on the stocks in one-two order, and in one-two-three order, and that in all probability has never been excelled" (Morrison, p. 121).

These multiple launchings occurred not just in the building of the clippers, but also with the many steamships that were also being built in New York, thus highlighting yet another clipper supply issue that New York builders had to contend with. This was the simple fact that, unlike what was going on in New England, the New York yards were not just concerned with sailing vessels, but also they had many contracts for building steamships, thereby adding to their heavy workload. As a result of these business conditions, only fifteen clippers were built at New York after 1853, as compared with the 82 clippers built in the greater Boston area (including Medford) from 1854 to 1859, equaling the number built at Newburyport, Massachusetts, and only three more than were built at Portsmouth, New Hampshire, during the same period. Further adding to the workload of the New York shipyards was the huge repair business in which they were also engaged. With, perhaps, the exception of San Francisco, no port was busier when it came to repairing and refitting clippers, either before they began their journeys, or after they arrived in port from San Francisco, the Far East, Europe, and all points in between. Indeed, this part of the shipbuilding trade, including hull repair, repairing or replacing metal work, and rigging work, was one of the most lucrative, and there were likely many builders engaged strictly in repair work who never built a clipper on their own. One such example is that of the firm of Sneden & Whitlock, which rebuilt the fire-damaged McKay clipper *Great Republic* in 1854.

Because of the time period when New York builders were most active, over half of the 67 clippers built here were of the extreme model, a true reflection of the early California boom years when speed was the overriding consideration. Of the fourteen builders of clipper ships in New York, the leader was William Webb, who put over fourteen clippers (ten of them of extreme model), closely followed by the Westervelt family, builder of twelve clippers (eight of them of extreme model), and the Bell family with nine clippers (all but one of the extreme type). The other notable clipper builders in New York include the firms of Roosevelt & Joyce, with seven to their credit, and Smith & Dimon and Perrine, Patterson & Stack, each with six clippers to their credit. The last listed of these firms is notable as the builder of the first medium clipper, the 1851-built *John Stuart*, built in the city, primarily for the European trade. Noticeably absent among the city's clipper builders after 1850 was the pioneering firm of Dimon & Smith, builders of *Rainbow* and *Sea Witch*; after launching several clippers in 1850, they were generally concerned with steamship production until their retirement from the shipbuilding business altogether. Similarly, while builder Thomas Collyer put over several clippers, two of them small barks, he was best known for his steamship production.

The honors for building New York's largest clipper go to Jacob Bell, whose 2,045-ton *Trade Wind*, an ill-fated ship, was only one of two clippers built here exceeding 2,000 tons in size, the other being Webb's 2,007-ton *Challenge*, also an ill-fated clipper. The smallest clippers built at New York were of the clipper bark class, they being the 350-ton *Flying Cloud* (Perrine, Patterson & Stack) in 1853 and the 387-ton *Dawn* (Thomas Collyer) in 1857, this last bark being little known today but somewhat famed in her day as a speedster. As to speed, much as already been discussed about the performance of the New York–built clippers, and though the Boston-built clippers of Donald McKay tend to overshadow their performance, there are many New York clippers in the record books that rank among the fastest ships of the decade. The following clippers are the most significant of the ships built here during the clipper ship era:

- *Sea Witch*: a pioneering clipper that set the all-time record on the Hong Kong to New York run even before the clipper ship era was in full stride.
- *Young America*: a well-designed clipper, the hallmark of builder William Webb, and a versatile ship that combined speed, carrying capacity, and a long lasting career.
- *Comet*: another outstanding Webb-built clipper that was one of the fastest clippers afloat.
- *Challenge*: yet another Webb-built clipper whose life story is perhaps the most interesting of all the New York clippers and one that illustrates in stark detail many aspects that defined the clipper ship era, both good and bad.
- *Contest*: though not as sharply built as many of her peers, this Westervelt production was also renowned for her speed.
- *Sweepstakes*: another fast ship from the Westervelts, this clipper made one of the fastest passages of all-time on the California run, bested by only six other ships.
- *Oriental*: this Jacob Bell production was a pioneer in the China–England tea trade, setting the bar for the later participation of American clippers *and* a great influence in the design of the British tea clippers of the 1850s.
- *N.B. Palmer*: one of the fastest and most long-lived of the American clipper fleet, and one of the consistently fastest vessels in the China trade.
- *Ino*: this diminutive and long-lived clipper is indicative of the ships built in New York by her lesser-known builders. This clipper was rakish in look, heavily sparred, and quite fast, very active in the Far East trade.
- *David Brown*: this Roosevelt & Joyce production was a fast one on the California run, making a maiden voyage passage in under 100 days.
- *Rainbow*: this pioneer ship, considered by many to be the first clipper ship ever, was fast in her day and embodied the principles, sharp built and heavily sparred, of the California clippers that succeeded her.

Borough of Manhattan

William Webb (1816–1899) was the premier shipbuilder in the entire greater New York area, renowned for his well designed and fast sailing ships. His career has previously been discussed at length, but it is here appropriate to state that he ranks, with Donald McKay, as the one of the greatest clipper ship builders ever, and was certainly the more technically proficient of the two builders. Webb was very active in the early 1850s, when he built eleven clippers (five of them in 1851), but from 1854 onward he produced only three such vessels.

- *Celestial*, 1850, 860 tons, of extreme model, built for Bucklin & Crane of New York. Intended for the California–Far East trade, maiden voyage to San Francisco made in 104 days, her cargo including 5,000 cigars loaded just before her sailing date. Later active in the China–England tea trade in 1852 and 1853, and last in 1857; sold foreign to Spanish interests in 1858. Still afloat and operating out of New York in 1861; further career details unknown.

- *Gazelle*, 1851, 1,244 tons, of extreme model, the sharpest ship launched by Webb (against his own advice), built for and on a model proposed by her owners, Taylor & Merrill (both former sea captains) of New York. Maiden voyage to California made in 135 days, her best subsequent California run was 114 days in 1854. During 1852 California run collided with a Spanish ship but continued on under jury rig. In late 1854 while bound San Francisco to Hong Kong was hit by a typhoon and nearly sunk, 16 of her 189 Chinese passengers being drowned, proceeded under jury rig and severely reduced provisions, finally towed into Hong Kong a floating wreck, condemned and sold for $13,500. Subsequently repaired and renamed *Cora* and sold to Peruvian interests, later put in the guano and coolie trade. By 1861 was sold to British interests and renamed *Harry Pudemsey*, hailing port Liverpool, later career unknown.
- *Challenge*, 1851, 2,007 tons, of extreme model, built for N.L. & G. Griswold of New York. Intended for the California and Far East trade, said to have been "fitted with too much sail at the dictation of her first commander" (Dunbaugh & Thomas, p. 186), Captain Robert Waterman. First voyage to California made in 109 days, a passage highlighted by a mutiny and the deaths of many crewmen. Subsequently voyaged to Hong Kong, coming back to San Francisco with over 550 Chinese coolies. Late in 1852 employed in the China–England tea trade, later employed in the coolie trade to Australia and Cuba. Late 1861 sailed from Hong Kong to Bombay, India, via Singapore, arriving in a leaking condition, sold foreign to British interests and renamed *Golden City*, homeport Hong Kong and continued in China and India trade. Later sold and homeported in South Shields, England. In 1876 wrecked on the French coast after her rudder was damaged and she went adrift in the English Channel while bound UK to Calcutta, India.
- *Comet*, 1851, 1,836 tons, of extreme model, built for Bucklin & Crane of New York. Intended for the California–Far East trade, maiden voyage to San Francisco 1851 and 1852 made in 103 days; in 1853 and 1854 made a 76 day, 7 hour passage from San Francisco to New York, the fastest on record to that port ever and the second fastest on record from San Francisco to an East Coast port. In 1854 carried coal from Liverpool to Hong Kong, 1857 put in the guano trade. In early 1863 sold at London and acquired by James Baines & Co. for operation in their Australian Black Ball Line and renamed *Fiery Star*. Lost in 1865 when bound Moreton Bay, Australia, for London after cargo of wool was discovered to be on fire, 18 crewmen perished aboard the burning ship, while a lifeboat with 80 other crew and passengers was lost at sea.
- *Invincible*, 1851, 1,769 tons, generally considered of extreme model though described by Webb as being of medium model, built at a cost of $120,000 for James Phillips of New York. Intended for the Liverpool trade but first put in the California–Far East trade. Forced to put into Rio de Janeiro due to a leaking water tank. On four subsequent California runs her best time was 109 days. Collided with an American ship near Hong Kong in 1855 and was beached with a hold full of water but was repaired. In 1860 sold to Spofford & Tileston for operation in their Liverpool line of packets and so operated for three years before being sold to Boston interests. Laid up at Brooklyn, New York, in early 1867, later in September 1867 was discovered by a watchman to be on fire, was subsequently beached on Governor's Island, a total loss.
- *Swordfish*, 1851, 1,036 tons, generally considered of extreme model, built for Barclay & Livingston of New York. Maiden voyage on the California run in 1851 and 1852 made in 94 days, one of the fastest passages on record. After her second California run in 1853, 107 days, continued on to Hawaii in several hours over eight days, an all-time record, and then to Shanghai, total voyage made in under 33 days, also a record. In 1859 and 1860 made a voyage from Shanghai to New York in a record 81 days. Lost in July 1862 while departing Shanghai for Amoy after going ashore due to her anchors becoming fouled.
- *Australia*, 1852, 1,447 tons, a packet ship built for Williams & Guion of New York.

Employed in the transatlantic and New Orleans trade. In early 1865 departed the Delaware Capes after loading at Philadelphia for Port Royal and was subsequently wrecked on Frying Pan Shoal, North Carolina, in March 1865, a total loss.
- *Flying Dutchman,* 1852, 1,257 tons, of extreme model, built for George B. Daniels of New York and intended for the California trade. Maiden voyage out in 1852 and 1853 made in 104 days. Her final voyage out to San Francisco took 102 days in 1857. Departed San Francisco for New York in November 1857. Subsequently went ashore at Brigantine Beach, New Jersey, in early February 1858 when close to her destination, a total loss.
- *Young America,* 1853, 1,961 tons, of extreme model, built for George B. Daniels of New York, cost $140,000; was William Webb's "conception of what a well-designed and built sailing ship should be. She will be fast and handy ... the ship of the future should be like this one" (Dunbaugh & Thomas, p. 194). Largely involved in the California trade or that with England, maiden voyage to California made in 110 days; her best run to California was 103 days in 1874 when twenty-one years old. Dismasted during her California run of 1859 and had to put into Rio de Janeiro for repairs. In 1877 made the run from San Francisco to New York in 92 days. Later owned by George Howes & Co. of San Francisco, sold foreign to Austrian interests in 1883 for $13,500 and renamed *Miroslav,* subsequently put in the oil trade between New York or Philadelphia and Europe. Final voyage loaded at Philadelphia over 407,000 gallons of crude oil bound for Europe in February 1886 and went missing with all hands after departure from Delaware Breakwater.
- *Flyaway,* 1853, 1,274 tons of medium model, built for Schiff Brothers of New York. Designed for the California trade, maiden voyage out to California made in 110 days, followed by a 106 day run in 1855. Sold by her original owners for $50,000 in 1858; in 1859 sold foreign to Spanish interests and renamed *Conception.* Still afloat in 1875 and re-rigged as a bark under British ownership and renamed *Bothalwood.* Lost in early 1880 after stranding on the island of Jersey in the English Channel while bound Cartagena, Columbia, to Scotland.
- *Snapdragon,* 1853, 619-ton bark, built for Wakeman, Dimon & Co. of New York. Employed on her owner's coastal line running between New York and Galveston, Texas. Later career unknown, still American owned in 1863; disappears from American registry after 1865.
- *Intrepid,* 1856, 1,173 tons, of medium model, built for Bucklin & Crane of New York. Intended for the California and Far East trade, lost on her third homeward voyage from the Far East, departing Macao in early 1860 with a large cargo, valued at over $500,000, of tea, silk, firecrackers, and other items; ran aground on Belvidere Reef in the Gaspar Straits and her crew subsequently had to fight off Malaysian pirates, losing one man before being picked up and taken to Anjer by the French clipper *Gallileo.*
- *Uncowah,* 1856, 988 tons, built for Wakefield, Dimon & Co. of New York. Maiden voyage was on the California run, passage 116 days, another in 1859 made in 143 days; in 1865 sailed New York to Shanghai. Later in 1865 sold to Peruvian interests and employed in the coolie trade. Lost in late 1870, while bound Macao to Callao, Peru, with over 500 coolies when they rebelled and set fire to the ship, captain, crew, and 112 coolies saved, at least 425 coolies "perished in the flames" (Dunbaugh and Thomas, p. 310).
- *Black Hawk,* 1857, 1,175 tons, a medium or half-clipper, built for Bucklin & Crane of New York. Mostly involved in the California and the transatlantic trades, from 1857 to 1880 made twenty runs to California, best time 107 days in 1861. In early 1881 sold foreign to German interests and employed in the oil trade between New York and German ports. In May 1888 collided with a barge while under tow, outward bound from Bremen, Germany, to Baltimore; 1889 sold to Norwegian interests and renamed *Christiana,* damaged by fire and condemned in early 1891.

The Westervelt family of clipper ship builders got their start in shipbuilding early on, with family patriarch Jacob Westervelt (born 1800 in New Jersey). Jacob's father was a shipbuilder and

The Westervelt Shipyard. Jacob Westervelt was the most prolific builder of his time at New York and launched some of the finest clippers of the 1850s (*Harper's Weekly*, August 31, 1861).

so, too, would his son become one, but not before going off to sea and learning what it was like to sail before the mast. Afterward, Jacob Westervelt served an apprenticeship under the leading New York shipbuilder of the day, Christian Bergh, and later worked for Bergh on the many packet ships he built in the 1820s through 1836. He even went to Charleston, South Carolina, to build ships on Bergh's behalf while still an apprentice but returned to New York by 1822 to enter into a formal partnership with Bergh. In 1836 Jacob Westervelt started his own shipyard, first building several ships on his own, and later in partnership with Marshall Roberts, and, by 1841, with William Mackey (born 1804) at a newly established shipyard on Corlear's Hook. This partnership was ended by late 1851 but had been a very profitable one. Both Mackey, identified as a merchant ship builder in the 1860 Federal Census with assets totaling $120,000, and Westervelt made a good living building well-regarded ships, including three clippers in 1851 before dissolving their partnership likely due to the fact that Jacob's sons, Daniel (1827–1896) and Aaron (1829–1879), were coming of age and Jacob wanted them to take over the business. The Westervelt sons apprenticed under their father and likely played a role in building the Westervelt clippers after Mackey left the firm, though in 1851 Aaron Westervelt built one clipper on his own. Before Jacob Westervelt retired from shipbuilding he would build one clipper with his sons as Westervelt & Sons, and later Daniel and Aaron built one clipper on their own, independent of their father. However, the Westervelt sons' careers in wooden shipbuilding were rather short-lived; perhaps sensing that their craft was a dying trade, Aaron by 1860 was a contractor and later, by 1870, was self-employed as a dock builder, while Daniel by 1870 had moved to Chicago and was working as a drygoods salesman. As for Jacob Westervelt, he did not live a quiet retirement by any means, serving as mayor of New York from 1853 to 1855, and later as dock commissioner from 1870 until his death in 1879. The Westervelt yard would continue in operation, building small craft, lightships, steamboats, and naval vessels until its final dissolution in 1868. By the end of his career Jacob Westervelt, alone and in partnership with others, built more vessels than any other shipbuilder of the day, even besting his friend and closest rival, William Webb.

- *Hornet*, 1851, 1,427 tons, of extreme model, built by Westervelt & Mackey for Chamberlain & Phelps of New York. First employed in the California–Far East trade, maiden voyage out heavily loaded with nearly 50 tons of equipment for a steamship which had to be jettisoned during a gale, arrived after a long passage of 155 days; in nine other California runs her best time was 106 days. By the 1860s put in the bulk cargo trades, carrying nitrate of soda from Chile to Philadelphia in 1862, wheat from San Francisco to Liverpool and coal from there to New York in 1863. In 1866 departed New York for San Francisco carrying a large cargo of case oil and candles, subsequently accidentally caught fire in early May 1866 while in the Pacific and was abandoned by her crew and passengers in several lifeboats, sixteen men were ultimately lost when their lifeboat was never seen again.

- *Mercury*, 1851, 1,350 tons, of medium model, built by Westervelt & Mackey for Boyd & Hincken's Second Line of Havre packets, employed on the New York–Havre route from 1851 to 1869, fastest passage was 23 days. Later owned on the West Coast, homeport San Francisco; last surveyed there in 1892, out of registry after 1900.
- *N.B. Palmer*, 1851, 1,400 tons, of extreme model, built by Westervelt & Mackey for A.A. Low & Brothers of New York. One of the fastest and most popular of all the clippers built, first put in the California–Far East trade for three voyages, her best run being 107 days; thereafter made fifteen voyages New York to Hong Kong, her fastest run out being 88 days in 1858, while her fastest homeward passage from China was 62 days. Sold foreign in 1873 and thereafter engaged in the case oil trade between New York and European ports. Later sold to Norwegian interests, abandoned in a sinking condition in January 1892.
- *Aramingo*, 1851, 760 tons, of medium model, built by Aaron Westervelt for Chamberlain & Phelps. Made two California–Far East passages to begin her career; collided with a British bark in the South Pacific in June 1853. Later put in the triangular trade between the U.S., West Indies, and England, suffering a number of mishaps. Sold foreign to German interests in 1863 and renamed *Matador*, homeport Bremen; out of register after 1878.
- *Eureka*, 1851, 1,041 tons, of extreme model, built by Jacob Westervelt for Chambers & Heiser of New York. Operated in the California–Far East trade, said to be an unlucky and unpopular ship, partially dismasted on her maiden voyage to California and put into Valparaiso for repairs; on third California run made a passage of 120 days. Sold to the Griswolds of New York in 1859 for $25,000 and repaired; sold foreign to Canadian interests in 1863 without a name change and in 1866 was condemned and scrapped at Calcutta, India.
- *Golden Gate*, 1851, 1,341 tons, of extreme model, built by Jacob Westervelt for Chambers & Heiser. Put in the California–Far East trade, maiden voyage to California in 115 days, made another California passage of 104 days in 1852–53. Early 1855 chartered by the French government for use as a troop and supply ship during the Crimean War. In April 1856 while bound New York to India put into Brazil partially dismasted, repaired and nearly ready for sea in May when she caught fire, probably set by one of her officers, and burned to the water's edge, a complete loss.
- *Contest*, 1852, 1,099 tons, designed by Daniel Westervelt, built by Jacob Westervelt for A.A. Low & Brothers. Employed in the California–Far East trade, made a fast California run of 100 days on her maiden voyage, and on her return to New York made the run in just several hours over 80 days, the second fastest run from San Francisco to the East Coast on record. On her 1861 California run suffered severe weather and put into St. Thomas in a leaking condition, discharged her cargo and returned to New York in ballast for repairs; subsequently departed again for California, from there went to Foo Chow to load tea for New York, making a fast passage home. Departed New York for Hong Kong in early 1863, from there went to Yokohama to load for New York, departing October 1863; subsequently captured and burned by the Confederate raider *Alabama* near the Straits of Sunda November 1863.
- *Golden City*, 1852, 810 tons, of extreme model, built by Jacob Westervelt for Chambers & Heiser. Put in the California–Far East trade, maiden voyage to San Francisco in 118 days. In 1853 suffered damage in a collision with a Spanish ship at Manila. Sold to Boston interests in early 1860s and put in the European trade; subsequently sold to British interests in 1863 and based out of London, later home-ported in Sydney, Australia, and renamed *Tokatea*. After 1873 employed in the Puget Sound lumber and coal trades. Wrecked on Wollstock Island in the South Pacific December 1879 while bound Australia to Hawaii with coal; her largely Chinese crew reached Tahiti in the ship's lifeboats.
- *Golden State*, 1853, 1,363 tons, of extreme

model, built by Jacob Westervelt for Chambers & Heiser. Put in the California–China trade, partially dismasted on her maiden voyage to California and had to put into Rio de Janeiro for repairs. In 1858 had a mutiny aboard while bound New York to Hong Kong and first mate killed. Later in the early 1860s put in the grain and guano trades. After 1864 largely in the China–Far East trade, arriving at New York May 1867 with the largest cargo of tea, valued at $1 million, ever received here. In 1869 underwent major overhaul at New York, continued in same trades; later re-rigged as a bark. In early 1883 was bound New York to Far East but encountered severe weather and developed a leak, forcing her to put into Rio de Janeiro in distress, sold there to Canadian interests, renamed *Anne C. Maguire* and put under the Argentine flag, operated in north Atlantic trade. Lost in December 1886 after going ashore at Cape Elizabeth, Maine.

- *Kathay*, 1853, 1,438 tons, of extreme model, built by Jacob Westervelt for Goodhue & Co. of New York. Intended for California–China trade but put on transatlantic run for maiden voyage; later would make only two California runs, one in 1854, the other in 1859. In 1863 sold to British interests at China, later put in the guano trade, departing Bombay, India, for Howland's Island in late 1866; in January 1867 was wrecked there while loading and was a complete loss.
- *Resolute*, 1853, 787 tons, built by Westervelt & Sons for London interests, said to be the first clipper built for English owners, but sale was never made and instead sold to A.A. Low & Brothers. Operated almost entirely in the China trade except for one California run in 1856. Sold to British interests by early 1859, continued in same trade. Sold to Spanish interests in 1871, named *Resoluda*, homeport Barcelona; out of register after 1876.
- *Sweepstakes*, 1853, 1,735 tons, of extreme model, built by Daniel & Aaron Westervelt for Chambers & Heiser; damaged on launching day and subsequently had to be repaired at the Brooklyn Navy Yard. Maiden voyage to California commenced in September 1853 during which she collided with a Danish vessel. In 1856 made her third California run, arriving at San Francisco, with Jacob Westervelt aboard as a passenger, after a 95-day run, the eighth fastest passage on record. Later in 1857 put in the Indian and Far East trades; in late 1860 departed New York for Australia and the Far East. Early 1862 went ashore on a reef in the Straits of Sunda, subsequently got off and went into drydock at Batavia, Indonesia, found to be severely damaged and sold for scrap.
- *Zephyr*, 1855, 534-ton bark, built for Chamberlain & Phelps of New York. Made one California passage of 168 days, slow time; career details uncertain, sold foreign to London interests in 1867. Out of registry after 1872.

The third most influential firm of clipper ship builders in New York was that involving Jacob Bell (born 1794 in Connecticut). Just who he may have apprenticed with to learn the shipbuilding trade is uncertain, but it was likely at the yard of Adam and Noah Brown sometime between 1810 and 1820. By 1821 Jacob Bell was building packet ships with David Brown (born 1793 in Connecticut, an adopted son of Noah Brown) and by 1825 they established the firm of Brown & Bell, taking over the shipyard of Adam & Noah Brown located at the foot of Stanton Street. While David Brown was one of the best ship designers of the day, Jacob Bell was equally capable. The partnership of Brown & Bell was a long and profitable one lasting until Brown's death in 1850 after having retired two years prior. While Brown & Bell built two early clippers, the *Houqua* and *Samuel Russell*, in the 1840s, Jacob Bell would continue on, building three more clippers until his death in 1852. Thereafter, Bell's son, Abraham (often referred to as A.C.) Bell (born 1827) continued to operate the Bell shipyard, building four more clippers from 1852 to 1854. Soon thereafter, Abraham Bell got out of the shipbuilding business altogether, whether by choice or due to financial difficulties is unclear, and he may be the same man that was later operating a clothing house in New York.

- *Houqua*, 1844, 583 tons, built by Brown & Bell for A.A. Low & Brothers of New York. Originally built as a warship and intended as to be sold to the Chinese government, but was deemed too small; used almost entirely in the China trade except for two

California runs, one in 1850, the other in 1853. Totally dismasted in early 1848 while bound New York to Hong Kong. In 1857 re-rigged as a bark, departed Yokohama, Japan, for New York in August 1864 and went missing with all hands, likely lost in a typhoon.
- *Samuel Russell*, 1847, 957 tons, built by Brown & Bell for A.A. Low & Brothers, who owned her for her entire career. Sailed to Hong Kong on her maiden voyage. Sailed from New York for California January 1850, "loaded as deeply as a sand barge" (Howe & Matthews, p. 537), arrived in 109 days, fastest passage to date. Thereafter in the California–Far East trade until early 1856, thereafter in the New York–Far East trade. Wrecked in the Gaspar Straits November 1870.
- *White Squall*, 1850, 1,119 tons, of extreme model, built by Jacob Bell for William Platt & Sons of Philadelphia, ready for sea cost, including provisions, $90,000. Put in the California–Far East trades, partially dismasted on her maiden voyage to California and had to put into Rio de Janeiro for repairs. Carried a tea cargo from Canton, China, to the UK in late 1851. Made a second California run of 111 days in 1852 and 1853; caught fire while docked at New York December 1853 due to a warehouse fire and burned to the water's edge, subsequently sold for $5,500 and raised and rebuilt by Thomas Stack as a barkentine (Griffiths, *The Monthly Nautical Magazine*, vol. 1, pg. 139) intended for the China trade, new tonnage 896. In December 1854 departed New York for San Francisco, suffered major storm damage and put back to New York for repairs; sailed again February 1855 but was dismasted during a storm and put into Rio de Janeiro for repairs; later returned to New York in early 1856, sailing yet again in mid–1856 for California but had to put into Montevideo in distress, sold to French interests and renamed *Splendide*, home port of Marseilles. Still afloat in 1875, probably the ship of the same name which was put ashore at Gibraltar in a sinking condition while bound Rouen, France, to Barcelona, Spain, in 1877.
- *Trade Wind*, 1851, 2,045 tons, of extreme model, built by Jacob Bell for Booth & Edgar of New York. The largest and longest sailing ship ever built in America up to that time; made three California runs, the best being 102 days. The vessel caught fire in mid–1852 while bound San Francisco to Panama, and again in late 1852 while bound New York to San Francisco. In June 1854 loaded cotton at Mobile, Alabama, subsequently collided with the ship *Olympia*, both ships later foundered, the clipper going down with her captain and fifteen men.
- *Messenger*, 1852, 1,350 tons, of extreme model, built by Jacob Bell for Slate & Co. of New York, cost $105,000; made one voyage then sold to William Platt & Co. of Philadelphia, employed in the California, China, and Indian trades, her fastest time in the former being 109 days in 1866. Made one coolie voyage in 1860 from Macao to Havana, Cuba. Sold to Boston interests in 1869, made several guano voyages; also in the grain trade in 1873, making a voyage from San Francisco to Queenstown, Ireland. In 1875 employed in the Puget Sound lumber trade, then again in the Far East trade. Condemned at Mauritius in May 1879 after arriving there from New York in distress with a cargo of case oil. Subsequently sold to New Zealand interests and re-rigged as a bark; later that year went ashore on Farewell Spit, coast of New Zealand, a total loss.
- *Jacob Bell*, 1852, 1,381 tons, of extreme model, designed by Jacob Bell prior to his death, built by A.C. Bell for A.A. Low & Brothers. Employed in the California–Far East trade, after 1856 almost exclusively employed in the China trade except for one California run in 1860. Driven ashore at Canton, China, during a typhoon in July 1862 but suffered only minor damage. Departed Foo Chow, China, for New York in November 1862 with a large cargo of tea and other items valued at $1.5 million; subsequently captured and burned by the Confederate raider *Florida* in February 1863.
- *North Wind*, 1853, 1,041 tons, of extreme model, built by A.C. Bell for Grinnell, Minturn & Co. of New York. Maiden voyage to California, subsequently made one guano voyage, a New York–Le Havre round-trip with over 300 passengers. Later in the Indian and Far East trade, in 1860

voyaged London to Australia, 1862 and 1863 made several coal voyages from Cardiff, Wales. Ashore at Singapore in late 1863 but got off without major damage, sold there to British interests. Later career uncertain, out of registry by 1868.

- *San Francisco*, 1853, 1,307 tons, of extreme model, built by A.C. Bell for New York interests. Departed New York for California in October 1853 on maiden voyage, arrived February 1854 after a 105 day passage. Subsequently went ashore at Rialto Cove while entering San Francisco harbor under control of a pilot, ship a total loss.
- *Adelaide*, 1854, 1,831 tons, of medium model, built by A.C. Bell for Thomas Wardle of New York. Intended for the transatlantic packet trade but was first put on the California run, making two voyages in 1855 through 1857, on the second manned by an African American crew. Later put in the guano and transatlantic trade. Possibly sold foreign to British interests in 1863, still afloat in 1874, homeport Liverpool. Subsequently lost in 1875, details uncertain.

The firm of Roosevelt & Joyce "succeeded in 1853 to the business and shipyard of the Browns and the Bells" (Fairburn, p. 2790), though just when this transition took place is uncertain. A.C. Bell launched his last clipper in 1854 at the Bell yard at the foot of Stanton Street, while Roosevelt & Joyce launched their first in 1853 from their yard located on the eastern side of Houston Street, about a block away. Presumably, Roosevelt & Joyce either expanded their yard to the Bell site in 1854 or moved their operations there altogether. The members of the firm, whose prior experience is unknown, were shipbuilder Solomon Roosevelt (born 1807) and ship carpenter Jonathan Joyce (1817–1866). After building their last clipper in 1857, the firm continued in operation, with a change in partners, until 1866, launching a number of steamers and ferry boats.

- *David Brown*, 1853, 1,715 tons, of extreme model, built for A.A. Low & Brothers of New York. Intended for the California–Far East trade, maiden voyage to California made in 99 days, subsequently continued on to Hong Kong; second California voyage in 1856 was made in 103 days. In late 1860 loaded a cargo of grain at San Francisco for Liverpool, encountered stormy weather after rounding Cape Horn and began to leak, subsequently abandoned on January 6, 1861, all crew and passengers saved.
- *Rapid*, 1852, 1,115 tons, built for James Bishop & Co. of New York. Employed in the California and Far East trade, maiden passage to San Francisco in 135 days; in 1856 and 1857 made a 220 day passage after experiencing strong storms and cold weather, resulting in the loss of ten men, forced to put back into Rio de Janeiro for repairs. In 1859 sold to Danish interests without a name change and continued in Far East trade; in 1866 listed as owned by the Danish Consul at Hong Kong. Subsequently sold to Chinese interests, likely with a change in name.
- *Monarch of the Seas*, 1854, 1,971 tons, built for Lawrence, Giles & Co. of New York. Likely involved in the transatlantic trade but little is known of her career. Sold to British interests in 1865, departed Liverpool March 1866, destination uncertain, and went missing with all hands.
- *Titan*, 1855, 1,985 tons, of medium model, built for Daniel Bacon of Boston. Sailed to Europe on maiden voyage and then chartered by the French government for use as a troop and supply transport during the Crimean War. Afterwards in 1857 put in the transatlantic cotton trade for one voyage, then chartered to the White Star Line of England for an Australian voyage. Final voyage was in the guano trade bound Peru for Ireland when abandoned in a sinking condition in February 1858.
- *Fairy*, 1856, 629-ton barkentine, built for Gordon, Talbot & Co. of New York. Employed in the China–England tea trade through 1860 and showed a good turn of speed that rivaled that of other, larger ship-rigged clippers; later career unknown.
- *Glad Tidings*, 1856, 898 tons, built for William Nelson & Son of New York. Built for the New Orleans transatlantic trade. Career details uncertain, out of registry after 1874.
- *Hotspur*, 1857, 862 tons, of medium model, built for Frank Hathaway and others of New York. Employed in the New York–China trade, fastest passage homeward in 85 days in 1859 and 1860. Lost in February 1863 while bound from Foo Chow, China,

for New York with a cargo valued at one million dollars after striking Paracels Reef and was a total loss.

The pioneering shipyard of Smith & Dimon, with John W. Griffiths employed as one of their primary designers, built five early clippers between 1844 and 1850. As previously discussed, Stephen Smith (born ca. 1797 in Connecticut) served his apprenticeship under famed New York builder Henry Eckford and was a renowned designer in his own right and was in charge of new construction contracts, while his partner, John Dimon, was responsible for the repair end of their business. The Smith & Dimon shipyard was located at the foot of East Fourth Street and began building ships, many for the packet trade, in 1821; after it was done building clippers, the firm concentrated on steamship construction before the retirement of its partners by the late 1850s.

- *Rainbow*, 1844, 752 tons, built for Howland & Aspinwall of New York. Employed entirely in the China–Far East trade for three round-trip voyages; partially dismasted on her maiden voyage out to Hong Kong in 1845. Fastest passage out from New York was 99 days, while her fastest homeward passage was 86 days. Went missing in early 1848 while bound New York for China via Valparaiso, thought to have been lost off Cape Horn.
- *Sea Witch*, 1846, 908 tons, built for Howland & Aspinwall. First employed in the China–Far East trade, first two voyages New York to Hong Kong; on second voyage homeward arrived at New York in all-time record run of 77 days, on sixth voyage made a California run of 111 days, followed by another of 109 days. In 1855 her commander, Captain Gordon Fraser, was murdered by his chief mate while bound New York to Hong Kong. Subsequently loaded coolies at Amoy for Havana, Cuba. Lost March 1856 after striking a reef just twelve miles off Havana.
- *Memnon*, 1847, 1,068 tons, the first clipper to bear this name (a second was built at South Boston in 1858), built for F.A. Delano of New York. Maiden voyage New York to Liverpool, the first American clipper to appear at that port. April 1849 departed New York for San Francisco, arriving in 120 days, the first clipper to arrive at that port prior to 1850. Subsequently sailed to China and was later among the first American clippers to take part in the China–England tea trade. Lost in the Gaspar Strait September 1851, going ashore near Alceste Rock while bound from Canton, China, to London with a valuable cargo of tea, the ship was subsequently plundered by pirates but her crew got off safely in several lifeboats.
- *Nicholas I*, 1850, 596 tons, of extreme model with 26 inches of deadrise and a flat-floored hull design, built for Weston & Goodhue and others of New York for the Russo-American Fur Company, the first American clipper expressly built for foreign ownership; subsequently delivered to her owners at Kronstadt, Russia, located on the Gulf of Finland, in mid-1850 and said to be a fast sailor. No further career details known.
- *Mandarin*, 1850, 776 tons, of extreme model, built for Goodhue & Co. of New York. Made ten round-trip voyages in her career, including three California runs, the fastest being 115 days; all other voyages were from New York to China and back, including several very fast runs. On final run departed Canton, China, for New York in mid-1864 but struck an unknown reef off Batavia, Indonesia, and was subsequently lost.
- *Universe*, 1851, 1,297 tons, the first clipper packet built for the North Atlantic trade, built for Williams & Guion's Liverpool Line. Full career details unknown. Hit by lightning with minor damage while bound Liverpool to New York with over 600 passengers in March 1854. By 1870s was sold foreign to British interests, still afloat in 1878. Historian William A. Fairburn incorrectly attributes this ship to William Webb.

Thomas Collyer (born 1822) was part of a shipbuilding family from Ossining, New York, on the Hudson that included his brothers George, Samuel, and William, who also had their own shipyards either alone or in partnership with others. Thomas Collyer's yard was located at the foot of 12th Street and employed about sixty men in 1853. Collyer was more famed for the steamships he built and also worked with William Brown, who launched a 1,300-ton steamer from Collyer's yard in 1853. However, Thomas Collyer did build several clippers, two of them barks, which were noted for their speed, and was also in the repair business, repairing the fire-damaged *White Squall* in 1854 (see above) and converting her to a barkentine, probably the first and largest clipper ship ever to be so rigged.

- *Panama*, 1853, 1,139 tons, of extreme model, built for N.L. & G. Griswold of New York. Originally to be named *Spirit of the Times*, but changed because a Baltimore clipper was already so named. Designed specifically for the China and California trade but first put in the European–China trade and the Australian trade. Made several fast California runs among her six such passages, including those of 101 days in 1864 and 108 days in 1866, her last such run. In 1867 while bound from Bangkok to Brazil with rice put into port with a bad leak and seven feet of water in her hold, subsequently condemned and sold.
- *Roebuck*, 1856, 456 ton bark, built for Reynolds & Cushman of New York. Made one long California passage. Merchant career details unknown, sold at New York in July 1861 to the government for use as a warship, primarily used in blockading squadrons. While employed off Indian River, Florida, in 1863 and 1864 captured or burned nine Confederate blockade runners; later went to Tampa for repairs and subsequent duty as a store ship. Sent north to Portsmouth, New Hampshire, late 1864 when a yellow fever epidemic broke out, there decommissioned and sold in mid–1865, later career details unknown.
- *Dawn*, 1857, 387-ton bark, built for George Savory and others of New York. Employed in the South American trade in which she made consistently fast passages between Buenos Aires and New York of less than forty days in 1860, including a 36 day passage that was one of the fastest on record (Cutler, p. 373). Later owned in Salem, Massachusetts, and thereafter at Boston and San Francisco, still in service as of 1900.

Borough of Brooklyn-Williamsburg

The firm of Perrine, Patterson & Stack was the predominant one in this village, located

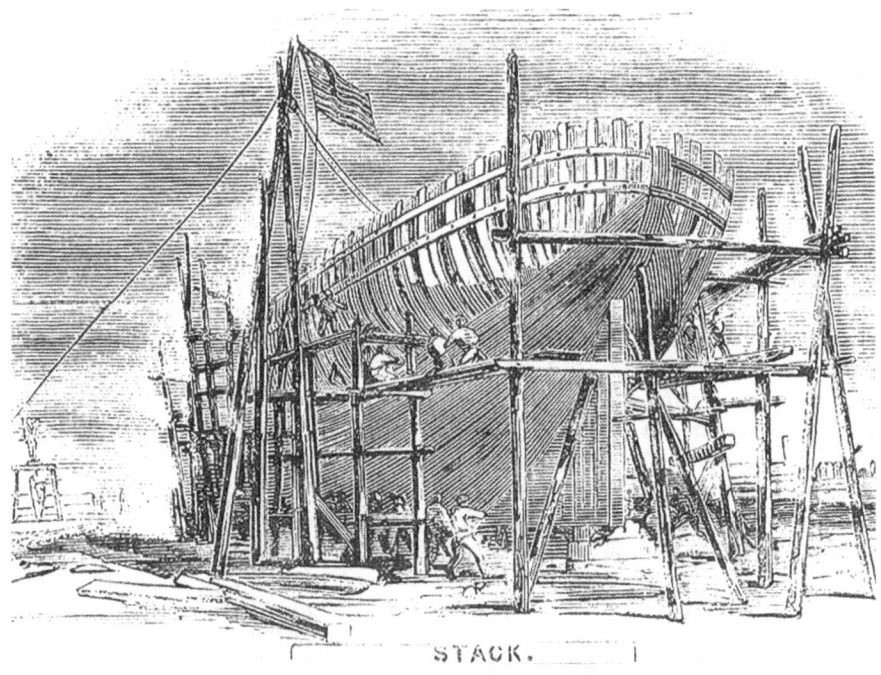

The Stack Yard. The firm of Perrine, Patterson, and Stack built six fine clippers, including the heavily sparred *Ino*, at their Williamsburg shipyard from 1851 to 1853 before dissolving their partnership. This woodcut shows a later view of Stack's yard where he rebuilt the fire-damaged clipper *White Squall* and built numerous others vessels into the 1870s (*Harper's Weekly*, August 31, 1861).

across the East River from Manhattan. The principal was former sea captain William Perrine, while Ariel Patterson (born 1807) and Thomas Stack (born 1821 in Quebec Province, Canada, immigrated to the U.S. in 1830) rounded out the group. This partnership was established in 1845 and originally operated at a yard in Manhattan, but by about 1850 they had moved their primary operations across the river to Williamsburg, located at the foot of North Second Street, and a short time later moved to the site where fellow shipbuilder Jabez Williams' yard was located. However, while there is some indication that Perrine, Patterson & Stack also operated two yards simultaneously, by 1853 the firm had dissolved, with Perrine & Stack continuing to work together to build two clippers in 1853, while William Perrine built one clipper on his own in 1854. As for Ariel Patterson, he continued on his own, establishing a yard prior to mid-1853 at the foot of North Sixth Street, adjacent to the newly established yard of Perrine & Stack. In 1853 Patterson had one so-called clipper schooner intended for the San Francisco–Hawaii trade on the stocks. The most prolific of the three builders, and probably the most skilled, was certainly Thomas Stack, who had apprenticed at the Brown & Bell shipyard; his building career continued well into the 1870s, his yard in 1870 being valued at some $250,000.

- *Eagle,* 1851, 1,296 tons, of extreme model, built for Henry Harbeck & Co. of New York. First employed on the California route, making a 104 day passage in 1853 and 1854; later in the Far East trade, repaired and refitted at New York in late 1862, then sailed to India where she was sold at Calcutta and her name changed to *Turkey.* Disappears from register after 1870.
- *Ino,* 1851, 895 tons, of extreme model, built for Sifkin & Ironsides of New York. Started career by making three California runs, best time 111 days. From 1854 to 1861 employed in the Far East trade. In 1861 sold to the U.S. government for use as a warship, employed in hunting down Confederate raiders and commanded by Josiah Cressy, made a record run in that service in 1862 from Boston to Cadiz, Spain, in 12 days. In 1867 sold by the government to Samuel Reed of Boston and renamed *Shooting Star,* subsequently put in the guano and West Coast coal trade and re-rigged as a bark, in 1876–77 employed carrying iron ore and oil. Thereafter sold foreign, registered in 1886 as the bark *Ellen* of Russia, home port Wasa, out of registry after 1892.
- *John Stuart,* 1851, 1,654 tons, of medium model, built for New York parties. Employed in the transatlantic trade, subsequently made four California runs from 1853 to 1860, her best time 125 days. Sold to Boston interests in 1859 for $36,750, later put in the coal and guano trades. June 1863 sold at Bombay, India, to British interests and home-ported there with no name change; out of registry after 1870.
- *Antelope,* 1852, 1,186 tons, of extreme model, built for Henry Harbeck & Co. Originally employed on the California–Far East trade routes, making a 97-day California run in 1855 and 1856, thereafter put in the China and India trade. In early 1863 sold to British interests at New York without a name change and still in the same trade; still in British registry in 1870, later career details uncertain.
- *Flying Cloud,* 1853, 350-ton bark, built by Perrine & Stack for Henry Harbeck & Co., not to be confused with the McKay ship-rigged clipper of the same name. Career details unknown, not in registry after 1858, possibly sold foreign with a change in name.
- *Wide Awake,* 1853, 758 tons, built by Perrine & Stack for Sifkin & Ironsides. Maiden voyage on the California route of 112 days, subsequently put in the New York–Far East trade; last sailed from New York in 1857 for Bangkok, Thailand, sold there to local interests.

Jabez Williams (1788–1870, born in Stonington, Connecticut) was another prominent builder in New York. His independent career was well underway by the early 1820s in Manhattan, where he built both steamships (his first vessel) and sailing vessels, both alone and for a time as junior partner in the firm of Thorne & Williams. In 1845 Williams moved his yard across the East River to Williamsburg, where he would build one of his three clippers before moving his operations yet again by mid-1852 to nearby Greenpoint. Williams' last clippers, his final ships before retirement, were in fact built at Greenpoint (Silka, p. 24), though one newspaper account states that the Jabez Williams shipyard in Williamsburg, located at the foot of Clinton Street, was still active and employed thirty men building a coastal packet schooner in mid–1853. Williams' shipyard was sometimes referred to as Jabez Williams & Son because he worked with his son, John T. Williams (a master builder by 1852), on the building of at least one clipper, while another son, Edward F. Williams, also had his own shipyard. Jabez Williams' ties to the shipbuilding industry in the area ran even deeper, as his daughter Susan married fellow Greenpoint shipbuilder Samuel Sneden (see below). After Jabez Williams' retirement from shipbuilding by 1853, he would later become a director in the Ship Timber Bending Company, along with noted designer John W. Griffiths, and worked as a marine surveyor at the Port of New York, employed by American Lloyd's. No matter what end of the building business he was active in, Williams must have been highly regarded, as one early historian refers to him as "honest old Jabez Williams" (Felter, p. 32).

Jabez Williams (1788–1870). This long-time shipbuilder's work is often overshadowed by that of other New York clipper builders, but was certainly their equal. He built three clippers altogether at his shipyards in Williamsburg and Greenpoint, including the famed *Tornado* and the long-lived *Simoon*. After his retirement from shipbuilding, Williams continued to play a major role in the maritime commerce of New York by serving as one of the city's first surveyors for American Lloyd's (photograph courtesy Robert J. Alesbury and A. William Alesbury).

- *Eclipse*, 1850, 1,223 tons, of extreme model, built for Thomas Wardle and Booth & Edgar of New York. Put in the California trade, with subsequent voyages from there to the west coast of South America and the Far East; best California run was 109 days in 1852. Driven ashore during a hurricane and wrecked in October 1853 while loading wood at Ypal Road, Mexico, a total loss.

George Steers (1820–1856, born in Washington, D.C.) and his older brother James R. Steers (1808–1896, born in Plymouth, England), also a shipwright, were the sons of an English shipwright, Henry Steers, who emigrated to the U.S. in 1819. George Steers learned the trade by apprenticing with his brother, who was employed in New York at several shipyards, including Smith & Dimon, where he was their shipyard superintendent by 1829. George Steers was designing fast pilot boats by the early 1840s and in 1843 was the junior member of the firm of Hathorne & Steers. The brothers later formed their own company, the George and James Steers Co., or George Steers & Co. as it was usually called. Their most famous production, designed by both, was the schooner yacht *America*, the first winner of the America's Cup in 1851. One historian, in describing the Steers brothers' rela-

tionship, refers to George as "the designer-promoter" and James as "the practical builder" (Fairburn, p. 2832). After the success of the *America*, George promoted the design and model for a 2,500 ton clipper to be built on the lines of their famed yacht, but such a ship was never built as the times were rapidly changing. After building his one clipper, a beautiful ship that looked like she had good potential, but turned out to be a poor performing vessel, Steers died unexpectedly just two years later at a young age.

- *Sunny South*, 1854, 776 tons, of extreme model with 28 inches of deadrise, built for Napier, Johnson & Co. of New York. Maiden run to California took 141 days, her only long distance voyage; subsequently put

The Williams Shipyard. This rare photograph likely records a launching day of a vessel at the shipyard of Jabez Williams. Neither the date of the photograph nor the identity of the vessel to be launched is known, although it appears to be a bark-rigged vessel. One of the figures in the foreground, perhaps one in the top hat, is almost certainly Jabez Williams (photograph courtesy of Robert J. Alesbury and A. William Alesbury).

in the South American trade, 1859 outfitted as a slave ship at New York, subsequently sold to Cuban interests at Havana for $18,000 and renamed *Emanuela*. Captured in August 1860 in the Mozambique Channel by the British warship *Brisk* with over 800 slaves aboard, subsequently condemned by a British prize court and intended to be taken into the Royal Navy as a cruiser but wrecked in the Mozambique Channel in 1861.

Borough of Brooklyn-Greenpoint

Jabez Williams, as discussed above, built his final two clippers at his new yard in Greenpoint, established in 1851, though he had bought land there some three years earlier.

- *Tornado*, 1852, 1,802 tons, built for W.T. Frost & Co. and Benjamin Mumford of New York. Made first two voyages to California, the second in 111 days; later put in the guano trade. Final California run in 1856 took 112 days; later in the coal and Far East trades. Sold to British interests in 1863 for 12,750 pounds without a change in name; subsequently hailed from Liverpool and sailed in the transatlantic trade. Burned at New Orleans in 1875.
- *Simoon*, 1852, 1,436 tons, of extreme model, built for Benjamin Mumford & Co. of New York. First put in the California trade for one voyage, later as a general trader to South America in the guano trade. In 1855 and 1856 served as a French transport during the Crimean War; later in transatlantic and Indian trade, 1861–62 carried sheep

from the UK to Australia and continued in the Indian trade. Sold foreign to British interests in October 1863 and continued in Indian trade. Sold foreign again to Norwegian interests in 1874 and re-named *Hovding* and re-rigged as a bark, still afloat in 1912.

Eckford Webb (born 1823), the brother of famed builder William Webb, built one clipper at his yard here. Webb apprenticed with his father and was named after the famed New York builder Henry Eckford, under whom Isaac Webb, their equally famed father, had served his apprenticeship. In 1850 Webb was the junior partner in the newly established Greenpoint firm of Collyer & Webb, working with George, the brother of Thomas Collyer, located at the foot of G Street. Here they built small steamers and schooners, but by mid–1851 the partnership had dissolved, with Eckford Webb carrying on the business alone. By 1860 Webb was the principal in the shipbuilding firm of Webb & Bell, with assets worth $50,000 and employing some thirty hands in shipbuilding and repair operations.

- *Sting Ray*, 1854, 985 tons, of medium model, built for Wakefield & Dimon of New York. Made one California passage of 132 days in late 1854. Subsequently voyaged to the Far East, departed Hong Kong for New York September 1855. Subsequently went ashore at Fire Island, New York, during a storm on the night of January 12, 1856, and was a total loss, including a cargo of over 275,000 pounds of tea.

Edward Lupton (born ca. 1823), built one clipper ship and one clipper brig here, of which little about the former is known. The half brig included here, the only vessel of this type included in this work, was deemed a clipper by none other than pioneer clipper designer John W. Griffiths. Lupton began his operations at Greenpoint in 1851, after having previously worked in New York shipyards. Once at Greenpoint, Lupton worked with another builder named John McDiarmid for a time (Silka, pgs. 21–22). By 1860, Edward Lupton's yard had assets of $10,000, employed thirty men, and was primarily engaged in ship repair and the building of smaller sailing craft.

- *Balear*, 1854, 222-ton half brig (also called a hermaphrodite brig), which was a two masted vessel, square rigged on the foremast and fore and aft rigged on the mainmast, of sharp model, heavily sparred with a 50 foot foremast and a 48 foot foreyard, length 105 feet, her hull pierced for two guns on each side, figurehead a sea-green serpent, built for Sheirs & Oliver of New York, first commander Captain Filetti. Intended for the trade with Mexico and South America, career details unknown. In 1859 commanded by E. Lapton (possibly a reference to the same man that built her), owned her entire career at New York, wrecked in July 1878.

- *Black Sea*, 1855, 791 tons, built for Funck & Meincke of New York. Career details unknown, likely engaged in the transatlantic trade. Repaired at Nova Scotia in March 1860, sold foreign to London interests in 1863 and renamed *Jupiter*. Continued in transatlantic trade, out of service after 1872.

The firm of Sneeden & Whitlock was important for its role in rebuilding the Donald McKay clipper *Great Republic* after she caught fire and burned to the water's edge at New York in December 1853. While this firm built no clippers, it was active in the repair business and was well known for its steamship production. The principals were steamboat builder Samuel Sneden (also spelled "Sneeden," born 1816) and Elisha Whitlock (born 1822 in New Jersey), they joining up in early 1853. In early 1854 they were hired by A.A. Low & Brothers to rebuild the *Great Republic*, which they had purchased as was from the ship's insurance underwriters. Under the guidance of Captain Nathaniel B. Palmer, the burned clipper was raised, her cargo partially salvaged, and was towed to Sneden & Whitlock's Greenpoint yard and rebuilt over the course of a year's time.

- *Great Republic*, 1853, 4,555 tons, built for own interests by Donald McKay at East Boston, burned at New York December 26, 1853, and scuttled, subsequently sold to A.A. Low & Brothers of New York; raised by the use of steam pumps in early 1854 and towed to Greenpoint for rebuilding. Original upper deck was not replaced, making the second *Great Republic* a three-decked ship, tonnage reduced to 3,556, depth of hold reduced, lightning conductors and

Howe's topsail rig installed, spars cut down by over 10 percent. Sailed on first overseas voyage for Liverpool in February 1855 and that same year chartered by the French government for use as a transport in the Crimean War. Subsequently made a near record California run of 92 days in 1856 and 1857, one of the fastest on record. Later put in the guano and grain trades and also made several other California passages, 1861–62 under charter to the U.S. government as a military transport, 1862–62 made another fast California passage of 102 days. Laid up at New York due to slow business in 1865, sold foreign in 1866 to Yarmouth, Nova Scotia, and put in the lumber trade; later sold in 1868 to British interests and renamed *Denmark* and continued in the lumber trade. Lost while bound South America to Saint John, New Brunswick, in January 1872, abandoned in a leaking condition off Bermuda during a storm.

Sag Harbor, Long Island

The firm of Willets & Bishop, heavily involved in the whaling business, built two clipper barks here in 1852; similar in tonnage size, they were likely built off the same model. While this town was more noted for the whaling ships it built, one of the small clippers built here was a fast ship that could keep up with the big boys. When the bark *Storm* arrived at San Francisco after a quick passage on her maiden voyage, her commander, Captain John Roberts, proudly wrote in his log that he had "beaten every clipper that sailed about the time I did" (Cutler, p. 250), which included the larger and ship rigged clippers *Golden West* (124 days), *John Stuart* (136 days), *Flying Childers* (113 days), *Red Rover* (117 days), and *Jacob Bell* (123 days).

- *Storm*, 1852, 545-ton bark, built for Slate, Gardner & Howell of New York. Maiden passage to California in 1852 and 1853 made in 110 days; also operated in the China and Far East trade, later career details uncertain.
- *Line Gale*, 1852, 536-ton bark, likely built on speculation and sold with a change in name, further details unknown.

New Jersey and Pennsylvania

These two mid–Atlantic states were largely unimportant when it came to not only the building of clipper ships, but also any large scale wooden sailing ship construction after the 1830s. All but one of the four New Jersey–built clippers were built on the Hudson River, just opposite New York City and are generally included as part of that city's shipbuilding activities. The other New Jersey–built clipper can barely be considered as such as it was built on an island in the Delaware River by a Pennsylvania shipbuilder, albeit on the New Jersey side of the river. While New Jersey shipyards were building ships elsewhere outside of the greater New York area on its southern coast and on the Delaware, these were, as they had been in the past, small fishing vessels, local craft, and small barges and riverboats.

In regards to the state of Pennsylvania, only three clippers were built here, all by the William Cramp yard in the Kensington District of Philadelphia on the Delaware River. Though the city of Philadelphia had had a long and storied maritime past, building many important vessels for the packet, China, and whaling trades, as well as the U.S. Navy, by the 1850s this had greatly changed. Interestingly, while the Philadelphia customs district ranked fourth nationwide in the amount of tonnage built in 1852 and 1853, only one of these vessels was a ship, most of the remainder being small sloops, canal boats, schooners, and steamers, thereby demonstrating, as one historian states, "the degeneracy of the Philadelphia type of marine construction" (Fairburn, p. 2770). While Pennsylvania would later build some iron sailing ships, the state was most prominent in the building of naval vessels from the Civil War through the World War II era.

The most important of the clippers built in these two states was the *Hurricane*. This sharp-built ship may have been the most extreme clipper ever built and was a fast vessel, albeit one that later proved to be an economic albatross around the neck of her owners.

——— *New Jersey* ———

Hoboken

Isaac C. Smith & Sons worked in this city on the Hudson River, across the way from Manhattan, from the late 1840s to the late 1850s, but I've been unable to discover much about Smith's background. If Isaac Smith was from the greater New York–New Jersey area, he likely apprenticed at a New York shipyard before establishing his own yard. The firm not only built several clippers, but also some steamboats, barks, and other small craft.

- *Hurricane*, 1851, 1,608 tons, of extreme model with 40 inches of deadrise, built for C.W. Thomas of New York. Partially dismasted on her first California voyage, subsequent fastest passage to California made in 112 days in 1854; later sailed in the Far East and Indian trade. Laid up in New York in 1858 due to poor business conditions, back in service January 1859 on the California route; subsequently voyaged from San Francisco to Singapore in November 1859, sold foreign there in early 1860 for $30,000, name changed to *Shaw-Allum*, still in operation in 1876.
- *Gravina*, 1853, 818 tons, built for Loring Brothers of Hingham, Massachusetts, and Malaga, Spain. Damaged in December 1853 by the same fire that burned the *Great Republic* at New York, subsequently cut down in size by one deck. Maiden voyage carried missionaries to Shanghai; later in the Far East trade and once attacked by pirates but they were driven off by the ship's two deck guns. Made voyages to Manila and Batavia from London and Amsterdam, and later still operated in the South American trade. Sold at Valparaiso, Chile, in the early 1860s, still in operation there in 1866, further details unknown (Sprague & Sprague, pgs 18–19).
- *Tejuca*, 1854, 470-ton bark, built for William Sale, Jr., of New York. Employed in part in the transatlantic trade, commanded by Captain William Gregory of Marblehead, Massachusetts. Final voyage departed New York late December 1855 bound for Queenstown, Ireland, with a load of sugar, subsequently experienced a hurricane on January 4 and 5, 1856, which caused her hold to fill with water, her pumps failed and provisions were ruined, bark abandoned on January 7; her crew rescued by the ship *Excelsior* of Kennebunk, Maine, all hands saved except one man badly injured, later died, who was crushed between the sides of both ships in the heaving waters, crew subsequently landed at Le Havre, France.

Petty's Island

Philadelphia shipbuilder William Cramp (see below) built one clipper on this island, located between the cities of Philadelphia and Camden, New Jersey. Now uninhabited and used as an industrial site, it was once the site of several shipyards over the years.

- *Manitou*, 1855, 1,401 tons, built for Stilwell S. Bishop of Philadelphia. Made one California run of 168 days; went missing in 1859 while bound New York to San Francisco.

——— *Pennsylvania* ———
Philadelphia

William Cramp (1807–1879) established his shipyard in the Kensington District of Philadelphia in 1830 and by the time of his death operated one of the most important shipyards on the East Coast, famed for the iron vessels it had constructed over the years both for the U.S. Navy and private mercantile trade. Interestingly, family tradition has it that Cramp originally studied to become a minister, but due to poor health it was recommended that he pursue an outdoor trade, whereby he chose shipbuilding. He apprenticed with Philadelphia builder William Grice, also a resident of the Kensington District, beginning in 1823, and, once married to his wife, Sophia, was no doubt aided by his new father-in-law, Henry Miller, who had also worked as a shipwright and shipping merchant. In 1857, after he was done constructing clippers, Cramp took his sons into the business, thereby creating the firm of William Cramp & Sons. After Cramp's death, his sons continued the business until it was eventually sold in 1919, thereafter ceasing operations in 1927 when the demand for warships dried up after World War I. Though the Cramp family was no longer directly associated with the yard, it was later reopened by the navy in 1940 and put to work building submarines during World War II until its final closure in 1947. Without a doubt the Cramp shipyard has the distinction of being the longest lasting shipbuilding firm of all the clipper builders. In addition to his last clipper, *Manitou*, built on Petty's Island in New Jersey territory, Cramp previously built three other clippers in Philadelphia, all owned by local interests.

- *Stilwell S. Bishop*, 1851, 595 tons, built for Henry Simons Jr. of Philadelphia. First put in the California trade where she made five such voyages from 1851 to 1856 and averaged 119 days. In 1856 sold to Baltimore interests and renamed *Grey Eagle*, operated in the South American trade. Rebuilt at Noank, Connecticut, in 1870 and by 1878 re-rigged as a bark. Disappears from registry after 1889.
- *Morning Light*, 1853, 938 tons, of extreme model, the second clipper to bear this name (the first being built at Portsmouth, New Hampshire), built for Bucknor & McGammon of Philadelphia. Employed as a general trader making several California runs as well as those in the coal and guano trades; sold in 1859 for $26,000. In 1861 purchased by government agents for $37,500 and converted into a naval vessel armed with eight cannons, destroyed off the coast of Texas during an engagement in early 1863.
- *Isaac Jeanes*, 1854, 843 tons, built for Isaac Jeanes & Co. of Philadelphia, later owned by Adams, Bliss & Co. Primarily engaged in the Mediterranean trade early in her career; made one California voyage of 129 days in 1855, also later worked as a transatlantic packet and immigrant ship. Wrecked in March 1876, details unknown.

Maryland

All of the clippers built in this state were built at **Baltimore**, the birthplace of the Baltimore clipper, but by the 1850s that port's significance as a builder of fast vessels had waned considerably. Within a decade after the War of 1812, the port of New York eclipsed all other American ports when it came to the production of fast merchant ships and few significant vessels utilized in the packet and China trades were being built at Baltimore by the 1830s. Additionally, Baltimore, and the Chesapeake Bay region in general, was handicapped by the fact that the port's location was several extra days' sailing farther from Europe than New York and Boston, and also because northern merchant ship owners had turned to the shipyards of New England, not southern shipyards, for their packet ships when New York yards were full up with work. However, Baltimore was by no means an unimportant port, for it was here in 1833 that Kennard & Williamson built the famed proto-clipper *Ann McKim* for merchant Isaac McKim, a 494-ton beauty that was one of the fastest ships of her day. By the 1850s the port of Baltimore was still significant in several aspects of maritime commerce, including the South American trade (perfect for the many smaller clippers built here), as well as for its shipments of coal, flour and other regional agricultural commodities.

Given the region's size and significant maritime past, the Chesapeake's contributions to the clipper ship era overall were rather small in terms of numbers and performance. Only twenty-eight clippers were built here (including three built in 1848), the same as were built in the much smaller Piscataqua Region of New Hampshire and but eight more than were built on the Mystic River in Connecticut. Of these clippers, less than half of them exceeded 1,000 tons in size and a third came in at under 600 tons. In addition, whatever speed the Baltimore clippers of the past were famous for did not materialize in the Baltimore ship-rigged clippers of the clipper ship era. As one historian notes, as a group these clippers had "a poor average speed record" (Fairburn, p. 2753), making only one passage out of a total of thirty-six in under 110 days on the California run, and but another six under 120 days, while 48 percent of all the Baltimore clipper passages on the California route took over 130 days, not a great showing. Still, some of these slow passages were, as with any clipper, not the fault of her model itself, but were often due to poor weather conditions and storm damage that forced them to put into foreign ports for repair. In fact, as noted below, some of the Baltimore clippers had a good reputation for speed, some of them despite their small size. As to the owners of the Baltimore clippers and their builders, all but a few of them were built for either local owners or for those based at Philadelphia, though a few did go to New York interests or were built on speculation and quickly sold foreign. The Gardner family of shipbuilders led the way in numbers, building seven clippers from 1850 to 1855, including the 460-ton bark *Paladin* and the 1,811-ton *Napier*. Next in line was John J. Abrahams, who built, both alone and in partnership with others, five clippers from 1848 to 1855, three of them sizeable clippers including the largest ever built at Baltimore, followed by George R. Cooper, builder of three clippers, and Adams Gray and Richard and Edward Bell, who built two clippers each. In fact, Baltimore is rather unusual for the multiple business arrangements among its clipper-building fraternity; Cooper had three different partners, one for each clipper he built, James Gardner worked both on his own and in a partnership to build multiple clippers, as did John Abrahams, while Adams Gray built two clippers on his own after employing another builder to construct his first. No doubt the Baltimore shipbuilding scene was a competitive one, but it also seems to have been one that was collaborative in nature. Finally, being the only southern state to build a significant number of clippers, it may be wondered whether any of these clippers were built expressly for the slave trade. Though evidence is meager on this account, at least one clipper, Adams Gray's *Lady Suffolk*, was possibly intended for this trade, and did in fact, very early in her career, become outfitted as a slave ship. Whether or not slave labor was employed in the building of any Baltimore clipper is unknown for certain, though the possibility does exist.

Among the clippers built at Baltimore, Maryland, the following are the most notable:

- *Architect*: one of a trio of small, early clippers built before the gold rush, this vessel made some very creditable passages on the California route and in the China–England tea trade.
- *Mary Whitridge*: a well-built and long lived ship, this clipper also was a fast vessel, making the run from the Chesapeake to Rock Light, Liverpool, in 13 days, 7 hours.
- *Seaman*: made the fastest California run, a passage of 107 days, of any Baltimore clipper.
- *Carrier Dove*: this medium clipper made a fast passage from England to Australia of 78 days in 1858.

The following builders launched twenty-eight clippers at Baltimore from 1848–1858:

William (born 1805) and George (born 1811) Gardner were native Marylanders who were very active shipbuilders in Baltimore from the 1820s through the 1850s. In fact, many of the Gardner family were active in the shipbuilding and allied trades; Jacob Gardner was a ship carpenter, Isaac Gardner a sailmaker. Another builder in the family, though whether he was a brother or a cousin is uncertain, was James Gardner (born 1818). He worked alone to build a clipper but also built one in partnership with William Gardner and in another non-family partnership with a man named Palmer (possibly lumber merchant John N.) to build yet another. Among William and George Gardner's early vessels was the *Venus*, built in 1838.

- *Paladin*, 1850, 460-ton bark, built by James Gardner, possibly on speculation; sold to Buenos Aires interests, no further details.
- *Atalanta*, 1852, 1,289 tons, built by Gardner & Palmer for Montell & Co. of Baltimore. Partially dismasted on maiden voyage to New York; put in California and Far East trade, best California run out of her three was 124 days. Went ashore on Romer's Shoals off New York while bound from Whampoa to New York. Arrived at Spain from New York in late 1856 and sold there, name changed to *Marguerita*.
- *Sirocco*, 1852, 1,130 tons, of sharp model, built by William and George Gardner for Damon & Hancock of Philadelphia. Mostly employed in the South American trade; made two California runs, the best being a 125 day passage from Philadelphia in 1855. Sold foreign to British interests by 1861 without a name change, subsequently lost at sea in 1873.
- *Euroclydon*, 1853, 1,410 tons, built by William and James Gardner for Hancock & Dawson of Philadelphia. Little is known about this ship, probably employed in the European trade and sold foreign by 1862, likely the same ship, now owned by the British, that was wrecked off the Irish coast at Greenore Point while carrying a load of lumber from Quebec for Liverpool in 1864.
- *Napier*, 1854, 1,811 tons, of medium model, built by William and George Gardner for Hancock & Dawson of Philadelphia at a cost of $140,000. First put in the California trade and made three such runs, the best being 119 days in 1859 and 1860; also employed in the guano trade. Sold foreign at New York in 1862 to British interests for

Clipper ship *Atalanta*. This woodcut shows the fine Baltimore clipper stuck on Romer's Shoals off New York in 1853 upon her arrival from Canton, China. Here the clipper was stuck for nine days before getting free with the assistance of tugboats and after discharging part of her cargo (*Illustrated News*, March 26, 1853).

$55,000; wrecked at Baker's Island April 1871 while loading guano.

- *Whistling Wind,* 1855, 1,800 tons, by William and George Gardner at Fell's Point, possibly on same model as that of *Napier*, possibly built on speculation and sold foreign; nothing is known about this ship.
- *Union,* 1851, 1,012 tons, built by William Gardner, the largest vessel built at Baltimore up to that time, built for S. Lurman & Co. of Baltimore. Her maiden passage to California made in 119 days. Later put in the China trade. After arrival at New York from Rio de Janeiro in early 1863 was sold foreign to French interests from Marseille and renamed *Eugene & Adele*. Put into Rio de Janeiro in a leaking condition August 1872 while bound from Marseille to San Francisco, condemned.

John J. Abrahams (born 1818, last name often incorrectly listed as Abraham) built four clippers at Baltimore from 1848 to 1855. His yard was located at the corner of Wolfe and Thames streets and Thames and Phipps streets. In the building of one clipper he partnered with ship carpenter Robert Ashcroft (born 1810), while on his first clipper he teamed up with ship carpenter George R. Cooper (born 1822). Abrahams worked as a shipbuilder well into the 1860s.

- *Grey Eagle*, 1848, 479 tons, built by Abrahams & Cooper for John McKeever and others of Philadelphia. First put in the California trade and made passages of 119 days in 1849 and 121 days in 1852; later career uncertain.
- *Flora Temple*, 1853, 1,916 tons, of medium model, built by John Abrahams, owned by Abrahams and Ashcroft. Made two California passages, the fastest being 129 days in 1857; also employed in the guano and coolie trades. Wrecked October 1859 after striking an uncharted rock while bound Macao for Cuba with 850 coolies, all of whom were lost.
- *Canvasback*, 1854, 731 tons, of medium model, built by Abrahams & Ashcroft for Oelrich & Lurman of Baltimore. Employed first in the South American trade, then the China trade; sold foreign to London interests in 1863 for $28,000, still in operation in 1875.
- *Carrier Dove*, 1855, 1,694 tons, of medium model, built by John Abrahams for Montell & Co. of Baltimore. Maiden voyage on the

California run, partially dismasted in a hurricane and forced into Rio de Janeiro for repairs that took two months. In 1858 made a passage from Liverpool to Australia and then around the world in ten months; later employed in the transatlantic trade. In 1863 ashore on the Irish coast off Valentia, got off and repaired, subsequently sold. In June 1865 carried a cargo of coal from Shields, England, to New York, went ashore on Governor's Island while making port; in the early 1870s made several California runs. Final voyage early March 1876 bound Liverpool to Tybee Island, Georgia, ashore on Stone Horse Shoal near Tybee, a total loss.

- *Cherubim*, 1855, 1,796 tons, of medium model, built by John Abrahams for David Currie and others of Richmond, Virginia. Largely employed in the South American and transatlantic trade. In September 1856 ran down the American emigrant ship *Ocean Home* off Lizard Point, UK, seventy-seven passengers lost. In 1859 made one and only California run in 193 days, forced to put into Valparaiso, Chile, due to her water supply being deliberately contaminated by one of the crew. After 1859 laid up and idle at London due to the Civil War and her southern ownership. In 1863 sold foreign at London, homeport Dundee, Scotland, renamed *Lochee*; out of registry after 1872.

Adams Gray (born 1791 in Maine) was a ship captain and owner who later built two clippers and commissioned another, all for his own interests. All were small ships, likely built on the same or similar model, measuring from 520 to 530 tons. Gray's family was a maritime one through and through, and his sons (all born in Maine) may even have helped crew and manage the Gray clippers; sons John (born 1820) and Horatio (born 1829) were both shipmasters, while Andrew (born 1822) was a commission merchant.

- *Sea Nymph*, 1850, 526 tons, built for own account. On maiden voyage made a quick passage to New York in just 74 hours, then made a California run of 157 days before continuing on to Hong Kong; in 1852 made a second California run of 124 days. By 1854 sold, possibly foreign, and employed carrying rice between Siam and China. By late 1850s was re-rigged as a bark and owned by the Germans. Totally dismasted during a voyage from British Columbia to Hong Kong in late 1860 and there condemned.
- *Lady Suffolk*, 1852, 530 tons, built for the owner's account and commanded by Gray. In late November 1852 reported as being in Cuba and outfitted for the slave trade with Captain Gray and crew under arrest based on British advice, though the American consul there protested that the ship had been sold to Spanish interests; by early December 1852 Gray and his crew were released, but the ship was likely condemned and sold.

Richard (born 1773) and Edward Bell built a pair of clippers here in the early 1850s, both for Thomas Handy of New York, a merchant with close ties to Baltimore. Richard Bell, worth a substantial $9,000 by 1850, has the distinction of being the oldest known of all the American clipper ship builders.

- *Seaman*, 1850, 546 tons, of extreme model. Put on the California route for her maiden voyage and made the passage in 107 days in 1850 and 1851, the fastest such run made by any Baltimore-built clipper; made one more California run in 1852, thereafter in the South American trade. Struck by lightning and burned February 1855 while bound from New Orleans to Marseille, France, crew saved.
- *Seaman's Bride*, 1851, 668 tons, of extreme model. Damaged on maiden voyage to California and forced to put into Valparaiso, Chile, for repairs, later continued on to China; second California passage made in 1853 took 120 days, while another in 1854 took 119 days. Subsequently went from San Francisco to the Far East and from there back to New York. Sailed from there to Hamburg, Germany, in early 1855 and there sold, her name changed to *Carl Staegoman*; no further details known.

George R. Cooper built three clipper ships in Baltimore in three different partnerships, his first being with John Abrahams, the 1848-built *Grey Eagle* (see above). He built two others, the first with Edward J. Slicer (born 1810), and the second with ship carpenter Samuel Butler. Cooper and Butler had worked together since the early 1850s, previously going by name of

Butler and Cooper, and built the last clipper to be launched here.

- *Spirit of the Times*, 1853, 1,206 tons, of sharp model with 14 inches deadrise, built by Cooper & Slicer for Aymar & Co. of New York. Maiden voyage to Liverpool, made one long passage, 160 days, to California in 1855; operated in the South American trade and also to the Far East, arriving at Hong Kong from London in 1858 and at New York from Bombay, India, in 1861. Thereafter sold foreign to German interests and continued in the China trade, sold again to British interests about 1864 and renamed *London*, sold again at Chile and renamed *Christine* in 1865, sold foreign yet again to Macao interests and renamed *Nina* by 1868. Condemned and scrapped in 1871.
- *Sirius*, 1858, 851 tons, built by Cooper & Butler, likely built on speculation and soon sold foreign to German interests, no further details known.

The firm of Hunt & Waggner built two clippers here at Fell's Point, the principal in this partnership being ship carpenter and Virginia native William Hunt (born 1818), while ship carpenter and Maryland native William Waggner (born 1811) was his junior. The Waggner family was active in the maritime trades in Baltimore, with Lemuel working as a ship carpenter while Isaiah, George, Francis, and John Waggner all worked together as block and pump makers.

- *Kate Hooper*, 1853, 1,489 tons, of medium model, built for J. Hooper of Baltimore. Made three California runs, the fastest being 130 days. Later put in the Far East and Australian trade, in 1857 made a coolie voyage from China to Cuba with 600 aboard, during which the coolies took partial control of the ship, the clipper later being towed to Melbourne by a Dutch warship at the request of her sick captain. In late December burned at Melbourne, Australia, while unloading cargo due to arson, the hulk being later sold, raised, repaired, re-rigged as a bark and renamed *Salamander*, out of registry by 1874.
- *Mary Whitridge*, 1855, 978 tons, of medium model, built for Thomas Whitridge & Co. of Baltimore. Made a maiden voyage from Cape Charles to Rock Light, Liverpool, in 13 days, 7 hours, the fastest passage on record from the Chesapeake; later made two California passages, the best being 114 days in late 1855. Subsequently employed in the Far East trade between San Francisco and Hong Kong; underwent repairs in New York in 1865 and then served as a New York China packet for nearly fifteen years. In the early 1880s was converted to a barge, lost off the coast of New Jersey in February 1902 while carrying a load of coal.

The firm of Foster & Booze has three clippers to their credit. Ship carpenter James M. Foster (born 1810 in Virginia) was the principal, while ship carpenter Thomas H. Booz was his junior. Their yard was located in the Canton District of Baltimore, east of Harris's Creek. Their first clipper was one of the very first to be sold to West Coast owners.

- *Rover's Bride*, 1853, 383 tons, of extreme model, built for J.D. Nason of San Francisco; career details unknown, sold to Australian interests in 1854, final fate unknown.
- *Pride of the Sea*, 1854, 1,600 tons, built for James Hooper & Co. of Baltimore. Employed in the transatlantic trade. Stranded on St. Patrick's Causeway off the coast of Wales while bound New Orleans to Liverpool, subsequently caught fire and was a total loss, year uncertain.
- *Rattler*, 1854, 794 tons, of medium model. Not in the California trade, sold to Italian interests in the early 1860s, homeport Palermo. Not to be confused with the Maine clipper of the same name, built in 1852, or a previous Baltimore vessel of the same name built in 1842 and wrecked while bound from Callao, Peru, to Baltimore in December 1853.

Virginia native Langley B. Culley (born 1790) was the builder of Baltimore's first famous clipper of the 1850s. He was likely assisted by his son Daniel Culley, who was a ship carpenter by 1850. By 1860 Culley was no longer building ships, though he was still active in maritime affairs, serving as the port warden for Baltimore at the City Yard.

- *Architect*, 1848, 520 tons, built for Adams Gray of Baltimore and intended for the South American trade. Sailed from New Orleans for San Francisco in January 1849 under command of Captain Gray with twelve crewmen and 56 passengers, made a long passage and forced to put into Rio de Janeiro due to an outbreak of cholera. By late 1850 sold by Gray for $24,000 and intended for the California trade; later in 1853 put in the China tea trade where she commanded high freight rates. In 1854 sold foreign at Hong Kong to British interests for $23,000 and continued in the China trade; out of registry by 1857, fate unknown.

John A. Robb (ca. 1792–1867) was a shipbuilder with one clipper to his credit; he had an impressive resume even before he adopted Baltimore as his home. Census records give his place of birth as Nova Scotia, Canada, while other sources call him a native of Scotland (Dudley, p. 66). Whatever the case, Robb arrived in New York at a young age and apprenticed under the great New York shipbuilder Henry Eckford; he was later one of Eckford's most trusted shipwrights and, prior to 1826, was sent to Baltimore to work on a warship there being built for the Brazilian navy. Robb must have liked the area, for here he eventually stayed and did quite well in his trade. By 1850 his holdings, including his shipyard on Thames Street, were worth over $18,000.

- *Frigate Bird*, 1853, 567 tons, built for C.H. Cummings & Co. of Philadelphia. Put on the California run for her maiden voyage, making the passage in 150 days, subsequently put in the China trade; in 1857 made a California passage of 165 days. Sold foreign to British interests in 1861 at Liverpool and sailed in the coal and lumber trade. Ashore at Puget Sound in 1864 but got off without damage. Later sold to Norwegian registers without a name change and re-rigged as a bark; last in the registry in 1869 with Bergen, Norway, as her homeport.

Ship carpenters Henry Meads (born 1805 in Virginia) and Maryland native Thomas Horney (born 1815) built one of the trio of Baltimore's first pre-gold rush clippers at Atlantic Wharf in the Canton District of Baltimore.

- *Grey Hound*, 1848, 536 tons, built for wholesale grocery merchant David Stuart and others of Baltimore. First employed in the California trade and here made three runs from 1849 to 1853, her best being a 129 day passage in 1852. Later career details uncertain, sold foreign to Chilean interests in 1856.

Two other clippers were built at Baltimore by builders unknown. These are as follows:

- *Eliza F. Mason*, 1851, 582 tons, built for Philadelphia interests, later owned at New Bedford, Massachusetts, by E.M. Robinson and put in the whaling trade. Sold foreign to Chilean interests at Hong Kong in 1865, later re-rigged as a bark and renamed *Emanuela*.
- *Kate Napier*, 1852, 700 tons, no further details known.

── *Virginia and Florida* ──

The southern states in general were not involved in large scale merchant ship production by the 1840s, and were instead more concerned with small local craft used in the coasting, freighting, and fishing trades. Virginia was, however, an important state when it came to naval construction, as the government owned Gosport Shipyard (established in 1767 and now called the Norfolk Naval Shipyard) was located here on the tidewater region known as Hampton Roads. In fact, there was no shortage of good southern pine and live oak from which to build clippers, and there were certainly men of talent capable of building such clippers. However, the south in general was not patronized in the shipbuilding business by northern ship owners, with the state of Maine instead being the preferred provider both before and after the clipper ship era had ended. As a result of these factors only two clippers were produced in the southern states; the one put over in Virginia is even said to have been built on plans provided by New York shipbuilder William Webb, for which claim, however, there is only supposition based on her owners and no clear documentary evidence. This Virginia clipper also has the distinction of being the only such ship to be commanded by a woman. Likewise, the most southerly of all the clippers built in America at Key West, Florida, is also an interesting vessel; she was, rather ironically, named after the man who would later become the Confederacy's secretary of the navy during the Civil War, and was almost certainly the only clipper constructed of mahogany wood, possibly harvested in the upper Florida Keys.

Portsmouth, Virginia

The shipbuilding firm of Allen & Page (reported as such in local newspapers, but usually given in most clipper works as Page & Allen) built one clipper here, but I've been unable to discover anything certain about the men involved. One of the partners in this firm may have been ship carpenter Thomas D. Allen, a resident of neighboring Norfolk in 1860. There is a bit of mystery surrounding this clipper; tradition states that she was built to order for a New York firm, based on plans drawn up by William Webb. However, Webb, who published comments on all his clippers, never claims this ship as being his design, nor is this discussed in any local news accounts. If this clipper was New York designed, John Griffiths is a more likely candidate, as he had formerly worked at the navy yard in Norfolk and possibly knew the shipwrights Allen and Page. It is also likely that this clipper was built on speculation, and only then, months later, sold to New York interests. When the clipper was launched on April 14, 1853, there was a slowdown in the California trade and she thus remained idle except for one transatlantic voyage until a buyer could be found.

- *Neptunes Car*, 1853, 1,617 tons, likely built on speculation, keel laid on November 15, 1852, subsequently completed in about 110 working days (not including Sundays. Made one round-trip voyage to England in 1853, sold in early September 1853 to Foster & Nickerson of New York for $83,000 and soon loaded for California, chartered for $55,000, loading at 55 cents (*American Beacon Daily*, April 5 and September 5, 1853), arrived at San Francisco February 1854, Captain Josiah Patten in command, passage 101 days. On the clipper's second California run in 1856 Captain Patten became ill and the ship was subsequently commanded during most of the voyage by his wife, Mary Ann Patten, and the second mate. Later sold foreign to British interests at Liverpool in February 1863, employed in the transatlantic trade; out of registry after 1869.

Key West, Florida

Bowne & Curry built Florida's only contribution to the clipper fleet. George Bowne (born 1821 in New York) was active in the wrecking and salvage business off the Keys and entered into a partnership in 1855 with William Curry (born 1822 in the Bahamas), a former fisherman, U.S. Navy quartermaster, and merchant active in the salvage business. By 1860 Bowne had amassed a fortune valued at $70,000, while Curry was worth $75,000. Their shipyard was located on Front and Simonton streets in Key West and remained in operation for many years. George Bowne retired due to poor health in 1861, but Curry & Sons continued the business. The constructor of the Bowne & Curry clipper was master ship carpenter John Bartlum (born 1815), a native of the Bahamas who built ships at Key West from the 1850s until his death in 1870 (Mueller, pgs. 2–3).

- *Stephen R. Mallory*, 1856, 959 tons, a clipper of medium model, built for the builder's account at a cost of $80,000. Made one long California passage in 1858 and 1859. Dismasted and severely damaged while voyaging from London to Key West in October 1860. By 1862 owned primarily in New York, though her builders still retained an interest; sold foreign to London interests in early 1864, name likely changed, final fate unknown.

Bibliography

Albion, Robert G. *Square Riggers on Schedule*. Princeton, NJ: Princeton University Press, 1938.

Anderson, Isabel. *Under the Black Horse Flag*. Boston: Houghton Mifflin, 1926.

Baker, William Avery. *A Maritime History of Bath, Maine, and the Kennebec River Region*, Vol. 1. Bath, ME: Marine Research Society of Bath, 1973.

Bank of the Manhattan Company. *Ships and Shipping of Old New York*. Boston: Walton, 1915.

Bolster, W. Jeffrey. *Black Jacks: African American Seamen in the Age of Sail*. Cambridge, MA: Harvard University Press, 1997.

Boyd, Scott, and Jeff Carr. "The War-Hawk Ship Wreck." http://www.boydski.com/diving/photos/wrecks/WarkHawk/Warhawk_Wreck.htm.

Bray, Mary Matthews. *A Sea Trip in Clipper Ship Days*. Boston: Gorham Press, 1920.

Brewington, M.V. *Shipcarvers of North America*. New York: Dover, 1972.

Briggs, Lloyd Vernon. *History of Shipbuilding on North River, Plymouth County, Massachusetts*. Boston: privately printed, 1889.

Brighton, Ray. *Clippers of the Port of Portsmouth and the Men who Built Them*. Portsmouth, NH: Randall, 1985.

Brookline Historical Society. *Proceedings of the Brookline Historical Society*. Brookline, MA: Brookline Historical Society, 1908.

Bruzelius, Lars. "North American Built Clipper Ships." The Maritime History Virtual Archives, http://www.bruzelius.info/Nautica/Ships/Clippers/American_clipper_ships.html.

Chamberlain, Tony. "Record 'round the Horn is eclipsed." *Boston Globe*, April 8, 1993, p. 30.

Chapelle, Howard I. *The Search for Speed Under Sail, 1700–1855*. New York: Bonanza Books, 1967.

Cheney, Robert K. *Maritime History of the Merrimac: Shipbuilding*. Newburyport, MA: Newburyport Press, 1964.

Clark, Admont G. *They Built Clippers in Their Back Yard*. Yarmouth Port, MA: Parnassus Book Service, 1963.

Clark, Arthur H. *The Clipper Ship Era*. Riverside, CT: 7 C's Press, 1970.

Comstock, Cyrus B. *Some Descendants of Samuel Comstock*. New York: Knickerbocker Press, 1905.

Comstock Family. "Comstock Family Business Records, 1833–1890 (inclusive), 1833–1876 (bulk): A Finding Aid." Mss: 766 1833–1876, Baker Library Historical Collections, Harvard Business School.

Crothers, William L. *The American-Built Clipper Ship, 1850–1856*. Camden, ME: International Marine/McGraw-Hill, 1997.

Cutler, Carl C. *Five Hundred Sailing Records of American Built Ships*. Mystic, CT: Marine Historical Association, 1952.

_____. *Greyhounds of the Sea: The Story of the American Clipper Ship*. New York: Halcyon House, 1930.

Dean, Nicolas, and David C. Switzer. *Snow Squall: The Last American Clipper Ship*. Gardiner, ME: Tilbury House Publishers — Maine Maritime Museum, 2001.

Delgado, James P. *Encyclopedia of Underwater and Maritime Archaeology*. London: British Museum Press, 1997.

Dictionary of Canadian Biography Online. "Cameron, Sir Roderick William," http://www.biographi.ca/009004-119.01-e.php?&id_nbr=6009.

Dillon, Richard H. *Shanghaiing Days*. New York: Coward-McCann, 1961.

Dunbaugh, Edwin L., and William DuBarry Thomas. *William H. Webb, Shipbuilder*. Glen Cove, NY: Webb Institute of Naval Architecture, 1989.

Evans, Robert, Jr. "Without Regard for Cost: The Returns on Clipper Ships." *Journal of Political Economy* 72, no. 1 (February 1964), pp. 32–43.

Fairburn, William Armstrong. *Merchant Sail*. 6 volumes. Center Lovell, ME: Fairburn Marine Educational Foundation, 1945–1955.

Felter, William L. *Historic Greenpoint*. Greenpoint, NY: Greenpoint Savings Bank, 1919.

Forbes, Allan, and Ralph M. Eastman. *Yankee Ship Sailing Cards*. Boston: State Street Trust, 1948.

_____. *Other Yankee Ship Sailing Cards*. Boston: State Street Trust, 1949.

_____. *Yankee Ship Sailing Cards*. Vol. 3. Boston: State Street Trust, 1952.

Forbes, Robert B. *An Appeal to Merchants and Ship Owners, on the subject of Seamen*. Boston: Sleeper & Rogers, 1854.

_____. *Means for Making the Highways of the Ocean More Safe*. Boston: Eastburn, 1867.

_____. *Notes on Navigation*. Boston: Cotter, 1884.

_____. *Notes on Ships of the Past*. Boston: privately printed, 1885.

_____. *Notes on Some Few of the Wrecks and Rescues during the Present Century*. Boston: Little, Brown, 1889.

_____. *Remarks on China and the China Trade*. Boston: Samuel Dickinson, 1844.

Gerber, James. "The Gold Rush Origins of California's Wheat Economy." http://www.scielo.org.mx/scielo.php?pid=s1405-22532010000200002&script=sci_arttext.

Gibson, Greg. "Clipper Ship Cards." http://www.tenpound.com/clipper.html.

Gleason, Hall. *Old Ships and Ship-Building Days of Medford*. Medford, MA: Medford Co-operative Bank, 1998.

Goodman, Jordan. "Guano Happens." http://findarticles.com/p/articles/mi_hb3120/is_11_78/ai_n29312399/pg_2/?tag=content:coll.

Griffiths, John W. *The Monthly Nautical Magazine and Quarterly Review*, vols. 1–7. New York: Griffiths and Bates, 1854–57.

_____. *The Progressive Ship Builder*. New York: privately printed, 1876.

_____. *Treatise on Marine and Naval Architecture*. New York: Appleton, 1854.

Hall, Henry. *Report on the Ship-Building Industry of the United States*. Washington: Government Printing Office, 1884.

Hassell, Martha. *The Challenge of Hannah Rebecca*. Sandwich, MA: Sandwich Historical Society, 1986.

Howe, Octavius T., and Frederick C. Matthews. *American Clipper Ships*. New York: Argosy Antiquarian, 1967.

Howe, Oliver H. *A Narrative History of the Town of Cohasset*. West Hanover, MA: Halliday, 1970.

Jackson, Joe. *A Furnace Afloat: The Wreck of the Hornet and the Harrowing 4,300-mile Voyage of its Survivors*. New York: Free Press, 2003.

Johnson, Rossiter. *The Twentieth Century Biographical Dictionary of Notable Americans*. Vol. 8. Boston: Biographic Society, 1904.

Kingston, Christopher. "Marine Insurance in Britain and America, 1720–1844: A Comparative Institutional Analysis." Seminar paper, Amherst College, Amherst, MA, March 24, 2005.

Kingston, George C. *The U.S. Consul at the Court of Siam: James Madison Hood*. Jefferson, NC: McFarland, 2013.

Kinney, Joyce E. *The Vessels of Way Down East*. Bangor, ME: privately printed, 1989.

Kittredge, Henry C. *The Shipmasters of Cape Cod*. Hamden, CT: Archon Books, 1971.

Lindsey, Benjamin J. *Old Marblehead Sea Captains and the Ships in which They Sailed*. Marblehead, MA: Marblehead Historical Society, 1915.

Low, Captain Charles P. *Some Recollections*. Boston: Ellis, 1906.

Lubbock, Basil. *The China Clippers*. Glasgow, Scotland: James Brown & Son, 1914.

_____. *The Colonial Clippers*. Glasgow, Scotland: James Brown & Son, 1921.

MacLay, Edgar S. *A History of American Privateers*. New York: Appleton, 1899.

MacLean, Duncan. "The New Clipper Ship *Lightning* of Liverpool." *Boston Daily Atlas*, January 31, 1854.

Macmillan, Joe. "House Flags of U.S. Shipping Companies." http://flagspot.net/flags/us-hf.html.

The Maritime Heritage Project. "Clipper Ships in San Francisco." http://www.maritimeheritage.org/ships/clippers.html.

Matthews, Frederick C. *American Merchant Ships 1850–1900*. Ser. 1. Mineola, NY: Dover, 1987.

_____. *American Merchant Ships, 1850–1900*. Ser. 2. Mineola, NY: Dover, 1987.

McClary, Daryl C. "The *SS Pacific* Founders off Cape Flattery." http://www.historylink.org/index.cfm?DisplayPage=output.cfm&file_id=8914.

McKay, Richard C. *Some Famous Sailing Ships and Their Builder, Donald McKay*. New York: Putnam, 1928.

Mel Fisher Maritime Heritage Society. "The Last Slave Ships." http://www.melfisher.org/exhibitions/lastslaveships/slaveships.htm.

Mendell, Charles Jr. *Shipbuilders of Mattapoisett*. Dartmouth, MA: Old Dartmouth Historical Society, 1937.

Milne, John. "Bow of Long-Sunken Clipper Completes a Journey Home." *Boston Globe*, March 13, 1987, pgs. 17 and 23.

_____. "Clipper Relocation Likely." *Boston Globe*, July 2, 1995.

Morison, Samuel Eliot. *Maritime History of Massachusetts, 1783–1860*. Boston: Houghton Mifflin, 1921.

Morrison, John H. *History of New York Ship Yards*. New York: Sametz, 1909.

Mueller, Edward A. "Florida's Clipper Ship." *Tequesta*, http://digitalcollections.fiu.edu/tequesta/files/1967/67_01.pdf.

Narvaez, Benjamin Nicolas. "Chinese Coolies in Cuba and Peru: Race, Labor, and Immigration, 1839–1886." Dissertation, University of Texas at Austin, August 2010.

Northrop, Everett H., ed. *Florence Nightingale of the Ocean: Patten Hospital at King's Point is Named in Honor of Mary A. Patten. This is the Reason*. King's Point, NY: U.S. Merchant Marine Academy, 1959.

O'Donnell, Dan. "The Pacific Guano Islands: The

Stirring of American Empire in the Pacific Ocean." *Pacific Studies* 16, no. 1, March 1993.
Peters, Fred J. *Clipper Ship Prints by Currier and Ives.* New York: Antique Bulletin, 1930.
Plowman, Robert J. "The Voyage of the 'Coolie' Ship *Kate Hooper*, October 3, 1857–March 26, 1858." *Prologue* 33, no. 2 (Summer 2001).
Roberts, Bruce. "Clipper Ship Cards." http://www.tradecards.com/article/br/.
Rothstein, Morton. "Multinationals in the Grain Trade, 1850–1914." *Business History Conference* 12, 1983. http://www.thebhc.org/publications/BEprint/vol2/p0085-p0093.pdf.
Rowe, William Hutchinson. *The Maritime History of Maine.* New York: Norton, 1948.
Samuels, Captain Samuel. *From the Forecastle to the Cabin.* New York: Harper & Brothers, 1887.
San Francisco Maritime National Historic Park. "The Grain Trade." http://www.nps.gov/safr/historyculture/balclutha-history.htm.
Sargent, Henry Jackson Jr. *The Captain of the Phantom.* Mystic, CT: Marine Historical Association, 1967.
Scott, Gregory Adam. "Finding Aid for D.W.C. Olyphant Papers, 1827–1851." Missionary Research Library Archives, The Burke Library Archives, Columbia University, Union Theological Seminary, New York, 2010.
Sechrest, Larry J. "American Shipbuilders in the Heyday of Sail: Entrepreneurs and the State." *Libertarian Alliance*, Historical Notes No. 50, 2007.
Semmes, Admiral Raphael. *Memoirs of Service Afloat during the War Between the States.* Baltimore: Kelly, Piet, 1869.
Sharp, Paul. "The Long American Grain Invasion of Britain: Market Integration and the Wheat Trade between North America and Britain from the Eighteenth Century." Discussion Paper, Department of Economics, University of Copenhagen.
Shaw, David W. *Flying Cloud: The True Story of America's Most Famous Clipper Ship and the Woman Who Guided Her.* New York: William Morrow, 2000.
Shockley, Megan Taylor. *The Captain's Widow of Sandwich.* New York: New York University Press, 2010.
Silka, Henry. "Shipbuilding and the Nascent Community of Greenpoint, New York, 1850–55." *The Northern Mariner/Le marin du nord* 16, no. 2 (April 2006), p. 15–52.
Smerz, Courtney. "Red D Line records, 1861–1936 ISM.Red D finding aid." Independence Seaport Museum, J. Welles Henderson Archives and Library, Philadelphia, 2010.
Sonne, Conway B. *Saints on the Seas: A Maritime History of Mormon Migration, 1830–1890.* Salt Lake City: University of Utah Press, 1983.
Spears, John R. *Captain Nathaniel Brown Palmer: An Old Time Sailor of the Sea.* New York: Macmillan, 1922.
Spence, Mary Lee. "Coleman, William Tell." American National Biography Online, October 2003.
Sprague, Francis William, and Leavitt Sprague. *Barnstable and Yarmouth Sea Captains and Ship Owners.* Brookline, MA: privately printed, 1913.
Starbuck, Alexander. *History of the American Whale Fishery.* Secaucus, NJ: Castle Books, 1989.
State Street Trust Company. *Other Merchants and Sea Captains of Old Boston.* Boston: State Street Trust, 1919.
_____. *Some Merchants and Sea Captains of Old Boston.* Boston: State Street Trust, 1918.
_____. *Some Ships of the Clipper Ship Era.* Boston: State Street Trust, 1913.
Stewart, David J. *Combination Atlas Map of Cumberland County, New Jersey.* Philadelphia: Stewart, 1876.
Svardskog, Karl-Eric. *Jenny Lind and the Clipper Nightingale Figurehead.* Portsmouth, NH: Randall, 2001.
Taber, Forest. "Spitfire." http://www.penobscotmarinemuseum.org/spitfire.html.
Taylor, Bayard. *A Visit to India, China, and Japan in the Year 1853.* New York: Putnam, 1891.
Train, George Francis. *An American Merchant in Europe, Asia, and Australia: A Series of Letters.* New York: Putnam, 1857.
Wallace, Frederick William. *Wooden Ships and Iron Men.* Boston: Lauriat, 1937.
Webster, C.B. & Co. *Old Ships of New England.* Boston: Lauriat, 1923.
Whipple, A.B.C. *The Challenge.* New York: Morrow, 1987.
_____. *The Clipper Ships.* Alexandria, VA: Time-Life Books, 1980.
Wilson, James Grant, and John Fiske. *Appleton's Cyclopaedia of American Biography.* Vol. 2. New York: Appleton, 1888.
Wooley, Fred H.C. "Old Ship Street: Some of its Houses, Ships, and Characters." *Medford Historical Society Papers*, Vol. 4, 1901.

Period Newspapers and Magazines

The American Beacon Daily, Norfolk, VA, 1852–53, microfilm records at Norfolk, VA, Public Library.
Ballou's Pictorial Drawing-Room Companion, Boston: Ballou, 1855 (author's collection).
Boston Daily Atlas, 1850–56, the primary source for Duncan MacLean's articles about newly launched clippers at Boston and New York, microfilm records at Boston Public Library.
Boston Daily Evening Transcript, microfilm records at Boston Public Library.
Brooklyn Eagle, accessed online at http://eagle.brooklynpubliclibrary.org.
Daily Alta Californian, 1850–56, accessed online at http://cdnc.ucr.edu/cdnc.
Gleason's Pictorial Drawing Room Companion, Boston: Gleason, 1850–55 (author's collection).
Harper's Weekly, New York, 1859–1867 (author's collection).

The Illustrated London News, London, 1850–1860 (author's collection).

New York Daily Times, 1852–54, accessed online at http://newspaperarchive.com/new-york-daily-times.

The New York Times, 1852–1865, accessed online at http://www.nytimes.com/ref/membercenter/nytarchive.html.

Whalemen's Shipping List and Merchant Transcript, 1852–54, accessed online at National Maritime Digital Library, http://nmdl.org/wsl/wslindex.cfm.

Shipping Registers

These registers are available online from the Mystic Seaport Museum, G.W. Blunt White Library, E-Register at http://library.mysticseaport.org/initiative/VMSearch.cfm.

American Lloyd's Register of American and Foreign Shipping, 1859–1883.

New York Marine Register, 1857–58.

Record of American and Foreign Shipping, 1871–1900.

Federal Census Records

United States Federal Census Records, 1840–1900.

United States Federal Census Non-Population Schedules, 1850–1880.

Accessed online at www.ancestry.com.

City and Business Directories

Baltimore City Directories, including *Matchett's Baltimore Directory* (1847–1856) and

Wood's Baltimore Directory for 1856–57, accessed via Maryland State Archives online at http://www.aomol.net/html/officials.html.

Boston City Directories, 1845–1875, accessed online at http://www.damrellsfire.com/cgi-bin/directory_search.pl.

New York City directories 1840–1870, accessed online at http://search.ancestry.com/search/db.aspx?dbid=8773.

Index

Note: All merchant vessels listed herein are designated as clippers except for those preceded by an asterisk (*), while military vessels are denoted by their country of origin (i.e., USS or CSS). Foreign-built clippers are denoted with their country of building. Multiple clippers with the same name are designated with the state in which they were built. Page numbers in ***bold italics*** indicate pages with illustrations.

A.A. Low & Brothers 12, 28, 54, 82, 129, 133, 167
A. & G.T. Sampson & Co. 35, 77, 314–315
Abbott Lawrence 308
Abrahams, James 68
Abrahams, John J. 70, 350–51
Abrahams & Ashcroft Shipbuilders 70, 178
Achorn, Edwin 78, 265
Adelaide 57, 63, 106, 110, 112, 118–119, 140, 175, 191, 233, 339
Admont, Clark 39
Adriatic 308
Aetos 90, 260
African American crew 112–116
CSS *Alabama* 174, 241, 242–243, 246
Alarm 19, 56, 87, 149, 160, 216, 218, 319
Alboni 58, 169, 212, 213, 330
Alert 78, 86, 131, 168, 266
Alexander 294
Alhambra 308
Allen & McFarland Shipbuilders 270
Allen & Page Shipbuilders 36, 170, 354
Allen & Stimson Shipbuilders 168, 237, 326
Alma 284
Alpheus Hardy & Co. 116–117, 164
America 343
American Guano Co. 152
American Navigation Club 194
Amos Lawrence 308
Amphitrite 310
Andalusia 177
Andrew Jackson 19, 37, 57, 67, 69, 87, 89, 140, 175, 178, 180, 184, 199, 201, 202–203, 216, 218, 246, 327, 329, 330
Andrews, Gen. Joseph 166
Andrews, Sarah 119
Andrews, Capt. Thomas 119
Anglo Saxon 63, 146, 182, 242, 263
Ann McKim 26, 173, 247, 348
Antelope (Boston) 67, 162, 297
Antelope (New York) 67, 70, 172, 181, 201, 217, 219, 342
Anti-Coolie Act of 1862 155
Aquilla see *Aetos*
Arabian (Canada) 250
Aramingo 37, 71, 142, 175, 336
Archer 19, 43, 88, 89, 122, 168, 184, 185, 220, 221, 228, 324–325
Architect 15, 67, 127–128, 135, 177, 230, 349, 352–353
Arey 175, 261
Arey, Captain James 24, 258, 261
Arey, Captain John 90, 116, 170
Arey, Ruth 116
Argonaut 15, 67, 166
Arthur the Great (Canada) 250
Asa Eldridge 57, 161, 166, 319
Aspasia 169, 179, 330
Asterion 63, 72, 153, 165, 169, 183, 292
Atalanta 38, 56, 106, 177, 181, 214, 349, ***350***
Atlantic Insurance Co. 188
Atmosphere 67, 174, 223, 224, 329
Aurora 56, 64, 67, 106, 157, 166, 184, 187, 291
Austin & Hall Shipbuilders 266–267
Australia 175, 333–334
Australian Black Ball Line 199–200, 205, 211, 250
Australian gold rush 135–136, 233

Australian Pioneer Line 181–182
Autocrat 291
Babcock, Charlotte N. 118
Babcock, Capt. David 87, 89, 195, 200
Babcock, Washington I. 87
Bacon, Capt. Daniel C. 165, 194, 210
Badger, Samuel, Jr. 52, 71, 279–280
Balch, John W. 260
Bald Eagle 42, 58, 67, 82, 86, 156, 208, 218, 235, 304
Baines, James 59, 65, 75, 177, 199, 248, 307
Baker, Capt. Ezra 164
Baker & Morrill Co. 160
Balear 345
Balkans, James M. 79, 258
ballasting 52
Baltic 308
Baltimore clipper ***7***
Bangs, Benjamin 166
bark rig 21
Barney, Mason 71, 325
Barstow, Gideon 322
Barstow, Capt. Wilson 322–323
Bartlum, John 354
battens 40
Beacon Light 292
Bearse, Capt. Frank 88
Bearse, Capt. Richard 88
Bearse, Capt. Warren 88
Beaver see *Miss Mag*
Bell, Abraham C. 72, 168, 172, 175, 200, 210, 233, 337, 338–339
Bell, Jacob 71, 175, 176, 200, 223, 229, 331, 332, 337–338
Bell, Richard 71
Bell Bros. Shipbuilders 70, 178, 349, 351
Belle Hoxie 69

359

Belle of the Sea 166, 187, 289
Belle of the West 35, 39, 40, 53, 57, 67, 88, 162, 166, 184, 228, 321
Belle Wood 174, 329
Belvedere 313
Benjamin, W.N. 166
Bergh, Christian 335
Besse, William 147
betting practices 193
Beverly 161, 300
B.F. Hoxie 179, 242, 330
billetheads 54
Billings, Capt. Samuel 100
Bingham & Reynolds Line 185
Bingjian, Wu 133
binnacles 54
Bishop, Stilwell S. 176
Black Ball Line 9–10, 11, 30, 89, 129, 136, 138, 199, 248, 249, 250, 307
Black Hawk (Connecticut) 228, 330
Black Hawk (Massachusetts) 288
Black Hawk (New York) 20, 155, 168, 184, 334
Black Prince 78, 106, 118, 161, 181, 184, 207–208, 288
Black Sea 345
Black Squall 274
Black Warrior 63, 177, 266–267
Black X Line 138
Blanche Moore 306
"Blow the Man Down" (sea chantey) 89
Blue Jacket 35, 37, 58, 136, 154, 163, 204–205, 212, 233, 283, 312
*Blue Jacket 256
Bolster, W. Jeffrey 112
Bone and Muscle Society 61
Bonita 37, 60, 137, 164, 318
Boole, Albenia 32
Boole, John 32
Boomerang (Canada) 250
Booth & Edgar Co. 176
Boston Light 68, 88, 106, 116, 154, 164, 184, 317
Boston Marine Insurance Co. *188*
Boston–New York rivalry 193–194
Bostonian 315
Bounding Billow 164, 292
Bourne & Kingsbury Shipbuilders 275
Bowen, Capt. Francis 239
Bowne & Curry Shipbuilders 354
Boyd, George 39
Boyd & Hinckens Second Line 139
Brewster 252, 286
Bridgeo, Capt. John 88
Briggs, Harrison 79
Briggs, J. Edwin 79
Briggs Bros. Shipbuilders 19, 35, 37, 40, 70, 71, 76–77, 160, 200, 281, 282, 283, 316–319
British-built clipper ships 246–249
Brown, Alexander 102
Brown, Capt. Charles 118
Brown, George 354
Brown, Capt. George W. 176
Brown, Capt. Richard 88
Brown, William 111
Brown & Bell Shipbuilders 12, 28, 32, 64, 83, 138, 337–338

Brown & Lovell Shipbuilders 316
Bucklin & Crane Co. 168–169, 179, 237
Bucknor & McCammon Co. 176
builder ownership 74–76
building costs 60–64
Burgess, Hannah Rebecca 91, 114–115, 117–118, 119–121
Burgess, Capt. John 86, 87
Burgess, Capt. William 91, 114, 117–118, 119–121
Burgess & Clark Shipbuilders 262
Burnham, Andrew 316
Bursley, Capt. Francis 86–87
Bush, Frederick T. 161, 162
Bush & Comstock Co. 161, 187
Butler, Alford 36, 72, 79, 258, 274
Butler, Cornelius 72, 79, 258, 274
Buttersworth, J.E. 53

cabin accommodations 46–47
California 184
California Gold Rush 12–15
California trade 14–15, 130–132
Callaghan, Mrs. 116
Cameron, Roderick W. 181–182, 233
Canadian-built clipper ships 249–251
Canvasback 38, 58, 67, 178, 350
Captain James Huckins & Sons Co. 164
captain tenure 87
captain's pay 92
cargo capacity 19–20
cargo rates 131–132
Carrier Dove 38, 70, 14, 177, 183, 187, 215, 349, 350–351
Carrier Pigeon 58, 160, 209–210, *272*
Carter, Columbus 19, 261–262
case oil trade 147
cathead decorations *54*–55
Cathedral 125, 139, 163, 280
caulking 46
Celestial 15, 16, 68, 87, 134, 135, 168, 332–333
Celestial Empire 68, 187, 228, 319–320
Celestial Line 184–185
Challenge 42, 45, 47, **48**, 53, 55, 58, 59, 63, 67, 82, 89, 92, 96, 105, 106, 107–**108**, 109–111, 13, 157, 175, 179, 191, 194, 198, 225, 245, 332, 333
Challenger 35, 57, 60, 67, 114–115, 117, 120–121, 145, 157, 160, 166, 183, 311
Chamberlain & Phelps Co. 175
Chambers, Heiser & Co. 169–170, 175
Champion of the Seas 46, 54, 58, 59, 68, 136, 154, 204, 248, 282, 302
Chapelle, Howard 6, 8, 17
Chapman & Flint Shipbuilders 265
Charger 54, 60, 72, 87, 165, 184, 191, 197, 216, 218, 281
Chariot of Fame 40, 56, 67, 136, 139, 154, 162, 224, 305
Charles Brewer & Co. 147
Charles Brewer & Co,'s Line of Boston and Honolulu Packets 186

Charles H. Cumming & Co. 176
Charles Mallory 146, 154, 178, 328
Charmer 50, 58, 60, 111, 116, 149, 161, 162, 187, 287
Chase, Capt. Josiah 116
Chase, Sarah 116
Chase & Davis Shipbuilders 175, 326
Cherubim 38, 68, 70, 143, 351
CSS *Chickamauga* 242
Chief of Clippers 228
China Mutual Insurance Co. **189**
China trade 11–12, 133–135
Chincha Islands 151, *152*–153, 155
Chinese Exclusion Act of 1882 (California) 155
Chisling, Henry 115–116
Chrysolite (British) 135, 194, **246**, 248
City of Adelaide (British) 248
Civil War (American) 189, 240–245
Clark, Capt. Arthur H. 3, 17, 97, 99, 100
Clark, Capt. Joseph 85
Clark & Wood Shipbuilders 53, 75, 127
Clarke, Andrew 125
Clay, Henry 68
Cleopatra 58, 67, 166, 190, 215, 312–313
Climax 58, 67, 157, 162, 295
coal hulks 145, 252
coal trade 144–145
Coeur de Lion 43, 52, 58, 59, 223, 224, 233, 276, 278
Coffin, Laban 127
Coghill, Alexander 108–110
Cole, Capt. 219
Coleman, William T. 15, 182–183
Coleman's California Line 180, 181, 182–183
Collyer, Thomas 175, 199, 332, 340–341
Colt, John 47
*Columbia 199
Columbian Insurance Co. 188
Comet (Maine) 73, 259
Comet (New York) 44, 67, 87, 131, 154, 168, 181, 183, 184, 187, 200, **212**–213, 236, 246, 332, 333
Commerce Insurance Co. 188
Commercial Insurance Co. 188
Competitor 53, 58, 60, 67, 116, 157, 158, 161, 252, 297–298
Comstock, Cornelius 187
Comstock, William O. 161
Comstock's Line of California Clippers 179, 187
Condry, Dennis 33
Connecticut-built clipper ships 327–331
Connell, Charles 248
Conquest 164, 184, 187
USS *Constitution* 59
Contest 29, 63, 67, 167, 187, 195, 200, 201, 242, 332, 336
Continent 271
Conway (Canada) 250
Cooley, Randolph M. 184, 187
coolie trade 154–158

Index

Cooper, Caroline C. 177
Cooper, George R. 349, 350, 351
Cooper, James Fenimore 67
Cooper & Butler Shipbuilders 351, 352
Cooper & Slicer Shipbuilders 351, 352
coppering **48**–50
Coquette 35, 88, 93, 308–309
Coringa 301
Corn Laws (Britain) 148
*Cornelius Grinnell **10**, **98**
Cossack 318–319
Cotter, Col. Cyrus 267
cotton trade 141
*Courier (Currier & McKay) 33, 142
Courier (Currier & Townsend) 286
Courser 64, 219, 300
Cox, James W. 74, 243
Creesy, Eleanor 121–122, 127
Creesy, Capt. Josiah 12, 89, 92, 94–95, 121–122, 199, 202, 244
Creesy, Capt. William 88
*Cremorne 256
Crest of the Wave 67, 178, 225, 226, 230, 265
crew: burial at sea 102; discipline of 105; duties of 100–105; feeding of 104–105; mutiny of 106–112; origins of 95; procurement of 96; size 84, 93
Crimean War 129, 165, 233, 235
crimps 96, 97
*Crisis 327
Criterion 165, 187, 267
Crocker & Warren Co. 168
Crooker, Charles 272
Crooker, William 272
Crosby, Capt. 183
Crothers, William 4
Crowell, Capt. Elkanah 88
Crowell, Isaiah, Jr. 162
Crowell, Nathaniel 162
Crowell, Prince S. 84, 157–158, 162, 166
Crowell, Capt. Sturgis 87, 88, 106
Crowell & Brooks Co. 162
Crystal Palace 166, 260
Cudworth, William 49
Culley, Langley B. 177, 352
Cummings, Capt. George 85
Cunningham Bros. Co. 165
Cunningham's Roller Reefing System 27
Currier, John, Jr. 32, 78, 79, 281, 288
Currier, William 33
Currier & Ives Printmakers 53
Currier & Townsend Shipbuilders 39, 43, 78, 214, 252, 281, 283, 284–286
Curry, William 354
Curtis, James O. 19, 35, 70, 77, 78, 79, 160, 164, 174, 252, 281, 282, 283, 284, 296–298
Curtis, Paul 35, 52, 55, 64, 73–74, 161, 172, 201, 221, 281, 282, 283, 293, 299–300, 312–314, 316
Curtis & Peabody Co. 165
Cutler, Carl 3–4, 17, 196, 233–234

Cutty Sark (British) 248
Cyclone 67, 165, 183, 318

Dale, Capt. Frank 216
Damon & Hancock Co. 176
Dana, Richard Henry, Jr. 115, 206
Daniel Bacon & Co. 165
Daniels, George B. 175
Daring 58, 78, 161, 162, 187, 192, 287
Darling, Grace 67
Dashaway 71, 187, 256, 268
Dashing Wave 20, 37, 54, 67, 78, 88, 106, 143, 165, 186, 216, 276, 278–279
Dauntless 57, 60, 166, 207, 302
David, John 261
David Brown 29, 149, 167, 224, 228, 229, 332, 339
David Crockett 55, 56, 63, 67, 86, 87, 145, 154, 171, 175, 183, 187, 189, 232, 327, 329
Davis & Company 66
Dawn 332, 341
Dawson & Hancock Co. 176
De Abranches, Georgia 237
De Abranches, J.W. 237
Dean, Nicholas 106, 254
deck fittings 54
deck supports 45–46
Defender 67, 143, 307
Defiance 19, 35, 67, 71, 72, 151–152, 192, 204, 262–263
Delano, Benjamin 281, 301–302, 320
*Delia Walker 32–33
Derby 67, 166, 183, 291
Dictator 74, 171, 242, 243, 258
Dillingham, Capt. James, Jr. 84, 243, 254
Dillingham, Capt. John 244
Dixie, Capt. Richard 88
Doane, Capt. Alfred 87
Doane, Capt. Azariah 210
Doane, Capt. Seth 87–88, 223
Don Quixote 47, 60, 87, 116, 154, 166, 283, 301
Donald McKay 55, 127, 136, 145, 147, 204, 248, 252, **307**
Douglass, James 108–111
Dow, Oliver 259
Dragon 285
Dramatic Line 11, 28, 138
Dreadnought 43, 54, 58, 78, 81, 82, 112–113, 15, 140, 147, 172, 173, 174, 185, **198**, 199, 225, 283, 285, **286**
Dred Scott Decision 235
Drew, Nathaniel 320–321
Driver 43, 78, 126, 140, 173, 174, 209, 286
Drummond, James 271
Drummond, William 78, 271
Dubois, Caroline Worrell 121
Dumaresq, Capt. Phillip 82, 86, 90
Dunham, George 260–261
Dunham, Capt. Isaac 69, 260–261
Dutch East India Co. 68
Dutton, Benjamin 72, 166, 281, 288–289
Dyer, Joseph W. 275
dyewood trade 142

E. Buckley & Sons Co. 175
Eagle 58, 102, 131, 172, 342
USCGC *Eagle* 253
Eagle Line 185
Eagle Wing 52, 67, 86, 184, 208, 297
East India Co. 247
East Indian 165, 286
Eckford, Henry 37
Eclipse 142, 190, 191, 343
Eclipse Line 183
Eddystone 286
Edith Rose 295
Edwin Forrest 57, 77, 208, 315
Eldridge, Capt. Asa 11, 88, 197
Eldridge, Capt. John 88
Eldridge, Capt. Oliver 88
Electric 140, 329
Electric Spark 40, 67, 149, 166, 220, 221, 295
Eliza F. Mason 176, 353
Eliza Mallory 328
Elizabeth F. Willets 147, 178–179, 328
Elizabeth Kimball 143, 145, 150, 166, 288–289
Ellen Foster 46, 55, 56, 67, 162, 166, 299
*Ellen Sears 321
Elliott, Mrs. G.W. 116
Eloisa de Valparaiso 285
*Emerald 199
Emerald Isle 38, 78, 140, 181, 183, 258, 271
Emery, Rufus 261
*Emily C. Starr 217
Emily Farnum 67, 187, 278
Empire 72, 170, 264
Empire Line 185
Empress 48, 52, 172, 313
Empress of the Seas 57, 63, 67, 75, 154, 177, 185, 200, 304–**305**
Endeavor 37, 67, 87, 165, 312
*Enoch Train 69
Enoch Train & Co. 162–163
Eringo 316
Essex (black steward, no last name) 113–114
*Eternal 69
Eureka 67, 170, 175, 184, 189, 336
Euroclydon 67, 176, 225, 349
Euterpe 78, 170, 183, 228, 229, 244, 264
Evans, Capt. Richard 88
Ewell, Henry 73, 288, 311
Ewell, Isaac 72, 73, 259
Expounder 145, 186, 290
Express 141, 151, 279

Faben, Capt. Samuel A. 82, 89
Fair Wind 67, 145, 166, 180, 319
Fairburn, William A. 4, 257
Fairy 339
Falcon 287
Fanny McHenry 176, 314–315
fastening methods 44
Fatherland 315
Fearless 35, 53, 67, 77, 144, 161, 198, 314
Ferguson, Henry 127

Ferguson, Samuel 113, 127
Fernald, Frederick 35
Fernald & Pettigrew Shipbuilders 37, 40, 213, 216, 276, 278–279
Fernie Bros. Red Cross Line (British) 250
Ferrin, George H. 72, 217, 270
Field, George 111
figureheads **55**–58
fire losses 210–213
Fish, Reuben 322, 323
Flaherty, Ann K. 125
Fleetwing 58, 67, 87, 142, 295
Fleetwood 67, 215, 216, 279–280
Flora Temple 157, 178, 183, 350
Florence 86, 137, 310
CSS *Florida* 151, 179, **241**–242
Flyaway 44, 58, 67, 334
Flying Arrow 20, 54, 67, 69, 85, 166, 190, 230
Flying Childers 58, 77, 145, 149, 185, 246, 309–310, 346
Flying Cloud (Massachusetts) **18**, 19, 33, 56, 64, 67, 68, 69, 89, 92, 95, 121–122, 127, 130, 131, 144, 159, 163, 172, 180, 187, 194, 195, 199, 201, **202**–203, 204, 225, 235, 236, 245, 251–252, 281, 282, 302, 303
Flying Cloud (New York, bark) 332, 342
Flying Dragon 38, 58, 67, 145, 154, 160, 220–221, 232, 258, 271
Flying Dutchman 44, 67, 68, 142, 149, 175, 179, 334
Flying Eagle 58, 63, 64, 67, 145, 165, 184, 215, 267
Flying Fish 58, 67, 93–94, 97, 160, 181, 195, 201, 220, 222, 283, 303–304
Flying Mist 55, 57, 154, 225, 226, 298
Flying Scud 38, 63, 67, 88, 90, 182, 183, 204, 246, 258
Flying Yankee 67, 261
Forbes, Robert Bennett 86, 94, 95, 99, 104–106, 213
Forbes Double Topsail Rig 23
foreign sales 245–246
Forsyth, Peter 37
Fortuna 314
Foster, Daniel 72
Foster, Joshua T. 77, 281, 290, 298–299
Foster, S.C. 259
Foster & Booze Shipbuilders 70, 352,
Foster & Nickerson Co. 36, 170
Fountain, George 259–260
Fowler's Line of New York–San Francisco Packets 186
framing details **42**
Francis A. Palmer 70, 79, 258
Frigate Bird 67, 71, 145, 176, 353

Galatea 53, 54, 56, 60, 90, 161, 184, 187, 289
Game Cock 23, 34–35, 47, 60, 129, 165, 174, 185, 309
Ganges 82, 90, 315

Gardner, Capt. E.C. 87, 168
Gardner, James 71, 349
Gardner Bros. Shipbuilders 37, 70, 71, 349–350
Garrick 11, 28
Gates, Capt. Gurden 88, 179
Gauntlet 67, 78, 129, 145, 269
Gay Head 323
Gazelle (Connecticut) 330–331
Gazelle (New York) 36, 58, 67, 134, 157, 174, 224, 333
Gem of the Ocean 49, 54, 67, 143, 150, 162, 225, 294
Gem of the Sea 326
Gemsbok 312
George E. Webster 160, 293
George Howes & Co. Dispatch Line 180, 183–184
CSS *Georgia* 171
George McHenry & Co. 176
George Peabody 161, 183, 187, 297
Gitana 203
Glad Tidings 339
Gleason, George 265
Gleason, William 55
Glidden, John A. 162
Glidden, William T. 151, 162
Glidden & Williams Co. 162, 221
Glidden & Williams Line of San Francisco Clippers 180, 184
Glory of the Seas 34, 56, 68, 87, 90, 217, 256, 302
Goddard, Nathaniel 166
Goddess 187, 296
Golden Age (Canada) 250
Golden City 67, 170, 210, 225, 336
Golden Eagle 58, 82, 146, 154, 162, 166, 174, 244, 293–294
Golden Era (Canada) 250
Golden Fleece (I) 52, 67, 161, 187, 220, 221, 316
Golden Fleece (II) 58, 67, 107, 150, 161, 210, 313
Golden Gate 77, 129, 170, 336
Golden Horn 53, 67, 75, 268
Golden Light 37, 58, 60, 67, 164, 190, **209**, 210, 317–318
Golden Line 250
Golden Racer 65, 67, 69, 78, 88, 222, 264
Golden Rocket 67, 242, 256, 260
Golden Rule 165, 267
Golden State 67, 77, 106, 135, 149, 167, 170, 189, 336–337
Golden West 35, 58, 162, 184, 312, 346
Goldfinger (Canada) 250
gone missing 207–209
Good Hope 174, 225, 298
Goodhue & Co. 175
Goodwin, Ichabod 66
Gorham, Capt. Josiah 157
Governor Morton 43, 87, 141, 157, 175, 183, 187, 211, 283, 324
Grace Darling 57, 67, 143, 149, 160, 184, 209, 318
Granite State 52, 68, 100, 225, 280
Grapeshot 85, 93, 257, 258, **273**–274
Graves, David 114–115, 120

Gravina 218, 347
Gray, Capt. Adams 128, 177, 236, 349
Great Admiral 256, 311
Great American II 200
Great Republic 21, 29, 33, 45, 47, **49**, 55, 59, 67, 69, 74, 75, 76, 83, 90, 93, 111, 129, 142, 149, 167, 176, 187, 188, 190, 196, **201**, 204, **210**, 281, **228**, 229, 232, 244, 283, 302, 305, 306, 331, 345–346
Great Western Insurance Co. 188
Green, Charles R. 171
Greenfield 149, 324
Greenman, George 70, 174, 210, 326, 327, 328–329
Greenman, Silas, Jr. 326
Gregory, Hugh 113
Gregory, Capt. Michael 87, 88
Grey Eagle 15, 142, 176, 350, 351
Grey Feather 67, 87, 90, 121, 151, 257, 258, 259
Grey Hound 15, 67, 353
Griffiths, John 12, 25–27, 62, 172
Grinnell, Minturn & Co. 64, 159, 171–172, 200, 252
Guano Islands Act of 1856 152
guano trade 142, 151–154
Guiding Star (Canada) 250
Guthrie, Lt. John 239–240

Haidee 168, **235**, 236, 237–238, 326
Hall, Alexander 247, 248
Hall, Capt. Christopher 166, 321
Hall, Samuel 17, 34–35, 37, 39, 59, 77, 165, 168, 175, 195, 201, 207, 210, 281, 282, 283, 284, 308–310
Hall, William 315
Hall & Teague Shipbuilders 228, 330
Hall, Snow & Co. Shipbuilders 271–272
Hallett, Henry 166
USS *Hancock* 9
Handy, Thomas J. 178
Handy & Everett Line 171, 175
Hanscomb, Samuel, Jr. 35, 66, 166, 276
Harbeck & Co. 172
Hardy, Alpheus 164
Hardy, Samuel 115
Hare, Second Mate 123–124
Harford, Capt. John 121
Harper, George 102
Harriet Hoxie 179, 329
Harriman, Capt. 245
Harry Bluff 171, 187, 292
Harry of the West 68, 184, 312
Harvey Birch 175, 185, **240**, 242, 329
Hastings, Henry 165
Hathaway, Frank 166
Hatch, Clara 116
Hatch, Capt. Freeman 12, 116, 164, 200
Hatch, Capt. James 116
Hatch, Lydia 116
Hatch, Mabel 116
Hawaiian Packet Line 186
Hayden & Cudworth Shipbuilders

35, 40, 70, 77, 160, 162, 281, 282, 283, 293–296
Hayes, Capt. John 215
Hazard 309
Haze 179, 187, 328
*Helena **12**, **31**
Henry, Capt. William 195
Henry Hill 307
Herald of the Morning 35, 56, 87, 111, 149, 153, 184, 215, 216, 283, 294
Hesperus 145, 299
Highflyer 43, 140, 173, 174, 219, 285
Hill, Mason 169, 330
Hinckley, Capt. Francis 87
Hippogriffe 40, 145, 166, 217, 218, 321
Hitchcock, William 64, 71, 267
Holmes, Jonathan 323
Holmes, Josiah 323
holystoning, practice of 103
Homan, Capt. William 88
Hood, Capt. James 43, 70, 79, 168, 174, 194, 211, 281, 282, 283, 323–325
Hood, Walter 248
Hoogly 57, 165, 190, 210, 220, 222, 309
Hornet 77, 90, **114**, 115–116, 127, 132, 147, 175, 180, 183, 184, 210, 211, 335–336
Horney, Thomas 353
Hotspur 67, 166, 216, 219, 339–340
Houghton, Levi 272
Howard, Capt. William 125
Howe, Frederick, and Matthews, Octavius 3, 17, 202
Howes, Capt. Allison 88
Howes, Jerusha 116
Howes, Capt. Levi 88
Howes, Capt. Moses, Jr. 116
Howes, Osborne 162
Howes, Capt. Thomas 87
Howes, Capt. William F. 88
Howes Patent Rig 23
Howland, Capt. William 83, 102, 171, 213–214
Howland & Aspinwall Co. 26, 62, 161, 172
Hound 178, 185, 328
Houqua 12, 15, 24, 28, 81, 84, 85, 86, 94, 103, 111, 113, 114, 133, 134, 196, 208, 218, 224, 251, 337–338
Hoxie, Benjamin F. 179
Huckins, Capt. James 37, 164, 195, 209
hull color 53
hull models 23–24
Hunt, Thomas 94
Hunt & Waggner Shipbuilders 352
*Huntsville 11, 28
Hurricane 37, 54, 59, 67, 89, 180, **234**, 346, 347
Hussar 161, 287
Huston, Caleb 70, 90, 259–260
Hyperion see *Golden Racer*

ice trade 52, 150–151
immigrant trade **125**, 126, **139**–140
Importation Act of 1846 (Britain) 148

India Fire & Marine Insurance Co. 188
Indiaman 68, 160, 315
Indian Queen (Canada) 250
Indian trade 138
Industry 248
Ino 37, 47, 70, 89, 145, 147, 160, 244, 251, 332, 341, 342
insurance losses 190–191
insurance practices 187–190, 245
Intrepid 67, 87, 123, 133, 168, 187, 218, 219–220, 334
Invincible 54, 55, 59, 63, 67, 140, 211, 333
iron bracing 44
Irons & Grinnell Shipbuilders 37, 69, 175, 179, 327, 329–330
Isaac Jeanes 77, 140, 176, 348
Island City 298

Jack, William 238
Jackman, George W., Jr. 78, 79, 162, 281, 286–288
Jackson, General Andrew 69
Jackson, Robert E. 35, 37, 68, 69, 70, 73, 77, 79, 164, 204, 211, 282, 283, 288, 310–312
Jacob Bell 54, 68, 82, 86, 167, 168, 197, **241**, 242, 338, 346
James Baines 47, 57, 59, 136, 198, 199–200, 204, 211–212, 233, 248, 281, 282, 306
James Bishop & Co. 169
James Hooper & Co. 177
Jeanes, Isaac 176
John Bertram 23, 58, 59, 68, 73, 162, 184, 283, 311
John E. Thayer 73–74, 153, 163, 313
John Gilpin 46, 60, 67, 146, 166, 184, 195, 201, 215–216, 283, 310
John H. Brower & Co. 175
John Land 68, 146, 160, 228, 229, 318
John Milton 67, 106, 166, 225, 226–227, 322, **323**
**John Quincy Adams* 183
John Stuart 22, 145, 173, 342, 346
John Wade 57, 68, 77, 160, 216, 217, 293
Johnson, Capt. 206
Joseph Peabody 68, 145, 165, 319
Josephine 166, 280
Juniper 79, 259

Kate Hayes 260
Kate Hooper 67, 157, 177, 352
Kate Napier 353
Kathay 51, 68, 153, 175, 185, 337
keel assembly 43–44
keel components 45
Kelly, Daniel D. 77, 315
Kennard & Williamson Shipbuilders 173, 348
Keyes, Samuel B. 262
Kimball, Edward 166, 288, 289
Kimball, Mrs. Harlow 116
King Lear 312
King of Clippers 69
King of the Forest 69
King Philip (Maine) 253–254, **268**

King Philip (Massachusetts) 72, 77, 184, 187, 320
Kingfisher 54, 77, 129, 149, 160, 162, 183, 187, 192, 244, 294
Kit Carson 39, 40, 84, 157–158, 166, 321–322
Kittredge, Henry 88, 121
Knight, Capt. Elias D. 116
Knight, Mary 116
Knight & Blanchard Shipbuilders 68, 258, 274–275
Knot, Mrs. William 116
Knowles, Capt. Elijah 111–112
Knowles, Capt. Josiah 87, 217
Kremlin 300

Lady Franklin 315–316
Lady Suffolk 177, 236, 351
Land, Capt. John 12, 26, 109, 110, 196
Lane, Fitz Henry 53
Lane, Capt. George 197
Lane & Jacobs Shipbuilders 330–331
Lantao 207, 309
Lapham, Samuel, Jr. 70, 281, 283, 300–301
Larrabee, Stephen 273
launching day 48–50
launching mishaps 51–52
Law, George 85
Lawrence, Giles, & Co. 170–171
Leading Wind 87
Leah **174**, **210**, **329**
Lecraw, Capt. David 88
Lee, Thomas Conrad 250
Levanter 67, 266
Lewis, Capt. J. 111
Lightfoot 63, 67, 72, 225, 311
Lightning **22**, 57, 60, 67, 119, **135**, 136, 200, 204, 211, 212, 217, 23, 248, 281, 282, 302, 306
lightning protection 213
Limeburner, Capt. Joseph 90, 93, 196
Lind, Jenny 55
Line Gale 346
Linnell, Capt. Eben 86
Live Yankee 52, 67, 78, 157, 170, 171, 263
Living Age 166
Lloyds of London Co. 191–192
Lodge, John E. 166
Logan 72, 320
logwood trade 142
Lookout 67, 145, 147, 149, 175, 180, 184, 185, 187, 216, 218, 232, 325, 326
Lotus 165, 290
Low, Capt. Charles P. 82, **84**, 85, 86, 89, 94, 103, 106, 111, 113–114, 167
Loyd, Capt. Thomas 107
Ludwig, M.R. 178
lumber trade 143–**144**, 252
Lupton, Edward 345
Lyon, Ellen 127
Lyon, Sarah 127

MacKey, William 335
Maffitt, Capt. John N. 242

Index

Magoun, Joshua 164, 208, 282, 290–291
Magoun, Thatcher 282, 296, 299, 300
Maid of the Sea 273
Maine-built clipper ships 256–275
Malay 58, 94, 166, 187, 252, 283, 290
Mallory, Charles 37, 52–53, 71, 75, 77, 88, 169, 178–179, 201, 327–328
Mameluke 87, 319
Mandarin 15, 134, 175, 199, 217, 218, 340
Manila trade 136–137
Manitou 77, 176, 184, 207, 347
Manning & Stanwood Co. 166
Manton, Capt. Benjamin 107
Marco Polo (Canada) 136, 200, **249**, 250
Mary 48, 67, 72, 88, 166, 228, 229, 289
Mary Bangs 67, 313
Mary Kimball 88
Mary L. Sutton 56, 77, 179, 328
Mary Ogden 175, 326
Mary Robinson 67, 166, 183, 271
Mary Whitridge 89, 140, 146, 157, 178, 349, 352
Maryland-built clipper ships 348–353
Mason, John 56
Mason, William 176
Massachusetts-built clipper ships 281–325
Mastiff 58, 187, 206, 307
masting and rigging details 41–42, 47–48
Matchless 67, 71, 166, 292
Matthews, Capt. 115
Matthews, Capt. George 117
Matthews, Mary 117
Maury, Lt. Matthew F. 25, 122
Maxon, Fish. & Co. Shipbuilders 179, 330
Mayo, Capt. David 245
McCerren, Capt. Robert 152
McDonald, John 250
McDonnell, Capt. Charles 200
McGaw, John A. 174, 210
McKay, Donald 10, 19, 24, 29, 31–**32**, 34, 39, 40, 43, 55, 59, 60, 63, 64, 68, 69, 70, 72, 73, 74, 76, 78, 79, 126, 138, 142, 161, 163, 172, 177, 190, 195, 197, 198, 199, 200, 201, 202, 203, 204–205, 211, 222, 233, 281, 282–283, 302–308
McKay, Hugh 316
McKay, Hugh R. 315
McKay, Capt. Lauchlan 75, 83
McKay, Simon 238, 284
McKeever, John 176
McKim, Isaac 173
McLaughlin, Capt. Daniel 87, 90, 121
McLean, Duncan 51
McLoon, Capt. William 102
McNulty, Edward 100
Meads, Henry 353

Mechanics Shipbuilding Co. 61, 280
medical epidemics 230–231
Mediterranean trade 141, 164
Memnon (New York) 12, 15, 340
Memnon (Newburyport) 285
Memnon (South Boston) 319
Mercantile Mutual insurance Co. 188
Merchants Express Line 180, 184
Mercury 139, 336
Mermaid (Canada) 250
Mermaid (Maine) 272
Mermaid (Massachusetts) 34–35, 309
Merriam, Horace 78, 263–264
Merrill, Orlando 23–24, 33
Messenger 67, 106, 107, 143, 147, 149, 157, 175, 176, 187, 225, 338
Messenger Bird 321
Metcalf, Benjamin 79
Metcalf & Norris Shipbuilders 37–38, 70, 78, 168, 257, 266–267
Meteor 37, 56, 87, 165, 317
Midnight 56, 63, 68, 116, 147, 165, **183**, 184, 279
Miller, Capt. James 207
Miller, Capt. Lewis F. 66, 116
Miller, Martha 116
Minnehaha 56, 160, 182, 307–308
Minott, Charles V. 259
Mischief 65, 68, 174, 185, 325
Miss Mag 269
Mitchell, Capt. Josiah 90, **114**, 115–116, 211
mold loft 40
Monsoon 38, 67, 166, 187, 271
*Montauk 12, 31
Montell, Capt. F. 106
Montell & Co. 177
Morgan, Governor Edwin D. **172**, 173
Morning Glory 61, 78, 280
Morning Light (Canada) 250
Morning Light (New Hampshire) 37, 51, 52, 58, 60, 63, 67, 116, 162, 184, 210, 232, 246, 279
Morning Light (Pennsylvania) 67, 145, 154, 176, 244–245, 348
Morning Star (Canada) 250
Morning Star (Massachusetts) 67, 106, 107, 166, 187, 242, 243, 299
Morton, Charles 70, 71, 75, 78, 264
Morton, Joshua C. 69, 70, 71, 75, 78, 222, 264
Moses Kimball **19**, 262
Moulton, Daniel 78, 280
Mountain Wave 54, 67, 116, 164, 246, 289
Mumford, Benjamin A. 173
Mumford, Capt. Oliver 11, 173, 226

Nabob 58, 145, 149, 166, 196, 233, 291
naming practices 66–69
Napier 38, 63, 153, 176, 184, 349–350
CSS *Nashville* **240**, 242
*Natchez 11, 106, 108, 196
National Eagle 58, 67, 77, 88, 117, 141, 225, 228, 299
Naturalization Act of 1870 155
N.B. Palmer 29, 54, 68, 86, 106, 130, 147, 167, 196, 217, 218, 228, 332, 336
Neesima, Joseph H. 164–165
Neptune Insurance Co. 188
Neptune's Car 35, 36, 67, 90, 122–124, 170, 190, 232, 246, 354
Neptune's Favorite 67, 183, 291–292
New Hampshire–built clipper ships 275–281
New Jersey–built clipper ships 346–347
*New World 33
New York & California Line 187
New York–built clipper ships 331–346
New York Insurance Co. 190
New York Journeyman Shipwright's and Caulkers Benevolent Society 61
New York Journeyman Shipwright's Society 61
New York Yacht Club 81
New Zealand trade 136
Nicholas I 340
Nickels, Capt. Edward 97, 107
Nickerson, Frederick 165
Nightingale 35, 52, 55, 60, **65**, 66, 69, 119, 134, 135, 144, 160, 166, 181, 182, 183, 186, 187, 194, 228, 236, 239–240, 245, 251, 252, 275, 276, 280
N.L. & G.G. Griswold Co. 92, 174–175, 199
Nonpareil 63, 129, 228, 244, 261
Noonday 22, 40, 63, 64, 68, 165, 216, 279
Norseman 77, 165, 312
North Atlantic trade 138
North Wind 67, 145, 154, 172, 200, 224, 338–339
Northern Eagle 316
Northern Light 35, 36, 56, 67, 72, 87, 116, 164, 195, 200, 223–224, 283, 316–317
Nor'Wester 67, 87, 88, 136, 145, 230, 301
Nott, Capt. William 87

occuli 55
Ocean Chief 35, 63, 67, 75, 78, 200, 264
Ocean Express 19, 58, 67, 106, 107, 144, 154, 160, 180, 184, 228, **242**, 244, 298
Ocean Herald 67, 129, 267
Ocean Monarch (Canada) 250
Ocean Pearl 54, 67, 164, 289
Ocean Rover 67, 74, 141, 186, 225, 279
Ocean Spray 67, 261
Ocean Telegraph 35, 57, 60, 67, 144, 160, 187, 246, 252, 284, 298
Oelrichs & Lurman Co. 177–178
officer positions 93–94
Ogden, John 181
Ogden & Associates Co. 173–174
Ogden & Haynes Co. 184
Olyphant & Co. 169
*Oneida 89, 122
Onward 57, 59, 160, 181, 186, 244, 297

Opium War 129
Oracle 265
Oriental 12, **29**, 64, 68, 134, 167, 196, 220, 248, 332
Oriental Mutual Insurance Co. 188
Orpheus 53, 87, 145, 161, 184, 191, 224, 225, 293
Osborne Howes 149, 154, 162, 183, 295
Owens, Henry W. 272
Owens & Duncan Co. 250

Pacific Guano Co. 162
packet trade 9, 11, 17, 138–139
Paine, Capt. John 116
Paine, Reliance 116
Paladin 348, 349
Palmer, Capt. Alexander 28, 89
Palmer, Capt. Nathaniel B. 11, 12, 19, 24, 27, **28**–30, 81, 82, 86, 89, 111, 167, 327
Palmer, Capt. Theodore 28, 89, 134
Pampero 37, 67, 77, 169, 198, 244, 328
Panama 68, 134, 137, 175, 184, 199, 341
Panic of 1857 234, 235
Panther 44, 137, 145, 184, 187, 300
Parritt, Capt. J.W.C. 199
Pathfinder 184–185, 325
Patten, Capt. Joshua 90, 122–124, 170, 190
Patten, Mary Ann 122–124, 170, 253
Patten & Sturdevant Shipbuilders 70, 269–270
Patterson, Edwin 265
Patterson, Joshua 265
Paul, Capt. Josiah 111
Paul Jones 12, 28
Pedrick, Capt. Knott 88, 117
Pedrick, Ruth 117
Peerless (Maine) 70, 77, 161, 270
Peerless (Massachusetts) 314
Penhallow, Pearce 81
Pennsylvania-built clipper ships 347–348
Perrine, William 70
Perrine, Patterson & Stack Shipbuilders 37, 70, 172, 173, 201, 331, 332, 341–342
Pettigrew, William 78
Phantom 54, 154, 165, 168, 184, 217, 219, 283, 300–301
Phoenix 22, 63, 68, 138, 224, 258, 274–275
Phoenix Insurance Co. 188
Pickering, Capt. McLauren 74
Pickett, W. B. 33
Pierce, Elbridge G. 72, 79, 276, 281
Pierce, George 269
Pierce, Hiram 261
Pierce & Hunnewell Co. 166
Pike, Capt. Samuel 87
Pile, William 248
Pilkington & Wilson Co. 250
pilot losses 220–221
pilotage practices 85–86
Pioneer Line 181, 185
pirate attacks 218–220
Pocahontas 272
Pointer 274

Polar Star 323
Polynesia 154, 166, 184, 190, 310
Pook, Samuel H. 24, 34–36, 59, 197, 204, 216, 257–258, 261, 308, 327
Portland 275
Post, Smith & Co. 179
Pratt, Jairus 315–316
Pride of America 67, 70, 228, 270
Pride of the Ocean 67, 72, 326
Pride of the Sea 67, 70, 177, 352
Prima Donna 58, 174, 184, 187, 189, 245, 329
Prince de Neufchatel 8
Prince of the Seas (Canada) 250
privateers 8–9
Progressive 263

Queen of Clippers 37, 56, 67, 69, 129, 163, 185, 186, 311
Queen of the East 67, 78, 168, 187, 266
Queen of the Pacific 67, 73, 145, 150, 160, 187, 259
Queen of the Seas 22, 55, 56, 67, 157, 162, 184, 208, 300
Quickstep (Maine) 67, 187, 275
Quickstep (Massachusetts) 67, 310
Quinlan, Capt. Charles, Jr. 253

Race Horse 15, 34–35, 87, 134, 218
Race Horse Line 185
Racer 22, 43, 58, 59, 67, 81, 140, 173, 199, 214, **215**, 285
Radiant 55, 160, 184, 187, 213, 218, 313
Raduga 65, 147, 165, 186, 285
Rainbow 12, 16, 26, 62, 173, 196, 207, 332, 340
Rambler 295
Ranlett, Capt. Charles A. 88, 111
Ranlett, Capt. Charles, Jr. 88
Rapid 67, 169, 339
Rattler (Maine) 63, 72, 88, 129, 138, 142, 187, 262
Rattler (Maryland) 352
Raven 43, 54, 131, 168, 194–195, 283, 324
Raynes, George 10, 37, 43, 55, 70, 138, 169, 171, 215, 224, 233, 276–278
Raynes, George, Jr. 72, 276
Red Cross Line 43, 140, 172, 173–174, 185, 198, 209
Red D Line 320
Red Gauntlet 74, 119, 145, 150, 187, 242, 243, 258
Red Jacket 35, 36, **42**, 52, 58, 67, 72, 77, 88, 136, 145, 163, 164, **197**, 198, 200, 204, 232, 233, 252, 257–258, 263
Red Rover 51, 52, 67, 174, 224, 278, 346
Red Star Line 138
Reed, Wade & Co. 160, 209
Reindeer 15, 160, 217, 303
Reporter 51, 58, 63, 141, 151, 161, 165, 313
resale prices 64–65
Resolute 67, 337
Reynard 137, 161, 162, 187, 288

Rhoades, Francis W. 263
Rhode Island–built clipper ships 325–326
Rhodes 8
Rice, Edmund 102
Rice & Mitchell Shipbuilders 225, 293
Richard Busteed 320
Richards, Enos B. 265
Richardson, Capt. Josiah 23, 139
Rideout, Johnson 71, 268
Ringleader 88, 115, 142, 154, 162, 187, 210, 219, 235, 295
Rip van Winkle 324
Rising Sun 270
Rival 162, 208, 296
Robb, John 37, 71, 353
Robin Hood 58, 67, 88, 153, 162, 184, 224, 295
Robinson, Edward M. 166, 174
Rock City (Canada) 250
Rocket **302**
Roebuck (Maine) 214, 275
Roebuck (New York) 341
Rogers, Capt. William C. 89
Romance of the Seas 57, 67, 68, 82, 86, 123, 183, 198, 201, 208, 283
Roosevelt & Joyce Shipbuilders 165, 166, 168, 169, 171, 201, 229, 331, 332, 339–340
Ropes, Capt. John 216
Rosario 324
Roscius 11, 28
Rover's Bride 70, 352
Russo-American Fur Company 340

S. Lurman & Co. 177–178
sail cloth 47
sail decorations 54
sail plans **20–23**
sailing card advertisements 180–181
Salter, Capt. Charles 81, 90, 101, 195
salting 41
Sampson & Tappan Co 157, 160, 194
Samuel Russell 12, 15, 29, 81, 82, 84, 86, 90, 111, 167, 196, 217, 338
Samuels, Capt. Samuel **81**, 82, 112–113, 174, 198
San Francisco 68, 188, 190, 191, 210, 220, 221, 339
San Francisco, port of **13**, **14**–15
Sanchez, Emilio 237
Sancho Panza 67, 166, 185, 301
Santa Claus 58, 154, 184, 228, 306
Saracen 58–59, 318
Sarah Cowles 69
Sargent, Capt. Henry, Jr. 93, 94, 97, 217
Sawyer, Capt. Charles 225
Schomberg (British) **247**, 248
Scottish Maid (Scotland) 247
Sea Lark 160, 242, 260
Sea Nymph (Maryland) 15, 67, 137, 177, 351
Sea Nymph (Massachusetts) 67, 166, 183, 191, 322
Sea Serpent 23, 37, 43, 53, 58, 59, 67, 83, 87, 90, 102, 113, 130, 134, 171, 180, 184, 187, 196, 213–214, 235, 252, 276, 277

Sea Witch 12, 15, 16, 26, 58, 62, 67, 81, 86, 105, 106, 108, 114, 131, 133, 134, 156, 157, 173, 190, 194–195, 201, 215, 332, 340
Seaman 15, 17, 71, 178, 349, 351
Seaman's Bride (Maine) 262
Seaman's Bride (Maryland) 58, 67, 71, 178, 186, 351
Sears, Capt. Joshua 90–91, 164
Seccomb & Taylor Co. 163–164
*Seminole 256
Semmes, Capt. Raphael 242, **243**
Shalimar (Canada) 250
shanghaiing, practice of 96–97
*Sheridan 11, 28
Shining Sea Foundation 253
ship timber 40–**41**, 43
Shipper's Line of San Francisco Packets 186–187
shipyard labor practices 61–62
Shiverick, Paul 70
Shiverick Bros. Shipbuilders 35, 39, 40, 162, 166, 281, 284, 321–322
Shockley, Megan Taylor 121
Shooting Star (Massachusetts) 57, 67, 72, 134, 160, 181, 196, 283, 296–297
Shooting Star (New Hampshire) 160, 242, 243, 276, 278
*Siddons 11, 28
Sierra Nevada 37, 45, 58, 59, 67, 69, 81, 154, 162, 184, 187, 199, 201, 221, 224–225, 246, 276, 279
Sillsbee, Stone & Pickman Co. 166, 253
Silver Star 60, 153, 160, 298
Simons, Henry, Jr. 176
Simonson, Robert 187
Simoon 62, 67 136, 173, 191, 198, 214, 252, 343, 344–345
Simpson, Thomas 272–273
Sirius 352
Sirocco 38, 67, 71, 176, 349
Sise, Edward 81
Sitzer, Capt. Isaac 210
Skolfield, George 270
Skylark 86, 146, 154, 168, 184, 206, 325
Slade & Co. 175
slave trade 235–240
Smith, Isaac 37, 346–347
Smith, James 250
Smith & Dimon Shipbuilders 12, 13, 24, 26, 55, 62, 83, 173, 175, 201, 331, 332, 340
Snapdragon 31, 334
Sneeden & Whitlock Shipbuilders 331, 345
Snow, David 165–166
Snow Squall 36, 58, 63, 67, 72, 102, 106, 107, 171, 187, 192, 199, 243, **253**, 254, 258, 274
Snow Squall Project 254
Soule, Capt. Enos 275
South American trade 141–142
Southard, Thomas J. 53, 70, 75, 78, 79, 269
Southern Cross 40, 58, 60, 67, 87, 142, 160, 317
Sovereign of the Seas **21**, 42, 53, 58, 69, 75, 83, 107, 127, 129, 146, **205**, 217, 230, 283, 304, 306
Spark of the Ocean 265
Sparkling Sea 265
Sparkling Wave 65, 67, 71, 214, 246, 325
Spear, David, Jr. 258, 273–274
Spears, Gilbert 258–259
Spirit of the Times 66, 67, 68, 352
Spitfire **24**, 35, 58, 90, 116, 149, 154, 166, 183, 246, 258, 261
Sportsman 182, 261
Stack, Thomas 342
Staffordshire 60, 68, 69, 126, 139, 163, 197, 214, 219, 283, 303, **304**
Stag (Canada) 250
Stag Hound 23, 34, 58, 60, 67, 106, 130, 134, 145, 160, 212, 283, 302, 303
Stanhope, Capt. Phillip 238
Star of Empire 40, 139, 163, 305
Star of Hope 67, 78, 137, 280–281
Star of Peace 67, 78, 87, 242, 288
Star of the East (Canada) 250
Star of the South (Canada) 250
Star of the Union 58, 60, 63, 67, 160, 180, 223, 240, 297
Starlight 58, 67, 88, 116, 141, 157, 160, 183, 184, 246, 318
Starr King 154, 160, 225, 287
Steele, Capt. Henry 81, 199
Steele, Robert 248
Steers, George 60, 239, 343–344
Steers, James 343
Stephen Crowell 262
Stephen Mallory 41, 243, 354
stern construction 20
stern quarter embellishments **57**, 58–60
Stetson, Abner 72, 73, 267, 292
Stetson, Jotham 70, 71, 281, 291–292, 301, 319–320
Stevens Bros. Shipbuilders 61, 269
Stingray 134, 175, 190, 345
Storm 346
Storm King 42, 58, 67, 77, 137, 154, 165, 290
Stornaway 262
Stornoway (Britain) 194, 248
Strelna 270
Sumatra 291
CSS *Sumter* 242
Sun Insurance Co. 188
Sunny South 58, 60, 87, 88, 236, **237**, 238–239, 343–344
*Sunrise 256
Surprise 15, 16, 17, 34–35, 58, 59, 67, 86, 88, 111, 134, 147, 167, 168, 194, 196, 201, 220–221, 283, 309
Sutton & Company Dispatch Line 180, 181, 183–184, 245
Swallow 37, 57, 77, 87, 149, 157, 162, 163, 228, 283, 312, 337
Sweepstakes 21, 37, 51, 67, 71, 136, 170, 197, 201, 204, 217, 332
Swordfish 31, 65, 87, 89, 118, 168, 189, 195, 196, 197, 220, 222, 333
Syren 56, **76**, 77, 131, 145, **146**, 147, 166, 181, 183, 187, 251, 252–253, 283

Talisman 38, 87, 168, 242, 243, 266
Tam O Shanter 228, 275
Tay, Capt. Benjamin 89
Taylor, Bayard 213
Taylor, Capt. Isaac 71, 163, 292, 320
Taylor, John 77, 79, 147, 166, 233, 253, 282, 283, 290–291, 292, 293, 299, 300
Taylor & Merrill Co. 36, 174
tea trade 134
Tejuca 347
Telegraph 35, **50**, 57, 63, 67, 77, 116, 131, 144, 157, 160, 210, 296
Templar 299
Thatcher Magoun 40, 58, 60, 67–68, 154, 166, 184, 296
Thatcher Magoun & Sons Co. 166
Thayer & Warren Co. 163
Thomas, Deacon George 19, 35, 71, 72, 77, 78, 79, 197, 204, 257, 262–263, 320
Thomas Whitridge & Co. 178
Thorndike, Capt. Ebenezer 72, 264
*Thursday's Child 203
Tilton Bros. Co. 165
Timothy Davis & Co. Line 183
Tinqua 58, 60, 90, 181, 214–215, 277–278
Titan 67, 88, 129, 141, 154, 165, 228–229, 339
Titania (British) 248
Tobey & Littlefield Shipbuilders 37, 74, 78, 201, 221, 276, 279
Tornado 67, 106, 107, 173, 191, **226**, 246, 343, 344
Townsend, James L. 79
Trade Wind 67, 141, 176, 190, 223, 332, 338
Train, Enoch 33, 64, 68, 69, 138, **163**, 172, 304
Train, George F. 68, 69, 156
Treadwell, Capt. Charles 85
Troubador 88, 285
Trowbridge, Robert 79, 264
Trufant, Gilbert 71
Trufant & Drummond Shipbuilders 37, 70, 166, 256, 258, 270–271
CSS *Tuscaloosa* 243
Twain, Mark 116
Twilight 37, 53, 68, 88, 154, 157, 179, 183, 187, 201, 235, 327, 328
Tudor, Frederic 150
Tudor Ice Co. 150
Typhoon 35, 45, 58, 59, 67, 78, 81, 90, 101, 194–195, 212, 213, 246, 276, 278

Uncle Sam 274
Uncowah 157, 334
Undaunted 67, 89, 107, 184, 192, 244, 272
Union 67, 178, 350
Universe 55, **57**, 340
Upton, George B. 86, 160

Valentine, William 100
Van Dolan, Charles 102
Very, Capt. Samuel 89
Victory (1851) 67, 72, 288
Victory (1857) 67, 174, 286

Viking 58, 78, 154, 166, 271
Virginia 258
Vitula 160, 319
Volunteer 184
Vose, Peter L. 258
Vose, Thomas 258
voyage-ready costs 64
*Voyageur de la Mer (Egypt) 314

W. & F.H. Whittemore Co 166
Wade, Capt. John 160
Wakeman, Adelaide Seaborn 118–119
Wakeman, Capt. Edgar 110, 112, 118, 191
Wakeman, Mary 118
Wakeman & Dimon Co. 175
War Hawk 19, 58, 60, 143, 156, 161, 184, 187, 253, 287–288
Warner 274
Warren & Co. 163
Washington, Joseph A. 113, 115–116
watch system 98
water tanks 45
Water Witch 57, 60, 143, 156, 161, 184, 187, 253, 287–288
Waterman, Capt. Gordon B. 174, 219
Waterman, Capt. Robert 11, 12, 81, 89, 92, 105, **106**, 107–111, 114, 172, 175, 191, 195, 225
Waters, T.B. 166
Waverly 208, 289
Webfoot 40, 67, 149, 166, 192, 197, 322
Webb, Eckford 134, 345
Webb, Isaac 25, 30, 32, 60
Webb, William 10, 12, 13, 30–31, 39, 43, 61, 65, 68, 70, 75, 76, 79, 107, 138, 168, 174, 175, 195, 196, 197, 200, 201, 208, 211, 212, 218, 222, 224, 331, 332–334, 353
Webster, Daniel 58
Weld & Baker Co. *see* William F. Weld & Co.
Wells and Emmanuel's Empire Line 178, 185
Wendell, Capt. George B. 90
West Wind 54, 60, 67, 77, 87, 88, 116, 166, 299
Western Continent 259
Western Empire 72, 267
Westervelt, Aaron 37, 71, 170, 197, 335
Westervelt, Daniel 71, 170, 197, 335

Westervelt, Jacob 71, **77**, 79, 138, 335
Westervelt & MacKey Shipbuilders 139
Westervelt Shipbuilders 37, 51, 170, 201, 204, 331, 332, 334, **335**–337
Westward Ho 58, 67, 156, 157, 160, 184, 304
Weymouth, Dennett 268
whale oil trade 146
wheat trade 147–149
Whipple, A.B.C. 108
Whirlwind 56–57, 59, 67, 91, 113, 117, 118, 119, 129, 142, 166, 197, 199, 218, 297
Whistler 67, 161, 185, 225, 287
Whistling Wind 71, 350
White, Capt. John 88, 115
White, Capt. Otis 88, 115
White Diamond Line 138, 139, 163, 304
White Falcon 61, 129, 154, 157, 269
White Squall 15, 17, 23, 64, 176, 190, **210**, 228, 338, 341
White Star (Canada) 250
White Star Line 129, 136, 140, 165, 200, 250
White Swallow 57, 60, 106, 111–112, 154, 162, 180, 184, 187, 228, 294
White Wing 320
Whitlock Line 138
Whitmore, Capt. Jacob 90
Whitney, Capt. F.G. 237
Wiard Rifled Gun 245
Wide Awake 37, 67, 342
Wild Duck 52, 58, 60, 67, 169, 181, 190, 220, 222, 278
Wild Gazelle 298
Wild Hunter 40, 87, 90–91, 133, 141, 157, 166, 187, 284, 322
Wild Pigeon 37, 55, 58, 60, 169, 181, 187, 228, 246, 276, 277
Wild Ranger 58, 77, 223, 224, 297
Wild Rover 141, 143, 164, 187, 266
Wild Wave 67, 72, 87, 166, 217, 270
Wildfire **236**, 237, 239, 283, 284
Willets & Bishop Shipbuilders 346
William Appleton & Co. 166
William C. Annan & Co. 185
*William Chamberlain **256**
William Cramp & Sons Shipbuilders 77, 79, 175, 346, 347–348
William E. Roman 169, 276, 277

William F. Weld & Co. 107, 160–161, 252
William Lincoln & Co. 162
William Platt & Co 176
William Wilson & Sons 177
Williams, Jabez 62, 70, 79, 173, 191, 226, 342, **343–344**, 345
Williams, Capt. John (Jack) 11, 69, **87**, 89, 105, 199, 202–203
Williams, John M.S. 162
Williams & Guion Co. 175
Wilson, Capt. George H. 88
Windward 182, 225, 271
Winged Arrow 67, 88, 136, 137, 149, 160, 180, 184, 198, 317
Winged Hunter 87
Winged Racer 35, 58, 67, 137, 149, 156, 157, 160, 163, 174, 242, 283
Wings of the Morning 67, 68, 78, 265
Winsor, Capt. Charles 209
Winsor, Henry 120–121
Winsor's Regular Line 186
Witch of the Wave 37, 43, 46, 52, 55, 57, 63, 67, 89, 116, 119, 134, 162, 184, 187, 197, 276, **277**
Witch of the Wave (II) 278
Witchcraft 23, 35, 58, 89, 130, 154, 166, 184, 201, 214, 215, 283, 290, 293
Wizard 37, 58, 60, 63, 137, 145, 175, 246, 310
Wizard King 53, 75, 78, 183, 269
Woodcock 78, 265
wreck salvaging 191
W.T. Frost & Co. 173

Yankee Ranger 79, 264
*Yorkshire 11, 31, 199
Young America 31, 54, 59, 63, 85, 87, 89, 118, 136, 149, 154, 174, 175, 183, 184, 187, 189, 200, **208**–209, 232, 332, 334
Young Brander 88, 291
Young Mechanic 24, 67, 102, 145, 150, 263

Z Line of Packets 308
Zephyr (Massachusetts) 77, 303, 315
Zephyr (New York) 175, 337